A2 Business Studies

John Wolinski & Gwen Coates

Philip Allan Updates
Market Place
Deddington
Oxfordshire
OX15 0SE

Tel: 01869 338652
Fax: 01869 337590
e-mail: sales@philipallan.co.uk
www.philipallan.co.uk

ISBN 13: 978-0-86003-754-5
ISBN 10: 0-86003-754-1

This textbook has been written specifically to support students studying AQA Advanced Business Studies. The content has been neither approved nor endorsed by AQA and remains the sole responsibility of the authors.

All efforts have been made to trace copyright on items used.

All website addresses included in this book are correct at the time of going to press but may subsequently change.

Printed by Raithby, Lawrence & Co Ltd, Leicester

Environmental information
The paper on which this title is printed is sourced from managed, sustainable forests.

P00488

Contents

Module 5 People and Operations Management

People in organisations

Operations management

Module 6 External Influences and Objectives and Strategy

External influences

Objectives and strategy

Introduction

This textbook has been written specifically to meet the needs of students taking the AQA A2 Business Studies course and provides comprehensive coverage of the subject content of the AQA A2 specification, module by module, section by section, as it is laid out in the specification document. It follows on from the authors' AS textbook, *AQA AS Business Studies* (Philip Allan Updates), subsequently referred to as 'the AS textbook'.

Up-to-date examples and illustrations from real-life organisations and situations are used throughout this book in order to help you to recognise the dynamic and changing nature of business studies and its relevance to society.

The AQA specification does not require real-life cases for its examinations (although real-life cases will normally be used for Unit 6), but we have tried to use real-life case studies as much as possible. For this reason, students are encouraged to read the case study articles as a development of the specification content, even if they do not attempt to answer the questions that accompany them.

Course coverage and how to use this book

Terminology

All A-level specifications use the following terms:

- a **module** is a body of learning (that is, the content of the specification)
- a **unit** is the method of assessment (for example, an examination or a piece of coursework)

Structure

This book follows the order of the AQA A2 Business Studies specification. The specification is divided into three modules, each of which is split into two parts.

- **Module 4:** 'Marketing' is covered in Chapters 1 to 5; 'Accounting and Finance' is covered in Chapters 6 to 18.
- **Module 5:** 'People in Organisations' is covered in Chapters 19 to 28; 'Operations Management' is covered in Chapters 29 to 32. Chapters 33 and 34 offer advice on how to approach Unit 5 (the written report or the coursework).
- **Module 6:** 'External Influences' is covered in Chapters 35 to 45; 'Objectives and Strategy' is covered in Chapters 46 to 54.

Unlike the AQA AS examinations, the A2 units of assessment are not necessarily based on the modules bearing the same number. See the section on assessment (pp. xi–xiii) for details.

For each module, the order of the chapters in this book provides a logical progression of learning, with the later chapters building on the theory and understanding acquired in the earlier chapters. Some questions at the end of chapters also assume an understanding of work in previous chapters.

Special features

This book contains several special features designed to aid your understanding of the requirements of the AQA A2 Business Studies course.

Key terms

These are clear, concise definitions of the main terms needed for the course. An accurate understanding of the definitions of key terms will reduce the chances of you producing an irrelevant answer.

Examiner's voice

Both authors have over 20 years' experience of examining and have used this to provide snippets of advice that will help you to present your ideas effectively and to avoid potential pitfalls. Some of this advice is specific to a particular topic; the remainder is general advice on how you should approach the examinations.

Fact files

Topical examples from the world of business are included at regular intervals in order to increase interest and to help you to develop your application skills by showing how the business ideas that you have studied can be applied to real-life situations. These fact files will also help you to increase your awareness of current developments and practices.

Did you know?

These boxes are placed throughout the book. They provide useful insights into the ideas and concepts covered in the A2 course and their use in businesses. The comments will help you to improve your understanding of business activities.

What do you think?

On occasions, facts or comments on business activity are presented in the form of a challenge — what do you think? There is often a range of possible solutions to business problems or many differing consequences to an action. These boxes will get you thinking about possible alternative solutions or consequences.

Group exercises

These are included when a part of the specification lends itself to discussion or a cooperative approach to study.

Practice exercises

Over 75 different practice exercises are provided to help you check your understanding of the topics you have covered within each chapter. Many of these exercises are geared towards testing knowledge, but several are based on relevant articles. You can use the latter type to test your higher-level skills, such as evaluation. Although individual questions within a practice exercise may match the style of AQA A2 questions, overall the practice exercises do not adopt the AQA examination style — the case studies perform this role.

Case studies

A common problem facing both teachers and students is finding suitable material for examination practice. The examinations are based on the whole of the specification and so, on completion of a particular topic, it is not possible to find a past examination paper that sets a realistic challenge. To fill this gap over 50 examination-style questions have been included in this book. The heading 'case study' is used wherever the style of the questions is the same as in the AQA A2 examinations.

Assessment

The hierarchy of skills

Every mark that is awarded on an A2 paper is given for the demonstration of a skill. The following five skills are tested:

- **Knowledge and understanding** — demonstrating knowledge and understanding of the specified content of the course, such as clear definitions or explanation of theories.
- **Application** — relating or applying your knowledge and understanding to a specific organisation or situation. An example might be advising a business to recruit and train a specific category of employee based on recognising the shortage of suitable staff for that business.
- **Analysis** — using theory or business logic to develop a line of thought in relation to the solution of a business problem. An example might be showing how a particular strategy may cause personnel difficulties and low morale in the short term, but more efficient production and higher profit margins in the long run.
- **Evaluation** — making a judgement based on weighing up different evidence and, possibly, recognising the strength, quality and reliability of the evidence before making a decision.
- **Synthesis** — assessing the relative importance and significance of information from a variety of sources. This skill is only assessed in Unit 5 (the examination or the coursework alternative) and is considered to be equivalent to evaluation. In Unit 5C (coursework) and Unit 5W (examination), students will acquire more information than is necessary to complete

their tasks. Synthesis rewards students for the skill shown in deciding on the relevance and importance of different information.

All questions are marked according to this hierarchy of skills, with knowledge being the easiest, progressing on to evaluation and synthesis as the most difficult. In Unit 4 you may be given:

- **questions asking you to 'explain'.** These require you to display both knowledge and application.
- **questions requiring analysis.** These have marks allocated for knowledge, application and analysis.
- **questions requiring evaluation.** In these cases, marks are awarded for all four skills. You cannot evaluate (make a judgement) effectively without showing knowledge, applying it to the situation and then developing the argument (analysing).

To reflect the relative difficulties of the four skills, the A2 examinations allow for progression. Greater emphasis is placed on the skill of evaluation in the final papers, Unit 5 and Unit 6.

Always ensure that your answers are linked to the situation in the article. This will gain you application marks and will also make it easier for you to evaluate, as judgements (evaluation) in examinations are based on your ability to assess the particular situation in the question.

Recognising the skills required

How do you know what skills are being asked for by the examiner? There are two ways in which you can identify the skills that are being tested:

- trigger words
- mark allocations

Trigger words

The majority of questions in the AQA A2 Business Studies examinations use the same trigger words employed in the AS papers. However, unlike the AS examinations, there is no guarantee that these trigger words will be used.

Analysis

The following trigger words indicate that analysis is required:

- 'Analyse...'
- 'Examine...'
- 'Explain why...'

It is worth noting that 'explain' on its own means that application is needed.

Evaluation

If evaluation is expected, the three triggers are:

- 'Evaluate...'
- 'Discuss...'
- 'To what extent...'

Mark allocations

At A2 the mark allocation is an excellent guide to the skills needed.

- Questions worth **fewer than 10 marks** will require application or analysis.
- Questions worth **exactly 10 marks** will require analysis or evaluation.
- Questions worth **more than 10 marks** will require evaluation.

This rule applies to all AQA A2 Business Studies papers.

There is no set pattern for mark allocations of individual questions, as the skills weighting for Unit 4 is very different from those for Units 5 and 6. However, Tables 1 to 3 show how a 'typical' A2 examination paper might be assessed.

Table 1 *Typical mark allocations for a Unit 4 examination*

	Skills				
Question	Knowledge	Application	Analysis	Evaluation	Total
1 (a)	2	3	5		10
1 (b)	2	2	3	3	10
2 (a)	2	2	4		8
2 (b)	2	3	3	4	12
3 (a)	2	2	2		6
3 (b)	3	3	4	4	14
4	3	6	6	5	20
Total	**16**	**21**	**27**	**16**	**80**

Unit 5 is assessed through coursework (Unit 5C) or a written examination (Unit 5W). Unit 5W is divided into two parts — a business report and an essay.

Table 2 *Typical mark allocations for Unit 5*

	Skills					
	Knowledge	Application	Analysis	Synthesis	Evaluation	Total
Unit 5C	**16**	**16**	**16**	**10**	**22**	**80**
Business report	8	8	8	5	11	40
Essay	8	8	8	–	16	40
Unit 5W total	**16**	**16**	**16**	**5**	**27**	**80**

Table 3 *Typical mark allocations for a Unit 6 examination*

	Skills				
Question	Knowledge	Application	Analysis	Evaluation	Total
1	3	2	4	5	14
2	3	2	4	5	14
3	4	2	4	6	16
4	3	3	4	8	18
5	3	3	4	8	18
Total	**16**	**12**	**20**	**32**	**80**

Demonstrating the skills required

Avoid the temptation to show off your knowledge by listing lots of different points. The AQA examinations reward quality, not quantity. As a general rule of thumb, in Units 4 and 6 it is best to focus on two or three points only per question, but to develop them in great depth. For Unit 5, a single question will take 45 minutes to complete and so a much broader coverage is expected, although quality is still the key requirement.

For an evaluation question, you should identify the appropriate number of relevant ideas, explain their relevance using arguments that are specific to the situation or organisation featured in the question, and then draw a conclusion or make a decision based on your arguments. If, and only if, time permits, you can add and develop further ideas. In short, move up the skills levels from knowledge to application and analysis and on to evaluation as quickly as possible.

The A2 examinations

Scheme of assessment

Each examination unit is tested in a separate 90-minute examination. There is a coursework alternative for Unit 5. *Note that, unlike in the AS examinations, the units of assessment at A2 do not correspond to the modules of study.*

- Unit 4 tests both Modules 4 and 5.
- Unit 5 tests the whole specification through *either* coursework (Unit 5C) *or* a written examination (Unit 5W).
- Unit 6 tests Module 6. Note that, although Module 6 is based on 'external influences' and 'objectives and strategy', it can draw on elements of all six modules of study. It is thus the synoptic paper that draws together the whole specification.

The marks awarded for each unit paper are weighted. As Unit 6 is the synoptic paper, building on the whole A-level specification, it has a higher weighting. The weightings for each paper are detailed in Table 4.

Unit	Topics	Weighting
4	'Marketing', 'Accounting and Finance', 'People in Organisations' and 'Operations Management'	15% of A-level
5	Whole specification	15% of A-level
6	'External Influences' and 'Objectives and Strategy'	20% of A-level

***Table 4** Weightings of each A2 paper*

As you progress through the A2 papers, a greater proportion of marks is given to the higher levels of skill, especially evaluation. In Unit 4, only 20% of the marks are awarded for evaluation, whereas Unit 5 and Unit 6 both award 40% of the marks for the higher skill levels (evaluation or synthesis).

The skills demonstrated in all three units are marked out of 80. Table 5 shows the AQA guidelines for the number of marks awarded for each skill in each of the three units.

Table 5 *Marks awarded for each skill at A2*

Unit	Skills: Knowledge	Application	Analysis	Evaluation/ Synthesis	Total
4	16	21	27	16	80
5	16	16	16	32	80
6	16	12	20	32	80

Note: 'quality of language' is awarded a maximum of 4 marks for each paper.

The case studies in this textbook are devised to reflect the AQA examinations. Thus the questions in Unit 4 are designed to include a smaller proportion of tasks requiring evaluation (20% of the marks), while the tasks in Units 5 and 6 include a larger proportion of evaluation and synthesis (40% of the marks). Each of the other skills is tested in exactly the same way as in an actual examination.

Unit 4

The topics covered in both Modules 4 and 5 are tested in Unit 4. The examination consists of a single case study based on a business decision. Unlike in Units 2 and 3 at AS, you will not see the stimulus material and questions before the examination. In this respect, the paper is similar to Unit 1. The case study is approximately 900 to 1,000 words in length, plus additional appendices. These are likely to include graphical or numerical data. The case study is followed by six or seven questions based on the case study.

The aim of the examination is to test equally all four sections of the specification: 'Marketing', 'Accounting and Finance', 'People in Organisations' and 'Operations Management'. However, the specification encourages you to see business studies as an integrated whole, so there may be tasks that require you to integrate two aspects of the specification (e.g. looking at the implications of a decision for the marketing and the financial situation of the business).

The structure of this book means that a series of marketing questions is followed by a series of accounting and finance questions, and so on. The actual examinations will integrate all four sections. On completion of the Unit 4 content, you are advised to use the Unit 4 sample examination paper (pp. 323–326) as final preparation for the examination.

During your revision you are also advised to practise answering actual past papers. AQA A2 Business Studies past papers are available (in pdf format) from the AQA website: www.aqa.org.uk. Mark schemes for these examinations can also be downloaded.

Unit 5

There are two options for Unit 5: a written examination or coursework. There is no specific content for these options. Consequently, this book contains no chapters that focus on the content requirements of Unit 5. However, to help prepare you for Unit 5, some general advice is given in Chapters 33 and 34.

The written examination

The AQA specification for Unit 5W, the written examination paper, states: 'This unit contains two sections and questions assess any module(s) of A2 subject content.' As Module 6 (the final A2 module) is synoptic, this description means that, in effect, Unit 5W can use concepts from any part of the AS or A2 specification. Some general advice on how to approach Unit 5W is given in Chapter 33.

Coursework

The AQA specification for Unit 5C, the coursework element, states: 'The project should be approximately 3,000 words in length, excluding tables, figures and appendices, and can be based on subject content from any module of this specification.' Given that the planning stages of the project should begin before the start of Year 2, it is probable that coursework will rely significantly on topics drawn from the AS specification. Some general advice on how to approach Unit 5C is given in Chapter 34.

Unit 6

The topics covered in Module 6 are tested in Unit 6. This 90-minute examination consists of a single, previously unseen case study, almost certainly based on a real company, although this is not a specific requirement.

The examination is based on 'External Influences' and 'Objectives and Strategy', but with questions that encourage students to draw on the other five modules of the AQA A-level specification in their answers.

The case study is approximately 900 to 1,000 words in length and is followed by five questions, with a focus on evaluation throughout. Mark allocations for each question usually range between 14 and 18 marks. Consequently, five extended answers are required. On the basis of the 'mark a minute' rule, students should devote just over 15 minutes to a typical answer.

How to approach the course and examination

Study advice

Keep up to date

This book contains many topical examples for you to use, but business studies is constantly changing. Although a textbook provides you with the theory, reading newspapers and magazines, and using other topical media such as the internet, will help you to keep pace with changes.

Build your own business studies dictionary

As you progress through the book, build up your own glossary/dictionary of terms. This will ease your revision and help to ensure that you can define terms clearly. Knowing the exact meaning of terms will also help you to write relevant answers.

Read each chapter thoroughly

On completion of a topic, make sure that you have read the relevant chapter and use the questions at the end to test yourself. If you adopt this approach for every chapter of the book, then your revision will be just that: revising what you have already learned rather than learning material for the first time.

Complete the practice exercises and case studies

Tackle the practice exercises and case studies at the end of each chapter, even if not asked to do so by your teacher. Completion of the practice exercises will help you to check that you have understood the basic ideas in the chapter. Completion of the case studies will give you useful examination practice and help you to learn what you can achieve. It will also enable you to develop the best approach to answering business studies questions. Through providing information about actual businesses, the case studies will improve your understanding too.

Develop your communication and data-handling skills

The A2 course expects you already to have developed skills in communication and the ability to use, prepare and interpret business data. You should be able to understand and apply averages (the mean, median and mode), prepare and interpret tables, graphs, histograms, bar charts and pie charts, and use index numbers.

Focus on the higher-level skills

It is tempting to focus chiefly on the facts when you are revising. In both the Unit 5 and Unit 6 examinations, 40% of the marks are awarded for the higher-level skills — evaluation and synthesis. Include scope for this within your revision, so that you are able to earn the marks given for evaluation.

Read the Chief Examiner's report

This report will alert you to the strengths and weaknesses shown by previous students and will help you to refine your approach. Along with previous examination papers and mark schemes, these reports are available in pdf format from the AQA website: www.aqa.org.uk.

Examination advice

Advice is provided throughout the book in the 'examiner's voice' boxes. Some of the key points are noted here:

- **Practice makes perfect.** Examination practice will help you to establish the best approach for you to take in the exam itself.

- **Plan the length of your answers.** After allowing for reading time, you will have approximately 1 minute for every mark awarded. Use this as a guideline to the timing of your answers (6 marks = 6 minutes; 10 marks = 10 minutes, etc.).
- **Use the mark allocations and wording of the question.** For most questions the AS trigger words are used for the A2 examinations. For Unit 4 the mark allocation is a good guide (below 10 marks means that evaluation is not required; 10 marks and above means that evaluation is needed). For Units 5 and 6, *all* questions require evaluation.
- **Move up the hierarchy of skills as quickly as possible.** Do not spend an excessive amount of time on stating points when application, analysis and evaluation are required. For Units 5 and 6 in particular, you should try to allow 40% of the time for evaluation.
- **Read the wording of the question carefully.** Half a minute spent on deciding exactly what is needed by the examiner can save you 10 to 20 minutes of wasted effort.
- **Do not be tempted to show off unnecessary knowledge.** Be prepared to accept that your favourite topic is not relevant to this examination if there are no questions on it.
- **State the obvious.** Some explanations might seem to be too easy, but they need to be included in your answer. The examiner can only reward what you have written.
- **Leave a space at the end of each answer.** If time permits, you can then add more detail at the end of your answer.

We wish you well in your studies and examinations, and hope that this book helps to provide you with the understanding needed to succeed. Good luck!

Acknowledgements

The authors would like to express their thanks to numerous individuals who have contributed to the completion of this book. Particular gratitude is shown to Philip Cross for the initial idea, unstinting support, good humour and patience. Thanks are also due to Chris Bessant and Patrick Fox, whose suggestions have greatly improved the final version.

John owes a debt of gratitude to Yvonne for her stoicism and tolerance during the writing, and to Lara, Nina, Marje, Joe, Tricia and Martin for their support over many years.

Gwen is grateful to John and Jessica, both of whom are always calm, relaxed and supportive, allowing her the time and space to complete this work.

Module 4

Marketing

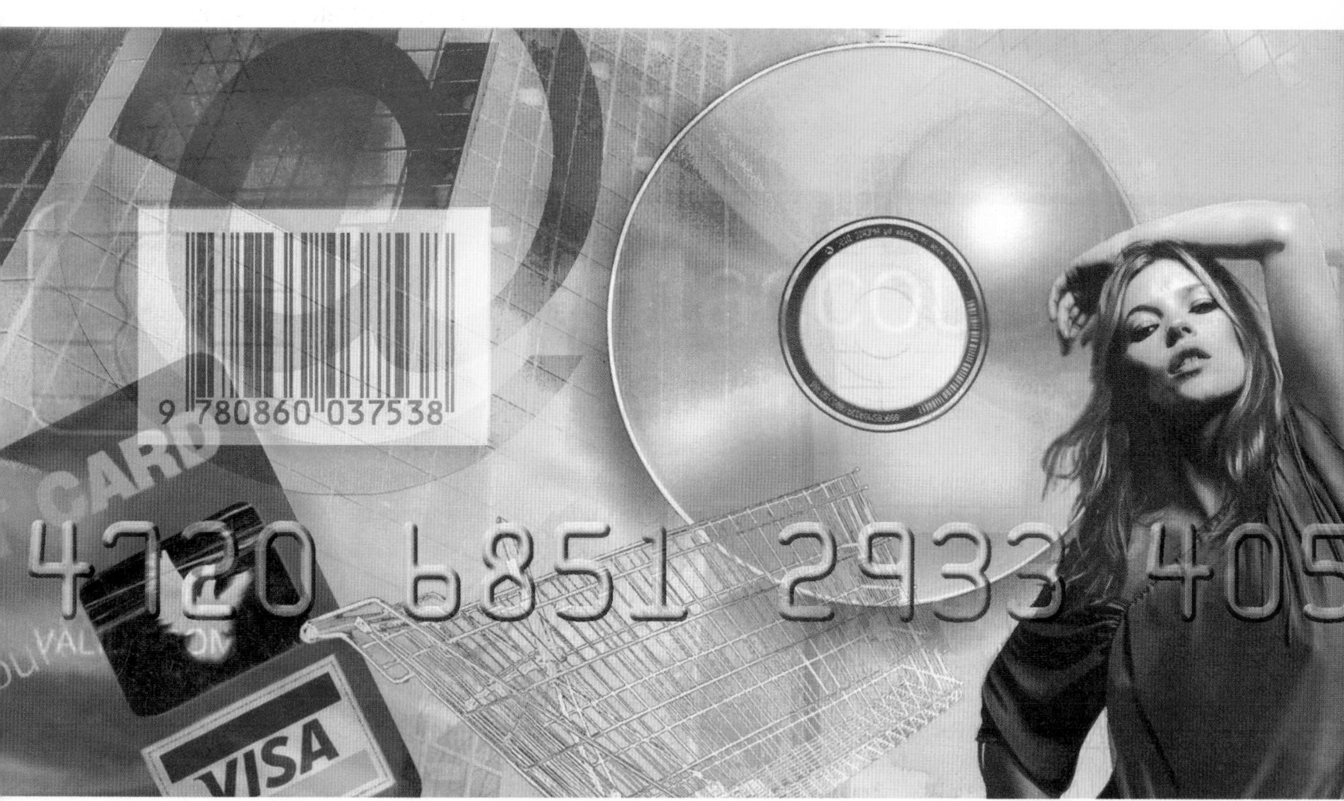

> "The purpose of a business is to create a customer."
>
> Peter Drucker

Asset-led and market-led marketing

This chapter introduces and defines 'asset-led' and 'market-led' marketing. The benefits of each approach and the circumstances in which they are used are discussed. The chapter concludes by examining the factors that influence the decision to use 'asset-led' or 'market-led' marketing.

Asset-led marketing

TERM

asset-led marketing: where a company uses its strengths or assets as the key element of its marketing.

In asset-led marketing, the business in effect concentrates on promoting its strengths and involving itself with products that it can deal with efficiently. The business might use its well-known brand name or image to promote itself, or concentrate on particular skills that it possesses as an organisation. In some cases, it may use a major tangible asset that it owns as an important aspect of its marketing: for example, a new ride in a theme park or a prestigious building that is owned by the company. In some organisations, the skills of the staff are a considerable asset, although a company should be careful about relying on this asset in its marketing as there is no guarantee that staff will stay with the firm. For example, the performance of the advertising agency Saatchi and Saatchi declined when the Saatchi brothers, who founded the business, left and formed a new agency.

EXAMINER'S VOICE

In accounting terms, the word 'asset' has a precise meaning — items that are owned by the organisation. However, in asset-led marketing the word 'asset' has a much broader meaning and could be more accurately described as an organisation's 'strengths'.

Excellent profit levels or cash-flow positions can also help a business to market itself more effectively, especially in situations where promotion or expensive research and development is needed to stay ahead of competitors. For many businesses, their location or address may be a significant asset. Examples include a location in Paris for a cosmetics business or a Harley Street address for a doctor's surgery in London. Many industries become associated with a particular place and this association becomes an asset for the business. Staffordshire is still famous for its pottery and Milan is an ideal location for a business involved in the fashion industry.

TOPFOTO

BIC

Why might a business use asset-led marketing?

- The business may wish to play to its strengths. BIC established that its main strength was 'working with plastics', so when it decided to diversify from ballpoint pens to other products, it was a natural choice to move into disposable razor blades. Ironically, one of the competitors that suffered most from BIC's move into the razor-blade market was Wilkinson. It had originally made swords, but in identifying its main asset as the ability to create sharp-edged metal, it had used an asset-led marketing approach in deciding to move into the manufacture of razor blades.
- By using asset-led marketing, the business is less likely to make mistakes. The approach may therefore appeal to firms that do not want to take risks. By concentrating on its strengths, the firm should be able to provide a good-quality product or service because it is staying within its area of expertise. However, this will not eliminate risk, especially if consumers are no longer interested in the products or activities in which the firm excels.
- Asset-led organisations should be able to retain customer or brand loyalty. If it focuses on its strengths, a firm's activities will correspond to the actions that created consumers' goodwill in the first place. Consequently, customers will trust the firm to deliver a good product or service, and are thus more likely to continue buying its products. A firm trying to move into a new area of business may lack credibility. Even Microsoft, with all its expertise, found that customers were sceptical when it moved into the computer console market with the launch of the Xbox.
- Business strategy in the early years of the twenty-first century has continued to encourage businesses to focus on their core activities in order to benefit from specialisation and their greater understanding of the market. Moving away from areas of expertise will involve additional expenses, such as market research and capital expenditure, with no guarantee that the firm will succeed in its new area of activity.
- Since asset-led marketing is often based on brand strength and brand loyalty, there is usually scope for the firm to use its strengths in order to achieve higher sales volume and often a higher price. This combination means greater overall profitability.
- In the case of location, the firm might wish to benefit from the prestige associated with its location or address. Many industries become associated with a particular place and this association becomes an asset for the business. Bordeaux is still famous for its wine and the City of London is an ideal address for a business involved in financial services. A nightclub in Ibiza may possess natural advantages over other locations, but organisations must be certain that the benefits remain. People setting up bars and nightclubs in Falaraki on the island of Rhodes may have mistimed their actions, as it is reported that there has been a 40% fall in income since

the Greek police started to crack down on drunken behaviour in the resort in 2004.

Asset-led marketing is often preferred by firms because it involves less immediate risk. However, it must be used with caution. If a brand or firm assumes that its strengths will remain, it is likely to be overtaken by events in the market (and by competitors whose market-led approach keeps them more in tune with the needs of the market).

FACT FILE

Asset-led marketing must be used with caution, as a current strength may cease to be a strength in the future if circumstances change. The business book with the greatest volume of worldwide sales, *In Search of Excellence*, by Tom Peters and Robert Waterman, was based on identifying 'excellence' in over 40 leading businesses throughout the 1960s and 1970s. Peters and Waterman identified the main factors common to these excellent companies. However, although these were considered to be the most successful firms at the time, many no longer continue to trade successfully and relatively few remain among the world's leading businesses. Those that remain tend to be within industries that have experienced relatively low levels of change in their markets. In his more recent publications, Peters has emphasised the need for constant adaptation in order to keep up with changes in the market. Although his work is much broader in its scope, to some extent it reflects a change in emphasis from asset-led to market-led marketing.

FACT FILE

Ferrari is an example of the use of asset-led marketing in which the product itself is the asset that is central to the firm's marketing. Fiat (the owners of Ferrari) uses the Ferrari name to generate profit. In addition to its sale of cars or income from Formula 1 motor racing, each year Ferrari is able to generate more than €30 million profit just from royalties paid in return for allowing other firms to use the Ferrari brand on their products.

Product-led marketing

Product-led marketing is a specific example of asset-led marketing, where the asset in question is a particular product. Companies with a particularly well-known product may use this product or its reputation in order to market other elements of their business. For example, Kellogg's original product — cornflakes — enabled the firm to become established as a cereal manufacturer and this provides reassurance to customers when deciding whether to try a new food product released by the company.

Market-led marketing

KEY TERM

market-led marketing: when businesses conduct regular market research in order to analyse consumers' needs and ensure that they fulfil them.

Market-led marketing requires an organisation to be continually alert to changes occurring in the marketplace, and ready to respond to threats and/or opportunities that might occur.

Why might a business use market-led marketing?

- Accurate anticipation of market changes will enable a business to react quickly to any changes when they take place. As a rule, the first company to introduce a new product has an advantage over companies that follow, since the first example of the product is associated more strongly with the new development than are the followers. Sometimes this even leads to the brand name replacing the generic product name in people's minds, such as Hoover rather than vacuum cleaner or, more recently, Dyson rather than cyclonic cleaner. Ironically, although these two brands became well known by using a market-led approach, they have been able to sustain their popularity by using their brand name as an 'asset'.

- Usually, a market-led approach allows the firm to launch new products with much greater confidence, as the chance of failure is reduced. In addition to the reassurance provided by market research results, the organisation will have had time to assess the feasibility of the project rather than being rushed into a decision as a reaction to other firms' actions.
- Market-led marketing enables the firm to respond promptly to any changes, thus satisfying the needs of the customers rather than the firm itself. Customers may be more inclined to buy a product or service that they have influenced, rather than an asset-led product that may have been developed to suit the needs of the business rather than its customers.

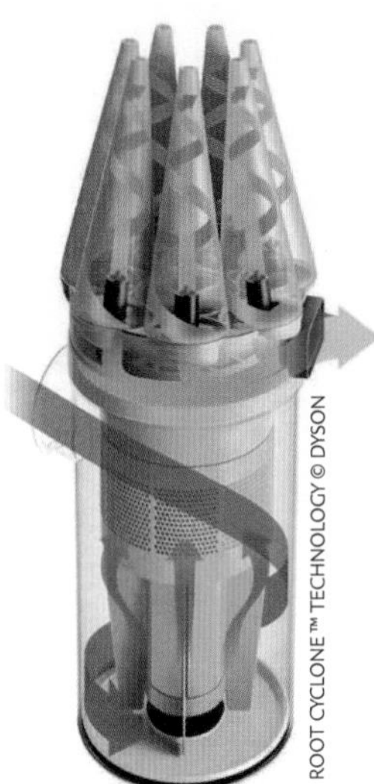
ROOT CYCLONE™ TECHNOLOGY © DYSON

Choosing between asset-led and market-led marketing

A number of factors influence the choice between asset-led and market-led marketing.

The pace of change in the market

In industries where rapid change is taking place, it is crucial that a firm keeps alert to any changes in consumer tastes and the marketplace, as new opportunities and threats will be continually emerging. Although this will involve careful scrutiny of the business's assets and their suitability, it is more likely to require the firm to research its customers regularly. Consequently, market-led marketing is more suited to such a situation.

The assets of the business

Some firms will possess specific assets of which they should take as much advantage as possible. A cash-rich business will want to take advantage of its situation in order to introduce or promote products. Similarly, if a firm has a very favourable image because of recent events, it should cash in on that image while it remains intact. The film industry has a tendency to cash in on successful films with sequels that build on the goodwill established by the first film. The movie *Rocky* led to four sequels; recent examples include *Spiderman 2, Shrek 2* and a second *Bridget Jones* film.

The extent to which the business is prepared to take risk

In the short term, asset-led marketing is less risky because the business is playing to its strengths. However, eventually there is a greater danger that the firm will lose contact with its customers.

The accuracy of market research

In theory, rapidly changing markets are best suited to a market-led approach. However, market-led marketing depends on correct forecasting of the future. This is not an easy task in any situation but is particularly difficult in rapidly changing markets. It may be very expensive to monitor the market, so firms may be less inclined to adopt a market-led approach if accuracy cannot be guaranteed.

The cost of change

Ultimately, the approach used will depend on the finances of the firm. Market-led marketing will probably enable the business to keep pace with the market and thus generate more income. In contrast, asset-led marketing will probably require less change in the business's activities and thus fewer costs. The firm will be able to compare these approaches and select the most profitable option (or the one that more closely meets its objectives).

The degree of competition in the market

The more competitive the market, the more a business must listen closely to the needs of its customers. In an industry with many competitors, a firm that is not market-led will lose market share to a business that meets the needs of consumers. However, a monopolist can focus on providing what it does best and know that sales are not going to be affected so much — the only alternative to the customer is to go without the product. It is alleged that Stagecoach has been much more market-led in providing bus transport in areas where competition exists than it has been in its provision of rail transport, where it is invariably a monopolist. A lack of competition has been particularly crucial in companies not using a market-led approach in situations where the product is a necessity. Water suppliers have little incentive to improve the quality of their service, as they know that people will still purchase from the local supplier, regardless of quality.

TOPFOTO

The ability of the company to relate customer tastes to its own business strengths

Some businesses are very skilled in recognising that customers' wishes can be met by playing to one of their strengths. For example, supermarkets have introduced a wide range of new products, including clothing products such as socks and underwear, recognising that customers buy these according to convenience and price rather than as a result of a planned shopping expedition. Other businesses, such as Coca-Cola, have the marketing skills to persuade people that their products are attractive and thus influence consumer taste. In both cases, asset-led marketing is being used.

Conclusion

In general, analysts recommend a market-led approach because 'consumer sovereignty' suggests that firms must meet the needs of their clients.

However, a successful business will benefit from playing to its strengths, so a combination of the two approaches may yield high profits. It is also possible for firms to influence the market. Is the taste of cola drinks so much better than all other flavours, or have the world's taste buds been influenced by the quality of the marketing?

EXAMINER'S VOICE

Business terms are not always universal. A market-led approach is sometimes described as 'market orientation'. The term 'product orientation' is sometimes used to refer to a product-led approach.

PRACTICE EXERCISE — Total: 40 marks (35 minutes)

1 Distinguish between asset-led marketing and market-led marketing. *(6 marks)*

2 Identify five different assets that a business might use as the basis of asset-led marketing. *(5 marks)*

3 What is meant by product-led marketing? *(3 marks)*

4 Explain three reasons why a firm might use market-led marketing. *(9 marks)*

5 List two disadvantages of asset-led marketing. *(2 marks)*

6 List three disadvantages of market-led marketing. *(3 marks)*

7 Explain four factors that will influence whether a firm decides to use asset-led marketing or market-led marketing. *(12 marks)*

WHAT DO YOU THINK?

Is it always possible to recognise the difference between asset-led marketing and market-led marketing? It is unlikely that somebody not involved with a firm will know the details of its products' introduction and marketing. Therefore, it might be impossible to tell the difference. A new cosmetic from Boots plc may be the result of intensive market research (market-led) or have arisen from research in a laboratory (asset-led). While Lemon Coke appears to have been created by Coca-Cola from observing that the two flavours were often combined in the market, it is possible that Vanilla Coke was introduced because a Coca-Cola executive thought it might be a good idea and play to the firm's strengths. It might also have been a combination of the two — using the firm's assets, but also conducting market research that confirmed its probable success.

CASE STUDY 1 Asset-led marketing in horse racing

Horse racing is an unusual industry. Owners of horses place their animals in the care of a specialist trainer whose stables will feed and care for the horses and train them for racing. Prize money is offered to winners of races, but few owners ever make a profit, as the costs of stabling are usually much higher than the prize money gained.

This is not a major issue for most owners. Their motivation comes from the joy of owning a horse and the extra excitement that owning a horse gives when watching the races, especially if the horse is successful. Thus, when deciding on which trainer's stables to use, most owners try to balance the costs of stabling with the chances of success for their particular horses.

For the trainers it is a different matter. Training horses is their business and like other businesses they need to make a profit to survive. A typical trainer needs fixed assets, especially stables and large areas of land on which the horses can train. With high fixed costs it is vital that a trainer is able to attract as much revenue from horse owners as possible. A successful trainer attracts more horse owners and is able to charge higher fees.

In horse racing, Newmarket in Suffolk and Lambourn in west Berkshire are arguably *the* places to locate your stables. This was the challenge facing Martin Pipe when he established his stables at Nicholashayne in Devon in 1975. This location, on the Devon–Somerset border, was a long way from the established centres of horse racing in Britain. How could he persuade horse owners to stable their horses in his yard?

Martin Pipe used asset-led marketing. Success in horseracing was traditionally achieved through horses winning major races such as the Derby, the Oaks or the Cheltenham Gold Cup. Stables that were successful in major races gained publicity and found it easier to attract new customers. Pipe realised that he lacked the resources to compete in this way, but he did have other assets.

His years of experience in horse racing had given him the ability to assess what was needed for a horse to win a wide variety of races, including minor races at the smaller racecourses such as Wincanton and Chepstow. Through a meticulously prepared training programme, and by carefully selecting lower key races in which his horses had a realistic chance of success, Pipe was able to build a very successful business. Many owners recognised that his stables were more likely to provide the training and race selection needed to achieve a winning performance for their horses, so growing numbers of owners placed their horses in his care.

TOPFOTO

This enabled Martin Pipe to develop his assets still further. His enquiring and quizzical mind was always striving to find improved techniques, and as his income increased, he was able to introduce pioneering facilities. In addition to normal facilities such as outdoor gallops, his base, Pond House Racing Stables, boasts an all-weather gallop, indoor training areas, swimming pool and solarium, horse-walker and treadmills. These amenities are enhanced further by a specialist laboratory and full-time veterinary support.

As a consequence, Pipe has gone from strength to strength and, in terms of the number of winners in a season, he has been the number one UK trainer for an unprecedented 19 years in succession.

Of course, it could be argued that this is market-led marketing. Pipe was one of the first trainers to recognise that owners wanted winners rather than unsuccessful performances in more prestigious races. He has certainly identified the needs of the smaller, less affluent horse owner. However well a business uses its assets, the end product must appeal to the market or the business will fail.

Source: Martin Pipe website:
http://64.225.202.76/facilitiesdetail.htm

Questions

Total: 20 marks (25 minutes)

1 Explain two reasons why it could be argued that Martin Pipe uses market-led marketing rather than asset-led marketing. *(8 marks)*

2 Evaluate the main assets that Martin Pipe might have used to market his stables. *(12 marks)*

CASE STUDY 2 Market-led marketing in tourism

Tourism is an industry that tends to use a market-led approach. Table 1.1 shows the major destinations for UK holidaymakers on package trips.

Despite the growing number of independent travellers, the package holiday market continues to display certain characteristics. Holidaymakers want:

- a high probability of sun
- services conveniently laid on to increase the scope for relaxation
- cheap, all-in-one prices
- scope to speak English at all times
- availability of English food and drink

Spain and Greece dominate the list, as their resorts are prepared to meet the demands of the UK tourist market. France was the main destination in the era that preceded the introduction of the package holiday, but its reluctance to adapt to the needs of the new market led to a fall in its popularity as a destination for UK holidaymakers. This was a conscious decision by France, which traditionally has a much stronger sense of its own identity and, in any case, is much less reliant on tourism for its economic wealth than Spain and Greece, which both rely greatly on revenue from holidaymakers.

Many UK tourists visit other countries independently and, in general, these tourists are more likely to

TOPFOTO

wish to see their destination in a more natural state. Details of destinations for independent travellers are shown in Table 1.2.

Independent travellers are a growing force in the overseas holiday market. Although they represent a smaller number of travellers, in most cases they represent much higher levels of spending per head and provide scope for higher profit margins for travel agents. This was once a niche market with firms such as Travelbag, specialising in Australasian trips, and Saga, providing holidays for consumers aged 50+.

Travel agents were and are often a part of a company that provides 'package' tours, but this link is weakening as travel agents are reacting to the market and seeking to provide more individually tailored holidays for their customers. A recent survey

Destination	Market share (%)
Spain (including Canaries and Balearic islands)	35
Greece	12
France	7
USA (mainly Florida)	6
Cyprus	5
Italy	4
Portugal and Madeira	4
Turkey	4
Caribbean	4
Other European	3
Others	16

Source: Mintel.

Table 1.1 *Destinations for UK holidaymakers on package trips, 2003*

Destination	Market share (%)
Spain (including Canaries and Balearic islands)	25
France	19
USA	11
Italy	7
Eire	5
Greece	4
Other European	4
Australia/New Zealand	3
Portugal and Madeira	3
Cyprus	3
Others	16

Source: Mintel.

Table 1.2 *Destinations for UK independent travellers abroad, 2003*

showed that UK tourists agreed that the part of their holiday they enjoyed least was the experience of sharing their holiday with other British tourists. If this trend continues, the market for independent travel will continue to grow and successful businesses will be those that adapt to this change.

The desire for 'last-minute' holidays and short breaks is a growing feature of the industry. Companies such as lastminute.com and Expedia have taken advantage of these developments.

Source: Mintel.

Questions

Total: 20 marks (25 minutes)

1 Explain why certain organisations in the tourist industry might use asset-led marketing. *(8 marks)*

2 Is the holiday trade for independent travellers more market-led than the provision of package holidays? Justify your opinion. *(12 marks)*

CASE STUDY 3 The UK banking industry: asset-led or market-led?

Banking before 1986

Before 1986 the banking industry was characterised by a division between two main types of organisation: banks and building societies. Banks concentrated on providing current accounts and savings accounts, and lending, mostly to businesses. Building societies existed almost solely to offer savings accounts and to provide mortgages for property. Building Societies were non-profit-making 'Friendly Societies', while the main banks were plcs seeking to make profit for their shareholders.

Customer loyalty was incredibly high — very few people changed their banks or building societies. Cash transactions tended to take place within banks prior to the introduction of ATMs (cash machines) and there were few different types of account. Hence the convenience of the branch was the main selling point for the banks. The opening of new branches became the way to get new customers and, with the high degree of brand loyalty, it was crucial to get to customers who did not yet possess bank accounts. Consequently, branches were set up on university campuses to attract 18-year-old students, most of whom did not have bank accounts before leaving school.

Traditionally, employers paid their staff in cash, so many individuals had no bank account. However, more and more businesses began to pay their workers by direct payment into bank accounts. Banks marketed their services to these businesses, encouraging them to get their employees to open accounts in the same branch as the company's account. Financial benefits were often offered to workers who opened a new account.

Banking since 1986

This stability in banking changed with the Building Society Act (1986), which allowed building societies to become banks and so provide a much wider range of services. Although they were smaller than banks, their low overheads enabled them to compete by offering favourable rates of interest to customers. This created much more competition in the banking industry.

Consumers began to expect wider choice and became more prepared to look around for accounts that suited their needs or loans with competitive interest rates. Banks started to provide more accounts and made it easier and cheaper for individuals to get loans. With high property prices, many homeowners felt secure and became much more willing to borrow money to improve their lifestyles, and banks were quick to cash in on this trend.

Longer working hours meant that people could no longer visit their branches. In response, more and more cash machines were introduced and banks started to open on Saturday mornings. As changes in lifestyle took people away from high street shopping to out-of-town shopping areas, the banks started to set up cash machines in these areas. This suited all parties: customers could pick up cash close to where they wished to spend it; and the banks and shops filled the machines from their daily cash takings and so saved money on employing security firms to transport money between the shops and the banks. Over half of all cash machines are now located away from bank premises.

The use of credit cards increased dramatically as people recognised their convenience for making purchases without carrying cash. Banks were able to use their customer databases to encourage customers to use debit cards or acquire the banks' own credit cards, so they had a natural advantage over rival credit-card suppliers such as MBNA and Capital One.

During the 1990s, fewer customers were using bank branches as cash machines, credit cards and internet banking grew. Another change in the market was the growth in communications, partly fuelled by the internet. This gave customers much better information on alternative offerings within the industry, and much of the marketing of banking services in recent years has concentrated on comparisons of interest rates and special offers. In order to deliver the cheapest loan or the highest rate on savings, the big banks have followed a policy of branch closures. Currently 55% of cash withdrawals are from cash machines. By 2012 this is predicted to exceed 75%.

However, the closure of bank branches has not gone smoothly. While the majority of customers were content to use cash machines, many valued the personal contact provided by people working within the branches. Table 1.3 shows the breakdown of cash machine users by age.

Age of customer	% of age range who are regular users
Under 25	88
25–34	91
35–44	73
45–54	55
55+	42
Average	**67**

Source: www.link.co.uk.

Table 1.3 *Customers who are regular users of ATMs, 2003*

The table shows that older people are less inclined to use ATMs. This fact was used by the NatWest bank in its marketing. It halted its plans to close branches and introduced a series of adverts showing images such as an old lady bewildered by the fact that her bank has been converted into a 'trendy wine bar'. (Ironically, NatWest had already closed a quarter of its branches in the 5 years previous to the marketing campaign.) These images were deliberately aimed at older customers, who are most likely to use bank branches.

Despite evidence that customers are becoming less happy with their banks, customer loyalty remains high. Less than 10% of all customers have changed their bank in recent years, despite dissatisfaction caused by bank charges, the quality of service and branch closures. The main reason for this inertia is fear of mistakes being made when an account is transferred.

Source: www.link.co.uk.

Questions

Total: 40 marks (45 minutes)

1 Based on the case study, indicate whether you believe the banking industry was asset-led or market-led in its approach *before 1986*. Justify your conclusion. *(20 marks)*

2 Based on the case study, indicate whether you believe the banking industry is asset-led or market-led *at present*. Justify your conclusion. *(20 marks)*

CHAPTER 2

Sales forecasting techniques

> **EXAMINER'S VOICE**
> Sales forecasting is a crucial part of **marketing planning**. However, in the AQA specification, the main quantitative techniques for sales forecasting are detailed under 'Market Analysis' in the section on extrapolation and correlation. To avoid repetition, the whole of sales forecasting has been incorporated into this chapter because all of the techniques require analysis of the market

In this chapter we look at the need for forecasting and the differences between qualitative forecasting (based on human judgement or opinion) and quantitative forecasting (based on statistical data). The different methods of forecasting are described with particular emphasis on the two main quantitative techniques: extrapolation and correlation. In looking at extrapolation, we identify the importance of trends and show the significance of seasonal variations. When considering correlation, the importance of high correlation and the pitfalls in using this technique for forecasting are considered. The difficulties associated with particular methods and of forecasting in general are also discussed.

Sales forecasting

KEY TERM

sales forecast: a prediction of the level of sales revenue for individual products or for the organisation as a whole.

Sales forecasting serves a number of purposes. As with any target, it can be used by the managers of an organisation to:

- measure the performance of an individual or department
- motivate staff by presenting them with a realistic but challenging target
- monitor achievements against targets in order to put into place remedial action if necessary, or to adopt a successful technique in other areas of the business

More specifically, its main use within an organisation is to coordinate the activities of a range of departments:

- Once agreed, the sales forecast allows the production department to plan its schedules and the ordering of raw materials. It also enables this department to identify any additional capital equipment that will be required.
- It helps the personnel department in its workforce planning, so that it can identify any potential shortages or surpluses of labour, requiring more recruitment or possibly redundancy. It also identifies the training needs of the organisation, where new skills are required by certain staff in order to reach the sales targets.
- It enables the finance department to finalise its cash-flow and profit and loss planning. This ensures that enough funds are available to each department and also assists the business in confirming the financial viability of the sales targets.

- It gives the marketing department itself confirmation of the strategies that it must employ in order to hit the sales targets.

Qualitative forecasting

KEY TERM

qualitative forecasting: methods of prediction that are based on personal opinions. These are often described as 'hunches', but are influenced by the personal knowledge and experiences of the individuals who are involved in the forecasting.

In business, trends do not tend to follow smooth patterns, so any forecasting techniques based on observing statistics from the past (quantitative forecasting) will have limitations. Qualitative forecasting attempts to overcome these limitations by introducing human understanding.

Methods of qualitative forecasting

The Delphi/Oracle technique

Named after the home of the oracle of ancient Greece, this approach relies on the firm asking individual experts for their views. These expert opinions are then collated into an overall consensus of future events, allowing a more accurate prediction of future sales to be made.

Brainstorming

This method involves all of the individuals concerned with the product or service. A relatively unstructured meeting is conducted in which all ideas are noted and then the more feasible suggestions are considered in depth. Brainstorming tends to be used most often for problem solving, but ideas from brainstorming sessions can be useful in predicting future sales.

Individual hunch

Ultimately, a particular manager will be held responsible for the product or service being considered. Based on his/her own understanding of the market, the manager may feel that sales will increase or decrease at a particular rate, even if other evidence suggests otherwise. As a result, some forecasts will be based on individual hunch, although this hunch may be based on customer feedback or qualitative market research.

Reasons for using qualitative forecasting

Most forecasting is based on a mix of qualitative and quantitative methods. Qualitative forecasting is more likely to be relied on when:

- the forecast concerns a new product or business, so there is no previous information on which to base predictions. In these circumstances, people's opinions are the most reliable predictor of the future. Alternatively, the firm may possess only a limited amount of data, so predictions will lack accuracy.

- there is no clear statistical indication of future sales. It is possible that quantitative methods (see pp. 15–27) are unable to produce a reliable forecast. Past sales may have fluctuated considerably with no obvious pattern, or there may be no evidence to suggest a link between a particular variable (such as price) and actual sales revenue.
- trends may have changed, so it would be unwise to predict on the basis of past statistics. For example, it may be known that a product has entered the maturity stage of its life cycle, so the predicted rate of growth needs to be adjusted downwards.
- the factors influencing sales may not be easy to quantify (measure in terms of numbers). Fashion items and the entertainment industry are often difficult to predict, and an experienced manager may be able to deliver a more accurate forecast than any attempt based on statistical data.
- the character of the individuals is important. In this case, a particular individual will be responsible for the forecast and will therefore want to make the final decision. This is also more probable if the manager has a mistrust of statistics or operates in an autocratic manner and so would want to make the decision.

EXAMINER'S VOICE

Note that all of these reasons for qualitative forecasting are limitations on the use of quantitative forecasting or reasons why a firm would *not* want to use quantitative forecasting.

Limitations of qualitative forecasting

- Experts may be knowledgeable, but it is unlikely that they will understand all aspects of a market.
- Many trends and relationships are broadly consistent over time, so forecasts based on quantitative data are more accurate than hunches or opinions.
- It is easier to persuade a more senior manager if your forecast is based on scientific methods.

FACT FILE

Qualitative forecasting has always played a major role in the toy market. Sudden crazes defy more scientific methods of analysis. Even long-established products such as Barbie can suddenly lose favour to new products such as Bratz dolls, which have recorded worldwide sales of 80 million dolls in 3 years and contributed to a major decline in sales of Barbie products.

More generally, there have been two significant changes in the UK toy market. Children are growing up more quickly, with girls as young as 7 rejecting dolls as being 'too childish'. By the age of 13 most children have totally abandoned the toy market. This trend has partly been offset by parents buying more toys. The divorce rate has increased and this may have led to more expensive and extra present-giving by both parents, perhaps based on feelings of guilt.

Source: www.keynote.co.uk.

- Ignoring statistical information may leave a manager open to criticism if predictions turn out to be incorrect. Managers may avoid qualitative forecasting to protect themselves from such criticism.

Conclusion

In general, new businesses (which lack backdata and market research) and managers in small firms (where time might be seen to be crucial and where there are no senior managers to whom the decision-makers must justify their decision) are more likely to use qualitative forecasting.

Quantitative forecasting

quantitative forecasting: those methods of prediction that are based on statistical information.

Quantitative forecasting usually relies on the assumption that the past will provide an accurate prediction of the future.

Methods of quantitative forecasting

The main methods of quantitative forecasting are:

- using backdata
- forecasting based on market research
- analysis of trends and extrapolation
- correlation

We will look at each of these in detail.

Using backdata

backdata: data taken from the past.

A firm can use backdata to predict the future. For example, a canteen may know from backdata that on Tuesdays typically 80% of the workers from the factory buy a meal, but only 60% of the office staff do so. Thus if there are 100 factory workers and 50 office workers, it will expect to sell 110 meals (80% of 100 plus 60% of 50 = 80 + 30 = 110).

TOPFOTO

Similarly, firms may know that a certain level of sales in test marketing is needed in order to obtain a successful launch of a new product, or that a two for the price of one special offer will usually increase sales by a certain amount.

Forecasting based on market research

Market research is carried out before a product is launched. By collecting together consumers' opinions, a business can gain awareness of how many consumers will buy the product and in what quantities. Market research can also be used to find out what the firm can do to get the best chance of success.

TOPFOTO

However, market research tends to be more accurate with existing products than with those that are totally new. It is difficult for consumers to know whether they will buy a product before it is launched. Moreover, new products are often heavily marketed at launch, so they enjoy high sales for a short period.

Secondary market research can also be used to forecast possible sales. For example, some market research organisations have developed sophisticated models that identify the types of customer who prefer specific supermarkets. These data are then sold to supermarkets to help them decide on their new store locations. When Morrisons bought Safeways, the Competition Commission allowed Morrisons to buy Safeways only if it agreed to sell certain Safeways stores (those in close competition with Morrisons). This type of market research is being used by Tesco, ASDA and Sainsbury's to decide which are the best stores for them to buy.

Analysis of trends and extrapolation

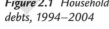

KEY TERMS

trend: the underlying pattern of change indicated within a set of numerical data.

extrapolation: using the previous patterns of numerical data in order to predict values in the future.

Figure 2.1 Household debts, 1994–2004

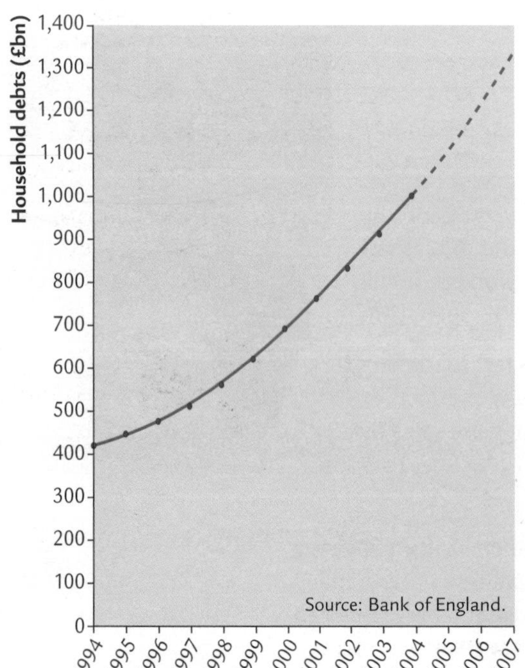

Predicting future sales using extrapolation

In effect, trend analysis examines the pattern of historic data and assumes that this pattern will continue in the future. If sales of a product have increased at 5% per annum in the recent past, the process of extrapolation will forecast that sales will continue to rise by 5% a year.

Extrapolation can be carried out visually or by calculation, although the latter method is recommended for greater accuracy.

Figure 2.1 shows the increase in household debt in the UK between 1994 and 2004. A business might wish to forecast future levels of debt, as the amount that people are prepared to borrow is a key factor in consumers' decisions to buy major items, such as houses, vehicles, household appliances (white goods) and furniture.

Visually, it is easy to see how the level of household debt is expected to increase in the future. The line shows that total debt in 2004 was £1,000 billion. The dashed line continues this pattern into the future (extrapolation). From this extrapolated line we can predict that household debt in the future is likely to be as follows:

2005: £1,100 billion
2006: £1,210 billion
2007: £1,331 billion

Where there is a clear pattern of change (as in Figure 2.1), it is easy to calculate the trend by calculating the average change for a period of time and extrapolating data into the future, on the assumption that this trend will continue. Household debt has been increasing at the rate of 10% per annum in recent years. Based on the 2004 level of £1,000 billion and adding 10% each year we can predict that household debt in the future is likely to be as follows:

2005: £1,100 billion
2006: £1,210 billion
2007: £1,331 billion

Table 2.1 shows the number of mobile telephone handsets sold globally between 2001 and 2004.

Year	Global sales (millions of handsets)
2001	404
2002	479
2003	573
2004	677

Source: DrKW.

Table 2.1 *Global sales of mobile telephone handsets, 2001–04*

To forecast sales for 2005 and 2006 we need to calculate the trend (the average increase per annum). Between 2001 and 2004 (3 years), sales rose from 404 million to 677 million, an increase of 273 million. The annual increase is therefore 273 million divided by 3 = 91 million per annum.

Projecting the trend therefore gives us the forecasts for the next 3 years shown in Table 2.2.

Year	Global sales (millions of handsets)
2004	677 (actual sales)
2005	677 + 91 = 768
2006	768 + 91 = 859
2007	859 + 91 = 950

Table 2.2 *Sales forecast for mobile telephone handsets, 2004–07*

Of course, this is only an estimate. Using quantitative analysis it could be argued that the rate of growth is increasing (+75 million between 2001 and 2002 but +94 million between 2002 and 2003 and +104 million between 2003 and 2004). Our method takes the average of these three increases, so it does not take into account the increase in the rate of growth.

EXAMINER'S VOICE

In an examination, it is vital that you can justify your answer. Therefore it is essential that you use a specific method of forecasting. You may wish to add a comment on its lack of reliability, but make sure that the examiner can see that your answer came from a particular method.

In both of the above examples there was a clear pattern of steady change. However, many sets of statistics have a less clear pattern. There may be an overall fall or rise, interspersed with fluctuations. To predict sales, the trend must be separated from the fluctuations. The techniques for doing this are known as moving averages and seasonal variations.

Qualitatively, it is argued that the global mobile telephone market is reaching maturity. This information would lead us to predict a slowing down of the rate of growth in the next few years.

For these reasons, the actual forecast may be based on a combination of methods.

Predicting future sales based on moving averages and seasonal variations

KEY TERM

moving averages: statistics used to analyse trends in the recent past so that a firm can predict future sales (through extrapolation).

Moving averages are calculated by combining data over a period of time in such a way that changes caused by fluctuations are eliminated or at least reduced. For example, many data are affected by the seasons of the year. If the trend is based on sets of numbers all representing exactly a year, then any seasonal effect will be eliminated.

KEY TERM

fluctuations or variations: periods of time when sales are above or below the trend.

Although sales may be increasing at an average rate of 5% per annum, there are periods of time when the rate of growth fluctuates above or below this level of growth. There are three main types of fluctuation:

- **Cyclical.** Sales of most products fluctuate according to the business (trade) cycle, with above average increases in boom periods and below average rises (or even falling sales) in downturns and recessions.
- **Seasonal.** Very few products sell consistently throughout the year. It is possible to measure seasonal variations by looking at the level of sales at a particular time of the year, in comparison to the trend figure.
- **Random.** Sales can vary for a wide range of reasons, such as changes in fashion or taste, production difficulties, favourable or adverse publicity, and changes in the weather.

FACT FILE

Fluctuations are not always unpredictable. In June 2004 there were dramatic changes in shopping habits while England played in the Euro 2004 football championship. However, market research organisations that use **footfall**, a technique that measures the total number of people in a shopping centre at any one time, were able to draw on experience of previous football championships to inform retailers of the probable changes in the shopping habits of customers during the tournament. As a consequence, the retailers were more able to cope with the sudden changes to normal shopping patterns that took place.

Source: www.footfall.com.

Moving averages allow an organisation to calculate a trend scientifically using a series of calculations designed to eliminate fluctuations within a series of data. The use of moving averages should smooth out the impact of random variations in data and longer-term cyclical factors, and thus highlight the trend. If the fluctuation is cyclical, the moving averages should be based on the span of the business/trade cycle (4 or 5 years). If the fluctuation is caused by seasonal factors, the moving average should be based on a period of exactly 1 year. It is not possible to use this method reliably if the fluctuations are random.

By predicting trends, firms are able to forecast future sales. This information is invaluable in helping to plan production and draw up human resource plans, and is the basis of much financial planning.

Table 2.3 overleaf shows the international sales of Nike products between the third quarter of 2001 and the second quarter of 2004. Although there has been a clear increase in sales, this has not been spread evenly over each quarter. Nike sells many winter products, such as basketball equipment, and trades in the southern hemisphere more than most firms. However, on balance its sales are slightly higher in quarters 2 and 3 because these tend to be the warmer months (April to September) in the northern hemisphere, where it records most of its sales.

In order to predict future sales, it is necessary to calculate:

- the trend (the overall pattern of change in the sales over time)
- seasonal variations (fluctuations in sales caused by the time of year rather than the general trend)

Table 2.3 shows how it is possible to separate these two factors in order to forecast future sales.

Columns 1–3 present the actual sales achieved by Nike in the recent past. Thus, in the third quarter of 2001 it gained international sales of $2.56 billion; by the second quarter of 2004 it was achieving sales of $3.48 billion, and so on.

If there were no seasonal variation, it would be acceptable to use these two figures (the beginning and end of the time period) in order to calculate the trend. However, the first figure in column 3 represents Nike's sales in the summer (July, August and September) of 2001 and the last figure in column 3 gives Nike's sales in the spring (April, May and June) of 2004, so we would not be comparing like with like.

This problem is overcome by calculating the four-quarter totals shown in column 4. By adding together four successive quarters, we are covering the whole year and so there is no seasonal effect. This four-quarter figure is excellent for showing the overall trend, as the seasonal variations have been eliminated.

However, if we add all of the sales for four successive quarters, there is a problem when we try to compare this figure to our quarterly sales. In Table 2.3 the first four quarters are from quarter 3 of 2001 to quarter 2 of 2002. On a graph we would plot this figure halfway through the year — this is the point at which we reach the end of quarter 4 of 2001 and the beginning of quarter 1 of 2002.

(1) Year	(2) Quarter	(3) Sales ($bn)	(4) Sales: four-quarter total ($bn)	(5) Sales: eight-quarter total ($bn)	(6) Sales: trend figures ($bn)	(7) Seasonal variation ($bn)
2001	3	2.56				
	4	2.31				
			9.67			
2002	1	2.26		19.60	2.45	-0.19
			9.93			
	2	2.54		20.07	2.51	+0.03
			10.14			
	3	2.82		20.38	2.55	+0.27
			10.24			
	4	2.52		20.94	2.62	-0.10
			10.70			
2003	1	2.36		21.70	2.71	-0.35
			11.00			
	2	3.00		22.30	2.79	+0.21
			11.30			
	3	3.12		23.10	2.89	+0.23
			11.80			
	4	2.82		24.08	3.01	-0.19
			12.28			
2004	1	2.86				
	2	3.48				

Source: Nike company reports.

Table 2.3 *International sales of Nike products, 2001–04*

To calculate the seasonal variations, we need to compare the trend to the sales figure for a particular quarter. To do this we need to use a process known as **centring**. In this case, the eight-quarter sales figure is used. By adding the first two four-quarter totals, we are in effect adding the following eight figures:

2001 quarter 3
2001 quarter 4 (twice)
2002 quarter 1 (twice) ← midpoint of the data
2002 quarter 2 (twice)
2002 quarter 3

This gives us an even spread of data across the calendar year (two figures from quarter 1, two figures from quarter 2, two figures from quarter 3 and two figures from quarter 4), thus overcoming any seasonal variations. The midpoint of these figures is clearly 2002 quarter 1. In other words, the data are *centred* around 2002 quarter 1.

Column 5 covers eight quarters (equivalent to 2 years) of sales. If we divide the column 5 figures by 8, we get a figure that represents one quarter's sales, shown in column 6. The figures in column 6 represent the **trend** — these are the sales figures we would expect to achieve having eliminated the effect caused by seasonal variations.

The trend is calculated by working out the average change per quarter. In column 6 we started with a trend figure of 2.45 in quarter 1 of 2002 and ended with a figure of 3.01 in quarter 4 of 2003. However, as we are starting with the first quarter and ending at the eighth quarter, the changes, in effect, span seven quarters.

The trend per quarter is measured by the total change in the trend divided by the change in the number of quarters.

$$\text{trend per quarter} = \frac{3.01 - 2.45}{7} = \frac{+0.56}{7} = +0.08 \text{ per quarter}$$

It is important to put this back into the units of measurement being used: 0.08 does not seem to be very much, but this means that Nike's international sales are increasing by \$0.08 billion (\$80,000 million) per quarter.

We can now compare column 6 (the figure we would expect if there were no seasonal variation) with column 3 (the actual sales figures achieved by Nike). (Note that we cannot do this for the first pair and final pair of quarterly figures.)

seasonal variation = actual sales – trend figure sales

Thus for quarter 1 of 2002 the seasonal variation is:

\$2.26 billion – \$2.45 billion = –\$0.19 billion

Table 2.4 summarises the seasonal variations.

Quarter	2002	2003	Average variation
1	–0.19	–0.35	–0.27
2	+0.03	+0.21	+0.12
3	+0.27	+0.23	+0.25
4	–0.10	–0.19	–0.15

Table 2.4
Seasonal variations in sales of Nike products, 2002–03

Seasonal factors are rarely consistent and it can be seen that there are differences between 2002 and 2003. For future predictions, the average variation is used. For quarter 3, for example, this is the average of +0.27 and +0.23, which is +0.25.

(Technically, a further adjustment can be made to make the total seasonal variations equal to zero, but for sales predictions this is not really necessary.)

Predicting future sales using the trend and seasonal variation

Based on our calculations, we would expect sales to increase by \$0.08 billion for every quarter, plus or minus the seasonal variation for that quarter.

Table 2.5 shows predicted sales for 2005 and 2006 based on the above calculations.

(Column 3 starts with the final trend figure (3.01 for quarter 4 of 2003). It then adds the quarterly trend figure of 0.08 to each quarter. Therefore, future trend figures are:

2004 quarter 1: 3.01 + 0.08 = 3.09
2004 quarter 2: 3.01 + (2 × 0.08) = 3.17
2004 quarter 3: 3.01 + (3 × 0.08) = 3.25, etc.

Table 2.5
Predicted sales for Nike products, 2005–06

(1) Year	(2) Quarter	(3) Predicted trend	(4) Seasonal variations	(5) Predicted sales
2003	4	3.01		
2004	1	3.09		
	2	3.17		
	3	3.25		
	4	3.33		
2005	1	3.41	–0.27	3.14
	2	3.49	+0.12	3.61
	3	3.57	+0.25	3.82
	4	3.65	–0.15	3.50
2006	1	3.73	–0.27	3.46
	2	3.81	+0.12	3.93
	3	3.89	+0.25	4.14
	4	3.97	–0.15	3.82

Column 4 shows the seasonal variations that must be added (or subtracted), as calculated in Table 2.4. For each future quarter 1, we would expect actual sales to be 0.27 below the trend; each quarter 2 will be predicted to be 0.12 above the trend.

Adding columns 3 and 4 gives us the prediction for each quarter (column 5). Although Nike is increasing sales by an average of $80,000 million for each quarter, it is worth noting that sales are predicted to fall at times because of the seasonal decline in sales in quarters 1 and 4.

DID YOU KNOW?

Centring is needed when there is an even number of sets of figures within a cycle. Thus for most seasonal variations it is essential, as the seasons are measured as either 4 quarters or 12 months. However, for odd-numbered sets of data it is not necessary. If the business cycle is treated as a 5-year cycle, the average of years 1–5 is plotted against the midpoint (year 3), so no further adjustments are needed; similarly, years 2–6 are plotted against year 4.

In the same way, as there are 7 days in a week, any fluctuations can be calculated without centring.

Weaknesses of extrapolation

Extrapolation suffers from a number of weaknesses:

- It is less reliable if there are fluctuations. Seasonal and cyclical changes are rarely repeated exactly and random fluctuations are very unpredictable.
- It assumes that past changes will continue into the future and thus does not take into account changes in the business environment that will influence sales, including changes within the business itself.
- It ignores qualitative factors.
- Trends do not often follow a straight line, so extrapolation can be open to interpretation if the changes are uneven.

Figure 2.2
Sales of DVD players in the UK, 1998–2003

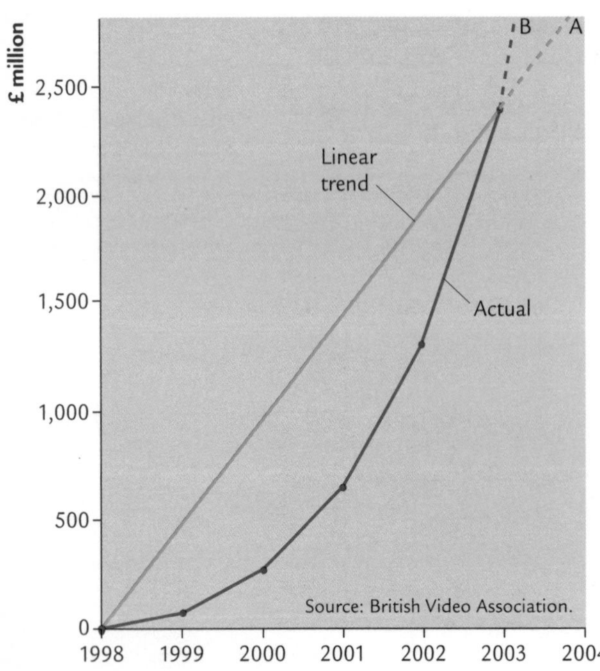

However, extrapolation is useful as a guideline and is widely used in business as a reliable tool in sales forecasting. Figure 2.2 shows the UK sales of DVD players since 1998.

If a linear (straight-line) extrapolation is used, the sales forecast is likely to be an underestimate. This is because the straight-line extrapolation (line A) is based on the average increase, which includes years such as 1999 when actual growth was quite low.

In these cases it is best to use a non-linear extrapolation, as shown by line B. (However, this must be used with caution, as most rapidly increasing trends will diminish as market saturation is reached.)

Correlation

correlation: a statistical technique used to establish the strength of the relationship between two sets of values.

Correlation can be a useful technique for sales forecasting, as it can show (statistically or graphically) the degree to which factors such as price, the advertising budget or even external factors, such as the proximity of competitors, are linked to sales of a product.

Graphically, the correlation between two sets of data is shown in a scatter diagram or scatter graph. The independent variable (the one causing the other to change) is plotted on the horizontal, x-axis. The dependent variable (the one being influenced) is plotted on the vertical, y-axis. So if we are trying to look at different factors that influence sales of a product, we plot sales on the y-axis and the other factor on the x-axis.

Once the points have been plotted, a line of best fit (or regression line) is added. The line can be drawn graphically 'by eye' but is more accurate if calculated mathematically. (An Excel spreadsheet will construct a scatter graph and will then calculate and add the regression line to any pairs of data that need to be compared.)

The line of best fit (regression line) is used to forecast. For any value of x a line is drawn vertically until it meets the regression line. From this point a line is then drawn horizontally to the y-axis in order to read the forecast value of the dependent variable. For example, in Figure 2.3(a) if $x = 20$, we would forecast $y = 4$. In Figure 2.3(b) if $x = 20$, our forecast for y would be 12.

Figure 2.3 shows the seven different examples of correlation.

Figures 2.3(a), (b) and (c) show **positive** correlation. This means that as x increases in value, the value of y also increases.

Figures 2.3(d), (e) and (f) show **negative** correlation. This means that as x increases in value, the value of y decreases.

Figure 2.3(g) shows no apparent correlation between the two sets of data.

Figures 2.3(a) and (d) show **perfect** correlation. All of the points plotted lie on the line of best fit. This means that we would expect 100% accuracy in our predictions. In the business world, it is unlikely that any sets of data would ever be linked as closely as this.

Figures 2.3(b) and (e) show strong or **high** correlation. The line of best fit is fairly close to the points plotted on the graph, so we could be confident that our forecasts were fairly reliable.

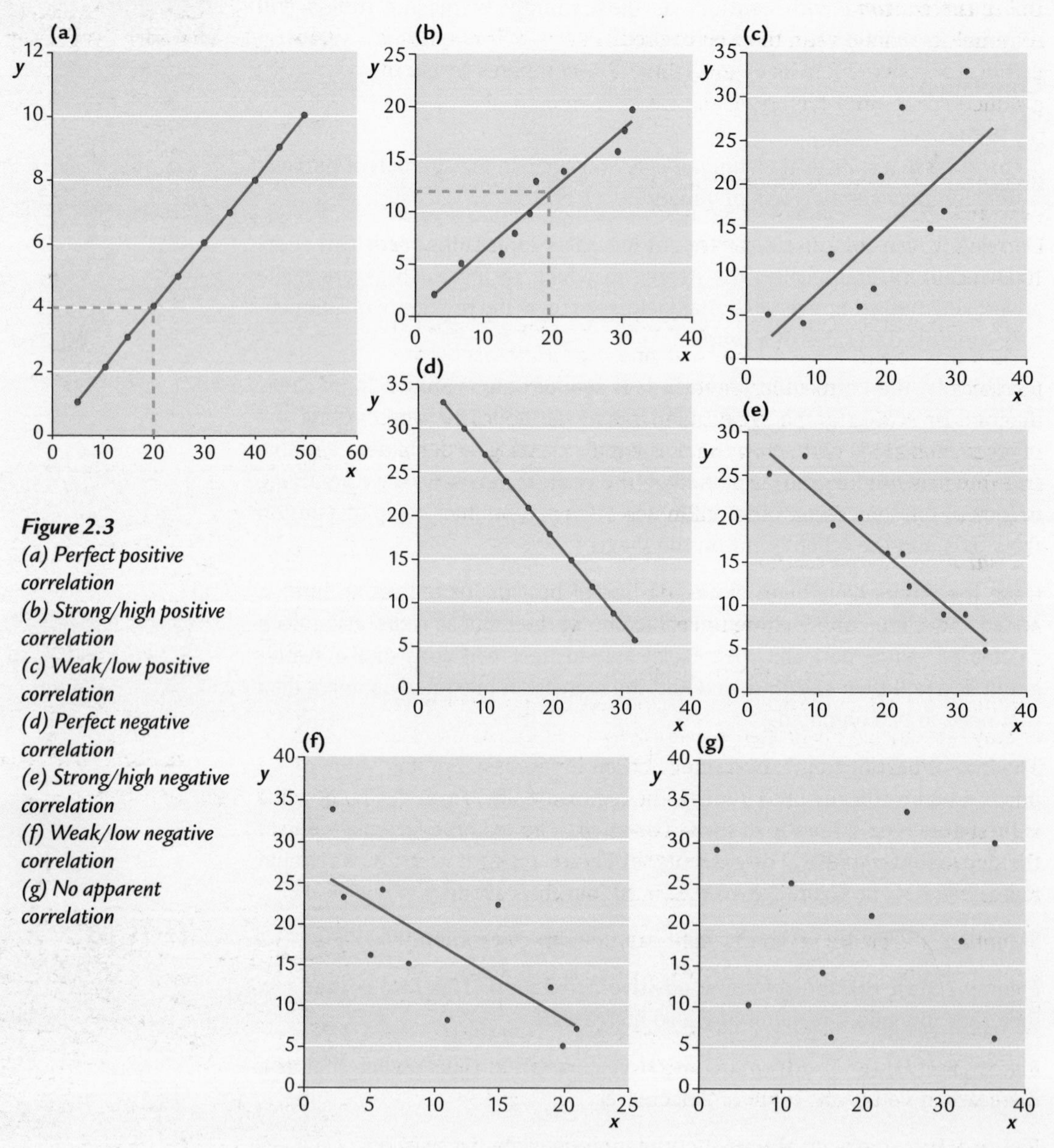

Figure 2.3
(a) Perfect positive correlation
(b) Strong/high positive correlation
(c) Weak/low positive correlation
(d) Perfect negative correlation
(e) Strong/high negative correlation
(f) Weak/low negative correlation
(g) No apparent correlation

Figure 2.3(c) and (f) show weak or **low** correlation. The line of best fit is not close to all of the points, although there is some link between the sets of data. We might wish to use the line of best fit to make forecasts, but these forecasts would not be reliable.

Figure 2.3(g) shows no apparent correlation between the two sets of data. Forecasts should not be made because there is no detectable link between the two variables.

Using correlation

Although correlation can be used to predict sales, it is employed in other aspects of business too. Table 2.6 compares levels of production within a factory to the number of staff absent on a particular day.

Figure 2.4 shows this information on a scatter diagram. As expected, the graph shows a high negative correlation. We would be able to make confident forecasts, as long as we did not expect 100% accuracy.

From the regression line, the firm can forecast that if 5 members of staff are absent, then 17 units of production are likely to be produced; if only 1 member of staff is away, then production is likely to rise to 31 units. Each person absent is likely to lead to a fall in production of 3.5 units. However, it is worth reflecting on the fact that these are only generalisations. On the day on which only one person was absent, actual production was 28 units (not 31).

Date	Units of production	Number of staff absent
5.9.2005	15	5
6.9.2005	18	4
7.9.2005	30	2
8.9.2005	28	1
9.9.2005	11	7
12.9.2005	12	6
13.9.2005	32	2
14.9.2005	25	3
15.9.2005	24	3
16.9.2005	10	8

Table 2.6 *Impact of staff absence on production*

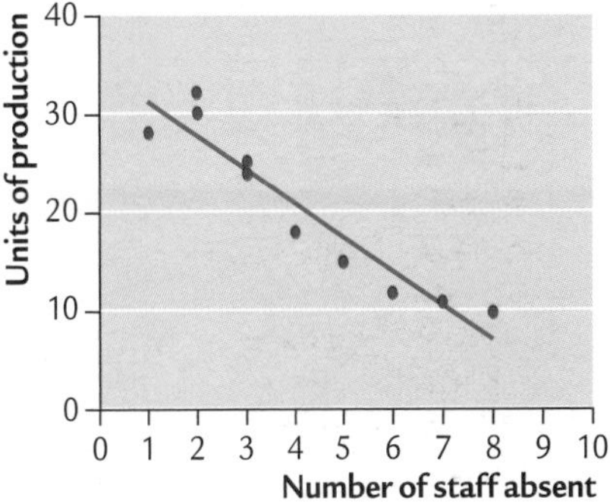

Figure 2.4 *Impact of staff absence on production*

Causal links in correlation

It has been said that 'There are lies, damn lies and statistics.' The speaker was probably looking at correlation at the time!

It is highly probable that one set of statistics will correlate with another. After all, over time a set of numbers can go up or down or stay the same. This limited set of alternatives means that it is possible to find apparently close connections between sets of data purely by coincidence. The rise in obesity in the UK correlates very strongly with the increase in medals for the UK in recent Olympics. However, it is unlikely that the two could be connected, at least until sumo wrestling is introduced into the Games.

Sometimes there is a third factor that influences the two apparently linked sets of data. For example, a school found a high degree of correlation between feet sizes and IQ test results. However, as the same IQ test was given to all pupils in the school, it was 'age' that led both to better IQ scores and to bigger feet; there was no proof that children's brains are in their feet.

Before drawing any conclusions that there is a link between two sets of information it is essential that a **causal link** is discovered. It is logical to expect that higher sunshine will cause people to consume more ice cream because of the desire to eat something cool. However, if it was found that more people bought overcoats in the summer, there would be no logic in suggesting that the temperature rise caused this behaviour. Instead we would need to look for other factors (such as shops selling overcoats cheaply at this time to get rid of old stock).

Once a causal link is discovered, correlation can be useful to identify the extent of the link between the two series of data.

On rare occasions, it can be difficult to distinguish between cause and effect. It is well known that price rises and wage increases are strongly correlated, but it is not easy to decide which is the dependent variable and which is the independent variable. Looking for causal connections, it can be concluded that price rises (and thus inflation) lead workers to demand higher wages so that their living standards are protected. However, high wages cause company costs to increase and so force businesses to put up prices. Furthermore, wage rises encourage people to spend more money and can make people more prepared to pay a higher price as they feel richer. The only logical conclusion is that they both influence each other.

FACT FILE

The popular Atkins diet is based on people eating specific products and avoiding carbohydrates. Research has shown high levels of correlation between the growing numbers of people following the Atkins diet and sales of certain food products. Sales of low-carb Miller Lite increased so dramatically that overall sales of SABMiller increased by 41%. The beef industry has also profited from people switching their diets and eating more meat.

In the UK, the Atkins diet is blamed for a 10% fall in purchases of potatoes and Unilever has seen sales of its Slim-Fast range plummet. However, firms are responding: Heinz has launched a low-carb tomato ketchup and TGI Fridays is offering an Atkins-friendly menu.

There is a tendency to assume that a company would prefer a high correlation to a low correlation. This may be true for the purpose of forecasting, but accurate forecasts are not everything. Compare Figures 2.5 and 2.6.

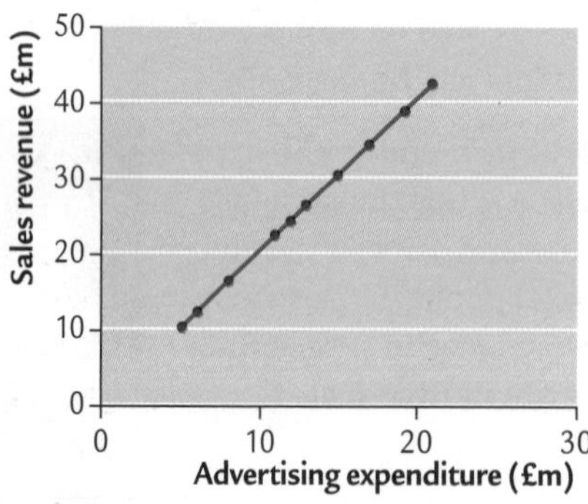

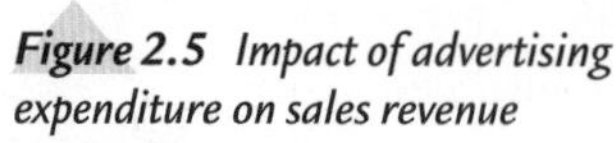

Figure 2.5 Impact of advertising expenditure on sales revenue

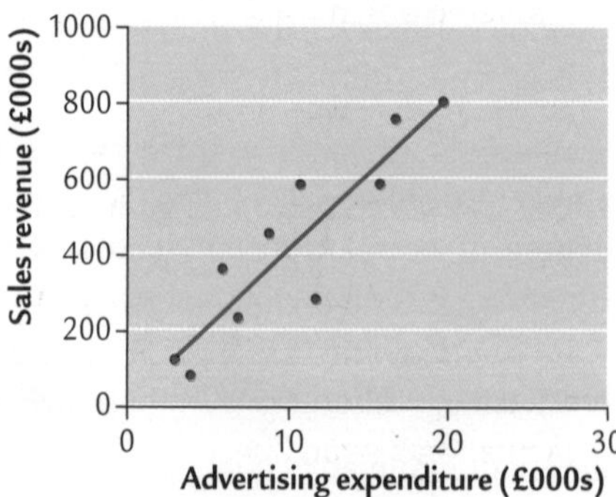

Figure 2.6 Impact of advertising expenditure on sales revenue

Figure 2.5 shows perfect positive correlation, indicating that extra advertising is likely to increase sales revenue by an exact amount. In this case, for every extra £1 spent on advertising, sales rise by £2. Although this is high correlation, it is not successful advertising. With all of the other costs involved, it is unlikely that a firm can make a profit if half of the sales revenue is going on advertising.

In contrast, Figure 2.6 shows a much lower level of positive correlation. However, look at the regression line and the scale on the y-axis. In this example, the gradient is much steeper. This shows that every extra £1 spent on advertising is linked to a possible increase in sales of revenue of £40. Although the forecast is much less certain, it shows that advertising is probably much more effective in creating extra sales.

The regression line (line of best fit) is every bit as important as the level of correlation. Do not ignore its importance.

Can you think of similar examples from the business world? Try to find real-life examples of Figures 2.5 and 2.6.

Limitations of quantitative forecasting

Quantitative forecasting makes sure that businesses scrutinise their predictions carefully and use a scientific form of analysis in their planning. However, there are a number of potential limitations that need to be considered when using it:

- Past trends do not always continue into the future.
- Correlation changes over time. For example, the major influence on sales might change from the price to the amount spent on advertising.
- External influences such as competitors' actions, consumers' tastes or the stages of the business cycle can vary over time.
- Corporate objectives may be amended, so that the sales target becomes more or less important.
- Internal policies or actions may change. For example, Kellogg's follows a policy of promoting a specific brand heavily for 6 months. It then focuses attention on other brands for the next 2 or 3 years.
- Market research used for forecasts may lack reliability. There may have been a small or biased sample, or the information may have become out of date by the time it was used.
- Forecasts become more difficult the further they project into the future. Thus, organisations tend to be less accurate with long-term forecasts than with short-term predictions.
- Quantitative techniques ignore the special understanding of the market possessed by the staff of a business. This awareness of the market may help a business to forecast changes that are different from those suggested by the factual data available.

The implications of incorrect forecasting

Businesses rely on accurate forecasting in their business planning.

If sales are overestimated, there is likely to be a waste of resources as the firm will produce too much. The cost to the firm depends on whether the products are perishable and how expensive they are to store. It also depends on whether the firm is flexible or not; a flexible workforce may be able to adjust

production levels quickly or, if the production is subcontracted, the firm may be able to shift the problem to a supplier.

Underestimation also causes problems. The opportunity cost of lost sales is high, especially if customer goodwill is undermined. If competitors have estimated correctly, the implications will be more severe than a situation in which the whole market has been wrongly forecast.

Mobile telephone companies lost money by overestimating the sales of third-generation (3G) mobiles. All of the main providers paid huge sums for licences to offer 3G services and only one operator, (3), has managed to get the system operating within a year of the start of the licences. All of these operators borrowed large sums of money based on forecasts of high sales and only one has received any returns (and most of its sales have been based on special offers of traditional mobile phone services rather than 3G services).

Conclusion

Although sales forecasts cannot be relied upon, they do give direction and targets for an organisation. Ideally, they should arise from a blend of qualitative and quantitative techniques.

Sales forecasts are more likely to be correct when:

- the product is well established and the market known
- external factors are predictable and there is stability in tastes and competitor actions
- the forecasts are made by, and agreed with, those involved in day-to-day contact with the market
- the organisation has undertaken detailed and reliable market research
- test marketing and/or backdata give the firm a clear understanding of the market

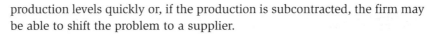

PRACTICE EXERCISE 1 — Total: 40 marks (35 minutes)

(These questions are based on pages 12–16.)

1 Explain how a production department would benefit from accurate sales forecasts. *(4 marks)*

2 Explain how a finance department would benefit from accurate sales forecasts. *(4 marks)*

3 Briefly explain two problems facing a personnel department if sales forecasts prove to be inaccurate. *(6 marks)*

4 Identify and describe three methods of qualitative forecasting. *(9 marks)*

5 Explain three reasons why a business might use qualitative forecasting. *(9 marks)*

6 What is meant by the term 'backdata'? *(2 marks)*

7 Analyse two possible benefits to a furniture store of using market research for forecasting sales. *(6 marks)*

PRACTICE EXERCISE 2

Total: 50 marks (55 minutes)

(These questions are based on pages 16–22.)

1 Figure 2.7 shows milk consumption in the UK between 1975 and 2002.

a Extrapolate the lines in the graph in order to forecast consumption levels in 2006 for:
(i) milk and cream
(ii) whole milk only
Show your workings. *(4 marks)*

b Calculate the trend for whole milk (the average fall per annum) for the period 1975 to 2002. Show your workings. *(4 marks)*

c Based on your answer to **b**, predict the year in which sales of whole milk will fall below 0.3 litres per person per week. Show your workings. *(4 marks)*

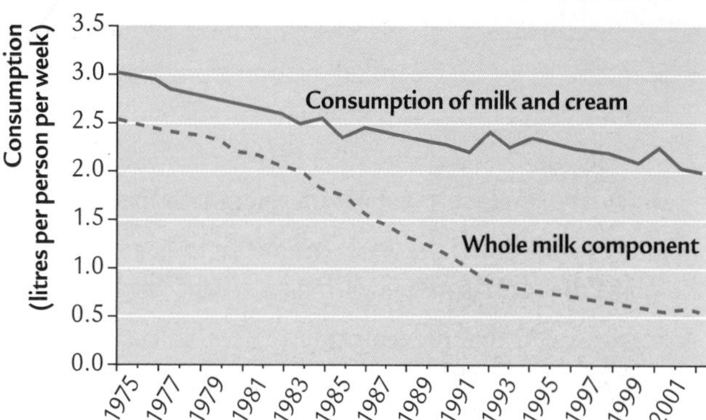

Figure 2.7 *Trends in average household milk consumption in the UK, 1975–2002*

Table 2.7 *Quarterly sales of hats in the UK (£000s), 2000–03*

Year	Quarter 1	Quarter 2	Quarter 3	Quarter 4
2000	14,623	12,133	14,763	12,822
2001	15,188	13,111	13,771	12,059
2002	11,851	11,212	11,318	10,776
2003	10,266	8,892	8,555	8,451

Source: Office for National Statistics.

2 Table 2.7 shows the quarterly sales of hats in the UK from 2000 to 2003.

a Plot these figures on a graph. *(6 marks)*

b Using moving averages, calculate the trend. *(8 marks)*

c Calculate the seasonal variations for each quarter. *(6 marks)*

d Use these calculations to forecast sales of hats in quarters 1 and 2 of 2005. *(6 marks)*

e Use the graph or your calculations to predict when the trend will fall below quarterly sales of £7 million. *(3 marks)*

f Explain three reasons why your forecast in part **e** may prove to be incorrect. *(9 marks)*

PRACTICE EXERCISE 3

Total: 15 marks (15 minutes)

(These questions are based on pages 23–27.)

1 Look at the seven charts in Figure 2.3 on page 24. Ignore Figures 2.3(a) and (d), which show perfect correlation. If the y-axis measures sales of a type of washing powder, identify an independent variable that would show high positive correlation (as in Figure 2.3(b)). Then identify a different independent variable that would show a low positive correlation (as in Figure 2.3(c)), and so on for Figures 2.3(e), (f) and (g). *(5 marks)*

2 Briefly justify each of your answers in question 1. *(10 marks)*

PRACTICE EXERCISE 4 Total: 20 marks (25 minutes)

Study the data on Unilever's ice cream sales in case study 1 (p. 31) and then answer the following questions.

1 Statistically, are ice cream sales more strongly correlated to the average temperature or hours of sunshine? Briefly explain your answer. *(4 marks)*

2 Study Figure 2.8. If the weather forecast indicates an average temperature of 4°C, what will be the forecast revenue from ice cream sales? *(2 marks)*

3 Study Figure 2.8. If the weather forecast indicates an average temperature of 16°C, what will be the forecast revenue from ice cream sales? *(2 marks)*

4 For every 1°C that the temperature rises, calculate the forecast increase in sales revenue for Wall's ice cream. *(2 marks)*

5 Study Figure 2.9. If the weather forecast indicates monthly sunshine of 50 hours, what will be the forecast revenue from ice cream sales? *(2 marks)*

6 Study Figure 2.9. If the weather forecast indicates monthly sunshine of 150 hours, what will be the forecast revenue from ice cream sales? *(2 marks)*

7 For every extra hour of sunshine, calculate the forecast increase in sales revenue for Wall's ice cream. *(2 marks)*

8 Identify two other factors that would have a positive correlation with ice cream sales. *(2 marks)*

9 Identify two factors that would have a negative correlation with ice cream sales. *(2 marks)*

CASE STUDY 1 The influence of the weather on sales

Sales levels of many products are influenced by the weather. A business that is able to establish this correlation is likely to be more exact in its forecasts than firms that are unaware of the link. Research by the French insurance giant AXA has found that beer sales increase by 3.2% for every 1°C rise in temperature. The research has even identified variations across the country: the 3.2% average conceals regional variations between 1.2% in the northeast and 5.2% on the south coast.

Of course, this assumes that weather forecasts are accurate. The Met Office claims that predictions are becoming more accurate. Today's 72-hour forecasts match the accuracy of the 24-hour forecasts of the previous decade and the number of accurate forecasts is continuing to rise as a greater understanding of weather patterns is established.

Sales figures also depend on the efficiency of firms' operations management. The record-breaking summer of 2003 saw acute shortages of fans, ice cream and lager. Carlsberg was able to benefit from this shortage by getting extra supplies from Denmark, and Currys profited from the fact that a European supplier had built up high stock levels of fans. But for most ice cream makers and organisations relying on just-in-time suppliers, the high temperatures represented a lost opportunity as the retailers ran out of stock.

As a result, businesses were well prepared for a sweltering summer in 2004. Unfortunately, the weather had other plans. On 19 August 2004, Nestlé identified poor weather conditions as a key cause of its failure to meet its growth targets. ASDA reported that spending patterns in August were close to the patterns normally witnessed in October. Boots reported a major decline

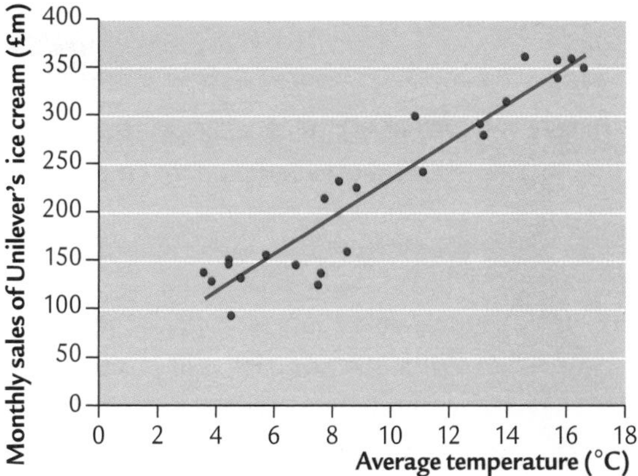

Figure 2.8 Correlation between sales of Unilever's ice cream and temperature, 2002–04

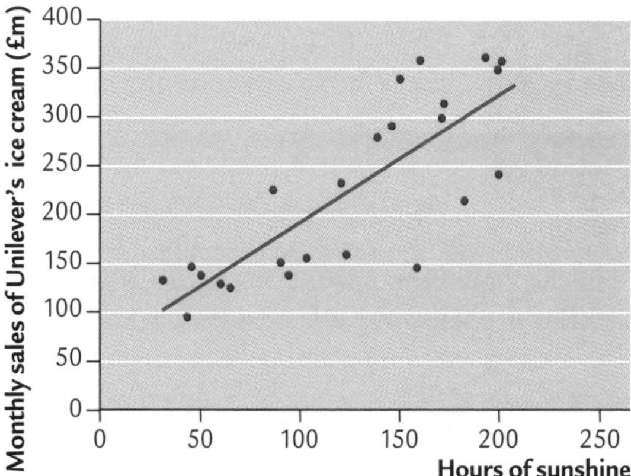

Figure 2.9 Correlation between sales of Unilever's ice cream and hours of sunshine, 2002–04

Month	Average temperature (°C)	Sales of Unilever's ice cream (£m)	Hours of sunshine
August 2002	15.7	340	149
September 2002	13.2	280	138
October 2002	8.8	226	86
November 2002	7.6	138	50
December 2002	4.8	133	31
January 2003	3.8	129	60
February 2003	3.5	138	94
March 2003	6.7	146	158
April 2003	7.7	215	182
May 2003	10.8	300	170
June 2003	14.6	362	192
July 2003	16.2	359	159
August 2003	16.6	350	198
September 2003	13.1	292	145
October 2003	8.2	233	120
November 2003	7.5	125	65
December 2003	4.4	147	45
January 2004	4.5	95	43
February 2004	4.4	152	90
March 2004	5.7	156	103
April 2004	8.5	160	123
May 2004	11.1	242	199
June 2004	14.0	315	171
July 2004	15.7	358	200

Source: Unilever and the Met Office.

Table 2.8 Sales of Unilever's ice cream compared to weather conditions

in sales of suntan lotion (but a 20% rise in fake tan products). Clothing retailers reported a 21% drop in sales of men's polo shirts and an 8% fall in sales of women's summer tops. Sales of weatherproof clothing, such as raincoats, were double their normal levels.

So how important is the weather to a traditional ice cream maker such as Unilever, which owns brands such as Wall's?

People expect ice cream sales to depend on the weather, but is there statistical proof of this link?

Table 2.8 shows the sales of Unilever's ice cream and weather information over a period of 2 years between August 2002 and July 2004. This information is plotted graphically in Figures 2.8 and Figure 2.9.

Sources: Unilever and the Met Office.

Question

Total: 20 marks (25 minutes)

Study the data in Table 2.8 and Figures 2.8 and 2.9. Evaluate how useful this information would be to Unilever in forecasting its ice cream sales.

CASE STUDY 2 The National Lottery

Since the first draw in November 1994, Camelot Group plc, the company that runs the lottery, has enjoyed mixed fortunes.

After very strong sales in the early years, sales peaked in 1997 and then fell. Having decided on a basic **price** of £1 for most of its products, Camelot concentrated on **place** and **promotion** as the key elements of its early marketing mix. Terminals were set up in a wide range of retail outlets, providing access for most potential customers. Before its opening, there was an intensive promotional campaign focused on two main messages: the charitable donations that the lottery would provide and the chance for participants to become millionaires. The crossed-fingers logo became one of the most widely recognised symbols in the UK.

Under the terms of the lottery agreement, Camelot is restricted in the amount of money it can spend on sales promotions. Consequently, it was unable to mount a huge advertising campaign in 1998 when sales started to fall (see Table 2.9).

Table 2.9 shows the following figures from 1995 to 2004:

- Camelot Group's promotions expenditure
- sales of all Camelot products

Figure 2.10 shows the actual sales of tickets, and the 3-year moving average, from 1995 to 2004. Figure 2.11 shows the correlation between Camelot's marketing expenditure and its total sales.

Camelot decided to focus more on **product**. A much broader range of scratch cards was brought out and additional draws such as 'Thunderball' were introduced. This period of decline coincided with adverse publicity surrounding the relatively low percentage of money going to good causes (approximately 29% of revenue), players becoming disillusioned by their lack of success in becoming millionaires, and newspaper headlines announcing the huge bonuses being paid to the senior executives of Camelot.

Much of the marketing budget has been spent on trying to restore Camelot's image. Between 2003 and 2004 the proportion of positive publicity about Camelot rose from 28% to 80%. Camelot's image has been helped by a successful 2004 Olympics for the Great Britain team. Many of the Olympic athletes received financial support from the lottery. Camelot has been actively providing press releases to the media on sports and community projects that have been supported by the lottery, most notably the building of the new Wembley Stadium.

Place has not been ignored. An additional 1,400 terminals have been opened in the last 2 years and Camelot is piloting the sale of lottery tickets on Sky Active and through mobile telephones and electronic point of sales (EPOS) checkouts in supermarkets.

A change to Camelot's **promotion** strategy began in the autumn of 2004. Camelot has started to broaden its use of the marketing mix. **Promotion** is now targeted

Financial year ending	Spending on promotions (£m)	Total sales (£m)
1995	93	4,721
1996	71	4,742
1997	75	5,500
1998	83	5,312
1999	92	5,127
2000	85	5,093
2001	89	4,983
2002	84	4,834
2003	83	4,575
2004	105	4,615

Source: Camelot Group plc.

***Table 2.9** Camelot Group marketing expenditure and sales, 1995–2004*

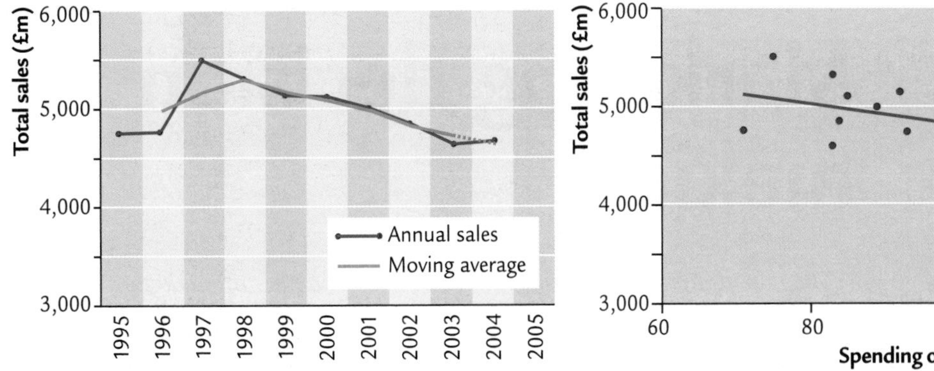

Figure 2.10 *Camelot lottery sales, 1995–2005*

Figure 2.11 *Correlation between Camelot promotions expenditure and total sales, 1995–2004*

at specific games and until recently emphasised the £16 billion raised for good causes. Since its inception, a significant amount of Camelot's promotions has been firefighting, trying to restore public faith at times when it has received negative publicity. However, Camelot is no longer responsible for publicising the good causes funded by the lottery – this has been taken over by an independent body. As a consequence, Camelot's future promotions are free to concentrate on the prizes element.

Questions

Total: 40 marks (45 minutes)

1 **a** Analyse the reasons why Camelot's expenditure on promotions did not always lead to an increase in sales. *(8 marks)*

b Using Figure 2.10, forecast national lottery sales for 2009. *(2 marks)*

c Why is Camelot less likely to be affected unfavourably by incorrect forecasting than a company such as Wall's? *(10 marks)*

2 **a** Camelot will spend £100 million on promotions in 2006. Based solely on Figure 2.11, what level of sales would be forecast? *(2 marks)*

b Which method of forecasting would you advise Camelot to use in order to predict future sales? Justify your answer. *(18 marks)*

Marketing decision making

The importance of marketing objectives and a number of marketing strategies were studied in the AS course: niche versus mass marketing; strategic use of the product life cycle; product portfolio analysis; and adding value. This chapter builds on the AS work on objectives and marketing strategies by looking at market decision making. The importance of scientific decision making in marketing is examined through the marketing model. The chapter also examines decisions based on hunch or gut feeling, and evaluates the relative merits of scientific decision making and decisions based on hunches.

EXAMINER'S VOICE

For Module 4 (Marketing and Accounting and Finance) the AQA A2 specification on 'marketing decision making' only requires an understanding of the marketing model; there is no direct reference to Ansoff's matrix. However, in the Objectives and Strategy part of Module 6 there is a requirement to study both the marketing model and Ansoff's matrix as approaches to strategic decision making in general. This means that there will be no question on the Unit 4 examination paper that specifies or needs an understanding of Ansoff's matrix (but you may be able to use it to enhance or improve an answer). Questions with a direct reference to Ansoff's matrix can appear in Unit 6.

For this reason there is no reference to Ansoff in this part of the book. However, we believe that it is a useful tool to illustrate and explain marketing strategy, and relevant reference to it in a Unit 4 examination should receive credit. If time permits, you are encouraged to read the section on Ansoff's matrix in Chapter 51 (pp. 476–79). The article on Tesco in this chapter includes an optional question on Ansoff's matrix.

The marketing model

KEY TERMS

marketing strategy: long-term or medium-term plans, devised at senior management level and designed to achieve the firm's marketing objectives.

marketing model: a decision-making process that ensures that marketing decisions are taken on a scientific basis. This scientific approach is an alternative to managers taking decisions on the basis of hunches or guesses.

scientific marketing decisions: policies that are based on the use of a logical, researched approach, such as that shown in the marketing model.

The **marketing model** involves a number of stages:

1 setting marketing objectives

2 gathering the data needed to decide on a strategy

3 assessing alternative marketing strategies and implementing the favoured choice
4 planning and implementing the marketing mix in accordance with the marketing strategy
5 controlling and reviewing the outcome of marketing decisions

An essential element of the marketing model is the existence of constraints. Internal factors (strengths and weaknesses) and external factors (opportunities and threats) are continually monitored at every stage in order to assess their impact. These factors can lead to changes at any stage of the model. For example, feedback gained from stage 2 may help a firm to recognise that its objectives are unrealistic and so stage 1 may be modified. Similarly, control and review (stage 5) might indicate that the wrong strategy was chosen (stage 3) or that the marketing mix was implemented incorrectly (stage 4).

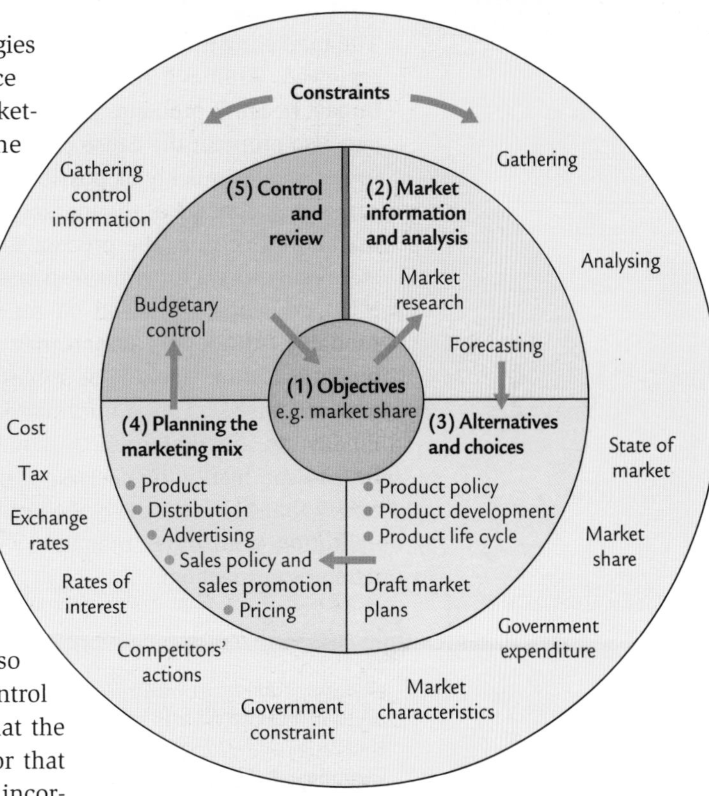

Figure 3.1
The marketing model
Source: P. Tinniswood, *Marketing Decision Making.*

For these reasons, the marketing model is often represented as a circle surrounded by constraints, to emphasise that marketing decisions do not necessarily follow a set of routine stages every time (see Figure 3.1).

Benefits of using the marketing model

A scientific approach to decision making brings a number of advantages:

- It provides a clear sense of direction. By emphasising the need to set objectives, it helps to ensure that people involved in the decision-making process are aiming towards the same goals. **SMART** (specific, measurable, agreed, reasonable and timed) objectives, in particular, will help the firm to make decisions that clearly match the aims of the organisation.
- Decisions are based on business logic, involving comparisons between alternative approaches. This makes it less likely that a decision will be made without its pros and cons being examined first, so weak ideas should be eliminated and the best suggestion adopted.
- It is probable (but not certain) that more than one person will be involved in the process. This will reduce the possibility of bias, which is especially important if an individual has a personal interest in one of the strategies or tactics, perhaps because they suggested it originally or might benefit from it financially.

- The marketing model ensures that decisions are monitored continually and reviewed. Although this will not prevent mistakes, it should limit their impact because problems can be identified quickly. A good review process can also pinpoint the cause of the problem, so that a different approach is introduced as quickly as possible.
- A major advantage of the marketing model is its flexibility. At any stage in making a decision, the process can be reviewed and changed if circumstances require a different response.
- If all decisions are based on rational thinking, overall success is more probable. Although a hunch may pay off occasionally, in the long run a business is more likely to be successful if its decisions are made in a logical manner, based on good information.
- Finally, an individual manager may prefer a scientific approach, so that he/she can justify the decision if things go wrong. It is easier to defend a policy that has been developed on the basis of good planning (and in co-operation with other managers) than one that is based solely on one person's gut feeling.

FACT FILE

Jill Barker, founder of Green Baby, set up her business on the basis of scientific decision making. With 13 years experience in City banking and background knowledge of the North American market, Jill recognised the potential for organic, environmentally friendly baby products. Barker chose the first outlet in Islington, North London because 'We were in the kind of area where mothers cared about green issues.' Having expanded into mail order and supply to other 'green' stores, Green Baby now has a mailing list of 50,000 customers and its products are distributed to 250 stores.

Source: adapted from an article by Elizabeth Judge in *The Times*, 17 April 2004.

Hunch and gut feeling

KEY TERM

hunch: a gut feeling held by a manager that is based not on scientific decision making but on the personal views of the manager. Hunches may or may not be based on past experience of the market.

FACT FILE

Wayne Hemingway and his wife Gerardine founded the Red or Dead fashion house in 1982 by sheer chance:

> We ran out of money one weekend so we emptied our clothes onto Camden Market. We took a load of money and that was it. You should always follow your gut instincts. We had more successes than failures and have never done any kind of market research, although the market is constantly in our minds.

Source: www.startups.co.uk

Benefits of using hunches

In general, hunches are used because of problems involved in using the marketing model:

- A scientific approach requires a large collection of data, initially, followed by the regular gathering of information to control and review decisions. This can be a very expensive process and will be hard to justify if there is very little risk involved and the eventual conclusion is seen to be obvious.
- Following the marketing model is time consuming. The constant checking and monitoring means that decisions may be delayed. In highly competitive industries, this delay may be fatal as a competitor can enter the market using your idea while you are still weighing up the pros and cons. A quick decision, based on gut feeling or a hunch, may be better in these circumstances.
- The data collected for the marketing model might be flawed. The information may be dated or the original sampling may have a bias. Customers may have just changed their minds. Any logical decisions based on invalid data will lead to an invalid strategy or plan, so a hunch is likely to be more effective.
- Invariably, scientific decisions are based on past information. If the nature of the market is changing, the firm should not rely on these data. Instead its decisions may be better if they rely on the instincts of a manager who has a 'qualitative' understanding of the market and can anticipate a change in the trend.

FILE

German multi-millionaire Knut Eicke has made a lot of money from hunches. His insurance company, Sir Huckleberry Insurance, offers the usual insurance policies but also provides the world's quirkiest alternatives. Based on a hunch, Knut started offering weird insurance policies against eventualities such as 'choking on pretzels', 'injuries from falling over at a beer festival' and 'being fired from work for playing computer games'. However, according to Knut, 'insurance against abduction by aliens is the big seller.' For additional premiums, people can also gain compensation for being whisked off to Mars (a payout of £2,500 for a policy that costs less than £20 per annum). Knut did not believe that scientific decision making would have revealed this opportunity. To date Knut has not paid out on the alien abduction policy (a big seller as a novelty gift).

Source: adapted from an article by Allan Hall in the *Evening Standard*, 31 March 2004.

Choosing between scientific and hunch-based decision making

The following factors are critical in deciding which approach to use:

- **The speed of the decision.** Where quick decisions are required, there may be insufficient time to analyse the situation and so hunches may be followed. If time is not an issue, a more scientific (but slower) approach can be adopted.

- **Information available.** Where detailed data are not available, hunches and guesswork are more likely to be used. However, if data are held, a more scientific decision is possible.
- **The size of the business.** As a rule, smaller businesses are more likely to follow a hunch. Larger firms have established approaches to decision making that are used by each department. Furthermore, larger firms face more complicated marketing decisions that need a more scientific approach.
- **The predictability of the market.** In an unpredictable situation, a hunch may be better than following a trend that will not continue. However, if past data are a reliable indicator of future changes, a scientific approach is ideal.
- **The character of the person or the culture of the company.** An entrepreneurial risk-taker is more likely to use hunches. A manager (or business) that tries to avoid risk or blame is more likely to use a scientific approach, in order to justify any decisions.

EXAMINER'S VOICE

When faced with a question about scientific decision making or hunches, try to identify any of the features listed here within the case study, in order to explain the reasons for the approach used by the business.

FACT FILE

The Body Shop was set up on a hunch because, according to its founder, Anita Roddick, 'We had no money — I was trying to pay the bills by doing what I was interested in. If I'd had a shed load of money, I'd have done everything wrong — marketing, focus groups, although they are more important now [that the business has grown].'

Source: www.startups.co.uk

TOPFOTO

FACT FILE

Marks and Spencer is an example of a company whose approach can be analysed by using the marketing model.

- **Objective.** The objective is to increase Marks and Spencer's share of the teenage fashion market by releasing a new range of clothing that is going head-to-head with Topshop and New Look.
- **Information/market research.** The financial year 2003/04 was a bad one for Marks and Spencer, which suffered a 10% fall in sales of its clothing. The Autograph range failed to inspire customers. The products received excellent reviews, but the prices, many in excess of £100, were too high for Marks and Spencer customers. David Beckham was paid handsomely to be the figurehead for a new range of boys' clothing, just before scandal tarnished his reputation as a family man.
- **Strategy.** Marks and Spencer responded by shifting its target market. In order to attract back its main customer segment, it recruited George Davies, the man behind ASDA's 'George' range of clothing. Davies introduced a new brand for women, Per Una, which was less fashion-led but also much cheaper. The Per Una range is targeted at 30- and 40-somethings. After some success, Marks and Spencer's response has been to launch another new range, Per Una Due, aimed at teenage girls seeking high-quality fashion clothes. The new range features the shortest skirt ever to bear the M&S label and boob tubes — a style that Marks and Spencer has never stocked before.
- **Tactics.** Marks and Spencer is hoping to appeal to mothers and daughters. A spokesperson for Marks and Spencer explained:

There is scope for mothers and daughters to shop together. The mothers can buy Per Una and the daughters can buy Per Una Due. Marks and Spencer hopes that the mothers will be impressed by the quality, which is far superior to rivals such as Topshop. The company also expects the daughters to enjoy the new 'boutique'-style layout of their shops. To keep the clothing fashionable, Per Una Due stock will be completely replaced every 8 weeks. Text marketing, where text messages advertising the brand are sent to target customers, is being used by Marks and Spencer for the first time.

- **Control and review.** The Per Una Due range is initially being offered in 65 stores. Close monitoring of sales, and comparisons with stores that are not offering the new range, will allow Marks and Spencer to determine the success (or failure) of its new strategy.
- **Conclusion.** Has Marks and Spencer achieved its objectives? Has its strategy and marketing plan been successful? At the time of writing it is too early to tell. A visit to Marks and Spencer may indicate whether this approach has worked.

Source: adapted from an article by Jess Cartney-Morley in the *Guardian*, 5 May 2004.

TOPFOTO

DID YOU KNOW?

Recent research by the Cranfield Management School supports the view that scientific decision making is the ideal approach. 'Strong' marketing strategies possess the following features:

- Market segments with similar needs are identified.
- Each segment is offered a unique proposition.
- Strategies are significantly different from those of competitors.
- Approaches show awareness of the organisation's strengths and competitors' weaknesses.
- The strategies lead to obvious tactics, thus reducing decision-making time.
- Sufficient resources are allocated.
- Strategies match corporate objectives.

PRACTICE EXERCISE 1 — Total: 45 marks (40 minutes)

1 What is meant by the term 'marketing model'? *(3 marks)*

2 What is the difference between scientific decision making and decisions based on hunches? *(6 marks)*

3 State the five stages of the marketing model. *(5 marks)*

4 Identify seven possible constraints on marketing decisions. *(7 marks)*

5 Explain two benefits of using the marketing model. *(6 marks)*

6 Explain two possible reasons for basing decisions on 'hunches'. *(6 marks)*

7 Discuss the factors that an insurance company might consider when deciding whether to use scientific decision making or hunches. *(12 marks)*

PRACTICE EXERCISE 2

Total: 15 marks (15 minutes)

Refer to the information in case study 2 on pp. 42–43.

1 Identify Coca-Cola's marketing objectives. *(3 marks)*

2 Describe the information that was used to assist the decision-making process. *(5 marks)*

3 Explain how Coca-Cola might control and review the success of its strategy. *(7 marks)*

CASE STUDY 1 Tesco stays hungry for overseas growth

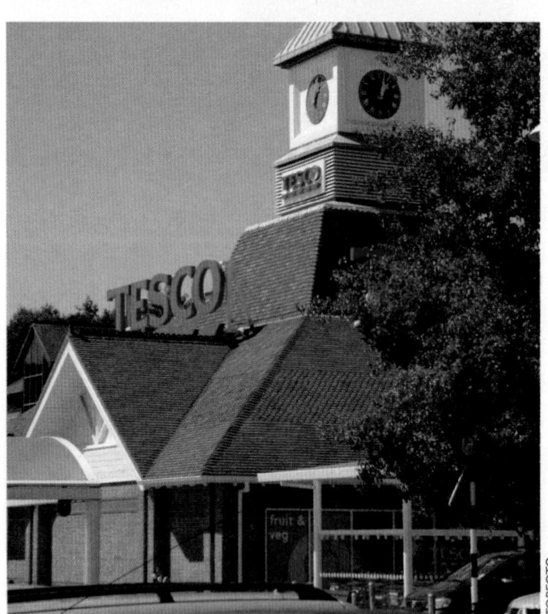

TOPFOTO

Many people attribute Tesco's success to the clarity of its objectives, but successful marketing requires integration between all of the stages of the marketing model. Tesco was quick to realise that it faced limitations to any plans to expand its market share in the grocery market. The Competition Commission had indicated that it would look closely at any proposed mergers (and in 2003 it did refuse to allow Tesco to bid for Safeways). As a result, Tesco targeted a three-pronged strategy for growth:

- consolidation — increasing its market share of the grocery market at the expense of its rival supermarkets
- product development — increasing the range of 'non-food' products that it sells
- market development — seeking new countries in which to establish retailing outlets

The first two strategies have worked well. Grocery sales have grown by 6% in the last year, taking Tesco's market share in the UK to over 30%. In 'non-food' items, Tesco has grown from 1% to 5% in only 5 years. Chief executive, Sir Terry Leahy, is excited about the prospects. 'We're not going to settle for 5% — there's 95% in which to make headway.'

However, Leahy recognises the constraints on domestic growth and is pursuing a strategy of market development through setting up new stores overseas. For many supermarkets, overseas ventures have proved to be difficult. Sainsbury's struggled in the USA after it took over Shaw's supermarkets. Cultural differences are very significant in the supermarket trade and throughout the world companies have found it difficult to make an impact when moving into new countries. The more successful attempts have usually involved purchase of a subsidiary, which is allowed to trade with a high degree of independence.

Commenting on Tesco's recent purchase of a chain of Japanese convenience stores, Leahy emphasised that overseas expansion need not be a problem.

> It has been good for Tesco wherever we have opened. Japan will be good for the business. One of the tricks Tesco has been able to pull off is to tailor stores to local consumers and take what we learn back into the group to improve how we operate.

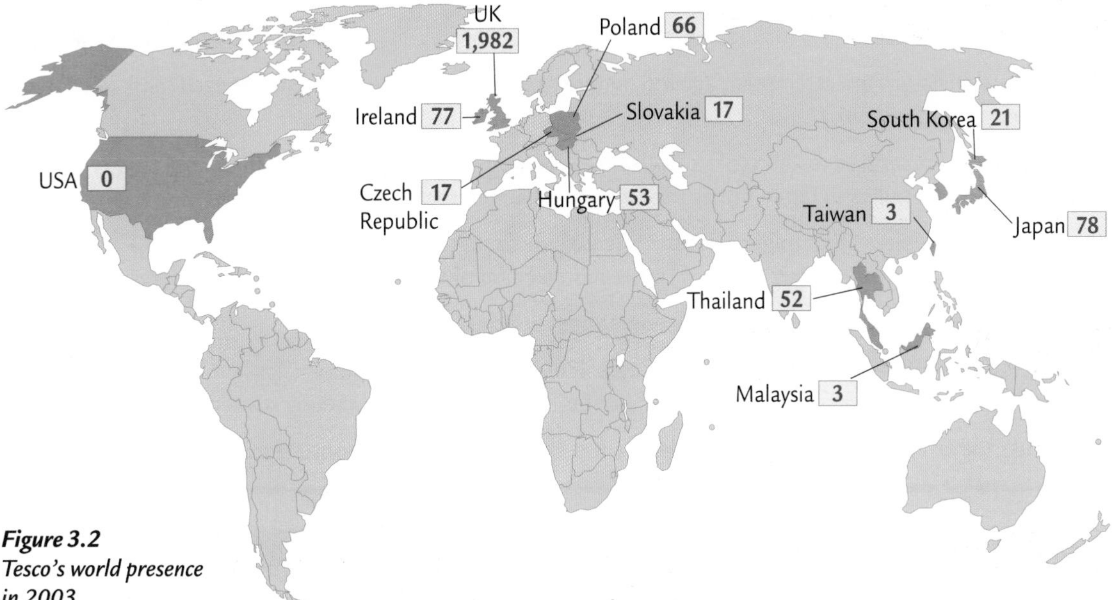

Figure 3.2
Tesco's world presence in 2003

Unlike French rival Carrefour, which is experiencing difficulties in Japan, Tesco is concentrating on a small-scale firm and building slowly, hoping to learn from others' mistakes. Overseas sales now account for 20% of Tesco's sales. Andrew Kasoulis, an analyst for CSFB, sees it as an 'interesting, earnings-enhancing way of conducting market research'.

Tesco is currently the world's seventh largest food retailer and Leahy believes that ultimately over 50% of the company's sales will come from abroad, but accepts that 'that day is some time away'.

Some industry experts think that Tesco needs to enter the USA to prove its worth, but Leahy says he has no plans to tackle America:

> I'd never rule it out or rule it in. We've looked at it for 22 years and never made a move. It's a big and competitive market and would be a big effort. Tesco is busy with its present strategy, which is creating a lot of growth. We would need to be sure that we had the spare resources needed to tackle the USA market.

To expand into the USA, analysts believe that Tesco would need to seek a partner such as a Safeway Inc., the American chain for which Tesco has provided software support, or Dutch rival Ahold, which has a major presence in the USA. Experts are divided on the best timing for entry into the USA. The advantage of waiting is that Wal-Mart's USA rivals are getting weaker; the disadvantage is that Wal-Mart is dominating the market more each year.

		Sales ($bn)
1	Wal-Mart (USA)	147
2	Carrefour (France)	39
3	Ahold (Netherlands)	36
4	Kroger (USA)	31
5	Metro (Germany)	29
6	Target (USA)	26
7	Tesco (UK)	24
8	Costco (USA)	23
9	Albertsons (USA)	21
10	Rewe (Germany)	21

Kasoulis believes that there is plenty of scope for Tesco to expand its UK operations through increasing its number of hypermarkets from 60 to 80, by extending its opening of Tesco Express convenience stores and through growth of sales of non-food items.

Source: adapted from an article by Matthew Goodman in the *Sunday Times*, 15 June 2003.

Questions

Total: 60 marks (65 minutes)

(If only some questions are attempted, allow 5 minutes' reading time plus 1 minute for each mark allocated to the questions attempted.)

1 Analyse two advantages to Tesco of its decision to concentrate on taking over a chain of small, local retailers in Japan rather than a chain of larger, national Japanese stores. *(8 marks)*

2 Analyse two problems that might arise from Tesco's decision to concentrate on taking over a chain of small, local retailers in Japan rather than a chain of larger, national Japanese stores. *(8 marks)*

3 Discuss whether Tesco should extend its operations into the USA. *(12 marks)*

4 (This is an optional question. Please read pages 476–479 before attempting it.) Show how Ansoff's matrix can be used to describe Tesco's different marketing strategies. *(12 marks)*

5 Discuss the extent to which Tesco uses the marketing model in its marketing strategy. *(20 marks)*

CASE STUDY 2 Coca-Cola sets out lifestyle stall

- In 2004, Coca-Cola UK president, Charlotte Oades, outlined its 'active lifestyle' strategy, aimed to counter the obesity epidemic. The strategy is built on four pillars:
- providing customer choice
- giving customers information to make choices
- responsible sales and marketing
- continuing support for active lifestyles, particularly among young people

Her remarks closely followed McDonald's announcement that it would spend £1 million on an educational campaign aimed at encouraging children to eat a balanced diet and take more exercise, through a series of 2-minute commercials.

'We're suddenly seeing food companies keen to promote a healthier message,' said Food Commission spokesman, Ian Tokelove. However, Labour MP Debra Shipley was sceptical about the motives of brand owners such as Coca-Cola and McDonald's. 'They have been dragged into this position reluctantly because of huge pressure from health experts, politicians and the general public.'

In its defence, Coca-Cola can point out that it has hardly been rushed into a relationship with health and physical fitness. Coke was originally invented for medicinal purposes, but the business gambled on moving it into the 'soft drinks' market. The company has also anticipated change ahead of its competitors. It believed that it would benefit from association with the Olympic Games and has been an Olympic sponsor since 1928. Moreover, it has a policy of not advertising on any television channels aimed at under-12s. Coca-Cola also led the way with diet soft drinks, with the UK launch 21 years ago of Diet Coke. Diet Coke and related 'healthier' variations now account for over 40% of Coca-Cola brand sales in the UK. These decisions have been based on a mixture of market research and individual guesswork by managers.

Coca-Cola has changed its marketing to ensure that promotions give greater prominence to diet brands. An example of this in action was the sponsorship of *Ant and Dec's Saturday Night Takeaway* on ITV1, in which both Coke and Diet Coke were featured.

In addition, the company announced that it was removing its branding from vending machines in secondary schools. However, this may not harm sales as design experts believe that

Coke is so strongly associated with vending machines that the logo on the machine is unimportant.

Oades admits that there is more that Coca-Cola could do. The company intends to develop an even wider range of low-calorie and low-sugar products. Its new citizenship website will contain nutritional information on all the company's products and its sales force has been given information to increase its understanding of balanced diets and active lifestyles.

But how will consumers react? As a company, Coca-Cola has been skilled in anticipating the future, but John Mathers, chief executive of consultancy firm Enterprise IG, believes that the company may have misinterpreted its customers. 'Consumers are seeing initiatives like these in a cynical way. The danger is that they will be seen as attempts to divert attention from the main issues.'

There are other signs that Coca-Cola is beginning to rely on unsupported ideas rather than thorough research. The failure of its bottled water in the UK showed a lack of awareness of the character of UK consumers, who expect bottled water to come from a natural source. The comment, by a senior executive of the company, that it would not have used bottled water in France did not help Coca-Cola's image in the UK.

Source: adapted from an article by Robert Gray in *Marketing*, 14 July 2004.

Questions

Total: 40 marks (45 minutes)

1 Coca-Cola's 'sales force has been given information to increase its understanding of balanced diets and active lifestyles' (lines 62–64). Explain why this is an important element of the company's new approach. *(6 marks)*

2 Coca-Cola's marketing strategy is based on four pillars (lines 3–9). Which of these pillars is most important to the success of the new strategy? Justify your choice. *(14 marks)*

3 To what extent is Coca-Cola's marketing strategy based on hunches rather than scientific decision making? *(20 marks)*

CHAPTER 4

Marketing planning and the marketing mix

This chapter examines the process of devising a marketing plan and the benefits of marketing planning. It revisits the marketing mix to see how and why organisations might emphasise particular elements and how they coordinate their marketing activities. The need to coordinate the marketing mix with other business functions is also scrutinised.

Marketing planning

Marketing planning is concerned with decision making and so developing the plan involves a similar process to marketing decision making. However, whereas the marketing model that we looked at in Chapter 3 focuses on individual decisions, marketing planning looks at the overall marketing of the organisation.

TERM

marketing plan: a statement of the organisation's current marketing position and future strategies, and a detailed examination of the tactics that it will use to achieve its objectives.

Stages of marketing planning

The stages followed in marketing planning are as follows:

1 Undertaking an audit of the factors that influence the marketing of a business. In effect, this audit looks at internal **s**trengths and **w**eaknesses and external **o**pportunities and **t**hreats (a **SWOT analysis**).
2 Setting SMART marketing objectives based on the SWOT analysis and considering the capabilities of the other functional areas of the organisation, such as the production department.
3 Agreeing the most appropriate marketing strategies to meet these objectives.
4 Allocating a marketing budget in order to finance the actions.
5 Implementing marketing tactics through a marketing mix that fits the budget.

Advantages of marketing planning

- It sets clear objectives and thus gives direction to the staff involved. This may also motivate staff if they are given responsibility for an element of the plan.
- The plan arises from a consideration of all functions of a business. This makes managers think strategically and forces them to coordinate marketing

actions with the activities of other departments. In this way, the different functions of the business should work together more cooperatively.

- Departmental plans such as the marketing plan allow senior managers to compare alternative demands for resources. This enables the firm to allocate resources to the activities that are likely to benefit the business to the greatest extent.
- Managers can assess efficiency by comparing actual outcomes with the plan and discovering the reasons for any differences. This also acts as a motivator to staff, who will be assessed on their ability to meet targets.
- Continual review of the marketing plan enables the firm to remain aware of any developments in the marketplace, allowing it to stay ahead of competitors and reap the benefits of adapting quickly to any changes.
- A well-constructed plan will take into consideration the budget allocation and so ensure that the activities to be carried out can be funded.

However, the usefulness of market planning will be limited if:

- it takes up excessive time in both the planning and reviewing stages, and thus becomes a brake on progress
- there are constant changes in the market, leading to an inability to assess the effectiveness of the planning process
- there is a lack of coordination between the different functional plans
- the plans are too ambitious or complicated — some plans become so detailed that the key features are hidden and the review process takes so long that problems continue for a much longer time than is desirable

The marketing mix

At AS we looked at the marketing mix — the **four Ps** of product, promotion, price and place. In the A2 specification, the focus is on the integration of the four Ps and their application to specific situations. You should revisit Chapters 6–9 of the AS textbook before answering any questions on the marketing mix.

EXAMINER'S VOICE

Make sure that you relate the four Ps to the case that is being studied. Avoid the temptation to talk about the marketing mix in general terms. You will need to use the information in the case to show which elements of the marketing mix are most critical. As the Unit 4 examination is centred on a business decision, you may be required to advise an organisation on its marketing mix.

Integrating the marketing mix

A good marketing mix needs to be coordinated so that each element supports, and is consistent with, the other parts of the mix. If a promotional campaign is based on the excellence of a product, the quality and design of that product must match the expectations of the promotion. Such a campaign would be consistent with a high price and an upmarket place where wealthy consumers are likely to buy the product.

Similarly, a supermarket would want its low-price, economy range of products to be packaged simply so that consumers can see that money is not wasted on packaging. Consumers would also not expect to see expensive advertising campaigns for such products.

Product

When deciding on its products, businesses should consider the following factors:

- **Suppliers.** Does the organisation have access to sufficient supplies and enough bargaining power to acquire raw materials at a reasonable price? In the UK, banana supplies are in the hands of a few suppliers who can dictate the price to small grocers. However, the large supermarkets can bargain for a much lower price than small grocers.

TOPFOTO

- **Number of buyers.** If a product has only a limited number of buyers, it may weaken the seller's position. In the past, most milk was sold to millions of individual customers through doorstep deliveries, allowing the dairies to set a higher price (partly because the customers were paying a premium for the convenience of delivery). At present, most milk is sold through supermarkets. In 2004, the major supermarkets used their power as buyers to renegotiate (and in some cases cancel) their contracts with the dairies. As a result, more of the profit from milk supply is now made by supermarkets rather than the dairies or the farmers, who are in a weaker bargaining position. With this in mind, farmers and others involved in the dairy industry are moving into other activities, or trying to sell their products directly to consumers through farm shops.
- **Competition.** In very competitive industries, a business needs to differentiate its product from those of competitors. This is achieved through branding, patenting original ideas and constantly developing new products to replace those in decline. In some industries, such as telecommunications, barriers to entry can limit the level of competition, as new firms cannot afford the huge capital costs involved.
- **Substitutes.** Businesses must look beyond their own market and appreciate that other industries can impact on their success. Bus companies are in competition with trains and the car industry. In some areas, companies such as Stagecoach operate both the bus and train routes, thus overcoming the risk of competition.

TOPFOTO

- **Consumers.** Ultimately, this is the most important factor. A firm's products must appeal to the customers, so continuous market research is needed. With greater scope for targeting, there is now a tendency for more variety in the product range, with each variation targeted at a different market segment.

Promotion

There are many issues that a business should consider when deciding the type of promotion to use:

- **The marketing budget and the cost of promotions.** Firms generally base promotional decisions on cost effectiveness. This is often measured by the cost per thousand (CPT). Thus a promotional campaign costing £60,000 and reaching 600,000 people would have a CPT of 10p per consumer.
- **Differentiated or undifferentiated marketing.** If the product is aimed at a niche market, promotions will be placed in media that are used by the consumers within that niche. If the mass market is targeted, media with a broad coverage, such as national newspapers and ITV, will be used.
- **The market segment.** Some target markets may be easier to reach through certain media. Specialist magazines are used to promote products such as cosmetics and computer games because the profile of the magazine's readership matches the market segment that the business is trying to attract.
- **The organisation's database.** If a business has acquired information on specific customers, it is more likely to use direct mail or internet contact to attract them. Organisations such as Sainsbury's (through its loyalty card) and Expedia and Trainline (through previous bookings) gain an understanding of consumers' tastes and are able to target specific offers to them.
- **The quality of the promotion.** There is a chance element in any promotional campaign. Some campaigns have failed because they were not cost effective — both Hoover and McDonald's ran campaigns that were stopped because of the financial difficulties they caused. Hoover offered expensive flights to people purchasing a product and McDonald's offered 'two meals for the price of one'. Other campaigns have captivated consumers and been very successful in generating extra sales (for example, Scottish Widows and Tesco's Dottie advertisements). Occasionally, external circumstances have affected success, as with Marks and Spencer's use of David Beckham's image as a family man shortly before he received negative publicity.

TOPFOTO

FACT FILE

A recent example of unfortunate timing was Barclays' advert to promote the fact that it had taken over sponsorship of the Football Premiership. The advert superimposed the face of Sir Bobby Robson, manager of Newcastle United and one of the most recognisable faces in football, on hundreds of fans as they travelled to the big match. The campaign had been described as 'a stroke of genius' and attracted a great deal of attention. After four matches without a win, however, Newcastle United sacked their manager and Barclays stopped showing the advertisement.

EXAMINER'S VOICE

Don't assume that organisations always want to use the media that reach most consumers — notably television. The CPT for television advertisements may be high when measured in relation to targeted customers. Specialist magazines or local media can be much more cost effective.

Price

Factors that need to be considered when setting a price include:

- **Price elasticity of demand.** If demand is price inelastic, an increase in price will lead to a relatively small fall in the quantity demanded. If demand is price elastic, an increase in price will lead to a relatively large fall in the quantity demanded. If no information on elasticity is provided, the nature of the product should be examined — is it a necessity (probably price inelastic) or does it have many substitutes (in which case it is likely to have price-elastic demand)?
- **The target market.** Who is the product targeting? Are they wealthy and/or desperate for the product? Factors such as these will allow a higher price to be charged.
- **The pricing method used.** If there is evidence that the firm is using cost-plus pricing, costs will serve as a guide to the selling price. If the business is following a price leader, it will set a similar price to the market leader.
- **The nature of the product.** There is an obvious connection between the quality of the product and the price that is set. Thus the price may be used to indicate the level of quality of the product.
- **The reputation of the business.** Some firms will deliberately avoid price cuts because they may adversely affect their upmarket image; others, with a reputation for value-for-money, will deliberately emphasise lower prices.
- **What the market will bear.** Ultimately, prices are set by supply and demand. In 2004 and 2005, oil prices rose because of a shortage in the supply of oil. Similarly, a popular item with a high demand, such as the iPod, will fetch a high price.

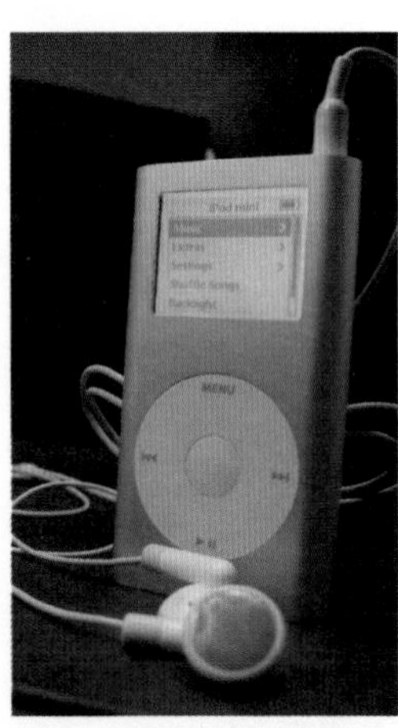

EXAMINER'S VOICE

Be cautious when applying price elasticity of demand in an answer. Two common mistakes are:

- 'If demand is price inelastic, a change in price will not lead to a change in demand.' This is not true — it will lead to a smaller percentage change in demand. Only perfect price inelasticity leads to no change in demand.
- 'If demand is price elastic, it is best to lower price.' It is true that this will increase total revenue, but it will also increase the quantity that needs to be made and thus the total costs. Therefore, cutting price may or may not increase profit. Information on costs is needed to draw this conclusion.

Place

The importance of place in the marketing mix is often underestimated. How might place make a critical difference to the success of a marketing plan?

- **The geographical location.** Convenience to consumers is vital. For a corner shop, this may mean that it is away from larger competitors; for an electrical retailer, it may mean being close to competitors, as consumers like to compare prices in as convenient a way as possible. For a growing number of consumers, convenience means being able to make your decisions at home, via the internet or telephone.

- **The layout of the place.** Supermarkets pay consultants millions of pounds to plan the layout of their stores. For any retailer, the impression given by the layout of the store will influence consumers' opinions and thus affect the retailer's popularity.
- **The distribution channels.** An efficient supply chain improves the frequency of deliveries, enabling a retailer to offer fresh or up-to-date items and to avoid empty displays and being out of stock.
- **The cost of distribution.** Lower costs will enable a firm to remain price competitive.

EXAMINER'S VOICE

Be careful when commenting on location as a factor in the marketing mix. A remote location may not matter to a factory supplying industrial goods, unless it increases costs. It may actually reduce costs if it is in a low-wage area or close to raw materials. However, a remote location will be a problem if the organisation expects consumers to visit the site in order to purchase goods.

The impact of place varies considerably between businesses. In general, it is more important to firms that supply the general public directly.

Coordinating the marketing mix with other business functions

Any business must ensure that each of its functional areas works cooperatively with other areas. A new recruitment drive must be coordinated between the personnel department, which organises the advertising and interviewing, the finance department, which must agree on the financial commitment needed, and the department within which the new recruits will be working.

When compiling its marketing plan, a business must liaise closely with the other departments within the organisation to ensure that each department is working towards the same goals and adopting consistent strategies. The sections below provide some examples of ways in which the marketing plan must coordinate with the other business functions.

The marketing plan and operations management

The marketing objectives must be consistent with the production department's approach. If the marketing plan is aiming to create an upmarket, quality image, it is vital that the products being manufactured meet this requirement. High-quality after-sales service will also be necessary if this target is to be achieved, especially if the marketing department has emphasised this as a key element of its plan. More simply, the two departments must coordinate production levels to make sure that a successful marketing campaign does not cause frustration for consumers because insufficient products have been manufactured. On occasions, the marketing department will need to constrain or delay its ideas and plans if the operations function is not in a position to deliver what the customer needs.

The marketing plan and finance

Similar cooperation is needed between finance and marketing. If the marketing plan is ambitious, it may be necessary to curtail certain marketing activities if there is insufficient funding. However, if the marketing department can justify the expenditure, the finance department will investigate alternative sources of funding. The finance department must also allocate sufficient money to each department that is supporting the marketing effort. Ultimately, the marketing budget (outlined in Chapter 5) and all other budgets must be agreed with the finance department.

The marketing plan and personnel

Successful marketing strategies need people to deliver. Consequently, personnel and marketing need to coordinate their activities. Staff in the marketing department must be recruited effectively and the workforce planning of the business is essential if each department is to have the right number of suitably qualified staff with the required skills. Changes in the marketing plan may well need changes in staffing and/or training. Customer service training is a specific example of personnel activities that will impact on the marketing function.

Although each functional area has to compete with the other areas of the business for resources, ultimately they are all striving to achieve the same (corporate) objectives. The following Fact File on the Co-op provides an example of a marketing strategy that depends upon cooperation between marketing, operations, finance and personnel for its success.

FACT FILE

The Co-op is an example of a business that has developed an integrated marketing mix in order to target a large niche market — the UK's 2 million blind and partially sighted people. The Co-op pioneered the use of Braille on packaging for certain medicines in 2001, and by January 2005 it had extended Braille labelling to 300 own-brand products.

The Co-op has signed up to the Guide Dogs for the Blind Association's high-street charter and is relying on word-of-mouth advertising — a strategy based on the close-knit network of blind people. The Co-op is guaranteeing that prices will be the same as its usual own-brand range, in keeping with its stance on ethical and socially responsible behaviour. The other main focus is on 'place'. To assist blind and partially sighted people, the supermarket is training its staff on the new labelling and on the charter, which advises shops on ways to assist blind people, such as offering explanations of store layout, store guides and helping to pack their shopping.

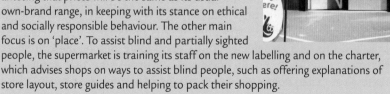

Source: adapted from an article by Rachel Barnes in *Marketing*, 14 July 2004.

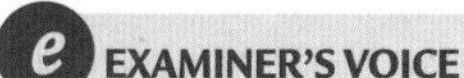

EXAMINER'S VOICE

When answering questions on marketing strategy or marketing planning, you should look for evidence of approaches that have been successful or unsuccessful and use any reasons behind this in your answer.

PRACTICE EXERCISE

Total: 55 marks (50 minutes)

1 What is meant by the term 'marketing plan'? *(3 marks)*

2 Identify five stages in the marketing planning process. *(5 marks)*

3 Explain two advantages of marketing planning. *(6 marks)*

4 Explain two reasons why a marketing plan might not be useful to an organisation. *(6 marks)*

5 Explain two factors that would help a firm to decide on the type of media to use for its promotions. *(6 marks)*

6 Explain one example of a good or service for which price is the most important element of the marketing mix. *(4 marks)*

7 Explain one example of a good or service for which product is the most important element of the marketing mix. *(4 marks)*

8 Explain one example of a good or service for which promotion is the most important element of the marketing mix. *(4 marks)*

9 Explain one example of a good or service for which place is the most important element of the marketing mix. *(4 marks)*

10 How does the price elasticity of demand influence a firm when it is considering whether to change its price? *(5 marks)*

11 Explain one implication of a successful marketing campaign for the personnel function of a business. *(4 marks)*

12 How might the production department of a business be affected by a successful marketing campaign targeted at lower-income consumers? *(4 marks)*

CASE STUDY 1 Barbie's mid-life crisis

The world's number-one fashion doll is 44 years old this year. Despite sales of over 1 billion Barbies worldwide, the US icon is facing some serious competition for her fashion-doll crown. In April 2004, her makers, Mattel, announced a 73% cut in profits and a 13% fall in global Barbie sales for the quarter, following on from a 25% fall in the previous quarter.

Barbie's main competitors are Bratz dolls — a range designed to be more streetwise and funky than Barbie. MGA Entertainments, the makers of Bratz dolls, describe them as coming in a range of different ethnicities and wearing fashions described as 'totally dangerous, totally ferocious and totally funkadelic'. Launched just 3 years ago in the USA, over 80 million Bratz dolls have been sold globally.

In the UK, Bratz has over 30% of the fashion-doll market. Nick Austin, Bratz's UK distributor, is confident that their share will grow. 'If you asked children a few years ago, it was always Barbie, Barbie, Barbie, but that was because there was no competition,' he says. 'This is the first time that little girls have had a real choice.'

But it's not just Bratz that wants a share of the UK's £100 million fashion-doll market. Barbie's old rival Sindy is planning to relaunch. Sindy originally came on to the market in the 1960s as a very British doll

with a girl-next-door look. She triumphed among British girls in the 1980s but was trounced by Barbie in the 1990s. Denise Deane, design and development director of Sindy, says: 'Twenty-first-century Sindy is different. She is more flexible than ever before and she will be marketed as a doll who is "just like me".'

Mattel is not taking this lying down. While Barbie's target market is 3 years old and upwards, Bratz appeals to older girls. Mattel has brought out a much funkier range to appeal to this older age range: 'My Scene'. So far, the strategy appears to be working. The range was launched in 2002 and sales grew by 380% in 2003. However, Barbie is still a much bigger brand than My Scene, and Mattel is determined to keep her at number one.

Mattel has also responded by updating Barbie. She has acquired a tan and split up with Ken, her boyfriend for 43 years. Barbie now uses computers and sends text messages on her mobile phone. But some of these changes have upset some customers, with letters of complaint to the *New York Times* about her lack of commitment to Ken. Although the split raised Barbie's profile, it did not lead to more sales.

More positive early signs have come from the launch of a Barbie-branded range of designer clothes for girls and a Barbie-branded perfume.

Remedies

What should Mattel do? *Marketing* magazine asked for remedies from two experienced toy industry marketers. These are outlined below:

Remedy 1: Ben Green, Chairman of the British Association of Toy Retailers

- Focus on appealing to both parents and girls by balancing the current strengths of the Barbie brand with innovation and changes based on existing trends.
- Make her more relevant to older girls by making her more risqué and upmarket. At present, most Barbie buyers are aged 4–7; Bratz attracts more girls aged 11+.
- Keep changing Barbie in line with the market.
- Remember that Barbie is still the ultimate fantasy for many girls.

Remedy 2: Martin Thomas, Partner in Nylon, Lego's strategic planning agency

- Accept that older children are moving away from dolls and target them with alternative, non-toy products.
- Don't copy Bratz's more streetwise characteristics; Barbie needs to retain her unique selling point.
- Focus on how to make Barbie more appealing to children under the age of 8.
- Target parents and grandparents. They grew up with Barbie and remain her strongest supporters.

Sources: article in *Marketing*, 4 August 2004; news items on the BBC website: www.bbc.co.uk in March and July 2004; *The Money Programme*, BBC2, 21 July 2004.

Questions

Total: 40 marks (45 minutes)

1 Analyse the impact of Barbie's fall in sales on the personnel function of Mattel. *(8 marks)*

2 The case study describes two possible remedies to Barbie's mid-life crisis, suggested by toy industry experts. Which of the two remedies would you adopt and why? *(12 marks)*

3 Discuss the features of a marketing mix that will enable Mattel to overcome the problems created by Barbie's decline in popularity. *(20 marks)*

CASE STUDY 2 Water torture for Coca-Cola

TOPFOTO

Coca-Cola has got itself into a product crisis that could cost the business $2 billion. It had planned a £10 million advertising budget for the March 2004 UK launch of Dasani, a bottled water that is the second biggest selling brand in the USA. However, it has now decided to stop the launch and cancelled plans for Dasani's release into Europe.

Until this month Coca-Cola had ambitious plans for water with worldwide sales growing by 50% per annum for each of the previous 3 years. In the UK, over £1 billion per annum is spent on this rapidly growing product, while the French consume 140 litres per person per annum. The company had planned to follow its launch in the UK with a European launch commencing in France.

The failure of the launch is being blamed on a mixture of arrogance and ignorance. With safe tap water the norm in the UK, bottled water has often been sold on the basis of its origins as much as its purity, with Volvic and Malvern being particularly well-known sources of mineral water. Dasani bottled water came from the mains water supply of a factory in Sidcup, Kent. Coca-Cola's declaration that it had never promoted Dasani as a mineral-water brand did not help. However, the final straw came 2 weeks after this news broke, with the discovery of excessive levels of bromate in the water. Bromate is a chemical that can increase the risk of cancer. The company immediately recalled all of its bottles.

This may not be the end for Coca-Cola, which already owns Malvern in the UK and Bon Aqua in Germany. However, its market share in Europe is only 2%, well short of the two market leaders, Danone (owners of Evian and other brands) and Nestlé (which includes Perrier in its portfolio). Rival executives are delighted: 'It's typical Coke arrogance — they think they can just copy ideas that have worked in the USA, but they can't.'

Media analysts give credit to the UK press, which is quick to pick up on any potential scandals. Coca-Cola also made matters worse by announcing that the Sidcup factory had been 'uniquely designed for the UK market' and that in France 'the water would have come from a genuine mineral source'.

Comparisons have been drawn with the company's largest ever product recall in 1999 when Belgian-produced Coke became contaminated. Coca-Cola blamed it on the cans, but many observers believe that the company's image was damaged more by the firm's reluctance to apologise.

Sources: adapted from an article by David Yelland in *The Times*, 5 March 2004 and an article by Dominic Rushe in *The Sunday Times*, 28 March 2004.

Question

Total: 20 marks (25 minutes)

Evaluate the main reasons for Coca-Cola's failure to launch Dasani successfully in the UK market.

CHAPTER 5

The marketing budget

This chapter examines the marketing budget, studying the different methods that are used to set the level of spending on marketing within an organisation. It also considers the factors that influence the size of the marketing budget.

EXAMINER'S VOICE

Don't confuse the marketing budget (which plans expenditure on marketing activities) with the sales budget (which is a revenue budget that details expected income from sales).

KEY TERM

marketing budget: the amount of money that a firm allocates to spend on marketing activities. This money may be used for activities such as advertising and sales promotions.

Methods for setting the marketing budget

The most common approaches to setting a marketing budget are as follows.

Budgeting according to marketing objectives

The more ambitious the objectives, the greater the budget that is allocated. Mars allocated a £7.5 million marketing budget to try to halt the fall in sales of the Mars Bar. In 2004, Scottish and Newcastle Breweries increased its marketing by 12% to achieve its objective of increasing sales by 6% and persuading customers to accept a slight price increase.

Budgeting according to competitors' spending

In order to stay competitive, a business may have to match the spending of its rivals. The mobile network '3' mounted an aggressive marketing campaign in 2004 to establish itself in the UK market. This led to a large increase in the marketing budgets of O_2 and Orange to protect their market share, and a loss of market share for Vodafone, which did not react to the same extent. This method is also common for new firms, for whom matching the expenditure of rival firms may enable them to stay competitive.

Marketing budget as a percentage of sales revenue

Although this is less scientific, it is commonly used because it is seen to be fair. If a firm matches the national average by spending just under 2% of its sales revenue on advertising, then a product with sales of £100 million per annum will be given a budget of just under £2 million and one with sales of £100,000 will receive almost £2,000. In the UK's liqueur market, advertising budgets for products such as Baileys and Tia Maria equate to 3% of sales revenue, while for Unilever, marketing costs are over 13% of its sales revenue (and much higher than this for its soaps and washing powders).

INGRAM

Zero budgeting/budgeting based on expected outcomes

In effect, this method allocates a budget on the strength of the case presented by the product manager. It is ideal for marketing budgets, as the dynamic nature of marketing means that a budget can be quickly agreed to suit a sudden event. In June 2004, Carlsberg anticipated a great deal of interest in the Euro 2004 football tournament among its target market and mounted a £5 million promotional campaign. This led to a massive 48% increase in sales of its main brands. In July 2004, Scottish and Newcastle Breweries increased the marketing budget for Fosters by £8 million because market research indicated that this level of spending was needed to restore recognition of the brand to its previous high levels. One reason for the decline of Fosters was the increases in sales gained by Carlsberg.

Budgeting according to last year's budget allocation

Although it is less scientific than the other methods, it is common practice for budgets to be set according to last year's allocation plus an allowance for inflation. The logic behind this approach is that, if it was suitable last year, it will be suitable this year. In markets experiencing little change this may be appropriate, so the method is used widely in public services such as the health service and education.

Factors influencing the size of the marketing budget

Some of the factors affecting the size of the marketing budget have already been dealt with in the previous section. The overall size of the budget will depend on:

- the marketing objectives
- the actions of competitors and the usual level of advertising for that industry
- the benefits to be gained from the spending
- last year's allocation

In addition, the marketing budget will be influenced by the following factors.

The organisation's financial situation

If an organisation is experiencing losses or cash-flow problems, it will tend to look more closely at any budget allocations. As the benefits of marketing are often long term and difficult to predict, marketing budgets are vulnerable in times of financial hardship. Similarly, businesses in a strong financial position are often inclined to put more money into marketing.

The cost of advertising in particular media

To some extent, the marketing budget is influenced by the cost of advertising in the media that the organisation wishes to use. Traditionally, television advertising is more expensive than other media, and if a firm feels that television advertising is essential, its budget must be set so that it can afford to use this medium. In recent years, the high cost of television advertising has been blamed for a decline in its use, and as a result the costs have fallen. However, the recent merger between Granada and Carlton has reduced competition and is expected to lead to an increase in television advertising charges.

The relatively low cost of internet advertising has allowed many firms to cut their marketing budgets. Internet advertising now represents 3% of all advertising spending.

The nature of the market

A monopoly may have less need to spend money on marketing, although monopolists do need to advertise in order to increase consumer awareness and prevent consumers moving to different products or services. For example, a train operator may advertise to try to prevent consumers shifting to buses or cars.

Consumer expectations

In some markets, consumers anticipate that marketers will communicate with them in certain ways and through certain media. Although a firm may use a different approach in order to distinguish itself from competitors, it may be difficult for the firm to promote itself differently. For example, many supermarkets offer price reductions on petrol as a reward for expenditure in the store. Any supermarket not making this offer may alienate consumers. Similarly, margarine producers tend to advertise on television, as this is the norm within the industry.

The level of change in the market

In a static market, businesses can rely on long-established reputations to sell products. However, in more dynamic markets, consumers need more information and persuasion in order to keep buying, so a larger budget is required.

The potential return compared with other activities

Marketing is in competition with other functions for the finances in a business. If a firm believes that a new production plant is necessary, it may divert money towards this project. Similarly, a business that believes that new product development is essential may put more money into research and development, leaving less for activities such as marketing that may be seen to offer lower returns. Of course, the business may see all of these activities as profitable and decide to raise additional finance in order to increase all of these expenditure budgets.

PRACTICE EXERCISE

Total: 20 marks (20 minutes)

1 What is the difference between a marketing budget and a sales budget? *(4 marks)*

2 Explain three different ways of setting a marketing budget. *(9 marks)*

3 Analyse two factors that might influence the size of the marketing budget that W.H. Smith plc would allocate to its magazines section. *(7 marks)*

CASE STUDY Marketing budgets in the liqueur industry

Background

The liqueur market is one of the more fragmented in the alcoholic beverages market. Historically, liqueurs have been regarded as an after-dinner tipple, but brands are aiming to promote a wider range of drinking occasions. It is a market that is heavily influenced by the latest fads.

The market

According to Quentin Rappaport of the Wine and Spirits Association, liqueurs are different from other alcoholic drinks. 'They are often bought and kept for a long time.' According to Mintel, the market research organisation, only 25% of consumers drink liqueurs. The market is evenly split among ages, but women are 50% more likely to drink liqueurs than men. Another feature of the market is its bias towards the middle classes, with social groups A, B and C1 dominating purchases. Brands are keen to attract more working-class consumers by changing the current 'stuffy' image of liqueurs.

The market is broadly split into three sectors:

- cream liqueurs, such as Baileys Irish Cream
- traditional liqueurs, such as Cointreau
- shooters (a relatively recent introduction) such as After Shock

Market data

Table 5.1 gives data on the market share of each sector of the liqueur market for 2003.

Liqueur sector	Market share by volume (%)	Market share by value (%)
Cream liqueurs	61	42
Traditional liqueurs	33	40
Shooters	6	18

Source: Mintel.

Table 5.1 *Market share of liqueur sectors, 2003*

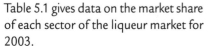

Marketing expenditure

Nearly three-quarters of marketing expenditure takes place in the run-up to Christmas. In recent years, marketing expenditure has been focused on cream liqueurs. The introduction of miniature bottles of cream liqueurs has led to 80% of all liqueur marketing being spent on cream liqueurs. This followed high marketing budgets for shooters, which led to sales of shooters rising by over 670% from 1999 to 2004.

Table 5.2 gives information on certain marketing budgets within the liqueur market in 2003. The table features the seven largest brands and Baileys Minis, a product about to be launched at the time.

The strategy

The makers believe that they can increase sales by encouraging drinkers to consume liqueurs on a regular basis. Currently, most of the consumption (and marketing) takes place around Christmas. Fiona Lovatt, director of marketing at First Drinks Brands, cites

Father's Day, bank holidays, barbecues and summer as examples of occasions that represent opportunities for liqueur drinking.

A recent trend has been to mix liqueurs in cocktails. This now represents 10% of all liqueur drinking (but 20% among those aged 18–24). Producers see trained bar staff as an important part of any strategy to develop this range.

Source: adapted from an article by Samuel Solley in *Marketing*, 4 August 2004.

Product	Sales (£m)	Market share (%)	Marketing budget (£000s)	Share of marketing spending (%)
Baileys Irish Cream	181	28.9	4,173	33.7
Tia Maria	83	13.2	374	3.0
Cointreau	30	4.8	389	3.1
Drambuie	23	3.7	776	6.3
Disaronno	21	3.3	572	4.6
Amarula	19	3.0	894	7.2
Tia Lusso	16	2.6	2,036	16.4
Baileys Minis	0	0	1,701	13.7
Others	254	40.5	1,478	12.0
Total	**627**	**100**	**12,393**	**100**

Sources: Mintel and Nielsen Media Research.

***Table 5.2** Marketing budgets by brand, 2003*

Questions

Total: 40 marks (45 minutes)

1 Calculate the average marketing budget as a percentage of sales in the liqueur industry in 2003. *(3 marks)*

2 What evidence is there to suggest that firms in the liqueur industry do not set their marketing budgets as a percentage of sales revenue? *(5 marks)*

3 Discuss the methods of setting marketing budgets that appear to have been used in the liqueur industry in 2003. *(12 marks)*

4 How might a liqueur producer plan its marketing expenditure in order to encourage consumers to drink liqueur all the year round, instead of just at Christmas? *(8 marks)*

5 Evaluate the possible reasons why the small firms described as 'Others' in Table 5.2 account for 40.5% of sales but only 12.0% of marketing expenditure. *(12 marks)*

Marketing

Unit 4 consists of a case study built around a 'decision'. The four elements of Modules 4 and 5 are tested equally. Thus, questions totalling 20 marks are based on Marketing. Questions on Accounting and Finance, People, and Operations Management are also worth 20 marks each.

There may be a single 20-mark question or two questions totalling 20 marks, one of which involves some evaluation. It is possible that a single question will test a mixture of two elements. The case study examination will be 90 minutes in duration, of which 10 minutes should be used as reading time. All questions are compulsory.

At this point in the textbook, only 'Marketing' has been covered, so it is not possible to provide a case study that integrates all four elements of the modules. Instead, this case study provides an opportunity to tackle a Unit 4 exam-style case study that is based only on Marketing, but which covers the whole of the A2 Marketing specification.

Unit 4 is based on a fictional business. However, this case study and others in the textbook are based on real businesses. These real-life case studies should be viewed as a part of the subject background, as well as the basis for certain questions.

CASE STUDY How Sainsbury's has lost the store wars

Justin King, chief executive of Sainsbury's, faces a challenge. How can he turn around the fortunes of a company that appears to have lost its way? The chief executive has already announced that one-fifth of head-office jobs will be cut in an effort to save costs and put more staff on to the shop floors. Mr King's predecessor spent over £3 billion on automated warehouses and IT systems that are not working properly and have led to shortages on shelves.

The latest profit forecasts show what might appear to be a healthy profit of £200 million, until it is compared with rival Tesco's £2 billion profit. In 8 years, Sainsbury's has fallen from the market leader to number 3 — a position that is now threatened by Morrisons. In recent years, Sainsbury's has lost ground by not retaining as high a level of profits as rivals, such as Tesco. These lower profits will increase the significance of the problem.

King has declared that his immediate focus will be on increasing sales, in contrast to his predecessor Sir Peter Davis, who concentrated on cutting costs and increasing profits. King expects profits to fall even further while he implements his strategy to refurbish 'tired' stores and regain customers through a series of price cuts. King has started already and, according to *The Grocer* magazine, a typical basket of shopping has fallen in price from £49.03 to £41.94 over the past 3 months. Analysts believe that Sainsbury's has not even been getting the basics right and that King's strategy will take until next year to start producing results, particularly as the new lower prices do not seem to be encouraging more shoppers into the stores.

The mammoth task facing King is underlined by a *Sunday Times* survey that shows that the average Sainsbury's store has 10% of its items out of stock (or '90% availability' in retailing terms). The industry average is half the Sainsbury's figure and shows some of the problems caused by the firm's difficulties with supply. Sainsbury's has experienced many difficulties with its distribution network, resulting in many failures to deliver the right stock at the right time. However, depleted stock is also seen as a reflection of demoralised staff. In some stores surveyed, stock was lying around unpacked. A lack of stock not only prevents a sale but also loses customer goodwill, and previously loyal Sainsbury's customers are going to other supermarkets.

Commenting on Sainsbury's relative decline, Richard Hyman, a retail consultant, says:

> Retailing is much more complex than it used to be. It has always been a combination of art and science, but the scientific approach is now playing a larger role and the art of guessing customer wants is becoming less common. The economics of retailing is changing too. Retail used to be dominated by the product, especially the big brand names. Customers have become much more important. There is so much choice nowadays that retailers have to understand their customers and stimulate them.

Recent surveys have shown an increasing trend towards shopping as a leisure pursuit, so the retailers must excite their customers by offering them more.

Some analysts blame store layout for Sainsbury's problems. Sainsbury's appears to shy away from the 'wow' factor of clear, price-led displays. A former director says:

> Customers judge a store in the first 20 feet. What message is Sainsbury's giving out with flower displays? Customers should find themselves in front of something saying 'fantastic value'.

Sainsbury's tendency to stock many versions of a particular item means that it cannot benefit from purchasing economies of scale. Furthermore, this approach leads to more wastage of stock. Other retail experts blame a lack of consistency in Sainsbury's approach. Simon Threadkell of Fitch, the design consultancy that created Sainsbury's Local shops, says:

> One minute you go in and the store is plastered with promotional offers and the next time you go in it is all about quality. It has a schizophrenic approach.

Crispin Tweddell, a former retail consultant, gave the following verdict on Tesco and Sainsbury's as a way of highlighting Sainsbury's challenge:

Tesco **Overall rating: 5 stars**	**Sainsbury's** **Overall rating: 2.5 stars**
• Cheap and cheerful • Packaging and branding are simple and clear • The first aisle shows everything (fruit and vegetables) colourful and in abundance • Large offer signs with no more than four words show where the offers are located • Crisps and snacks feature heavily • There is a complete balance between quality and price from the 'Finest' range to the 'Value' products • Store staff appear to be happier in their jobs	• No sign of food on entry; flowers, wine and cards are featured, sending out an ambiguous message • Fruit and vegetable displays are untidy, making the aisles appear small, and many products show no prices or are placed against the wrong price • In some sections, many shelves are empty • There are too many signs with different messages • Random 'save' signs fail to specify the products • Packaging is too fussy

In the light of this background and the data provided in the appendix, Justin King needs to find a new strategy that will help Sainsbury's to regain some of the ground that it has lost to rival supermarkets.

Sources: articles by Sarah Butler in *The Times*, 12 and 16 October 2004; article by Richard Fletcher in *The Sunday Times* on 17 October 2004; other sources.

Appendix

Year	Market share (%)	Expenditure on new stores/extensions (£m)	Expenditure on refurbishments (£m)	Expenditure on promotions (£m)
1999/2000	18.5	420	90	110
2000/01	18.3	455	25	130
2001/02	17.6	385	220	215
2002/03	16.8	500	85	195
2003/04	16.0	100	25	380

Table 1 *Sainsbury's market share and marketing expenditure, 1999–2004*

Year	Sales revenue (£m)
1999/2000	13,403
2000/01	14,048
2001/02	15,025
2002/03	15,147
2003/04	15,517

Table 2 *Sainsbury's sales revenue, 1999-2004*

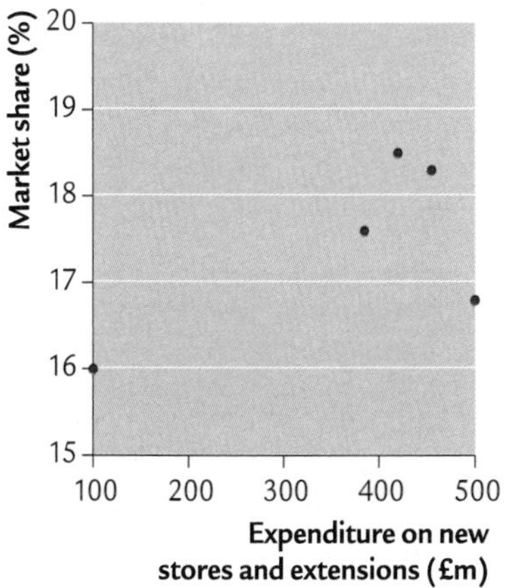

Figure 1 *Sainsbury's market share compared with expenditure on new stores/extensions, 1999–2004*

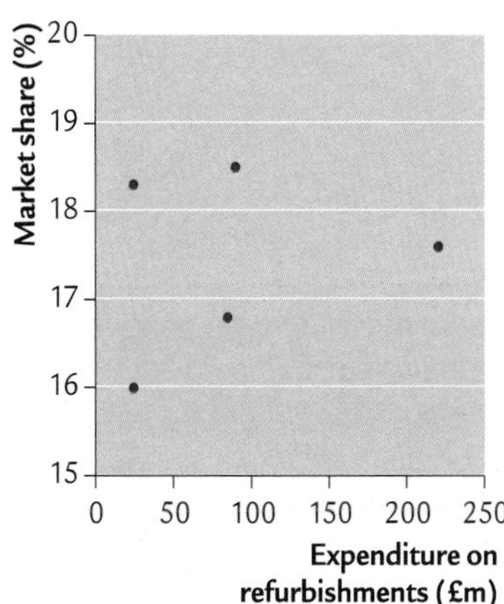

Figure 2 *Sainsbury's market share compared with expenditure on refurbishments, 1999–2004*

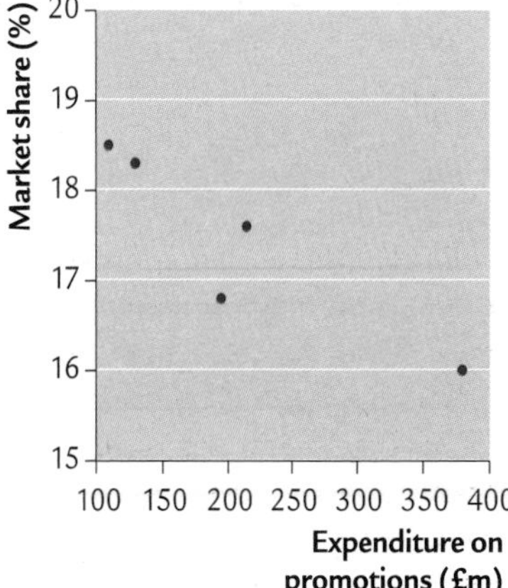

Figure 3 *Sainsbury's market share compared with expenditure on promotions, 1999–2004*

Questions

Total: 80 marks (90 minutes)

1 What evidence is there to suggest that supermarkets are now using scientific decision-making techniques more than in the past? *(6 marks)*

2 Using the data in Table 2, forecast Sainsbury's sales level for the financial year 2004/05. Show your workings. *(4 marks)*

3 Discuss possible reasons why the key elements of Sainsbury's marketing expenditure (shown in Table 1 and Figures 1–3) showed such wide variations in spending during the 5-year period from 1999 to 2004. *(10 marks)*

4 Using the scatter graphs in Figures 1–3, show:

a the market share (%) that Sainsbury's might gain if it spent £170 million on promotions *(3 marks)*

b the level of expenditure on new stores/extensions that might give Sainsbury's a market share of 18%. *(3 marks)*

5 Evaluate the reasons why any forecasts based on the appendix (such as those in question 4) are likely to be unreliable. *(14 marks)*

6 To what extent has Sainsbury's difficulties resulted from poor planning of its marketing mix? *(20 marks)*

7 What strategy or strategies should Sainsbury's adopt in order to increase its market share? Justify your views. *(20 marks)*

Module 4

Accounting and finance

“We didn’t actually overspend our budget. The allocation simply fell short of the expenditure.”

Keith Davis

CHAPTER 6

Interpretation of profit and loss accounts and balance sheets

All businesses keep financial documents to help run the organisation and to comply with legal requirements. Of particular significance are the balance sheet, the profit and loss account, and the cash-flow statement. These documents are required by law in order to show people the financial strengths and weaknesses of the organisation's recent performance and current situation. This chapter introduces company accounts by studying the people who use accounting information and scrutinising the reasons for using it. We then look specifically at the profit and loss account and its purposes. The structure of the profit and loss account is described and the reasons for the structure are explained. The concept of profit quality and the significance of profit utilisation are examined. The chapter then scrutinises the balance sheet, focusing on its layout and its main components. The purposes of the balance sheet are considered and the reasons why it balances are outlined.

Company accounts

The three key financial documents kept by firms are:

- the balance sheet
- the profit and loss account
- the cash-flow statement

KEY TERMS

balance sheet: a document describing the financial position of a company at a particular point in time, by comparing the items owned by the organisation (its assets) with the amount that it owes (its liabilities).

profit and loss account: an account showing the revenue and expenditure (and thus the profit or loss) of a firm over a period of time (usually a year), and the use made of the profit by the firm.

cash-flow statement: a financial document showing the flow of cash into and out of a business over a period of time.

All three documents are based on historical data and show what has happened in the recent past.

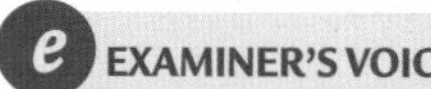

EXAMINER'S VOICE

Do not confuse the cash-flow *statement* with the cash-flow *forecast*. The cash-flow statement shows how the organisation has raised and disposed of cash over a period of time, usually the past 12 months. The cash-flow forecast predicts what the firm expects to happen in the near future, so that it can take any action necessary to avoid a future cash-flow problem.

Purposes and users of company accounts

KEY TERMS

management accounting: the creation of financial information for use by *internal users* in the business, in order to predict, plan, review and control the financial performance of the business.

financial accounting: the provision of financial information to show *external users* the financial position of the business; it concentrates on historical data.

Financial accounts are also used internally as a part of an organisation's control and review policy. In particular, they help managers to assess the effectiveness of their policies.

Accounting information serves many purposes and these depend on who is using the accounts. The main users and purposes are summarised in Table 6.1.

INGRAM

At AS, the main focus in the Accounting and Finance part of the course was on management accounting, through examining breakeven analysis, sources of finance, cash-flow forecasting and budgeting.

The A2 course continues the study of management accounting by extending and developing the study of breakeven analysis and introducing investment appraisal. However, at A2 there is greater emphasis on financial accounting through the study of company accounts and their significance (see Chapter 10 on ratio analysis).

***Table 6.1** Purposes of accounting information*

Users	Purpose
Internal users	
Managers	Managers use information to record financial activities, plan appropriate courses of action, control the use of resources, and analyse and evaluate the effectiveness of actions and decisions taken in financial terms.
Employees	Employees can assess the security of their employment and the ability of the firm to provide them with reasonable wages by examining the financial position of the business.

Users	Purpose
External users	
Government	The government wants to know that the business has met its legal requirements and that it has paid certain levels of tax. In addition, UK firms collect some taxes, such as VAT and the income tax payments of their employees, and pass them on to the tax authorities. Government also uses this information to assess the impact of its economic policies on the sales revenue and profits of businesses, and to plan future policies.
Competitors	Competitors are able to compare their performance against rival companies and benchmark their performances. Government encourages the publicising of results so that firms can learn from each other's strengths and errors.
Suppliers	Suppliers want information about a firm's financial situation before agreeing to supply materials. This may help them to decide if the firm is likely to continue operating. Closer scrutiny may help the supplier to identify the sort of payment terms that are being offered to other suppliers.
Customers	Customers want to know if the company is financially sound and that guarantees and after-sales servicing agreements are secure. Business customers want to establish whether it is advisable for them to draw up long-term supply contracts with this company.
The local community	The local community relies on businesses for employment and wealth creation. The local council may need to modify its housing or road-building plans if a local firm is getting into financial difficulties and likely to close down or reduce staff. (It may also need to consider the possible consequences if a local firm is becoming very successful and wishes to expand.)
Owners and investors	Investors want to compare the financial benefits of their investment with alternatives, such as shares in different companies or placing their savings in a bank. Invariably, the financial benefits to owners and investors are closely related to the financial success of the business.

The profit and loss account

Profit (or loss) is the difference between a firm's revenue and its costs. If revenue exceeds costs, a profit is made. If costs are greater than revenue, a loss is recorded. For many organisations, making a profit is their main objective. Even if other aims, such as growth, image, workforce welfare and social responsibility are pursued, financial success is needed to fund these objectives.

Purposes of the profit and loss account

- Regular calculations of profit throughout the year help managers to review progress before the final end-of-year accounts are completed, while the final accounts allow the firm to assess the success of its policies.

- To satisfy legal requirements, the Companies Act requires firms to publish their profit and loss account.
- Publication allows stakeholders to see if the firm is meeting their needs.
- Comparisons can be made between different firms (inter-firm comparisons) in order to measure relative performance.
- Comparisons can be made over time to see if the firm is improving its performance, or to compare the effectiveness of different divisions or branches within the firm (intra-firm comparisons).
- The profit and loss account can be used to show potential investors that the firm is successful and able to repay loans or provide a good return on investments.

FACT FILE

The details provided in the company accounts depend on the legal structure of the business. The government requires more detail from a public limited company than from a private limited company. Accounts of sole traders only need to meet the needs of the tax authorities.

Structure of the profit and loss account

The profit and loss account is divided into three sections, each of which provides useful information for users of the accounts. These are:

- the trading account
- the profit and loss account
- the appropriation account

The trading account

This account records the turnover (sales income) of the company and the 'cost of sales' (costs that can be linked directly to the provision of the product or service). 'Cost of sales' includes items such as raw materials and wages of production-line workers for a manufacturer, or the cost of purchasing stock and warehousing and transporting the stock to shops for a retailer. This account calculates the **gross profit**.

TOPFOTO

KEY TERM

gross profit: revenue minus cost of sales. The gross profit shows how efficiently a business is converting its raw materials or stock into finished products. It is useful to compare the gross profit with that of competitors, but as overheads are excluded from the calculation, gross profit is of limited use as a measure of performance.

The profit and loss account

This account takes the gross profit and deducts those costs that are not directly related to producing the product or service, such as marketing expenditure,

general administration costs, rent and depreciation. These costs are termed 'expenses' or 'overheads'. This account calculates the **operating profit**.

KEY TERMS

operating profit: the revenue earned from everyday trading activities minus the costs involved in carrying out those activities.

net profit: gross profit minus expenses or overheads.

EXAMINER'S VOICE

The AQA A2 specification makes no direct reference to operating profit, as net profit is declared as the actual profit made. However, in exceptional circumstances net profit may rely on unusual, one-off items. In these circumstances, operating profit provides a useful measure of success.

Net profit takes all revenues and costs into consideration, not just those related to everyday trading activities. It is deemed to be a reliable indicator of a firm's performance because it shows the actual profit made. However, it is possible that 'exceptional' or 'extraordinary' items (see below for details) are included in the accounts. These affect net profit but are not included in the calculation of operating profit. These items may give a misleading impression of performance. In these situations, operating profit is a better indication of the efficiency of the business.

In addition, the profit and loss account includes information on any interest payments made by the business and any tax paid on the profits made.

The appropriation account

This statement shows what happens to the profit (how it is used or distributed). Typically, the appropriation account shows how much of the profit is retained by (or 'ploughed back' into) the business and how much is distributed to shareholders. Tax paid is often shown as an element of the appropriation account, but such a format is not used in this book.

EXAMINER'S VOICE

Always remember to compare like with like when analysing a given profit or loss. The profit recorded may be the net profit or the operating profit and it might be shown before or after interest payments and/or tax. Comparing net profit before interest and tax with operating profit after interest and tax would lead to an inappropriate conclusion.

Additional information

The summaries above are brief and only intended to give a guide to the layout of a profit and loss account. In the UK it is common practice not to provide a detailed breakdown of the 'cost of sales' in the published accounts, but most companies include a separate reference to any 'one-off' factors that have influenced the overall profit level. These are known as:

- **extraordinary items.** These are very rare events that are not a normal part of trading, such as Kingfisher's sale of Comet. This inflated the income and overall profit of Kingfisher in the year in which it occurred, but it must be shown by law, so that investors know the reason for the final profit figure.
- **exceptional items.** These events are more in line with everyday activities but are separated because, like extraordinary items, they have had a one-off effect on profits that will not be continued. In 2003 Bunzl plc (see example below) undertook a major rationalisation process that involved the closure of a division. The cost of £54 million was entered as a one-off exceptional cost/loss, as in future years it was expected to increase profit levels.
- **profit (loss) from other activities.** These are activities separate from the main business, such as a shareholding in a joint venture with another company. These items are listed separately because they do not relate to the main focus of the business.

Reasons for the structure of the profit and loss account

The profit and loss is structured into three sections for the following reasons:

- The trading account enables a business to see how efficiently it is turning materials into sales revenue. A high gross profit level suggests that costs of sales are being kept low or that the business is achieving a high **value added** by creating a product that fetches a high price. However, it is vital that comparison is made with similar businesses so that the conclusion is based on the norm for that industry.
- The profit and loss account shows the efficiency of a firm in controlling its overheads/expenses. If expenses are low, the firm should be able to secure a high net profit. Again, it is necessary to compare its performance with its competitors before drawing a conclusion.
- The appropriation account is of particular interest to shareholders. A business that is using most of its profits to pay high dividends will please shareholders looking for a quick return. However, shareholders with a long-term interest in the business may prefer to see higher retained profits, as these will be reinvested into the business to boost profits in the future.

The layout of the profit and loss account

It is customary to publish the latest profit and loss account alongside the profit and loss account from the previous year (or the equivalent period from the previous financial year if the account covers less than 1 year). It is usual for firms to publish 6-month or 3-month profit and loss accounts.

Example: Bunzl plc

Bunzl plc is the leading supplier and distributor of materials and products to retailers and caterers. It specialises in providing packaging for finished food products. It also makes and transports finished products, such as sandwiches and ready-made salads, to supermarkets, caterers and hotels.

Table 6.2 shows the profit and loss account for Bunzl plc for the financial years ending in 2003 and 2004. Note that it is traditional to place the latest year on the left and the previous year on the right.

Table 6.2 Profit and loss accounts for Bunzl plc

		Years ending:	31.12.04 £m	31.12.03 £m
Trading account		SALES REVENUE	2,916	2,728
	minus	COST OF SALES	1,694	1,522
	equals	GROSS PROFIT	1,222	1,206
Profit and loss account	minus	EXPENSES/OVERHEADS	996	940
	plus (minus)	Exceptional items	–	(54)
	equals	OPERATING PROFIT	226	212
	plus (minus)	PROFIT (LOSS) FROM OTHER ACTIVITIES	(20)	(17)
	equals	NET PROFIT BEFORE INTEREST	206	195
	minus	INTEREST	5	2
	equals	NET PROFIT BEFORE TAX	201	193
	minus	CORPORATION TAX	72	69
	equals	NET PROFIT AFTER TAX	129	124
The uses to which the profit is put are shown below:				
Appropriation account		NET PROFIT AFTER TAX	129	124
	minus	DIVIDENDS TO SHAREHOLDERS	60	54
	equals	RETAINED PROFIT	69	70

Profit quality

Although all businesses aim to make a profit, it is possible to distinguish between high-quality profit and low-quality profit.

KEY TERM

profit quality: a measure of whether profit is sustainable in the long run — high-quality profit is profit that will continue; low-quality profit arises from exceptional or extraordinary circumstances that are unlikely to continue.

When analysing accounts, profit is used to assess performance and so it is vital to know if there are any unusual or one-off circumstances that are affecting the accounts in the year being studied. For example, if a firm sells many of its fixed assets, this will increase its net profit for this year because of this one-off source of income. However, the sale of these fixed assets may reduce future performance, as fixed assets produce the goods and services that help the business to make a profit. We can conclude that in this case the profit shown in that year is of low quality.

In contrast, a firm may be undergoing a major restructuring programme, which in the short term could lower profit, as the firm adjusts to the new systems. However, this could lead to greater profit in the long term.

WHAT DO YOU THINK?

In 2004, Tesco reported a record annual profit of £2,000 million (£2 billion) as a result of greater efficiency than its competitors. This level of profit is high quality because it is likely to continue into the future.

TOPFOTO

In the same year, Shell announced profits of £2.4 billion for the first quarter of the year and a plan to earn £2 billion from the sale of some subsidiary companies, in order to reward shareholders. Clearly Shell's planned £2 billion profit is of lower quality than its reported £2.4 billion profit. However, there are differences of opinion about the £2.4 billion. Some people see it as a short-term, low-quality profit arising from current shortages in oil supply; others believe that these shortages will remain a permanent feature of the oil market and that companies such as Shell will be able to rely on them into the future. What do you think?

FACT FILE

'Profit quality' can also apply to lower than expected profits. In July 2004, Morrisons, the supermarket chain, issued the first profits warning in its 37-year history, and then gave a repeat warning early in 2005. These were blamed on teething problems as a result of its takeover of Safeways. In the long run, Morrisons expects to benefit from economies of scale resulting from the takeover, and believes that eventual profits will be much higher as a result.

Profit utilisation

KEY TERM

- **profit utilisation:** the way in which a business uses its profit or surplus.

Profit utilisation is shown in the appropriation account. It is common for a business to use its profit in one of two ways.

Dividends paid to shareholders

Every 6 months, public limited companies usually pay a dividend to their shareholders. This dividend payment represents the share of the profits allocated to shareholders. Shareholders tend to buy shares for three different reasons: to earn regular dividends; to receive capital gains from selling their shares at a higher price than the purchase price; and to receive voting rights at the company's annual general meetings (AGMs). Voting rights are sought mainly by those wanting to obtain control of the business, but are increasingly being sought by pressure groups to get their views across at the AGM.

Some shareholders depend on the dividend payment as a source of income, particularly retired people who rely on their shares to provide a steady flow of money. These shareholders may have a greater interest in making sure that a high dividend is paid.

Retained profits

In order to fund expansion plans and capital investment, the company directors will wish to keep some of the profits in the business. This avoids the need to pay interest on borrowed money or to sell more shares in order to finance expansion. Retained (or 'ploughed-back') profits increase the assets of a business and should therefore increase the value of the company. Furthermore, retained profits should help the business to increase its future profits (and thus increase future dividends). Consequently, shareholders often support requests to increase the level of retained profit. In practice, most firms will strike a balance between paying dividends and retaining profits.

On occasions, profit may be utilised in different ways. As indicated on page 71, Shell recently used some profit to reward shareholders. It did this by giving them £2 billion through buying back some of its shares.

FACT FILE

Decisions to retain profit or pay dividends often depend on recent history and corporate aims. Table 6.2 shows that Bunzl plc has recorded steady profits and has thus been able to keep a consistent balance between dividend payments and retained profits. In contrast, Rolls-Royce's policy (see Table 6.4 on p. 81) arises from 2002 (the year before the accounts shown) when it made a loss of £53 million but paid dividends totalling £133 million. This was possible because of retained profits from earlier years. Having drained some of the company's funds in 2002, shareholders agreed to a lower dividend in 2003 and received no dividend in 2004 when the company recorded a good profit level. It is perhaps no coincidence that Bunzl, a US company, retains a higher percentage of its profits than most UK companies. US companies have a reputation for retaining much of their profits in order to fund future expansion. UK companies are often accused of taking short-term decisions to satisfy the immediate needs of shareholders.

PRACTICE EXERCISE 1 — Total: 40 marks (35 minutes)

1 Identify three purposes of a profit and loss account. *(3 marks)*

2 Explain the differences between the trading account, the profit and loss account and the appropriation account. *(9 marks)*

3 How is gross profit calculated? *(2 marks)*

4 What is the difference between net profit and operating profit? *(4 marks)*

5 Identify the two deductions from net profit that are usually made before the appropriation account is compiled. *(2 marks)*

6 Identify the two uses to which profit is appropriated. *(2 marks)*

7 Using the figures below, calculate:
   a the gross profit *(3 marks)*
   b the operating profit *(3 marks)*

Show all of your working.

Cost of raw materials	£400,000
Marketing expenditure	£125,000
General administration	£200,000
Sales revenue	£980,000
Wages of production-line workers	£110,000

8 A company must pay corporation tax of 30% on its profit of £200,000. If it plans to use 60% of its profits (after tax) to build an extension to its factory, how much of its profit will be paid to shareholders? *(4 marks)*

9 Explain the meaning of profit quality. *(4 marks)*

10 Why might shareholders allow a business to keep all of the profit for its own use? *(4 marks)*

Balance sheets

The balance sheet looks at the accumulated wealth of the business and can be used to assess its overall worth. It lists the resources that a business owns (its **assets**) and the items that it owes (its **liabilities**). In addition, it shows the capital provided by the owners (the shareholders in a limited company). Capital is provided through either the purchase of shares or the agreement to allow the company to retain or 'plough back' profit into the business, known as **reserves**, rather than using it to pay further dividends to the shareholders. If a business ceases trading, the shareholders receive the value of the company's assets after liabilities have been paid in full to the creditors.

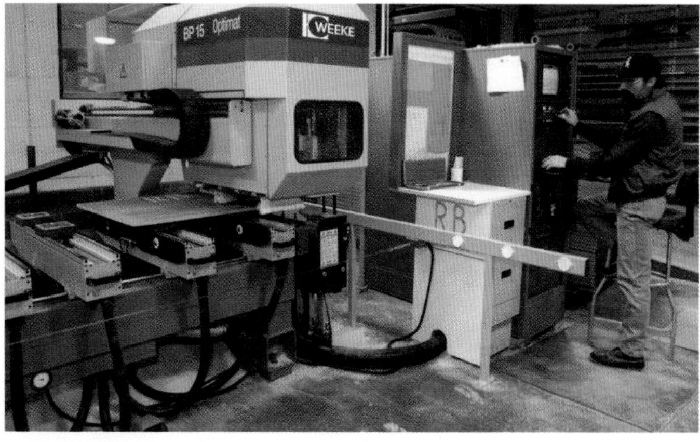

TOPFOTO

Elements of the balance sheet

In order to understand the layout of the balance sheet, it is important to understand the different elements listed in it.

Assets

KEY TERM

- **assets:** items that are owned by an organisation.

Assets can be divided into two main categories according to time:

- **Fixed assets** tend to be owned by an organisation for a period of more than 1 year.
- **Current assets** tend to be owned for less than 1 year.

KEY TERMS

fixed assets: resources that can be used repeatedly in the production process, although they do wear out (depreciate). Examples are land, buildings, machinery and vehicles.

tangible assets: fixed assets that exist physically.

intangible assets: fixed assets that do not have a physical presence, but are nevertheless of value to a firm, e.g. a brand name or patent.

In general, **fixed assets** are purchased to allow the business to operate continually. Land and buildings are acquired so that the firm has the premises from which to operate. Machinery and equipment enable organisations to manufacture and/or sell their goods and services, and to administer their business. Vehicles are required for delivery and staff transport, as appropriate.

DID YOU KNOW?

The balance sheet only shows those fixed assets that are owned by the business. In summer 2004, HBOS sold its headquarters in central London for £145 million and it now rents the property from the new owners. As a consequence, HBOS's fixed assets fell by £145 million (but its cash reserves rose by £145 million).

FACT FILE

The three biggest owners of trains and railway carriages in the UK are banks! Abbey, HSBC and Royal Bank of Scotland added £4.2 billion of trains and railway carriages to their fixed assets between 1996 and 2004. Why? The government typically offers train operators a franchise (the right to run a service) for 7 years. However, the trains usually have an economic life of 30 years. It is a big gamble for a train operator such as Stagecoach to buy trains to run a 7-year franchise. As a result, the three banks have set up rolling stock companies that lease the trains to the operators. This reduces the risk to the operator and provides a nice source of profit for the banks — an average of £1 billion per annum in recent years. Typically, the train operators will not possess trains as one of their fixed assets.

TOPFOTO

The main intangible asset is **goodwill** and includes the value of a firm's brand names, patents and copyrights. The value of intangible assets is difficult to assess objectively and so it is customary to exclude them from the balance sheet.

DID YOU KNOW?

Although accounting regulations indicate that businesses should not include intangible assets, such as the value of a brand name, in their balance sheets, there is a major exception to this rule. A business that buys another firm invariably pays for the goodwill/intangible assets belonging to that firm. As money has been paid for these intangible assets, they are included as a fixed asset in the balance sheet.

The value of each tangible fixed asset is reduced annually; this is known as **depreciation** (see Chapter 7). Similarly, businesses must reduce the value of their goodwill over time; this process is known as **amortisation**.

In recent years, Bunzl plc has bought a number of other businesses, spending £255 million in 2004 with the aim of getting hold of brands, processes and expertise. As a consequence, its intangible assets are valued at a higher level than its tangible assets, and amortisation of goodwill in 2004 was a massive £102 million.

KEY TERM

current assets: short-term items that circulate in a business on a daily basis and can be expected to be turned into cash within 1 year.

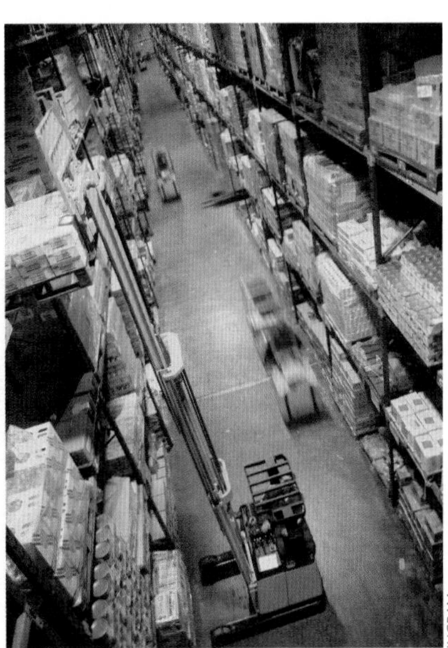
INGRAM

Examples of **current assets** are stocks, debtors (people who owe the business money — usually customers who have been given credit terms), the bank balance and cash.

Stocks consist of finished products, work-in-progress (partially completed goods) and raw materials. In order to meet the accounting concept of prudence, stocks are valued at the cost paid, rather than the price they are expected to fetch. Firms regularly update the value of their stock. If stock has been damaged, is past its sell-by date or has gone out of fashion, its value is reduced. Similarly, the value of debtors is reduced if any debtor is behind schedule and unlikely to pay. (Most firms value their debts at slightly below their face value to allow for **bad debts**: that is, debts that are not paid.)

Liabilities

KEY TERM

liabilities: debts owed by an organisation to suppliers, shareholders, investors or customers who have paid in advance.

Liabilities are classified according to time, in a similar way to assets:

- **Long-term liabilities** are debts due for repayment after more than 1 year.
- **Current liabilities** are debts scheduled for repayment within 1 year.

Examples of **long-term liabilities** are debentures and long-term or medium-term loans. Debentures are fixed-interest loans with a repayment date set a long time into the future. The holder of a debenture certificate may sell it to another investor, who will then receive the interest and repayment. Loans are usually provided by banks. These long-term liabilities must be repaid, but they mean that a company does not need to issue more shares to raise funds to purchase fixed assets.

Examples of **current liabilities** are creditors, bank overdrafts, corporation tax owing and shareholders' dividends due for payment. Creditors are people or organisations that are owed money by the firm. Often these are suppliers awaiting payment, but they may be trade creditors who have supplied services, such as gas, electricity and telephone systems.

FACT FILE

Information on current assets and current liabilities in isolation is of limited use. However, when current liabilities are subtracted from current assets, the figure provided, known as **working capital**, gives a strong indication of the firm's ability to pay its liabilities. In August 2004, Euro Disney had €63 million in cash and at the bank, but its current liabilities were so high that it forecast that it would be unable to meet its debts after the end of September 2004. (Do not despair if you are a Mickey Mouse fan — it managed to get help in order to survive.)

TOPFOTO

Capital

KEY TERM

capital: funds provided by shareholders to set up the business, fund expansion and purchase fixed assets.

Capital takes two main forms:

- **Share capital** — the funds provided by shareholders through the purchase of shares.

- **Reserves** — those items that arise from increases in the value of the company, which are not distributed to shareholders as dividends, but are retained by the business for future use.

Most reserves arise because shareholders have voted at the annual general meeting to allow the firm to keep some of the profit, rather than distribute it to shareholders as dividends.

EXAMINER'S VOICE

Remember, reserves are not cash. Usually they are an entry in the accounts that shows how much profit the firm has retained, but invariably the purpose of this action is to purchase fixed assets. Any cash held by the business is shown under current assets. Technically, reserves are included to recognise the fact that there is a liability to shareholders, not an asset. Reserves represent the sum that shareholders could have taken as dividends, but which was retained in the business for its own use.

Purposes of the balance sheet

The details provided in the balance sheet help stakeholders to assess the financial strength of a business. As with the profit and loss account, the balance sheet should be studied over time and a comparison made with the balance sheets of competitors in order to draw valid conclusions.

Studying a balance sheet serves the following purposes:

- **Recognising the value of a business.** Adding fixed assets to working capital (see Table 6.3) gives the net worth of a business. This figure can be compared with other firms or previous years. It can also be used to see if the share price is an accurate valuation of the business's wealth.
- **Gaining an understanding of the nature of the firm.** The structure of a firm's assets may give information about the nature of the business:
  - Primary industries, such as agriculture and mineral extraction, often own large areas of land in comparison to other firms, although high street organisations may own expensive land.
  - Shops tend to possess high levels of stock, as they need to display their goods to attract customers. Lower levels of stock tend to be held by firms providing personal and financial services, as they are often selling expertise rather than an item that can be stocked. Manufacturers operating just-in-time methods of production also carry low levels of stock.
  - Low levels of debtors are shown on the accounts of firms providing personal and financial services, as there is a tradition of immediate payment rather than credit facilities being provided.
- **Identifying the company's liquidity position.** Comparing liquid or current assets (those that can be turned into cash quickly) with current liabilities (those that must be paid back soon) shows whether a firm is going to be able to avoid cash-flow problems. (We will return to this in Chapter 8: 'Working capital'.)

TOPFOTO

- **Showing sources of capital.** A company raising its finance from retained profits (shown as reserves) is in a stronger position than one that has not benefited from this source. In contrast, a business that relies heavily on long-term loans may be vulnerable if interest rates rise.
- **Recognising the significance of changes over time.** Continual scrutiny of the balance sheet can identify undesirable changes and allow a business to take appropriate action to prevent difficulties (such as a shortage of stock or a rise in bad debts). The balance sheet also shows if the business is growing in value compared with other businesses.

The layout of the balance sheet: the vertical format

The vertical format allows the value of a company (its **net worth**) to be calculated, by adding **fixed assets** to **working capital** or **net current assets** (current assets minus current liabilities), or by taking total assets and subtracting current liabilities (see Table 6.3).

***Table 6.3** Balance sheets of Bunzl plc, 31 December 2004 and 2003*

	As at:	31.12.04 (£m)	31.12.03 (£m)
Fixed assets			
Intangible assets		541.3	290.9
Fixed assets		218.4	196.5
TOTAL FIXED ASSETS		**759.7**	**487.4**
Current assets			
Stocks		275.2	215.6
Debtors		468.5	374.7
Short-term investments		29.3	111.3
Bank balance and cash		78.4	47.5
TOTAL CURRENT ASSETS		**851.4**	**749.1**
minus			
Current liabilities			
Creditors (less than 1 year)		786.3	499.1
equals			
WORKING CAPITAL			
(net current assets)		**65.1**	**250.0**
NET ASSETS EMPLOYED/net worth/			
total assets less current liabilities		**824.8**	**737.4**
minus			
Long-term liabilities			
Creditors (more than 1 year)		297.8	220.2
Other long-term liabilities		95.2	82.4
		393.0	**302.6**
TOTAL NET ASSETS		**431.8**	**434.8**
Capital and reserves			
Share capital		209.8	205.3
Reserves		222.0	229.5
		431.8	**434.8**
TOTAL CAPITAL EMPLOYED		**824.8**	**737.4**

Why the balance sheet always balances

The balance sheet balances because:

assets = liabilities + capital

The balance sheet always balances because of the way it is constructed. The compilation of a balance sheet is based on the **dual aspect concept**, which states that any recording of an asset must also record a claim against it of equal value. Claims against assets are shown as liabilities or capital. Occasionally, the balance is achieved by increasing the value of one asset and decreasing the value of another asset by an identical amount.

Accounting transactions are recorded by a system known as **double entry**, which balances assets against liabilities or capital. The following three examples illustrate this system, which ensures that the balance sheet remains in balance:

- **A company raises £5,000 from issuing shares.** This action increases a current asset (cash) by £5,000 and increases capital (in the form of share capital) by £5,000.
- **The company buys £1,000 of goods on credit.** This transaction increases an asset (stock) by £1,000 and this is matched by an increase in a short-term liability (creditors) of £1,000.
- **The company sells £3,000 of stock on credit.** This transaction decreases an asset (stock) by £3,000 and increases another asset (debtors) by £3,000. The balance sheet therefore remains balanced.

INGRAM

What happens if the stock valued at £3,000 is sold for £4,000? In this instance, overall assets will increase by £1,000. However, this profit belongs to the shareholders, so it is also recorded as an increase of £1,000 in a capital item (reserves).

Any loss is dealt with in a similar way. If stock worth £6,000 is 'written off' (deemed to be worthless), the reduction of £6,000 in stock (an asset) is matched by a fall of £6,000 in the reserves (a capital item).

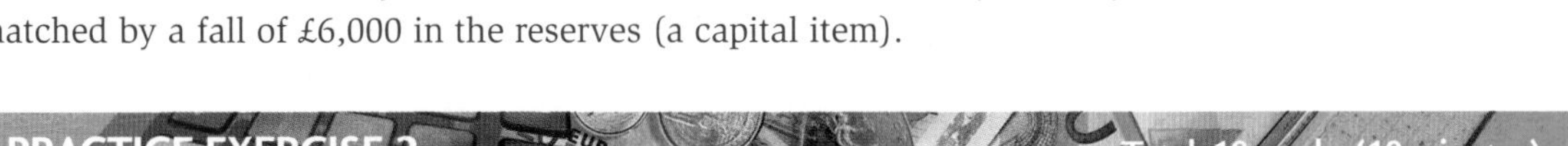

PRACTICE EXERCISE 2 Total: 10 marks (10 minutes)

Refer to the profit and loss account for Bunzl plc for the year ending 31 December 2004 (see Table 6.2 on p. 70). Rewrite the profit and loss account to take into consideration the following changes:

- Sales revenue: increase by £40 million
- Raw materials: decrease by £15 million
- Marketing: increase by £16 million
- Corporation tax: equal to 30% of net profit before tax
- Dividend to shareholders: equal to 40% of net profit after tax

PRACTICE EXERCISE 3 — Total: 35 marks (30 minutes)

1 What is meant by a 'balance sheet? *(3 marks)*

2 What are the differences between assets, liabilities and capital? *(6 marks)*

3 Identify three fixed assets. *(3 marks)*

4 Identify three current assets. *(3 marks)*

5 Why is it important to distinguish between fixed assets and current assets? *(4 marks)*

6 Identify three current liabilities. *(3 marks)*

7 Explain three uses of balance sheets. *(9 marks)*

8 Why must the balance sheet always balance? *(4 marks)*

PRACTICE EXERCISE 4 — Total: 20 marks (20 minutes)

Using the data in the table, calculate the following values:

1 Fixed assets *(3 marks)*

2 Current assets *(3 marks)*

3 Current liabilities *(3 marks)*

4 Working capital *(3 marks)*

5 Total net assets *(3 marks)*

6 Long-term liabilities *(2 marks)*

7 Capital *(3 marks)*

	£m
Intangible assets	68
Cash	4
Creditors	23
Share capital	74
Debtors	34
Bank overdraft	3
Bank loans (over 1 year)	16
Land and buildings	88
Stock	19
Vehicles	11
Reserves	132
Plant and machinery	24

CASE STUDY Rolls-Royce gearing up for take-off

To remind us of its pedigree, Rolls-Royce celebrated its one hundredth anniversary at the 2004 Farnborough air show with a display of aircraft powered by Rolls-Royce engines — from Spitfires to the Airbus A340.

After the disposal of its car division, Rolls-Royce basically had one role — manufacturer of aircraft engines. However, its main product — the Trent engine — has been adapted for ships and power generators. After GE of America, Rolls-Royce is the second biggest engine-maker in the world. Few UK companies can claim such status.

The future looks bright for Rolls-Royce. It had forecast a decline in sales and profits for 2004, but as shown in Table 6.4, both showed increases in comparison to 2003. With its two main customers, aircraft manufacturers Boeing and Airbus, both predicting sales increases of 10–15% for 2005, Rolls-Royce is expecting further growth. Its engines are on both of the next generation of commercial aircraft — Airbus's A380 superjumbo and Boeing's 787 dreamliner. Furthermore, it has received advance orders for a further 50 commercial and military projects. In total, the company's order book stretches to £19.7 billion — a very secure level for a company with annual sales of less than £6 billion.

Replacement parts and upgrades on its existing products account for 55% of its total sales, so the order book suggests a significant growth in sales in the near future.

Rolls-Royce has spread its risks well — no single contract accounts for more than 3% of its sales. Furthermore, the company is gaining so much cash that it is likely to have paid off its debt by the end of the year. For the year ending 31 December 2005, the directors are forecasting sales of £6,200 million and net profit before tax of £400 million.

Source: based on an article by Philip Aldrick in the *Daily Telegraph*, 30 July 2004, and recent annual reports of Rolls-Royce plc.

***Table 6.4** Profit and loss accounts for Rolls-Royce plc*

		Years ending:	31.12.04 (£m)	31.12.03 (£m)
Trading account		SALES REVENUE	5,939	5,645
	minus	COST OF SALES (direct costs)	4,812	4,714
	equals	GROSS PROFIT	1,127	931
Profit and loss account	minus	EXPENSES/OVERHEADS		
		Research and development	282	281
		Marketing and product support	252	181
		General administration	273	140
			807	602
	plus (minus)	Exceptional items	–	(54)
	equals	OPERATING PROFIT	320	275
	plus	PROFIT (LOSS) FROM OTHER ACTIVITIES	(56)	(5)
	equals	NET PROFIT BEFORE INTEREST	376	270
	minus	INTEREST	70	90
	equals	NET PROFIT BEFORE TAX	306	180
	minus	CORPORATION TAX	102	64
	equals	NET PROFIT AFTER TAX	204	116
The uses to which the profit is put are shown below:				
Appropriation account		NET PROFIT AFTER TAX	204	116
	minus	DIVIDENDS TO SHAREHOLDERS	0	53
	equals	RETAINED PROFIT	204	63

Table 6.5 Balance sheets of Rolls-Royce plc, 31 December 2004 and 2003

	As at:	31.12.04 (£m)	31.12.03 (£m)
Fixed assets			
Intangible assets		911	863
Fixed assets		1,882[a]	2,015
TOTAL FIXED ASSETS		**2,793**	**2,878**
Current assets			
Stocks		1,081	962
Debtors		2,410[b]	2,606
Short-term investments		730	174
Bank balance and cash		758[c]	794
TOTAL CURRENT ASSETS		**4,979**	**4,536**
minus			
Current liabilities			
Creditors (less than 1 year)		2,774[d]	2,853
equals			
WORKING CAPITAL (net current assets)		**2,205**	**1,683**
Total assets less current liabilities		**4,998**	**4,561**
Long-term liabilities			
Creditors (more than 1 year)		1,904[e]	1,623
Other long-term liabilities		787	795
		2,691	**2,418**
TOTAL NET ASSETS		**2,307**	**2,143**
Capital and reserves			
Share capital		443	435
Reserves		1,864	1,708
		2,307	**2,143**
TOTAL CAPITAL EMPLOYED		**4,998**	**4,561**

Questions

Total: 40 marks (45 minutes)

1 Referring solely to Table 6.4, to what extent can it be concluded that 2004 was a more successful year for Rolls-Royce plc than 2003? *(15 marks)*

2 Study the changes in Rolls-Royce's balance sheet between 31 December 2003 and 31 December 2004 (Table 6.5). Briefly describe the possible reasons for each of the five changes labelled a to e. *(10 marks)*

3 Based on the article and the accounts, discuss whether Rolls-Royce's financial position is likely to improve or worsen between 2004 and 2005. *(15 marks)*

CHAPTER 7

Capital expenditure, revenue expenditure and depreciation

This chapter examines the distinction between capital expenditure and revenue expenditure and the implications of these concepts for the two main sets of company accounts: the balance sheet and the profit and loss account. The concept of depreciation is introduced and the calculation of straight-line depreciation is explained. The chapter concludes by looking at the purposes of depreciation, its implications, and the mix of objectivity and subjectivity in its use.

Classifying business expenditure

Business expenditure can be classified as either revenue expenditure or capital expenditure.

KEY TERMS

revenue expenditure: spending on day-to-day items such as raw materials, stock, wages and power to run the production process.

capital expenditure: spending on **fixed assets** — those assets used over and over again in the production process, such as buildings, vehicles and machinery.

Capital expenditure exists when the spending is on an item that will be used time and time again. For accounting purposes, if the expenditure on an asset continues to help the business in future years, then it is capital expenditure.

DID YOU KNOW?

As with many business classifications, the distinction between revenue spending and capital spending is open to interpretation. The key distinction is the length of time that the business benefits from the spending. For marketing spending it is often argued that this year's marketing can help to build a brand for the future. However, for the sake of simplicity, marketing is taken to be revenue expenditure. Similarly, a business that rents its property is undertaking revenue expenditure but an organisation that buys its property is making a capital expenditure.

CHAPTER 7 Capital expenditure, revenue expenditure and depreciation

The main categories of revenue expenditure and capital expenditure are listed in Table 7.1.

Table 7.1 Categories of revenue expenditure and capital expenditure

Revenue expenditure	Capital expenditure
■ Wages and salaries to employees ■ Office consumables such as stationery and ink cartridges ■ Operating expenses such as power and petrol for vehicles ■ Marketing expenditure ■ Raw materials and stock ■ Rental payments	■ Freehold property or extensions to premises ■ Machinery for production purposes ■ Office equipment and furniture ■ Vehicles

The significance of the distinction between capital and revenue expenditure

When constructing accounts, accountants follow certain agreed principles. One of the basic rules of accounting is the **matching** or **accruals concept**. This states that, when calculating a firm's profit, any income should be matched to the expenditure involved in creating that income. What are the implications of this convention?

For **revenue expenditure**, the implications are reasonably clear. Any wages paid to production-line workers and payments for raw materials are deducted from the income earned from selling the final product. It is assumed that the sales revenue and expenditure take place in the same financial year. Thus, wages and power are always treated as a cost in the year in which the payment is made. In general, payments for raw materials are treated in the same way. However, if there are some raw materials left over at the end of the year, the value of those raw materials is transferred to the next year's accounts, as that is when they will be used. This meets the requirements of the 'matching' principle, because raw material costs are matched to the time period in which they are used to make the finished products.

For **capital expenditure**, the situation is very different. Fixed assets are used over a long period, so any capital expenditure needs to be spread over the lifetime of the fixed asset in order to 'match' the spending to the income that it creates. For example, a machine that costs £50,000 and lasts for 5 years could be deemed to cost £10,000 a year for the next 5 years. It should not be charged as £50,000 in the year in which it is purchased because it will continue to create income in all 5 years.

Another accounting convention (that of **prudence**) states that accounts should ensure that the worth of the business is not exaggerated. This means that a firm must be careful and therefore slightly pessimistic in estimating the value of its assets.

These two conventions (matching and prudence) lead to a system that reduces the value of any fixed asset by a sum equal to the figure that has been agreed as the cost of the item for that year. In the above example, the value of the £50,000 asset will fall by £10,000 per year for 5 years so that at the end of the 5 years it is worth nothing. This process is known as **depreciation**.

Depreciation

TERMS

depreciation: the fall in value of an asset over time, reflecting the wear and tear of the asset as it becomes older, the reduction in its economic use or its obsolescence.

obsolescence: when an asset is still functioning but is no longer considered useful because it is out of date.

Causes of depreciation

Assets depreciate for a number of reasons. The main ones are as follows.

Time

Assets such as machinery wear out over time, although some last much longer than others. For reasons of prudence, a business will want to be pessimistic when depreciating an asset, so a shorter period of time is used if there is doubt. An established firm will know from experience the likely useful lifetime of an asset. Remember, it is the *useful* lifetime of an asset that is important.

Use

The more an asset is used, the quicker it will wear out. Although careful use and regular maintenance can extend the useful life of an asset, there is still a correlation between the amount that an asset is used and the level of depreciation. A dishwasher that is constantly in use will probably wear out faster than one that is used only occasionally. Similarly, company cars may depreciate through use rather than over time, as the loss in value will relate closely to the number of miles driven.

Obsolescence

Changes in technology may mean that an asset needs to be replaced as it becomes inefficient in comparison with newer alternatives; this occurs

frequently in the field of information technology. Changes in the market, particularly in industries or firms whose products are subject to changes in fashion, may lead to an asset becoming obsolete. A common cause of obsolescence is the ending of a contract. If a firm wins a 5-year contract to supply a customer, any equipment that it buys to meet the needs of that contract should be depreciated over 5 years. Even if the equipment is still operating efficiently, the *economic lifetime* of the asset may be over because the firm may not be able to use it for its other activities.

These three factors help a firm to calculate the time over which an asset should be depreciated. Table 7.2 shows the time periods over which specific assets are depreciated by three different organisations.

Table 7.2* *Depreciation in three real-life organisations

Organisation	Asset	Period of depreciation	Comment
London Transport	Tunnels	100 years	All of these assets will last a very long time, although some maintenance will be required. The lack of any real threat of competition means that each of these assets will have a long economic lifetime too. Recently, London Transport replaced some 50-year-old buses because of poor disabled access rather than because of wear and tear.
	Buses and trains	30 years	
	Signals	15 years	
Wincanton Transport	Lorries	5–10 years	Wincanton Transport purchases specialist lorries for different contracts (e.g. liquids, chemicals, livestock), so although the lorries will last longer, they are depreciated over the length of the contract. For image reasons, company cars are replaced more regularly.
	Office equipment	3–5 years	
	Company cars	3 years	
Next plc	Warehouses	10 years	The recent introduction of just-in-time deliveries from factories means that Next depreciates its warehouses over 10 years (25–40 years is common practice). Office equipment needs updating every 3–5 years and stock over 3 months old is probably unfashionable or out of season.
	Office equipment	3–5 years	
	Clothing stock	3–6 months	

TOPFOTO

Calculating depreciation

The two most widely used calculations are the **straight-line** and **reducing balance** methods. The AQA A2 Business Studies specification only requires an understanding of the straight-line method of depreciation. This can be calculated as follows:

$$\text{annual provision for depreciation} = \frac{\text{initial cost} - \text{residual value}}{\text{expected lifetime (in years)}}$$

For example, if a piece of equipment costs £100,000 and the company expects to receive £40,000 when selling it after 4 years (its expected lifetime), then:

$$\text{annual depreciation} = \frac{£100{,}000 - £40{,}000}{4} = £15{,}000 \text{ per annum}$$

EXAMINER'S VOICE

The AQA specification requires no understanding of the reducing balance method of depreciation. However, it is worth noting that this method reduces the **book value** of the asset (the value of the asset in the balance sheet) by a greater amount than the straight-line method in the early years, but by a smaller sum in later years. Therefore, the depreciation cost in the profit and loss account is higher at the beginning and lower towards the end of the asset's lifetime. In the example above, the reducing balance method would have calculated the depreciation at £20,000 for the first year, falling to £10,200 by the fourth year.

FACT FILE

The straight-line method is used to reflect more accurately the annual expense charged in the profit and loss account. The asset is likely to yield similar levels of revenue in each year, so the annual provision for depreciation is the same each year.

The reducing balance method tends to reflect the fact that an asset's value declines more in the early years of its lifetime, so it portrays the book value in the balance sheet more accurately.

Although there is debate about the impact of depreciation on the accounts in the short term, ultimately it makes no difference. Historically, the total allowance for depreciation of an asset over its actual lifetime is equal to its initial cost minus any residual value achieved from its disposal. This is a fact and is not affected by people's judgements.

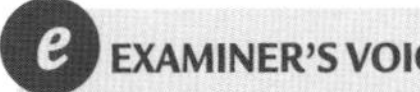

EXAMINER'S VOICE

Remember, depreciation is a non-cash expense. Only in the year of purchase will any cash leave the firm.

The purposes of depreciation

Depreciation is used to ensure that the accounts meet the principles of accounting. The purposes can be seen by the impact of depreciation on the main accounts.

In the **profit and loss account**, depreciation spreads the cost of an asset over the lifetime during which it is helping to create income. This overcomes the problem of exaggerating a firm's costs in the year in which an asset is bought, and thus reducing the firm's profits considerably in that year. This meets the requirements of the accruals (matching) convention, as the cost is spread over a number of years.

In the **balance sheet**, depreciation shows the reduction in an asset's value over its lifetime. This helps the company to show a true and fair valuation of each asset in its balance sheets over the years. Rather than showing the cost of the asset, the balance sheet shows a steady lowering of the asset's book value over time.

In the **cash-flow statement**, the company shows an outflow of cash in the year in which an asset is purchased and an inflow of cash in the year in which it is sold. Using the figures given in the example above, the cash-flow statement shows an outflow of £100,000 in the year of purchase (assuming this was a cash purchase). Using the same logic, the cash-flow statement at the end of year 4 will show an inflow of cash of £40,000 if it is sold for its estimated disposal value.

Table 7.3 shows how the asset used in the example would be treated in the main accounts.

***Table 7.3** Example: impact of depreciation on financial accounts*

Financial year	Annual charge to profit and loss account (£000s)	'Book value' of asset in balance sheet Start of year (£000s)	End of year (£000s)
1 (year of purchase)	15	100	85
2	15	85	70
3	15	70	55
4	15	55	40

WHAT DO YOU THINK?

Depreciation is one of the reasons why the profit and loss account does not show the cash position of a business. In our example above, the cash-flow statements show an outflow of £100,000 at the beginning and an inflow 4 years later of £40,000: a net outflow of £60,000. The profit and loss accounts shows 4 successive years in which depreciation has cost £15,000. This represents a total cost of £60,000 over the 4 years, but the figures in each individual year's accounts are very different.

Can you think of any other reasons why cash flow can be very different from levels of profit or loss?

The implications of depreciation

Depreciation is important because its incorrect application can lead to misleading information for users of the firm's accounts. If the residual value of an asset or its lifetime is wrongly estimated, this can affect the accuracy of the accounts. In our example of a £100,000 asset, what would happen if the residual value were only £25,000 and the lifetime of the asset were only 3 years? In this case, the annual depreciation would be:

$$\frac{£100{,}000 - £25{,}000}{3} = \frac{£75{,}000}{3} = £25{,}000 \text{ per annum}$$

Table 7.4 shows the impact on the accounts.

***Table 7.4** Example: impact of incorrect application of depreciation on financial accounts*

Financial year	Annual charge to profit and loss account (£000s)	'Book value' of asset in balance sheet Start of year (£000s)	End of year (£000s)
1 (year of purchase)	25	100	75
2	25	75	50
3	25	50	25

These figures show a different picture for the first 3 years:

- The profit and loss account shows an extra £10,000 of costs each year.
- The balance sheet shows a lower book value for the assets.

The second set of accounts would show that the business made a smaller profit (and hence paid less tax) in the first few years. However, this lower profit might discourage investors and other stakeholders from getting involved. It might also discourage lenders, who often look at the value of a firm's assets as a way of assessing whether a loan should be made. On a large scale, these factors can make a big difference in the short term.

Any information that relies on depreciation calculations should be treated with caution. The calculation itself is based on both facts (**objectivity**) and personal opinions (**subjectivity**). Taking in turn each element of the formula:

$$\text{annual provision for depreciation} = \frac{\text{initial cost} - \text{residual value}}{\text{expected lifetime (in years)}}$$

- **Initial cost.** This figure is objective, as it is the sum that the firm actually pays for the asset.
- **Residual value.** This is subjective, as it is an estimate of how much the asset will be worth in the future. The longer the lifetime of the asset, the less accurate this prediction is likely to be. The degree of accuracy will depend on circumstances. An experienced manager in a business in a relatively stable market may be able to predict the figure very accurately. In industries in which rapid changes are taking place, an asset may lose its value more quickly than expected.
- **Expected lifetime.** Again this is a matter of opinion. If the business has a set policy of replacing an asset after a fixed period, then a figure can be relied upon. However, it is very difficult to know how long an asset, such as a piece of furniture, will last and the lifetime may depend on how well the company is performing, as much as the condition of the furniture.

TOPFOTO

There is no widespread agreement on depreciation. Table 7.2 shows that London Transport depreciates its vehicles over 30 years, while Wincanton Transport uses 5–10 years for its lorries (and only 3 years for its cars). Matters are complicated further by the fact that there are different methods of calculating depreciation, each of which gives a different result. There is thus scope for using depreciation to 'window dress' the accounts (see Chapter 8) in order to make matters appear more favourable than they are.

DID YOU KNOW?

If the actual residual value at the end of the life of an asset is higher than expected, the difference is added to the profit. If the actual residual value at the end of the life of an asset is lower than expected, the difference is subtracted from the profit.

CHAPTER 7 Capital expenditure, revenue expenditure and depreciation

PRACTICE EXERCISE 1 Total: 15 marks (15 minutes)

1 What is the difference between capital expenditure and revenue expenditure? *(4 marks)*

2 Which three items from this list of six purchases would be classified as capital expenditure?

- buildings
- machinery
- raw materials
- rent
- vehicles
- wages *(3 marks)*

3 Explain why revenue expenditure is treated differently from capital expenditure in the profit and loss account and in the balance sheet, but not treated differently in the cash-flow statement. *(8 marks)*

PRACTICE EXERCISE 2 Total: 50 marks (45 minutes)

1 Explain what is meant by the term 'depreciation'. *(3 marks)*

2 Explain three factors that cause assets to depreciate. *(9 marks)*

3 An asset is bought for £6,000 and is expected to last for 6 years, at which point it will be sold for £900. Calculate the rate of depreciation using the straight-line method. *(3 marks)*

4 What is the residual value after 5 years of an asset whose initial cost is £800 and which depreciates by £130 per annum? *(3 marks)*

5 An asset has a residual value of £24,000 and has been depreciated by £18,000 per annum for 4 years, using the straight-line method. Complete the table below.

Year	Depreciation charge in profit and loss account	Book value in balance sheet at end of year
1		
2		
3		
4	£18,000	£24,000

(4 marks)

6 Why is the calculation of depreciation a mixture of subjectivity and objectivity? *(6 marks)*

7 Discuss the view that depreciation is not important because in the long run the final figure must be the difference between the initial cost and the actual disposal value of the asset. *(10 marks)*

8 The table below shows the value of fixed assets and the annual depreciation levels of four different organisations in 2004.

Name of organisation	Description of business	Book value of fixed assets (£m)	Level of depreciation (£m)	Depreciation as a % of fixed assets
AstraZeneca	Large-scale pharmaceutical company	7,564.6	660.8	8.7
London Transport	Provider of bus and underground rail transport	3,246.1	135.3	4.2
Dixons Group plc	Electrical retailer trading as Dixons, Currys and PC World	440.8	114.5	26.0
Wincanton Transport plc	Haulier, supplying lorry transport for businesses	247.3	38.3	15.5

Discuss the possible reasons for the differences in the level of depreciation of fixed assets in these four organisations. *(12 marks)*

CHAPTER 8

Working capital

This chapter examines the concepts of working capital and liquidity. The working capital cycle is considered and the factors that influence the level of working capital in an organisation are explained. The chapter also investigates the possible causes of working capital difficulties and the ways in which an organisation can solve its working capital problems. The chapter concludes by comparing the historic cost and net realisable value methods of stock valuation.

What is working capital?

KEY TERM

working capital (or **net current assets**): the day-to-day finance used in a business, consisting of current assets (such as cash, stock and debtors) minus current liabilities (such as creditors, overdrafts, dividends owed and tax owed).

The formula for calculating working capital is:

working capital = current assets – current liabilities

As a general rule, firms wish to have working capital equal to current liabilities (that is, twice as many current assets as current liabilities), although in many industries a lower ratio is acceptable.

KEY TERMS

liquidity: the ability to convert an asset into any form (usually cash) without loss or delay.

liquid assets: items owned by an organisation that can be converted into cash quickly and without a loss of value. The most liquid asset that a business can possess is cash.

The working capital of a business provides an indication of the firm's scope to pay its short-term debts, as it includes the most liquid assets (the current assets). Fixed assets may take a long time to sell, or may be sold at a loss if the business tries to sell them immediately.

The working capital cycle

KEY TERM

working capital cycle (or **cash operating cycle**): the inflow and outflow of liquid assets and liabilities within a business (see Figure 8.1).

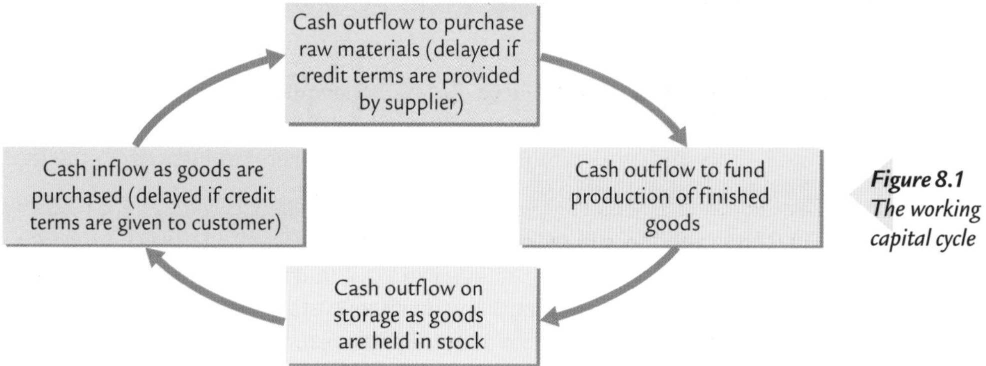

Figure 8.1 *The working capital cycle*

The length of the working capital cycle can be calculated by studying the three main elements of working capital:

- stock
- debtors
- creditors

The formula is:

$$\text{length of working capital cycle} = \text{length of time that goods are in stock} + \text{time taken for debtors to pay} - \text{period of credit received from suppliers}$$

Here is an example of calculating the working capital cycle:

- Goods are held in stock for an average of 14 days.
- Debtors are given 30 days to pay, on average.
- Suppliers (creditors) give the firm 28 days to pay for the supplies that they purchase.
- The working capital cycle is: 14 + 30 – 28 = 16 days.

In effect, the company has to wait 16 days after it has paid for its supplies before it receives payment from the sale of its goods.

TOPFOTO

Although it is often said that current assets should be twice as much as current liabilities, this is certainly not necessary in some industries. A newsagent traditionally receives cash from customers and holds stock for 1 day only. Usually the newspaper wholesaler expects payment at the beginning of the next week — an average credit period of 4 days. In this case, the working capital cycle is: 1 day + 0 days – 4 days = –3 days. This means that, on average, the newsagent receives payment for the goods 3 days *before* he or she pays for them.

FACT FILE

At certain times of the year, a business must possess a higher than usual level of working capital, as it must hold sufficient liquid assets to pay outstanding short-term liabilities, such as dividends to shareholders and corporation tax payments to the government.

Factors influencing the level of working capital

The example of the newsagent shows that the level of working capital varies considerably between different firms. Consequently, any judgement of a firm's working capital situation should be based on comparisons with competitors and/or previous years. There are several influences on the level of working capital held.

The time taken to sell stock

A range of factors affect the number of days that stock is held:

- **The nature of the product.** Items such as clothing that must be displayed in order to entice customers require higher stock levels than those that do not need display.
- **The durability of the product.** Companies try to have lower levels of stocks of perishable items or finished products that may become unfashionable.
- **Efficiency of suppliers.** If suppliers can supply large quantities at short notice, a business will be able to reduce its stock levels.
- **Lead time.** If it takes a long time to make a product, companies will be more likely to hold them in stock.
- **Customer expectations.** If the customer is prepared to wait, it may be unnecessary to hold stock; if the customer wants the item immediately, stocks should be kept.
- **Competition.** A business needs to match its rivals, so stock levels are influenced by the policies of competitors.

TOPFOTO

The time taken by customers to pay for goods

Factors that lead to delay in receiving payment will lead to the need for greater working capital:

- **The nature of the market.** Commercial products (sold to other businesses) are usually sold on credit, with 28 or 30 days being common credit periods.
- **The type of product.** Expensive, durable items such as vehicles, white goods and electrical products are often offered on credit. Smaller, everyday items are normally paid for immediately.

- **Bargaining power.** The offer of credit may depend on the relative bargaining power of the supplier and the buyer. A large supermarket may demand (and get) a credit period from a small supplier that is desperate for the contract. A small supermarket may be forced to pay immediately for supplies from a major supplier such as Coca-Cola.

The credit period offered by suppliers

The longer the period of credit offered to the business the better, as this means delaying the payment made. The factors influencing the credit period are the same as those listed above. However, the impact on the business is exactly the opposite because in this case the firm is the debtor. Businesses want to reduce their need to hold working capital, so the best-case scenario is a situation in which they receive immediate payment from their customers but can delay payment to their suppliers. The worst-case scenario is when they have to wait for their customers to pay but are expected to pay their suppliers immediately.

DID YOU KNOW?

The term 'white goods' refers to domestic appliances such as washing machines, fridges and dish-washers, even though they may come in a variety of colours.

Causes of working capital difficulties

In general, working capital problems are caused by weak management of the firm's current assets and current liabilities. The main causes are as follows.

Failure to control stock levels

This worsens a firm's working capital position as high levels of stock 'tie up' resources unnecessarily and cost the business money in storage costs. However, a business must balance this factor against the dangers of running out of stock and upsetting customers.

Poor control of debtors

A firm that allows debtors to delay payments needs to hold higher levels of other current assets, such as cash, as a precaution. This reduces the funds available for other activities.

Poor control of creditors

A firm that pays creditors too quickly will damage its working capital. Ideally, businesses will try to delay payments to creditors for as long as possible.

Cash-flow problems

A failure to manage cash flow will cause working capital difficulties, as cash is a major component of working capital (see Chapter 13 of the AS textbook for causes of cash-flow problems).

Poor internal planning and coordination

If individual departments of a firm are unable to meet targets, working capital problems will occur. Examples of poor internal planning are the personnel department being unable to recruit or train workers, causing production levels to fall and leading to inadequate stock levels, and the finance department failing to chase up debtors who do not pay on time. Poor coordination may happen if the sales achieved by marketing do not match the number of products being manufactured.

External factors

Unforeseen changes can affect consumers' tastes. If the business is not able to adapt quickly, this may lead to unsold stock or low levels of cash.

Solving working capital problems

Solutions to cash-flow problems were outlined in Chapter 13 of the AS textbook. Other solutions relate to **stock control** and **debtor control**.

Stock control

In the short term, it is ideal that stock levels are maintained at a low level, as it means that less money is tied up in stock. However, the firm wants stocks of finished products to meet customer demand and stocks of raw materials to keep production flowing. The company must consider factors such as the potential loss of customer goodwill if there is ever a shortage of stock. If a loss of goodwill is possible, higher levels of stock should be held.

INGRAM

Low stock levels reduce the need for storage space, and the chances of damage, deterioration and obsolescence. **High stock levels** allow companies to benefit from bulk-buying discounts and minimise the risk of lost sales and lost goodwill through a failure to meet customer needs. Firms will calculate the most cost-efficient quantity of stock to order and hold, balancing the relative merits of high and low stock levels. Firms that operate **just-in-time** systems of supply can exist with low levels of stock, but these companies need efficient suppliers that can meet tight deadlines.

Details of stock control systems are provided in Chapter 32 of the AS textbook.

Debtor control

Debtors should be kept to a minimum, as they mean a delay in receiving cash. However, the offer of credit may help to increase sales, particularly in markets in which buyers expect credit facilities. The company will balance the benefits of increased sales as a result of offering credit against the loss of liquidity and the risk of late or non-payment.

If credit is offered to customers, the company must ensure prompt payment. This can be achieved by:

- managing credit control so that customers are invoiced promptly and reminded of the need for payment towards the end of the credit period

- chasing up late payers and being prepared to take debtors to court if payment is not received. In practice, responsibility for this is often passed to specialist companies — this can help a firm to avoid a breakdown in its relationship with a debtor who might be a regular customer but who has failed to pay on this occasion.
- obtaining a credit rating, which indicates the capability of the potential debtor to finance the debt. This allows the company to refuse credit to customers who might not pay.
- controlling the quality of the service or product, as a satisfied customer is less likely to delay or dispute payment
- scrutinising the provision of credit to check that it is cost-effective (that is, that the extra profit gained from offering credit exceeds the additional costs of providing it)

Finally, a company can turn its debtors into cash by **factoring**. This means selling the right to collect the debts to another business, usually at a discount. Less money is received, but cash is received much more quickly and the risk of bad debts is reduced.

FACT FILE

Firms will not want excessive, 'unproductive' working capital. In 2003, Bunzl plc found itself accumulating high levels of working capital. As a result, it used this high level of liquidity to buy back £91.7 million of shares. This action will reduce the value of dividends that it needs to pay to shareholders in future years.

EXAMINER'S VOICE

There are other methods of stock valuation such as LIFO and FIFO. However, an understanding of these methods is not required for the AQA A-level in Business Studies.

Stock valuation

Stocks are much more valuable when sold as finished products, but the convention of prudence indicates that they should be given a pessimistic, but realistic value. Two possible methods of valuation are **historic cost** and **net realisable value**.

KEY TERMS

historic cost: a method of stock valuation that values stock at the price that the organisation paid for it.

net realisable value: a method of stock valuation that values stock at the price for which it can be sold.

INGRAM

For most stock, the net realisable value is higher than the historic cost. The concept of prudence means that the lowest value should be taken — invariably this will be the historic cost. However, if stock becomes obsolete and is worth less than its purchase price, it should be valued at the price for which it can be sold (the net realisable value).

Using the historic cost method

Stock is often purchased over time at a variety of prices, so the organisation cannot use one price for all of its stock when seeking to put a value on it. A common approach to stock valuation is the **average cost method**. A weighted average of the costs is calculated to find the value of stock.

Example

12 units were purchased at £10, 48 units at £11 and 60 units at £12. These would not be valued at £11 (the average of 10, 11 and 12), as this would ignore the fact that relatively few units were purchased at £10 and half of the units cost £12.

$$\text{average cost} = \frac{\text{total cost}}{\text{units of stock}}$$

In this example the stock value would be

Units		Cost (£)		Total cost (£)
12	×	10	=	120
48	×	11	=	528
60	×	12	=	720
120	×		=	1,368

The value of the 120 units of stock is £1,368.

$$\text{average cost} = \frac{\text{total cost (£)}}{\text{units of stock}} = \frac{\text{£1,368}}{120} = \text{£11.40 per unit}$$

PRACTICE EXERCISE — Total: 40 marks (35 minutes)

1 How is working capital calculated? *(2 marks)*

2 What is meant by the term 'liquidity'? *(3 marks)*

3 Calculate the working capital cycle based on the following information:
- Goods are held in stock for 23 days.
- Debtors are given 15 days to pay.
- Creditors give the firm 28 days to pay. *(3 marks)*

4 Explain one factor that might increase the level of working capital in a firm. *(3 marks)*

5 Briefly explain three possible causes of working capital problems. *(6 marks)*

6 Explain how stock control might improve a firm's working capital problems. *(6 marks)*

7 Explain how debtor control might improve a firm's working capital problems. *(6 marks)*

8 Why is it sensible for a firm to make sure that its level of working capital is not too high? *(3 marks)*

9 Explain the difference between historic cost and net realisable value. *(4 marks)*

10 The data below show the number of kettles in stock at an electrical retailer's warehouse:
- 25 kettles purchased at £20
- 15 kettles purchased at £18
- 60 kettles purchased at £23

What is the value of each of the 100 kettles in stock, using the average cost method? *(4 marks)*

CASE STUDY Stashing the cash

A survey in 2004 by Morgan Stanley shows that companies are holding record levels of cash, with some firms operating at particularly high levels of working capital. The top cash-rich companies in 2004 are shown in Table 8.1.

The Morgan Stanley survey reveals that there are three main causes of these high cash levels:

- The operations of some firms (such as Stagecoach) lead naturally to high cash levels as customers pay cash and stocks of products are not required. Although Stagecoach has high levels of cash, it has a very low level of working capital.
- Deep cost-cutting during the global downturn has led to high profit levels as the economy has grown.
- Companies face dilemmas in deciding how to use high levels of cash or working capital.

This latter point has become more significant as companies have begun to question the accepted view that excess liquid assets should be converted into fixed assets in order to improve profitability.

The Morgan Stanley report shows the dilemma facing cash-rich companies. During the 15 years from 1988 to 2003, companies that reinvested money in capital investment performed less well than those that cut back on investment or focused on high dividend growth. In many cases, retained profits were invested in less profitable activities than the firm's core business.

This is a particular issue for Hanson. In the 1970s and 1980s, this business used its profits from supplying raw materials for the construction industry to finance a policy of diversification – buying a wide range of different companies. However, Hanson found that its construction industry activities were much more profitable than its new activities. Consequently, it then sold most of its non-construction divisions and has re-established itself as a successful business. However, it has found it difficult to find profitable uses for its cash, so it has used its high levels of cash and working capital to repay shareholders in the form of high dividends.

Tate and Lyle has benefited from the dramatic success of its new range of sugar-based, non-fattening sweeteners, which have been adopted as a healthy ingredient in many foodstuffs. With no major new products in the pipeline, Tate and Lyle has found itself in the unusual position of high working capital but no obvious use for the money that has been made.

Source: adapted from an article by Gary Duncan in *The Times*, 9 April 2004.

Table 8.1 *Cash-rich companies, 2004*

Name of company	Net value (£m)	Working capital (£m)	Working capital (% of company value)	Cash holding (% of company value)
Hanson	4,894	1,359.1	27.8	11.9
Tate and Lyle	1,016	327.0	32.2	11.7
Stagecoach	874	42.5	4.9	11.1

Questions

Total: 20 marks (20 minutes)

1 Explain how Stagecoach, a business that operates bus and train services, can have a very high level of cash but a very low level of working capital. *(6 marks)*

2 Discuss the reasons for Hanson and Tate and Lyle possessing such high levels of working capital. *(14 marks)*

CHAPTER 9

Window dressing

This chapter describes the concept of window dressing of financial accounts. The various reasons why a business might wish to use window-dressing techniques are explained. The chapter then examines the techniques that are employed and the implications of each of these for the business in the short term and the long term.

What is window dressing?

KEY TERM

window dressing: when a business prepares its financial accounts in a way that presents the business in the most favourable way possible.

FACT FILE

Window dressing is not illegal. It is merely a process that takes advantage of the flexibility that firms have in how they present their accounts. Most firms have no wish to adjust their accounts in this way.

Window dressing can be conducted by amending the actual figures in the accounts or by taking a short-term action that is designed deliberately to make the accounts appear more favourable than they would have been if that action had not been taken.

EXAMINER'S VOICE

Don't exaggerate the importance or scope of window dressing. There is a temptation to get carried away with the amount of window dressing that firms carry out. Even if accounts are window dressed, they are unlikely to hide effectively a firm's financial problems.

Reasons for window dressing

Firms undertake window dressing of their accounts for several reasons.

To encourage potential shareholders to buy shares in the firm

Potential shareholders choose to put their money into businesses that appear to have the potential to succeed in the future. Consequently, firms are tempted to take measures that boost the profit figures, so that there is a greater demand for shares. Usually shareholders want to see evidence of growth too, so figures may be 'dressed' to give an appearance of sustained increases in sales and profits.

To appeal to banks and other lenders

The measures described above also encourage banks and other lenders to provide finance for the firm. However, in most cases the lenders take a more short-term view of their investment in the firm. As a result, they also want reassurance about the firm's working capital and liquidity, and the value of the company's fixed assets. A company may find that favourable working capital and security provided by ownership of fixed assets are sufficient to get a loan.

To increase the apparent scale of the firm

Most businesses pursue objectives linked to size. Window dressing may allow a firm to increase its apparent size and therefore attain its objectives. Valuing intangible and other fixed assets highly can make a company appear larger than it is. More importantly, size may increase a firm's reputation and enhance its status within an industry. It may thus be tempting to window dress accounts to make a firm look larger than it is.

To give the impression that a company's future is secure

To many stakeholders, it is the future of a business that is most important. Thus, a firm might take steps to create an impression of future success. For example, Shell exaggerated its oil reserves in order to give a more favourable view of its future. This action can reassure customers and suppliers too.

To appease analysts and stakeholders

Sometimes a firm needs to match the performance of competitors, or register an improvement in its own performance, in order to reach the expectations of stakeholders or 'experts'. Quite often analysts compare firms with their most successful rival. By most objective standards, Sainsbury's financial performance was quite strong until 2004, but it was deemed to have failed because it was falling further and further behind Tesco.

Window-dressing techniques

Although accounting principles and regulations apply, they are not rigid and so basic accounting data may be interpreted differently when compiling the accounts. This creates a situation in which window dressing can take place. However, it should be recognised that window dressing is limited by the need for firms to follow consistent approaches in compiling their accounts.

Revaluation of land and buildings

Unlike most fixed assets, land and buildings tend to increase (appreciate) in value over time. A business should usually set a prudent value for these assets, in order not to exaggerate, and most organisations do not regularly update property values in the balance sheet. This means that a business can show a sudden increase in the value of its assets simply by obtaining an updated valuation of its property. However, once this action has been taken, the business will be unable to use this window-dressing technique again for a while.

INGRAM

FACT FILE

'You can be sure of Shell' is no longer a slogan that reassures stakeholders in the oil giant. Shell's reputation for prudent estimations of its worth was destroyed in January 2004, when it was discovered that its oil reserves had been window dressed to the tune of 1 billion barrels of oil and gas — one-fifth of Shell's entire reserves. Richard Brackenhoff, an analyst for Kempen and Co., estimates that this overstatement exaggerated Shell's value as a company by £4 billion, roughly 10% of the company's worth. The revelations have since led to a major upheaval and restructuring of Royal Dutch Shell, which blames the situation on a lack of control rather than a deliberate attempt at window dressing. In effect, Shell was exaggerating the value of a major asset — its oil reserves.

Depreciation of fixed assets

The level of depreciation depends upon three variables: the initial cost of the asset, its residual value and its expected lifetime. A firm trying to put the most favourable 'spin' on its accounts may estimate a very high residual value and a long lifetime for an asset. This means that depreciation of the asset (a charge in the profit and loss account) is low, thus boosting profits. It also keeps the asset value high, so the company appears to be more valuable.

However, this type of window dressing should be treated with caution. If the asset becomes worthless before its expected lifetime is over, the business must 'write down' the value to zero. This will cause a big drop in both the profit and the net value of the business, and therefore have a very unfavourable impact on the firm in that year.

Ultimately, the fixed asset will be depreciated in full, so this approach to window dressing may have short-term benefits but over time there will be no difference.

Amortisation of intangible assets

A firm can include intangible assets (such as goodwill and the value of brand names) in its accounts *if* it has purchased them. In the same way that depreciation can be reduced each year in order to keep up the value of a tangible asset, it is possible for a firm to spread amortisation over a longer time than the norm. Consequently, in the short term, the accounts may be window dressed to give a more favourable impression, but in the long run, any short-term gains will be lost and so the benefit will not be permanent.

Sale of fixed assets

A company with low levels of liquidity or low levels of working capital can obtain cash by selling some of its assets. This will, of course, reduce the value of the fixed assets but it will enable the business to show that it has sufficient cash to pay its immediate liabilities. This is a more questionable approach to window dressing, as it reduces the level of fixed assets, which are often the basis on which the company generates its income. There is a particular danger that the firm will lose the use of its fixed assets. This risk can be limited by using sale and leaseback.

Sale and leaseback

In this case, the firm sells the assets but then leases (rents) them back from the new owner. This gives a more secure situation than merely selling the assets, as the company continues to use them. However, it should be recognised that the new owner will charge a rent that is high enough to make a profit, so it may be an expensive decision for the firm to take in the long run.

> **FACT FILE**
>
> Travelodge, the budget hotel operator, cashed in on its fixed assets in autumn 2004 by agreeing the sale and leaseback of its hotels in a £400 million deal. Travelodge is leasing its former properties for periods of between 25 and 45 years.

Bringing forward sales or delaying expenditure

The balance sheet and profit and loss account are compiled at the end of the financial year. If the business feels the need to window dress the accounts, it may try to persuade customers, perhaps by offering a discount, to place an order at the very end of the financial year, rather than the beginning of the following year. This may give a favourable but misleading impression of the company's finances (and will, of course, mean that next year's performance will be adversely affected). Similarly, revenue expenditure on items such as newspaper advertisements can be agreed but the invoices delayed until the beginning of the next financial year.

TRAVELODGE PRESS CENTRE

Acquiring cash

A firm that is having liquidity problems can borrow in order to get hold of cash. This might create future difficulties, but its immediate effect is to overcome any doubts over its ability to pay its creditors.

Defining assets as capital or revenue expenditure

In Chapter 7 we examined the difference between capital expenditure and revenue expenditure. While this distinction is clear-cut in most instances, there are items of expenditure, such as office equipment, where the classification is open to debate. Staplers, printers and computer software could all be classified as items that will be used up within the year (revenue expenditure) or as ones that will be used time and time again over a longer period. A business seeking to boost this year's performance might therefore spread the cost over more than 1 year (capital expenditure) whereas a firm that is doing well but anticipates that next year will be more difficult might want to classify the spending as revenue expenditure, so that it is all charged to the accounts in the first year.

INGRAM

Conclusion

Although there are many ways to 'window dress', they nearly all have one factor in common. Any apparent improvement in financial performance will be offset in the future by a fall in performance relative to what would have happened without the window dressing.

It is not always possible to identify window dressing. Recently, Marks and Spencer revalued many of its properties because it believed that they were undervalued in its balance sheet and that this undervaluation could lead to Marks and Spencer shareholders accepting a takeover bid by Philip Green (the chief executive of Arcadia and BHS). Marks and Spencer saw this revaluation as a way of improving the accuracy of its balance sheet. The original balance sheet estimate of its property value was £2.2 billion; an independent valuation by DTZ revalued its property at £3.6 billion.

PRACTICE EXERCISE — Total: 30 marks (25 minutes)

1 What is meant by the term 'window dressing'? *(3 marks)*

2 Is window dressing legal or illegal? *(1 mark)*

3 Explain three reasons for window dressing. *(9 marks)*

4 Explain four methods of window dressing. *(12 marks)*

5 Why is window dressing unlikely to help a business in the long run? *(5 marks)*

CASE STUDY Does window dressing exist in the mobile phone industry?

The lack of clear direction in reporting procedures is demonstrated in the mobile telephone industry. In May 2004, the main networks provided the figures in Table 9.1 to show the average revenue per user in the UK.

Table 9.1 *Average annual spending by customers on mobile phones (by network)*

Mobile network	Average spend per customer (p.a.)
Vodafone	£303
Orange	£273
O_2	£264 (gross); £245 (net)
T-Mobile	£241

Source: Bear Stearns, May 2004.

The figure declared by O_2 is £264, but unlike all of the other networks, this figure includes commission paid to 'distributors'. As a consequence, analysts relying on company figures have inadvertently exaggerated O_2 potential sales by 8%.

The situation has arisen because the publication is at the discretion of the networks and no guidelines on standard practice have been issued. In fact, until March 2001, Vodafone used the same method of calculation as O_2 but then changed its approach to bring its method into line with other networks and to provide a more realistic figure.

However, this factor is likely to lead to only minor differences in the figures released by the networks. Of much greater significance is the way that the networks are treating the costs of licences for third-generation mobile services.

In 2000, European governments granted licences for third-generation phone networks that would offer the mobile internet, with scope to download news, videos, music and other forms of entertainment directly onto mobile phones. The excitement about this opportunity persuaded the main network providers to pay £22.5 billion to the government for the 3G licences (see Table 9.2).

Problems with network technology and delays in producing suitable mobile handsets led to doubts about the viability of third-generation phone services. By May 2003, only one network (3, owned by Hutchison Whampoa) had started to operate services, and difficulties in providing reasonably priced handsets and good customer service meant that only 10,000 customers had signed up in the UK. (3's subsequent growth in 2003/04 was based on excellent deals on second-generation phones rather than its

Table 9.2 Cost of UK third-generation licences and write down (amortisation) per operator

Operator	Licence cost (£bn)	Write down (£bn)
Vodafone	6.0	0
3 (Hutchison Whampoa)	4.4	0
Orange	4.1	0
O_2	4.0	2.1
T-Mobile	4.0	1.6

Source: annual reports, 2004.

third-generation offering.) Only in Japan were there significant numbers of third-generation customers (420,000 people) using the new technology.

As a result, O_2 and T-mobile decided to write down (amortise) the value of this 'intangible' asset in their balance sheets. On 21 May 2003, O_2 announced that it was following the lead of T-mobile in reducing the value of this asset. Peter Erskine, chief executive of O_2, said: 'In hindsight, the £4 billion we paid in the UK was too much, and frankly £6 billion [the sum paid by Vodafone for the fast internet licence in the UK] was even more to pay.' Mr Erskine announced that O_2 was writing off over half of the value of its UK licence and three-quarters of the cost of its German licence. These two items alone led to a loss in O_2's value of £5.9 billion.

Unlike O_2, Vodafone believes that the £14 billion it paid across Europe still represents good value for money. It plans no write-offs. Chief executive, Sir Christopher Gent, has resisted making any amortisation of this nature, arguing that this would be an admission that shareholders' money was wasted on the licences.

Certainly there are no unanimous opinions on the value of 3G licences. While some accountants want greater consistency in valuing such major assets, one City analyst, who asked not to be named, indicated that companies should be free to make their own judgement in cases such as this: 'I don't think that this would have been an issue, had O_2 not conducted these write-offs. Nobody is expecting Vodafone to start doing it now.'

In fact, Vodafone's belief in third generation has increased as the technology and quality of handsets have improved. The company put a further £6 billion into the launch of its third-generation phones in November 2004, four and a half years after paying for the licence. Orange is also launching its third-generation mobile through its 3G Peasy campaign in March 2005. The three companies that have launched third-generation phones are the ones maintaining the value of this intangible asset in their balance sheets.

Two things are certain:

- It is still too early to tell whether third-generation phones will be a success, although some telecommunications experts believe that the value has been eroded as the technology has become a bit dated during the four and a half years since the licences were bought in 2000.
- Comparisons of company value and profit have become more difficult, with the five main networks following different approaches in valuing the licences.

Sources: adapted from articles by Dan Sabbagh in *The Times*, 22 May 2003 and 4 May 2004, and an article by Paul Durman in *The Sunday Times*, 7 November 2004.

Questions

Total: 20 marks (25 minutes)

1 Accounting procedures allow firms to adopt their own approach to asset valuation. Analyse one benefit and one problem of allowing individual mobile phone networks to choose how much value they allocate to the licences they own, rather than imposing a common system on all firms. (8 marks)

2 On the basis of the evidence provided in the case study, to what extent do you believe that window dressing takes place in the mobile phone industry? *(12 marks)*

CHAPTER 10

Ratio analysis

This chapter introduces the concept of ratio analysis. The importance of comparing ratios is explained and the main users of ratio analysis are identified. The chapter describes the main categories of ratios, explains their significance and provides data on the key ratios for UK firms in recent years.

The concept of ratio analysis

KEY TERM

ratio analysis: a method of assessing a firm's financial situation by comparing two sets of linked data.

Ratio analysis is based mainly on data extracted from the firm's financial accounting records — usually the balance sheet and profit and loss account. However, for some ratios, information needs to be extracted from the management accounting information or other sources.

FACT FILE

A ratio is a comparison of a figure with another figure where the relative values of the two numbers can be used to make a judgement. Ratios are expressed as, for example, 2.5:1. In this example, the first digit is two and a half times the second digit. In ratios, the second digit is always 1. Despite the name of this technique, many of the 'ratios' featured in ratio analysis are actually stated as percentages.

As indicated in Chapter 6, different groups of people use the information provided in a company's accounts in order to judge a firm's situation. Some actual figures in the accounts, such as net profit, can be used to draw conclusions about a company's performance. However, much more meaningful conclusions can be drawn by comparing this figure with another. If a business has doubled its profit in the last decade, is this an indicator of success? Most people would conclude that this does show good performance, but what if the sales of the business have trebled in that time? Should its profits have trebled too? Ratio analysis allows us to compare two sets of data (in this case, profit and sales) in order to try to draw more meaningful conclusions.

Ratio analysis also allows a business to compare itself with other firms, taking into consideration differences in size or circumstances. Similarly, it can be used to compare the relative efficiency of different parts of a business, such as departments, stores or factories. However, no two businesses or departments operate in identical circumstances and so, at best, ratio analysis can only act as a guide to performance.

EXAMINER'S VOICE

In the A2 course you will be expected to interpret ratios. Many students calculate the ratios but fail to explain their significance. Make sure that you comment on the conclusions that can be drawn from the ratios that you have calculated, with particular reference to any limitations to the conclusions that you have drawn.

Stages in using ratio analysis

If ratios are to prove useful, careful selection and organisation are needed. The following process will help businesses to take full advantage of ratio analysis:

1 Identify the reason for the investigation. Is the information needed to decide whether to become a customer or an employee, or is it being used by the organisation itself to improve its own efficiency?
2 Decide on the relevant ratio(s) that will help to achieve the purpose of the user(s).
3 Gather the information required to calculate the ratio(s).
4 Interpret the ratio(s). What is the meaning of the results that have been obtained?
5 Make appropriate comparisons (see the next section) in order to understand the significance of the ratio(s).
6 Take action in accordance with the results of the investigation.
7 Apply the above processes again, to measure the success of the actions taken in stage 6.

Comparisons

Ratios in isolation are rather meaningless. To interpret a ratio, it should be compared with other results, so that the company can be judged in relative terms. The main bases for comparison are as follows:

- **Inter-firm comparisons** — comparisons *between* companies. A company should compare itself with rival companies, in order to assess its relative performance. Ideally, the company should select those competitors with which it has most in common, as any external factors that are helping (or hindering) the company should be having a similar effect on those competitors.
- **Intra-firm comparisons** — comparisons *within* the company. The efficiencies of different divisions or areas of a company can be compared. Again, comparisons should be made between similar areas of the company. A retailer should compare stores in similar towns where the size of population and levels of competition are matched.
- **Comparisons to a standard.** Certain levels of performance are recognised as efficient within the business community. A company can compare itself with these standards in order to assess its performance objectively. It is often easy to obtain comparable data from other companies too, if such standards are widely used.

EXAMINER'S VOICE

Ratios must be used in context. A firm's ratio may compare unfavourably to the 'standard' or to its performance in previous years, but look at the background to the firm. Is there a reason for this unfavourable result? Ensure that you refer to any such reasons in your answer.

- **Comparisons over time.** Whatever basis is used, a company's ratios should be compared over time in order to register trends in efficiency and to allow for exceptional circumstances in a particular year. A boom or recession may last for years. Similarly, a firm may take a long time to reap the benefits of a restructuring or to devise suitable strategies to fight off a new competitor. For these reasons, it is important to use ratios to identify trends in performance as well as the performance in one particular year.

Types of ratio

Ratios can be categorised under five headings, as shown in Table 10.1.

***Table 10.1** The main types of ratio and their meanings*

Type of ratio	Meaning of ratio type
Profitability ratios	These compare profits with the size of the firm. As profit is often the primary aim of a company, these ratios are often described as **performance ratios**.
Liquidity ratios	These show whether a firm is likely to be able to meet its short-term liabilities. Although profit shows long-term success, it is vital that firms hold sufficient liquidity to avoid difficulties in paying debts.
Gearing	Gearing focuses on long-term liquidity and shows whether a firm's capital structure is likely to be able to continue to meet interest payments on, and to repay, long-term borrowing.
Financial efficiency ratios	These generally concentrate on the firm's management of its working capital. They are used to assess the efficiency of the firm in its management of its assets and short-term liabilities.
Shareholders' ratios	These focus on drawing conclusions about whether shareholders are likely to benefit financially from their shareholding in a company.

EXAMINER'S VOICE

There is a wide variety of ratios that can be used to judge a firm's performance (Figure 10.1). The philosophy behind the AQA A-level specification is that students should understand the significance of ratio analysis and be able to interpret and apply sufficient ratios to draw valid conclusions on a firm's operations.

For these reasons, ten specific ratios have been incorporated into the specification. There are other ratios that can be used to assess a company. This book includes an explanation of the **current ratio** (which is not included in the AQA specification) because it assists understanding of another ratio, the acid test ratio, which is included. However, with the exception of this one ratio, only those ratios that are identified in the AQA specification are considered in this chapter.

Figure 10.1 provides a summary of the types and classification of the ratios used.

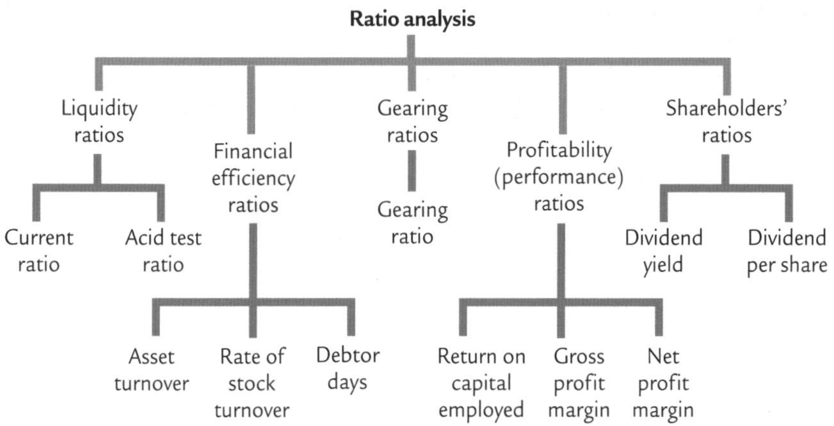

Figure 10.1 *Classification of financial ratios*

Users of ratios

Ratios serve a number of purposes, which will be outlined in detail in subsequent chapters as each ratio is examined. Different ratios meet the needs of a variety of users of accounts. Table 10.2 shows the main groups of users and their reasons for using ratio analysis.

Table 10.2 *Users and their reasons for using ratio analysis*

Users	Reasons for using ratio analysis
Managers	To identify the efficiency of the firm and its different areas, to plan ahead, to control operations and to assess the effectiveness of policies
Employees	To find out whether the firm can afford wage rises and to see if profits are being allocated fairly
Government	To review the success of its economic policies and to find ways of improving business efficiency overall
Competitors	To compare their performance against rival firms and discover their relative strengths and weaknesses
Suppliers	To know the sort of payment terms that are being offered to other suppliers, and whether a firm can afford to pay
Customers	To know if the future of the firm and therefore any guarantees and after-sales servicing agreements are secure
Shareholders	To compare the financial benefits of their investment with other alternatives, such as shares in a different firm or placing savings into a bank

Using ratios

The majority of ratios are based on information from the profit and loss account and the balance sheet. Each of the 11 ratios explained in this book is calculated using the figures from the accounts of GlaxoSmithKline plc (GSK plc), a global pharmaceutical company and one of the UK's largest businesses. To allow *intra-firm* comparisons,

NEWSCAST

the accounts shown are from two successive years — the financial years ending on 31 December 2003 and 31 December 2004.

In Chapter 16, *inter-firm* comparisons will be made with another global pharmaceutical company, AstraZeneca plc.

Tables 10.3 and 10.4 show extracts from the accounts of GlaxoSmithKline plc.

***Table 10.3** Profit and loss accounts for GlaxoSmithKline plc (GSK plc)*

Years ending:	31.12.04 (£m)	31.12.03 (£m)
SALES REVENUE	20,359	21,441
COST OF SALES (direct costs)	4,309	4,188
GROSS PROFIT	16,050	17,253
EXPENSES/OVERHEADS		
Research and development	3,839	2,770
Selling, general and administration	7,061	7,563
	9,900	10,333
TRADING PROFIT	6,150	6,920
Exceptional items	(60)	(133)
OPERATING PROFIT	6,090	6,787
PROFIT (LOSS) FROM OTHER ACTIVITIES	232	93
PROFIT BEFORE INTEREST	6,322	6,880
INTEREST	203	161
PROFIT BEFORE TAX	6,1119	6,719
TAX	1,701	1,848
PROFIT AFTER TAX	4,418	4,871
OTHER POST-TAX PAYMENTS	116	106
NET PROFIT AFTER TAX (EARNINGS)	4,302	4,765
EARNINGS PER SHARE	75.0 pence	82.1 pence
Appropriation account		
NET PROFIT AFTER TAX	4,302	4,765
DIVIDENDS TO SHAREHOLDERS	2,402	2,333
PURCHASE OF GSK SHARES*	-	980
RETAINED PROFIT	1,900	1,452

FACT FILE

*Many companies are now using their profit to buy back shares in the company on the open market. In 2003, GSK spent £980 million on buying back its own shares. This process must be agreed at the annual general meeting but is usually supported by shareholders because it means that future profits are shared among fewer shareholders, leading to larger dividends. It is used most often when share prices are low and the business cannot find a profitable alternative use for the profit if it is retained.

There are concerns about this policy in some quarters. BSkyB has followed the practice despite opposition from minority shareholders. Their opposition is based on the fact that Rupert Murdoch, whose shareholding remains the same, is increasing the percentage of shares that he owns as the company is reducing the number of shares. In effect, company money is being used to conduct a policy that is increasing his control over the business.

V. CRUDGINGTON

Table 10.4
Balance sheets of GlaxoSmithKline plc (GSK plc), 31 December 2004 and 2003

As at:	31.12.04 (£m)	31.12.03 (£m)
Fixed assets		
Intangible assets	2,142	1,840
Fixed assets	6,471	6,441
Long-term investments	332	294
TOTAL FIXED ASSETS	**8,945**	**8,575**
Current assets		
Stocks	2,192	2,109
Debtors	7,309	6,897
Short-term investments	2,971	2,657
Bank balance and cash	1,161	962
TOTAL CURRENT ASSETS	**13,633**	**12,625**
Current liabilities		
Short-term loans and overdrafts	1,582	1,452
Creditors (less than 1 year)	7,140	7,019
	8,722	**8,471**
WORKING CAPITAL (net current assets)	**4,911**	**4,154**
Total assets less current liabilities	**13,856**	**12,729**
Long-term liabilities		
Creditors (more than 1 year)	4,625	3,883
Other long-term liabilities	3,029	3,042
	7,654	**6,925**
TOTAL NET ASSETS	**6,202**	**5,804**
Capital and reserves		
Share capital	2,065	1,993
Reserves	4,137	3,811
	6,202	**5,804**
TOTAL CAPITAL EMPLOYED	**13,856**	**12,729**
Additional information		
Share price:	1250 pence	1206 pence
Number of shares issued:	5,762 million	5,804 million

FACT FILE

The accounts used in this book so far all show years ending 31 December. This is purely coincidental. Financial years represent 12 successive months and invariably span over two calendar years, in which case they are shown as 2003/04, 2004/05, etc. As the tax year ends in early April, many businesses have a financial year ending 31 March. Other popular days for the end of a company's financial year are 30 June and 31 July.

PRACTICE EXERCISE — Total: 25 marks (20 minutes)

1 What is meant by the term 'ratio analysis'? *(3 marks)*

2 Identify five different users of ratio analysis. *(5 marks)*

3 Select two of the five users identified in question 2 and explain the reasons why they might use ratio analysis. *(6 marks)*

4 Distinguish between inter-firm comparisons and intra-firm comparisons. *(4 marks)*

5 Identify two other types of comparison. *(2 marks)*

6 Identify the five main types of ratio. *(5 marks)*

CHAPTER 11

Liquidity

In Chapters 11–15 we consider the financial ratios introduced in Chapter 10, show how they are calculated and explain their purpose. Sample calculations, based on the accounts of GlaxoSmithKline plc given in Chapter 10, are used to assess the company's financial position. In this chapter, we look at two liquidity ratios — the current ratio and the acid test ratio — in order to assess their role in examining the ability of the organisation to meet its short-term liabilities.

Liquidity ratios

Although profit is the main measure of company success, firms can be vulnerable to cash-flow problems, so the ability of a firm to meet its immediate payments is a key test. Liquidity ratios concentrate on balance sheet information. Examination of a firm's short-term (current) assets and its current liabilities allows an observer to analyse a firm's ability to stay solvent in the short term.

KEY TERM

solvency: a measure of a firm's ability to pay its debts on time. A firm that can meet its financial commitments is described as 'solvent'; a firm that cannot meet its financial commitments is described as 'insolvent'.

It is estimated that as many as 30% of all business failures can be attributed to insolvency. Consequently, liquidity ratios are vital in analysing a firm's financial position. A profitable firm may still be in danger of liquidation if its liquidity is weak.

EXAMINER'S VOICE

The current ratio is not required for the AQA A-level. It is included here because it is closely related to the acid test ratio and because it allows more comparisons with other organisations.

Current ratio

In order to meet its liabilities, a firm can draw upon its short-term (current) assets. Cash and bank balances are the most liquid current assets. However, debtors will be paying their debts to the company, thus providing a steady source of cash. Similarly, stock will be sold continually, providing the business with an additional means to pay its current liabilities.

The ratio is calculated as follows:

current ratio = current assets:current liabilities

If a company has between £1.50 and £2 of current assets for every £1 of current liabilities, it is unlikely to run out of cash. Therefore, the 'ideal' current ratio is between 1.5:1 and 2:1.

It should be noted that a maximum as well as a minimum ratio is recommended. Too many current assets will limit a firm's ability to purchase the fixed assets that are needed to produce the goods that provide the company's profit. Consequently, a high current ratio may be an advantage in the short run but will inhibit the long-term profitability of the company.

Based on Table 10.4 on p. 111, calculation of these ratios for GSK plc gives the following results:

2003: 12,625:8,471 = 1.49:1
2004: 13,633:8,722 = 1.56:1

Acid test (quick) ratio

The current ratio assumes that stocks and debtors are liquid assets. This is likely to be true of debtors, as any debtors who are deemed to be unlikely to pay will be classified as 'bad debts' and not included in the balance sheet. However, for stock the situation is less clear. Firms cannot be certain that their stock will sell quickly, so the acid test ratio is used as an alternative to the current ratio. The calculation of the acid test (quick) ratio ignores stock in its calculation, considering only cash, bank balances and debtors as liquid assets.

The ratio is calculated as follows:

acid test ratio = (current assets – stock):current liabilities

Again, there is an ideal maximum and an ideal minimum ratio, as explained for the current ratio. If a company has between £0.75 and £1 of current assets (excluding stock) for every £1 of current liabilities, it is unlikely to run out of cash. Therefore, the 'ideal' acid test ratio is between 0.75:1 and 1:1.

Based on Table 10.4, the acid test ratios for GSK plc are as follows:

2003: 10,516:8,471 = 1.24:1
2004: 11,441:8,722 = 1.31:1

WHAT DO YOU THINK?

The 'ideal' levels of the liquidity ratios are based on historical research. Some years ago, an examination was undertaken of the balance sheets of leading companies over a period of years. It found that a number of businesses whose liquidity ratios were below the advisable (ideal) levels went into liquidation. Similarly, those with excessive liquidity tended to make less profit over time because they were not putting enough money into fixed assets.

'Ideal' ratios were set as a result of these observations, but do they still apply today? With businesses using just-in-time stock control, and having much easier access to funds, many accountants feel that these 'ideal' levels are too high. Retailers that benefit from a constant flow of cash receipts can survive with very low levels of liquid assets. Peacocks, the clothing retailer, has a current ratio of 0.71:1 and an acid test ratio of only 0.24:1. Tesco's ratios are also low at 0.66:1 and 0.42:1 respectively. These ratios are well below the minimum 'ideal' levels of 1.5:1 and 0.75:1 respectively.

A quick glance at Table 11.1 supports this view — the average current ratio of UK companies in 2004 was 1.19:1, well below the recommended minimum level of 1.5:1. However, business liquidations increased in 2004, so this may be proof that businesses at present are holding too little liquidity.

Table 11.1 Current ratio of UK firms, 1999–2004

	Year					
Ratio	1999	2000	2001	2002	2003	2004
Current ratio	1.17:1	1.16:1	1.14:1	1.06:1	1.15:1	1.19:1

Note: data show the average of UK companies' financial positions at the end of the second quarter of each year.

Source: Experian.

PRACTICE EXERCISE — Total: 30 marks (30 minutes)

1 Ideally, the acid test ratio should be between x:1 and y:1, where x and y are numbers.

a What is the ideal value for x? *(1 mark)*

b What is the ideal value for y? *(1 mark)*

2 Why should a firm try to avoid a low acid test ratio? *(4 marks)*

3 What is the disadvantage of a high acid test ratio? *(4 marks)*

4 The following information is extracted from the accounts of Dixons Group plc. The Dixons Group consists of three main retail outlets: Dixons, Currys and PC World.

As at:	1.5.2004 (£m)	1.5.1999 (£m)
Balance sheet:		
Current assets	2,304	1,220
Stock	793	581
Current liabilities	1,566	1,126

Based on this information, calculate the following ratios for the year ending 1 May 2004 and the year ending 1 May 1999.

a current ratio *(6 marks)*

b acid test ratio *(4 marks)*

5 In the light of Table 11.1 and your calculations in question 4 above, discuss how well Dixons has managed its liquidity. *(10 marks)*

CHAPTER 12

Financial efficiency

Financial efficiency ratios measure the efficiency with which the business manages specific assets and liabilities. They allow the business to scrutinise the effectiveness of certain areas of its operation. This chapter analyses the three financial efficiency ratios included in the AQA A2 Business Studies specification: asset turnover, rate of stock turnover and debtor days.

Financial efficiency ratios

For all of the financial efficiency ratios covered in this chapter, a business will compare itself with similar businesses in the same industry, as standards vary significantly between industries. Businesses will also use the ratios in order to compare the performance of individual branches, departments and divisions within the firm, and thus to assess their relative efficiency.

Asset turnover

This ratio measures how well a company uses its assets in order to achieve sales revenue. A key purpose of a company is to maximise its sales. Companies organise their finances in order to create an efficient balance of fixed assets and working capital. Fixed assets, such as machinery and retail premises, enable a firm to generate sales revenue from providing and selling goods and services. A healthy level of current assets within the firm's working capital also helps it to increase sales revenue. Current assets, in the form of stock, must be held to meet customers' needs and, for retailers, to entice buyers. The existence of debtors also helps to increase sales, as many customers are attracted by the offer of credit when they buy goods.

Asset turnover is calculated by the formula below. It should be noted that it is measured as a number and not as a ratio or percentage.

$$\text{asset turnover} = \frac{\text{annual sales (turnover)}}{\text{assets employed}}$$

A *high* figure shows that the business is using its assets efficiently to achieve sales. A *low* figure shows that the business is not using its assets efficiently to achieve sales. However, care needs to be taken when using the asset turnover ratio, as it can be misleading. Capital-intensive firms will have lower asset turnover figures than labour-intensive firms. This is because any capital owned by a business will be included in its assets, thus lowering the value of the ratio. In contrast, labour-intensive firms do not own their labour forces, so their net assets figures will be lower.

If comparisons are made between firms with similar asset structures, however, a valid conclusion can be drawn. For this reason, asset turnover is used by firms to make intra-firm comparisons between branches. Supermarkets, for example, use this ratio to see which branches are the most efficient at generating sales. In this way, underperforming branches can copy the techniques used by the more efficient ones.

From Tables 10.3 and 10.4 on pages 110–111, GSK plc's asset turnover figures are:

2003: 21,441/12,729 = 1.7 2004: 20,359/13,856 = 1.5

Table 12.1 *Asset turnover of UK firms, 1999–2004*

	Year					
Ratio	1999	2000	2001	2002	2003	2004
Asset turnover	2.2	2.3	2.4	2.6	2.8	3.0

Note: data show the average of UK companies' financial positions at the end of the second quarter of each year.
Source: Experian.

FACT FILE

Uniquely among the financial ratios studied in this book, Table 12.1 shows consistent improvement in efficiency for UK firms between 1999 and 2004.

Rate of stock turnover (stockturn)

This measure of financial efficiency indicates how quickly stock is converted into sales. A high figure means that stock is sold quickly, thus bringing money into the company more quickly.

$$\text{rate of stock turnover} = \frac{\text{sales (valued at cost)}}{\text{average stock}}$$

Sales must be valued at cost to provide a fair comparison, as stock values are based on cost. This provides accuracy, but it does mean that it is difficult to use published accounts to calculate this ratio.

The rate of stock turnover (RST) figure represents the number of times in a year that the firm sells the value of its stock. An RST of 3 means that it sells its stock three times a year (that is, once every 4 months). Thus it will take 4 months, on average, to convert stock into cash (if no credit is given).

An alternative method of calculation is to measure the average number of days taken to sell an item of stock:

$$\text{average no. of days to sell one item} = \frac{\text{average stock}}{\text{sales (valued at cost)}} \times 365$$

INGRAM

Factors influencing the rate of stock turnover

The main influences on stock turnover are:

- **the nature of the product.** Perishable products or products that become dated (such as newspapers) have very high rates of stock turnover. In contrast, some products, such as antiques, sell slowly and so have a low rate of stock turnover.
- **the importance of holding stock.** Some businesses, such as clothes retailers, need to hold high stock levels to encourage shoppers. However, commercial customers are less likely to expect a good to be already in stock when they decide to purchase.

- **the length of the product life cycle/fashion.** Fashionable products will be expected to sell quickly and products with very short life cycles (such as chart records and computer games) must also have a rapid turnover.
- **stock management systems.** Companies that use just-in-time stock control have very low stock levels, so their rate of stock turnover will be high.
- **quality of management.** Poor market research may lead to inappropriate stock being displayed and therefore low rates of stock turnover being achieved.
- **the variety of products.** An organisation with 20 varieties of a product will inevitably be holding higher stock levels than an organisation with only one version of a product. The firm with 20 varieties will thus have lower stock turnover and higher costs of stock holding. However, this should be balanced by the fact that the additional variations of the products may attract extra sales.

It is not possible to calculate the rate of stock turnover from published accounts. In order to give sample calculations for GSK plc, based on Tables 10.3 and 10.4, it has been assumed that the 'cost of sales' is equal to the value of stock at cost. It is also assumed that the stock level on the date of the balance sheet is equal to the average stock held during the year. In practice, both of these assumptions are likely to provide only an estimate, with the cost of stock being particularly unreliable.

2003: $\frac{4{,}188}{2{,}109} = 1.99$

2004: $\frac{4{,}309}{2{,}192} = 1.97$

These results suggest that GSK plc takes 365/1.76 = 207 days to turn over its stock. It is highly unlikely that this is a reliable result for a pharmaceutical company, which would expect to sell stock much more rapidly.

Debtor days (average age of debtors)

This shows the number of days that it takes to convert debtors into cash.

$$\text{debtor days} = \frac{\text{debtors}}{\text{annual sales}} \times 365$$

Firms that provide long-term credit for their customers may expect a high figure, but companies such as Papa John's Pizza receive cash payments, so their debtor days are very low.

Standards vary between industries, but in general terms a firm will want to have as low a value as possible, meaning that debtors are paying promptly. Although the finance department will wish for prompt payment, the marketing department may want to offer generous credit facilities to attract customers. Retailers of furniture traditionally offer long credit terms, so high debtor days may be a feature of that trade. Car manufacturers provide garages with credit to encourage the garages to display a wide range of stocks, leading to high average debtor days.

EXAMINER'S VOICE

The **return on capital employed**, which we will look at in Chapter 14, is identified in this book as a profitability ratio. However, because it measures the overall financial efficiency of the business, it can also be categorised as a measure of financial efficiency.

The calculations for GSK plc based on Tables 10.3 and 10. 4 are:

$$2003: \quad \frac{6,897}{21,441} \times 365 = 117 \text{ days}$$

$$2004: \quad \frac{7,309}{20,359} \times 365 = 131 \text{ days}$$

FACT FILE

Firms tend to compare debtor days with another ratio known as **creditor days**. In general, a firm trying to remain solvent will benefit from a situation whereby its payments to its creditors (its suppliers) take longer to make than the time it takes to receive payment from its debtors (that is, its creditor days exceed its debtor days).

DID YOU KNOW?

Many firms that provide credit for their customers 'factor' their debts to a specialist bank. Banks such as HFC and GE Capital thus 'own' the debts. Consequently, retailers such as Currys and Comet will not have as high levels of debtors as might be expected.

PRACTICE EXERCISE

Total: 50 marks (50 minutes)

1 Many businesses are now leasing their properties. Why does this reduce the reliability of asset turnover as a measure of financial efficiency? *(4 marks)*

2 How has just-in-time stock control affected the value of the rate of stock turnover? *(4 marks)*

3 Explain two other factors that influence the rate of stock turnover of a product. *(6 marks)*

4 Briefly explain the benefit of a high rate of stock turnover. *(4 marks)*

5 Explain one advantage and one disadvantage to a business of having a high value for debtor days. *(6 marks)*

6 The following information is extracted from the accounts of Dixons Group plc.

Years ending/as at:	1.5.2004 (£m)	1.5.1999 (£m)
Profit and loss account:		
Sales revenue (turnover)	6,492	3,914
Sales (valued at cost)	1,280	1,133
Balance sheet:		
Assets employed	2,308	1,846
Debtors	507	475
Average stock	793	581

Based on this information, calculate the following ratios for the year ended 1 May 1999 and the year ended 1 May 2004:

a asset turnover *(4 marks)*

b rate of stock turnover *(4 marks)*

c debtor days *(6 marks)*

7 Discuss the financial efficiency of Dixons plc in 1999 and 2004. *(12 marks)*

CHAPTER 13

Gearing

Gearing examines the capital structure of a firm and its likely impact on the firm's ability to stay solvent. There is one relevant measure of gearing, known as the gearing ratio (or capital gearing), and we shall consider it in this chapter. The chapter also considers the relative merits of high capital gearing and low capital gearing.

INGRAM

Gearing ratio

The gearing ratio is measured by the following formula:

$$\text{gearing (\%)} = \frac{\text{loan capital}}{\text{total capital employed}} \times 100$$

If the gearing ratio is greater than 50%, the company is said to have *high* capital gearing. If the gearing ratio is below 25%, the company is said to have *low* capital gearing. Usually, capital gearing between 25% and 50% would be considered to be low, but the interpretation of 'high' and 'low' gearing can vary over time.

A high capital gearing ratio shows that a business has borrowed a lot of money in relation to its total capital. A low capital gearing ratio indicates that a firm has raised most of its capital from shareholders, in the form of share capital and retained profits.

Based on Table 10.4 (see p. 111), the gearing ratios for GSK plc for 2003 and 2004 are:

$$2003: \quad \frac{6{,}925}{12{,}729} \times 100 = 54.4\%$$

$$2004: \quad \frac{7{,}654}{13{,}856} \times 100 = 55.2\%$$

EXAMINER'S VOICE

The most commonly used formula for gearing is:

$$\text{gearing (\%)} = \frac{\text{loan capital + preference shares}}{\text{total capital employed}} \times 100$$

The AQA specification does not refer to preference shares, as relatively few companies issue them. Therefore, calculations of the gearing ratio in this book are based on loan capital without any reference to preference shares.

FACT FILE

Table 13.1 shows the average gearing ratio in the UK in recent years. In 2002 and 2003 interest rates fell to record low levels. At the same time, the economy was growing steadily. Consequently, businesses were eager to take advantage of the opportunity to borrow money at low rates of interest and lenders were eager to lend, confident that businesses could repay any money that was lent. This led to an unprecedented rise in gearing ratios in 2002 and 2003, which ended in 2004 when interest rates started to rise again.

Table 13.1 Gearing, 1999–2004

	Year					
Ratio	1999	2000	2001	2002	2003	2004
Gearing (%)	47.9	53.5	49.8	64.6	73.3	60.4

Note: data show the average of UK companies' financial positions at the end of the second quarter of each year.

Source: Experian.

DID YOU KNOW?

Gearing may also be expressed as the ratio:

loans:share capital

Using this formula, a business with equal levels of loans and shareholders' capital would have a gearing ratio of 1:1. (This is equivalent to a gearing of 50%.)

Benefits of high and low gearing

Benefits of high capital gearing

- There are relatively few shareholders, so it is easier to keep control of the company.
- The company can benefit from a very cheap source of finance when interest rates are low.
- In times of high profit, interest payments are usually much lower than shareholders' dividend requirements, allowing the company to retain much more profit for future expansion.

Benefits of low capital gearing

- Most capital is permanent share capital, so the company is at less risk of creditors forcing it into liquidation.
- A low-geared company avoids the difficulties facing high-geared companies, which have to pay high interest rates on their borrowed capital when interest rates are high.
- The company avoids the pressure facing highly geared companies that must repay their borrowing at some stage.

We can conclude that there is no ideal gearing ratio. The best gearing percentage will depend on circumstances.

- A highly profitable company will prefer high gearing, as its dividend payments usually exceed its interest payments on loans. High gearing will also be advantageous if interest rates are low and if the owners of a business want to limit the number of new shareholders.
- Low gearing will tend to exist if companies are less profitable, if interest rates are high and if the business is prepared to expand its number of shareholders. Companies that have retained high levels of profit in the past will tend to have low levels of gearing.

DID YOU KNOW?

Recent high profits have encouraged some businesses to buy back shares and thus increase their gearing ratios. In some cases, these firms have taken advantage of low interest rates to borrow funds, further increasing their gearing ratios.

CHAPTER 13 Gearing

PRACTICE EXERCISE

Total: 25 marks (25 minutes)

1 Capital gearing is considered to be 'high' if it exceeds what percentage? *(1 mark)*

2 Briefly explain two possible disadvantages of high capital gearing. *(6 marks)*

3 Briefly explain two possible advantages of high capital gearing. *(6 marks)*

4 The following information is extracted from the accounts of Dixons Group plc.

As at:	1.5.2004 (£m)	1.5.1999 (£m)
Balance sheet:		
Capital employed	2,272	2,542
Long-term liabilities/loans	804	1,475

Based on this information, calculate the gearing ratio for the year ending 1 May 2004 and the year ending 1 May 1999. *(6 marks)*

5 Refer to Table 13.1 on p. 121. Explain why the high levels of capital gearing in 2003 coincided with the UK's lowest levels of interest rates in 40 years. *(6 marks)*

CHAPTER 14

Profitability and performance

Most firms aim to make a profit. In order to assess the efficiency of the business in achieving this major objective, three profitability (or performance) ratios are used: the return on capital employed, the gross profit margin and the net profit margin. This chapter examines each of these ratios in turn.

Profitability ratios

Each of the three profitability ratios covered in this chapter relates profit to the size of the firm. In all three ratios, a high percentage represents a better performance than a low percentage.

Return on capital (employed)

The return on capital employed (ROC or ROCE) ratio shows the net profit (operating profit is also used) as a percentage of capital employed; capital employed equates to the net worth of the firm.

Net profit is normally used, as it is always declared. However, operating profit is considered to be the best measure of performance, as it focuses only on the company's main trading activities, whereas net profit can include exceptional items that are not a reflection of efficiency. For example, a firm that sells some fixed assets will increase its net profit, but this gives a misleading impression of its efficiency and in fact may reduce future profits. In such instances, operating profit may be more useful than net profit.

Profit *before tax* is used because tax rates vary between countries, so profit after tax is a less reliable measure of the company's performance.

Capital employed is generally considered to be the best measure of a firm's size. It is not a totally reliable guide, as firms are tending to lease many assets rather than purchase them, but in general, capital employed is a good basis for comparing the scale of companies' operations.

Return on capital employed is measured as a percentage, using the following formula:

$$\text{return on capital employed (\%)} = \frac{\text{net profit before tax (or operating profit)}}{\text{capital employed}} \times 100$$

(Operating profit can be used if net profit does not show accurately the profit quality.)

Based on Tables 10.3 and 10.4 (see pp. 110–111), the ROCE (%) for GlaxoSmithKline (GSK) plc is:

$$2003: \quad \frac{6{,}719}{12{,}729} \times 100 = 52.8\%$$

$$2004: \quad \frac{6{,}119}{13{,}856} \times 100 = 44.2\%$$

FACT FILE

Table 14.1 shows the average ROCE (%) for all UK companies in recent years. Companies can use these figures as a benchmark to see if they are making a good profit. GSK plc would conclude that its ROCE (%) shows success relative to other firms (in general and in the pharmaceutical industry) both in 2003 and 2004. However, the fall in the ratio between 2003 and 2004 is a sign of a slight decline. In fact, it would be more useful to use figures based on the same industry. For example, in 2004 GSK plc would compare its ROCE (%) with the average for the pharmaceutical industry (24.7%) rather than the national average of 5.4%.

It should also be noted that there are considerable variations in performance between regions and industries. For example, the average return on capital of 5.2% in 2003 incorporates regional variations from 12.0% in Yorkshire and Humberside and 11.1% in the Southwest to 4.5% in the Northwest and 1.4% in Wales. Similarly, the average return on capital was 24.7% in pharmaceuticals but only 1.2% in engineering and 1.3% in media.

***Table 14.1** Profitability ratios for UK firms, 1999–2004*

	Year					
Ratio	**1999**	**2000**	**2001**	**2002**	**2003**	**2004**
Return on capital employed (%)	14.0	12.5	10.8	7.6	5.2	5.4
Net profit (%)	8.0	7.6	7.1	5.6	3.9	4.1

Note: data show the average of UK companies' financial positions at the end of the second quarter of each year.

Source: Experian.

Gross profit margin

Gross profit margin calculates the gross profit as a percentage of sales (turnover). Again, gross profit is a measure of profitability and the sales of a company are a reliable indicator of the size of the company.

Gross profit margin is calculated as follows:

$$\text{gross profit margin (\%)} = \frac{\text{gross profit}}{\text{sales (turnover)}} \times 100$$

Based on Table 10.3, the gross profit margin figures for GSK plc are:

$$2003: \quad \frac{17{,}253}{21{,}441} \times 100 = 80.5\%$$

$$2004: \quad \frac{16{,}050}{20{,}359} \times 100 = 78.8\%$$

This ratio must be treated with caution, as gross profit in the profit and loss account is sales minus direct costs. Since all of the overheads are ignored in this calculation, it is not as important a measure of success as net profit.

However, the gross profit margin is useful in assessing a firm's ability to control its direct costs (the cost of sales) and also its ability to maximise sales revenue by creating value added. As long as these factors are noted, comparisons of gross margins are useful for a business.

Firms in industries with low rates of stock turnover (see p. 116), such as antique stores, must try to obtain as high a gross profit margin as possible. Supermarkets with high rates of stock turnover usually have lower gross profit margins, as profit is made from the higher volume of sales. As gross profit margins vary considerably between industries, inter-firm comparisons should only be made with firms in the same industry.

Net profit margin

This measures operating profit (or net profit) as a percentage of sales (turnover).

Operating profit is viewed as the best measure of the quality of a firm's profit, while sales turnover is an excellent measure of scale.

The ratio is calculated as follows:

$$\text{net profit margin (\%)} = \frac{\text{net profit before tax}}{\text{sales (turnover)}} \times 100$$

Based on Table 10.3, GSK plc's net profit margins were:

$$2003: \frac{6{,}719}{21{,}441} \times 100 = 31.3\%$$

$$2004: \frac{6{,}119}{20{,}359} \times 100 = 30.1\%$$

FACT FILE

Table 14.1 shows the average net profit margin for all UK companies in recent years. Firms with high rates of stock turnover tend to have lower profit margins, as their profit arises from the large numbers sold. Consequently, net profit margin may not be a reliable comparison between different industries. However, it is an excellent way of assessing the relative profitability of two firms competing with each other.

PRACTICE EXERCISE 1 — Total: 15 marks (15 minutes)

1 Explain why return on capital employed is considered to be the best measure of a firm's performance. *(4 marks)*

2 Explain two reasons why return on capital employed might not be a good indicator of a firm's success. *(6 marks)*

3 Why is the net profit margin a better indicator of profitability than the gross profit margin? *(5 marks)*

PRACTICE EXERCISE 2 — Total: 40 marks (40 minutes)

The following information is extracted from the accounts of Dixons Group plc.

Years ending:	1.5.2004 (£m)	1.5.1999 (£m)
Profit and loss account:		
Sales revenue	6,492	3,914
Gross profit	642	429
Net profit	366	215
Balance sheet:		
Capital employed	2,272	2,542

1 Based on the information above, calculate the following ratios for the year ending 1 May 2004 and the year ending 1 May 1999:

a return on capital employed *(6 marks)*

b gross profit margin *(6 marks)*

c net profit margin *(6 marks)*

2 Did Dixons plc improve its profitability between 1999 and 2004? Use the ratios above to support your views. *(10 marks)*

3 In the light of the data in Table 14.1 and your calculations in question 1, comment on Dixon plc's profitability in comparison with other companies in 1999 and 2004. *(12 marks)*

CHAPTER 15

Shareholders' ratios

Shareholders will judge the company on its ability to reward them for their input into the company. This means that shareholders' ratios will measure the benefit of a company's activities to its shareholders, rather than other stakeholders. Shareholders' ratios thus have a narrower focus than other ratios. Other stakeholders may not see a 'favourable' shareholders' ratio as a positive sign. This chapter examines two shareholders' ratios: dividend per share and dividend yield.

TOPFOTO

Dividend per share

A **dividend** is that part of a company's profit that is distributed to shareholders as their reward for holding shares. The term 'earnings' is used to describe the profits available for shareholders (the profit after tax). Usually, companies will retain a significant proportion of this profit for future investment or purchase of shares. Thus, only part of the profit is paid as dividends to the shareholders.

The dividend per share is calculated as follows:

$$\text{dividend per share} = \frac{\text{total dividends paid}}{\text{number of shares issued}}$$

If a business has issued 1 million shares and pays £150,000 in dividends, the dividend per share is: £150,000/1,000,000 = 15 pence per share.

This ratio is of limited usefulness as it lacks context. For example, it does not reveal how much the share cost to buy. A 15 pence dividend is excellent if the share cost 30 pence to buy, but it is a very poor return if the share price was £30. The dividend per share is thus used as the first stage of the calculation of the dividend yield (see the next section).

Referring again to Tables 10.3 and 10.4 on pages 110–111, the dividend per share for GSK plc in each of the years covered was:

$$2003\text{:}\ \frac{\text{£2,333m}}{\text{5,804m}} = 40.2 \text{ pence per share}$$

$$2004\text{:}\ \frac{\text{£2,402m}}{\text{5,762m}} = 41.7 \text{ pence per share}$$

Dividend yield

The dividend yield builds on the dividend per share by expressing it as a percentage of the current market price of the shares.

$$\text{dividend yield (\%)} = \frac{\text{dividend per share}}{\text{market price of share}} \times 100$$

This shows the annual percentage return on the money needed to purchase the share. Its significance is that it can be compared with the percentage return from other investment choices, such as a bank account or other shares. Thus, a dividend yield of 6% might be seen as a good return if banks are paying 3% interest on savings accounts, but it would be a poor return if banks were paying 9% interest.

These calculations ignore the gains or losses that can be made from owning shares. If share prices are increasing, the dividend yield will fall and yet owning these shares will be a more attractive proposition. In contrast, a fall in the share price will increase the dividend yield but may be seen as an unfavourable trend by shareholders. If share prices are relatively static, the dividend yield is a more relevant measure. However, it is still limited because it ignores the part of profit that is retained.

In conclusion, dividend yield is a good measure of the short-term rewards from owning shares, but it tends to ignore the long-term consequences.

From Table 10.4 and the earlier calculation of the dividend per share for GSK plc, the dividend yield was:

$$2003: \frac{40.2}{1206} \times 100 = 3.3\%$$

$$2004: \frac{41.7}{1250} \times 100 = 3.3\%$$

PRACTICE EXERCISE — Total: 35 marks (35 minutes)

1 Why is the dividend per share a key ratio for shareholders? *(3 marks)*

2 Explain two reasons why the dividend per share might not be a good measure of the success of the company as a whole. *(6 marks)*

3 Why would a shareholder use the dividend yield as a way of assessing the benefits of buying shares in a business? *(4 marks)*

4 Outline one reason why the 'dividend yield' might not be a good guide to whether a potential investor should buy shares in a company. *(4 marks)*

5 The following information is extracted from the accounts of Dixons Group plc.

As at:	1.5.2004	1.5.1999
Additional information:		
Dividends paid	£143 million	£129 million
Number of ordinary shares	1,959 million	1,925 million
Share price	155 pence	131 pence

a Calculate the dividend per share in 2004 and 1999. *(4 marks)*
b Calculate the dividend yield in 2004 and 1999. *(6 marks)*

6 In which year (1999 or 2004) would it have been more advisable for an investor to have purchased shares in Dixons plc? Justify your decision. *(8 marks)*

CHAPTER 16

Limitations of ratio analysis

Ratio analysis provides a scientific basis for decision making and is an excellent guide to a firm's current financial position. However, organisations have many different aims and objectives, so financial performance is not the only measure of an organisation's success. Because ratios are based on financial measures and are largely objective, there is a tendency to place too much reliance on them. Other, non-financial indicators (such as social audits) also have a part to play in assessing an organisation's performance. Ratio analysis should be used alongside these other indicators to assess a firm's success or failure. Trying to draw conclusions based solely on ratio analysis will give a limited focus. Some of the problems and limitations of ratio analysis are outlined below.

EXAMINER'S VOICE

This is an important area for evaluative questions. Ratios tend to give a definite view — a company's ratios are either better or worse than desired. Consequently, judgements based on ratios alone will have a limited focus. However, this is not the case if the limitations of ratio analysis are taken into account. Considering actual ratios alongside the reliability of the information, the possible objectives of the business, and the external factors that can influence performance, provides far more opportunities to demonstrate evaluation.

Reliability of information

The reliability of available information limits the usefulness of ratio analysis in several ways:

- The data on which ratios are based may be unreliable.
- Some figures, notably asset valuation, are subjective to some extent. Differences in values may be related to the views of the people estimating them. This is particularly true of intangible assets and fixed assets that have no alternative uses. For example, how valuable is a railway line and signalling system to an organisation if it decides to close the route?
- Different accounting methods may be employed. Straight-line depreciation generally provides higher book values for the balance sheet than alternative methods. This also means that costs of depreciation are lower in the earlier years, but higher in later years, compared with a business using other methods of calculation. It is difficult to make inter-firm

comparisons if businesses use different methods of depreciation. However, these differences may not be too significant when comparing the overall performance of the business.

- A firm's financial situation changes daily, and it may manipulate its accounts to provide a favourable view on the date on which they are prepared. This practice, known as window dressing, was examined in Chapter 9.

Historical basis

The historical basis of published accounts affects ratio analysis for the following reasons:

- Accounts indicate where a company has been, rather than where it is going. Past performance is not necessarily a useful guide to the future. A number of former 'blue-chip' companies (firms recognised as excellent performers) have fallen behind rivals in recent years. Sainsbury's and Marks and Spencer are examples of firms that failed to build on previously strong financial positions.
- Accounts show *what* has happened, rather than *why*, and so they can only serve to point out potential problems. Other methods must be used to rectify the difficulties. For example, despite record profit levels, Shell has recently had its credit rating reduced from the safest category (AAA) because of concerns about its levels of oil and gas reserves available for future extraction.

Comparisons

Ratios rely on comparisons, but they always involve difficulties because no two businesses or divisions face identical circumstances.

Intra-firm comparisons

When comparing branches of a company, consideration must be given to other factors. The size, location, age, appearance and position relative to competition of a branch will all affect its chances of success. A well-managed branch may appear to be performing poorly simply because it is in an inappropriate location, too small to benefit from economies of scale or in an area with a number of competitors with brand new premises. In contrast, a badly managed branch may appear to be performing well because external factors are all acting in its favour.

Inter-firm comparisons

It is difficult for a firm to find a competitor that is operating in exactly the same market and facing identical circumstances. Particularly in the case of global organisations, comparisons may be influenced by the state of the different markets in which they are operating rather than the efficiency of the firm. However, it should be noted that selecting the right products and markets in which to operate is a critical business decision.

Comparisons over time

Booms and recessions will influence a firm's success, and so historical comparisons may demonstrate the state of the marketplace rather than the efficiency of the company's management. Table 14.1 on page 124 shows how average performance varies considerably over time. For example, an average UK firm in 1999 recorded an ROCE of 14.0%, but by 2004 this had fallen to 5.4%. Consequently, a firm whose ROCE fell from 11% to 7% has actually improved its profitability compared with most other firms.

Comparisons with a standard

A standard only shows average or typical situations. These standards may not be applicable to all businesses. For example, standards for liquidity ratios were set before the introduction of just-in-time methods of production, which allow firms to hold much lower levels of stock than was previously the case. Averages for the economy as a whole may not be relevant for a firm that is facing a particularly difficult (or easy) trading situation.

Corporate objectives

Ratio analysis only looks at financial measures, and relies on the assumption that maximising profit is the only aim of all firms. It ignores other objectives that may be more important to a business:

- **Reputation.** A profitable company that is seen to be exploiting its customers may suffer a considerable loss of goodwill. This will make it harder for it to achieve the same level of sales in the future.
- **Human relations.** A company may experience a high rate of labour turnover and low levels of productivity if it does not meet the needs of its employees. Eventually these factors will reduce profitability.
- **Relationship with suppliers.** Low prices paid for materials can help profits in the short term but might upset suppliers, who may reduce the quality of their service or even seek out new customers to supply.
- **Product quality.** This may be essential for long-term customer loyalty. Reducing quality as part of a cost-cutting exercise may increase profits in the short term, but in the long run this can lead to a decline in the number of customers.
- **Future profit.** It may pay a company to make decisions that do not lead to or produce profit in the short term, in order to create profit for the future. Research and development (R&D) is an example of an activity that may reduce current profit in order to help future profit levels.

External factors

Company performance is very dependent on outside factors. A PESTLE analysis will show the external factors (opportunities and threats) that affect performance. Examples include:

- the stage of the economic cycle (for example, boom or recession)
- government legislation, which may add costs or create markets
- changes in taste — in favour of or against the firm's products
- new technology leading to new products or processes in the market
- the level of competition, which can affect the ability of a firm to make money

It is vital that these and other factors are considered before conclusions are drawn.

Conclusion

Ratios must not be ignored. They are still an excellent guide to performance. However:

- conclusions should be based on the specific circumstances. In some cases, profitability ratios may be the most important measure, but in emergencies, liquidity ratios may be more significant.
- the problems and limitations involved in ratio analysis should be borne in mind.

PRACTICE EXERCISE 1 — Total: 45 marks (45 minutes)

1 For a firm such as BP, analyse two factors that may cause the information used in its ratio analysis to be unreliable. *(6 marks)*

2 State the four main types of 'comparison' used in ratio analysis. *(4 marks)*

3 Explain four reasons why comparisons of ratios may provide misleading results. *(12 marks)*

4 Identify two external factors that can affect company performance. Using a particular ratio, show how it might be affected by the two external factors that you have identified. *(6 marks)*

5 Analyse how changes in corporate objectives might influence the ways in which a car manufacturer might use ratio analysis. *(8 marks)*

6 'Ratio analysis is of limited use because it shows the past, not the future.' To what extent is this statement valid? *(9 marks)*

PRACTICE EXERCISE 2 — Total: 60 marks (65 minutes)

(This exercise is for self-assessment — the answers are provided in the case study on pages 136–137.)

Tables 16.1 and 16.2 show extracts from the accounts of AstraZeneca plc.

***Table 16.1** Balance sheets of AstraZeneca plc, 31 December 2004 and 2003*

As at:	31.12.04 ($m)	31.12.03 ($m)
Fixed assets		
Intangible assets	2,826	2,884
Fixed assets	8,083	7,536
Long-term investments	276	220
TOTAL FIXED ASSETS	**11,176**	**10,640**
Current assets		
Stocks	3,020	3,022
Debtors	6,274	5,960
Short-term investments	4,091	3,218
Bank balance and cash	1,055	733
TOTAL CURRENT ASSETS	**14,440**	**12,933**
Current liabilities		
Short-term loans and overdrafts	142	152
Creditors (less than 1 year)	7,640	7,543
	7,782	7,695
WORKING CAPITAL	**6,658**	**5,238**
(net current assets)		
Total assets less current liabilities	**17,834**	**15,878**
Long-term liabilities		
Creditors (more than 1 year)	2,285	2,318
Other long-term liabilities	1,030	303
	3,315	2,621
TOTAL NET ASSETS	**14,519**	**13,257**
Capital and reserves		
Share capital	961	951
Reserves	13,558	12,306
	14,519	**13,257**
TOTAL CAPITAL EMPLOYED	**17,834**	**15,878**
Additional information		
Share price	2,283 pence	2,400 pence
Assuming exchange rate of £1 = $1.85	4,224 cents	4,440 cents
Number of shares issued	1,762 million	1,709 million

Table 16.2 Profit and loss accounts for AstraZeneca plc

Years ending:	31.12.04 ($m)	31.12.03 ($m)
SALES REVENUE	21,426	18,849
COST OF SALES (direct costs)	5,150	3,789
GROSS PROFIT	16,276	15,060
EXPENSES/OVERHEADS		
Research and development	3,803	2,341
Selling, general and administration	8,018	8,808
	11,821	11,149
TRADING PROFIT	4,455	3,911
Exceptional items	-	-
OPERATING PROFIT	4,455	3,911
PROFIT (LOSS) FROM OTHER ACTIVITIES	630	291
NET PROFIT BEFORE INTEREST	5,085	4,202
INTEREST	0	0
NET PROFIT BEFORE TAX	5,085	4,202
TAX	1,254	1,143
NET PROFIT AFTER TAX	3,831	3,059
OTHER POST-TAX PAYMENTS	18	23
EARNINGS	3,813	3,036
EARNINGS PER SHARE	$2.28	$1.78
Appropriation account		
NET PROFIT AFTER TAX	3,813	3,036
DIVIDENDS TO SHAREHOLDERS	1,555	1,350
RETAINED PROFIT	2,258	1,686

Based on the above data, calculate the following ratios for AstraZeneca for the financial years ending 31 December 2003 and 31 December 2004:

1 Return on capital employed (%) *(6 marks)*
2 Gross profit margin (%) *(6 marks)*
3 Net profit margin (%) *(4 marks)*
4 Current ratio *(6 marks)*
5 Acid test ratio *(4 marks)*
6 Gearing (%) *(6 marks)*
7 Asset turnover *(4 marks)*
8 Rate of stock turnover *(6 marks)*
9 Debtor days *(6 marks)*
10 Dividend per share *(6 marks)*
11 Dividend yield (%) *(6 marks)*

CASE STUDY Financial ratios in the pharmaceutical industry

Study the data in Table 16.3 and read the extracts on recent events in the pharmaceutical industry before answering the questions that follow.

Ratio	GSK (2003)	GSK (2004)	AstraZeneca (2003)	AstraZeneca (2004)
Return on capital employed (%)	52.8	44.2	26.5	28.5
Gross profit margin (%)	80.5	78.8	79.9	76.0
Net profit margin (%)	31.3	30.1	22.3	23.7
Current asset ratio	1.49:1	1.56:1	1.68:1	1.86:1
Acid test ratio	1.24:1	1.31:1	1.29:1	1.47:1
Gearing (%)	54.4	55.2	16.5	18.6
Asset turnover	1.7	1.5	1.2	1.2
Rate of stock turnover	1.99	1.97	1.25	1.71
Debtor days	117	131	115	107
Dividend per share	40.2 pence	41.7 pence	79.0 cents	88.3 cents
Dividend yield (%)	3.3	3.3	1.8	2.1

***Table 16.3** Financial ratios for GlaxoSmithKline plc and AstraZeneca plc, 2003 and 2004*

Drugs firms hit by safety scares

Drugs companies are worrying about the health of their own businesses after the US authorities issued a list of drugs requiring further scrutiny. Among the drugs that may be banned from sale in the USA is GlaxoSmithKline's Serevent, a treatment for asthma. This drug is a minor part of GSK's product range, but the same cannot be said for AstraZeneca. The USA is considering a ban of its cholesterol-cutting drug, Crestor, which is expected to account for 12% of the company's sales in the near future.

The news follows recent negative publicity for GSK, which has been fined for failing to reveal negative clinical trial results for one of its drugs.

After a rip-roaring 1990s, the pharmaceutical industry is having a more difficult time in the twenty-first century. Prices are being forced down in the USA and, globally, politicians are angry that ageing populations and governments are finding that they are unable to buy enough of the expensive medicines that they need. However, the most significant development has been the growth of generic drugs companies. These companies produce cheap copies of patented drugs, notably in countries such as India. They are racing to push out more cheap copies of the patented drugs that provide the main profits for the large pharmaceutical businesses — undercutting the main producers in the marketplace.

Sources: article by William Lewis in *The Times*, 12 September 2004, and BBC News, 19 November 2004.

GlaxoSmithKline (GSK)

For GSK, the main problem has been a lack of new medicines coming out of its R&D. GSK has responded by splitting its R&D operation into lots of small, specialised drug-development centres. Early signs are promising, with a number of new ideas being developed and tested. Chief executive Jean-Pierre Garnier is optimistic. Not only is the new system more cost effective, but also it is more productive than the previous approach. Analysts believe that it will have to succeed — new drugs are becoming more and more vital for the company as competition grows. Generic alternative drugs have led to a fall in sales revenue of £1.2 billion for two major products: Paxil (down 51%) and Wellbutrin (down by 30%). In general, the large pharmaceutical businesses are finding that they have less time to cash in on their patented products. However, for GSK there has been good news too: sales of the Avandia diabetes drug and Advair (an asthma treatment) have been leading GSK's fight back. The latter is now the fifth biggest-selling pharmaceutical product in the world.

Source: www.citywire.co.uk.

AstraZeneca plc

AstraZeneca is also suffering from generic competition, especially in the treatment of ulcers, where its patent on Prilosec has expired. AstraZeneca is anticipating future growth from new heart and cholesterol treatments, although the latter has received a setback in the USA, where authorities are demanding more testing before agreeing to its release. A similar problem has occurred in France, where the government is reviewing its existing approval of the company's blood-thinning medicine, Exanta. Problems have arisen from extending the use of the drug beyond the normal 2-week period. If the drug is withdrawn in France, it will also be withdrawn across Europe as part of an EU agreement.

The company has a number of the world's leading drugs in its product portfolio, including treatments for cancer, asthma and heart disease. It is constantly seeking sources of new products, spending $3.5 billion per annum on R&D. In response to its USA setback, it announced that it has bought a 20% share of Cambridge Antibody Technology and is providing financial support to the business to allow it to develop its products. The market for antibody drugs is expected to increase from $6 billion in 2005 to $45 billion in 2009. Furthermore, the treatments are more complex and thus it is harder for generic companies to provide alternatives. With less competition, AstraZeneca sees this as a potentially profitable market to enter.

Source: article by Mike Verdin in *The Times*, 22 November 2004.

Questions

Total: 80 marks (90 minutes)

1 Based solely on the data provided in Table 16.3, discuss the relative efficiency of GlaxoSmithKline and AstraZeneca in terms of their profitability, liquidity and gearing. *(20 marks)*

2 Based solely on the data provided in Table 16.3, discuss the relative efficiency of GlaxoSmithKline and AstraZeneca in terms of their financial efficiency. *(10 marks)*

3 Based on the shareholders' ratios *and* the information in the extracts, advise a shareholder on which company he or she should buy shares in. Justify your view. *(10 marks)*

4 Based on the extracts, evaluate the likely future profitability of:
a GlaxoSmithKline *(10 marks)*
b AstraZeneca *(10 marks)*

5 Evaluate the limitations of ratio analysis in assessing the performance of *either* GlaxoSmithKline *or* AstraZeneca. *(20 marks)*

CHAPTER 17

Contribution and breakeven analysis

In the AS course, the concept of 'contribution' was introduced and simple breakeven analysis was examined. This chapter extends the study of breakeven analysis to consider the impact of changes in fixed costs, variable costs per unit and selling price on the breakeven output, profit levels and margin of safety of a business activity. It also considers the problems and limitations of breakeven analysis in examining changes to a firm's breakeven situation. 'Special order' decisions are considered by looking at situations in which short-term strategies are adopted based on contribution rather than the long-term profit that might arise. The chapter contrasts the quantitative and qualitative factors that are involved in special order decision making. (You are advised to read Chapter 12 of the AS textbook before reading this chapter.)

Breakeven analysis

TERM

breakeven analysis: study of the relationship between total costs and total revenue to identify the output at which a business breaks even (that is, makes neither a profit nor a loss). A business can also use this to discover the impact of changes in output on its profit levels.

Assumptions of breakeven analysis

- The selling price is not affected by the number of units sold.
- Fixed costs remain the same, regardless of the number of units of output.
- Variable costs per unit are the same at all levels of output.
- Every unit of output that is produced is sold.

Calculating breakeven output

Remember that breakeven output can be worked out in three different ways:

- using a table showing revenue and costs over a range of output levels
- using a formula to calculate the breakeven quantity
- using a graph that shows revenue and costs over a range of output levels

In the examples that follow, the original values are as follows:

selling price = £16 per unit

variable costs = £6 per unit

fixed costs = £80

Table 17.1 Breakeven data in tabular form

Units of output	Sales revenue (£)	Fixed costs (£)	Variable costs (£)	Total costs (£)	Profit (£)
0	0	80	0	80	(80)
1	16	80	6	86	(70)
2	32	80	12	92	(60)
3	48	80	18	98	(50)
4	64	80	24	104	(40)
5	80	80	30	110	(30)
6	96	80	36	116	(20)
7	112	80	42	122	(10)
8	128	80	48	128	Zero
9	144	80	54	134	10
10	160	80	60	140	20
11	176	80	66	146	30
12	192	80	72	152	40

In the above table, the breakeven output is 8 units. Below 8 units the firm makes a loss. Above 8 units the firm makes a profit.

The formula below shows how to calculate the breakeven output.

$$\text{breakeven output} = \frac{\text{fixed cost (£)}}{\text{contribution per unit (£)}}$$

In our example, the breakeven output is:

$$\frac{£80}{£16 - £6} = \frac{£80}{£10} = 8 \text{ units}$$

EXAMINER'S VOICE

Remember, contribution per unit is the difference between the selling price and the variable costs per unit.

In Figure 17.1 it can be seen from the gradient of the sales revenue line that the selling price per unit is £16. Similarly, the gradient of the variable costs line shows that variable costs per unit are £6. The fixed costs are £80 (at all levels of output).

In the diagram, the breakeven point is marked. The output required to break even is 8 units, at which level the sales (total) revenue and total costs are both equal to £128.

The margin of safety is the difference between the actual output and the breakeven output. If actual output is 12 units, the margin of safety is 12 – 8 = 4 units.

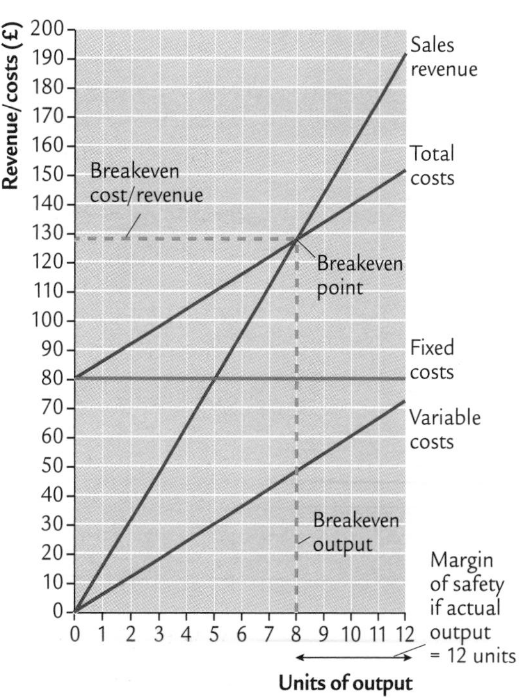

Figure 17.1 Breakeven in the form of a graph

Changes to the breakeven chart

There are six possible individual changes that can occur to a breakeven chart. These are shown in Figure 17.2 (a–f).

The possible changes are:

- an increase in the selling price
- a decrease in the selling price
- an increase in the variable cost per unit
- an increase in fixed costs
- a decrease in the variable cost per unit
- a decrease in fixed costs

In all parts of Figure 17.2, line A shows the original value and line B shows the new value, after the change.

How do the changes shown affect breakeven output? Two examples are given on page 142:

- Figure 17.3 shows the change in breakeven output brought about by an increase in fixed costs, with no other changes.
- Figure 17.4 shows the change in breakeven output caused by a decrease in variable costs *and* an increase in the selling price, but with no change in fixed costs.

Figure 17.2 (a–f) Possible changes to the breakeven chart

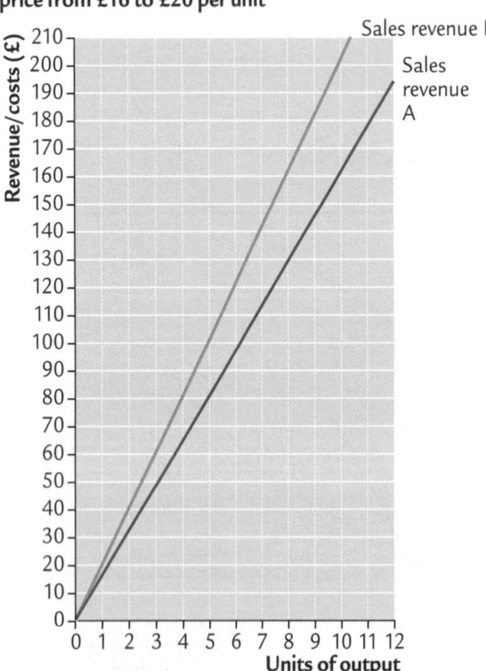

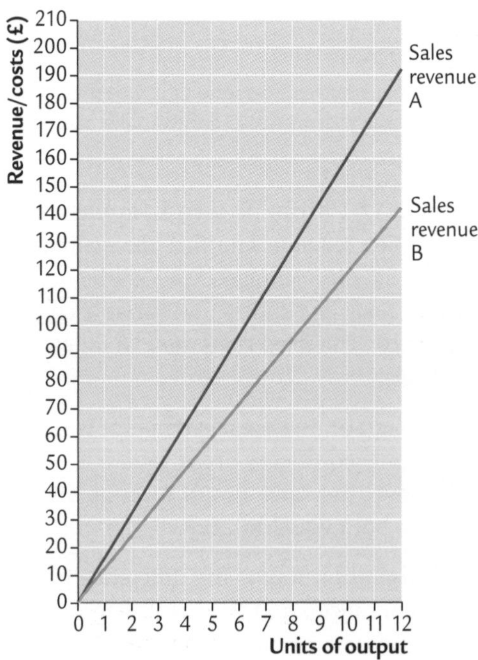

(c) Effect of an increase in variable costs from £6 per unit to £9 per unit

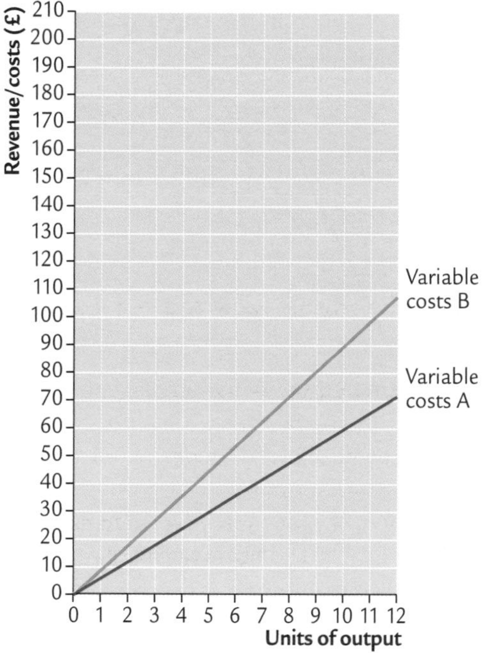

(d) Effect of a decrease in variable costs from £6 per unit to £4 per unit

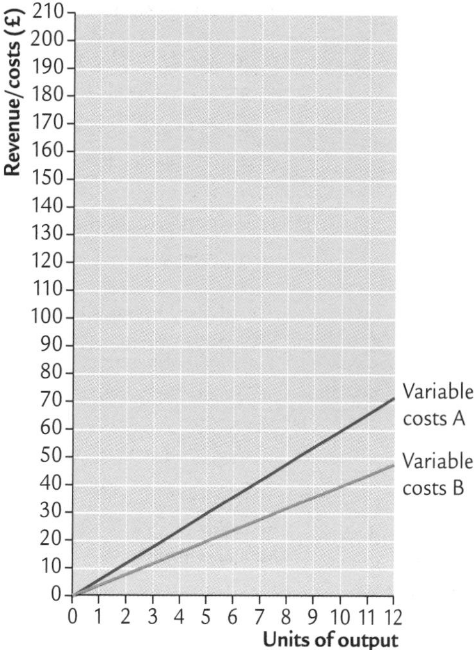

(e) Effect of an increase in fixed costs from £80 to £110

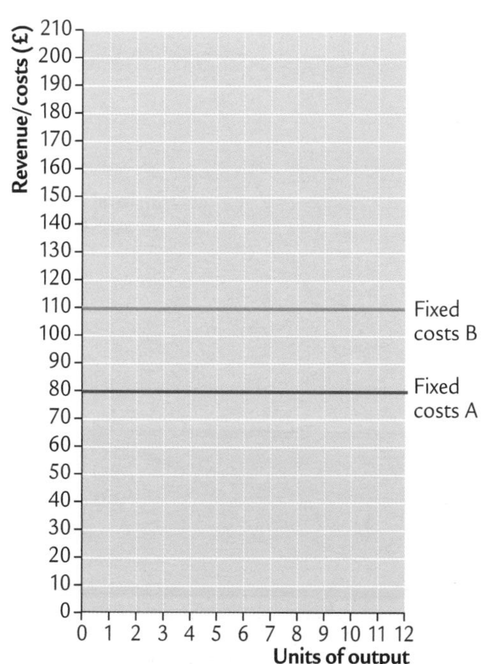

(f) Effect of a decrease in fixed costs from £80 to £60

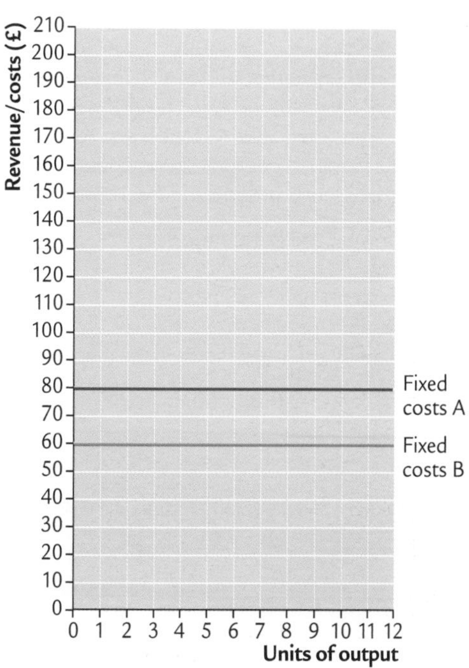

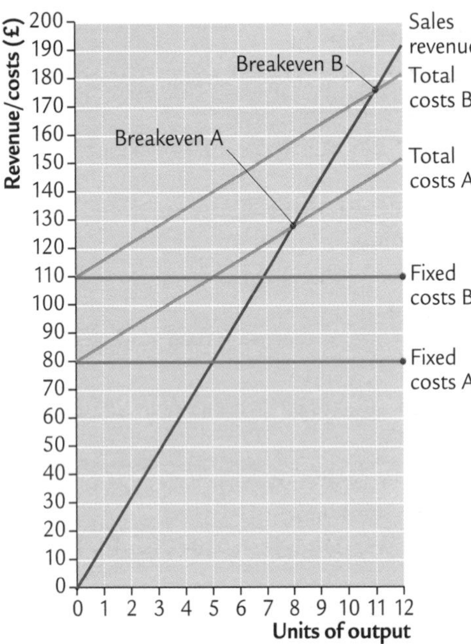

Figure 17.3 Change in breakeven point resulting from an increase in fixed costs from £80 to £110

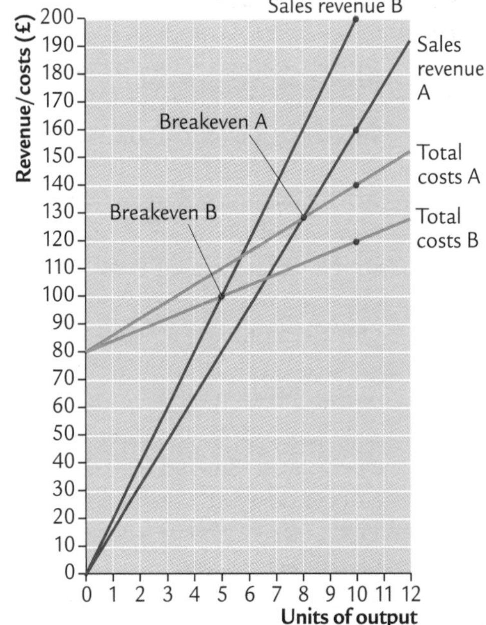

Figure 17.4 Change in breakeven point resulting from a decrease in variable costs from £6 per unit to £4 per unit and an increase in the selling price from £16 per unit to £20 per unit

WHAT DO YOU THINK?

Figure 17.5 shows changes that lead to a change in the breakeven output. Sales revenue A and total costs A show the original position. Sales revenue B and total costs B show the modified position after changes in selling price, variable costs per unit and fixed costs.

1 Identify the original and the modified:

a selling prices

b variable costs per unit

c fixed costs

that have caused the changes shown in the diagram.

2 What is the change in the breakeven output?

1 a Selling price: increases from £5 per unit to £20 per unit.

b Variable costs: increases from £1 per unit to £5 per unit.

c Fixed costs: increases from £40 to £90.

2 Breakeven output changes from 10 units to 6 units.

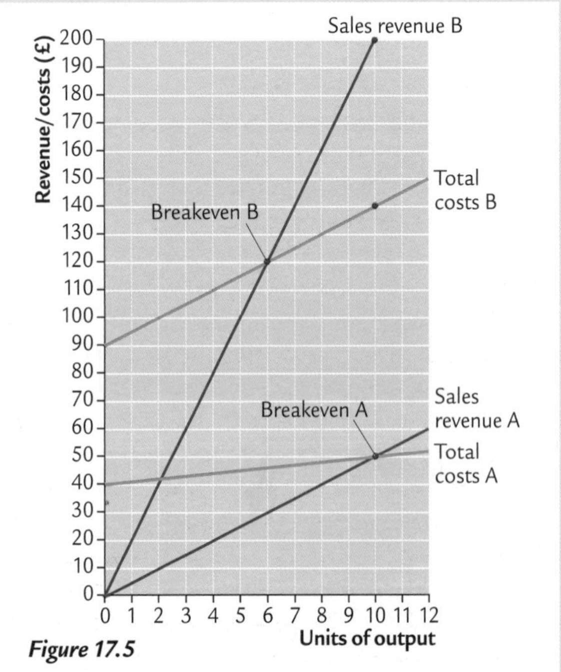

Figure 17.5

Benefits of breakeven analysis

- Breakeven analysis shows the different levels of profit achieved from the various levels of output that might be produced. This allows the business to predict its profit levels if it knows the number of units that it is going to sell. This knowledge may help a business to plan its future objectives and strategies.
- A new firm can use the breakeven output to calculate how long it will take to reach the level of output needed to make a profit. This will help it to assess whether its business idea is feasible. Given the tendency for new firms to experience cash-flow problems, it is helpful for the owners to estimate when they can expect to reach a profit level.
- Breakeven analysis is quick and easy to complete, thus saving time. Although the method can be criticised for possible inaccuracy, it provides businesses with a quick estimate before they need to proceed with a decision.
- Many firms have a target to earn a certain level of profit. Breakeven analysis can be adapted to discover at which point a company can reach a particular profit level. This assesses the contribution needed to pay both the fixed costs and the target profit figure.
- Breakeven analysis allows a firm to use 'what if?' analysis to show the different breakeven outputs and the changes in levels of profit that might arise from changes in its price, variable costs and fixed costs. This will help the firm to plan strategies for each of its products.
- Businesses that foresee future changes (such as higher wage costs or lower prices) can examine the impact on individual products within their range. This can help them to identify products that may be successful now but vulnerable in the future (or vice versa).

Problems of breakeven analysis

- All breakeven analysis is based on predictions. Chapter 2 explains some of the difficulties involved in forecasting the future. In some markets, such as those for raw materials, costs are prone to major fluctuations within short periods of time. In competitive markets it is difficult to be certain of prices.
- The assumption that sales will equal output is a major weakness of breakeven analysis. It is likely that some output will remain unsold, particularly in the case of perishable goods. Furthermore, there is likely to be some wastage of raw materials.
- The selling price will probably need to fall in order to persuade customers to buy larger quantities. Although many firms set a fixed price for their products, others will find that the sales revenue line is not straight but curves below the line assumed in breakeven analysis.
- Fixed costs may not stay the same as output changes. At particular levels of output, new machines and even new buildings may need to be purchased. This will lead to a sudden step up in fixed costs. It is misleading to believe that fixed costs will never change.

- The analysis assumes that variable costs per unit are always the same, ignoring factors such as economies of scale. In practice, firms will find that variable costs per unit fall as they increase output, leading to a variable cost line that curves below the line shown in previous breakeven charts. Similarly, diseconomies of scale will lead to an increase in variable costs per unit.

EXAMINER'S VOICE

Breakeven analysis can be categorised as 'simple' or 'complex'. The AQA A-level specification only requires an understanding of simple breakeven analysis. Complex breakeven analysis looks more critically at the problems identified above. Although this is not directly relevant to the specification, it is an indication of the limitations of using simple breakeven analysis to try to make business decisions.

PRACTICE EXERCISE 1

Total: 25 marks (25 minutes)

The following information applies to a product:

Units of output:	500
Variable costs:	£20 per unit
Fixed costs:	£3,900
Selling price:	£33 per unit

1 Calculate the contribution per unit. *(4 marks)*

2 Calculate the breakeven quantity. *(5 marks)*

3 How much profit is made if all 500 units are sold? *(4 marks)*

4 What is the margin of safety if 500 units are sold? *(2 marks)*

5 Calculate the breakeven quantity if the variable costs rise to £22 per unit and the fixed costs increase to £4,400. *(5 marks)*

6 Calculate the breakeven quantity if the variable costs remain at £20 per unit with fixed costs changing to £4,200 and the selling price is £35 per unit. *(5 marks)*

PRACTICE EXERCISE 2

Total: 30 marks (35 minutes)

The following information applies to a product:

Units of output:	10,000
Variable costs:	£8 per unit
Fixed costs:	£60,000
Selling price:	£16 per unit

1 Plot the breakeven chart based on this information, mark the breakeven point and show the margin of safety based on output of 10,000 units. *(10 marks)*

2 Amend the diagram to show the effects of a new price of £20 per unit. *(2 marks)*

3 Show the new breakeven point and margin of safety. *(4 marks)*

4 Plot a new breakeven chart based on the new price of £20 and a change in fixed costs to £75,000. Mark the breakeven point and show the margin of safety based on output of 10,000 units. *(8 marks)*

5 Amend the diagram to show the effects of a new variable cost of £5 per unit. *(2 marks)*

6 Show the new breakeven point and margin of safety. *(4 marks)*

Contribution and special order decisions

The concept of contribution was introduced in Chapter 11 of the AS textbook.

KEY TERMS

contribution per unit: selling price minus direct or variable cost per unit.

total contribution: total revenue minus total direct costs or total variable costs.

e EXAMINER'S VOICE

The concept of contribution was also covered in Chapter 7 of the AS book, when considering pricing methods. Certain pricing methods are based on costs. The most widely recognised of these pricing methods is **cost-plus pricing**. This method calculates the average cost (or average total cost) of production (combining the average variable costs and the average fixed costs). A percentage (the **mark-up**) is then added to set the price. The logic behind cost-plus pricing is that it ensures that the price set leads to a profit, as all costs are covered.

An alternative method of pricing is **contribution pricing**. This method takes the average variable costs only and adds a percentage (to help towards fixed costs and profit).

KEY TERM

special order decision: a business decision relating to a one-off contract. Usually the special order decision is needed in response to a request to supply a fixed quantity of a product at a particular price (invariably a lower price than usual).

In the long run, it is necessary to cover all costs. Consequently, 'cost plus' will be used as a long-term method of pricing. If all products are sold, a profit is secure. However, what happens if a one-off (special) order is received, at a lower price than usual? It may be worthwhile to accept this order as long as it leads to extra profit for the business. A firm's fixed costs are assumed to be unrelated to output. Logically, therefore, a special order to make additional items will not make any difference to the firm's *fixed* costs. However, additional output will lead to extra *variable* costs.

Using the data in Table 17.1 (p. 139) we can examine the financial implications of a special order decision. From Figure 17.1 we can see that fixed costs were £80 and variable costs were £6 per unit. The selling price was £16. Based on the assumption that fixed costs will not be affected by a special order to supply more units, it can be assumed that each additional unit will only add £6 to total costs (as variable costs will be £6 per unit).

A 'one-off' order will increase profit if the price exceeds £6, even though the normal price is £16. Ideally, the firm would like to receive £16 (its normal price), but should it accept a lower price? If the price offered is £13, the contribution per unit is £7 (£13 – £6). Thus the firm's profit will increase by £7 for every unit sold. Even a price of £8 will increase profit by £2 (£8 – £6) for every unit sold.

Special order decisions are therefore based on variable costs only, and use contribution pricing to set the price. These are one-off, short-term decisions.

In the long run, fixed costs will be due for payment. At this point, the firm must ensure that its products earn sufficient contribution to cover these fixed costs, before it is able to accept further orders based on variable costs alone.

Examples of special order decision calculations

1 A firm sells a product for £33. Variable costs are £20 per unit and fixed costs are £6,000. Existing sales have already covered the firm's fixed costs. Should it accept an offer from a customer to buy 100 items at £25 per unit? Answer: *yes*. The special order provides a contribution of £5 per unit (£25 – £20). Although this is lower than the usual contribution of £13 (£33 – £20), it will still contribute towards the firm's profit. Total contribution is 100 × £5 = £500. If a better offer is not available, this offer should be accepted, as it will increase profit by £500. (Note that the normal selling price and fixed costs are irrelevant to this calculation.)

2 A firm sells a product for £57. Variable costs are £44 per unit and fixed costs are £9,600. Should it accept an offer from a customer to buy 80 items at £40 per unit? Answer: *no*. The contribution per unit is *minus* £4 (£40 – £44). Thus, every additional item leads to a further loss of £4 to the firm's overall profits.

The decisions above are based solely on short-term financial factors. However, special order decisions may have long-term implications that should be considered. Furthermore, there will be non-financial factors that should be scrutinised before a decision is taken. These factors are considered in the next section.

Qualitative factors to consider in special order decisions

In practice, a special order decision would not be taken on the basis of its direct financial consequences. The firm would need to look at the implications for its objectives and its impact on other aspects of the firm. Factors to consider include the following:

- **The effect that the decision has on production.** The first step a business must take is to examine its capacity utilisation. If there is plenty of spare capacity, the special order may improve efficiency as the firm will be producing closer to full capacity. However, if the business is already close to full capacity (or the special order is large and will take the firm beyond its capacity), it may prevent other, more profitable orders from being accepted.
- **The impact on costs.** It is usually assumed that a special order does not affect fixed costs. However, the terms of an order may require additional spending on fixed costs in order to meet the specific requirements of the new customer. Unless the business has plenty of under-used resources, there is likely to be some increase in variable costs per unit, such as the need to pay overtime or purchase new components.

- **How will the company's reputation be affected?** The new customer may see the firm as flexible and helpful, but existing customers may experience delays and thus the company may lose some goodwill.
- **What happens if existing customers find out?** Existing customers will react badly if they discover that a new customer is receiving preferential treatment. In the long run, this could lead to a considerable loss in customer loyalty, with previously loyal customers either demanding price reductions too or taking their custom elsewhere.
- **Possible 'leakage' of special order products into existing markets.** The new customer may sell on to existing customers, undercutting the normal price. Shortly after its patent for photocopiers expired, Xerox decided to sell old versions of its photocopiers (it had previously only rented them to customers). It then discovered that its main competitors were companies that had bought its old copiers and were renting them out more cheaply than Xerox.
- **Is there potential for future (profitable) orders?** Although the special order may make a loss, it can build up a relationship with a customer. A satisfied customer may return in the future with many large, profitable orders.
- **The effect on staff.** If workers are under pressure, a special order may add to the stress and pressures on the workforce. However, if the workforce is feeling insecure because of a lack of orders, a special order may prevent redundancies and boost morale and productivity. The nature of the special order may increase variety and interest among the workforce (or add to boredom and monotony).
- **External factors.** Current and projected economic indicators should be examined. In a boom it is probable that demand will rise, so the firm may refuse a special order (unless it is offered a high price). In a recession the firm may be relieved to be offered a short-term contract that provides the chance to earn some additional revenue.

The firm may also want to consider individual issues based on the product itself. For example, it might help to achieve other objectives such as market diversification or social or ethical objectives.

Ultimately, the firm will need to balance these 'qualitative' issues with the financial consequences. If the profit to be made is large, the above factors may not be significant. If the financial benefits are small or non-existent, these factors may dominate the decision-making process.

EXAMINER'S VOICE

The financial (quantitative) calculations involved in a special order decision are fairly straightforward. If price exceeds variable costs, the order should be accepted. Consequently, special order decisions in examinations are likely to require consideration of the 'qualitative' factors. If an exam question is asked on this topic, look at the issues in the particular case study to find the factors that are of special significance.

PRACTICE EXERCISE 3 — Total: 30 marks (25 minutes)

1 What is meant by a special order decision? *(4 marks)*

2 Distinguish between contribution per unit and total contribution. *(5 marks)*

3 Explain the significance of contribution pricing in a special order decision. *(5 marks)*

4 Explain three qualitative factors that might be considered in a special order decision. *(9 marks)*

5 The following information applies to a firm:

Units of output/sales:	12,000 units per annum
Production capacity:	16,000 units per annum
Usual selling price:	£125 per unit
Fixed costs:	£50,000
Variable costs:	£100 per unit

The firm is approached by a potential customer that wishes to buy 2,000 units. The price offered is 10% lower than the usual selling price. Furthermore, modifications will need to be made to the raw materials used and the production methods employed. These changes will add 10% to variable costs per unit and will increase fixed costs by £7,000. Should the offer be accepted? *(7 marks)*

CASE STUDY 1 The fellowship of the rings

'It makes me chuckle sometimes,' says John Lundberg, gazing across a wheat field in central England. 'If somebody had said to me 10 years ago that today I'd be flying all over the world making crop circles for big companies and being paid for it, I'd have said they were mad.'

This is a deeply disturbing statement. Crop circles, as we all know, are supposed to be made by little green men from outer space. They arrive in flying saucers, make intricate patterns in wheat fields, and then go home to Planet Zog, leaving us simple Earthlings to argue over what it all means.

Mr Lundberg is certainly a man, but he is not green. For most of the past 13 years he has been making crop circles for fun, but in the past few years the commercial work, mostly advertising, has taken off. A project to promote *Big Brother* through crop circles was estimated to cost £250,000 and Orange recently spent £100,000 on its Wiltshire crop circle images.

Landowners are benefiting too, receiving payments for allowing their fields to be used for the work. However, it is not a simple calculation. Richard Cowan, an Oxfordshire farmer, has twice allowed Mr Lundberg's company to make crop circles on his land. The original agreement led to further requests for use of his land. A Wiltshire farmer indicates that the going rate is 'at least £500 per circle and sometimes much more'. Mr Cowan estimated that the damage to crops lost him £200, giving him a decent profit from the deal as more than one circle was constructed. However, it is not a reliable source of income and farmers run the risk of alienating their agricultural customers if they do not provide a regular supply of grain. There are also hidden costs involved, with disruption to farming and valuable time taken in crop circle planning. For those crop circles created for advertising purposes, the landowner may receive as little as 1% of the overall budget.

TOPFOTO

Most crop circles are not devised for advertising purposes. Since the 1970s they have been appearing mysteriously during the crop circle 'season' from April to September. About 250 are estimated to appear worldwide each year and the damage caused to the crops is sometimes worsened by the arrival of curious visitors trampling the wheat in order to view the mysterious circles. However, some enterprising farmers who wake up to find that they have been 'circled' make the most of it by charging visitors £1 or £2 to have a look. One Wiltshire farmer made £15,000 from charging people to view a particularly elaborate crop circle that inspired thousands of visitors.

Crop circles have boosted tourism, particularly in Wiltshire, which accounts for 80% of the UK's crop circles. However, the benefits are felt by local traders rather than farmers, who sometimes suffer hundreds of pounds of damage. The County Landowners' Association describes the night raids by circle-makers as 'rural graffiti' but is encouraging farmers to work with the circle-makers to generate income. 'It's innovative, entrepreneurial and good for rural businesses,' a spokesman said. However, there is a danger of market saturation. Already the market is changing from people interested in aliens to those who see crop circles as an art form.

It has been suggested that some farmers should consider hiring circle-makers. For example, a 'simple' crop circle might incur fixed costs of £400 and could attract 2,500 visitors over a period of 5 weekends (10 days), paying £1.50 each. An 'extravagant' crop circle would cost £800 to create but could attract 3,000 visitors paying £2.50 each. Farm workers would be prepared to work a rota at weekends in return for a payment of £1 per visitor.

Source: adapted from an article by David Harrison in the *Sunday Telegraph*, 25 July 2004.

Questions

Total: 20 marks (25 minutes)

1 Based solely on the financial information in the final paragraph, advise the farmers on whether they should produce a 'simple' or 'extravagant' crop circle. (8 marks)

PLUS EITHER

2 Discuss the other factors that farmers should consider before going ahead with projects to create crop circles on their land. *(12 marks)*

OR

3 A farmer wakes up one morning to find some crop circles on his land. Evaluate the limitations of using breakeven analysis to decide whether to charge the public to view the circles. *(12 marks)*

CASE STUDY 2 Dizzy Ltd

Table 17.2 shows the current financial position of three products made by Dizzy Ltd, which sells all of its products in the UK market. It has been approached by three different firms:

- Firm X is based in Germany and has had no previous contact with Dizzy Ltd. It has offered Dizzy a fixed price of £38 for 200 units of product A.
- Firm Y regularly buys product B on a small scale. It wishes to buy 450 items at a fixed price of £22.
- Firm Z is a company that has regularly purchased items from Dizzy Ltd's main competitor. The competitor has experienced difficulties in supplying Firm Z, which is desperate to find alternative supplies. Product C is the closest substitute to the competitor's product. Firm Z has offered £23 per unit in return for a set order of 300 items on a 'take it or leave it' basis.

***Table 17.2** Financial position of three Dizzy products*

	Selling price (£ per unit)	Variable costs (£ per unit)	Fixed costs (£ per unit)	Current output (units)	Capacity (units)
Product A	50	22	8,400	650	900
Product B	30	19	5,500	450	900
Product C	20	10	5,000	700	900

Question

Total: 20 marks (25 minutes)

Based on quantitative and qualitative factors, advise Dizzy Ltd on whether it should accept the orders from Firms X, Y and Z. Justify your recommendations in each case.

CHAPTER 18

Investment decision making

This chapter introduces the concept of investment decision making. It considers three quantitative methods of investment appraisal: payback, average rate of return and net present value. The calculations of each method and its relative merits as a form of investment appraisal are compared. The chapter also examines the significance of the source of the data and assessment of risk in such decisions. Finally, the qualitative factors that influence investment decisions are scrutinised and their significance is evaluated.

KEY TERM

investment decision making: the process of deciding whether or not to undertake capital investment (the purchase of fixed assets) or major business projects.

Reasons for capital investment and major business projects

Capital investment describes the process of purchasing fixed assets, such as new buildings, plant, machinery or office equipment. It considers the buying of any asset that will pay for itself over a period of more than 1 year.

Capital investment is undertaken for two main reasons:

- to replace or renew any assets that have worn out (depreciated) or become obsolescent. Investment appraisal informs a business when an existing asset is inefficient to the extent that it is cost-effective to replace it with a more productive replacement.
- to introduce additional, new assets in order to meet increased demand for the firm's products

TOPFOTO

Major business projects involve decisions that incorporate more than just capital equipment. Setting up new factories or stores, introducing new products, setting up a research laboratory and relocating to a new country are all examples of major projects to which investment appraisal techniques can be applied.

Sometimes businesses allow investment decisions to be based on the instinct of a manager, the firm's financial

position (for example, whether there are sufficient funds to buy an asset) or just a matter of routine (such as replacing computers every 3 years). These decisions may lead to financial difficulties. Investment appraisal ensures that decisions are subject to a rigorous scrutiny before agreement.

Investment appraisal

KEY TERM

investment appraisal: a scientific approach to investment decision making, which investigates the expected financial consequences of an investment, in order to assist the company in its choices.

EXAMINER'S VOICE

Investment appraisal can be applied to any major business decision. A firm considering a takeover or a new location can assess the financial implications by using investment appraisal. Chapter 32 shows how investment appraisal can be used to make location decisions.

Investment appraisal is a *quantitative* (numerical) tool in the decision-making process. Investment appraisal recommendations should be combined with an investigation of *qualitative* factors before a final decision is reached. These qualitative factors are considered later in the chapter.

The three investment appraisal techniques examined in this chapter base their recommendations solely on the following financial information:

- the initial cost of the investment
- the net return (revenue minus costs) per annum
- the lifetime of the investment

Methods of investment appraisal

There are three main methods of investment appraisal:

- payback period
- average rate of return or annual rate of return or average annual rate of return (ARR)
- net present value (NPV)

Each method provides a numerical calculation of the financial benefits of an investment. This result can be compared with the return required by the business and/or the results of alternative investment decisions.

The following scenario will provide the background information for investment appraisal by each of these methods.

Martin's Motors

Martin's Motors is a small garage on the outskirts of Basingstoke in Hampshire. The business offers servicing of certain makes of car for customers who do not wish to take their cars to the main dealerships.

Martin's key selling points are low overheads and a more flexible and personal service for customers, in comparison with local competitors. Most customers are recommended by friends, but in recent years a number of loyal customers have taken their cars back to the main dealers for their servicing. Martin has discovered that the main reason is the lack of certain technical equipment within his garage, as he is unable to afford the state-of-the-art machinery purchased by the large garages against which he is competing.

TOPFOTO

A particular weakness is the lack of a machine to recharge (service) the air-conditioning units in his customers' cars. He is looking at purchasing a Viper GT air-conditioning machine for carrying out this task. Martin has financial estimates based on prices in a Viper GT catalogue, comments from other garages, and his own estimates of the number of customers that he has lost through his failure to provide recharging of air-conditioning for his customers. These estimates are outlined below:

Cost to purchase a Viper GT air-conditioning machine: £5,000

Running costs:
- Air-conditioning liquid: £20 per treatment
- Wages and other costs: £5 per treatment

Charge to customers: £65 per treatment

Cost of a one-off advert in the *Thomson Local* directory (to alert customers to the new service): £250

Anticipated number of customers requesting the treatment:
- Year 1: 60
- Year 2: 45
- Year 3: 39
- Year 4: 34
- Year 5: 30

Martin is expecting to make money by attracting back customers for a full service of their cars. However, he wants to take a pessimistic view, so he is basing his decision on whether the Viper GT will pay for itself by attracting customers who only wish to service their air-conditioning. Any additional revenue is seen as a bonus.

The expected lifetime of the machine is anticipated to be 5 years, although this is probably a pessimistic estimate. As competition for air-conditioning recharging increases, the selling price is expected to fall from £65 to £50 or £60.

Table 18.1 shows the expected revenue, costs and net return on the Viper GT over its expected lifetime, based on the estimated costs, charges and customer numbers. For example, in year 1, revenue is 60 × £65 = £3,900 and costs are 60 × (£20 + £5) = £1,500.

Table 18.1 Expected revenue, costs and return on the Viper GT

Year	Annual revenue (£)	Annual cost (£)	Net return (£)
0*	0	5,250	(5,250)
1	3,900	1,500	2,400
2	2,925	1,125	1,800
3	2,535	975	1,560
4	2,210	850	1,360
5	1,950	750	1,200
Cumulative total	**13,520**	**10,450**	**3,070**

*It is traditional to denote the year in which the initial cost of an investment is incurred as year 0.

Payback

KEY TERM

payback period: the length of time that it takes for an investment to pay for itself from the net returns provided by that particular investment.

Payback is calculated by adding the annual returns from an investment until the cumulative total equals the initial cost of the investment. The exact time at which this occurs is the payback period. It is often measured in years, but for some investments months or weeks may be more appropriate. Firms will hope for as short a payback as possible.

An example calculation based on Martin's Motors is shown in Table 18.2.

Table 18.2 Predicted payback period for a Viper GT air-conditioning system for Martin's Motors

Year	Annual revenue (£)	Annual cost (£)	Net return (£)	Cumulative returns (£)
0	0	5,250	(5,250)	(5,250)
1	3,900	1,500	2,400	(2,850)
2	2,925	1,125	1,800	(1,050)
3	2,535	975	1,560	510
4	2,210	850	1,360	1,870
5	1,950	750	1,200	3,070
Cumulative total	**13,520**	**10,450**	**3,070**	

The final column shows the running total of revenues minus costs. When this column reaches zero, payback has been achieved. By the end of year 2, £4,200 of the £5,250 has been repaid. During year 3 the net return is £1,560, leading to a surplus of £510 by the end of year 3. Thus, the payback occurs at some time during the third year.

In payback calculations it is assumed that costs and income occur at regular intervals throughout the year. Therefore, the £1,560 net return in year 3 is evenly spread over the 52 weeks of the year. This means there are net returns of £1,560/52 = £30 per week. At this rate it will take exactly £1,050/£30 = 35 weeks of year 3 to reach payback. Thus, the payback point is 35 weeks after the end of year 2: that is, 2 years 35 weeks.

An alternative way to calculate the final part is to work out the fraction of the year that elapses before payback is reached. In the above example, £1,050 is still needed to reach payback after the end of year 2. The net return for year 3 is £1,560. Therefore, the payback point is reached 1,050/1,560 of the way through the year. This is 0.673 of a year. Thus the payback period is 2.673 years.

A simpler result is achieved by calculating in weeks:

$$\text{number of weeks before payback is achieved during the third year} = \frac{1{,}050}{1{,}560} \times 52 = 35$$

Therefore, the payback period is 2 years 35 weeks.

Average rate of return

average rate of return: total return divided by the expected lifetime of the investment (usually a number of years), expressed as a percentage of the initial cost of the investment.

Firms will want as high a percentage return as possible. A benchmark that is often used to see if the ARR percentage is satisfactory is the interest rate that the firm must pay on any money borrowed to finance the investment. If the percentage return on the project exceeds the interest rate that the business is paying, the project is financially worthwhile.

An example calculation based on Martin's Motors is shown below:

$$\text{ARR (\%)} = \frac{\text{net return or surplus from a project/no. of years}}{\text{initial cost}} \times 100$$

Calculations for Viper GT air-conditioning machine:

$$\frac{£3{,}070/5}{£5{,}250} \times 100 = \frac{£614}{£5{,}250} \times 100 = 11.7\%$$

At current interest rates, this ARR would mean that it is financially worthwhile to purchase the air-conditioning equipment.

Net present value

net present value (NPV): the net return on an investment when all revenues and costs have been converted to their current worth.

Given a choice between £1 now and £1 in the future, a rational individual (or firm) will choose £1 now. Implicitly, this suggests that money today has a greater value than money in the future. This arises because of the **opportunity cost** of the money. For example, £100 received today could be invested at, say, 10% and would be worth £110 in a year's time. Thus, in these circumstances, the **present value** of £110, receivable in 1 year's time, is £100.

The net present value method of investment appraisal takes this factor into consideration.

Any receipts (or payments) in the future are considered to be worth less than the equivalent sum received (or paid) today. In effect, future sums are

INGRAM

discounted (reduced) by a certain percentage to reflect their lower value. In our example, a 10% discount rate would be appropriate. A commonly used discount rate is the current rate of interest, as this is the opportunity cost of using money for a particular investment. The opportunity cost (next best alternative) is assumed to be the return that the firm could have made by just saving the money involved.

Discounted cash flow

The payback and average rate of return methods assume that the exact timing of the payments and receipts is not important. They ignore the **time value of money**. However, the net present value method of investment appraisal includes this factor in its calculation.

There is no single agreed percentage by which future values should be discounted, as companies face different circumstances. If a company can find a very profitable immediate use for its cash, it will place a much higher value on money in the present (as the opportunity cost of waiting will be the lost opportunity to make a high profit). Paradoxically, a firm suffering from cash-flow problems will deem a high discount rate appropriate: money received in the present may be necessary to keep the business operating. Conversely, a business that is secure but less profitable would consider a low discount rate to be valid.

Whatever the financial situation of a firm, the current market interest rate can be earned if money is received immediately. This acts as a guide to the loss or discount that should be applied to money in the future.

The process of reducing the value of future sums is known as **discounted cash flow**. As time progresses, the 'present' value of a given sum declines. The higher the discount rate, the lower is the value. Exact values can be determined from a 'present value' table.

Table 18.3 shows the present value of £1, based on three different discount rates.

***Table 18.3** Present value of £1 at selected discount rates*

		Discount rate	
Year	5%	7%	10%
0	1.0	1.0	1.0
1	0.952	0.935	0.909
2	0.907	0.873	0.826
3	0.864	0.816	0.751
4	0.823	0.763	0.683
5	0.784	0.713	0.621

The choice of discount rate may be critical in an investment appraisal. It can be seen that £1 received in 5 years' time is equivalent to £0.784 (78.4p) today, if a discount rate of 5% is applied, but only 62.1p (£0.621) if 10% is used.

EXAMINER'S VOICE

Do not try to remember discount tables. If you are required to calculate net present value, the discount rates will be provided. However, you may be provided with alternative rates, such as those in Table 18.3, and be required to select an appropriate discount rate based on circumstances (such as a note on current interest rates or the firm's expected percentage return on its investments).

Two example calculations based on Martin's Motors are shown in Tables 18.4 and 18.5.

Year	Net return (£)	Discount factor (5%)	Present value (£)
0	(5,250)	1.0	(5,250)
1	2,400	0.952	2,284.8
2	1,800	0.907	1,632.6
3	1,560	0.864	1,347.84
4	1,360	0.823	1,119.28
5	1,200	0.784	940.8
Total	**3,070**		**2,075.32**

Table 18.4 *Net present value of a Viper GT air-conditioning system for Martin's Motors, using a 5% discount factor*

The net present value of the investment is +£2,075.32. *On financial grounds only*, the project is worthwhile. Net present value gives a definite recommendation. If the NPV is positive, it is financially justified; if the NPV is negative, it is not worthwhile. However, the firm may wish to include other factors in its decision. These will be discussed later.

Note how the actual net return on this investment is +£3,070. However, the net present value is only +£2,075.32. This is because the main costs are incurred in year 0, whereas the returns are in the future when we are assuming that money is less valuable.

Table 18.4 uses a 5% discount factor. If Martin's Motors could earn a 10% return on its money, then a 10% rate might have been selected. Would the project still be worthwhile?

Year	Net return (£)	Discount factor (5%)	Present value (£)
0	(5,250)	1.0	(5,250)
1	2,400	0.909	2,181.6
2	1,800	0.826	1,486.8
3	1,560	0.751	1,171.56
4	1,360	0.683	928.88
5	1,200	0.621	745.2
Total	**3,070**		**1,264.04**

Table 18.5 *Net present value of a Viper GT air-conditioning system for Martin's Motors, using a 10% discount factor*

Table 18.5 shows that, at a 10% discount rate, the net present value is +£1,264.04. This is much lower than the net present value at 5%

FACT FILE

As no discounts are being applied to the first column (the net return), the total of this column (£3,070) is, in effect, the net present value at a 0% discount rate. With current interest rates of 0% in Japan, it is possible, in some circumstances, for this rate to be appropriate.

(+£2,075.32) and the overall net return of £3,070, but it is still a positive return and therefore the investment is worthwhile.

DID YOU KNOW?

The examples above show that the higher the discount rate, the lower the net present value. As discount rates become higher and higher, even projects with exceptionally high returns will eventually give a negative NPV. Some firms use this approach to calculate a fourth method of investment appraisal. The internal rate of return (IRR) is the discount rate needed to give a net present value of zero. For the Martin's Motors Viper GT investment, the IRR percentage is 20.4%.

FACT FILE

Investment appraisal can apply to decisions where no revenue is involved. The Home Office is planning to spend £500 million on four huge prisons in the southeast of England so that prisoners can be held closer to their homes, reducing transport costs for the government and for relatives visiting the prisoners.

TOPFOTO

Traditional, smaller-scale prisons cost the government £21,800 per annum for each prisoner held. These new prisons will reduce annual costs to £15,000 (saving £6,800) per prisoner. The jails will house 6,000 prisoners, giving an annual saving of £40.8 million. This gives a payback period of:

$$\frac{£500\text{m}}{£40.8\text{m}} = 12.25 \text{ years}$$

This would be a long payback for most private projects. However, for a long-term major government project with no real risk involved, this is an acceptable payback period.

Source: article by Richard Ford in *The Times*, 4 August 2004.

Strengths and weaknesses of investment appraisal methods

The three methods of investment appraisal outlined above use very different approaches in deciding whether an investment is worthwhile. Each method can also be used to compare alternative investments, where a firm has to decide between different projects. The methods have various strengths and weaknesses, as described below.

Payback

Advantages

- The payback period is easy to calculate. If many projects are being considered, this may save valuable time, especially in the initial process of eliminating the least likely investments.
- The concept of payback is easy to understand — it is how long it takes to get the money back. Accountants compile most investment appraisals, but managers or directors who may have no financial expertise invariably take the final decision on major investments. Consequently, it is useful to adopt a method that is easily understood by non-accountants.
- The payback method emphasises cash flow by focusing only on the time taken to return the money. As a result, it is a particularly relevant approach for organisations that have some cash-flow difficulties.
- By emphasising the speed of return, the payback period is popular with firms operating in markets that are experiencing rapid change. All investment appraisals are based on future estimates. Therefore, estimates for years in the distant future are going to be less reliable than those for the near future, especially if external factors can invalidate the assumptions made in the original predictions.

Disadvantages

- The calculation of payback ignores any revenue or costs that occur after the point at which payback has been reached. This means that it does not consider the overall net return from a project. As profit is usually considered to be the main aim of most businesses, this is a major weakness. The payback method may lead to a business ignoring the most profitable investment, simply because it takes slightly longer to achieve that profit.
- It is very difficult to establish a target payback time. Some major investments, such as a new factory, will take many years to pay for themselves. However, investment in a marketing campaign or a new recording will pay for itself in months or not at all. It is therefore very difficult for organisations to compare different types of investment using the payback method.
- Payback values future costs and revenues at the same value as current costs and revenue. Thus it does not consider the time value of money in the way that net present value does. Furthermore, in effect, it completely ignores any costs or income after the payback period.
- By focusing on payback, the business may be encouraged towards short-termism. UK firms are often accused of a failure to consider the long-term benefits of capital investment. A firm using the payback method would fail to look at the long-term consequences of an investment.

Average rate of return

Advantages

- The result (a percentage calculation) can be easily compared with the next best alternative (the opportunity cost). The opportunity cost will be either the percentage return on another project or the percentage interest earned from a savings account. This helps the organisation to make a clear, logical decision.

- The average rate of return shows the true profitability of the investment. It is the only method that takes into consideration every item of revenue and expenditure at its face value.
- Percentage returns, such as the average rate of return, are usually understood by non-accountants.

Disadvantages

- The average rate of return is harder and more time consuming to calculate than the payback method, so it may use valuable company time in compiling shortlists of potential investments.
- It considers all income and expenditure as equal in value. Thus, projections a long time into the future are given the same importance as predictions of present costs and incomes, even though the former are less reliable. As such, it does not consider the time value of money.

Net present value

Advantages

- Net present value is the only method that considers the time value of money. By discounting future figures, NPV recognises that people and organisations place a higher value on money paid/received now than in the future.
- As sums of money far into the future are discounted more heavily, this approach reduces the importance of long-term estimates. As long-term estimates are probably the least reliable predictions, NPV helps to make the conclusions more accurate.
- Net present value is the only method that gives a precise answer. A positive NPV means that, on financial grounds, the investment should be undertaken. A negative NPV indicates that the project should be rejected. If projects of a similar scale are being compared, the one with the highest positive NPV should be chosen. (However, if the investments are not on the same scale, it can be difficult to compare NPVs in a meaningful way.)

Disadvantages

- Net present value is time consuming and more difficult to calculate than the other methods. Given that the results of each method often lead to the same conclusions as to the best project, it is often considered that the additional time spent on calculating the NPV is not cost effective.
- It is more difficult to understand than the other approaches. This may mean that decision-makers distrust any conclusions drawn using this method.
- The calculation of net present value is based on an arbitrary choice of percentage discount rate. Although the method is calculated scientifically, the final conclusion often relies on the discount rate used. The higher the

discount rate, the more likely a project is to be rejected, but there is no common agreement on the percentage discount rate that should be used.

FACT FILE

Investment appraisal is often used by government when deciding on major projects such as the construction of new public roads. In these cases, the government conducts what is known as a **cost–benefit analysis**. In addition to the costs of construction, estimates are made of the value of social costs, such as the loss of agricultural land and the environmental impact of the new road. As the government receives no income from users of public roads, the main benefit that it considers is the travel time that the population saves by using the new road. Additional benefits that are valued include the removal of pollution from town centres and the reduction in accidents that tends to arise from new roads.

A recent example of a major project is the Millau Viaduct that crosses the river Tarn in the south of the Massif Central in France. This 3-kilometre-long viaduct was designed by Britain's Lord Foster and is built on seven pillars. The bridge was opened on 14 December 2004 and is the highest in the world, with the tallest pillar being 343 metres high — 43 metres higher than the Eiffel Tower.

A cost–benefit analysis by the French government concluded that the bridge, which will help the area to avoid regular summer traffic jams of 20–30 kilometres long, will pay for itself through quicker journey times and the opening up of this region for economic development.

The Eiffage Company, which is managing the project, grew out of the company that built the Eiffel Tower in the nineteenth century. The company has paid all of the £269 million construction costs in return for the right to charge a toll to all of the vehicles that use the bridge for the next 75 years. With an expected traffic flow in excess of 15,000 vehicles a day, paying tolls varying between £3.20 and £4.60 per crossing (and more for HGVs), the expected payback period is approximately 10 years.

Sources: adapted from articles by Paul Webster in the *Guardian*, 25 May 2003, Charles Bremner in *The Times*, 15 December 2004 and Henry Samuel in the *Daily Telegraph*, 15 December 2004.

Forecasting cash flows in a situation of market and cost uncertainty

©VIEW PICTURES LTD/ALAMY

The Millau Viaduct (right) is unusual in that its final costs were close to the budgeted figures. For many major projects it is very difficult for a firm to estimate the anticipated costs and revenue. The construction costs for the venues for the Athens Olympics in 2004 were budgeted at £3 billion, but its eventual costs were closer to £4.4 billion. The British Library was budgeted to cost £74 million but the actual cost was £511 million. London's two major millennium projects proved to be unpredictable too. The Millennium Dome was completed on time, but the actual cost of £780 million far exceeded the original estimate of

£399 million. Furthermore, the Dome fell short of its revenue targets. In contrast, the London Eye was not completed on time but has surpassed its expected income levels.

At least the Millennium Dome and the London Eye earned revenue in the year 2000. Portsmouth's millennium project — the Spinnaker Tower (left) — was agreed in 1995 and scheduled for completion in 1999, at a cost of £14 million. Its completion date was in fact July 2005, at a cost of £24 million. The Spinnaker Tower is an example of two major difficulties that often occur in investment appraisal:

- The tower is a unique piece of architecture, so it was difficult to draw on previous experience to get estimates of how much it would cost to build, how much it will cost to maintain, and the probable levels of revenue that might be earned from visitors.
- With any major project there is the chance that business logic may not prevail, as the decision-makers may wish to make their mark by providing a grand project. In this particular project, auditors have been critical of the decision-making process involved.

Even everyday projects can suffer from unexpected occurrences that lead to delays in investments and consequent increases in costs. Firms usually build in allowances or contingencies in case problems occur. Of course, this can lead to investments being unexpectedly cheaper than the budgeted costs if the project runs smoothly.

Investment appraisal also involves human nature. In any situation where estimates are used, it will be tempting for an individual manager to take a pessimistic or optimistic view of forecasts, in a way that favours one particular alternative.

The other uncertainty that may occur is the market. Most appraisals cover a period of years. Even in stable markets it is difficult to foresee the future. In rapidly changing markets, estimates may be no more than guesswork. Thorough market research, close scrutiny of similar investments in the past, and benchmarking data with other companies are all methods that can reduce the uncertainty. However, ultimately most figures in an investment appraisal are based on guesswork.

To cover these uncertainties, it is common practice to conduct further investment appraisals based on best-case and worst-case scenarios, to see if the investment is still worthwhile if estimates prove to be incorrect.

Finally, a business should use these scenarios to estimate the level of risk in a project. If a project only just meets the target payback period or achieves a satisfactory average rate of return or net present value, it would not be advisable to proceed if the worst-case scenario predicts a heavy loss. Even where there is no great risk involved, a firm should think carefully before agreeing to an investment that only just meets its targets, as a slight change can lead to failure rather than success.

Qualitative factors affecting decisions

Investment appraisal provides a scientific decision-making technique for managers and can improve the quality of decisions if used appropriately. However, financial data do not always show the full picture, so a firm must not base its decisions solely on investment appraisal results.

The other factors to be considered, and their relative importance, vary according to circumstances. Some of the key factors are described briefly below, but these are only an indication of some of the issues that may apply. Every investment project will raise its own issues to consider.

- **The aims of the organisation.** A profit-making firm will emphasise the quantitative (numerical) results of an investment appraisal, and is therefore likely to accept its results. A business experiencing liquidity problems will use quantitative data but will deem the payback method to be the most relevant measure, as it needs a quick return. However, a firm that places a high value on social issues might reject a profitable investment that is considered to exploit its workforce or damage the environment.
- **Reliability of the data.** Future costs and incomes rely on the accuracy of market research and an ability to predict external changes. For the more original investments and those of a longer duration, the predictions may be wildly inaccurate, undermining the use of investment appraisal techniques.
- **Risk.** High-return projects often involve high risk. A firm may prefer to choose a lower, but more certain, return. This will safeguard the company and avoid the possibility of upsetting shareholders if the risk does not pay off.
- **Production requirements.** The company must consider the compatibility of any new machinery with its existing range. A firm may also be reluctant to deal with a new supplier if it enjoys a good service from its existing supplier. The availability of spare parts, the promise of just-in-time deliveries, or the general benefits arising from the goodwill of another company may all prove to be more important factors than a minor financial gain.
- **Personnel.** Will the new equipment or method suit the company's staff? The ease of use; the level of training needed; the safety of the machine; the impact on the number of staff employed — these are all factors that should be considered. If these factors lead to a lowering of morale and poor motivation among the workforce, they may be deemed to be more important than the short-term financial situation.
- **The economy.** Interest rates will have a major impact. If interest rates are increasing, any investment will pose a greater risk, especially if the firm is using borrowed money to fund the project. Economic forecasts (for

example, predicting a recession or boom) must be considered in the predictions of future costs and revenues.

- **Image.** The firm should consider the influence of a project on its image and public relations. A high-technology project producing a quality product in a prestigious market will be preferred to an equally profitable project that leads to unemployment and damages the environment.
- **Subjective criteria.** All investment decisions are taken by individuals who have their own personal preferences. Sometimes a manager may have a 'gut feeling' that an investment will benefit the business.

Is investment appraisal worthwhile?

Although each method of investment appraisal can be criticised, investment appraisal in general is still a worthwhile process. It encourages organisations to research and evaluate carefully the possible financial consequences of potential investment decisions. A careful evaluation can help an organisation to avoid expensive mistakes or alert it to projects with tremendous potential.

However, it is vital that decisions are not based solely on quantitative factors. The organisation needs to consider the level of uncertainty in its financial forecasts. Furthermore, it is crucial that qualitative factors are taken into account in its decision making. With a thoughtful blend of quantitative and qualitative analysis, investment appraisal will help an organisation to make sound investment decisions.

PRACTICE EXERCISE 1 — Total: 35 marks (40 minutes)

1 Explain what is meant by the term 'investment appraisal'. *(3 marks)*

2 Identify the two main reasons for capital investment. *(2 marks)*

The following table shows the financial details of a new investment:

Year	Income (£m)	Costs (£m)	Annual net return (£m)	Present value of £1 at a 5% discount rate
0	0	50	(50)	1.0
1	30	20	10	0.952
2	40	20	20	0.907
3	50	20	30	0.864

3 Calculate the payback period. *(3 marks)*

4 Calculate the average rate of return. *(5 marks)*

5 Calculate the net present value based on a 5% discount rate. *(6 marks)*

6 On the basis of your answers to questions 3, 4 and 5, advise the business on whether it should go ahead with the new investment. Justify your decision. *(4 marks)*

7 Explain two advantages of using the average rate of return method of investment appraisal. *(6 marks)*

8 Explain two problems of using the net present value method of investment appraisal. *(6 marks)*

PRACTICE EXERCISE 2 Total: 25 marks (25 minutes)

1 Explain two reasons why it is difficult to provide reliable forecasts for major investment projects. *(6 marks)*

2 Explain how a business can reduce the risk of inaccurate forecasts. *(6 marks)*

3 Explain two reasons for choosing payback as a method of investment appraisal. *(4 marks)*

4 Explain three qualitative factors that might be considered in assessing an investment. *(9 marks)*

CASE STUDY 1 Maize mazes

Farmers and theme parks, predominantly in the UK and USA, are using maize mazes as tourist attractions. A specialist firm designs a maze and in the spring the maize is planted in accordance with its instructions. Once the maize is fully grown, it forms a maze that can be used from July to September. The following year a revised design can be created to present a new challenge to visitors. Because of the short life span of the maze, the field can be used to cultivate a winter growing crop and generate more profit.

Paul Swaffield, a Dorset farmer, is one individual who has been won over by the idea. The maize maze on his farm brought in 25 times as much revenue as the crop that he usually grew in that field. Furthermore, at the end of the summer the maize was used as cattle feed, providing additional revenue.

Jowett House Farm in Cawthorne, Yorkshire, is a farm that has taken advantage of this new source of revenue. The year 2004 marked its fourth maize maze. The maze is open for 50 days in the summer. The average ticket price is £3 per visitor and the maze is expected to receive an average of 220 visitors per day. However, the vast majority of these visits occur at weekends and heavy rainfall has a big impact on sales revenue. In 2004, the opening of the maize was delayed by over a week because of the weather in July.

TOPFOTO

A typical maize maze costs £20,000 to make, although running costs vary. For a maze such as the one at Cawthorne, where a 'Maze Master Team' is employed to help visitors, the running costs can amount to £100 per day. At the end of the summer, the maize is used to feed the 140 cows in the farm's dairy herd.

(Please note that all the figures in this case study are estimates.)

Questions

Total: 20 marks (25 minutes)

1 Calculate the payback period of the Cawthorne maze, based on the figures in the case study. (4 marks)

2 Analyse two additional items of financial data that would have helped you to make the decision on whether to construct a maze at the farm. *(6 marks)*

3 Discuss possible reasons why the average rate of return and net present value methods of investment appraisal are not as suitable as the payback method in assessing the Cawthorne maize project. *(10 marks)*

CASE STUDY 2 The Humbly Grove pipeline

This is a challenging case study based on an unusual industry. It may be worthwhile discussing the nature of the business, and revisiting the ways to calculate each of the methods of investment appraisal, before commencing the questions.

Not all of the UK's oil is found in the North Sea. A number of small-scale, onshore oilfields exist. One such oilfield is situated at Humbly Grove, near Alton in Hampshire.

Oil was discovered there in 1980 and full production at the oilfield began in 1986.

The site is set in a rural area. Many of the 100 jobs created are unique to the business, especially as the firm employs a relatively high percentage of graduates. The remote setting and effective landscaping of the site mean that relatively few people are aware of its existence.

In its natural state, the oil well is pressurised by the presence of gas overlying the oil. Over time the gas pressure falls, making it more difficult to extract the oil. Star Energy Ltd, the owner of the oil well, has responded to this challenge by planning a 25-kilometre gas pipeline that will connect the site to the national gas transmission system.

The pipeline will bring two major benefits to the company. First, it will allow the company to purchase gas from the national gas transmission system. This gas will increase the gas pressure at the existing oil well and increase the economic viability of the oil field. 'Without this project, the field is unlikely to be viable by 2010,' says Star Energy UK onshore managing director Roger Pearson. The pipeline will enable oil extraction to continue until 2020.

WWW.STARENERGY.CO.UK

Second, it will help Star Energy Ltd to enter the gas storage market. With its oil fields depleting and falling profit levels, the company has identified diversification as a key strategic aim. Gas storage is predicted to be a growth market. The UK has the lowest storage capacity for gas in Europe, largely because it has been self-sufficient in gas supply. However, between 2005 and 2012, the UK's imports of gas will rise from 10% of total consumption to 70%. The UK government is targeting an increase in UK gas storage capacity to levels similar to France (which can store 35% of its annual consumption). Star Energy will thus be providing a service to a number of stakeholders: the government, its shareholders (the gas can be bought cheaply in the summer and released at peak times in the winter when prices are higher), its workforce (currently 100 people are dependent on the firm restoring its profit levels) and the local community

***Table 18.6** Estimates of possible changes in gas and oil revenues and extraction costs arising from the pipeline/gas storage project*

Year	Increased revenue (£m)	Increased costs (£m)	Net return (£m)
2005	–	65.0	(65.0)
2006	13.0	1.0	12.0
2007	16.1	1.5	14.6
2008	19.2	2.1	17.1
2009	22.3	2.6	19.7
2010	22.3	2.6	19.7
2011	22.3	2.6	19.7

***Table 18.7** Present value of £1 at selected discount rates*

Year	Discount rate 5%	7%	10%
0	1.0	1.0	1.0
1	0.952	0.935	0.909
2	0.907	0.873	0.826
3	0.864	0.816	0.751
4	0.823	0.763	0.683
5	0.784	0.713	0.621
6	0.746	0.666	0.564

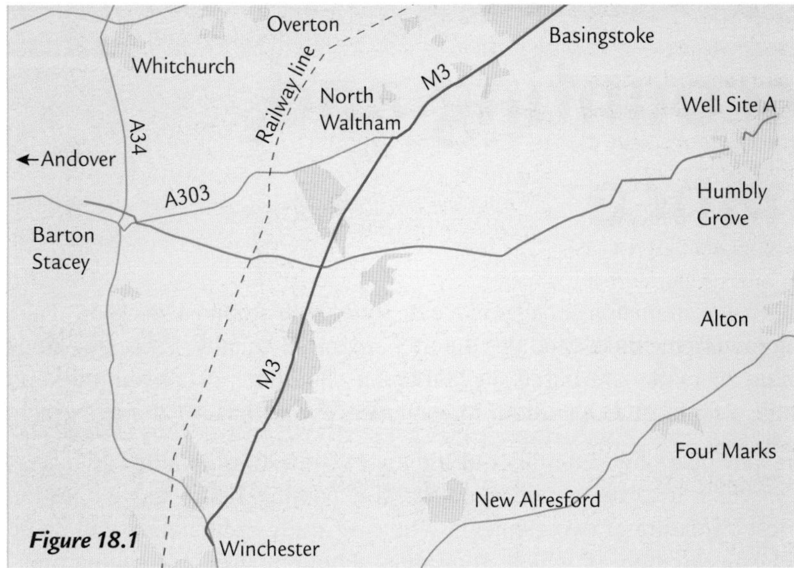

Figure 18.1

The completion of the pipeline and gas storage facility is scheduled for October 2005. Money has been raised from the sale of shares and a long-term loan on which an interest rate of 7% is payable. In total, the construction costs are estimated at £65 million. Income will be received from two sources: the sale of gas and additional oil revenue. The additional gas and oil revenues and additional costs are estimated to follow the pattern shown in Table 18.6.

Given the uncertainty of the gas and oil markets, the company wishes to base any investment appraisal on a 6-year lifetime. Table 18.7 provides information on discount rates.

(which will benefit from the wealth and jobs created).

The company has a strong cash-flow situation, but in 2004, after years of profit, Star Energy made an operating loss. Consequently, new profitable ventures are crucial to the company's long-term future.

The main aim of the company, during construction of the pipeline, is to minimise environmental damage. The pipeline is being built to the highest safety standards and the route has been planned to have the least impact on the environment (see Figure 18.1). Eight areas of archaeological potential have been identified and trial digging will lead to slight adjustments to the route if necessary.

Currently the company is dependent on oil for 89% of its revenue. As its reserves fall, the empty oil wells will provide an ideal opportunity to diversify, particularly as rival gas storage companies will need to spend large sums to create suitable storage. It is feasible that gas will eventually replace oil as its main source of income.

Sources: adapted from *Humbly Grove News*, published by Star Energy Ltd, and the Star Energy website, www.starenergy.co.uk.

Questions

Total: 50 marks (60 minutes)

1 Calculate the payback period for the Humbly Grove pipeline and gas storage project. (4 marks)

2 Calculate the average rate of return for the Humbly Grove pipeline and gas storage project. *(8 marks)*

3 Calculate the net present value of the project and explain the reason for your choice of discount rate. *(12 marks)*

4 The pipeline requires planning permission from both central and local government. Discuss the factors that government should consider in deciding whether to allow the pipeline to be constructed. *(10 marks)*

5 Basing your decision on both quantitative and qualitative factors, recommend to Star Energy whether it should undertake the pipeline/gas storage project. *(16 marks)*

INTEGRATED CASE STUDY

Accounting and finance

The Unit 4 examination consists of a case study built around a 'decision'. Each of the four elements of Modules 4 and 5 are tested equally. Thus, questions totalling 20 marks are based on Marketing. Questions on Accounting and Finance, People, and Operations Management are also worth 20 marks each.

There may be a single 20-mark question or two questions totalling 20 marks, one of which involves some evaluation. It is possible that a single question will test a mixture of two elements. The case study examination will be 90 minutes in duration, of which 10 minutes should be used as 'reading time'. All questions are compulsory.

This case study is included to provide an opportunity to tackle a Unit 4 exam-style case that is based only on Accounting and Finance, but which covers the whole of the A2 Accounting and Finance specification.

The Unit 4 examination is based on a fictional business. However, this case study and others in the textbook are based on real businesses. These real-life case studies should be viewed as a part of the subject background, as well as the basis for certain questions.

CASE STUDY BAA soars on passenger record

Airports operator BAA recorded a strong rise in profits, boosted by record passenger numbers and higher retail spending. BAA earns its income from charging airlines such as British Airways and Ryanair for using the facilities at its seven airports. The other major revenue earners are the charges and commission that it earns from allowing retailers and organisations such as car hire companies to operate from its airports.

In 2004, total traffic at the seven airports rose by 10%, with BAA's main airport, Heathrow, recording a 15% increase. Currently, BAA is planning to spend £6.2 billion on investment projects.

Mike Clasper, BAA's chief executive, said: 'We have made an excellent start to the year.' In particular, progress on the £4,000 million Terminal 5 at Heathrow 'has been good and the project remains ahead of schedule and on budget'. The new terminal, when completed, is predicted to provide an annual return of £650 million per annum. BAA's target is to achieve an ARR of 7% after 12 years. However, there has been considerable opposition to Terminal 5. Local residents have campaigned vigorously against the project, complaining about the increased noise levels and traffic congestion. In 2004, BAA paid £100 million in compensation to residents near Gatwick as a result of recent expansion; compensation demands from Heathrow residents could seriously affect any profit calculations. Environmentalists even question the need for expansion of air travel, and many analysts foresee

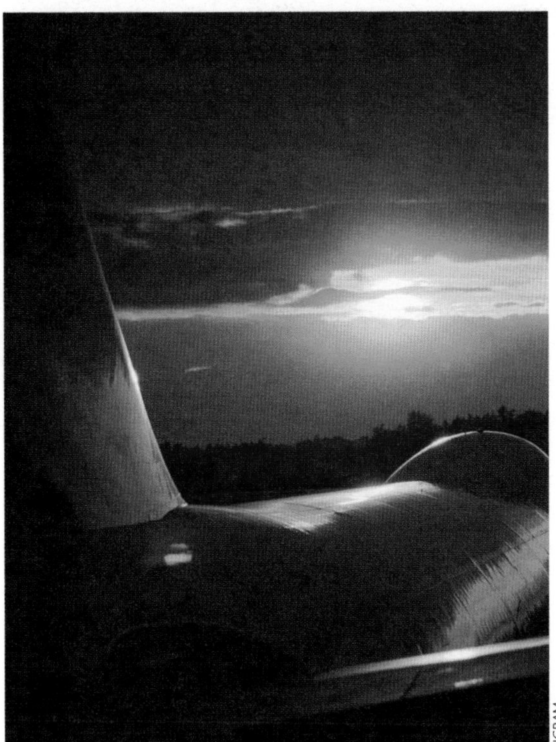
INGRAM

a future in which high energy costs lead to lower levels of air travel. Current government thinking is also against airport expansion. Regional airports are being used much more and are growing faster than the London airports. Southampton and Exeter airports experienced increases in passenger numbers in excess of 25% per annum.

BAA has now recovered from the fall in passengers arising from security fears following the 9/11 terrorist attack and, more recently, from the SARS epidemic in Asia. The firm has also benefited from improved facilities and passenger screening that has encouraged more travellers to use BAA airports. The average airline passenger spends £4.06 at airport shops.

Although most retail outlets are independent retailers, BAA is the sole owner of World Duty Free Europe Limited, which operates from its airports. Profit margins on perfumes are high. A typical perfume costs £20 to purchase but sells for £50. The fixed costs associated with a single brand of perfume are £450 per week. The lack of competition allows BAA to charge relatively high prices compared with high street stores.

Appendix 1: Profit and loss accounts for BAA plc, years ending 31 March 2003 and 2004

Years ending:	31.3.04 (£m)	31.3.03 (£m)
SALES REVENUE	1970	1882
OPERATING COSTS	1354	1295
OPERATING PROFIT	616	587
PROFIT ON SALE OF ASSETS	0	33
INTEREST	77	82
NET PROFIT BEFORE TAX	539	538
CORPORATION TAX	161	162
NET PROFIT AFTER TAX	378	376
The uses to which the profits are put are shown below:		
NET PROFIT AFTER TAX	378	376
minus		
DIVIDENDS TO SHAREHOLDERS	216	202
equals		
RETAINED PROFIT	162	174

Appendix 2: Balance sheet as at 31 March 2004

	£m
Fixed assets	
Intangible assets	10
Fixed assets	9,074
Investments	202
TOTAL FIXED ASSETS	**9,286**
Current assets	
Stocks	23
Debtors	270
Short-term investments	740
Bank balance and cash	150
TOTAL CURRENT ASSETS	**1,183**
minus	
Current liabilities	
Creditors (less than 1 year)	944
equals	
WORKING CAPITAL	
(net current assets)	**239**
Total assets less current liabilities	9,525
Long-term liabilities	
Creditors (more than one year)	2,760
Other long-term liabilities	1,747
	4,507
TOTAL NET ASSETS	**5,018**
Capital and reserves	
Share capital	1,294
Reserves	3,724
	5,018
TOTAL CAPITAL EMPLOYED	**9,525**

To some extent, BAA benefits from people expecting airport prices to be cheaper, as in previous years it was possible to buy tax-free products.

BAA is in dispute with Ryanair, which claims that BAA is taking advantage of its monopoly of airport ownership in the southeast of England. Ryanair is claiming that BAA is overcharging for its facilities, particularly the fuel that it provides for the aircraft. The government is considering an investigation of BAA's charges and has suggested that it may not be allowed to continue its ownership of Heathrow, Gatwick and Stansted airports.

Appendix 3: Notes to the accounts — depreciation policy

Depreciation applies to all fixed assets except land. Expected useful lifetimes of assets are set out below:

- Airport buildings: 60 years
- Escalators and lifts: 20 years
- Runway surfaces: 12 years
- Motor vehicles: 6 years

Source: adapted from an article by Alistair Osborne in the *Daily Telegraph*, 3 August 2004, and the BAA Annual Report, 2003–04.

Questions

Total: 80 marks (100 minutes)

(Although this case study matches the style of an AQA Unit 4 paper, the focus on financial content and calculations means that a 100-minute time allowance is more appropriate than the normal 90 minutes for this particular case.)

1 a Calculate the average rate of return (ARR %) over 12 years on the Heathrow Terminal 5 investment. *(6 marks)*

b Discuss the qualitative factors that should be considered in a decision on whether BAA should build Terminal 5 at Heathrow. *(14 marks)*

2 a Study the information on depreciation policy in Appendix 3. Using the straight-line method of depreciation, calculate the annual depreciation costs of a motor vehicle that costs £20,000 and has a residual value of £5,000. *(4 marks)*

b Many buildings are depreciated over 40 years. Briefly analyse one possible reason why BAA has chosen a longer expected lifetime and one possible reason why BAA should choose a shorter period. *(6 marks)*

c Using the information in Appendix 2, discuss whether BAA is suffering from a lack of working capital. *(10 marks)*

3 a Calculate the number of bottles of perfume that World Duty Free Europe Limited would need to sell per week in order to break even if the price per bottle fell to £45. *(4 marks)*

b Calculate BAA plc's gearing ratio. *(4 marks)*

c Discuss the implications of this gearing ratio, and any other information in the appendices, for BAA's plans to spend £6.2 billion on investment projects. *(12 marks)*

4 a Study the profit and loss accounts in Appendix 1. On the basis of this appendix, explain why the profit in 2003/04 would be considered to be of higher quality than the profit in 2002/03. *(4 marks)*

b Calculate the return on capital employed (ROCE %) for 2003/04. *(4 marks)*

c BAA's main corporate aims are growth and increased profit levels. Based on the information available, do you believe that BAA is achieving these aims? Justify your view. *(12 marks)*

Module 5

People in organisations

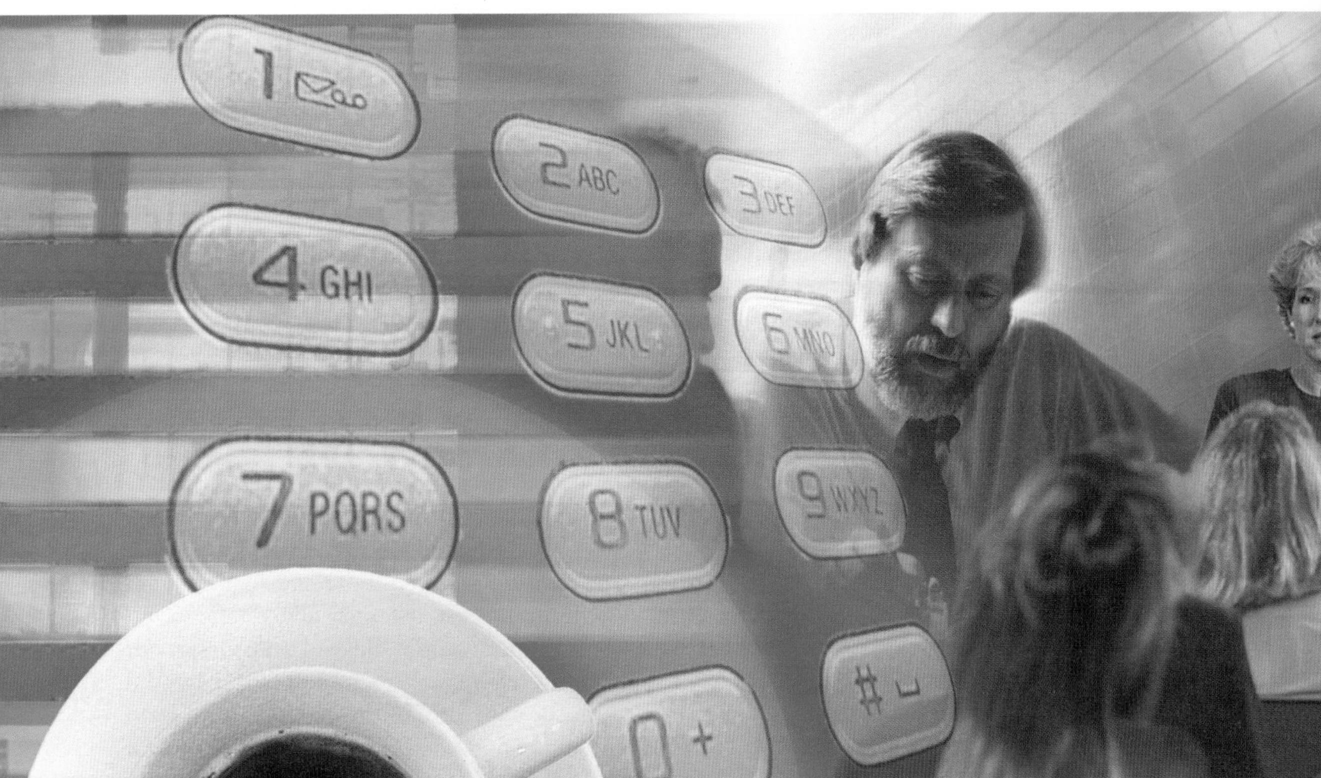

"You will never have so much authority as when you begin to give it away."

Anon.

CHAPTER 19

The importance of communication

This chapter looks at the importance of communication in a business context. It considers the importance of communication in relation to external groups and its influence on employee motivation. By considering the process of communication and the importance of feedback, the concepts of one- and two-way communication, formal and informal channels of communication, and vertical and lateral communication are explored.

EXAMINER'S VOICE

Refer back to your AS studies on mission statements and corporate objectives, and remember that clear communication of these to employees is vital, as is clear communication of targets for individual employees.

Internal and external communication

KEY TERMS

communication: the process of exchanging information or ideas between two or more individuals or groups.

internal communication: exchange of information that takes place within an organisation (for example, at departmental meetings, in team briefing sessions and in memos to staff).

external communication: exchange of information that takes place with individuals, groups and organisations outside the business (for example, via advertising material, telephone calls to suppliers and letters to customers).

INGRAM

Good internal communication is vital to the efficiency and success of a business. It ensures that employees know exactly what they are required to do and that different departments interact effectively. Good communication lies at the heart of effective management and is an essential aspect of successful decision making in relation to coordinating and controlling a business. It ensures that the various parts of a business work together in order to achieve corporate aims and objectives.

All businesses exist within a dynamic, external environment. Therefore, it is also important for organisations to communicate effectively with external groups, such as suppliers, customers, investors, pressure groups, the media and the local community. Good communication with external groups allows an organisation to monitor its operations and identify areas for improvements more effectively. For example, by listening to comments from customers, it should be able to monitor changes in the market and improve its products and services. Similarly, by establishing good channels of communication with the local community, it should be able to assess its local reputation and adjust its operations if necessary. Equally, the efficient operation of just-in-time (JIT) requires highly effective communication systems with suppliers.

Communication and employee motivation

Good communication is very important in motivating employees. It can make employees feel valued and an important part of the organisation. Motivational theories recognise the importance of effective communication in raising morale. It also forms the basis of the kaizen approach of continuous improvement, where change most often arises as a result of suggestions made by employees working in a corporate culture that encourages them to communicate their thoughts and ideas.

FACT FILE

Beaverbrooks, the jewellery retailer chain, came respectively second and third in *The Sunday Times 100 Best Companies to Work For* in 2004 and 2005.

Employees feel valued and respected, and say their suggestions are acted upon: only 20% say their manager does more telling than listening, 88% agree that their manager talks openly and honestly to them and 85% say their manager regularly expresses appreciation for good work – results bettered by no other company (in the survey). 'You constantly get praise,' says Zoë Osborne, a sales assistant in Belfast, 'and there's no hierarchy between people. You feel that we're all equal.'

Staff are impressed that Mark Adlestone, the chain's managing director, knows everybody by name and staff feel comfortable enough to phone him personally with any concerns. In fact, employees are encouraged to have direct contact with any executive by phone or e-mail.

One employee says: 'I feel I have an input in how things change and feel that, if necessary, I could approach the company director about anything, personal or professional.'

Source: *The Sunday Times 100 Best Companies to Work For*, 2004 and 2005.

Any organisation that tries to empower its employees and thus extend their roles and authority will need to ensure that effective communication systems are in place to support this. It is important that employees understand the objectives of their organisation, how their own job contributes to meeting these objectives and how well they are performing their job and hence contributing to the success of the organisation. Regular feedback on performance, both formal and informal, is an important aspect of employee motivation. By communicating effectively in this area, management is likely to have a much more focused and committed workforce.

Just as good communication can increase employee motivation, well-motivated employees are likely to communicate more readily with management by suggesting ideas, listening to advice and contributing their

opinions, and to be more willing to participate in decision making. Demotivated workers, on the other hand, are often reluctant to communicate with managers.

Communication and change

Effective communication is vital if an organisation is to introduce any form of change. Taking into account the opinions of employees and involving them in decision making is likely to encourage greater commitment to the change process. Similarly, canvassing the opinions of external groups, such as customers or the local community, is likely to ensure a smoother change.

DID YOU KNOW?

In a recent survey, employees were asked the following question: 'To improve your workplace environment, what would you like to see your executives/supervisors/managers do?' Sixty-nine per cent of the respondents replied: 'Be better at communicating.'

EXAMINER'S VOICE

Wherever possible, make use of the knowledge you gained in your AS studies and, in particular, in relation to communication, your knowledge of styles of leadership and motivation theories. For example, good communication is likely to mean that employees are praised for their efforts, which might, in accordance with Maslow's hierarchy of human needs, meet their ego needs and thus improve motivation. Similarly, good communication can help to make employees feel involved and meet their social needs.

The process of communication

Effective communication will happen only if the information sent is received and clearly understood. Although numerous types of communication might occur in a business context, certain features are common to them all:

- a **sender** or **communicator** — the person (or group) who is sending the message
- the **message** — the topic of the communication
- a **transmission mechanism** (also known as the **process**, **medium** or **channel**) by which a message is conveyed: for example, by telephone, by memo or in a face-to-face meeting
- a **receiver** — the person (or group) whom the message is aimed at
- **feedback** — the response from the receiver, whether written, verbal or even a facial expression, indicating that the message is understood. Without feedback, the communicator does not know whether the message has been received and clearly understood.

EXAMINER'S VOICE

Effective feedback is one of Herzberg's motivators.

Figure 19.1 illustrates the communication process. For example, if a particular organisation is experiencing a permanent fall in sales, senior management may decide that compulsory redundancies have to be made. They communicate this decision, and the reasons, to the employees of the organisation by individual letters sent to their home addresses and by a series of staff meetings at which senior management explains its decisions. Feedback is via questions posed by employees at the meetings, and employees' subsequent reactions (letters to, and meetings with, management, trade union response etc.).

A message that is not delivered effectively may lead to significant problems for a firm. For example, if the marketing department fails to inform the production department of the estimated demand for a product, insufficient stock may be produced, resulting in disappointed customers and adverse effects on the firm's reputation. Equally, if employees put in huge amounts of extra effort in order to satisfy a sudden increase in demand but receive no praise or recognition for this from senior management, they are unlikely to do the same thing again.

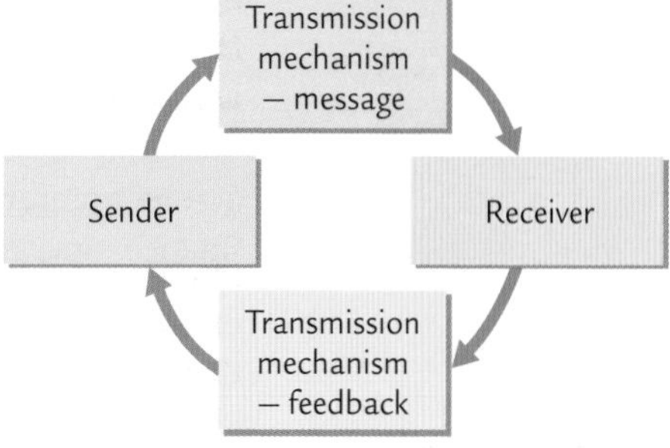

Figure 19.1
The communication process

One and two-way communication

TERMS

one-way communication: communication without any feedback (for example, putting a notice on a notice board, or giving instructions in an authoritarian manner that allows no comment or questions from the listener).

two-way communication: communication with feedback (for example, giving instructions in a manner that allows for questions to be asked or comments to be made, a discussion or a question-and-answer session).

In the context of one-way communication, the communicator can never be sure whether the message has been understood and therefore whether the communication was effective. One-way communication is often associated with autocratic or authoritarian management styles.

In contrast, two-way communication ensures that any communication has been fully understood and is therefore more effective. Effective two-way communication is a vital element of democratic management, effective delegation, empowerment, team working and the kaizen approach.

Communication channels

TERM

communication channel: the route through which communication occurs.

The most effective channels of communication vary according to the information that is being passed on. For example, team briefing sessions are usually held at the start of a working day or working week, and are likely to be used as a forum for communication between supervisors and their teams about production targets, new production methods and issues related to the quality of production. Another channel might be a works council, which allows discussion about company plans between management and employee representatives. This ensures that ideas and suggestions from the employees' points of view become an automatic element of company decision making.

Communication can take place up and down the chain of command in an organisation, with orders or instructions being passed down through the layers of hierarchy and ideas and suggestions being passed in the other direction. Alternatively, the communication channel might be horizontal across a hierarchy, as in a management meeting attended by the marketing, finance, operations and personnel managers.

Open and closed channels of communication

KEY TERMS

open channels of communication: any staff member is welcome to see, read or hear the discussions and conclusions.

closed channels of communication: access to the information is restricted to a named few.

In the previous example of a firm that is experiencing a permanent fall in sales, the initial discussions about the choice of strategy might be conducted through closed channels such as senior management meetings, with the minutes of the meetings being confidential. However, once the decision has been made, the staff meetings and the subsequent meetings with union representatives would be open in the sense that all employees would, in the case of the staff meeting, be able to attend or, in the case of meetings between senior management and union representatives, have access to the minutes or reports of the meetings.

Formal and informal channels of communication

Within any business there are both formal and informal channels of communication.

KEY TERMS

formal channels of communication: communication channels established and approved by senior management, within which any form of communication is regarded as formal (for example, meetings of departmental heads, personnel department meetings and production team briefing sessions).

informal channels of communication: means of passing information outside the official channels, often developed by employees themselves (for example, 'the grapevine' and gossip).

DID YOU KNOW?

Research has shown that the most effective communication requires both formal and informal channels.

Informal communication channels can both help and hinder formal communications and for this reason the grapevine is usually recognised by management as extremely important. Messages concerning, for example, rumours of redundancies or a takeover or the suspension of a senior executive often pass more quickly through informal channels than through established channels; however, they may not always be accurate. In some instances, firms have even issued 'leaks' on to the grapevine about a possible new development in order to assess the reactions of employees and then to make changes based on these reactions, before introducing the development to employees along the formal channels of communication. In general, though, the existence of large amounts of informal communication may suggest that the formal communication channels are not operating effectively.

EXAMINER'S VOICE

Students often confuse formal communication with written communication and informal communication with oral communication. Oral communication can be formal (a meeting or an interview) or informal (gossip by staff waiting by the photocopying machine). Similarly, written communication can be either formal (minutes of a meeting) or informal (a 'private' e-mail about the behaviour of a certain member of staff).

FACT FILE

Buying a coffee machine and water cooler could be the most important investments a company ever makes in its future, for it is at these social hubs of office life that the real business often gets done, as part of a casual chat or chance meeting.

But many managers are unaware that this seemingly pointless social networking does in fact play a crucial part in the way people interact with each other to get work done, according to Andrew Parker, a research consultant with IBM. He argues that official organisation charts underpinning the structure of a company ignore the hidden social networks that really drive performance. The rapid growth in remote working means it is now even more essential to acknowledge that they are a key factor in business success.

'More often than not, however, important networks don't exist on the formal chart and it can be hard to get busy executives to pay attention to these seemingly invisible structures,' says Parker, co-author of *The Hidden Power of Social Networks: Understanding How Work Really Gets Done in Organizations*.

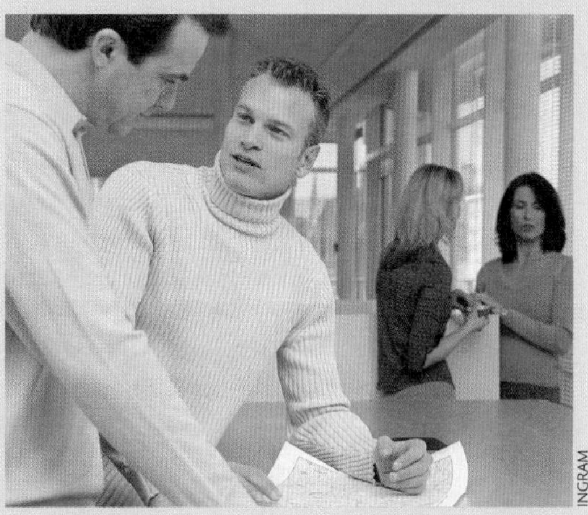
INGRAM

Source: adapted from *Professional Manager*, January 2005.

Vertical and lateral communication

Information can be communicated vertically, both up and down the chain of command, and laterally (horizontally across the chain of command). These different channels of communication are illustrated in Figure 19.2.

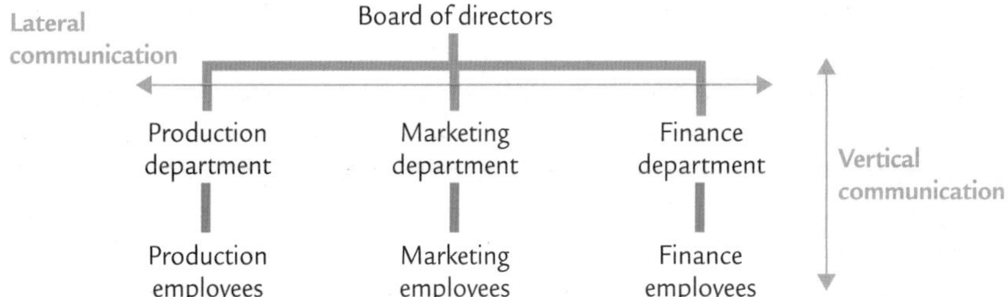

***Figure 19.2** Vertical and lateral communication*

vertical communication: when information is passed up and down the chain of command.

There are two types of vertical communication:

- **Downwards communication** (also known as **top–down communication**) is transmitted from the top of the organisation down to the bottom of the organisation or from superior to subordinate. This form of communication is generally used to tell employees about decisions that have already been made and to give instructions.
- **Upwards communication** (also known as **bottom–up communication**) is transmitted from the bottom of the organisation up to the top of the organisation or from subordinate to superior.

There is considerable evidence that upwards communication can be of great help in decision making. This is because:

- it helps managers to understand employees' views and concerns
- it helps managers to keep in touch with employees' attitudes and values
- it can alert managers to potential problems
- it can provide managers with the information that they need for decision making and gives feedback on the effects of previous decisions
- it helps employees to feel that they are participating and can encourage motivation
- it provides feedback on the effectiveness of downwards communication and how it can be improved

KEY TERM

lateral communication: when people at the same level within an organisation pass information to each other.

An example of lateral communication is a member of the finance department telling the marketing department about the budget available for a sales promotion, or a member of the marketing department informing the production department of the estimated sales for the coming year. Problems can arise if the different departments fail to understand each other's needs. For example, staff in the marketing department might promise a customer a large sales order within a specified time without discussing with staff in the production department whether they are able to meet the order in time. Thus effective lateral communication is vital for the efficient running of the firm.

Methods of communication

A number of methods can be used to communicate information in a business. These are either written or oral, or make use of information and communication technology (ICT).

Written communication

Table 19.1 identifies the main methods of written communication and provides a brief description of each.

Table 19.1 *Methods of written communication*

Method	Description
Letter	Flexible, provides a written record, usually for external communications
Memorandum	Flexible, provides a written record, used for internal communications
Report	Allows a large number of people to see complex facts and arguments
Form	Routine and can be filled in quickly, e.g. timesheet, stock request form
Notice board	Informs a lot of people cheaply, but relies on people reading them
Internal magazine or newsletter	Used in large firms to inform employees about staff changes, sports and social events, developments and successes

Oral communication

Oral communication, whether face-to-face in meetings or by telephone, has a number of advantages and disadvantages.

INGRAM

Advantages

- It enables feeling and emphasis to be conveyed by the communicator and the receiver more clearly. Facial expressions and the tone of someone's voice are powerful means of communication.
- It has the potential to generate far more immediate, accurate and powerful feedback, especially in relation to one-to-one or small-group communication.
- It creates no specific costs, such as the clerical work, paper, equipment and storage facilities involved in producing written communications.
- It can encourage more constructive criticism, more open exchanges of views and cooperation.
- It allows information to be spread more quickly.

Disadvantages

- As evidence of incidents, discussions and agreements, it lacks the legal status provided by written communication.
- It is less effective for conveying statistical information and detailed analysis of, for example, an organisation's performance.
- As with 'Chinese whispers', the message is likely to become distorted if it is passed through many intermediaries.

Communication using ICT

Communication using information and communication technology is considered in Chapter 21.

Which method of communication?

A variety of factors can affect which method of communication is used by a business in any situation. These include:

- **the nature of the message.** Some messages are best sent by more than one method of communication. For example, a meeting between a manager and a worker to discuss the worker's unsatisfactory performance should be confidential and face-to-face, followed up by a written report or warning, as evidence.
- **the costs involved.** In a 'paperless office', the use of e-mail and the posting of documents and reports on internal websites have saved firms huge amounts of money that would have gone into paper, photocopying and delivery costs.

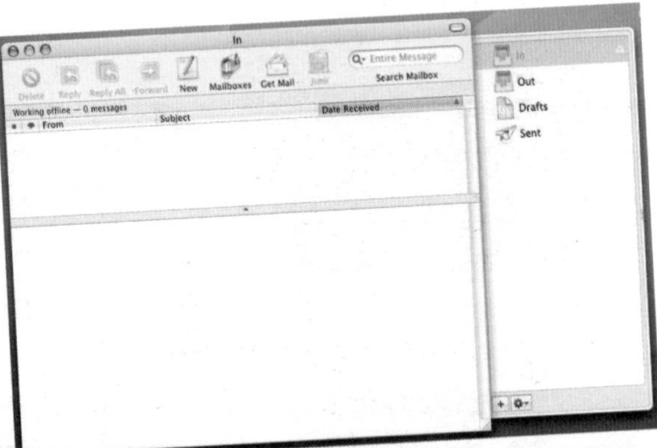

- **the speed of communication.** If something needs communicating immediately, verbal or electronic communications tend to be quickest.
- **the length and complexity of the message.** If the message is long, verbal communication may mean that the receiver does not remember everything that has been said and hence written communication is more appropriate. If a simple yes or no answer is needed, written communication might also be suitable.
- **the size of the organisation.** Much more use is likely to be made of verbal and face-to-face communication in very small organisations than in very large organisations, where formal procedures, written and, increasingly, electronic communication are likely to dominate.
- **the needs of the receiver.** Bankers and potential investors may require detailed written data on the firm's financial performance, whereas employees may only need the simple headline figures indicating the firm's overall sales and profitability.

Conclusion

Effective communication offers organisations a number of benefits:

- It allows the organisation to make more informed decisions based on better-quality information.
- It makes it easier to implement change because employees and other stakeholders understand and recognise the need for it.
- It encourages a more motivated workforce and develops commitment to the business from employees at all levels of the organisation.
- It helps to ensure that the business is well coordinated and that all employees pursue the same corporate objectives.

- It allows the organisation to be more competitive by improving efficiency and identifying opportunities.

Thus an organisation that communicates effectively is likely to be more in touch with consumers and other external groups, have a more motivated and committed workforce, make better decisions and find it easier to introduce change.

PRACTICE EXERCISE

Total: 50 marks (40 minutes)

1	Define the term 'communication'.	*(3 marks)*
2	Explain two benefits to a firm of good communication.	*(6 marks)*
3	Explain two problems that a firm might encounter if it has poor communication.	*(6 marks)*
4	Distinguish between internal and external communication.	*(4 marks)*
5	Distinguish between one-way and two-way communication.	*(4 marks)*
6	Identify the five common features that are involved in the process of communication.	*(5 marks)*
7	Identify and explain two channels of communication.	*(6 marks)*
8	Distinguish between formal and informal communication.	*(4 marks)*
9	Distinguish between vertical and lateral communication.	*(4 marks)*
10	Identify four methods of written communication that might be used in a business context.	*(4 marks)*
11	State two advantages and two disadvantages of oral communication.	*(4 marks)*

CASE STUDY It pays to be a good listener

According to this year's *Sunday Times 100 Best Companies* survey, employers should sit up and listen if they want a happy, successful workplace. Companies that listen to what employees have to say rather than just telling them what to do are likely to perform better across the board (see Figure 19.3).

Out of 66 questions in the survey, one had a closer relationship to a company's final overall ranking than any other. The question asked staff if they agreed that 'senior managers of this organisation do a lot of telling but not much listening'.

It is important to remember that listening alone will not make a difference if it is not acted upon. Indeed, listening and then ignoring could make things worse. Dialogue and agreement as opposed to the old-fashioned method of 'we tell you what to do and you go and do it' are what count.

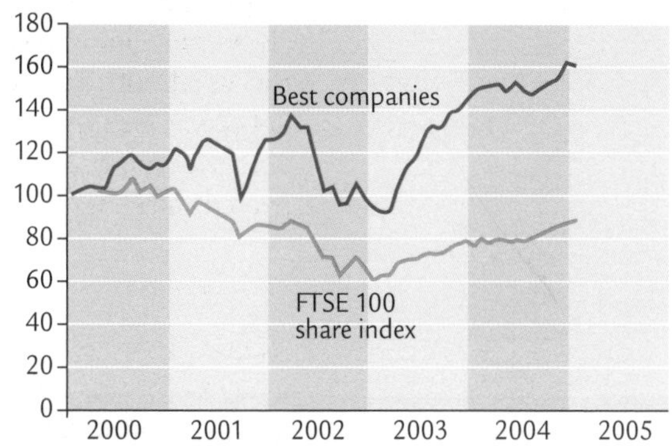

***Figure 19.3** Why 'best companies' are good for your workforce and your wealth*

Listening makes a real difference to how staff feel about their company leadership. In companies where workers reported lots of telling and not much listening, bosses got a positive score of just 54%, compared with 81% for companies where staff are listened to. Similarly, among those reporting that bosses do a lot of telling and not much listening, just 51% agreed with the statement: 'I have confidence in the leadership skills of the senior management team', but this figure was 94% among staff who are listened to.

A close connection also exists between being listened to and the stress levels of staff. The survey asked ten questions related to employee wellbeing, and this factor got a 73% positive score among companies where staff are listened to, compared with just 52% where they are not. 'If people are listened to, they are much more likely to have a sense of control. If senior managers never listen to you, then you will feel that you have no control and the stress will reduce your wellbeing very strongly,' says Dr Pete Bradon, one of the survey team.

The survey also indicates that where staff are listened to there is lower turnover and lower rates of absenteeism.

Source: adapted from *The Sunday Times 100 Best Companies to Work For*, 2005.

Question

Total: 20 marks (25 minutes)

Using your knowledge of communication and the information in the above case study, discuss the extent to which effective communication and feedback can influence employee motivation and a firm's performance.

CHAPTER 20

Barriers to communication

This chapter looks at the characteristics of the most common communication networks. Barriers to communication are then discussed. As well as physical barriers, attitudes, intermediaries and the lack of a common language or sense of purpose are also considered.

Communication networks

KEY TERM

communication network (or **net**): the communication structure, between individuals or departments, within an organisation.

A communication network can be represented diagrammatically. The following are the main types of communication network, but there are many variations on these.

Circle

A communication network in the form of a circle (see Figure 20.1) is where departments or individuals within an organisation can only communicate with two others. For example, in Figure 20.1, A can only communicate with B and F. This type of communication may occur between managers of different departments at the same level of an organisation. A major problem with this network is that decision making is likely to be slow and also less effective because of a lack of coordination and the difficulty of getting together.

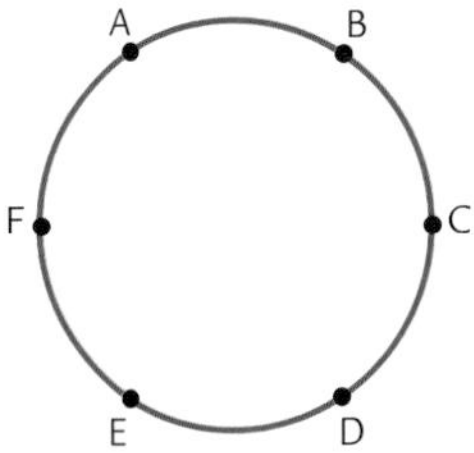

Figure 20.1
Circle network

Chain

A communication network in the form of a chain (see Figure 20.2) is where one person passes information to others, who then pass it on. This formal hierarchical approach is commonly adopted by large bureaucratic organisations such as the civil service and local government. A major problem with this type of network is the isolation and lack of motivation often experienced by those at the bottom of the hierarchy, who may not be part of any lateral communication flows. For example, in Figure 20.2, E, F and G can only communicate with D.

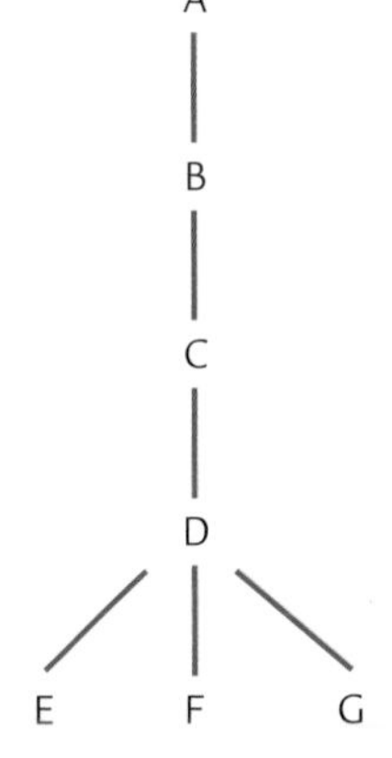

Figure 20.2
Chain network

Wheel

In the communication network in the form of a wheel (see Figure 20.3), one person or group occupies the hub or central position, with other groups or

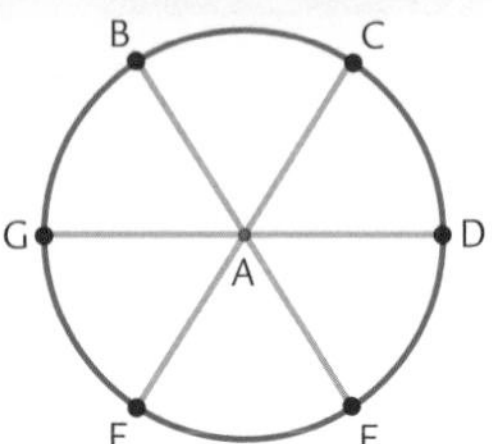

Figure 20.3
Wheel network

individuals occupying the spokes. The person or group at the centre has control, but there is some communication laterally for individuals or groups on the spokes. For example, in Figure 20.3, B can communicate with A, C and G. This type of network is particularly good at solving problems. For example, a regional store manager might be at the hub, communicating with individual store managers about how to reduce wastage or ensure stock meets the target market.

Fully connected circle

The fully connected circle or all-channel network (see Figure 20.4) ensures that all individuals or groups can communicate with everyone else. With its participatory and democratic style, and more open communication system, the connected network provides the best communication system for solving complex problems. This is most likely to be used in small-group situations: for example, when a department needs to 'brainstorm'. As a result, however, decision making in this situation tends to be slow.

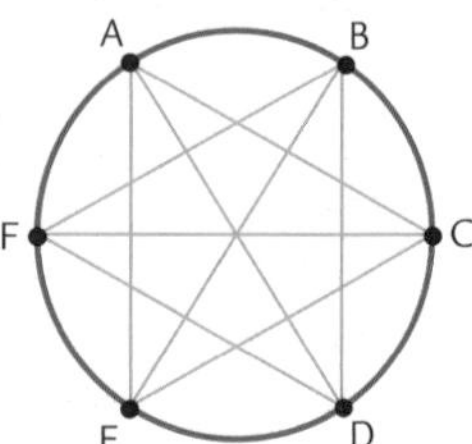

Figure 20.4
Fully connected circle network

e EXAMINER'S VOICE

When discussing these networks in the context of a particular business, try to relate them to the most appropriate leadership style.

Communication barriers

We have seen that effective communication will take place if the message is received and understood by the receiver. A number of barriers might prevent this from happening. Barriers to communication occur as a result of **noise**. The term 'noise' in this context is broader than the general meaning of noise, meaning a physical sound.

KEY TERM

noise: anything that can interfere with the receipt of a message, including physical problems or aspects of attitude or culture that get in the way of the communication.

Physical problems might include noisy environments that make conversation impractical, or geographical distance that causes a manager in, for example, an outlet in the north of England to be less well informed than one in London, where the head office is based. Attitudinal or cultural problems might include employees deciding not to pass on complaints that could adversely affect their department's status, or the reluctance of demotivated workers to listen clearly to new instructions.

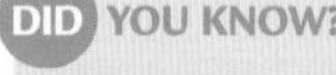
DID YOU KNOW?

One of Elton Mayo's findings was that the informal groups to which workers belong exert significant influence over their attitudes.

Attitudes

How employees perceive other people can affect how they interpret the messages that are sent. Employees are more likely to have confidence in people they trust, and hence are likely to be more receptive to any communication they receive from them, even if such communication includes bad news. On the other hand, if an employee has learned to distrust certain people, then what they say will be either ignored or treated with caution, even if it involves good news. In a similar way, stereotyping can influence the effectiveness of any communication and how one person interprets a message from another. For example, if male employees view a female manager as less rational or less able than a male manager, their initial reaction might be to have less respect for her authority. Thus they will treat any communications from her less seriously than they might treat communications from a male manager.

Intermediaries

intermediaries: individuals or groups within official communication channels through whom messages must be passed in order to reach the intended receivers.

The greater the number of intermediaries, and therefore the longer the chain of command, the less effective the communication system is likely to be. As Figure 20.5 illustrates, if employee J wants to communicate with manager A, the message has to go via intermediaries F, C and B. This will slow the message down and may lead to it becoming distorted. Even worse, F, C or B may either forget to forward it or decide it is not worth passing on.

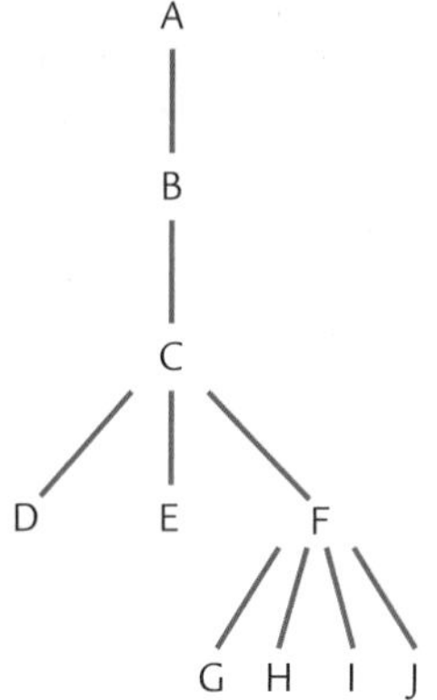

Figure 20.5 *Communication channel with intermediaries*

In contrast to this, **delayering** has been a feature of many organisations. This means that fewer intermediaries exist. In such a situation, managers have much wider spans of control and effective communication is vital to ensure the efficient running of the organisation.

Lack of a common language or sense of purpose

The skills of the sender and the receiver should be appropriate for the message. For example, if communication is to be effective, the sender must have the ability to send an appropriate message and the receiver must have the ability to understand it. Similarly, if **jargon** is to be used, it must be clearly understood by the recipient.

jargon: a word or phrase that has a technical or specialised meaning.

The terms understood by a certain group of people may be meaningless to those who do not have this technical or specialist knowledge. For example, technical information about a product that is not understood by the marketing department may result in misleading advertising and poor sales. Equally, if advice from sales staff or product instructions are too technical, this may be unhelpful for customers and lead to reduced sales.

People from different countries and cultures may experience problems in communication. Modern-day organisations possess multinational workforces operating globally. It is now commonplace for an employee based in London to spend more time liaising with a colleague or client in, for example, Berlin

than in Birmingham. This increasing internationalisation has brought new cultural challenges to many organisations. The ability of companies to interact successfully with people of different cultures is dependent on their capacity to understand their own cultural makeup as well as that of their counterparts.

FACT FILE

Communicaid is a training company offering Business Briefing sessions that provide employees with a greater awareness of overseas business cultures and help them to develop cross-cultural communication skills. The following is an outline of the content of its Japanese Business Briefing — *Working Successfully with the Japanese* — plus a comment by one of its clients.

Objective

To provide delegates with an understanding of key values that influence Japanese culture in order that the delegates are better prepared to work or conduct business with the Japanese.

Content

- A brief introduction to Japanese belief systems and cultural norms from a historical and religious perspective.
- Exploration of how Japanese values influence business. This section also discusses briefly the role of family and women within the workplace.
- A discussion on how the Japanese view the West, including western business and Europeans working in Japan.
- Japanese corporate culture, including hierarchy, the Japanese 'salaryman' and the Japanese work ethic.
- Practical advice on establishing good working relations with the Japanese:
  - first impressions (meeting and greeting) — handshake versus bowing, presenting one's business card, forms of address, concepts of time, dress codes, the business meeting, seating arrangements, recognising the head of the meeting, body language, how/when to contribute
  - building a relationship — concept of reciprocity, keeping 'face', understanding when 'yes' means 'no'/vice versa, socialising
  - taboos — unsuitable topics, sneezing

'The Japanese briefing, delivered to key De Beers LV personnel, provided not only an invaluable insight into working effectively with our Japanese counterparts but also an understanding of Japanese society and values — key to the success of our new operations in Japan.' (Claire Lamb, human resources manager, De Beers LV)

Source: adapted from www.communicaid.com.

Conclusion

To summarise, the sender of the message must ensure that any communication:

- does not contain too much information
- is not poorly written
- is not presented too quickly
- is not presented in a way that the receiver does not expect
- conveys the information that the sender actually wants to communicate
- is written in a way that the receiver will understand

PRACTICE EXERCISE 1 — Total: 40 marks (35 minutes)

1 What is a communication network? *(3 marks)*

2 Explain one major problem of a communication network in the form of a circle. *(3 marks)*

3 Explain one major problem of a communication network in the form of a chain. *(3 marks)*

4 Explain one major problem of a communication network in the form a wheel. *(3 marks)*

5 Outline two benefits of a fully connected communication network. *(6 marks)*

6 In the context of barriers to communication, what does the term 'noise' mean? *(3 marks)*

7 In what way can attitudes influence the effectiveness of communication in both a negative and positive manner? *(4 marks)*

8 Explain how the number of intermediaries can affect the quality of communication. *(3 marks)*

9 What is meant by the term 'jargon'? *(2 marks)*

10 Briefly explain one way in which the use of jargon might improve communication. *(2 marks)*

11 Briefly explain one way in which the use of jargon might create problems in a firm. *(2 marks)*

12 Explain two aspects of any communication that the sender needs to consider to ensure that it will be received effectively. *(6 marks)*

PRACTICE EXERCISE 2 — Total: 12 marks (15 minutes)

Refer to the Fact File on Communicaid (p. 186). Evaluate the barriers to communication that a business might encounter if it decides to set up a base in Japan.

CHAPTER 21

Communication and large organisations

This chapter reviews the difficulties of communication for larger organisations, particularly communication overload and the impact of many layers of hierarchy. It reviews possible solutions, such as decentralisation and the use of information technology.

Communication difficulties

Communication often becomes more difficult as organisations grow. Poor communication leads to diseconomies of scale because of reduced motivation, weak coordination and control difficulties. Inadequate understanding of corporate objectives, different languages and cultures, different time zones and too many intermediaries all make effective communication much more difficult for larger businesses (especially multinationals). These firms are likely to place much greater reliance on technological communication, which may improve speed and efficiency but does mean that the benefits of face-to-face communication are not as evident.

TOPFOTO

Communication overload

More communication does not necessarily mean better communication. It can lead to communication (or information) overload and adversely affect decision making.

KEY TERM

communication overload: when an individual becomes swamped by the sheer volume of communication and information.

EXAMINER'S VOICE

If you are not confident about your knowledge of the benefits and problems of delegation, refer back to Chapter 19 of the AS textbook.

Communication overload might apply to managers wanting to be kept fully informed of the activities of all their subordinates. As a result, they may miss key issues, fail to respond to urgent requests and generally become less effective in their role. At the same time, they may come under great stress as a result of their inability to cope. E-mail, which benefits an organisation because of its speed, immediacy and convenience, often adds to this problem of communication overload. The solution is to encourage managers to delegate more widely, reducing the need for so much upward communication.

Many layers of hierarchy

As firms grow in size, they tend to add more layers of hierarchy. This in turn means that communication becomes more difficult, as messages moving from the top of the organisation to the bottom have to go through more intermediaries. This slows down the decision-making process and makes it more likely that messages will get distorted or confused. It also means that communication from the bottom to the top of the organisation is more likely to be discouraged.

Similarly, as the number of people increases, face-to-face communication tends to decline and written or e-mail communication tends to increase. This means numerous messages passing back and forth, which slows down decision making and adds to communication overload. It is much less effective than face-to-face communication, when immediate feedback can be given and it is possible to check understanding instantly.

Solutions to communication problems

Possible solutions to the inevitable problems of communication associated with large organisations include decentralisation and the use of information technology.

Decentralisation

decentralisation: the delegation or passing of decision-making authority from head office to local branches.

EXAMINER'S VOICE

If you are not confident about your knowledge of the benefits and problems of decentralised organisations, refer back to Chapter 17 of the AS textbook.

Decentralisation reduces the volume of day-to-day communication between head office and the branches and thus gives senior managers more time to consider long-term strategy, while also empowering local managers and encouraging them to be more innovative and motivated.

Information and communication technology (ICT)

ICT can help improve communication but has to be used effectively. Rapid developments in technology have greatly changed the way businesses communicate with each other. It is now possible to deliver messages instantly, over great distances and to a large number of people at the same time. Thus developments in ICT create huge opportunities for improvements in communication, making it easier, quicker and cheaper, and providing quick access to data, such as stock availability and the latest sales figures. However, ICT systems quickly become outdated and need replacing, which is costly. ICT also requires costly staff training to ensure the technology is exploited as effectively as possible.

INGRAM

Here are a few examples of how the use of ICT improves communication within a business:

- Mobile phones allow employees who work outside the business to be in constant touch.
- Answer phones allow important messages to be stored and received while employees are away from their desks and outside normal office hours.

- Paging devices alert receivers to messages waiting for them on a prearranged telephone number.
- Videoconferencing allows individuals in different locations to communicate as if they were in the same room. Individuals can see each other on screens and talk to each other via telephone lines.
- Teleconferencing allows many people to be linked together via telephone lines, with each person being able to talk to all the others.
- Laptop computers allow people to work in different locations and to continue working during train journeys.

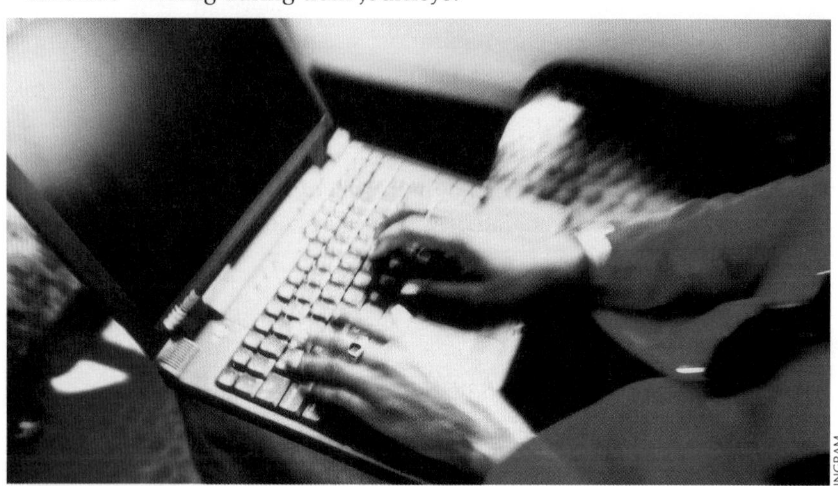

INGRAM

FACT FILE

One in five of the 30 billion text messages that will be sent this year will be about business. Many people prefer text messages to e-mail. According to research by Cable and Wireless, we read 85% of the texts we receive compared with only 20% of the e-mails. That might be because individually we do not get many text messages, and most e-mails are irrelevant.

- E-mail allows businesses and individuals to communicate immediately with others and permits lengthy documents to be sent promptly to people anywhere in the world.
- The internet is increasingly used as a means of selling products directly to customers as well as a source of information on virtually any topic for anyone who cares to access it.
- An intranet, on the other hand, contains information that is under the control of the company using it and is usually available only to the staff of that organisation. An intranet allows an organisation continually to make up-to-date information available to its staff. For example, internal phone numbers, diaries and details of meetings, which quickly become out of date, can be revised as soon as a change occurs and made available to all staff through an intranet site.

Although ICT can improve the speed, ease and cost of communication, there are problems resulting from information overload. In addition, for many people such developments have led to an increase in the time they spend on work-related tasks, often dealing with work-related e-mails at home, for instance.

ICT can lead to the introduction of more flexible working patterns and production processes: for example, part-time working, home working, job sharing, outsourcing, etc. These require more effort in coordinating communication.

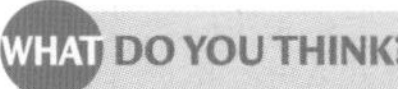

WHAT DO YOU THINK?

'In future, managers, who are growing up today, will not have the same need for face-to-face contact as they are used to running their lives largely through mobile phones, text messages and e-mail.' (Clive Radford, a senior construction manager in the leisure industry, quoted in *Professional Manager*, January 2005) Do you agree?

DID YOU KNOW?

Messages sent by e-mail and via the internet can often be seen by people other than the intended receiver. This can be a problem if the sender wants the message to remain confidential and is also a cause of security breaches that can involve customers as well as staff.

Conclusion

Communication problems, even in large organisations, can be resolved in a number of different ways if managers are prepared to:

- train employees in communication skills
- avoid the danger of generating too much information
- recognise that cultural and linguistic differences exist
- review the leadership style and the structure of the organisation
- ensure that corporate objectives are understood by all employees

EXAMINER'S VOICE

Communication is a genuinely integrative theme. Ensure that you understand its significance in relation to, for example, production techniques (such as lean production and empowerment), marketing (such as market research and promotional activities) and organisational decision making.

PRACTICE EXERCISE — Total: 45 marks (40 minutes)

1 What is communication (or information) overload? *(3 marks)*

2 Explain how communication overload can create problems for a business and explain one way in which it can be reduced. *(6 marks)*

3 Why might a large organisation with many layers of hierarchy experience less effective communication? *(4 marks)*

4 Define the term 'decentralisation'. *(3 marks)*

5 In what way might a more decentralised structure improve communication for large firms? *(3 marks)*

6 Explain two possible problems of decentralised structures. *(6 marks)*

7 Identify four examples of the use of ICT to improve communication in a business. *(4 marks)*

8 Explain briefly one advantage of each of the examples identified in question 7. *(8 marks)*

9 State one possible problem of each of the examples identified in question 7. *(4 marks)*

10 What are the possible consequences of increased flexible working patterns for the communication systems of an organisation? *(4 marks)*

CHAPTER 21 Communication and large organisations

CASE STUDY 1 Get the message!

INGRAM

What would get your attention — a printed letter telling you when the installer is coming to connect your broadband, or a text message the day before, reminding you not to go out? Since it started sending reminders by text message, NTL is finding a third fewer people are out when the engineer calls. This has lowered costs as well as making customers happy; some of them even reply with a thank you.

The increasing use of text messaging is shown in the following fields:

- Text messaging is reliable enough for both Britannia Airways and Gatwick Airport to use it for contacting their crisis response teams.
- Sending text messages from a central system leaves an audit trail. Three of the largest legal practices in the UK use a business texting system, not just to reach colleagues quickly but also to make sure messages are stored for evidence. As compliance regulations force companies to document who knew what and when, tracking texts is viewed as a less intrusive way of doing it.
- Text messages are ideal for getting information to employees who are rarely at their desk. The charter airline First Choice texts information to its staff about problems with their planes. Text messaging takes pressure off the operations team. It saves them having to ring lots of people individually or have people constantly ringing in to find out what is happening.
- Text messages can also connect you to the office diary when you are on the train, or extend an existing job scheduling system. RAC Auto Windscreens sends text messages telling fitters where their next job is. The fitters text back when they arrive and when they are ready to leave, keeping the scheduling system up to date.
- Incoming text messages are also more discreet than phone calls. Interrupting customers you are dealing with to take a call makes them feel less important.

Because text messages are very direct, they can be very intrusive and so timing is everything. If, for example, you have a production or shipping department that runs 24 hours a day, it is important that outgoing messages are scheduled to arrive during what other employees consider to be working hours.

Text messages do not replace real conversation and are not always appropriate, but used properly they can be a valuable business tool.

Source: adapted from an article in the *Guardian*, 10 March 2005.

Question

Total: 20 marks (25 minutes)

ICT is now a significant aspect of the communication process for most organisations. Discuss the extent to which businesses benefit from this development.

CASE STUDY 2 Mushroom management — don't keep your workforce in the dark

Ragbags is a producer of fine leather handbags. It has grown from a single small factory in Leeds to a much larger manufacturer with six new production sites throughout the UK and a headquarters based at its original site in Leeds. It sells its products to upmarket department stores and leather retailers only.

Initially the owner and managing director, Joe Watts, managed the small factory well. His approach was somewhat paternalistic, but he knew everyone and made a point of having an 'open door' policy as far as staff were concerned. All staff, regardless of their position, knew they could see him personally to raise issues and make suggestions about any aspect of their work.

As the company grew, the organisation adopted a more formal structure, with more layers between senior management and the workforce. The organisation chart for the growing organisation is shown in Figure 21.1.

The new structure meant that some directors were never seen at any one site for months at a time. In addition, issues that staff at one site might be concerned with were never communicated to other sites and there was a general feeling among staff of being left in the dark. Increasingly, tea breaks were spent moaning to each other and talking about looking for new jobs. Despite this general feeling of unhappiness, so far there had been no adverse effects on productivity rates and production levels.

Robina Smith was appointed to the business manager's post, which was a new appointment with responsibility for all administrative staff and procedures across all sites. Each of the six new sites had an administrative supervisor answerable to her. Robina saw her role as that of a strategic manager and did not feel that 'meeting the troops', as she put it, was an essential part of this – and anyway she thought that it could be done much better by the administrative supervisors. She did, however, believe in communicating with all her staff and she did this regularly – always by e-mail. Every week, staff received endless emails from her about new policies and procedures she was introducing. Many of these e-mails people just ignored because they knew the policies and procedures would never work.

The administrative supervisors were a bit put out by Robina's approach. They could tell that she was highly efficient and really keen to change and update their working practices, but they felt that it should be they who communicated changes to their staff. The six of them were required to travel to Leeds once a month for a meeting with Robina but had no other opportunity to meet each other or her. It was often difficult to raise issues of concern at these meetings because the agenda, set by Robina, was very tightly structured and

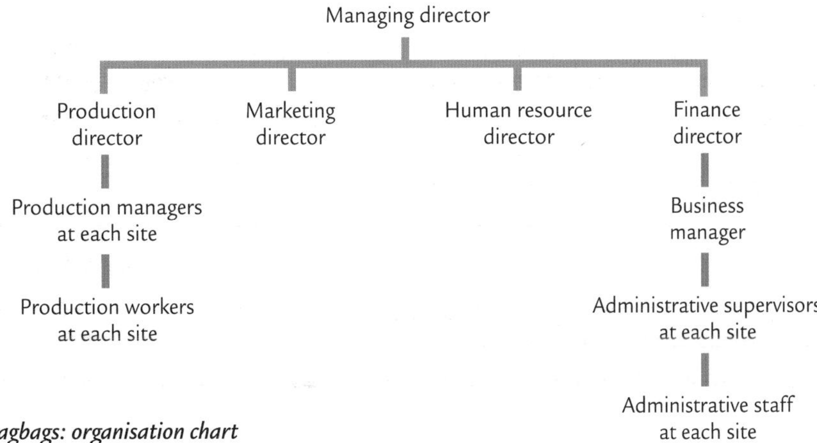

***Figure 21.1** Ragbags: organisation chart*

the meetings always kept to time.

Production staff at one of the sites were increasingly unhappy about the way their shift-working system was developing. A new system had been introduced recently, but although there had been consultation with the unions and general agreement that it would benefit the company and the workforce, staff did not feel that anyone had really talked it through with them. The production managers at the six sites were in the same position as the administrative supervisors, meeting once per month with the production director at headquarters (HQ). However, they did talk to each other a lot on the phone and correspond by e-mail, mostly complaining to each other about the lack of involvement of senior management in the operations of the six sites and the failure of anyone at senior management level to take their views and the views of their workers into account.

Joe Watts, the MD, had little idea of the discontent at the various sites. As far as he was concerned, the company was prospering, sales were high and growing, and profitability was excellent. He was currently setting up talks with a group of businesses in Japan to discuss the possibility of selling the company's products in department stores over there. The company had recently invested a significant amount of money in improving its ICT, including its communication systems, and all the directors had talked very positively about the beneficial impact of this in terms of communication with the different sites.

It came as something of a surprise to Joe when he met Bill Sykes, one of the production managers, by chance at HQ. Bill had been with the company from the start and Joe knew that he was a first-rate production manager who was loyal and hard working. Bill had come to HQ for one of his monthly production meetings. They got chatting and Joe learned that Bill was leaving at the end of the month. Joe assumed that Bill had got a promotion and congratulated him on 'moving up the ladder', as he put it. Bill said that it was not a promotion, just a sideways move to another firm. Joe got worried. He reasoned that unless it is to do with their personal circumstances, most people do not move sideways to another company unless they are unhappy with their present job. 'Quite honestly Joe, we feel — I feel — that I'm kept in the dark most of the time, and I don't like it so I'm going! The staff don't like it either, but they have no way of telling you.'

Joe decided that he needed to raise this at the next day's senior management meeting. As far as he knew, none of the directors was aware of any problems — which meant the problem was even more serious...

Questions

Total: 20 marks (30 minutes)

1 Examine the communication problems facing Ragbags as it has grown from a single-site producer to a multi-site producer. *(8 marks)*

2 Discuss the possible solutions that might be discussed at the senior management meeting. *(12 marks)*

CHAPTER 22

Approaches to workforce structures

This chapter considers the general trend away from a secure, full-time, salaried workforce to a more flexible approach that includes core and peripheral workers, along with temporary and subcontracted work. It analyses the impact of these changes on business and on employees.

Core versus peripheral workers

In a dynamic business environment, organisations need to have structures that can respond quickly to changes taking place in the external environment. One approach is to introduce more flexible workforce structures that allow organisations to expand or reduce capacity quickly and easily. An example of such an approach is to employ a core of permanent, full-time, salaried workers supported by other peripheral, temporary or part-time workers. The activities and responsibilities of core workers will be central to the organisation and such workers are likely to be fully committed to the aims and objectives of the organisation. Peripheral workers, on the other hand, are likely to be engaged in activities that are additional to the main purpose of the organisation. Their jobs will be less secure and they are less likely to be committed to the organisation's aims and objectives.

The shamrock organisation

Charles Handy, in *The Age of Unreason* (1990), developed this idea further and suggested that modern firms would increasingly be composed of three elements: the core, the contractual fringe and the flexible workforce. He called this the 'shamrock organisation' (see Figure 22.1).

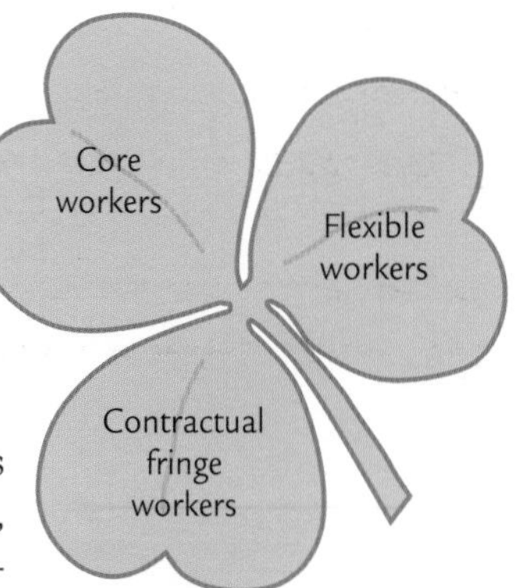

Figure 22.1 *The shamrock organisation*

The core

The core includes the professional, permanent employees who are essential to its continuity and have detailed knowledge of the organisation and its aims, objectives, practices and procedures. Workers in this core of essential, key professionals have skills and abilities to move the company's core capabilities forward. These permanent employees have to work hard and give commitment, but, typically, are very well paid for this.

The contractual fringe

There has been a strong trend for organisations to outsource their non-critical work to independent contractors, so that the organisation can concentrate on its core competences. As Handy puts it:

> All non-essential work, work which could be done by somebody else, is therefore sensibly contracted to people who make a speciality of it and who should, in theory, be able to do it better for less cost. Manufacturing firms are increasingly assembly firms, while many service organisations are, in effect, brokers, connecting the customer with some intervening advice.

Handy calls this element of the 'shamrock' the contractual fringe:

> This is made up of both individuals and organisations. These organisations, though often smaller than the main organisations, will have their own shamrocks, their own cores and their own subcontractors. It is a Chinese-box type of world (boxes within boxes). These individuals will be self-employed, professional or technicians.

These independent contractors are project experts who may be used, for example, for advertising, R&D, computing, catering and mailing services. They are rewarded with fees rather than with salaries or wages. Their contribution to the organisation is measured in output rather than in hours, in results rather than in time. Management chooses not to add these people to its permanent payroll and benefits plan, thus achieving a significant cost saving.

The flexible workforce

The third element of Handy's shamrock organisation is the flexible workforce, sometimes known as the **contingent** workforce. This comprises part-time, temporary and seasonal workers, who are often young and female. These people are brought in from outside to do individual, low-level, temporary tasks. Some may desire more permanent jobs; others (such as women with young families) may not, desiring only a job to supplement the family income, and with some outlet for meeting people.

The growth of flexibility

It is possible to argue that the three-level organisational structure described by Handy has always existed: firms have always, to some degree, been a mixture of permanent staff working with independent contractors and contingent, temporary workers. But what Handy has identified is the scale of the phenomenon today. The shamrock organisation is here to stay for the foreseeable future and so are the 'portfolio people' with their 'portfolio careers' that constitute the contractual fringe.

KEY TERM

portfolio career: a career in which income is derived from a variety of sources — perhaps a number of jobs, or a job and a business.

A portfolio career might consist of different working arrangements at different times. It typically includes periods of employment obtained through short-term contracts but could equally involve a permanent part-time job combined with short-term project or freelance work. Having a self-managed portfolio career is a cumulative process and replaces the traditional idea of promotion and progression within one organisation.

For many firms, this emphasis on being responsive to the external environment has led to a decline in the size of the core group of workers. Handy suggested that for many organisations, the 'permanent' core of highly skilled employed staff might amount to only 20% of the total activity, the remainder being accounted for by external suppliers, contractors and the self-employed. During the 1980s and 1990s, this core component of the large organisation typically declined as a result of a refocusing on core competencies and the 'downsizing' efforts that have accompanied this in a world of tougher international competition. Almost all functions other than those directly concerned with the organisation's primary business activity begin to take on a support role and are therefore candidates for outsourcing. This includes the bulk of the operations, administration, finance, personnel, legal, property and IT functions.

FACT FILE

Some commentators suggest that the approach of using temporary workers (the flexible workforce), which provides a cushion of 'disposable workers' in the case of an economic slowdown or cancellation of non-core projects, seems reasonable in principle. However, experience suggests that temporary workers cause tensions and jealousies with permanent employees during the good times because of the different terms under which they work and their lack of commitment to the company. Then when the temporary/flexible workforce is no longer required and is 'disposed of', the permanent employees feel just as exposed as if permanent employees were being cut. These findings emerged from the Watson Wyatt's Human Capital Index (HCI) research, which suggested that companies avoiding the 'disposable worker' approach deliver up to 5.6% more shareholder value than average-performing companies.

WHAT DO YOU THINK?

Self-employment has increased dramatically for both men and women, full time and part time, across a broad range of occupations, including banking, finance, IT and the professions. In addition, as well as a rise in self-employment among skilled trades such as construction, national statistics show increases in the number of taxi drivers, chauffeurs, child minders and farmers. Management writers might argue that this increase in self-employment is due to the fact that people are making choices about how to structure their working lives and are opting out of traditional work patterns. Statisticians, on the other hand, suggest that the growth is due to a lack of choice, noting that increases in the number of financial and investment analysts and advisers broadly coincide with media stories about City job losses, leading to people moving into self-employment.

Outsourcing and downsizing

The most usual method of achieving a workforce structure similar to that discussed above is by subcontracting work to other firms — now more commonly known as outsourcing.

KEY TERMS

outsourcing: where a firm uses sources outside the business to undertake functions that used to be done internally by a section of the business itself. These sources include marketing consultants, call centres, and production and assembly plants. Outsourcing is linked to the issue of 'downsizing'.

downsizing: reducing the size of a firm to make it more responsive to market conditions — for example, by removing 'back room' activities such as office functions and call centres or the production and assembly of parts, which are then contracted out to other agencies.

Subcontracted activities can then be increased or decreased at short notice, according to demand, without the need for expensive recruitment and selection processes or the difficult and expensive process of redundancies.

DC15 THE BALL™ © DYSON

FACT FILE

Production and assembly of Dyson household appliances is now carried out in Malaysia in the Far East. This is where a large part of the company's market is located, where its suppliers are and where, in comparison to the UK, labour is cheap. According to James Dyson, however, the UK is still the centre of the organisation and retains Dyson's most important function and its core competence – that of research, which requires the high-quality skills and ingenuity of UK engineers and scientists.

The impact of a more flexible workforce structure on organisations

Advantages

Advantages of a flexible workforce structure include the following:

- The organisation is able to respond more quickly to market conditions by expanding or contracting capacity.
- It can make more efficient use of resources by directing them to what the organisation's priorities or strengths are.
- It is able to cut down on costs — particularly labour, which for most businesses is their major cost.
- It can make more use of specialists — for example, Dyson's UK operation is focused on its high-quality engineers and scientists.

Disadvantages

Disadvantages of a flexible workforce structure include the following:

- Such an approach is likely to require a culture change for firms, which might be problematic, particularly in the short term.
- Organisations will be dependent on other organisations and agencies outside of their direct control.
- In the short term, if employees are laid off, this is likely to have a negative effect on workforce motivation and hence productivity. In the longer term, the peripheral workforce may be less motivated than the core workers.
- By downsizing and focusing on core activities, there may be less opportunity for future expansion as workers' skills and experience will be lost.

The impact of a more flexible workforce structure on employees

The move to a more flexible workforce can have a significant impact on employees, creating real concerns at the same time as opening up huge opportunities.

Traditionally, most people aim to have a job for life, with changes occurring only due to promotion or, very occasionally, a move to another firm. This is reinforced by the fact that most employees resist change and dislike uncertainty.

Outsourcing and downsizing are likely to lead to redundancy of some sections of the workforce. The threat of redundancy and a general lack of job security are likely to have adverse effects on motivation. However, for those employees who successfully embrace the move to a portfolio career, there can be huge gains in terms of flexibility, personal challenge and empowerment.

There is likely to be a need for on-going training as a result of the requirement to upgrade skills continuously. This is supported by government and its introduction of the concept of lifelong learning. This could be a threat or an opportunity. Many people enjoy and even thrive on new challenges. Learning new skills and updating them regularly may allow people to achieve Maslow's self-actualisation as employees pursue goals chosen by themselves. However, some people find constant change unsettling and stressful, which has quite the opposite effect on their motivation.

e EXAMINER'S VOICE

Always try to relate these ideas to your knowledge of motivation theories. For example, consider the issue of job security in relation to Maslow's hierarchy of human needs.

PRACTICE EXERCISE — Total: 45 marks (40 minutes)

1 Distinguish between the core and peripheral employees in an organisation. *(4 marks)*

2 How does Charles Handy split the peripheral employees in an organisation? *(3 marks)*

3 Explain two benefits to a firm of having such a flexible approach to workforce structure. *(6 marks)*

4 Explain two problems that such a structure might cause a firm. *(6 marks)*

5 Explain two opportunities that individual workers might have as a result of such an approach. *(6 marks)*

6 Explain two concerns that individual workers might have if such a structure were to be introduced. *(6 marks)*

7 Explain the term 'outsourcing'. *(3 marks)*

8 What does the term 'downsizing' mean? *(3 marks)*

9 Using illustrations from actual motivation theories, comment on how a change towards a more flexible workforce would affect the motivation of a firm's workers. *(8 marks)*

CASE STUDY The shamrock organisation

Dear Sir

Back in 1994, I worked for a near 200,000-strong organisation called British Telecom. How many of those people-factory, monolithic bureaucracies are around today? I was one of 20,000 managers, all of whom were just cogs in a wheel, following the same routine, nine-to-five office life, and doing whatever was in the procedures manual.

By the time I left BT 6 years later, I was leading a team of people that had a business plan, but otherwise no rules or procedures. The entire team was home-based, and we had as many relationships and partnerships outside of the organisation as within. We worked hard, motivated by both significant bonus and share-save schemes, but mainly because we felt more empowered and could make a difference at an individual level. Work had become more challenging and rewarding.

I recall Handy predicting the 'Shamrock organisation' as one that would have three layers. First, there would be the small core of key employees who develop the organisation, then the 'contractual fringe', comprising contractor and partner organisations that would be paid by results, and finally the flexible workforce, often freelance agents, who would be employed as and when required. This is the exact model for my organisation, a management consultancy, where we have outsourced IT, accounting and many marketing functions, and provide as much work for our partner (freelance) consultants as our own staff.

Is there an organisation that has not outsourced functions or is not using freelance support in some capacity?

Source: letter to *Personnel Today*, 30 November 2004.

Questions

Total: 20 marks (20 minutes)

1 In response to the above letter, write a reply that argues the case for a more traditional employment structure within organisations. *(10 marks)*

2 Examine the beneficial impact of a more flexible workforce structure on an organisation and its employees. *(10 marks)*

CHAPTER 23

Employee participation and industrial democracy

This chapter considers the general concept of industrial democracy and the different forms of employee participation, including works councils, employee shareholders and autonomous work groups. It identifies the practical problems and the benefits of working in teams, and assesses the general impact on motivation.

What are employee participation and industrial democracy?

KEY TERMS

employee participation: a general term referring to the extent to which employees are involved in the decision-making process.

industrial democracy: when employees have the opportunity to be involved in and to influence decision making. It can take the following forms: worker directors, who are elected to the board of directors by employees from the factory floor; works councils, which are discussed in detail below; and workers' cooperatives, where a firm's workers own a majority of its shares, such as in the John Lewis Partnership.

FACT FILE

The John Lewis Partnership is one of the UK's top ten retail businesses, comprising 26 John Lewis department stores and more than 160 Waitrose supermarkets. It is also the country's largest example of worker co-ownership. All of its permanent staff (over 60,000 people) are partners in the business, and the Partnership sees the commitment of its partners to the business as a unique source of competitive advantage.

The partners do not merely have the satisfaction of *working* in a good business — they have the enjoyment of *owning* it. That is the essential difference at the John Lewis Partnership. John Spedan Lewis, the founder, aimed to create:

- a business that was fair to all — its customers and suppliers as well as those who work in it
- a business that the partners really felt was their own
- a business that would challenge and beat the best of the competition and attract people from the top of their profession into its executive ranks

Its ultimate purpose was defined, by John Spedan Lewis, as the 'happiness' of those who work in the business. That remains its visionary aim. Above all, the founder wanted to instil in partners an awareness that any benefits for them would depend entirely on the quality of service they delivered to the customers and on the returns they were able to generate. He had no doubt of the need to maintain a tight commercial discipline and a sharp focus if the Partnership was to achieve its long-term objectives.

This vision and its ideals are the foundation of the written constitution, which is a framework defining the Partnership's principles and the way it should operate. The greater part of this constitution relates to how democratic ownership should work in practice, through the sharing of profit, knowledge and power. The constitution is built around three main pillars, known as the 'governing authorities':

- **The Partnership Council.** This is the Partnership's 'parliament', at least 80% of its members being directly elected. It represents partners as a whole and shares responsibility for the Partnership's health with the Partnership Board and the chairman (see below). Its role is to hold principal management to account and in doing this it has the power to discuss 'any matter whatsoever'. The chairman comes before the council twice a year to report and answer questions on his running of the Partnership. Other key directors report once a year. The council also plays a role in decisions concerning the use of profit (particularly in relation to those decisions that affect partners directly, like pensions and discounts), the development of the social life of the Partnership community and charitable giving.
- **The Partnership Board.** This has ultimate responsibility for issues of policy and for allocating the financial and other resources of the business. Its role is important in keeping the Partnership true to its principles – in terms of both the vitality of its commercial policies and its distinctive co-ownership objectives. There are 12 members – the chairman and the deputy chairman, five directors appointed by the chairman and, uniquely, five directors elected by the Partnership Council, who provide a direct link with the Partnership's democratic structure.
- **The chairman.** The chairman takes executive leadership of the Partnership and, as a 'governing authority' in his own right, carries personal responsibility for ensuring that the Partnership retains its distinctive character and democratic vitality. He is also ultimately responsible for its commercial performance.

All partners have a say in the business, through a system of councils and committees that feed opinion back to the Partnership Council, the Partnership Board and, ultimately, the chairman.

The Partnership-wide system of democracy is replicated at a local level within the organisation. The two trading divisions have elected Divisional Councils for John Lewis and Waitrose, each of which holds its divisional management board members to account. In addition, all of the operational units of John Lewis – shops, warehouses and factories – have their own Branch Councils that, like the Partnership Council, are elected by all who work in them. A further channel of representation is provided through the Committees for Communication. These are elected bodies that ensure that all those who are not involved in management can communicate directly with management and, ultimately, the chairman.

Figures 23.1 and 23.2 illustrate, respectively, how management policy is carried out and how partners' opinions are relayed back.

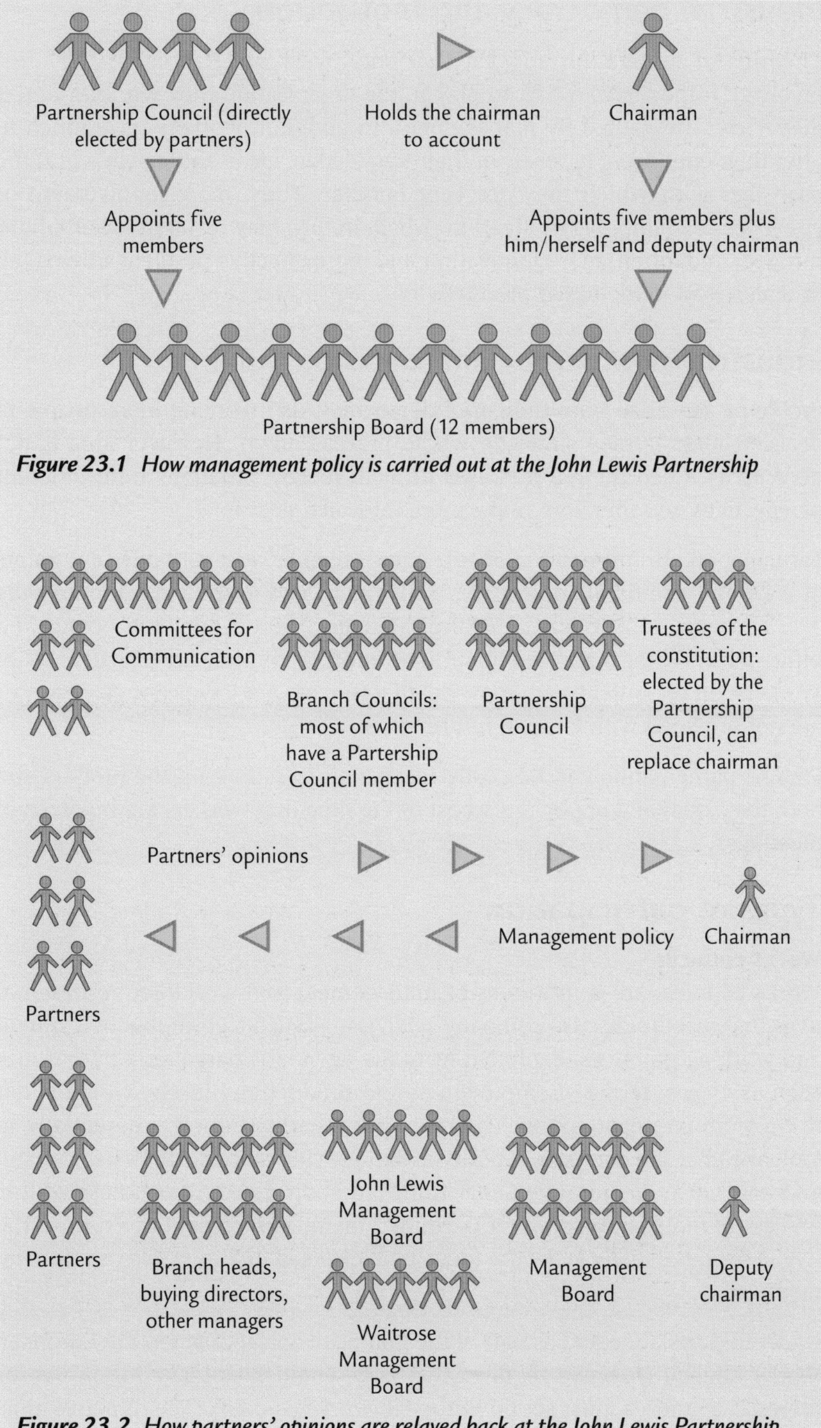

Figure 23.1 How management policy is carried out at the John Lewis Partnership

Figure 23.2 How partners' opinions are relayed back at the John Lewis Partnership

DID YOU KNOW?

In March 2005, the John Lewis Partnership announced that each of its 63,000 staff at John Lewis and Waitrose was to receive a bonus equal to 7 weeks' pay after the retail group increased profits by 24%.

WHAT DO YOU THINK?

Is the type of industrial democracy illustrated in the John Lewis Partnership always likely to have positive effects on employees' motivation?

Industrial democracy and motivation

Theories of motivation suggest that employees are happier if they feel involved, if they have a part to play in the organisation they work for and if their views are valued by management. In addition, workers have much to offer their employers in terms of their knowledge, ideas and insights into the processes with which they are very familiar. Thus, more involvement of employees can improve motivation, which in turn may result in lower labour turnover and, often, more innovation and more effective problem solving, all of which lead to increased productivity.

EXAMINER'S VOICE

Refer back to your AS work on Mayo's study of the Western Electric factory at Hawthorne and Maslow's hierarchy of human needs (see the AS textbook, pp. 179–181) to ensure that you can relate these ideas to motivation theory.

Industrial democracy and decision making

Problems can arise from industrial democracy, as involving more people in decision making may slow the whole process down. However, this is not necessarily a bad thing if it causes firms to review situations from different perspectives and therefore make more informed decisions.

Participation also means that people come together with very different points of view and conflicting objectives, which may lead to difficulties in arriving at a consensus in decision making. Managers may resent the power and influence of workers and the amount of information they are provided with. Workers, on the other hand, may feel that they do not have enough power or are not provided with enough information.

Finally, participation can be costly in relation to setting up the process and both the actual and opportunity cost of the time that workers are involved in meetings.

Types of participation

Works councils

Works councils are committees of management and workforce representatives that meet to discuss company-wide issues such as training, investment and working practices. Excluded from the agenda is bargaining over issues such as wages, terms of employment and productivity levels, which is left to trade union negotiations. The role of the works council is essentially to look ahead at the company's plans and to provide an opportunity to consult and gain ideas or improvements from the shop floor. A weakness of this process is that, because a works council includes representatives from the whole firm, it usually lacks the focus of a localised quality circle or improvement group.

Under EU legislation and as part of the European Social Chapter, the European Works Council Directive requires that large companies operating in two or more EU countries must set up European works councils. The directive aims to 'improve the right to information and to consultation of employees'. The intention is to restrict the power of multinationals and to provide their workers in different locations with the opportunity to discuss common concerns. A European works council (EWC) usually meets once a year and is made up of at least one elected representative from each country plus representatives of central management. Areas for discussion include corporate structure, the economic and financial situation, investment, the employment situation, health and safety, cutbacks and closures, acquisitions and new working practices. It is usually agreed that no single-country issues, including pay and conditions, are discussed. Most commentators agree that the process is worthwhile and encourages two-way communication.

How effective are European works councils?

At General Motors (GM), the European Works Council (EWC) coordinated European-wide action to challenge the company's restructuring plans. As a result, closure was averted and a restructuring framework agreement was established.

In December 2000, GM Europe told the EWC of plans to cut 6,000 jobs across Europe, 3,000 of them at the Luton plant in the UK, which was to close. Management informed the press at the same time, thereby violating both the EU directive and the General Motors EWS agreement, which requires timely and complete information to be given to the EWC. The decision to close the Vauxhall plant at Luton also violated a job security agreement signed in 1998 with the UK unions. In January 2000, the EWC presented a list of demands, which included:

- no closures or forced redundancies
- transferred workers to maintain all their benefits
- job cuts only on the basis of voluntary agreement or early retirement
- improved productivity through product and sales campaigns
- all existing agreements to be honoured

With the aim of securing an agreement covering all sites, the EWC called a Day of Action in January 2001 to pressure management to come to the negotiating table. There were work stoppages in the UK, Germany, Belgium, Spain and Portugal, with 40,000 people taking part in rallies. Knowing that more industrial action was planned, management agreed to negotiate. In March 2001, an agreement was signed that contained the following points:

- no redundancies from restructuring measures before 2005
- UK plants to be maintained with a guaranteed growth in capacity
- no disadvantages for workers transferred to other locations
- union recognition and employee representation to stay the same

Representatives from Unilever suggest that quality information in good time is the most tangible gain that has been won by their European Works Council. They have also achieved consistency of information from the company across Europe, which makes coordination and organisation of the union side much easier, while the fact of receiving timely information means they are able to negotiate better.

CHAPTER 23 Employee participation and industrial democracy

FACT FILE

Introduced in April 2005, the EU **Information and Consultation Directive** gives employees in organisations with 150-plus staff the right to be informed about the business's economic situation and prospects. In effect, the workforce must be notified of all changes that could affect the nature of staff's employment, such as work organisation, contractual relations, redundancies, mergers or takeovers. The new law includes a requirement to hold ballots to elect staff representatives, and gives staff in the UK extensive new rights to information and consultation. Companies that fail to comply face fines of up to £75,000. Smaller businesses will have a few more years to prepare.

The new law gives businesses an ideal opportunity to review their decision-making processes and to consider when or when not to consult and what to consult on. Management and human resource consultants seem to agree that the directive is likely to have a positive impact on business. If one accepts that mature adults respond best to consultation rather than to direction, then the more employees are involved, the better. Employee consultation not only helps to improve staff motivation, but can also enhance companies' effectiveness and success. Research has shown that organisations with a positive communication environment achieve superior business results over time. Higher job satisfaction and lower staff turnover may cause productivity levels to rise and other beneficial results to follow, such as improved customer relations.

Some consultants suggest that the 'inform' part of the legislation is better understood than the 'consult' part. Many businesses are unsure how to reconcile the need for rapid decision making with the new requirement to consult staff, which can slow down the process.

Changing management attitudes will be a huge challenge for many businesses. Consultants are suggesting that a good first step is to survey all employees and ask them exactly what they want to be consulted on. For example, in one mobile telecoms company, a survey found that people with customer-facing roles asked to be involved in product development, whereas others were more interested in HR issues and how the business was run.

Dr Patrick Gilbert, of Mercer Human Resource Consulting, believes that regular surveys can be an effective way to make the voice of the employee heard. 'When properly designed, surveys provide employees with a collective voice to communicate with management about their concerns,' he says. 'Attitude surveys allow management to measure employee reactions to proposed or actual business changes and to pinpoint issues that affect motivation and commitment.' However, surveys must be acted on or they will be dismissed as time-wasting formalities, Gilbert warns. 'It is vital that management takes clear and reasonable actions in response to employee feedback. If employee consultation is undertaken simply as a public relations exercise, it will lead to cynicism and will reduce motivation.' Research by Mercer indicates that employee surveys that result in action by management boost the proportion of employees ticking the 'highly committed' box to more than 80%, when asked about their attitude to the company. Where surveys are seen to be little more than window dressing, the figure drops to less than 40%.

'Staff may not be used to being consulted and to start with may want to discuss low-level issues like car parking or the state of the toilets,' says Ali Gill, a management consultant. 'They may have a lack of belief that anything will happen. You need to build trust by showing them that what they say will make a difference.'

Although the legislation envisages that companies will communicate with employees using face-to-face meetings with elected staff representatives or union leaders, the use of IT to communicate directly with all staff is also encouraged. Gill advocates the use of new technology, such as a video messaging system, where staff can message back their views and the data collected are published on the company intranet site, to speed up the consultation process.

Paul Gollan of the London School of Economics says that, if employees are happy with existing arrangements, there is no compulsion on the employer to do anything else. However, he warns that in the absence of a valid pre-existing agreement, a request for the establishment of an information and consultation procedure by 10% of staff will trigger a range of new statutory obligations.

Companies that pride themselves on being good employers realise they have to engage and collaborate more with their employees. This legislation is just one means of achieving this. However, implementing the directive will make greater demands on the softer management skills, and may create a need for more training in mediation, questioning and listening techniques, and learning how to deal with emotion in the workplace, as a means of building mutual trust.

Sources: adapted from *The Times*, 1 January 2005, and *Professional Manager*, March 2005.

Employee shareholders

In some companies, employees are given the opportunity to buy shares in the company at favourable rates. It is suggested that this encourages them to be more interested in company performance, to develop a sense of common purpose, to improve motivation and to be aware of how individual performance contributes to company performance.

DID YOU KNOW?

Companies that provide opportunities for employees to purchase shares and that have a high share take-up rate by employees include Punch Taverns plc, ASDA, Orange, Vodafone and Tesco. Tesco offers Save as You Earn (SAYE) schemes to its employees, who can purchase its shares at favourable rates. Employees who started the scheme 5 years ago were allowed to buy shares at 151p each, while those who joined 3 years ago could buy them at the 2001 price of 198p. Tesco's shares were valued at 304.75p in February 2005, when thousands of its workers shared a £110 million payout.

Source: adapted from an article in *The Times*, 22 February 2005.

TOPFOTO

Autonomous work groups

Job satisfaction, and therefore motivation, can be enhanced if employees work together in groups in order to achieve common goals. Giving employees more responsibility provides them with a sense of purpose and thus improves morale and possibly productivity. Autonomous work groups are teams of people who are given a high level of responsibility for their own work. This might include organising and scheduling their own work, making decisions about the allocation of tasks and, in some cases, recruiting new members of staff.

Teamwork

Increasingly, employees work in teams rather than in isolation — for example, in production teams via cell production or quality circles, or in project teams within a matrix organisational structure.

EXAMINER'S VOICE

Refer back to your AS notes to ensure that you are still confident in your knowledge of all of the concepts covered previously — for example, cell production, quality circles and matrix organisational structure.

Where successful, teamwork is likely to lead to improved morale, efficiency and productivity. More specific benefits for a business and for its employees include the following:

- Teamwork can lead to more efficient and effective production for the business as employees work together and complement each other's skills and experience, thus producing synergy.

KEY TERM

synergy: where the whole is greater than the sum of the individual parts. For example, the level of output resulting from 10 individuals working as a team, making use of their individual strengths most effectively, is likely to be much greater than the total output of the 10 individuals working in isolation.

- People often respond positively to working with others, as it satisfies their social needs and particularly their desire to belong. At the same time, where responsibilities are delegated to teams, this may satisfy people's ego and self-actualisation needs.
- Individuals gain from the strength and skills of others. The sharing of different skills helps to solve problems, which in turn benefits the firm.
- Working in teams might allow more variety of activities (job rotation) if members alternate tasks between them.

However, just as teamwork can benefit a business and its employees, it can also be problematic:

- Some people simply do not like working in teams, preferring to work on their own. Thus teamwork may reduce their motivation and efficiency, and may lead to increased labour turnover.

- Similarly, some people think that their own performance is better than that of the team or members of it, and that working in a team simply holds them back. Equally, team responsibility for a particular activity or target can often encourage 'free riders': that is, individual workers who put in less effort (knowing that they cannot be easily identified), while receiving the same benefits as other team members.
- Decision making may be slowed down as a result of needing to gain input from all team members, and more disagreements are likely to occur. Therefore, arriving at a consensus may be more difficult.

Other methods of encouraging employee participation include quality circles, worker directors, company newsletters, suggestions schemes and a democratic style of management, some of which you have covered in your AS studies.

Conclusion

Increased employee participation needs to be part of a cultural change involving greater trust and mutual respect between managers and workers. Any analysis of the benefits of participation is very much based on motivation theories. You should ensure that you are familiar with this area from your AS studies. Overall, greater employee participation may lead to competitive advantage for the firm, as a result of more ideas, improved motivation, greater efficiency and an increase in commitment from employees.

PRACTICE EXERCISE — Total: 40 marks (35 minutes)

1	Explain the term 'industrial democracy'.	*(3 marks)*
2	How might greater employee participation improve a firm's productivity?	*(4 marks)*
3	Explain two possible problems of greater employee participation for a business.	*(6 marks)*
4	What is a 'works council'?	*(3 marks)*
5	Under what circumstances must a business set up a European works council?	*(3 marks)*
6	How do employee shareholder schemes benefit a business?	*(4 marks)*
7	What are autonomous work groups?	*(3 marks)*
8	State two examples where employees might work in teams.	*(2 marks)*
9	Identify two advantages of teamwork for a business.	*(6 marks)*
10	Explain two possible problems for a business resulting from teamwork.	*(6 marks)*

CASE STUDY 1 The EU Information and Consultation Directive

Refer to the Fact File on the EU Information and Consultation Directive (pp. 206–07). Answer the following questions.

Questions

Total: 20 marks (25 minutes)

1 Consider the extent to which leadership style will affect the successful implementation of the new directive. *(8 marks)*

2 To what extent might the new directive and other methods of employee participation affect the performance of a company in the long term? *(12 marks)*

CASE STUDY 2 The John Lewis Partnership

Refer to the Fact File on the John Lewis Partnership (pp. 201–03). Answer the following question.

Question

Total: 15 marks (20 minutes)

Discuss the benefits and problems to the organisation of the type of worker co-ownership exemplified in the John Lewis Partnership.

CHAPTER 24

The role of trade unions and ACAS

This chapter considers the objectives, functions and organisation of trade unions. It explores the nature of industrial disputes and methods of resolution, including conciliation and arbitration. Single-union and no-strike agreements are explained and the role of ACAS is examined.

What are trade unions?

KEY TERMS

trade union: a pressure group that represents the interests of people at work. Trade unions have existed for over 200 years. Traditionally, unions were categorised as craft unions, industrial unions and general unions.

craft union: the oldest type of union, which developed from traditional crafts and skills — for example, the bakers' union (BFAWA).

industrial union: a union that looked after the collective interests of all types of employee within a specific industry — for example, the National Union of Mineworkers (NUM).

general union: a union made up of workers with a wide range of skills in many different industries — for example, the General, Municipal, Boilermakers and Allied Trades Union (GMB).

Mergers of unions in recent years have blurred many of these distinctions and an alternative categorisation of unions into those with more *open* and those with more *restricted* recruitment policies is probably more appropriate. The latter tend to recruit employees with certain skills — for example, Equity (actors) and the National Union of Teachers. For such trade unions, membership increases and decreases with the changing level of employees in the industry.

More open recruitment policies tend to be associated with larger unions that seek membership regardless of their members' jobs or industries (for example, the Transport and General Workers' Union, TGWU), or recruit from a wide variety of related industries such as the public service industries (for example, UNISON). Problems that arise for unions with such large, open recruitment policies include the difficulty of taking account of the needs of different groups of members and the conflict that can result when unions are accused of 'poaching' members from other areas.

Union	Membership
UNISON	1,298,000
Amicus	1,061,199
TGWU	835,351
GMB	703,970

Source: TUC data, January 2003, www.tuc.org.uk.

Table 24.1 Union membership in the largest general unions

The biggest unions in the UK include UNISON, Amicus, the TGWU and the GMB (see Table 24.1), each of which represents people working in a range of different occupations and industries in the public and private sectors. Such large general unions have emerged as a result of the amalgamation of smaller unions wishing to increase their membership and therefore their power and influence.

What do trade unions do and how do they benefit employees?

The main functions that trade unions provide for their members are negotiation and representation.

Negotiation

KEY TERM

negotiation: (also known as **collective bargaining**): where union representatives in a particular organisation discuss with management the issues that affect employees working in that organisation.

There are often differences of opinion between management and trade union members in relation to issues in the workplace. Negotiation involves the process of finding a solution to these differences. In many organisations, trade unions are formally 'recognised' by the employer, meaning that there is a formal agreement between the trade union and the organisation, giving the trade union the right to negotiate with the employer.

The following should be true for collective bargaining to take place:

- Employees must be free to join representative bodies such as trade unions.
- Employers must recognise such bodies as representative of workers and agree to negotiate with them.
- Such bodies must be independent of employers and the state.
- Bodies should negotiate in good faith, in members' interests.
- Employers and employees should agree to be bound by agreements without having to use the law to enforce them.

Representation

Trade unions also represent individual union members when they have problems at work. If employees feel they are being unfairly treated, they can ask their trade union representative to help sort out their difficulties with management. If the problems cannot be resolved amicably, they may go to an industrial tribunal, at which individual union members can ask their trade unions to represent them.

Trade unions also offer their members legal representation — for example, helping them to get financial compensation for work-related injuries.

Other functions

In addition to these two main functions, trade unions provide information, advice and member services. They can advise on a range of issues, such as how much holiday an employee is entitled to each year and how much pay a woman is entitled to while on maternity leave. During the last 20 years, trade unions have increased the range of services they offer members. These can include:

- education and training courses on employment rights and health and safety
- legal assistance on personal matters such as housing, wills and debts
- financial discounts on mortgages, insurance policies and loans
- financial help to members who are sick or unemployed

More generally, individual employees have very little power to influence decisions that are made about their jobs. In relation to negotiating pay and conditions, they are in a very weak position compared with a large employer. By joining together with other workers in a trade union, there is more chance of having a voice and therefore having influence. By collective bargaining with employers on behalf of their members, trade unions are able to improve the lot of their members at work in relation to issues such as rates of pay, work facilities, working conditions, bonuses and targets, job security, contracts, redundancy, dismissal, grievance procedures, job descriptions and job specifications.

Do trade unions benefit employers?

Media reporting tends to suggest that trade unions are something of an irritation to employers, disrupting their operations and preventing them achieving their objectives. However, in general, trade unions benefit employers as well as employees.

- They provide a valuable communication link between management and the workforce that has not been filtered by middle managers. Senior managers can expect straight talking about workers' opinions or grievances.
- The presence of a trade union means that management can avoid what would be very time-consuming bargaining and negotiation with each individual employee in relation to their pay and conditions.
- A strong union may encourage management to take workers' needs seriously and may thus improve employee morale, which in turn may have a positive influence on labour turnover, absenteeism and productivity.
- The presence of a trade union may ease situations that could cause difficulty for a firm, such as relocation, retraining for new technology, downsizing and redundancy, renegotiation of employment conditions and contracts. Trade union officials can be consulted at an early stage of the decision-making process, which may make the workforce more confident that management is acting properly and thoughtfully. It also gives the opportunity for the trade union to offer advice or objection at an early stage, thus promoting consultation rather than conflict.

Industrial disputes and industrial action

Most collective bargaining takes place quietly, away from media attention and with agreements being reached quickly and amicably by the union and the employer. However, disagreements can occur. In this case an industrial dispute might result. An industrial dispute might be resolved by successful conciliation or arbitration. If this does not occur, the union may ballot its members on whether to take industrial action.

TOPFOTO

KEY TERMS

industrial dispute: a disagreement between management and the trade union representing the employees, which is serious enough for industrial action to result.

industrial action: measures taken by employees to halt or slow production or disrupt services in order to put pressure on management during an industrial dispute — for example, a strike, an overtime ban, a work-to-rule or a go-slow.

strike: a form of industrial action involving the complete withdrawal of labour by employees.

overtime ban: a form of industrial action that attempts to disrupt the employer while keeping employees' basic wages unaffected.

work-to-rule: a form of industrial action in which employees refuse to undertake any work that is outside the precise terms of their employment contract.

go-slow: a form of industrial action in which employees keep on working, but at the absolute minimum pace required to avoid being subject to legitimate disciplinary action.

Strikes are only called as a last resort since both sides have a lot to lose: employers lose income because of interruptions to production or services, while employees lose their wages and salaries and may find that their jobs are at risk.

Work-to-rules, go-slows and overtime bans are similar in their impact on employees and the firm:

- In a work-to-rule, the workforce applies the employer's own rules and procedure 'to the letter', thus stopping overtime and many forms of participation and communication that are accepted practice. This behaviour cannot be criticised by the employer and may lead to considerable delay. Staff may prefer to work-to-rule rather than go on strike, since they are able to draw their basic pay.
- A go-slow will lose employees any bonuses, but will ensure that they receive their basic pay. If conducted at a time of high demand, a go-slow could be successful in applying considerable pressure upon an employer.
- An overtime ban can only be effective if a significant proportion of work in a key section is done on overtime. This is only likely to occur in seasonal production peaks.

Table 24.2 identifies the factors that influence the success of industrial action and the possible problems and benefits for employees and employers.

Table 24.2 *Industrial action*

Factors that influence the success of industrial action	Problems of industrial action for employers	Problems of industrial action for employees	Benefits of industrial action
• Nature and strength of union • Workforce concentration (e.g. lots of union members in one firm compared with a few members in many firms) • Management tactics (e.g. if stocks are available to meet demand during a strike) • Economic and legal climate • Public support	• Lost production, reduced revenue and lower profits • Continuing poor relationships and grievances that lead to poor motivation and communication • Shifts management's focus away from strategic planning for the future • Harms the firm's reputation with its customers	• Reduced or lost earnings • Closure of the business and redundancies • Stress and friction between levels of the hierarchy • If unsuccessful, workers are in a weaker position • Support from the public may decline if action affects them • Must conform to legislation or be liable for damages	• Resolves ongoing grievances and improves the atmosphere • Often leads to new rules about which all agree (e.g. regarding rates of pay or the need to consult) • Leads to greater understanding of each other's positions

Employers can also take industrial action by withdrawing overtime, introducing a lockout (that is, closing the factory and not allowing employees in to continue working), changing standard and piecework rates, closing the business and dismissing workers.

As Figures 24.1 and 24.2 illustrate, times have changed and industrial unrest in the form of days lost and stoppages (industrial action that involves employees stopping work) are much less frequent today. The main causes of disputes have not changed, however, and pay still dominates. Figure 24.3 shows the principal causes of working days lost in 2003: 84% of working days lost were due to disputes over pay, which accounted for 60% of all stoppages. In comparison, working conditions and supervision issues accounted for less than 0.5% of working days lost and 4% of stoppages. Staffing issues accounted for 1% of working days lost and 7% of all stoppages, while redundancy issues accounted for 1% of total working days lost and 6% of all stoppages.

Figure 24.1 *Working days lost in the UK, 1983–2003*

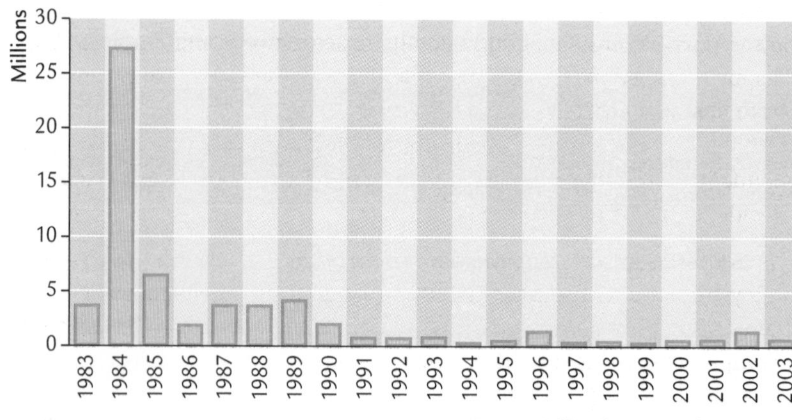

Source: Office for National Statistics.

Figure 24.2 *Stoppages in progress in the UK, 1983–2003*

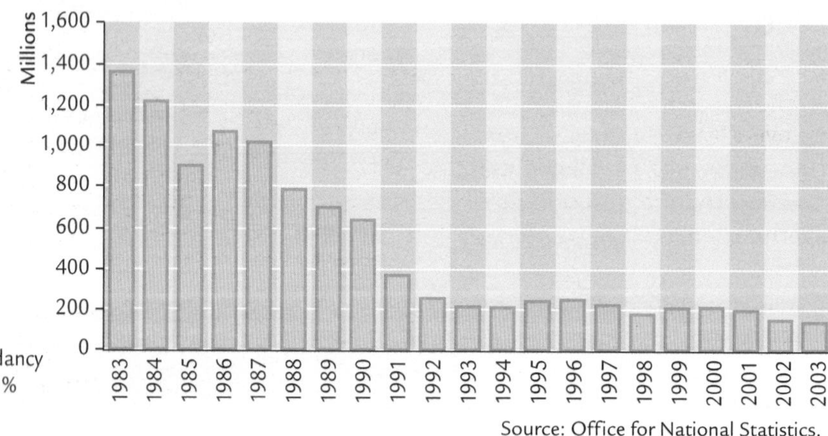

Source: Office for National Statistics.

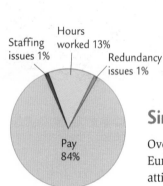

Hours worked 13%
Staffing issues 1%
Redundancy issues 1%
Pay 84%

Source: Office for National Statistics.

Figure 24.3 *Principal causes of disputes leading to working days lost in the UK, 2003*

Single-union and no-strike agreements

Over the last 20 years, the increasing importance of inward investment from European, American and Asian businesses has meant a new management attitude towards unions and the increasing establishment of **single-union agreements** (for example at Nissan).

KEY TERM

single-union agreement: the recognition by a firm of only one trade union for collective bargaining purposes.

The introduction of a single-union agreement removes the potential disruption caused by inter-union disputes and reduces the time spent on negotiations. Toshiba's agreement with the electricians' union (the EEPTU) in 1981 is believed to have been the first of its kind in the UK. Such agreements have been quite common with Japanese firms such as Nissan, but not all Japanese companies insist on them. Single-union agreements have sometimes added **no-strike agreements** and have often included **pendulum arbitration** clauses.

KEY TERMS

no-strike agreement: a contract, signed as part of a firm's negotiation and disputes procedure, which prevents the trade unions in a particular firm from calling a strike.

pendulum arbitration: a system of binding arbitration in which an independent person or panel (usually appointed by ACAS — see below) must decide in favour of one side or the other.

In pendulum arbitration, if a trade union claims a 7% pay rise while the employer offers 2%, the arbitrator must decide which is closest to the 'correct' or most appropriate outcome. If the arbitrator believes 3% to be appropriate, the employer's 2% offer will be imposed.

The Advisory, Conciliation and Arbitration Service

TOPFOTO

The Advisory, Conciliation and Arbitration Service (ACAS) was founded in 1974. Its 'ambition' is to improve organisations and working life through better employment relations. It is funded by the Department of Trade and Industry but is a non-governmental body, ensuring that it is fully independent, impartial and confidential. It is governed by a council made up of leading figures from business, the trade unions and academia, and operates in regional centres throughout England, Wales and Scotland, with a head office in London.

During the turbulent days of industrial unrest from the late 1970s to the mid-1980s (see Figures 24.1 and 24.2), ACAS became a household name. For example, during the miners' strike of 1984, the National Coal Board (the employer) and the National Union of Mineworkers (the trade union representing miners) were regular visitors to ACAS for over a year.

ACAS only becomes involved if both sides (employers and employees or their trade union representatives) believe that ACAS can help them make progress in the dispute. Once involved, representatives from ACAS will discuss the dispute with both sides and all will agree on how best ACAS can help. The role of ACAS can involve:

- sorting out the issues
- finding common ground between the two sides
- giving people the space to calm down and see the problems from the other side too (sometimes this means taking the dispute out of the media spotlight)
- having meetings with each side separately and together to discuss and explore the issues, and then starting to negotiate a solution
- repairing relationships and building trust

This type of process is called **conciliation**.

KEY TERM

conciliation: negotiation intended to reconcile differences between the parties to an industrial dispute.

The two sides try to reach an agreement that they both feel will work.

Sometimes conciliation does not lead to the dispute being settled. In these cases, ACAS may offer or be asked to appoint an independent expert arbitrator or mediator. The parties agree before the process begins whether the solution the independent expert puts forward will be binding or non-binding.

KEY TERMS

binding arbitration: where both parties agree in advance that they will accept the arbitrator's solution and the dispute ends.

non-binding mediation: where both sides at least consider seriously what the mediator suggests as a basis for resolving the dispute, but ultimately do not have to act on it. A non-binding mediation process was the basis of discussion suggested in the recent London Underground workers' dispute.

DID YOU KNOW?

The top ten topics that ACAS is asked about are:

1. Discipline and dismissal
2. Contracts
3. Layoffs/short-time working/redundancy
4. Holidays and holiday pay
5. Other employment matters
6. Wages
7. Maternity provisions
8. Working time regulations
9. Grievance procedure
10. Paternity rights

The approach that ACAS takes is: 'Don't get angry — get curious'. Its advice for a first step towards a solution in any kind of dispute is to find out why people are taking the positions they are and why they are angry.

ACAS still helps to solve high-profile labour disputes, such as the London Underground workers' strikes and the firefighters' dispute. However, as the employment world changes, so too does the role of ACAS. Since the early 1990s, much of the work of ACAS has focused on individual complaints to employment tribunals. These are passed to ACAS and, at present, 75% are settled or withdrawn at the ACAS stage, so preventing the need for an industrial tribunal hearing. Another growth area is in solving employment issues before they become problems at all. ACAS advisers give guidance to 750,000 callers a year on topics such as discipline and dismissal, contracts, layoffs, short-time working, redundancy, holidays and holiday pay, wages, maternity provisions, working time regulations, grievance procedures and paternity rights. They also promote good practice at training sessions and work in individual companies with employer, employee and trade union groups in partnership to find lasting solutions in the workplace.

FACT FILE

Major disputes in ACAS's history include:
1979 — public sector strike ('Winter of Discontent'); cause — pay
1984 — miners' strike; cause — pit closures
1986 — 'Wapping' dispute; cause — introduction of computer-aided technology
1996 — postal workers' dispute; cause — pay increases linked to productivity

How have trade unions changed in recent years?

Trade union membership has declined over the last two decades. In 1979, 13.3 million people were members of trade unions and the proportion of all employees who were union members (**union density**) stood at 55%. In autumn 2003, 7.4 million UK workers belonged to trade unions and union density was approximately 29%. As can be seen in Figures 24.4 and 24.5, the number of trade union members has remained stable in the last few years.

KEY TERM

union density: the proportion of all employees who are union members:

$$\text{union density} = \frac{\text{actual union membership}}{\text{potential union membership}} \times 100$$

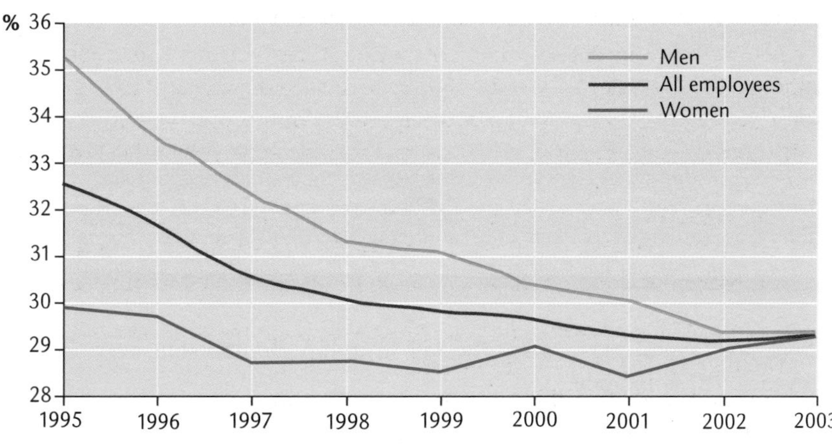

Figure 24.4 *Trade union density of UK employees by gender, 1995–2003*

Sources: Labour Force Survey (autumn quarters), Office for National Statistics.

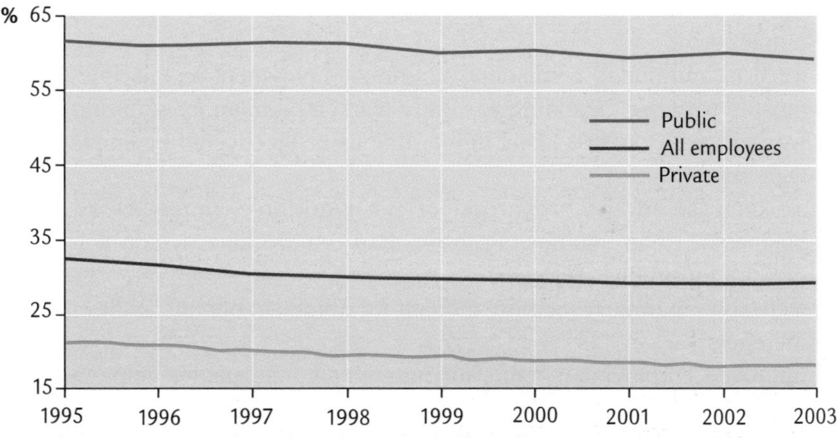

Figure 24.5 *Trade union density of UK employees by sector, 1995–2003*

Sources: Labour Force Survey (autumn quarters), Office for National Statistics.

Figures 24.4 and 24.5 show the overall figures, but union membership varies enormously by industry, region, sector, gender and age, and by whether

workers are full time or part time. Union density is slightly higher for men than for women and higher among older employees: more than a third of those aged 35 and over are union members, compared with a quarter of those aged 25–34. Full-time employees are more likely to be trade union members: 32% of full-time workers compared with 21% of part-timers.

DID YOU KNOW?

The typical union member today is likely to be a technician or skilled professional working in the public sector.

There are large regional differences in the proportion of employees who are union members. Union density ranges from 22% in the southeast to 39% in Northern Ireland. Less than 1 in 5 private-sector employees in the UK are union members (a union density of approximately 18%), while almost 3 in 5 public sector employees are union members (a union density of about 59%). Almost half of UK employees are in a workplace where a trade union is present. However, union presence is much lower in the private sector (approximately 35%). Around 36% of all employees are covered by collective agreements.

FACT FILE

Both low-paid and highly paid workers are less likely to be union members than those in middle income ranges. According to the Department of Trade and Industry, employees earning between £250 and £999 per week reported higher union density than those earning either less than £250 or more than £1,000 per week.

Source: *Trade Union Membership* (DTI, 2003).

There are several reasons for the fall in union membership over the last 25 years. These include:

- a dramatic fall in the number of jobs in manufacturing industries, where union membership was traditionally high — for example, shipbuilding, steel and mining
- the privatisation of major utilities, reducing the number of employees in the public sector
- a fall in traditional, permanent, full-time employment and an increase in flexible working, including part-time workers, temporary staff and home workers, who are less likely to join unions or be covered by employment legislation
- an increase in the proportion of the workforce employed by small businesses, many employing fewer than ten workers, where it is often difficult for unions to organise
- legislation that makes it more difficult for unions to operate and keep their members
- improved employment rights for individuals and greater employee participation in the workplace, causing people to feel that unions are less necessary
- a fall in collective bargaining agreements and an increase in deals between individual employees and management

The power of the trade unions has changed as a result of a number of factors:

- Reduced membership, discussed previously, is a major factor.
- Government legislation in the 1980s and 1990s severely limited the ability of trade unions to take industrial action.
- Changes have occurred in the approach of management, which is now more interested in human resource management and puts more emphasis on employee involvement and direct communication.
- The approach of many trade unions has changed. They recognise that international competitiveness in relation to cost and quality are the key to future success and jobs. This has meant that trade unions have been more willing to embrace change and the new technology and training that go with it.
- The economic and political climate, especially low inflation, has made it less likely, for example, that unions will push for higher wage claims.
- Smaller unions have merged to form larger unions with more diverse memberships. Such amalgamations have led to fewer unions but more powerful ones, representing a greater and more varied membership. These trade unions are in a far stronger bargaining position, with more finance to offer the range of services that members demand.

FILE

In February 2005, two of the UK's biggest unions agreed to start merger discussions in a move that could lead to the creation of a 2.5-million-member 'super union'. Amicus and the TGWU are to invite the GMB to join in the talks. Union bosses suggested that a merger would create a 'major force' to protect working people's interests and would allow them to avoid the pointless inter-union competition for members. It would also send a message to employers that the trade unions intend to match the power of capital with the power of united labour. Any merger would have to be approved by the unions' executives and their membership.

The Trades Union Congress

The Trades Union Congress (TUC) is the national organisation that represents trade unions in the UK. It has 67 affiliated (member) unions representing nearly six and a half million working people. Trade unions join the TUC because they know that they can be stronger and more effective if they work together with other unions to protect the rights of working people. One small union has little chance of achieving things alone, but by adding its voice to that of other unions, it has far more chance of success.

The TUC was formed in 1868 and has had periods of considerable influence on government decision making, particularly in the 1970s. In the 1980s and 1990s, its role diminished and it was excluded from consultation by the government. The TUC aims to:

- combat injustice in the workplace and promote equality of opportunity for working people and the unemployed

- help the UK have a strong economy by encouraging unions and employers to work in partnership to improve the competitiveness of organisations
- provide the affiliated unions with high-quality information, research and education programmes that help them take up issues that affect their members and that assist them to recruit and retain subscribers

Its functions are to:
- be the voice of the union movement as whole
- prevent or solve inter-union disputes
- promote international labour solidarity, especially within Europe
- act as a pressure group to influence government policy on labour and union issues

While TUC unions represent the vast majority of trade unionists in the UK, there are a number of unions that are not affiliated (i.e. not members). Most of these are small organisations representing specialist staff and, in many cases, employees of a particular organisation. There are, however, some substantial organisations that are outside the TUC. These include the Police Federation, which is barred by law from affiliating to the TUC.

Employers' associations

Just as trade unions represent employees, so employers' associations represent the views and interests of companies within a sector or industry — for example, the Engineering Employers' Federation. They are especially useful for small firms negotiating with large trade unions. Like trade unions, they are financed by members' subscriptions. Their functions include:
- providing advice to employers about collective bargaining
- acting as a pressure group influencing government policy in areas of interest to the sector or industry they represent
- researching and providing information, such as sales figures for the industry as a whole or guides on new procedures or legislation
- providing a negotiating team that can agree minimum pay and conditions with trade unions throughout the industry

FACT FILE

The **Confederation of British Industry** (CBI) was formed in 1965. It performs a similar role to the TUC. It is the main employers' association and includes most of the country's leading firms as members. Its main functions are to:
- lobby the government in order to influence legislation and economic policies favoured by the private sector
- promote the image of industry as a worthwhile career
- provide its members with well-researched reports, such as the CBI's *Quarterly Survey of Economic Trends*

The CBI works with the TUC on consultative bodies such as ACAS.

Improving industrial relations

KEY TERM

industrial relations: the atmosphere prevailing between a management and its workforce representatives — the trade unions.

Successful industrial relations result when both employers and trade unions compromise and recognise each other's objectives and needs. In situations where this does not occur, actions by one side often have adverse consequences for both sides. For example, if a union demanded a substantial pay increase for its members and this led to an increase in the firm's costs and the prices of its products, this might reduce the firm's competitiveness, lead to a fall in demand for its products and ultimately result in redundancies. Equally, a decision by management to increase the average weekly hours of work might lead to a reduction in employees' motivation, increased absenteeism and higher labour turnover, and eventually have an adverse effect on productivity.

EXAMINER'S VOICE

Consideration of the role of trade unions is likely to arise in case studies or essays about individual businesses. Ensure that you apply your knowledge effectively to the given context.

Many people still perceive trade unions to be a negative force. To counter this, both the TUC and the UK government have been promoting a new 'partnership approach' within the workplace, attempting to stress the benefits that cooperation rather than antagonism can bring. Trade unions have attempted to add value to business as well as enhancing the benefits provided to their members. These partnership approaches generally involve a far greater degree of employee involvement in key decisions (with the unions playing a vital coordinating role), together with much greater information sharing to eliminate any sense of a 'them-and-us' culture.

According to the TUC, a strong sense of worker participation in decisions, often coordinated through trade unions, seems in recent years to have enhanced business performance. One of its recent reports suggests that, while initiatives such as employee share ownership schemes have some impact on growth and profitability, employee involvement has been the key. One study reported that organisations that had strong employee involvement were growing four to five times as quickly as those that did not, even though both groups had share ownership schemes. Other research has suggested a link between employee representation and productivity.

It would be simplistic, however, to suggest that strong worker representation is, by itself, a benefit to businesses. The common factor in successful organisations has been a management team that is highly committed to including employees. This has given rise to the concept of partnership, where unions and employees work together with an open-minded management to generate positive change and growth for the business (see the Thames Water case study on page 224).

Recent strikes by firefighters, underground workers, train drivers and airport staff can leave us in no doubt that a partnership approach has been far from

universally adopted. However, it is clear that some businesses and unions have managed to overcome the distrust that employers and trade unions have traditionally felt for each other, and those that have done so have reported clear benefits.

PRACTICE EXERCISE — Total: 45 marks (40 minutes)

1 Explain three functions that trade unions carry out on behalf of their members. *(9 marks)*

2 State two benefits of trade unions for employers. *(2 marks)*

3 Identify three forms of industrial action that trade union members might take. *(3 marks)*

4 Why might industrial action have an adverse impact on employees? *(4 marks)*

5 State three factors that might influence the success of industrial action. *(3 marks)*

6 Explain the following terms:
 a no-strike agreement *(2 marks)*
 b single-union agreement *(2 marks)*
 c pendulum arbitration *(3 marks)*

7 What is the role of ACAS? *(4 marks)*

8 Explain the terms 'conciliation' and 'arbitration'. *(6 marks)*

9 Identify three reasons for the fall in union membership over the last 25 years. *(3 marks)*

10 Suggest possible consequences of further mergers between the UK's largest trade unions. *(4 marks)*

CASE STUDY Thames Water

A good example of the benefits that a partnership approach can bring is demonstrated by Thames Water. The company recognises four unions, and operates in a highly regulated environment. By 1999 it was coming under heavy pressure from the Competition Commission and shareholders simultaneously. The unions suggested that the way forward might be a partnership agreement. As discussions about this progressed, both sides realised that greater employee involvement might be a route by which changes to archaic working practices could be brought about. The central concept of the partnership is a 'Partnership Forum' with seven directors and seven elected representatives, but the real heart of it is changed approaches throughout the business in terms of the way decisions are taken, which have brought benefits to employees and business alike.

Pay negotiations

One example is the annual round of pay negotiations. In the past this had tended to be a prolonged process of offer and counter-offer, with neither side prepared to divulge key information. As a result, the negotiations were felt to be antagonistic. The most recent round of pay negotiations was very different. The partnership approach meant that the key information was known to both management and unions as a result of their shared approach to decision making on a day-to-day basis. Negotiations that had previously taken months were concluded in 2 days.

New shift system

Another example is a change in the shift system, which had previously created an annual £1 million overtime bill. Thames Water had attempted to change the system in the past, but with no success due to a complex system of local agreements and precedents. For the first time, shift workers (assisted by union representatives and managers) took part in the discussions about possible changes. Over a 3-month period, a new system was agreed that was expected to save Thames Water £380,000 a year but also gave employees more say over the hours that they worked.

Thus, in both cases, effective employee involvement, facilitated by constructive union support, has brought substantial business benefits as well as helping to improve terms and conditions for employees.

Source: adapted from Simon Harrison, 'Employee–employer relations in the UK', *Business Review*, November 2003.

Questions

Total: 20 marks (25 minutes)

1 Examine two benefits to Thames Water of a partnership approach between the trade unions and the employer. *(8 marks)*

2 'Trade unions are no longer necessary given the increasing emphasis on employee participation and the recent EU Information and Consultation Directive.' Discuss this statement in the context of Thames Water. *(12 marks)*

CHAPTER 25

Principles of employment law

This chapter considers both individual labour law and collective labour law, and explains the impact of employment legislation on business. It develops issues and discusses legislation first introduced in the AS specification.

Employment law falls into two main categories: individual labour law and collective labour law.

Individual labour law

Individual labour law aims to ensure that employees and employers act fairly in dealing with each other and relates to the rights and the obligations of individual employees. Since 1970, the amount of individual labour law has increased considerably, with the influence of the European Union being a significant contributory factor behind this trend. We will briefly look at the main legislation in this area.

Equal Pay Act, 1970 and Equal Pay Directive, 1975

The 1970 Act states that both sexes should receive equal pay and conditions for equal work. Thus a woman employed in the same job as a man must have the same pay and conditions.

This legislation has been strengthened by the EU's 1975 Equal Pay Directive, which established the principle of equal pay for work of equal value.

TOPFOTO

Sex Discrimination Acts, 1975 and 1986

In the employment field, the 1975 Act's main purpose is to outlaw discriminatory practices relating to recruitment, promotion, dismissal and access to benefits, facilities or services. It is not directly concerned with discrimination in relation to pay. The Equal Opportunities Commission was established in 1975 to enforce this legislation.

The 1986 Act enables the government to introduce a common retirement age for men and women.

Race Relations Act, 1976 and Race Relations (Amendment) Act, 2000

The 1976 Act makes it unlawful to discriminate, in relation to employment, against men or women on the grounds of sex, marital status, colour, race, nationality, or ethnic or national origin. These provisions apply to the recruitment of employees and to the way they are treated once employed. This legislation is enforced by the Commission for Racial Equality.

The 2000 Act strengthens but does not replace the 1976 Act, requiring public bodies, including schools, colleges and universities, to take positive steps towards racial equality in both their employment practices and the services they give to the public.

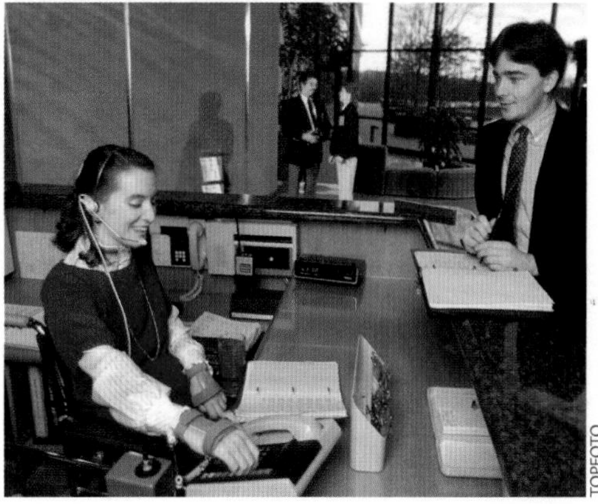
TOPFOTO

Disability Discrimination Act, 1995

The main employment-related provisions of the 1995 Act are to make it unlawful for an employer to treat a disabled person less favourably than others and to require employers to make reasonable adjustments to working conditions and to the working environment in order to help overcome the practical effects of disability.

The Working Time Directive, 1999

This Directive limits the average working week to 48 hours. At the moment, the UK has an opt-out arrangement. Employees can agree to work longer if they wish to. The European Commission is proposing to change this so that employers must negotiate the opt-outs with trade unions, rather than with individual employees.

FACT FILE

The 2003 Labour Force Survey found that 4 million people work more than 48 hours a week on average — 700,000 more than in 1992 when there was no legislation in place to protect workers from long hours.

DID YOU KNOW?

In 2002, the Department for Trade and Industry (DTI) found that twice as many UK employees would prefer working shorter hours to winning the lottery than the reverse.

The National Minimum Wage Act, 1998

This Act resulted from an EU Employment Directive and was introduced by the Labour government after it came to power. The minimum wage increases each year in line with the rise in the cost of living.

Recent changes in individual labour law

Additional legislation implementing EU employment directives to outlaw unfair discrimination came into force recently under the Employment Equality (Sexual Orientation and Religion or Belief) Regulations, 2003.

In December 2004, the government announced legislation to outlaw age discrimination in the workplace. This is part of the EU's Employment Directive and is scheduled to come into force in October 2006. It will set a default retirement age of 65, but also create a right for employees to request working beyond a compulsory retirement age, which employers will have a duty to consider. It will also allow employers to justify earlier retirement ages if they can show that these are appropriate and necessary.

FACT FILE

As a member of the EU, Ireland already has age discrimination legislation — approximately 19% of all formal discrimination claims in Ireland involve allegations of ageism. One high-profile case involved the budget airline Ryanair, which had advertised for a 'young, dynamic professional'. The airline claimed in its defence that the term 'young' meant 'young at heart', but evidence submitted showed that none of the 28 candidates who applied for the job was over 40. Ryanair was fined for contravening legislation.

In 2003, parents of young and disabled children were given the right to request flexible working arrangements. Representatives of smaller businesses said the resulting increase in costs would be crippling. Now there are proposals to extend paid maternity leave from 6 to 12 months and to raise paternity-leave pay. This would take the rate from the present £102 per week to 90% of earnings (the rate for maternity leave). Also under review is a plan to extend the right to request flexible working to people who look after elderly relatives.

DID YOU KNOW?

In relation to the maternity and paternity leave regulations, an anonymous food wholesaler said: 'How can you run a business if somebody is not there? Often it takes 6 months just to train up temporary staff. I try not to employ too many people who give me that sort of problem but these days you are not allowed to discriminate.'

Collective employment law

Collective labour law aims to influence industrial relations and control the activities of trade unions. The Conservative governments of the 1980s and 1990s generally believed that trade union power was excessive, especially in relation to wage negotiations, and that trade unions were disruptive and prevented changes in working practices. Governments during this period sought to reduce the influence of trade unions by introducing a series of acts of parliament that progressively limited their ability to take action. By restricting the power of trade unions and breaking down barriers and restrictions in the labour market, this legislation had the long-term effect of liberalising the economy.

Employment Act, 1980

Under this legislation, employers were no longer obliged to recognise or negotiate with a particular union or unions. The Act also restricted picketing to striking employees' own place of work, limited lawful secondary action to direct suppliers or customers, and introduced the first restrictions on closed shops, permitting the introduction of new closed shops only if 80% of the workforce voted in favour of them in a secret ballot.

KEY TERMS

picketing: when a group of striking workers involved in an industrial dispute gathers at the entrance of the premises and attempts to dissuade other workers, suppliers and customers from crossing the picket line and therefore breaking the strike.

secondary action: industrial action at a place other than where the dispute originated.

closed shop: where a union requires an organisation to employ only members of one union or requires individuals employed in that organisation to join that union.

The Act limited the number of picketing workers to six, making illegal the use of mass picketing, which can intimidate those thinking of going to work or doing business with the organisation. An example of mass picketing is **secondary picketing**, which means setting up a picket line at a place other then where an industrial dispute originated. All such forms of action were made illegal through a series of Employment Acts during the 1980s, culminating in the Employment Act, 1990.

TOPFOTO

Employment Act, 1982

This Act further tightened the rules introduced in 1980. It further restricted lawful industrial action by redefining the meaning of a 'lawful dispute'. The Act removed a trade union's immunity from damages if it authorised unlawful industrial action (making unions liable for damages of up to £250,000), and made it easier for an employer to dismiss striking workers. Closed shop union membership agreements were made harder to enforce by increasing the required vote in favour in a secret ballot to 85%.

Trade Union Act, 1984

This legislation made trade unions liable to be sued by employers if they authorised a strike without a secret ballot of the membership. In addition, it required trade unions to elect or re-elect voting members of their national executive every 5 years (or less) in order to improve democratic decision making.

Employment Act, 1988

This legislation further tightened the controls on trade unions by insisting that all voting members of the unions' national governing committees must be elected by postal ballot of the entire membership every 5 years. It also provided the specific wording to be used on voting papers in industrial action ballots, and introduced laws protecting union members from being disciplined by their unions for ignoring strike calls or for refusing to picket, even if the result of a ballot favoured industrial action.

Employment Act, 1989

This Act was designed to 'remove outdated, unnecessary barriers to women's employment and relieve young people and their employers of a mass of bureaucratic restraints'. Some critics argued that the 'barriers' were far from unnecessary or outdated. Its main provisions were to remove all restrictions on the hours of work of young people (previously night work had been prohibited), to remove discriminatory legislation against women (previously there had existed a ban on women working underground in mines) and to abolish the Industrial Training Boards.

Employment Act, 1990

The main provision of this Act was to make it unlawful for an employer to refuse to employ a non-union worker, which meant the end of the closed shop. The act also made unlawful any remaining forms of secondary action. It made trade unions liable for almost all industrial action taken by their members, and allowed employers to dismiss any worker for taking part in an unofficial strike without the worker having the right to complain of unfair dismissal to an industrial tribunal.

Trade Union Reform and Employment Rights Act, 1993

In passing this Act, the government's aims were to increase the rights of individual employees and trade union members, and to improve competitiveness. Critics argued that the act was, in fact, designed to weaken trade unions. Its main provisions included requiring trade unions to provide employers with at least 7 days' notice of official industrial action. It also abolished the remaining wages councils and their statutory minimum pay rates.

The above legislation, introduced by successive Conservative governments throughout the 1980s and the early 1990s, was designed to restrict trade union power, give employees choice and protect employers. The Labour government that came to power in 1997 retained much of this legislation but aimed to provide employees with more protection in the workplace and to encourage a partnership between unions and business.

Employment Relations Acts, 1999 and 2004

The 1999 Act aimed to increase employees' rights in relation to trade union membership and claims for unfair dismissal. Its key measures included reducing the employment qualifying period for those claiming unfair dismissal from 2 years to 1 year and increasing the maximum sum that courts can force firms to pay to a worker who has been unfairly dismissed from £12,000 to £50,000. It also introduced a statutory procedure for employees to obtain union recognition where there is clear support among the workforce. If 50% or more of the workforce is in a union, recognition cannot be refused by the employer. In other situations, employers have to recognise a trade union if at least 40% of workers eligible to do so take part in a ballot, and a majority of those voting are in favour of recognition.

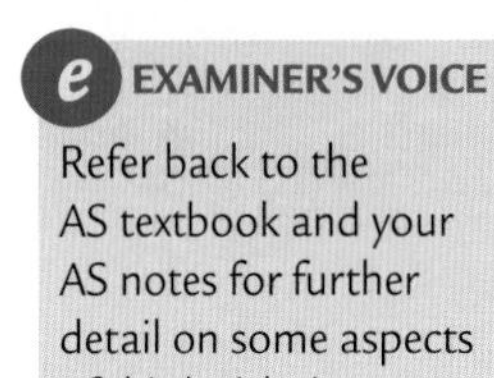

EXAMINER'S VOICE
Refer back to the AS textbook and your AS notes for further detail on some aspects of this legislation.

The 2004 Act amends and extends earlier legislation, paving the way for the implementation of information exchange and consultation between employers and employees.

The impact of employment law on business

Individual legislation is intended to protect employees, who are usually in a weaker bargaining position than their employers, and to reduce the possibility of an employer exploiting its employees through unfair practices. In general, collective legislation is intended to protect employers from the actions of powerful trade unions. Overall, the impact of employment legislation has both positive and negative consequences for business.

Impact on disruption

Fewer working days are now lost due to strike action (see Figures 24.1 and 24.2 on p. 216), which is likely to be a consequence of the progressive constraints imposed on trade union activity by legislation over the last 25 years.

Impact on costs

Business is likely to incur increased costs in order to implement legislation and provide for the rights of individual workers.

Impact on small businesses

Small businesses may suffer more from employment legislation. For example, large businesses can spread the risks of a request for maternity leave or can organise their working hours to fit in with the Working Time Directive relatively easily. Small businesses, by their nature, are sometimes much less flexible. There may be no one to stand in for an absent key person, or fulfilling an urgent order may be difficult with a small workforce if working time is limited. Taking on an extra person to cope temporarily will raise costs, which may mean a loss of profit; or if it means charging higher prices, the business may lose competitiveness and face reduced demand, again affecting profit. In addition, complying with the law means that one needs to know about it first. Here again, large businesses usually employ people whose entire job is to be familiar with current legislation and the changes it requires. In a small business, the owner has to study the regulations in between doing many other things.

FACT FILE

Stephen Alambritis, spokesman for the Federation of Small Businesses, wants a moratorium on new employment legislation. He says: 'The government has imposed 17 major pieces of new employment legislation since 1997. Owner-managers have to acquaint themselves with all of it, whereas a large company would have a legal department to deal with it. The vast majority of business start-ups are now sole traders because they are worried about employment legislation. The average small business spends 30 hours a month dealing with red tape.'

Impact on efficiency and productivity

Equal opportunities legislation should ensure that the 'right' person for the job is selected, resulting in an effective and efficient workforce, which in turn might have a positive impact on productivity.

Impact on motivation

If the relationship between employers and employees improves as a result of legislation, then motivation is likely to improve.

Conclusion

There are many different perspectives on employment legislation. Big businesses usually cope with new laws and regulations, although they may complain. Small businesses may despair of the red tape and the compliance costs. But many large and small businesses are unconcerned because their policies are at least as favourable to the employee as the minimum required by law. These firms ensure that they take good care of their employees, recognising that by doing so they are likely to secure the loyalty of their staff and have lower staff turnover.

EXAMINER'S VOICE

Ensure that you remember the terms introduced at AS so that you can use them effectively at A2. An example is 'corporate culture', meaning the code of an organisation (perhaps unwritten) that affects the attitudes, decision making and management style of its staff.

FACT FILE

Innocent Drinks, the fruit smoothie maker, gives each new parent on its staff a tax-free bonus of £2,000 towards the costs of the new baby. It routinely goes beyond the legal requirements in its employment practices. It thinks that the motivating effect of this and its other innovative staff benefits far outweighs the extra costs entailed. The company is seen by its employees as an exceptionally good employer and this has produced a highly positive corporate culture.

Regardless of the concerns of individual firms, the principle of the level playing field is highly significant in relation to employment legislation. By requiring that all businesses, whether large or small, have to abide by the same laws and regulations, the government ensures that they can all compete on equal terms. By harmonising employment legislation, the EU ensures common standards in all member countries and hence a level playing field across Europe.

PRACTICE EXERCISE — Total: 30 marks (25 minutes)

1 Distinguish between individual labour law and collective labour law. *(4 marks)*

2 What is the difference between equal pay for equal work and equal pay for work of equal value? *(4 marks)*

3 Identify three types of discrimination in employment that legislation seeks to outlaw. *(3 marks)*

4 Why is there a need for individual labour law? *(3 marks)*

5 Briefly summarise the impact of the collective labour legislation of the 1980s and 1990s on the actions of trade unions. *(3 marks)*

6 Explain one positive way in which employment legislation impacts on a firm. *(3 marks)*

7 Explain one negative way in which employment legislation impacts on a firm. *(3 marks)*

8 Why might the impact of employment legislation be much harsher on a small firm than on a large one? *(4 marks)*

9 What is meant by a 'level playing field' in relation to employment legislation? *(3 marks)*

CASE STUDY Just Chocolate

Just Chocolate is a small, private and limited family firm that makes fancy chocolates. It has three directors: the owner, who is managing director and responsible for strategy, including product and market development; the administration manager, responsible for general administration, purchasing, personnel and day-to-day finance; and the production manager.

Because of adverse market conditions in the past, including a high pound and cheap imports from Europe, the firm moved to a core and peripheral workforce structure. From 25 employees in the mid-1990s it now has five employees, supplemented, on a seasonal basis, by up to 25 agency staff.

The following comments about employment legislation were made by the owner of the business:

'I don't think that we need regulation. A business that forces people to work 60 hours a week is unlikely to prosper. What you get if people work too many hours is diminishing returns and productivity begins to fall off.'

TOPFOTO

'We've had no incidence of maternity leave since we reduced the staff to the core. A business of this size couldn't afford to keep someone on maternity leave.'

'All regulations are an intrusion.'

'Legislation has no positive impact. We would be better off without it because we never exploit our employees.'

'We don't want to employ people direct, because once we've had them for 12 weeks, we can't really get rid of them — we've got them for life.'

'One of the biggest problems is not knowing about all of the legislation — and then it's too late. I think somebody in government should ensure that all small businesses have a handbook that lists what they should do in relation to every piece of law.'

Question

Total: 20 marks (25 minutes)

To what extent do you believe that the owner's comments about employment legislation are justified?

CHAPTER 26

Human resource management and workforce planning

This chapter revisits and further develops aspects of human resource management and workforce planning studied at AS. It analyses two different approaches to human resource management (HRM): 'hard' HRM and 'soft' HRM. It then focuses on workforce planning as an integrated process, taking into account production, marketing and corporate plans.

Human resource management

KEY TERM

human resource management: the management of people at work in order to assist the organisation in achieving its objectives.

Human resource management is the strategic process of making the most efficient use of an organisation's employees. People are a vital resource for modern businesses, and planning their use must be part of strategic management if a business is to compete in global markets. HRM views activities relating to the workforce as integrated and vital in helping the organisation to achieve its corporate objectives. Thus, policies relating to recruitment, pay and appraisal should be formulated as part of a coordinated human resource strategy.

Human resource management versus personnel management

Since the 1980s, HRM has tended to replace personnel management in describing the function within business that focuses on the selection, appraisal, development and reward of people. Referring to people as 'human resources' might sound mechanical, but in fact the objective of the approach is really the opposite. The intention is to emphasise a total strategy related to a firm's most valued resource, rather than the set of functions that a personnel management department was commonly expected to undertake.

Personnel management regarded activities such as planning the workforce, recruitment and selection, training, appraisal, monitoring performance, and motivation and rewards as separate tasks to be done when necessary and in response to demand: in other words, it was *reactive*. HRM, on the other hand, regards all of these activities as being linked and integrated with all other areas and functions of the business and its development: that is, it is *proactive*.

Table 26.1 summarises the main differences between human resource management and personnel management.

Table 26.1

The personnel management approach	The human resource management approach
• is tactical	• is strategic
• is short term and responds to policies introduced in other areas of the organisation	• is long term and leads policies in other areas of the organisation
• tackles issues separately with no overall framework	• places issues within a clearly defined and integrated framework that benefits the organisation
• tends to operate in organisations with traditional ways of working, where there is little employee involvement in decision making	• emphasises the importance of involving employees in decision making
• may operate in traditionally unionised organisations	• encourages single-status agreements and places less emphasis on the role of trade unions
• focuses on getting identical rewards and conditions for groups of individuals	• focuses on individual contracts and payment and reward systems
• tends to specialise in all of the personnel function activities — recruitment, selection and training etc.	• tends to devolve personnel function activities, such as recruitment, selection and training, to departmental managers, concentrating instead on developing policies, planning, monitoring and evaluating

There are two different approaches to human resource management: 'hard' HRM and 'soft' HRM.

Hard human resource management

KEY TERM

hard HRM: human resource management that takes the view that employees are essential for a business to function but need to be controlled.

EXAMINER'S VOICE

Refer back to F. W. Taylor, one of the motivation theorists studied at AS. He viewed employees as a resource and believed that managers should manage and that workers should be told what to do and be paid according to their output — an approach that is not dissimilar to hard HRM.

Under this approach, the aim is to utilise employees as efficiently as possible by directing them. Hard HRM treats employees simply as another resource, like raw materials or fixed capital. Just like any other resource, employees need to be monitored, used efficiently and have their costs controlled, in order to achieve the strategic objectives of the organisation. This approach sees HRM as essentially a control mechanism. The style of management in organisations using hard HRM is likely to be authoritarian or autocratic, and because the approach requires that authority is kept in the hands of a few, it is likely to involve a centralised rather than decentralised organisational structure. This type of HRM includes workforce planning, analysing the current and future demand for and supply of employees, and predicting labour turnover.

Soft human resource management

KEY TERM

soft HRM: human resource management that views employees as valuable assets to be developed; because of their skills and expertise, they are a major source of competitive advantage for the firm and hence of vital importance in achieving the strategic objectives of the organisation.

Soft HRM focuses on motivational issues and organisational culture, leadership approaches and industrial relations. As it is essentially a strategy for the personal development of all staff, soft HRM is likely to be associated with a democratic management style. With this approach, managers will wish to pass authority throughout the organisation and are likely to favour delegation and decentralisation rather than centralisation. Equally, because firms that embrace a soft HRM approach recognise that they will benefit from employees' ideas, they are likely to encourage high levels of employee participation.

EXAMINER'S VOICE

Ensure that you are confident about the knowledge you gained at AS in relation to management/leadership styles.

Which approach?

Whether a company adopts a soft or hard approach to HRM depends largely on the history and culture of the firm, the approach and attitudes of managers and their management style, their relationship with recognised trade unions, the skills and attitudes of staff and the level of employee participation in decision making.

Today, employees are likely to react more favourably to the soft HRM approach than to the hard HRM approach. As employees become increasingly educated and skilled, they begin to expect greater involvement in business decision making. This is encouraged by trends in industrial relations in the workplace, such as the partnership approach that is being adopted by some organisations and their recognised trade unions, requirements for European works councils and the recent EU Information and Consultation Directive (see Chapter 23).

The possible benefits of effective HRM strategies for a firm are huge, including more motivated and committed staff, who contribute more ideas and exhibit greater loyalty. These factors, in turn, are likely to lead to lower labour turnover, less absenteeism and greater productivity, all of which can be used as indicators of effective HRM within an organisation (see Chapter 28).

Workforce planning

KEY TERM

workforce planning (or **human resource planning**): the method by which a business forecasts how many and what type of employees it needs now and in the future, and matches the right type of employees to the needs of the business.

Workforce planning is one of the central activities of human resource management and helps organisations to foresee change, to identify trends and to implement human resource policies. It is an important part of the overall strategic plan and should be centralised to ensure a whole-company view.

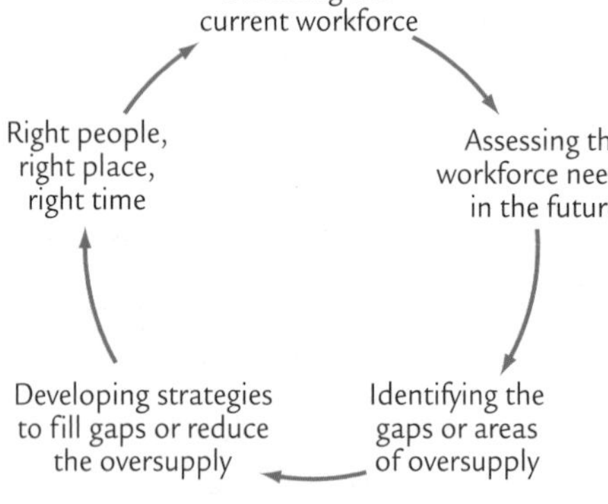

Figure 26.1 Workforce planning cycle

Efficient workforce planning requires managers to question the existing employment structure at every opportunity — for example when an employee leaves the firm, when an employee is promoted internally, when there is an increase in workload or when a new product or new technology is developed that requires employees with different skills.

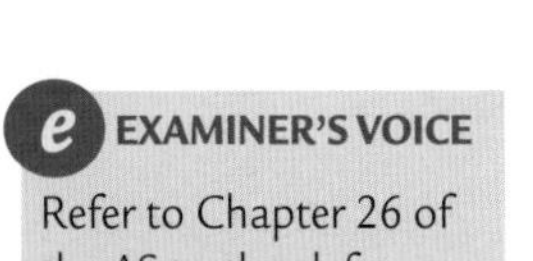

EXAMINER'S VOICE

Refer to Chapter 26 of the AS textbook for more detailed background on workforce planning.

Stages in workforce planning

Workforce planning involves a number of stages to ensure that the right people are in the right place at the right time in order to meet the organisation's objectives. These are summarised in the workforce planning cycle (Figure 26.1) and covered in more detail below:

- Examining the corporate objectives of the organisation and converting these objectives into human resource requirements.
- Making a judgement about the size and nature of the workforce required over the short, medium and long term in relation to these objectives.
- Estimating the future demand for skills and staff in relation to this judgement about the size and nature of the workforce required. Table 26.2 illustrates a stage in national workforce planning for dentistry in the National Health Service by identifying a range of factors and how they affect the supply of, and demand for, dental services in the future.
- Comparing the future demand for skills and staff with the organisation's current workforce and estimating the changes required in the existing supply of labour in the short, medium and long term, taking into account potential labour turnover and retirement.
- Estimating the future state of the labour market and the availability of staff with the required skills and attributes in the short, medium and long term.
- Developing an appropriate workforce plan for the short, medium and long term, involving recruitment and training, and possibly redeployment or transfers and redundancies, in order to match the current workforce with the desired one.

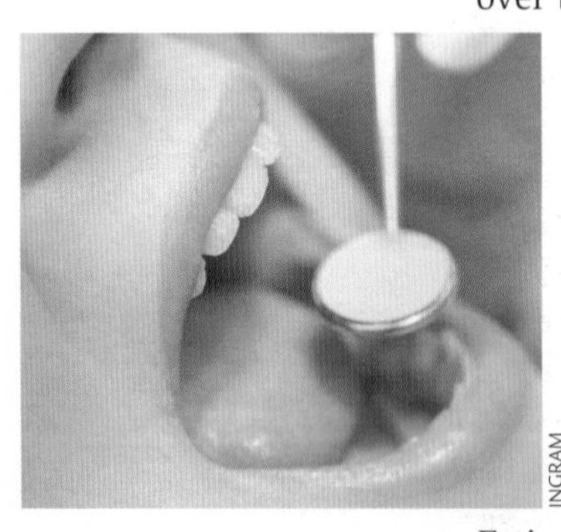
INGRAM

WHAT DO YOU THINK?

Approximately 31% of the total workforce, 53% of managers and supervisors and 65% of senior executives are eligible to retire in the next 5 years. What do you think are the possible consequences of this for the UK economy?

Demand factors	Estimated effect on demand
Trend of increased demand for all health services	Increase in demand
Increasing proportion of the elderly in the population	Increase in demand
Increasing number of individuals who have natural teeth	Increase in demand
Increasing number of more complex treatments available	Increase in demand
Increasing public expectations of dental treatments/services	Increase in demand
Increasing proportion of children with untreated decay	Increase in demand
Reduction in oral disease	Reduction in demand
Technological changes	Increase/reduction in demand

Supply factors	Estimated effect on supply
Predicted decline in number of registered dentists	Reduction in supply
Increased early retirements and part-time working	Reduction in supply
Increased availability of dentists from overseas	Increase in supply
Reduction in UK dental graduates	Reduction in supply
Loss of dental workforce to other countries	Reduction in supply
Increase in non-NHS working	Reduction in supply
Working Time Directive, conditions of service, e.g. maternity leave, etc.	Reduction in supply
Dissatisfaction with working conditions	Reduction in supply

Table 26.2 Factors influencing the supply of, and demand for, dental services

Construction of a workforce plan

Factors that influence the construction of a workforce plan and the number and type of employees required in the short, medium and long term include:

- the organisation's corporate plan, which includes overall objectives. It is vital that workforce planning is recognised as a part of the strategic plan and that its aim is to ensure that human resources are sufficient to facilitate the meeting of its overall corporate objectives
- the organisation's marketing and production plans, which respectively include the overall marketing and production objectives. Workforce planning needs to ensure that sufficient workers, in relation to skill and job level, are available to meet the requirements of the marketing and production departments
- the financial position of the organisation, in order to determine whether it is able to fund the requirements of the workforce plan
- external factors, including the state of the market and the economy, which are likely to affect the demand for products and services and therefore the actual need for workers, their availability and their cost

Reviewing the workforce plan

A workforce plan might prove inaccurate for a number of reasons:

- There may be changes in **corporate objectives**, following a change in ownership or as a result of a crisis or competition.
- Changes in **market conditions** might occur, causing demand for products to fall, thus leaving the firm with an oversupply of employees. Unless demand is expected to pick up, the organisation may have to consider issuing redundancy notices. Similarly, a firm may face a sudden huge

increase in demand for its products because a competitor has gone out of business. In such a situation, it may be faced with a sudden shortage of staff.

- Changes in the **labour market** might occur. For example, fewer young people may be available for full-time work if the government achieves its target of getting 50% of all young people into higher education. On the other hand, there may be more people over 60 available for work if changes are made to pensions and current retirement dates. Similarly, the concentration of particular **skills** may change; there may be insufficient people available with the skills required by the organisation, and the wages they demand may increase as a consequence. In such a situation, a firm may decide that it is more efficient to train its own staff rather than recruit trained staff from outside. The costs of labour may suddenly increase, as they did for some organisations when the government introduced the minimum wage.

TOPFOTO

Changes such as those indicated above suggest that effective workforce planning requires the constant review and update of forecasts in order to take full account of any changes in circumstances.

Benefits of workforce planning

Without effective workforce planning that takes into account appropriate forecasting of future trends, problems might occur. For example, there could be problems in recruiting and selecting appropriately skilled individuals, or staff could be inadequately trained for new processes that are introduced. Morale and motivation problems might occur if existing workers are expected to cover staff shortages. This in turn might lead to high levels of stress, more absenteeism and labour turnover, and increased costs for the business, which in the longer term may affect demand and competitiveness.

EXAMINER'S VOICE

Given the discussion of employee participation in Chapter 23, it is likely that employees and their representatives should be consulted in order to ensure effective workforce planning that is accepted throughout the organisation.

Without workforce planning, managers will simply react to events when they occur rather than being prepared for them, which may lead to hasty and poor-quality decision making when it comes to staffing.

Firms undergoing continual change may find workforce planning more difficult. However, such firms still need to recruit the right number of employees and ensure that staff have the right skills and attitudes. If anything, workforce planning is likely to be even more important for firms that operate in markets that are constantly changing than in other markets, since few firms can afford either to have too many staff or to be short of staff at critical moments.

The benefits of effective workforce planning are significant in that it ensures that an organisation has a sufficient and appropriately skilled workforce to meet its objectives. On a practical level, it enables an organisation to avoid labour shortages and thus to ensure that production continues. This means that customer demand is met on time, with products in sufficient quantity and of the right quality. It therefore allows an organisation to compete more effectively in the market.

DID YOU KNOW?

Workforce planning may involve the introduction of outsourcing, that is, the transfer of internal activity to a third party. Reasons for this might include:

- a chance to use expertise not otherwise available to the organisation
- offloading low-level administrative work
- freeing employees to undertake more interesting work
- reducing costs

Areas of work commonly outsourced include:

- recruitment (for example, initial stages of processing enquiries and applications, and carrying out standard assessments)
- training design, development and implementation
- personnel-related activities
- payroll
- pensions
- information systems
- security

PRACTICE EXERCISE 1 — Total: 40 marks (35 minutes)

1 Distinguish between human resource management and personnel management. *(5 marks)*

2 Explain one main characteristic of the 'hard' approach to human resource management. *(3 marks)*

3 Explain one main characteristic of the 'soft' approach to human resource management. *(3 marks)*

4 How might effective human resource management strategies benefit a firm? *(4 marks)*

5 Explain the term 'workforce planning'. *(3 marks)*

6 Identify four stages involved in workforce planning. *(4 marks)*

7 Explain how workforce planning is linked to the marketing and production plans of an organisation and to the overall corporate plan. *(6 marks)*

8 Explain two reasons that may cause a workforce plan to be inaccurate. *(6 marks)*

9 Identify two possible long-term consequences for a firm that does not have a workforce plan. *(6 marks)*

PRACTICE EXERCISE 2

Total: 20 marks (25 minutes)

1 Workforce planning is an important process for both public- and private-sector organisations. The following information provides brief details of the planning process in Tameside Metropolitan Borough Council.

> Tameside is located in the eastern part of the Greater Manchester conurbation. Tameside Metropolitan Borough Council has 9,100 employees and serves a community of 220,000 people.
>
> Workforce planning is seen as essential to ensure that the council can attract and retain people with the right levels of skills to support the needs of the community.
>
> Workforce planning is an embedded practice within the authority and is seen as an integral part of the overall business planning process. The HR function has a pivotal role in carrying out HR planning; this includes providing data collection and analysis.
>
> Typical data collection and analysis covers:
>
> - leavers (labour turnover)
> - employees aged 55 and over
> - employees due to retire (that is, those aged 65 within the planning cycle)
> - employees on fixed-term contracts
> - age and service profiles of employees during the planning cycle
>
> Source: www.lg-employers.gov.uk.

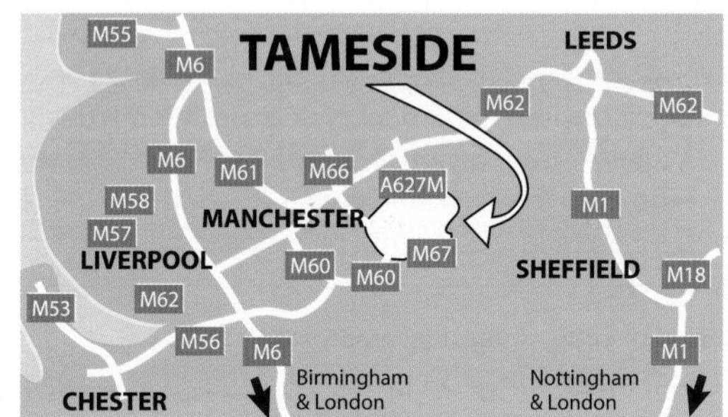

Briefly examine the consequences of not having a detailed workforce plan for a large organisation such as a local authority or a public limited company. *(6 marks)*

2 Refer to Table 26.2 on p. 239, which provides an analysis of a range of factors and how they affect the supply of, and demand for, dental services. Evaluate possible strategies that the government might consider in order to ensure that sufficient dentists are available in the NHS in the future. *(14 marks)*

CHAPTER 27

Human resource management and methods of remuneration

This chapter builds upon Chapter 23 of the AS textbook. It assumes that students are familiar with the various forms of financial incentive used in business (particularly time rates, piecework, performance-related pay, profit sharing, share ownership/share options and fringe benefits) and considers how methods of remuneration are linked to the goals of human resource management.

Remuneration and corporate objectives

KEY TERM

remuneration: the complete set of rewards offered by an organisation to its employees; it goes beyond actual pay and may include pension contributions, share options and other fringe benefits, including company cars.

Any decision to change or introduce a particular remuneration system has implications for different aspects of a business and its strategy. In relation to financial incentive schemes, consideration needs to be given as to how each type of incentive matches or contributes to the corporate objectives. For example, one objective of an organisation might be to achieve a national reputation based upon the quality of its products or services. In such an organisation, if financial incentives are high and very firmly based on *quantity*, such as the provision of generous piece rates, quality may be sacrificed in the drive to produce or sell more, with serious long-term consequences for the organisation.

This is easy to understand in a manufacturing situation where actual products are being produced. But it is also apparent in the service sector. For example, the substantial monetary incentives provided to salespeople in the financial services sector (pensions, mortgages and insurance) to encourage them to increase the sales of these products has resulted in customers finding, years later, that they have been sold inappropriate products for their particular needs and have as a consequence lost vast amounts of money. Complaints have been made to the ombudsman over the misselling of pensions, mortgages and insurance by financial services companies, resulting in huge customer relations problems that have seriously affected the companies' reputations.

If another objective is to build a committed and motivated workforce based on effective team working, then rewards based on individual performance may cause conflict between employees, especially where employees are doing the same job and their contributions cannot be measured objectively. There has been an ongoing debate in education about the pros and cons of introducing performance-related pay into the teaching profession. Most research suggests that performance-related pay, especially in the public sector, has an

INGRAM

adverse effect on motivation and has little effect on performance. It is very difficult to measure the contribution of an individual teacher. Exam results achieved by students are influenced by other teachers whom the student may have had in previous classes, by parents and by the motivation of the student themselves. In relation to teaching, it is suggested that performance-related pay adversely affects the 'collegiate spirit' of a school: that is, the commitment and responsibility of all staff for the common good of the school and its students.

Remuneration and other factors

In addition to the objectives of the organisation, other factors that might influence the effectiveness of a remuneration scheme include:

- the financial resources available to the organisation
- the planning and cost effectiveness of the scheme
- the ease with which the scheme can be administered
- how easy the scheme is for the workforce to understand
- the competitive environment of the firm (for example, remuneration for the manager of a product in a growing market might include a relatively small basic salary plus a substantial incentive element based on the market share of the product, whereas the manager of a product in a stable or declining market might have a greater element of basic salary)
- how motivating the scheme is for the workforce (this will depend on the type of work involved and the individual needs of employees, which are considered in more detail below)

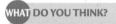

WHAT DO YOU THINK?

What factors do you think might be relevant when determining the remuneration offered to each of the following: a professional footballer, the chief executive of a major plc, a teacher, an assistant in a motorway service station?

In relation to the type of work involved, can individual effort be measured separately from the team's effort? If it can, individual bonuses might be more appropriate than a team bonus, but this may lead to tension and conflict between individual workers. On the other hand, if effort cannot be measured, a team bonus may be the most effective system, although this might lead to the **free-rider effect**, where some workers put in less effort, knowing that they will reap the same benefits as their more productive colleagues.

In relation to individual needs, consideration should be given to whether individual workers need the security of a salary or would prefer the relative uncertainty of payment on the basis of performance. Many payment systems include both, in order to provide workers with some security but also to provide an incentive for effort.

FACT FILE

A possible remuneration scheme for the staff of a large retailer might include:

- an annual salary, demonstrating that staff are trusted to use their time effectively
- performance-related pay, to encourage effort (although there may be disagreement about what type of performance should be measured, such as sales or customer satisfaction)
- hourly pay, which may lead to staff requesting to work more hours in order to increase their pay (but which may, as a consequence, require more supervision and monitoring)
- commission on sales (although this might mean that customers are harassed by employees who are overly keen to make a sale)

The scheme chosen will depend on what is easy to administer, what is cost effective and what achieves the desired objectives. It is likely that a combination of schemes will be chosen: one that provides a salary to give employees some security, supplemented by some kind of bonus, and which varies among different groups of staff — for example, sales staff and managers.

e EXAMINER'S VOICE

An important point to consider when deciding on appropriate motivational tools to employ in the workplace is the timescale. It is relatively easy to motivate people with financial incentives in the short term (or to create 'movement', according to Herzberg), but much harder in the longer term. Remember, Herzberg said that 'a reward once given becomes a right', meaning that employees can get used to financial rewards and take them for granted.

Conclusion

The remuneration system that is used by an organisation plays an important role in helping to encourage employees to behave in such a way that they assist the organisation in achieving its HRM aims and therefore its corporate objectives. Different types of payment system can be used to achieve different objectives. For example, piece-rate systems might be used to encourage more effort and thus achieve greater productivity, while bonuses can be paid for good attendance over a period of time in order to reduce absenteeism and labour turnover. Similarly, bonuses or skills premiums can be used to encourage employees to adopt new methods of production or engage in training.

WHAT DO YOU THINK?

Your study of motivation theory at AS suggested that money was not a good motivator. How can you reconcile this with the discussion here on how remuneration or financial incentives assists an organisation in meeting its HRM goals? Is the HRM approach to controlling the workforce through the remuneration system based upon a fundamental misunderstanding of motivation and human behaviour?

PRACTICE EXERCISE

Total: 35 marks (30 minutes)

1 Explain the term 'remuneration'. *(3 marks)*

2 Identify three different types of financial incentive. *(3 marks)*

3 Identify two financial incentives that a business might provide and explain how they might contribute to a firm's corporate objectives. *(6 marks)*

4 If a firm's objectives focus on quantity rather than quality of production, what type of financial incentive might be most appropriate for its workforce and why? *(3 marks)*

5 If a firm's objectives focus on individual effort rather than team effort, what type of financial incentive might be most appropriate for its workforce and why? *(3 marks)*

6 Identify three factors, other than the objectives of an organisation, that will influence the remuneration scheme offered to employees. *(3 marks)*

7 How and why might the remuneration package of someone managing a product in a growth market differ from that of someone managing a product in a declining market? *(5 marks)*

8 Outline one problem that may occur in paying employees a bonus based on their team effort. *(3 marks)*

9 Identify and explain the most appropriate type of financial incentive to bring about an increase in productivity. *(3 marks)*

10 Identify and explain the most appropriate type of financial incentive to bring about a reduction in absenteeism. *(3 marks)*

CHAPTER 28

Human resource management and measurements of personnel effectiveness

This chapter explains different measures of personnel effectiveness and their importance as indicators of personnel strategy. It focuses on measures of labour productivity, labour turnover, absenteeism, and health and safety, and demonstrates how they are calculated. It analyses the factors that cause the measures to change and evaluates the impact of such measures on business.

Labour productivity

TERM

labour productivity: a measure of the output per worker in a given time period.

Calculating labour productivity

Labour productivity is calculated as follows:

$$\frac{\text{output per period}}{\text{no. of employees per period}}$$

Calculation 1: example of a labour productivity calculation

If output in a given month is 20,000 units and 40 people are employed during that month to produce the goods, labour productivity is 500 units per worker (20,000/40).

How to increase labour productivity

Labour productivity may be increased by appropriate HRM policies such as:

- the recruitment and selection of suitably skilled and trained employees
- the provision of training to enhance skills and attitudes of existing employees
- appropriate remuneration and non-financial benefits that improve motivation and effort

Other factors that may increase labour productivity include:

- improved working practices
- improved technology and capital equipment

An increase in labour productivity means that output will be increased using the same number of employees. It also implies a lower labour cost per unit (assuming wages stay the same), which might enable the firm to charge a lower price and/or gain a higher profit margin.

Calculation 2: example demonstrating that an increase in productivity will lead to an increase in output using the same number of employees
From calculation 1, if improved machinery or new systems are introduced that cause output to increase to 30,000 units using the same number of employees, then labour productivity increases to 750 units per worker (30,000/40).

Calculation 3: example demonstrating that an increase in productivity will lead to lower labour cost per unit
In calculation 1, if labour costs are £1,000 per worker per month, total labour costs are £40,000 per month (£1,000 × 40). The original labour cost per unit is £2 (£40,000/20,000 units).

If labour productivity increases (as in calculation 2), labour cost per unit falls to £1.33 (£40,000/30,000 units).

EXAMINER'S VOICE

Many students assume that an increase in labour productivity always leads to an increase in output. This is incorrect. Output per worker (that is, labour productivity) may have increased, but the firm may be producing the same level of output as before the increase in productivity, while employing fewer workers. Make sure that you are fully aware of the difference between the level of **production** (the total units of output) and the level of **productivity** (units of output per worker).

A firm's efforts to increase productivity are likely to be more successful if it ensures that:

- employees recognise why the firm needs to increase productivity — for example, because it needs to reduce costs in order to become more competitive and therefore safeguard jobs in the long term
- employees are involved in the changes
- jobs are not lost
- employees gain extra rewards as a result

Where these conditions do not apply, employees may resist attempts to increase productivity. This is particularly the case if they know that the firm does not want to increase the total level of output but simply wishes to reduce costs and maintain output at its original level. Redundancies are then likely as, given the increased productivity, the firm will require fewer workers. Similarly, employees may feel that plans to increase productivity may involve a great deal of extra work on their part, and may therefore demand higher rewards. This is why the negotiation of both pay and productivity deals often take place at the same time.

FACT FILE

It is worth noting that, as a measure of efficiency, labour productivity is really only useful when all other factors are taken into account. For example, the introduction of new machinery could lead to an increase in output, so that the same number of workers is now producing a greater amount of output. This 'increase' in labour productivity is, of course, a reflection not of a more productive or improved workforce, but rather of more productive or improved capital equipment. On the other hand, if the new machinery means that workers have retrained and acquired new skills, it could be the case that the labour force has become more effective.

TOPFOTO

Conclusion

In many ways, labour productivity is the most crucial measure of all. There is a direct connection between the productivity of a workforce and the competitiveness of a firm, mainly because labour costs are such a high proportion of total costs for most companies.

Labour turnover

KEY TERM

labour turnover: the proportion of employees leaving a business over a period of time — usually a year.

How to calculate the rate of labour turnover

The rate of labour turnover is calculated as follows:

$$\frac{\text{no. leaving a business over a given period}}{\text{average no. employed over a given period}} \times 100$$

For example, if the average number of staff employed in a firm last year was 250 and the number of employees who left the firm last year was 10, the labour turnover would be $(10/250) \times 100 = 4\%$.

FACT FILE

A survey in 2003 by the Chartered Institute of Personnel and Development (CIPD) estimated that overall labour turnover averaged 16%.

EXAMINER'S VOICE

The average number of employees can be calculated by adding the number of people employed at the start of the year to the number of people employed at the end of the year and dividing the total by two. For example, if at the start of the year a firm employed 55 people and at the end it employed 47, the average number it employed over the year would be $(55 + 47)/2 = 51$.

Causes of high labour turnover

In general, labour turnover indicates how content the workforce is within a firm. If a company's labour turnover rate is increasing, it could be a general

sign of worker unrest or dissatisfaction. The causes of labour turnover could be internal or external. Factors internal to the firm include:

- ineffective leadership and management techniques
- poor communications
- wages and salaries that are lower than those being paid by firms offering comparable jobs in the area
- poor selection procedures that tend to appoint the wrong people to the wrong jobs
- boring and unchallenging jobs that lack career and developmental opportunities
- poor working conditions and unpopular working practices
- low morale and motivation as a result of the above issues

External factors include an increase in vacancies for more attractive jobs. This could be because they are more highly paid, offer better conditions and stronger training, are more interesting and challenging, are closer to home or offer easier transport links.

FACT FILE

Within the first 9 weeks of the opening of Euro Disney in Paris, 1,000 of the new employees appointed had left, about 50% voluntarily. Unreasonable working conditions, poor communication and lack of cultural awareness among managers were the main reasons given for the staff turnover. The rate of staff turnover at Disney World in Florida is between 200% and 300% per annum!

Problems of high labour turnover

High labour turnover may create problems for the firm, including:

- high recruitment and selection costs to replace staff who leave. These include the administrative and management costs incurred in advertising positions, conducting interviews, etc. Such costs are likely to be higher for senior management and professional positions
- high induction and training costs to ensure that new employees quickly become familiar with the practices of the firm and learn the necessary skills to carry out their job effectively. This process can take a great deal of time, especially if the job requires specialised skills
- in some industries, where labour turnover is a particular problem, a need to redesign jobs in order to keep them as simple as possible, so that it is easier to replace staff who leave
- reduced productivity due to the disruption caused by skilled staff leaving and new, usually untrained, staff joining the firm. This could result in loss of production or sales, especially if a worker plays an important role in a company or has key knowledge or skills that the firm will find difficult to replace
- low morale among existing workers as a result of the constant change of work colleagues and the unsettling feelings this engenders

DID YOU KNOW?

The CIPD estimated the cost per employee of labour turnover in 2002 by occupational group. The costs were high and especially so for more skilled or senior positions: for example, £6,807 for managers compared with £2,810 for administrative, clerical and secretarial employees. The average for all occupations was £4,301.

Variations in labour turnover

Labour turnover varies by occupation and by industry. Some industries and occupations are particularly prone to higher labour turnover than others. For example, the hotels and restaurants sector has an average labour turnover of just over 24%, which is high compared with the average for all industries of just over 16%. It is likely that this is related to the fact that this sector typically employs students and seasonal workers whose turnover is naturally higher. Labour turnover is much higher in less skilled jobs, particularly among sales and customer service occupations, where the average rate of labour turnover is just under 19%, compared with professional occupations, where it is just over 6%.

Whether such differences in rates of labour turnover matter depends to some extent on the overall impact labour turnover has on quality, costs and the ease of recruitment. For example, in a fast-food restaurant such as McDonald's, high rates of labour turnover certainly lead to higher recruitment and training costs. However, the disruption and effect on the quality of the service has to some extent been alleviated by the fact that McDonald's jobs are designed so that it can very quickly and easily train new recruits, and the fact that many of its staff are students and part-time workers ensures that wages tend to be low.

TOPFOTO

How to improve labour turnover

Better HRM practices are needed in order to reduce rates of labour turnover. Some of the key areas where improvements may be made are as follows:

- **Monitoring and benchmarking.** Currently, many firms are either not proactive in dealing with labour turnover or unaware of its cost implications. A monitoring system that includes knowing how labour turnover in the firm compares with the industry average, tracking trends in employee turnover over time, and identifying areas, departments and roles within the firm where labour turnover is particularly high, might be useful.

FACT FILE

A spokesman for the CIPD says that: 'Most employers are completely unaware of the savings that they might achieve by reducing labour turnover further, even by just a few percentage points. There seems to be no systematic approach to stemming the losses.' At present, only about 7% of human resource departments calculate the cost of labour turnover.

- **Exit interviews.** Exit interviews are a useful strategy in highlighting problem areas within an organisation and identifying any characteristics that may be common to leavers who have not been with the firm for long. Issues to discuss include: the job itself; supervision and management; pay and conditions of work; training and career prospects; and equal opportunities.

FACT FILE

The CIPD suggests that the reasons people give for their resignations are frequently untrue or only partially true. Although the use of exit interviews is widespread, they are notoriously unreliable, particularly when conducted by someone — for example, the line manager — who may later be asked to write a reference for the departing employee. In such instances, employees are understandably reluctant to voice criticisms of their managers, colleagues or the organisation generally, preferring to give a less contentious reason for their departure.

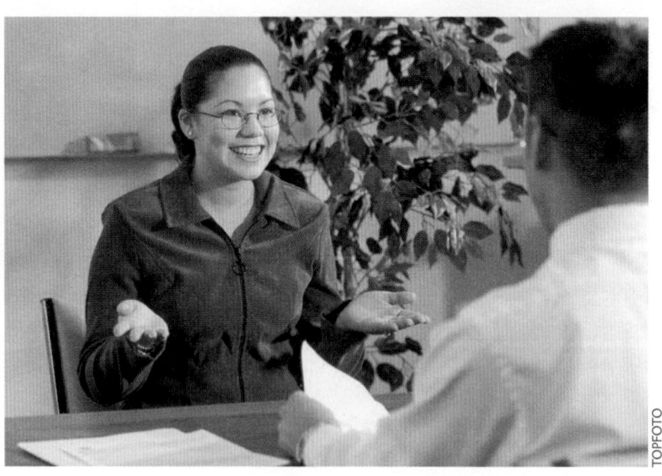
TOPFOTO

- **Recruitment and selection.** Money spent on ensuring that recruitment and selection procedures are effective will be more than saved on lower labour turnover later on.
- **Induction and training.** High-quality induction training to make the new employee feel a part of the firm is as important as well-directed, on-the-job training and supervision. It is important to make sure that the new employee is kept sufficiently motivated and that the work is neither unchallenging nor too challenging.
- **Reducing turnover of long-term workers.** Employees who have been with the firm for a long time accumulate a huge amount of firm-specific human capital, that is, knowledge and skills that are of direct relevance to the firm. If these employees leave, their knowledge and skills also disappear, so it is vital for the firm to try to retain them. This may involve ensuring that some kind of career progression is available to them and examining their remuneration to ensure it is not out of line with that provided by firms offering similar jobs.

Conclusion

The consequences for a firm of having a high labour turnover are usually negative. The cost of recruiting and training new staff can lead to a weaker competitive position and a fall in efficiency. Evidence suggests that, in general, most firms are either unaware of the costs of high labour turnover or do not have systems in place to monitor or deal with the problem. Better HRM practices are therefore necessary in dealing with the problem.

It is, however, worth noting that there is likely to be a 'natural' level of labour turnover which is unavoidable and which may vary from firm to firm.

Indeed, some labour turnover may be positive in bringing new ideas, skills, talents and enthusiasm to the labour force. Labour turnover can be healthy if it enables a firm to avoid complacency and an over-reliance on tried and tested ways of working, which may make it inflexible in response to changes in its environment. It can also allow a business to reduce its workforce slowly without having to resort to redundancies — this is often referred to as **natural wastage**.

There is a clear need for a balance to be struck in relation to labour turnover. Rather than aiming for as low a figure as possible, a firm needs to review its human resource management programme; how and why the rate of labour turnover is changing is probably as important as the figure itself.

Absenteeism

KEY TERM

absenteeism: the proportion of employees not at work on a given day.

How to calculate the rate of absenteeism

The rate of absenteeism is calculated as follows:

$$\frac{\text{no. of staff absent on 1 day}}{\text{total number of staff}} \times 100$$

For example, if 21 people out of a workforce of 300 are absent on a given day, the absentee rate is (21/300) × 100 = 7%.

Similarly, if a firm has an average daily absentee rate of 5% and a workforce of 300, the typical number of people absent per day is (5/100) × 300 = 15.

To calculate the absentee rate for a year, the following formula is used:

$$\frac{\text{total no. of days lost due to absence during the year}}{\text{total no. of days that could be worked} \times \text{no. of employees}} \times 100$$

For example, if the total number of days that could be worked is 250 (5 days × 50 weeks), the total number of employees is 80 and the number of days lost due to absence is 600, then the absenteeism rate for the year is (600/(250 × 80)) × 100 = 3%.

EXAMINER'S VOICE

Data such as those explained above can only give an overall view. When considering the problem of absenteeism in a particular firm, it is important to consider personnel data in more detail and ask pertinent questions, for example: Who is absent? How often are they absent? What reasons are given for their absences? When did the absenteeism start? Possible reasons could then be identified and hypotheses suggested that could be tested against the data. Any solution will depend on the causes and the resources available to the firm.

DID YOU KNOW?

According to the Confederation of British Industry (CBI), UK employees average 7.8 days absence per year, amounting to a total of 192 million days or 3.4% of total working time per year. Apparently, this is the equivalent of a working population of 861,000 people taking a year off! Public sector workers take more days off (average 10.2 days) than people in the private sector (7.6 days) and small businesses have the lowest rates of absenteeism — 5.9 days for firms with fewer than 50 workers compared with around 9 days in businesses with more than 500 employees.

Causes of absenteeism

A high rate of absenteeism tends to be an indicator of underlying problems either with the individuals involved or with the firm itself. Some absences are unavoidable: for example, those resulting from an illness or a transport strike. However, there are other times when absenteeism may be a consequence of poor levels of motivation and commitment, or ineffective management and communication within a firm. Thus when levels of absenteeism suddenly increase or are generally high, it may indicate that there are problems within the firm that require investigation and intervention. Such problems are usually linked to weaknesses in a firm's human relations system.

EXAMINER'S VOICE

Ensure that you review your knowledge and understanding of motivation theorists studied at AS and be prepared to make connections with the work covered at A2. For example, the causes of absenteeism may be linked to Herzberg's 'hygiene factors' (for example, poor working conditions), a failure to respect the individual as part of a team, over-supervision, inappropriate tasks leading to stress, or rates of pay that employees consider to be too low for the quantity or standard of work expected by the job.

FACT FILE

The possible business-related causes of absenteeism noted above are rarely mentioned by survey respondents. For example, in a survey on absenteeism by the Industrial Society, 91% of employees reported time off for flu and colds, 74% gave stomach upsets or food poisoning and 54% cited headaches or migraines.

FACT FILE

'Temp agencies' often provide clerical staff at very short notice to cover for absentees in the office. The firm requiring staff will pay the 'temp agency', which in turn pays the temporary clerical staff. The rate that the firm pays to the agency is usually at least twice as much as the standard hourly rate for the employee.

Problems of absenteeism

The impact of absenteeism on a firm depends largely on which employees are absent, how many are absent and the extent to which their work can be covered by those employees who are present. In general, however, absenteeism is enormously expensive for firms. It costs money to cover for those employees who are absent. This will be the case especially if deadlines are looming and other employees need to be paid overtime to cover for absent colleagues or if additional staff need to be recruited.

Staff absences can also mean that important work is not completed, leading to possible delays in production. On the other hand, if new and less skilled staff have to be deployed, productivity and quality may be sacrificed. Eventually, such absences may lead to dissatisfied customers and adversely affect the profitability of the firm.

DID YOU KNOW?

A CBI survey found that the average cost of absence per employee is estimated at £434, costing UK business a total of £10.7 billion when projected across the entire workforce. A spokesman for the Industrial Society said: 'Left unchecked, absenteeism hits productivity and erodes morale in organisations. Firms should regularly examine the cause of absence and take appropriate action — by promoting workplace well being or flexible working practices.'

Strategies to reduce absenteeism

A number of strategies can be introduced in an attempt to reduce absenteeism. These include:

- introducing more flexible working practices. This might involve flexitime, where workers have some control over how they organise certain parts of their working day: for example, between 7 a.m. and 10 a.m. and between 3 p.m. and 6 p.m. Thus an employee may wish to begin work at 7 a.m. and finish at 3 p.m. in order to pick a child up from school or attend a dental appointment

FACT FILE

A survey by the Industrial Society indicates that flexible working patterns can help to reduce absenteeism. Absence rates in the companies surveyed fell from an average of 8 days per employee to 6.5 days per employee; 49% of survey respondents linked this improvement to having flexible annual leave, 40% to the ability to work from home on occasions and 55% to flexible working hours.

- ensuring that jobs are interesting and challenging, so that people enjoy work and want to turn up. This could also involve flexibility in relation to annual leave, home working, part-time working and job sharing
- improving working conditions and thus reducing dissatisfaction
- improving relations between employers and employees, so that the latter feel valued and an essential part of the organisation

EXAMINER'S VOICE

Remember Herzberg's hygiene factors — those aspects of a job that need attention in order to prevent workers becoming dissatisfied.

FACT FILE

In the Industrial Society's survey, improving motivation and interviewing employees when they returned to work were cited by employers as the most effective ways of managing attendance.

- introducing attendance bonuses to provide an incentive for workers to attend regularly. Such schemes vary, but might involve a firm paying out between £100 and £1,000 for a period of 12 months without sickness. Some evidence suggests that, if these bonuses are set at attractive rates and if the scheme is carefully designed, attendance might improve. However, in

the above example, once a person has had one day off, they have lost the bonus and there is no incentive for them not to have more time off. In addition, if employees get used to a certain level of bonus, it ceases to have any impact.

Conclusion

Like labour turnover, absenteeism needs to be monitored. If it is seen to be a problem in a certain organisation, action needs to be taken to ensure that human resource management policies are working effectively. Without effective monitoring, employees may be absent without valid reason, knowing that no action is likely to be taken.

Health and safety

A final area that can be used to determine personnel effectiveness is the health and safety record of a firm. At first glance, there may seem to be little connection between health and safety and personnel effectiveness. However, accidents often happen because of a casual disregard for correct procedures and injuries, such as repetitive strain injury, are often the direct result of a poorly designed workstation, unrealistic workloads or poor training. Many such problems could be remedied by appropriate human resource policies.

How to calculate the rate of absenteeism due to health and safety

The rate of absenteeism due to health and safety reasons can be calculated as follows:

$$\frac{\text{no. of working days lost per year due to health and safety reasons}}{\text{total no. of possible working days per year}} \times 100$$

For example, if over a period of a year there are 250 actual working days and the number of days lost due to health and safety reasons is 5, then the rate is $(5/250) \times 100 = 2\%$.

TOPFOTO

If employees are managed effectively, they will know what they are supposed to do and how to do it. This should mean that the number of accidents and health and safety problems is reduced. If, however, employees have not had sufficient health and safety training and/or take little interest in their work, health and safety related accidents are more likely to occur. The consequences for the firm are significant. It may have to pay compensation to staff. There will be a need for greater investment in training to prevent accidents from happening in the future. Overall, health and safety accidents may adversely affect employer/employee relations and eventually lead to poor public relations and have a negative effect on demand and profits.

We have seen that there are several measures of personnel effectiveness (or the effectiveness of HRM policies) that can give a business some idea of how well it is managing its most valuable resource — people. The ones considered in this chapter are labour productivity, labour turnover, absenteeism and health and safety. In general, any measure of personnel effectiveness taken in isolation is relatively meaningless. However, looked at over a period of time and in the wider context of the business and its environment, these measures can provide a clear indication of what issues need to be addressed by the HRM programme in order to assist the business in meeting its corporate objectives.

PRACTICE EXERCISE 1 — Total: 45 marks (45 minutes)

1 Explain the term 'labour productivity'. *(3 marks)*

2 Outline two ways in which a firm might increase its labour productivity. *(4 marks)*

3 In a firm, output in a particular month is 60,000 units, 75 workers are employed and labour costs are £1,000 per worker per month. Calculate labour productivity and labour cost per unit. *(6 marks)*

4 Define the term 'labour turnover' and identify two problems that high rates of labour turnover might cause a firm. *(9 marks)*

5 In a firm, 190 workers were employed at the start of the year, 178 workers were employed at the end of the year and during the year 24 workers left. Calculate the rate of labour turnover for the year. *(3 marks)*

6 In a firm, the average daily absentee rate is 15% and the total workforce is 300. What is the average number of workers who are absent on any one day? *(3 marks)*

7 Identify two possible causes of a high rate of absenteeism for a firm. *(2 marks)*

8 Explain two consequences for a firm of a high rate of absenteeism. *(6 marks)*

9 Explain how a firm's health and safety absentee record might be a measure of personnel effectiveness. *(3 marks)*

10 How can the four measures of personnel effectiveness considered in this chapter indicate how well a human resource management programme is operating? *(6 marks)*

PRACTICE EXERCISE 2 — Total: 30 marks (30 minutes)

1 Discuss the possible reasons why labour turnover in the hotel and restaurants sector tends to be higher than in most other sectors. *(12 marks)*

2 Analyse the likely impact of this high labour turnover on those hotels and restaurants affected. *(8 marks)*

3 Evaluate the possible solutions that a hotel or restaurant might use to overcome this problem. *(10 marks)*

CASE STUDY Measuring personnel effectiveness

A small firm has available the personnel data shown in Table 28.1.

***Table 28.1** Personnel data for a small firm, 2002–04*

	2002	2003	2004
Total output (units)	6,700	6,800	6,900
Average number of employees	100	98	96
Number of employees leaving	10	15	20
Number of working days	250	250	250
Total number of days lost due to absence	500	520	735
Total number of days lost due to health and safety reasons	20	22	18

	Marketing			Production			Administration			Finance		
	2002	2003	2004	2002	2003	2004	2002	2003	2004	2002	2003	2004
Employees	20	20	20	62	60	58	10	10	10	8	8	8
Leavers	1	1	2	8	6	8	0	8	9	1	0	1
Absences	85	80	70	325	315	480	50	45	35	40	80	150
Health/safety absences	1	2	0	18	19	18	1	0	0	0	1	0
Age profile (2004)												
16–29			4			2			8			2
30–49			14			11			1			4
50+			2			45			1			2

Over the last few years, there have been relatively few changes in the operation of the business and the market for its product has been stable. Management has also been relatively stable, although a new office manager was appointed to the administration section 2 years ago — a 53-year-old woman who is the sister of the managing director.

Questions

Total: 20 marks (25 minutes)

1 Using the data provided, calculate the following measures of personnel effectiveness for each of the 3 years:

a labour productivity *(2 marks)*

b labour turnover *(2 marks)*

c absenteeism *(2 marks)*

d health and safety absenteeism *(2 marks)*

2 Discuss the issues that these indicators raise for human resource management policies within the firm. *(12 marks)*

People in organisations

This case study is included to provide an opportunity to tackle a Unit 4 exam-style case study that is based only on People in Organisations, but which covers the whole of the A2 People in Organisations specification.

Please note that this is significantly longer than the usual Unit 4 case study. This additional material is included to allow two sets of questions to be based on a single case study. Both sets of questions take the form of a typical Unit 4 examination.

CASE STUDY Vittoria's Deli

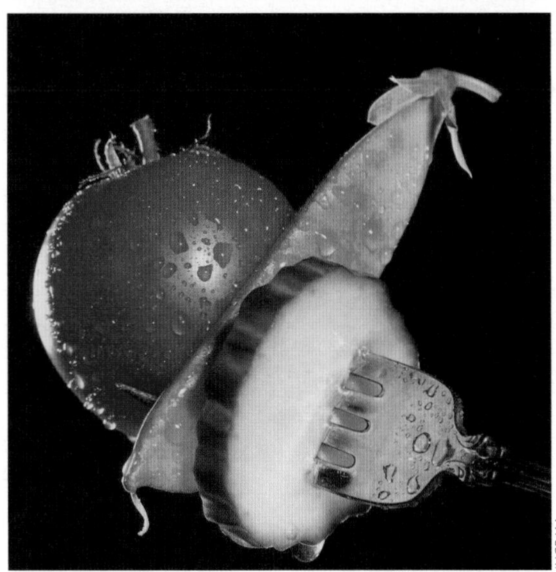

INGRAM

Vittoria's Deli is a large plc with 200 Italian restaurants, specialising in good-value, quality food and high standards of customer service in stylish settings.

The managing director has called for a full review of all human resource policies at the next meeting of the board of directors. This is part of a general review of company operations. The company's financial situation has been causing some concern and reviews have been taking place across all functional areas to ensure that operations are as efficient as they can be, without compromising quality. The purpose and agenda for the meeting are outlined in Figure 1.

Purpose	The board of directors requires evidence that the HRM approach is working to support business goals and targets.
Agenda item 1	Employee involvement and communication
Agenda item 2	Personnel effectiveness – rates of labour turnover and absenteeism
Agenda item 3	Methods of remuneration
Agenda item 4	Workforce planning

***Figure 1** Purpose of, and agenda for, the meeting*

In relation to each of the agenda items, the following information is available.

Agenda item 1

A system of employee forums was set up 2 years ago with the aim of creating a structure to enable effective and consistent communication with employees and to help feedback via employee representatives at local level. Management and decision making in the company operates at national, regional, area and

branch levels and the employee forums mirror this structure. Elected branch representatives, from below management level, are part of the area forums; elected representatives from the areas are part of the regional forums; and elected representatives from the regions are part of the national forum. The national forum meets regularly with the board of directors.

The development has been successful and the chief executive was quoted in the monthly newsletter as saying that the system of employee forums has helped Vittoria's Deli to 'appreciate the importance of excellent communication across all levels of employment within the organisation'. A representative in the national forum suggested that it 'has allowed employees to enlarge their self-esteem because management is listening to them and allowing them to be involved with the issues'. This view is further supported by a recent survey undertaken by the HR team, suggesting that employees feel valued and respected and say their suggestions are acted upon.

At present, Vittoria's Deli has a small number of restaurants in other European countries, which it runs as franchises. It expects to open some company-owned ventures during the next year and realises that, in line with these developments, the employee forums may have to evolve in order to take account of EU employment directives on works councils and the recent Information and Consultation Directive.

Two hundred restaurants throughout the UK and a total workforce of approximately 4,000 means that creating an effective communication structure is a challenge. The most persistent communication problem concerns branch managers. Branch managers report to area managers, who in turn report to regional directors, who have direct access to the board of directors. There is tension among branch managers about the fact that there are no means of communication between them and the regional directors and board of directors. Neither is there any formal opportunity for communication between one branch manager and another. From the branch managers' point of view, the employee forums ensure that restaurant staff have the ear of the board of directors and have effective lateral communication links, but branch managers somehow get left out of the chain, with only their area managers to communicate with.

Agenda item 2

The restaurant sector, in which labour is the major cost, is characterised by high rates of labour turnover and absenteeism. The majority of the workforce at Vittoria's Deli is young, aged between 18 and 30, and about 30% are students. Given this profile, rates of overall labour turnover and absenteeism are actually quite good and certainly lower than the average for the sector. However, labour turnover and absenteeism are major issues in some areas and for some branches. For example, there are staff shortages in many branches in the southeast region, and it is becoming more and more difficult to recruit and retain good staff in this area. It has been suggested that this is because of the relatively low unemployment situation in the southeast, but there may be other reasons. There is relatively low unemployment in a number of the regions in which the company operates its restaurants and these don't appear to suffer the same problems. Where possible, exit interviews were carried out by branch managers during 2003, in an attempt to gain evidence of reasons for staff leaving. Initial conclusions suggest that most staff gave 'personal reasons', with students suggesting 'study commitments' as their reason. HRM statistics for 2003 are provided in Table 1.

***Table 1** HRM statistics for Vittoria's Deli*

Number of employees at the start of 2003	4,000
Number of employees at the end of 2003	4,100
Number of employees leaving during 2003	810
Rate of labour turnover in the southeast region in 2003	25%
Rate of absenteeism across the company in 2003	20%
Number of days the business is open per annum	360

Agenda item 3

Teamwork is very important and encouraging effective teamwork is one of the major responsibilities of a branch manager. However, it does occasionally result in tension as a result of the remuneration systems.

Presently all restaurant staff are paid on an hourly basis, at a single rate that is just slightly above the minimum wage. Tips in each branch are shared out at the end of each shift among the staff who worked on that shift. This system suits students but fails to reward effectively those staff whom the company really needs to retain: that is, those who are slightly older and who view the job as a permanent position. At present, the company has no system in place to provide incentives to encourage attendance.

Branch managers are paid an annual salary and also have the opportunity to gain a bonus if their branch outperforms others. The bonus system in operation relates to branch performance in each area and, as the bonus is a fixed sum that goes to the highest-performing branch, it generates a form of competition between branches and discourages the sharing of ideas. This is reinforced by the way that personnel effectiveness data is summarised by the HR team and issued as a league table to all branches, which simply compounds feelings of competition rather than cooperation among branch managers.

Agenda item 4

Recently all regional directors attended a seminar on workforce planning. The impetus for this came as a result of two restaurants, both run by new managers. These restaurants had to close for a week because they suddenly found themselves without sufficient staff when most students left to begin their college and university courses in September 2003. The new managers had failed to plan to fill the gap that this would inevitably leave. Although this was an example of poor management on their part, it was widely recognised in the company not only that insufficient training is provided for new managers, but also that the company has no general planning system to overcome such problems.

Questions (set A)

Total: 80 marks (90 minutes)

1 a Examine the problems that might be caused by ineffective internal communication for a company such as Vittoria's Deli. *(8 marks)*

b Discuss the importance to Vittoria's Deli of employee involvement in decision making. *(12 marks)*

2 a Calculate the rate of labour turnover for Vittoria's Deli in 2003. *(3 marks)*

b Outline the possible costs to Vittoria's Deli resulting from high levels of labour turnover. *(5 marks)*

c Discuss possible strategies that could be introduced to reduce labour turnover at a company such as Vittoria's Deli. *(12 marks)*

3 a Examine the benefits of teamwork for Vittoria's Deli. *(8 marks)*

b To what extent might methods of remuneration encourage teamwork at Vittoria's Deli? *(12 marks)*

4 Discuss the value of workforce planning to an organisation such as Vittoria's Deli and the extent to which it might contribute to meeting overall company objectives. *(20 marks)*

Questions (set B)

Total: 80 marks (90 minutes)

1 a Explain how individual employment legislation might be important in creating a 'level playing field' for companies such as Vittoria's Deli. *(8 marks)*

b In the context of Vittoria's Deli, discuss the extent to which internal communication problems might affect the motivation of branch managers and the performance of the business. *(12 marks)*

2 a Calculate how many staff, on average, were likely to be absent on any one day in 2003. *(3 marks)*

b An attendance bonus of £200 for every individual who works for a period of 6 months with no absences has been suggested as a strategy to reduce absenteeism at Vittoria's Deli. Examine the possible impact of such a strategy on staff attendance. *(8 marks)*

c Analyse the consequences for a business such as Vittoria's Deli of high rates of absenteeism. *(9 marks)*

3 Discuss the role of incentives in reducing labour turnover and absenteeism and in meeting overall human resource objectives. *(20 marks)*

4 a Consider the consequences for a business such as Vittoria's Deli of a lack of workforce planning. *(8 marks)*

b Discuss how workforce planning might be linked to other planning mechanisms within the company, such as the marketing plan, the operations plan and the overall corporate plan. *(12 marks)*

Module 5

Operations management

"Quality is remembered long after the price is forgotten."

Gucci family slogan

CHAPTER 29

Research and development

This chapter introduces research and development (R&D), explaining its functions and the problems associated with its use. An examination of the ways in which a firm can help to ensure the success of R&D is undertaken and the importance of science and technology in R&D is considered. The need to integrate R&D with other activities and factors is studied through an investigation of its links with product design, the product life cycle and market research. The chapter concludes by looking at the factors that influence the level of spending on R&D.

KEY TERMS

research and development (R&D): the scientific investigation necessary to discover new products or manufacturing processes, and the procedures necessary to ensure that these new products and processes are suited to the needs of the market.

innovation: bringing in new methods. Once an idea has been researched and developed, innovation is needed to ensure that the new product or process is successfully implemented by the business.

EXAMINER'S VOICE

Do not confuse *research and development* with *market research*. Market research involves finding out what consumers want and developing a product to meet that need. R&D, which often starts in a laboratory, means that the product or process is invented or discovered and then its commercial applications are investigated. As a consequence, products developed from market research are often described as 'market led', while those arising from R&D are 'product led'.

Functions of R&D

R&D serves a number of purposes:

- It helps firms to develop products or services that have a unique selling point, allowing the business to achieve a higher degree of product differentiation. Products with a unique selling point usually sell in higher quantities and their uniqueness tends to lead to more inelastic demand, allowing the organisation to increase price and so earn a higher profit margin.
- If R&D discovers a new invention, this can be patented, giving the business a guaranteed monopoly of manufacture for a number of years. Analysis by

the UK and US governments shows a high correlation between the increase in sales achieved by a business, its level of R&D spending and the number of patents that the company acquires.

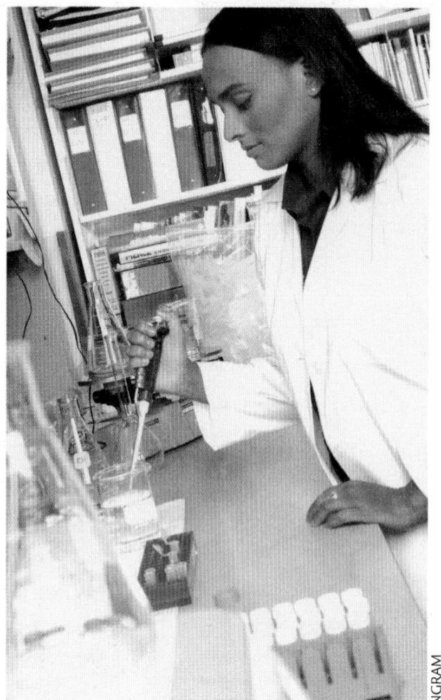
INGRAM

- R&D may focus on developing higher-quality products that will be more attractive to consumers, again allowing increased sales and added value. A reputation for quality can have beneficial effects throughout the company, as a firm's reputation is often based on its main products.
- Often R&D is designed to improve the efficiency of production methods. Innovative ways of producing reduce the average cost of production and may also improve flexibility.
- R&D allows a business to update its product range continually and stay ahead of competitors. In rapidly changing, technologically advanced industries, consumers are often unaware of the possible products that can be made and so R&D is vital in presenting new products to the market. R&D is a key element of product portfolio planning. It enables firms to balance their product portfolio through the creation of new growth products to take over from those that are approaching or have reached the decline stage of the product life cycle.
- The opportunity to create new products and ideas provides a stimulating working environment and therefore motivates employees. It also makes it easier for a firm to recruit workers.

Problems associated with R&D

Although R&D brings many benefits, businesses need to be aware of the potential pitfalls.

- There is no guarantee that R&D expenditure will lead to new products and processes. Some projects, such as research into the common cold, have still not generated successful outcomes. The level of uncertainty in R&D makes it much more difficult to justify the high levels of spending that are often needed.
- R&D spending may encourage rivals to undertake similar activities. This will merely lead to increased costs for both firms, but with no competitive advantage being gained.
- Operational difficulties are common with new products. Companies often suffer setbacks when new products are released, particularly if they are in a hurry to release them and have had to rush their testing processes. In industries where product safety is vital, a hasty action can destroy a firm's reputation and the trust of its customers.
- The new idea may have already been developed (and patented) by another organisation working on the same project.
- In industries such as pharmaceuticals, there is a growing tendency towards

'generic' products. These 'copies' are produced cheaply as soon as the patent expires. In industries where patent protection is more difficult to achieve, this can negate the benefits of R&D. A company may spend millions developing an innovative product only for a rival to produce a similar product at a much cheaper price because the rival has not had to spend so much money on R&D.

FACT FILE

Research in Germany indicates that big firms find it easier to block R&D and innovation than to support it. The researchers from the University of Bochum identify rigid business structures and organisation as the main obstacles to R&D. Innovation leads to change and managers fear that this may undermine their positions in the company. Even the successful projects survive only because they have been taken 'underground' by their supporters, with development happening almost in secret, to avoid blockage by other managers. The researchers found that, unless R&D is integrated into the mainstream of the firm's activities, it is less likely to receive the support necessary for it to succeed.

EMPICS

Square water melons were first developed in Japan because the managers of large western food producers were not prepared to risk producing foods that were so obviously modified by human intervention. Recent concerns about genetically modified food highlight western society's reluctance to take risks with its food products.

The research concludes that R&D is often more successful in small firms, where workers may be allowed more freedom to develop their own ideas.

According to the researchers, there are two distinct approaches that large firms can take to avoid this problem. The first solution is to involve all interested parties right from the start, including partner companies such as customers and suppliers. Professor Cornelius Herstatt and his colleagues at the University of Hamburg have found that this early cooperation considerably reduces misunderstanding and opposition later on. It also provides a much larger group of people with a sense of 'ownership' of the R&D, and who will therefore support it if its value is questioned.

The second idea is to mimic small firms by creating small R&D units that operate independently from the more formal business structures, with a brief to champion the cause of innovation. This approach has been adopted by the pharmaceutical giant GlaxoSmithKline plc. Back in 2000, the company had to postpone its traditional 'R&D Day' for discussing new drugs, because there weren't any. Frustrated by this lack of new products arising from its R&D programme, the company's new head of R&D, Tachi Yamada, set up 'centres of excellence in clinical development'. The aim was to recreate the entrepreneurial spirit of smaller organisations. According to Yamada, size is an advantage in the early stages of research, when expensive computers are needed to screen alternative drugs, and in the last stages of human trials. 'But in the middle, size is a barrier. That's when you need quick, entrepreneurial, independent, free-thinking, unencumbered people.'

Yamada has also signed agreements with small independent drug development companies that will compete with the firm's own R&D 'centres of excellence'.

He believes that these businesses will eventually account for more than half of GSK's new drugs.

Sources: based on articles by Brian Bloch in the *Daily Telegraph*, 15 July 2004, and Stephen Foley in the *Independent*, 20 November 2004.

DID YOU KNOW?

Have you ever dreamed of owning Harry Potter's invisibility cloak but thought it was a technical impossibility? Think again. Scientists in Japan have developed an invisibility cloak.

The cloak has cameras built into the back and front of the garment. The material acts as a screen and the image from the cameras at the front of the cloak is projected on to the rear of the cloak and vice versa.

The only problem is that passers-by see a disembodied head. The scientists are working on an invisibility balaclava to overcome this problem.

Unfortunately, commercial applications have not yet been identified.

Ensuring successful research and development

As indicated, R&D will always involve risk because there are no guaranteed results. However, a firm can help the potential success of its R&D by taking the following actions:

- Make sure that any results of R&D are protected as soon as possible and in as many countries as possible through the use of copyrights and patents. This protection will give the firm sole ownership of the idea and will also give it time to refine the product.
- Plan projects early rather than late. A business should be aware of its existing products, particularly those that are approaching (but not yet in) the decline stage of their life cycles. At this point, new R&D should be undertaken so that the firm always has a product in the maturity stage of the product life cycle.
- Create a business culture that is supportive of R&D and encourage all employees to use their initiative. Quality circles are a classic Japanese approach to development, encouraging lots of small changes rather than relying on a major discovery. This culture must include the management of finance. In times of difficulty, R&D is often the first area of spending to be cut because of the uncertainty of returns. However, successful R&D can be the ideal way to overcome problems.
- Pay careful attention to the attractiveness of the idea to consumers. Many inventions have not been developed further by their inventors because they did not recognise the potential or were unable to persuade consumers to buy the product.

The importance of science and technology

R&D is not confined to businesses based on scientific or technologically advanced products and processes. Many new products developed by companies in industries such as leisure and tourism and publishing require no scientific input. However, in various industries, science and technology are becoming increasingly crucial to successful innovation.

CHAPTER 29 Research and development

FACT FILE

Even the humble cup of tea is subject to rigorous research. Unilever, producer of PG Tips, undertook a major R&D programme investigating the ideal teabag shape for optimum infusion of the tea. This R&D led to the introduction of the pyramid teabag — a process that took 4 years to complete.

Unilever's latest tea R&D project focuses on its Lipton Iced Tea. In the USA, 80% of tea is consumed as iced tea. Bottled iced tea is expensive but is the preferred product for most Americans, as the alternative is to make a traditional cup of tea with hot water and wait an hour for it to cool down.

A team of scientists drawn from Brooke Bond tea plantations in Kenya and Lipton and Unilever's R&D base in Colworth has developed novel technology to overcome this delay. 'Cold tea infusion technology' is a modification of standard tea processing that allows the tea to be brewed with cold water straight from the tap. Unilever has patented both the product and the process, and is expecting a considerable advantage in the iced tea market.

Scientific research can also serve to improve product quality. Each of Unilever's projects has focused on two elements: the provision of a new, innovative product and the improvement of product quality for the consumers.

Source: Unilever website: www.unilever.com.

R&D spending in UK businesses

The importance of science and technology has been recognised in the DTI's annual *R&D Scoreboard*. This annual survey examines the role of R&D in improving UK business efficiency. The report shows that increased spending on R&D among firms in high-tech sectors of the economy is bolstering the UK's international competitiveness.

R&D in the UK is dominated by the pharmaceutical and biotech sectors, which account for almost 40% of annual R&D spending in the UK. However, the major change shown is in computer software. This industry has increased its competitiveness following rises in R&D spending. Between 1999 and 2004, R&D spending in this industry increased from 4.9% to 6.8% of sales revenue. Almost a third of the 108 UK firms identified as 'R&D intensive' are involved in the software business. The need for heavy R&D spending is driving many smaller software businesses out of the computer games industry. Eidos, creator of *Tomb Raider*, admitted in June 2004 that it was too small and could no longer afford the technology and expensive testing required to ensure the quality of its new games. The firm is seeking joint ventures with other companies so that it can continue to compete with larger-scale rivals.

Overall, the UK still lags behind countries such as the USA in terms of R&D spending. The UK's flagship firms invest only 2.3% of their sales revenue in R&D, compared with 4.9% for similar firms in the USA (see Figure 29.1 and Table 29.1).

(a)

(b)

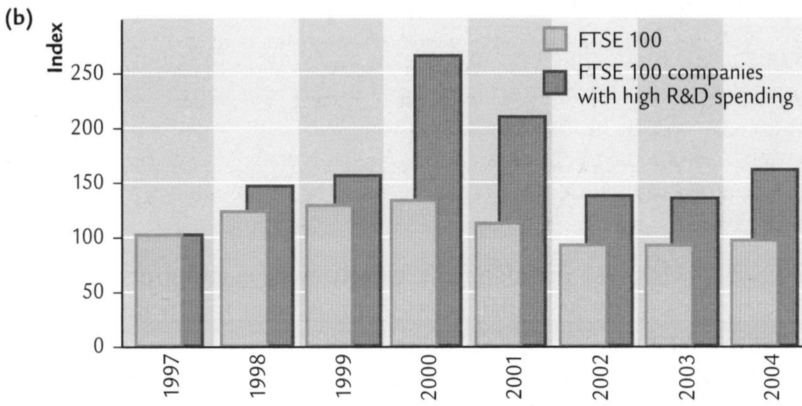

Source: *The Times*, 25 October 2004.

Figure 29.1 *(a) Number of UK R&D-intensive companies with research budgets of more than 4% of sales. (b) Relative share prices*

Table 29.1 *Annual R&D spending, 2004*

UK top 5	R&D spending (% of sales)	International top 5	R&D spending (% of sales)
GlaxoSmithKline	£2.8 billion (13.0%)	Ford	£4.2 billion (3.8%)
AstraZeneca	£1.9 billion (18.3%)	Pfizer	£4.0 billion (18.1%)
BAE Systems	£1.1 billion (13.1%)	DaimlerChrysler	£3.9 billion (5.1%)
Unilever	£0.8 billion (2.0%)	Siemens	£3.9 billion (17.7%)
BT	£0.3 billion (2.3%)	Toyota Motor	£3.5 billion (4.0%)

Source: *The Times*, 25 October 2004.

FILE

After years of concentration on 'business systems' that maximise efficiency and gear organisations to maximising productivity, many companies are now having to change the business culture that they have created in order to encourage more creative and innovative thinking by employees.

Throughout the 1980s and 1990s, General Electric (GE) achieved success through a programme of diversification and cost cutting, focused on short-term profits.

The firm that developed the light bulb and X-ray ended the twentieth century by leading the trend to buy back its own shares, partly because it lacked new product ideas to develop with any retained profit.

The firm is now working hard to change its culture in order to retrieve its reputation for innovation. In the same way that Hewlett-Packard draws attention to its focus through its 'Invent' mission, GE has changed its slogan to 'Imagination at Work'.

DID YOU KNOW?

Many UK universities are using their brainpower to develop new, innovative businesses. Science Parks have sprung up in cities such as Oxford and Cambridge, with firms being set up to take advantage of, and develop commercially, the scientific research emanating from the universities.

Many of these firms are involved in biotechnology, which is one of the UK's most R&D-intensive industries. Seabait, a small company in Ashington, Northumberland, grew out of research undertaken at Newcastle University in the 1980s. Seabait specialises in producing marine worms that are used as a high-quality diet for shrimp farms.

FACT FILE

The Apple iPod is a product that arose from R&D. However, rather than rest on its laurels, Apple increased the iPod's capacity from 5 gigabytes to 10 and then 40, and introduced a smaller model. Meanwhile, its competitors are still trying to catch up with the first iPod.

Integrating R&D with other functions

Although R&D is often pictured as a separate activity, with scientists working independently in laboratories in the hope of discovering a new product or process, in reality it must be integrated with the organisation's other functions. As noted earlier, researchers at the University of Bochum found that a lack of integration with other functions was one of the main reasons for the failure of R&D.

Successful R&D must therefore link closely with existing products and customer needs. Three particular factors that need to be incorporated into any R&D programme are:

- product design
- product life cycles
- market research

R&D and product design

As society becomes wealthier, consumers place greater importance on the design of the products that they buy. This trend means that firms must incorporate product design into their R&D activities. In some industries, such as fashion, the product design is arguably more important than any other factor. Stella McCartney Ltd is 50% owned by the Gucci Group and is in its third year of trading. In 2003/04 the Gucci Group invested £6.5 million in the company. The majority of this funding has gone into Stella McCartney Ltd's design and creative studios and a separate product development department. Between 2003 and 2004, worldwide sales of the McCartney label rose from £14 million to £21 million. The R&D expenditure also includes funding for the development of a new range of perfumes.

TOPFOTO/UPPA

However, good product design is important not just to clothes designers. If R&D can deliver a well-designed product, it can provide a number of benefits, such as:

- improving the durability and reliability of the product
- improving the appearance of the product and making it more fashionable
- enhancing the convenience of use for consumers

- allowing a firm to keep within the law by modifying products to meet new legislation, such as the need for more environmentally friendly products
- reducing the cost of manufacture by modifying production processes or designing a product that is easier to make.

DID YOU KNOW?

Formula 1 racing is very R&D intensive, as car manufacturers use their racing cars to test advanced techniques and equipment. Ferrari spends £220 million a year on Formula 1. Toyota has the second biggest Formula 1 budget — a total of £192 million in 2004. Of this, £139 million is spent on R&D activities.

FACT FILE

Shimano, the Japanese bike parts maker, celebrated Lance Armstrong's victory in the 2004 Tour de France. Armstrong was riding a bike powered by Shimano pedals and cranks, shifted with Shimano derailleurs and slowed (only occasionally, of course) by Shimano brakes. In the past 20 years, Shimano has become the dominant supplier of components for the higher-end range of bikes.

The keys to Shimano's success are R&D and market research. Every year it sends more than a dozen employees to work with manufacturers in order to discover changes in design that are taking place. It also holds regular meetings with top racers such as Armstrong to discuss products and prototypes. With its consistent focus on market research, a strategy that led to it identifying the 1980s trend towards mountain biking, Shimano is equipped to meet the changing needs of its customers.

Source: *Business Week*, 9 August 2004.

R&D and product life cycles

Timing is vital in research and development. Companies use the product life cycle to try to time the release of new products or product modifications.

Experience helps a firm to ascertain the normal time that it takes to modify a product or develop and release a new one. With this information, firms can plan the timing of extension strategies and new product launches.

Figure 29.2 shows the link between R&D and extension strategies. The company forecasts that, at point A, sales of its existing product will reach the decline stage of the product life cycle. The dotted line AB shows the forecast sales of the original product. Careful timing of an R&D programme will allow the firm to create a modified version of the product that will revitalise sales, keeping the product in the maturity stage. The line AC shows the sales of the modified product.

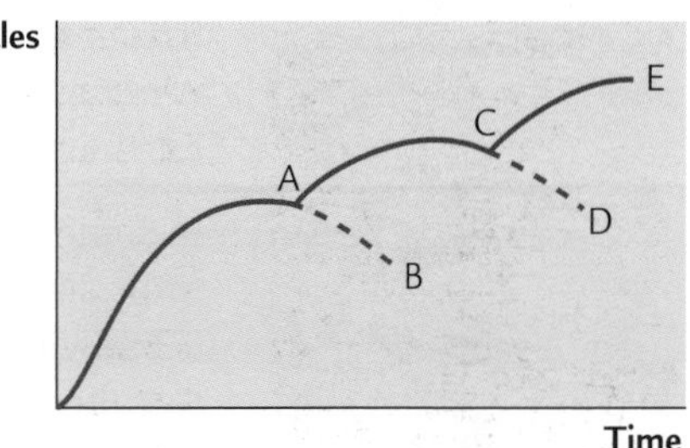

Figure 29.2 *R&D and product life cycle extension*

Again, at C a further modification is introduced in order to prevent sales falling (as shown by the line CD). This modification again prolongs the maturity stage of the product life cycle, allowing sales to grow from C to E.

Figure 29.2 shows the pattern when the process has worked well. However, the product life cycle is never easy to forecast and the success of R&D programmes is never guaranteed. In reality, attempts to use R&D to extend the life cycle are unlikely to work as smoothly as shown in Figure 29.2.

An alternative approach is to use research and development to launch new products at a time when it is considered that the original product is declining and beyond the help of an extension strategy.

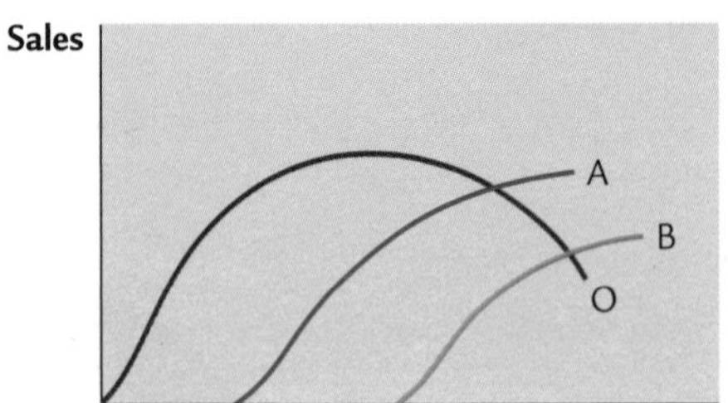

Figure 29.3 *R&D and early new product launch*

Figure 29.3 shows the product life cycles of three products. Line O shows the original product. In anticipation of the decline of product O, a new product (A) is launched onto the market. Note how, in this case, product A is launched while O is still in its growth stage. This is because product O is expected to have a relatively short maturity period. Most products spend much longer in maturity than the products shown in Figure 29.3, so new product development will not usually need to be planned until an existing product has reached maturity. However, this depends on the length of the R&D process, which can take many years in some cases. The diagram also shows the launch of product B, which will be needed to replace product A.

The timing of new launches is a major challenge to firms. In Figure 29.3, the relatively early launch of product A is likely to hasten the decline of product O, as customers will prefer a newer version.

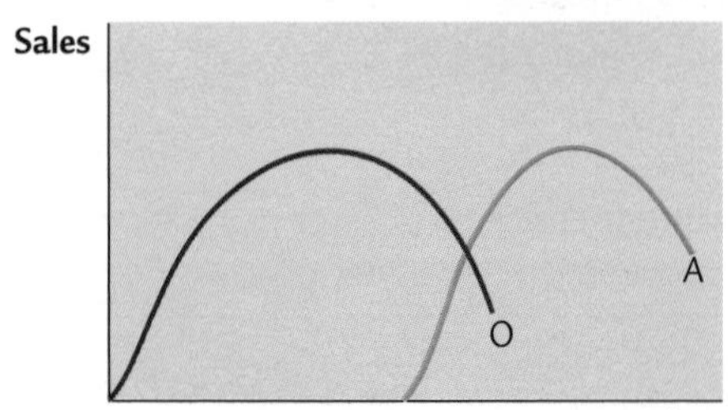

Figure 29.4 *R&D and delayed new product launch*

The alternative is to wait until product O has started to decline. Figure 29.4 shows the situation where the R&D is delayed, so that product O is already into its decline period before product A is launched. This prevents product A from 'cannibalising' (taking away) sales of product O, but it does mean that there is a period in which the company has no product with a high market share. This may open up opportunities for competitors to increase their influence in the market.

R&D and market research

Although R&D and market research are separate business activities, it is essential that they are coordinated.

In some industries, products are discovered. In the pharmaceutical industry, firms aim to meet market needs, focusing research on aspects that the market is known to want, such as cures for cancer and HIV. However, it is recognised that the curative properties of many drugs are identified in laboratories before their commercial applications are confirmed. In this case, R&D creates the product and market research is then used to find out whether it can be marketed profitably.

In other cases, market research is used to identify a market need. This information is then relayed to the R&D teams, who try to develop a product to serve that market need.

The Fact File on Shimano (p. 271) indicates the nature of this link. Shimano combines both R&D and market research in order to introduce new products. A successful product must meet consumer needs, but must also be produced at a cost that makes it financially viable.

FACT FILE

Even after the release of a new product, R&D is needed to monitor progress. This is particularly true in the pharmaceutical industry. In 2004, the industry suffered a number of setbacks involving drugs developing unforeseen side-effects. This led the USA's Food and Drug Administration, the authority responsible for scrutinising drugs that can be sold in the USA, to recommend the withdrawal of permission to provide these drugs. Among the companies and drugs affected were:

- AstraZeneca – Crestor, a cholesterol-lowering drug
- GlaxoSmithKline – Serevent, an asthma treatment
- Merck – Vioxx, an arthritis painkiller
- Pfizer – Bextra, a painkiller
- Roche – Accutane, an acne treatment

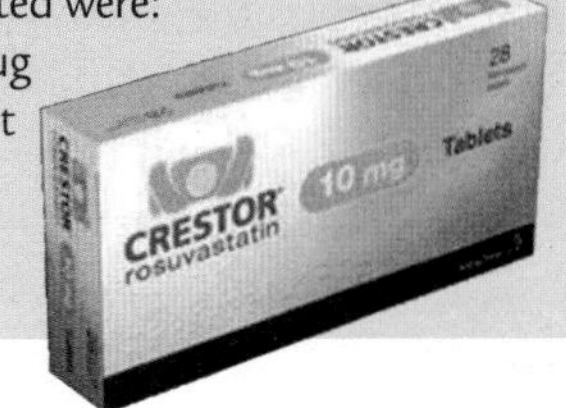

How much should an organisation spend on R&D?

The UK government believes that the UK is not spending enough on R&D. However, for individual organisations, the need for R&D varies considerably. The main factors that influence the need for R&D spending are as follows:

- **The nature of the product.** Technically advanced products offer scope for improvement through research and development. Among the most highly developed economies in the world there is a consistent pattern of high R&D spending in industries involved in the production of cars, pharmaceuticals and biotechnology, computer hardware and software, electronics and chemicals. In 2004, these industries accounted for 78.5% of the world's R&D spending.
- **Competition.** The need to keep ahead of rivals is often identified as the driving force behind R&D. UK businesses that export have a much greater tendency to spend money on R&D because they face higher levels of competition than firms that do not need to match overseas competitors.
- **The market.** Ultimately, R&D succeeds only if the firm provides products that are wanted by consumers. If customer tastes are continually changing, such as in computer software, the need for R&D is increased. In more static markets, such as clothing, there is less need for R&D.

The factors above identify the main influences on the need to spend money on R&D. The following factors are significant in determining *how much* is actually spent:

- **Finance.** R&D is expensive and cannot guarantee results. In times of financial difficulty, it is often cut back; in times of plenty, it may be generously funded.
- **Company culture.** Risk-taking firms are much more likely to involve themselves in R&D. A business that is more conservative in its culture will be more cautious in releasing funds for R&D and will also be more inclined to stop a project that is not appearing to bring in results. Another aspect of culture is whether the business takes a long-term or short-term view of its future. R&D rarely brings in profit in the short term, so it is not going to be encouraged in a business seeking immediate returns.
- **Chances of success.** Ultimately, R&D is a gamble. Research into the common cold has not increased in line with other pharmaceutical research because organisations are not optimistic that they will find a cure.
- **Efficiency of R&D.** Although R&D is subject to chance, businesses can take steps to improve the effectiveness of their R&D. GlaxoSmithKline plc is an example of a business that is introducing changes in its approach rather than in its overall spending levels. Thus, an effective programme of R&D may actually lead to a fall in the expenditure needed to achieve a firm's targets.

PRACTICE EXERCISE 1 — Total: 40 marks (40 minutes)

1. Briefly explain three functions of research and development. *(6 marks)*
2. Analyse two problems that a pharmaceutical company might experience in its research and development. *(6 marks)*
3. Explain two actions that a firm can take in order to improve the chances of success for its research and development. *(6 marks)*
4. Identify three UK industries that are major investors in research and development. *(3 marks)*
5. Indicate two ways in which the product life cycle influences the need for research and development. *(6 marks)*
6. Why is it important for research and development to be linked with market research? *(4 marks)*
7. Explain three factors that influence the level of research in a business. *(9 marks)*

CASE STUDY 1 The crinkly can built to indent new markets

This case study is based on topics covered in Chapter 29.

Francis Labbé, chief executive of Impress, the world's second biggest maker of non-beverage cans, thinks crinkly cans are a selling point. This thinking is based on five factors:

- They stand out on the shelves, providing product differentiation for the products that they contain.
- They are easy to grab and hold; of particular importance if one is standing on top of a ladder and the can contains paint or some form of decorating material.
- Production is technologically complex, so counterfeiting is difficult — a particular advantage in eastern Europe, where leading brands are often copied illegally.

- They could feature in company marketing as a talking point.
- Empty cans can be given to young children to play with.

The non-beverage can industry is worth £8.1 billion a year. This is a highly competitive market in which Impress has an 11% market share. It produces 8 billion cans a year in 20,000 different shapes, sizes and colours. It sells them at an average price of 11p. Its customers tend to be powerful consumer goods companies that can dictate the price paid to suppliers — few cans sell for more than 17p. The industry has suffered from higher raw material costs too. In 2004, steel costs rose by 100%.

This is where the crinkly can enters the story. Impress reckons that only a continual stream of new ideas will enable it to preserve its profitability. Richard Moore, head of strategy, says: 'Our customers are always wanting designs that will promote excitement.' The company's R&D effort employs 90 staff and accounts for 1% of the firm's costs. Currently, the firm is researching an 'easy to open' can.

The first corporate customer is ICI, the UK chemical company. The new crinkle can is being tested out in Poland. The product in the cans is ICI's Hammerite, a special paint used to rust-proof metal surfaces.

Labbé believes that R&D is essential to the company's future. 'Our profit margins right now are unsatisfactory. We need to get our margins up to at least 10%.' He is betting that these new products will help him achieve his goal.

Source: based on an article by Peter Marsh in the *Financial Times*, 5 November 2004.

Question

Total: 20 marks (25 minutes)

Discuss the advantages and disadvantages for Impress of the introduction of the crinkly can.

CASE STUDY 2 Executive euphoria fed by the sweet taste of success

This case study is based on topics covered in Chapter 29.

Tate and Lyle executives are ecstatic. A product discovered in their laboratories in 1976, and nurtured despite few signs that it would ever reach commercial production, has finally come good. Sales of sucralose, a no-calorie sweetener made from sugar, are 'going like the clappers'.

Food manufacturers, keen to take advantage of rising demand for diet products, want all the sucralose they can get because it performs better than other calorie-free sweeteners. For example, it can be heated to high temperatures and its shelf-life makes it suitable for even the longest-lasting foodstuffs.

For years Tate was known as a commodity producer, refining sugar and milling grain. Even the more unusual products developed by its R&D activities, such as sugar soap, tended to compete in mass markets. Faced with falling profit margins, Tate and Lyle stayed loyal to sucralose, convinced that one day it would form a part of a 'high value-added' business that would transform its profit margins.

Tate's strategy was twofold: cut back on its core activities and replace them with more unique, value-added products. This strategy required a successful R&D programme.

In addition, Tate and Lyle has discovered and patented three new products that, along with sucralose, now create over 50% of the company's profits. These products are:

- Bio-3G — a by-product of corn that can produce a fibre for use in clothes and carpets, and which is cheaper than polyester.
- Aquasta — a nutrient for fish farming that is renewable and replaces what was previously an oil-based non-renewable nutrient.

- Biogums — a product that provides texture and body to a wide range of food products, such as salad dressings.

Other products are in the pipeline. Tate is continuing to increase funding for R&D and has transformed its company culture from one of security, safety and dependability to one that thrives on innovation and creativity.

So what can go wrong? Analysts point out that Tate is still reliant for most of its sales on commodities such as sugar and grain, and thus at the mercy of highly volatile agricultural prices. However, Tate is confident that this agricultural basis is needed to assist the development of its new products. With patents secured and technological know-how not possessed by its rivals, Tate and Lyle is confident that it can maintain high profit margins on these new products.

Source: adapted from an article by Maggie Urry in the *Financial Times*, 5 November 2004.

Questions

Total: 40 marks (45 minutes)

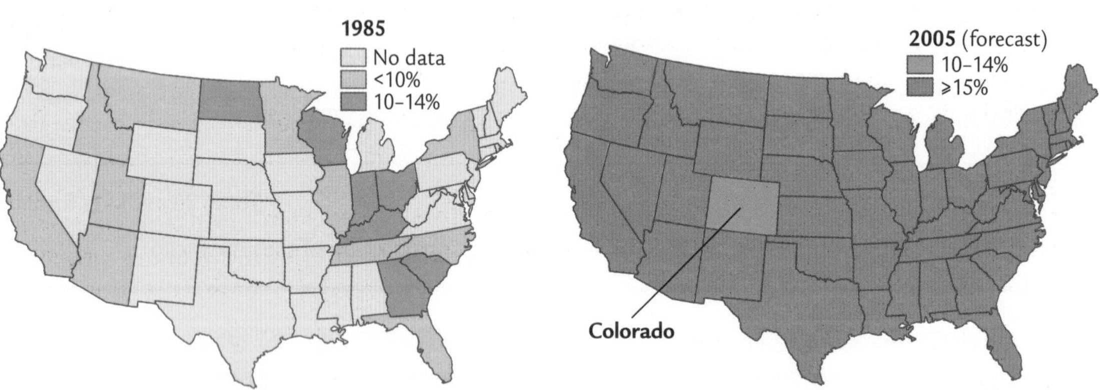

***Figure 29.5** Incidence of obesity among US adults*

1 a Study the maps shown in Figure 29.5. Analyse the likely impact on Tate and Lyle of increased levels of obesity among American adults. *(8 marks)*

b To what extent is Tate and Lyle's success the result of a long-term strategy based on research and development? *(12 marks)*

2 a Analyse the ways in which Tate and Lyle can protect itself from competition for the new products that it introduces as a result of its research and development. *(8 marks)*

b Evaluate the benefits and problems for Tate and Lyle of increasing its focus on research and development as a means of securing its future. *(12 marks)*

CHAPTER 30

Critical path analysis

This chapter introduces critical path analysis (CPA), describing the terminology used and showing how a network is constructed in order to represent a project. The notion of the critical path is explained. The implications of CPA for different aspects of business are discussed and the potential difficulties examined.

KEY TERMS

network analysis: a method of planning business operations in order to identify the most efficient way of completing an integrated task or project. The main form of network analysis is critical path analysis.

critical path analysis: the process of planning the sequence of activities in a project in order to discover the most efficient and quickest way of completing it.

critical path: the sequence of activities in a project that must be completed within a designated time in order to prevent any delay in overall completion of the project.

critical activity: any activity on the critical path.

Background

The roots of critical path analysis (CPA) lie in aircraft. During the Second World War, the US Air Force recognised that an aircraft on the ground was both ineffective as a fighting weapon and more vulnerable to attack. Consequently, critical path analysis techniques were employed to ensure that planes were serviced and overhauled as quickly as possible.

Ironically, one of the latest converts to CPA is the airline industry. Southwest Airlines in the USA and Ryanair in Europe have used CPA to excellent effect to reduce the turnaround time on a plane (the time between it touching down and taking off again) to 25 minutes — half the time of rivals such as British Airways. This increases the number of journeys that a plane can make.

TOPFOTO

Critical path analysis is widely used in industries such as construction, in which it is possible to operate a range of activities in parallel. By mapping out the network of different activities, the firm is able to see which activities can run concurrently (at the same time) in order to save time and thus complete complex projects as quickly as possible. CPA also allows a business to identify those activities that cannot be delayed without holding up the overall project.

Features of critical path analysis

Networks in critical path analysis are constructed in a specific way (see Figure 30.1). The features of a network are identified below:

- **Nodes.** These are circles representing a point in time, identified by the completion or start of an activity. Nodes are split into three. The left half of the node contains the **number of the node**. This serves to provide a unique identity for each node. The right half of the node is split into two. The top segment shows the **earliest start time (EST)** that an activity can commence, and depends on the completion of the previous activity. For the opening activity or activities the EST is always zero. The bottom segment shows the **latest finish time (LFT)** of the previous activity, or can be seen to represent the **latest start time (LST)** at which the next activity can commence without delaying the overall project.
- **Activities.** These are events or tasks that consume time and are shown as lines that link the nodes on the network diagram. Most network diagrams show activities moving from left to right, but for clarity arrows are usually shown on the lines to indicate the sequence of activities. A letter (or description of the activity) is placed above the line that represents that activity.
- **Duration.** This is the length of time that it takes to complete an activity. Depending on the nature of the project, the duration may be measured in months, weeks, days or minutes. The duration is shown as a number below the line that represents that activity.
- **Prerequisite.** This is the activity (or activities) that must be completed before our selected activity can commence. For example, 'reading the questions' should be a prerequisite of 'starting to answer questions in an examination', and 'getting dressed' should be a prerequisite of 'catching the bus in the morning'.
- **Dummies.** These are activities that do not consume time, but are incorporated into a network to show the true sequence of events. (Dummy nodes and activities may also be used to show more clearly the ESTs and LSTs/LFTs of non-critical activities.)

***Figure 30.1** Features of critical path analysis*

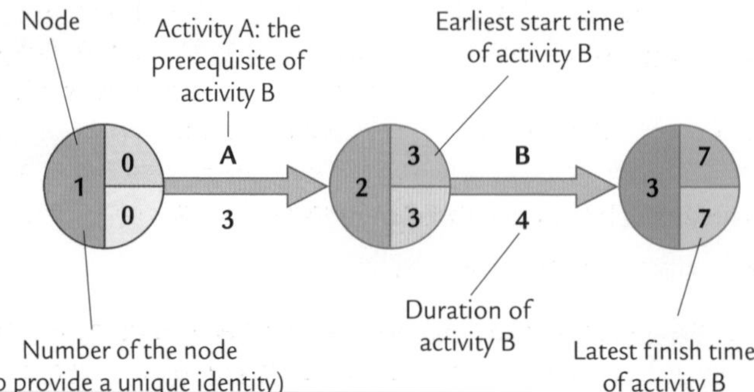

EXAMINER'S VOICE

There is no direct reference to the use of 'dummies' in the AQA specification and no examination questions to date have required their use. Consequently, their use is not featured in any of the example networks in this book.

Similarly, because the AQA specification refers to the latest finish time (LFT) rather than latest start time (LST) of an activity, any examples in this book will use latest finish times (LFTs).

Constructing a critical path network

Table 30.1 shows a series of activities that form a network. This table lays out the logic behind the sequence of activities that make up a project.

Once a table of this type has been constructed, the network is laid out by following the approach outlined below.

Activity	Duration (days)	Prerequisite(s)
A	6	–
B	7	A
C	5	A
D	3	C
E	8	C
F	4	B, D
G	2	E, F

Table 30.1 *Activities in a network*

1 Draw a node (circle) to represent the start of the network. (All networks must start and end at a single node.) See node 1 (the first node on the left) in Figure 30.2. Number each node as it is drawn.

2 Identify any activities that have no prerequisite. Draw lines from left to right, starting from the original node, for the activities that have no prerequisite. Do not draw any nodes at the right-hand end of these activity lines at this stage. See activity A in Figure 30.2.

3 Identify the activity line by placing a description of it immediately above the line in the diagram (either the letter or activity description). See activity A in Figure 30.2.

4 Put the duration of the activity immediately under the line. Activity A is represented by a 6, showing that it takes 6 days to complete.

5 Move on to the first activity that has a prerequisite (activity B in this example). Place a node (circle) at the end of the line that represents the prerequisite activity, as this activity must be completed before the next activity can begin. Draw a line starting at the node that you have just drawn to represent the new activity (see activity B in Figure 30.2). Do not place a circle at the end of this node at this stage. (If a new activity has two or more prerequisites, the lines representing these prerequisite activities must be drawn in such a way that they both lead into the same node. This node therefore represents the point of time at which both of the prerequisites have been completed and the new activity can begin. See activities F and G in Figure 30.2 for examples.

6 Repeat stages 3 to 5 for activity B.

7 Continue this process until every activity has been completed. (At this point there will be at least one line that has not been completed by a node.)

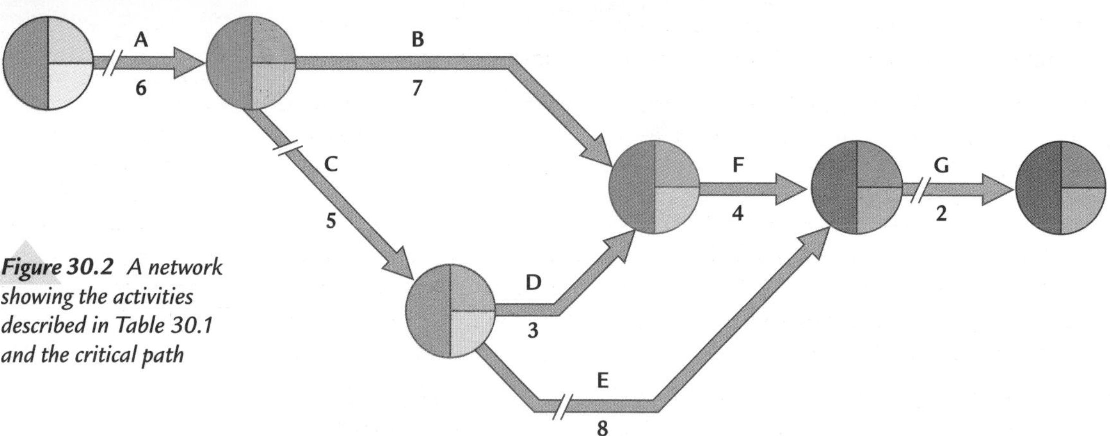

Figure 30.2 A network showing the activities described in Table 30.1 and the critical path

8 As all of the network's activities have now been plotted, bring any remaining lines together into a final node. This node represents the completion of the project that has been planned by the network. See node 6, the last node on the right, in Figure 30.2.

Completing the timings

Completing the earliest start times

Once the outline diagram has been completed, work forward (from left to right) to calculate the earliest start times (ESTs). The EST in the first node (the EST of activity A) is shown as a zero.

For subsequent activities, the EST is found by adding the sum of the durations of activities on the path that leads up to the node that represents the start time of that activity. For example, the EST in node 3 is 6 + 5 = 11 (see Figure 30.3). Thus both D and E cannot start before day 11 because activity A takes 6 days and activity C takes 5 days to complete.

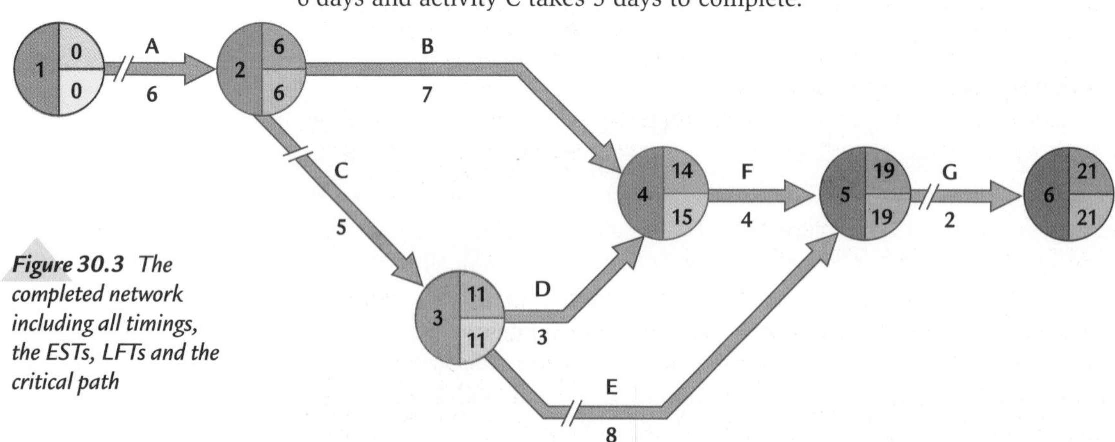

Figure 30.3 The completed network including all timings, the ESTs, LFTs and the critical path

If there is more than one path to a node, the highest total is taken as the EST. For example, activity F cannot begin until A and then B are completed (6 + 7 = 13 days). However, activity F also cannot start until activities A, C and D have been completed. These three activities take 6 + 5 + 3 = 14 days to complete. Therefore, the EST for activity F is 14 days rather than 13 days.

Insert the EST in the top right-hand corner of the node at the start point of that activity. The EST in the final node represents the earliest completion time for the project.

Completing the latest finish times (LFTs)

Once the ESTs have been completed, work backwards from right to left to calculate the latest finish times (LFT). The LFT in the final node must equal the EST because a final activity must be on the critical path. Place the LFT in the bottom right-hand quadrant.

Moving from right to left, deduct the duration of the activity in order to calculate the LFT of the previous activity. Keep moving from right to left inserting the LFTs in the bottom right-hand quadrants. For example, the LFT for activity F, shown in node 5, is 19. This figure is calculated by taking the LFT in node 6, 21, and deducting the 2 days that it will take to complete activity G: 21 – 2 = 19.

Be cautious where there are nodes that lead on to more than one activity. For example, the bottom right-hand sector of node 2 shows the number 6. This is because by working backwards from right to left on the path G to E to C, we arrive at a figure of 6 as the LFT for activity A (21 – 2 – 8 – 5 = 6). Thus the LFT shown in node 2 is 6. However, by moving backwards from right to left along the path G to F to B we also arrive at node 2. The calculation for the LFT via this path is 21 – 2 – 4 – 7 = 8. *If there is more than one path working backwards to a node, the lowest total is taken as the LFT.* In effect, the digit 6 in the bottom right-hand quadrant of node 2 means that the latest finish time for activity A is 6 days, if activity C is to be started on time. However, it is possible to start activity B on day 8 without delaying the overall project.

EXAMINER'S VOICE

For any activities, the node at the start of the activity line gives the EST in the top right-hand section and the node at the end of the activity line gives the LFT in the bottom right-hand section.

Plotting the critical path

The critical path is the sequence of activities that cannot be delayed without delaying the overall completion of the project. It is represented by those activities that:

- have LFTs identical to their ESTs *and*
- represent the longest path between the nodes

In Figure 30.3 the sequence A–C–E–G represents the critical path. For these critical activities, the ESTs and LFTs in each node are the same.

Non-critical activities are those that can be delayed without extending the completion time of the project. In Figure 30.3, these are activities B, D and F. Although both node 2 and node 3 show identical ESTs and LFTs, these arise because activities C and E are both on the critical path. We have seen already, by working back from right to left, that activity B can be delayed by 2 days without delaying the overall completion of the project. Similarly, activity D can be delayed by 1 day because the working-back process gives a figure of 12 for node 3.

In Figure 30.3, the critical path is shown by the symbol //. This is common practice, but the critical path may be shown in other ways, such as through the use of a highlighter or colour.

We can therefore see that, although individually the seven activities in Table 30.1 take a total of 35 days, by careful planning the project can be completed in 21 days.

Float times

KEY TERMS

float time: the amount of time that non-critical activities within a project can be delayed without affecting the deadline for completion of the project as a whole.

total float for an activity: the number of days that an activity can be delayed without delaying the project, measured by the formula:

total float for an activity = LFT – EST – duration of the activity

Thus activity D can be delayed by 15 – 11 – 3 = 1 day, without delaying the project.

Activity	Total float (days)
A*	0
B	2
C*	0
D	1
E*	0
F	1
G*	0

*Critical activity.

Table 30.2 *Float times*

The float times can be derived from the network and are set out in Table 30.2.

WHAT DO YOU THINK?

Be cautious when using total float to calculate how long activities can be delayed.

Table 30.2 shows that:

- Activity B can be delayed by 2 days without delaying completion of the overall project.
- Activity D can be delayed by 1 day without delaying completion of the overall project.
- Activity F can be delayed by 1 day without delaying completion of the overall project.

However, what happens in each of the following situations?

a Activity B is delayed by 2 days *and* Activity D is delayed by 1 day.

b Activity B is delayed by 2 days *and* Activity F is delayed by 1 day.

c Activity D is delayed by 1 day *and* Activity F is delayed by 1 day.

You should find that situation **a** is the only one that leads to no overall delay. Why do you think this happens?

EXAMINER'S VOICE

If you experience difficulties in constructing a network, remember the examiner's 'own figure rule'. The examiner will reward you for those parts of your answer that are logically correct, even if an earlier mistake means that the final answer is wrong. Do not leave your network incomplete. If you have a start node and bring together the final activities into a node to represent the finish of the project, you should be able to add together all of the timings and therefore find a critical path. You will be given credit for any relevant understanding shown within your network.

Constructing a critical path network from descriptive information

In real life, managers will not be given a table of activities with their prerequisites neatly defined. The first step in compiling a real network is to work out the logic behind the project in order to identify sequences of events.

The following activities represent the steps needed to introduce a new product that has just completed its design stage:

A Brief advertising agencies — 1 day
B Await ideas from agencies — 15 days
C Select advertising agency — 2 days
D Prepare advertising materials for launch — 40 days
E Order new production machinery — 3 days
F Await delivery of machinery — 20 days
G Install machinery — 12 days
H Production run for initial launch — 15 days
I Recruit production workers — 21 days
J Off-the-job training of production workers — 6 days
K Launch product — 1 day

Activity	Duration (days)	Prerequisite(s)
A	1	–
B	15	A
C	2	B
D	40	C
E	3	–
F	20	E
G	12	F
H	15	G, J
I	21	–
J	6	I
K	1	D, H

Table 30.3 *Network of activities needed to launch a new product*

Activities A to D form a logical sequence of events in the marketing department, with A being the first stage. Activities E to H are the sequence of production department activities, with activity E being able to start at the beginning of the network. Activities I and J are personnel roles. Activity I can start at the beginning of the project and is the prerequisite of activity J. However, J must be completed before activity H, as this stage requires trained workers. Once all of the marketing and production activities have been completed, the final activity (K) can take place.

The sequence of events based on the logic described above is shown in Table 30.3.

Figure 30.4 shows the network based on these data.

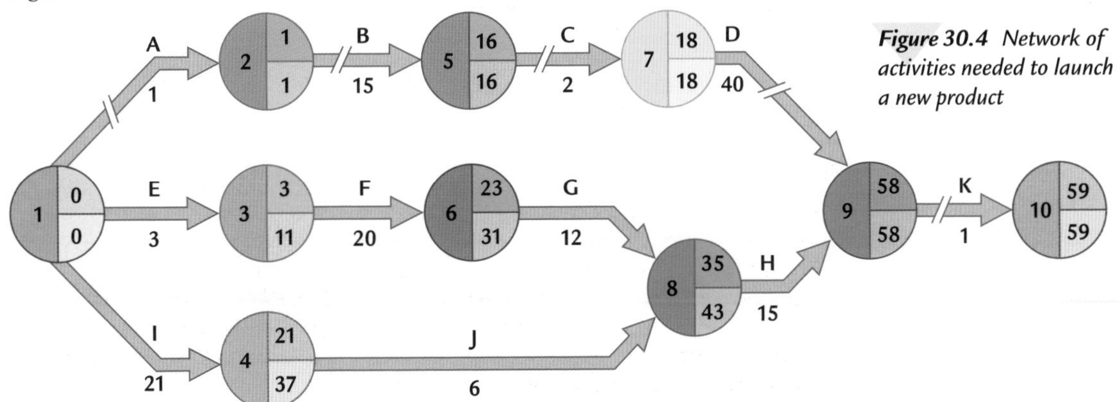

Figure 30.4 *Network of activities needed to launch a new product*

The critical path is A–B–C–D–K.

EXAMINER'S VOICE

Note that, although the sequence of events in the network may not change, the critical path can change because it is dependent on the timings of the activities. For example, in Figure 30.4 an increase in the duration of F from 20 days to 30 days will lead to a change in the critical path (from A-B-C-D-K to E-F-G-H-K). Overall, the duration of the project will increase from 59 days to 61 days.

Business implications of critical path analysis

Use of critical path analysis brings many advantages to a business, if the system operates smoothly.

Efficiency benefits

- Critical path analysis allows a business to improve the efficiency of its resources. If the business can reduce the time taken to complete a project, it can translate these savings in time into cost savings. In turn, this will increase the competitiveness of the business, particularly if cost or speed of completion is a vital factor in the eyes of the customers.
- The process lets a business know precisely when activities are scheduled to take place. This assists the business in its resource planning and stock ordering. This should improve the efficiency of resources, such as labour, as it enables the business to make sure that the use of labour corresponds to the available supply. It also helps businesses to manage their stock levels to prevent excess stock or insufficient stock being held.
- If necessary, the business can use CPA to investigate changes in resources or sequencing that would improve efficiency. For example, additional resources can be transferred from a non-critical activity to one on the critical path. This will reduce the time taken on the critical path and therefore reduce the overall duration of the project.
- CPA can be used to help control and review. Monitoring of progress against the original plan will identify any delays and allow the business to take steps to rectify the problem early (or take maximum advantage of the situation if activities are ahead of schedule).

Business decision-making benefits

- Critical path analysis forces managers to engage in detailed planning. This helps the business to reduce the risk of delays and other problems that may not have been anticipated without the careful planning demanded by network analysis.
- The business's relationship with its customers can be improved, as it can provide detailed information on the schedule for completion of a project.
- As indicated earlier, changes in scheduling can be implemented to change the allocation of resources or sequencing of activities, in order to improve efficiency.

- During the operation of the project, CPA can be used to calculate the likely impact of any delays that are unavoidable.
- The information from CPA assists managers in making high-quality decisions, by ensuring that all of the business's functions, such as marketing, production and finance, are integrated.

FACT FILE

Unilever is a company that has benefited from using CPA to provide an integrated view of its projects. A network constructed to plan the release of a new food product shows that, at different stages of the network, the critical path activities are, on the whole, marketing department responsibilities. However, at particular points of time, production, packaging and distribution activities are on the critical path. Consequently, Unilever managers know when it is most vital to monitor the progress of particular departments.

Time-based management benefits

- Critical path analysis helps the firm to estimate the minimum time within which it is possible to complete a project (through identifying the critical path).
- By identifying the (critical) activities that cannot be delayed without delaying the completion of the project, CPA gives a firm the opportunity to focus its attention on the more 'important' tasks.
- The network helps the organisation to calculate the extent to which other (non-critical) activities can be delayed. This reduces the possibility of a project failing because the delay in a non-critical activity suddenly becomes significant and causes that activity to be on the critical path.
- Resources needed for each activity can be made available at the appropriate time because CPA identifies the exact time when those resources are needed. This reduces costs.
- Time can be saved by identifying those activities that can be completed simultaneously.

INGRAM

Working capital benefits

- Critical path analysis allows a firm to plan when it needs particular resources. This means that the firm can avoid holding unnecessary stock and will be able to reduce its cash holdings to the level needed to purchase resources needed in the near future, as indicated by the network.
- Firms that want to use just-in-time methods of stockholding can do so because they know when stock is needed. Consequently, lower stock levels can be held.
- The impact of any delays on the firm can be calculated by adjusting the network. This will usually give the firm enough time to modify its approach in order to avoid running out of working capital.

Problems of using critical path analysis

Although critical path analysis is a useful tool, its use can lead to difficulties:

- It can encourage rigidity. On paper, CPA works best with fixed times for each activity and a fixed sequence of activities. This may encourage managers to see these timings and this sequence as unchangeable, so they may miss opportunities to reduce the overall time of a project by failing to identify the scope for flexibility.
- As every activity in a network is strictly timetabled, it can lead to greater inefficiency if a crucial activity is delayed. This can happen in projects such as the construction of a building, where subcontractors and suppliers will plan their workloads around the original network. Any delay can lead to the project coming to a halt because, for example, the crane hire company has agreed to hire the crane to another company or the electricians are working on another firm's building.
- Complex activities may be very difficult to represent accurately on a network. (In practice, businesses use computer modelling to construct highly complex networks, but these need to be understood by the manager.)
- There may be a tendency to believe that the hard work has been done when the CPA has been completed. However, the project must be managed and monitored thoroughly at every stage, as keeping to the initial network is more challenging, especially as external factors change.
- CPA relies on estimates of the expected duration of activities. If these are inaccurate, the whole process may break down. As major projects are often one-offs, it is possible that the firm has no experience in this field. Consequently, the probability of producing an accurate forecast of timings is low. Firms often provide ranges of estimates (best-case to worst-case scenarios) to allow for this uncertainty, but this approach can cause networks to become very complicated and unclear.
- CPA encourages businesses to focus on the speed of completion of a project, rather than other elements such as quality and flexibility to meet the customer's needs. As such, it may not increase profitability because it encourages thinking that is product-led rather than market-led.

e EXAMINER'S VOICE

Although most networks are large-scale projects, it is not possible to include a complex network in an examination. Any requirements to complete a network will involve a fairly small-scale project or the completion of details such as timings, the identification of the critical path and float time calculations.

Remember, critical path analysis is not just about drawing diagrams. Make sure that, for a particular project, you can present relevant arguments on the benefits that CPA brings and the limitations to its usefulness.

PRACTICE EXERCISE 1 — Total: 35 marks (30 minutes)

1 What is meant by the term 'network analysis'? *(3 marks)*

2 What is meant by the term 'critical path'? *(3 marks)*

3 In a network, what is represented by:
  a a node (circle)? *(2 marks)*
  b a line? *(2 marks)*

4 Distinguish between the EST and the LST. *(3 marks)*

5 What is a prerequisite? *(2 marks)*

6 What is meant by the term 'float'? *(2 marks)*

7 Explain three advantages to a business of using critical path analysis. *(9 marks)*

8 Explain three problems that may arise as a result of using critical path analysis. *(9 marks)*

PRACTICE EXERCISE 2 — Total: 45 marks (50 minutes)

The following table shows a network of activities.

Activity	Duration (days)	Prerequisite(s)
A	5	–
B	4	–
C	5	A
D	8	B
E	3	D
F	3	D
G	6	C,E
H	5	F

1 a Draw a fully labelled network diagram of the activities described in the table, including the numbered nodes, the duration of each activity, the earliest start times (ESTs) and the latest finish times (LFTs). *(12 marks)*
  b Show the critical path. *(2 marks)*

2 Based on the original network in each case, describe how the critical path and overall duration of the project will be affected by the following changes in the duration of individual activities:
  a Activity F increases from 3 days to 6 days. *(3 marks)*
  b Activity D decreases from 8 days to 4 days. *(3 marks)*
  c Activity C increases from 5 days to 12 days. *(3 marks)*

The following diagram shows a sample network. Questions 3 and 4 are based on this network.

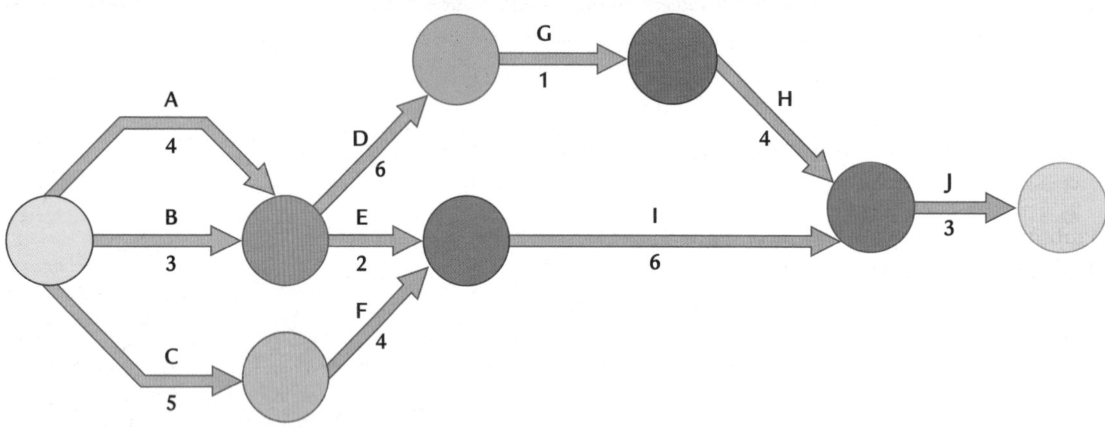

3 Complete the nodes, showing the earliest start times (ESTs) and latest finish times (LFTs), and show the critical path. *(6 marks)*

4 Copy the table below and complete the prerequisites column, based on the network shown in the diagram in question 3. *(6 marks)*

Activity	Duration (days)	Prerequisite(s)
A	4	
B	3	
C	5	
D	6	
E	2	
F	4	
G	1	
H	4	
I	6	
J	3	

5 Complete a network and show the critical path for the following project:

Ingredients are mixed for 15 minutes and then weighed (1 minute). At the same time, the container is cleaned for 5 minutes and labelled (2 minutes) before being transported to the production line (6 minutes).

Once all of the above processes have been completed, the ingredients are placed in the container (7 minutes). The finished product is then simultaneously checked for defects (2 minutes) while being placed on a conveyor belt that places the containers into boxes of a dozen products (4 minutes). The finished products then take 3 minutes to be loaded onto pallets, ready for delivery. *(10 marks)*

CASE STUDY Critical path analysis at Balfour Beatty

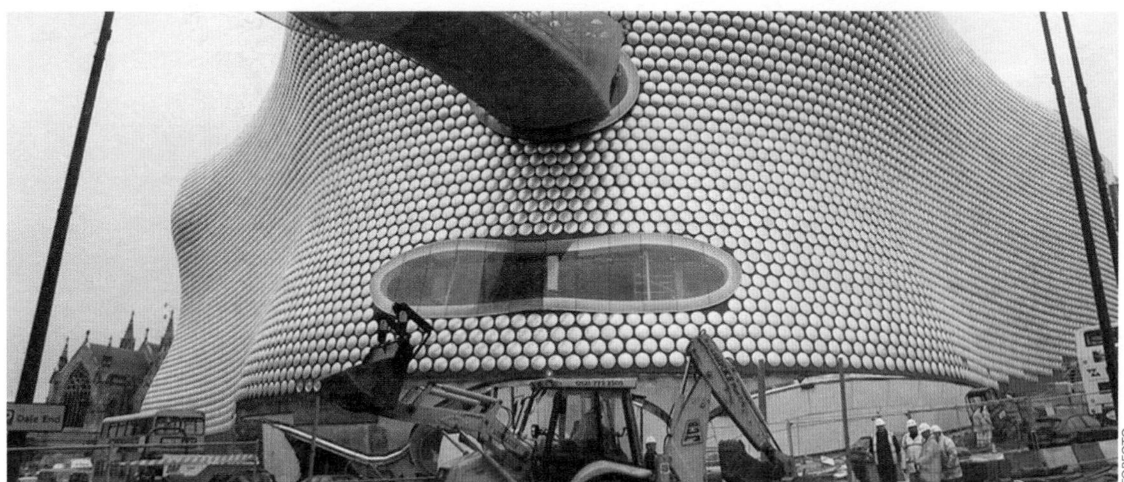
TOPFOTO

The construction industry is a major user of critical path analysis. In order to improve efficiency, construction firms use CPA to plan the most efficient method of construction and to monitor progress.

Balfour Beatty is a major construction company that uses CPA. In one recent project, the use of CPA enabled the company to design and build a new road within the budget of £35 million and considerably quicker than customer expectations. The customer requested completion in 124 weeks, but through careful planning using CPA, Balfour Beatty was able to plan the project for completion in 79 weeks.

Moreover, through close supervision and teamwork with its subcontractors, the company was able to take advantage of favourable external factors and complete the project 9.5 weeks earlier than its own estimate, despite some changes that increased the scope of the project.

Construction companies face particular problems in planning projects because they rely on other companies (subcontractors) to complete certain tasks. Furthermore, expensive earth-moving equipment is hired and any delays (or even improvements) in the schedule can make it difficult to acquire resources at the time they are needed. For this reason, companies tend to build large margins of error into their project timings.

A further complication that is often faced by construction companies is the need to keep existing facilities open. New roads or shopping centres can cause tremendous disruption to existing businesses. Most contracts now reward construction companies for planning projects that minimise disruption to existing facilities.

A project in which this was an important element was the construction of Birmingham's new Bull Ring Shopping Centre. Balfour Beatty was involved in this project, supporting the main contractor, Sir Robert McAlpine.

The following list gives the estimated timings of certain key aspects of the completion of the Bull Ring between 2000 and 2003:

- A Demolition of old Bull Ring – 8 months
- B Planning of new Bull Ring – 6 months
- C Agreement reached with key retailers – 4 months
- D Construction of West Mall – 25 months
- E Construction of East Mall – 23 months
- F Construction of 'flagship' stores – 18 months
- G Food Court constructed – 5 months
- H External work on Rotunda – 4 months
- I Completion of works – 1 month

These are represented in the critical path network shown in Figure 30.5.

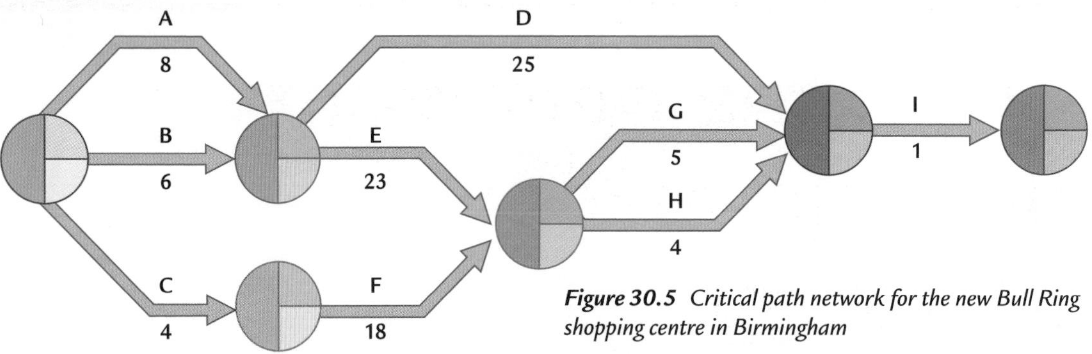

Figure 30.5 Critical path network for the new Bull Ring shopping centre in Birmingham

Sources: The Highways Agency website, www.highways.gov.uk; the Balfour Beatty website, www.balfourbeatty.com; and the Bull Ring website, www.bullring.co.uk.

Questions

Total: 40 marks (45 minutes)

1 Copy and complete the network for the construction of the new Bull Ring and use your completed diagram and timings to identify the following:
- **a** the earliest start time for activity G *(2 marks)*
- **b** the latest finish time for activity H *(2 marks)*
- **c** the 'float' time for activity F *(2 marks)*
- **d** the critical path *(2 marks)*
- **e** the prerequisites of activity E *(2 marks)*

2 Based on your network, briefly indicate the implications of a delay of 6 months in the completion of activity D. *(4 marks)*

3 Discuss the benefits to Balfour Beatty of using critical path analysis in order to plan its construction projects. *(14 marks)*

4 Evaluate the main difficulties faced by Balfour Beatty in its use of CPA to plan its projects. *(12 marks)*

CHAPTER 31

Controlling operations using information technology

The AS textbook introduced methods of controlling operations through the study of stock control and quality control. Brief reference was made to the role of information technology in controlling operations. At A2 the focus moves on to a scrutiny of the breadth of operations that are enhanced by the use of information technology (IT) and the ways in which IT can be used to improve efficiency. These benefits are contrasted with some of the problems associated with the use of IT.

The impact of information technology

KEY TERM

information technology (IT): the acquisition, processing, storage and dissemination of vocal, pictorial, textual and numerical information by a microelectronics-based combination of computing and telecommunications.

The role of information technology in the business world has increased dramatically in recent decades. The use of business software packages, the internet, automatic money transfers, bar codes and e-mail has transformed business activities. There is almost no part of a business that has not been affected by IT. Information technology has replaced manual systems in activities such as planning distribution, and office work has changed because IT can undertake routine activities far more effectively and flexibly than people. Marketing has been changed through improvements in the data held on customers, obtained using electronic point of sale (EPOS) technology and loyalty cards.

ISBN 1-84489-273-5

Particular aspects of business that have been changed through the application of information technology are described below.

Information technology and stock control

- IT enables businesses to improve their stock control. Computer programs linked to statistics on patterns of consumer purchases allow firms to anticipate changes in stock levels more accurately. This reduces the possibility that a firm will run out of stock or build up unnecessarily high levels.

Firms are now able to operate with lower levels of stock and so decrease their costs.

- Computerised systems allow organisations to recognise immediately their current stock levels, reducing the need for time-consuming manual checks (although these will still be needed on occasions to cover for problems such as pilferage).
- Retailers are able to link their tills to stock control. Every time an item is sold, the stock level is adjusted. These systems can also order new stock from suppliers automatically when the 'reorder level' is reached.
- Organisations with many branches can also use IT to establish the locations where stock is being held, so that, in emergencies, stock can be moved between branches.

FACT FILE

Argos, the catalogue retailer, allows its customers to access its stock control data in order to see if an item is in stock. By keying the product's code into a unit next to the catalogue, customers can modify their order if their first-choice product is unavailable – a convenience for both them and the retailer.

Comet uses its stock control system to identify nearby stores that are holding an item requested by a customer. As part of its customer service, managers at branches without stock are encouraged to liaise with branches that hold items requested by its customers, in order to transfer the stock to the branch at which it is needed.

Information technology and production

- New products have been created by IT. Traditional leisure pursuits, such as playing cards, have been hit by computer-based alternatives. The time spent using computers for relaxation has also hit other leisure activities. One of the most publicised toys for Christmas in 2004 was Robosapien, a programmable robot designed by a former NASA scientist.
- Production planning is another operational area that benefits from the use of IT. Networks are constructed and manipulated on the computer, and 'what if?' analysis is applied to examine the implications of any modifications to the network. By using this approach for all of its activities, the firm can plan the use of resources more effectively.
- Computer-based quality assurance systems can overcome the possibility of human error and also provide more rigorous scrutiny of quality.

FACT FILE

A Unilever factory that processes peas in Lowestoft, Suffolk, was the winner of Cranfield University's annual Best Factory competition in 2004. The factory invested £4 million a year on automated equipment. In addition to achieving cost savings of £10 million per annum, the factory is able to detect the progress of individual peas among the 120 million peas passing along the line and can detect 3 million different colours. Unilever claims that the system produces 'the cleanest pea in the world'.

- New manufacturing processes have been introduced as a result of information technology. Two particular examples of the role of IT in production are computer-aided design and computer-aided manufacture.

KEY TERMS

computer-aided design (CAD): the use of computers to improve the design of products.

computer-aided manufacture (CAM): the use of computers to undertake activities such as planning, operating or controlling production.

CADCAM: an approach that combines computer-aided design and computer-aided manufacture, using IT to aid both the design and the manufacture of an item.

Different ideas can be introduced and compared much more quickly in a CAD system than in a manual one. For many products, two-dimensional drawings can be transformed into three-dimensional images and rotated in order to demonstrate the whole range of possible views. Where appropriate, the CAD system can also include programmes to simulate testing, such as wind tunnel simulations. This can save considerable sums of money by eliminating the production and testing of expensive prototypes.

In computer-aided manufacture, the use of robots and fully automated production lines, controlled by computers, has increased productivity and reduced the problems arising from human error. With greater use of miniaturisation in production, many components are now too small for humans to manipulate. Flexible programming also allows a fully automated line to produce different varieties.

DID YOU KNOW?

A survey by Kwik Save in August 2004 revealed that the average woman now spends £200 a year on gadgets based on information technology, only £30 less than her male counterpart. Another survey of 6,000 people by Maplin, the electronics retailer, found that women spend 15 minutes a day longer than men at their computers. The average single person aged 25–35 wears or carries £1,762 of possessions when they leave the house, much of it in the form of technological accessories or gadgets.

Information technology and communications

- Information technology allows firms to improve both internal and external communications, improving efficiency and the firm's understanding of its market.
- Internal information can be processed and amended more quickly. By keeping employees up-to-date and facilitating two-way communication, IT improves the efficiency and motivation of staff.
- Company intranets enable employees and, where necessary, suppliers and customers to access company information continually. Individuals will not always be aware in advance of their information requirements, so a system that provides data at the press of a button will save considerable time.

- IT increases the speed of communication and the scope for greater responsibility. As such, it allows organisations to delayer and operate wider spans of control.
- The growing use of loyalty cards allows firms to accumulate information on the buying habits of their customers. Organisations can use these data to tailor services or products to customer needs. **Relationship marketing** arises from the data, whereby marketing techniques are based on the firm's understanding of its individual consumers.
- The internet has been arguably the most significant IT development in recent years. It has led to a whole new category of business (e-commerce or dot.com companies) and brings a number of specific advantages to firms that use it:
  - It can eliminate the need for expensive High Street premises. Operations can be moved to places where costs such as rent and wages are considerably lower.
  - It can reduce the need for staff. Organisations such as banks have closed many of their branches as people have moved to internet banking.
  - It adds flexibility to business operations, which no longer need to fit in with usual business structures. For example, 24-hour opening is possible and decisions such as credit card approval can be made on the basis of information that is accessible via the computer.
  - Data can be stored more cheaply and accessed more quickly if an individual needs to refer back to a previous communication.

FACT FILE

The effectiveness of using internet sites for advertising is a matter of debate. With software enabling computer users to delete 'pop-ups' there is doubt as to whether it is a sensible use of marketing budgets. However, some organisations have found that the scope for targeting can overcome these problems.

'Pay-per-click' advertising, used with internet search engines such as Google, is a system whereby advertisers pay a sum for every customer who visits their website from a link through a search engine page.

Divorce Online, which offers legal services to separating couples, has used this method to attract business. The firm's managing director, Mark Keenan, states: 'For every pound we spend on advertising, we get £40 of sales.'

Postoptics, the UK's leading contact lens mail-order business, achieves 60% of its £5 million of annual sales through 'pay-per-click' advertising. Trevor Rowley, who runs Postoptics, estimates that it costs £12 to attract a customer, but that customer will typically spend between £50 and £60.

However, not all users enjoy such success. The number of potential customers choosing to click on advertisers' sites fell from 20% in 1999 to 1% in 2003.

Source: adapted from an article by Paul Durman in the *Sunday Times*, 9 November 2003.

FACT FILE

One industry that has been transformed by the internet is gambling. Two major beneficiaries are, coincidentally, based in the same office block in Gibraltar. Cassava Enterprises, whose main brand name is www.888.com, was launched in 1996 and is now valued at more than £1 billion. Its rival, iGlobalMedia, has been even more successful. Launched in 1997, its www.partypoker.com and related websites have helped it to reach profit levels of £190 million. It has recently floated on the London Stock Exchange and immediately entered the FTSE 100 as one of the Stock Exchange's top 100 most valued companies.

Source: adapted from an article by Dominic Walsh in *The Times*, 26 October 2004.

Information technology and accounting

- Applications of IT in accounting allow for time saving and closer monitoring.
- IT greatly improves the budgeting process. The speed of processing data and the ability to access more information directly enables businesses to plan their budgets more rigorously. Alternatives can be scrutinised in order to make sure that the budgets are allocated efficiently. Perhaps the greatest benefit to the budgeting process is in budgetary control. With all of the actual expenditure being recorded on an integrated IT system, it is possible to monitor actual expenditure against the budget in order to identify areas of inefficiency. This helps the firm to take prompt action to resolve any problems.
- The wealth of accounting data now generated by IT systems allows for greater emphasis on strategic and tactical planning, rather than primarily control and monitoring. Managers can use the data to plan the firm's future strategies rather than spend time undertaking operational tasks.
- IT improves the scope for communicating accounting information to stakeholders. Public limited companies use their websites to improve 'investor relations', providing details of their accounts within their annual company report. Quarterly updates are also provided and many firms present information on their major strategies and the financial implications of those strategies.

Information technology and employment and location

- The introduction of IT has created new skills and jobs. Traditional workforce skills such as printing have been replaced by tasks requiring computer operators, and a number of new jobs requiring data handling have been introduced. The 'communication age' has increased the demand for data and been instrumental in shifting the balance of employment in the UK from the secondary sector to the tertiary (service) sector. Even within manufacturing companies themselves, there has been a shift towards more tertiary jobs, as computers have led to automated production lines that need fewer manual employees, while creating jobs in administration and planning.

- IT is allowing firms to benefit from the multiskilling of staff, creating jobs that are less rigidly defined and adaptable to changes in need. It has also been a key factor in the development of many small businesses operating from home or small premises.
- Changes in working practices have occurred as IT offers greater flexibility in terms of the place of operation. It is encouraging **teleworking**: that is, people working from home and other locations, and keeping in contact through IT. Occupations such as market research, design and software development can all be based away from the office. This change can motivate staff by giving them more independence and responsibility, while reducing adverse hygiene factors such as travel time and expense. However, projections that the typical office will cease to exist are probably unrealistic, as many teleworkers find that they miss the social aspects of working alongside colleagues. Moreover, some teleworkers find it difficult to separate work from leisure — a major factor in causing stress.
- In addition to removing some of the need to find a base for a firm's workforce, IT places the firm in immediate contact with its customers.

TOPFOTO

These factors, alongside the trend towards tertiary industry that requires no raw materials, mean that the key influences on location become less important. As a consequence, firms are able to choose from a much wider range of locations. Organisations such as call centres and firms based on e-commerce can choose to locate wherever they like, often away from the country in which they originated. Improved communications are also encouraging firms to set up many smaller bases rather than one major headquarters.

Conclusion

The sections above illustrate some of the benefits created by IT for firms. In turn, these benefits are passed on to society in the form of greater wealth accumulation and higher-quality products made at lower costs. IT also allows firms to meet their social, environmental and ethical responsibilities more readily, by reducing the need for materials and allowing businesses to respond more quickly to the needs of their stakeholders.

Although so far we have focused predominantly on the benefits of IT, its use can cause difficulties to firms. Some of the problems associated with IT are outlined in the next section. These problems relate to the firm. Stakeholders such as employees will have a different perception.

EXAMINER'S VOICE

Be cautious in answering any questions relating to the benefits or problems arising from IT. The question will probably be asked from the perspective of the business, but it may require a different focus, such as that of an employee, department, customer or supplier. This may radically alter the arguments that are relevant.

Problems caused by the growth of information technology in business

People are often concerned by change. IT can lead to job losses for workers in traditional skilled crafts. This causes stress for workers, as existing workers fear for their future. Consequently, productivity falls.

IT can undermine group morale by breaking up teams. In this instance, morale falls because workers are concerned for colleagues who have lost their jobs. Again, productivity falls as a result.

For many firms, the most significant problem is the cost of IT. Not only is it expensive to introduce, but it also needs regular updating. In some situations, it may be more cost effective to employ less advanced techniques, to avoid constant expenditure on updating IT. For some organisations, the cost of IT can make the firm uncompetitive and thus threaten its survival.

The nature of IT is changing constantly. Consequently, there is a constant need to replace hardware and software, and to provide continuous training for staff, again adding to costs and threatening efficiency if a business is unable to keep pace.

IT helps international communication, so firms can gain from the opportunities offered by the opening up of world markets. However, IT does pose a threat to some firms, as it reduces some of the barriers to entry in certain industries. As consumers can use the internet to compare prices, IT has the potential to force prices and profits down, especially in high-wage economies such as the UK.

FACT FILE

IT does not always operate smoothly. Website errors and manufacturing and distribution problems have led to delays in receipt of items. On 23 December 2004, Amazon.com announced to its customers that iPods ordered in November and promised for Christmas would not be delivered until February 2005. An Amazon spokesman also revealed that hundreds of other goods ordered online would miss delivery by Christmas. This led to a last-minute rush for alternative presents.

Problems were experienced by delivery firms too. Amtrak, the parcel carrier, suffered huge difficulties when its computer system failed in the run-up to Christmas. The Royal Mail estimated that it delivered 55 million items ordered online before Christmas 2004. The Office of Fair Trading said that complaints connected to online buying had more than doubled in the last year.

To compound consumer misery, the UK's largest bank, HSBC, suffered a breakdown in its IT systems on 3 January 2005. As a result, its customers were unable to withdraw cash to take advantage of the January sales.

EXAMINER'S VOICE

IT affects all firms, even those that do not use it directly. The extent of the impact depends on the situation. In the examination, you should look at the case study for any indications of benefits or problems that have arisen. Look also at the manner in which IT is used. Ultimately, its impact will depend on how well the firm has implemented IT.

CHAPTER 31 Controlling operations using information technology

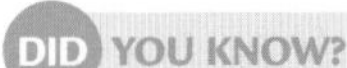

DID YOU KNOW?

The music industry is an example of a trade that is suffering from internet technology. Sales of singles in the UK fell by 30% in 2003, part of a £1.5 billion slump in worldwide music sales. Global sales peaked in 1999 and have fallen every year since.

A combination of music piracy and illegal file swapping is blamed, with only a small fraction of the decline arising from legitimate downloading. EMI cut its workforce by 1,900 in 2003 and 2004 and further cuts in its 9,000 workforce are planned.

PRACTICE EXERCISE — Total: 45 marks (40 minutes)

1 What is meant by the term 'information technology'? *(3 marks)*

2 What do the initials EPOS stand for? *(2 marks)*

3 Distinguish between CAD and CAM. *(3 marks)*

4 Explain two benefits of CADCAM. *(6 marks)*

5 Analyse two advantages to a retailer of using IT in its stock control. *(8 marks)*

6 Analyse two benefits of the internet to a car manufacturer. *(8 marks)*

7 Explain two changes to employment and business location caused by greater use of information technology. *(6 marks)*

8 Show three ways in which the use of information technology might create difficulties for a firm. *(9 marks)*

CASE STUDY 1 Information technology in Europe and the USA

Why can't Europe be more productive? From 1945 to 1995, Europe matched or surpassed US growth, but in the last 10 years the USA has grown faster than its European rivals. Europe now has an hourly output that is 20% below American levels.

Two theories are advanced for this trend. First, Europe spends less on research and development — about 2% of GDP in Europe compared with 3% of GDP in the USA.

Second, and most significantly, Europe lags behind the USA in its use of IT. In part this has been caused by Europe's barriers to competition and the inflexibility of its labour markets; these factors have meant that European firms find it more difficult to replace labour with new technology. Europe is seen as an area that is psychologically less suited to IT, as it places emphasis on survival rather than risk taking.

According to the OECD, IT spending in the USA is 4.42% of gross domestic product (GDP). This exceeds spending on IT in Europe's largest economies, where it accounts for 2.09% of GDP in Germany, 2.80% in the UK and 1.97% in France. Roger Fulton, an analyst at Garner Inc., believes that this partly reflects cultural differences. 'The USA is a "just do it" society, whereas Europe is more of a "let's think about it" society.' This results in a greater hesitancy to introduce IT in Europe.

Kasper Rorsted, managing director of Hewlett-Packard in Europe, sees European labour laws as a major cause. 'Employees in Europe are seen as more of a fixed cost – not something you can easily trim.' This makes European companies reluctant to introduce labour-saving IT. Rorsted is so concerned that he meets monthly with EU policy-makers in Brussels to investigate investment incentives and reductions in regulations that would assist IT development.

Europe simply does not have as large an IT sector as the USA. According to McKinsey and Co., the IT sector generates 2.3% of total GDP in the USA compared with 1.5% in Europe. More significantly, the IT sector of the USA economy contributed between 25% and 30% of recent US growth compared with less than 20% contributed by the IT sector in Europe.

The greater enterprise culture in the USA is a factor advanced by Dirk Pilat of the OECD in Paris. New companies – if they survive – contribute much higher productivity increases than established firms.

There is evidence to suggest that the greater scope for economies of scale is also a factor. Europe's largest economy, Germany, has matched the USA in the introduction of IT into its banking industry, but its productivity is still 13% lower than its US counterparts. This arises because IT involves high fixed costs and the larger scale of the US economy means that these costs can be spread over more customers. Movement towards the goal of a single European market with no barriers will, if successful, give Europe the advantage in this respect.

But is IT a guarantee of success? Research at the Massachusetts Institute of Technology casts doubt on assumptions of success. The MIT research suggests that the consumer is the main beneficiary of IT, followed by the users. The IT producers benefit least as competition drives down the price.

Nicholas Carr, author of *Does IT Matter?*, cites four main reasons for caution in the implementation of IT:

- Computer power is outstripping user needs. Users should thus be careful to avoid buying the top-of-the-range models. Even technology leaders such as Google and Amazon are cobbling together IT systems from cheap, generic components.
- Customers are driving hard bargains. Greater access to information increases the awareness of buyers who are able to negotiate lower prices from suppliers.
- New IT systems have often contained 'bugs'. Firms are learning to wait until the supplier has sorted out initial problems in IT systems before committing themselves to a package.
- Financial analysts are now taking a more pessimistic view of IT benefits. They have learned from experience that competition often quickly erodes any short-term gains from new IT systems.

Sources: article in *Business Week*, 9 August 2004; article by Nicholas Carr in the *Financial Times*, 16 August 2004.

Question

Total: 20 marks (25 minutes)

Discuss the reasons why European businesses are less likely to use information technology than companies in the USA.

CASE STUDY 2 Cottage industry has big ideas

Rachel Thomas used to help on her family's 500-acre dairy farm in Wales by hand-feeding the newborn calves. 'I had a bout of 'flu and when I came back my husband had replaced me with a machine.' She used her time to form the ultimate cottage industry – renting country cottages as holiday homes.

Thomas and her business partner, Liz Davies, set up the business by renting two local properties that they owned. Within a year of setting up they had made contact with 35 people with properties to let.

The big break came in 2000 when the business – Coast and Country Cottages – launched a website and began taking bookings online. Today more than half of its business comes from the website and this excludes many customers who discover the business via its website but then choose to book through a brochure. 'People can see far more properties and get much more detail online than from a brochure,' says Thomas.

The internet meant that the business could spread from its origins in Pembrokeshire to the neighbouring counties of Cardiganshire and Carmarthenshire. A particular benefit has been a disproportionate increase in off-season bookings. The adaptability of the website in comparison with the brochure means that marketing messages can be adapted, for example, in winter to 'selling the romantic notion of a rural cottage with a roaring log fire and long walks along the beaches'.

Today Coast and Country Cottages, which employs 11 full-time staff, has fully embraced technology.

With computerised booking systems, and targeted marketing through the customer database that it has developed over 14 years, operations run more smoothly than the earlier paper-based booking systems.

The growth of the business has enabled it to attract more cottages and a greater variety of properties. Its 260 properties include a disused mill and a lighthouse. The owners vary from local people to Premiership footballers. The lower costs from using IT have helped to make 'buying a property to let a good investment', according to Liz Davies. Costs of ownership can be met by letting the property for 7 months in a year. The company has a £2.2 million turnover and takes a 20% commission on each booking. Marketing and postage are the major costs — £150,000 a year — in this low-cost business. These costs are kept down by e-mail marketing and booking.

IT has also helped the firm to improve the quality of its marketing. It uses digital photography, downloading pictures of each property onto the website. The web also allows a greater variety of images to be presented — a service valued by the customers.

Some 70% of properties are booked all year round. As not all cottages are booked in advance, there is a need for a late-booking service. 'We have just launched lastminute-wales.com,' says Thomas. In addition to details on late availability and special offers, the website is being used to promote Wales as a holiday destination. The site provides information on places to eat and what to see.

As a result of its use of e-commerce, Coast and Country Cottages was one of the winners in the 2003 DTI/Interforum E-commerce awards.

Source: *The Sunday Times Enterprise Network*, 25 July 2004.

Question

Total: 20 marks (25 minutes)

Evaluate the extent to which the success of Coast and Country Cottages has depended on its use of information technology.

CHAPTER 32

Location

This chapter discusses the business approach to decisions on location. The key factors that influence regional location — costs, resources, infrastructure, the market, government intervention and qualitative factors — are considered and their relative importance assessed. Further factors influencing international location, such as protectionism and the scope for economies of scale, are then studied. All of these factors are considered as elements of business decision making, using analytical techniques such as breakeven and investment appraisal.

The main factors influencing regional location

EXAMINER'S VOICE

The AQA A2 Business Studies specification distinguishes between factors that influence regional location and those additional factors that just affect international location. The heading above is consistent with the descriptions used in the specification. However, it should be noted that *all* of the factors that influence regional location will influence international location decisions too.

Business decisions concerning location are influenced by a range of factors. The main assumption made about such decisions is that firms will locate at the least-cost site.

KEY TERM

least-cost site: the business location that allows a firm to minimise its costs (and hence its selling price).

For businesses in which the selling price is vital in achieving sales, the least-cost site will greatly increase their competitiveness. However, as there is a greater tendency for consumers to purchase products on the basis of quality and other criteria, it is possible that other factors, such as the reputation of an area, will be more important. For example, cities such as Paris and Milan are attractive locations for fashion houses because of their image, although they are not the least-cost locations.

We will now consider the main factors determining the location of businesses.

Costs of factors of production

Within the UK there are significant variations in **wage levels** between regions. The southeast of England is the most expensive region and those areas that are the greatest travel time from London generally have the lowest wage levels. On its own, this factor would suggest that low-wage areas should be

THIS PHOTOGRAPH IS REPRODUCED WITH THE PERMISSION OF ROLLS-ROYCE PLC, © ROLLS-ROYCE PLC 2005

TOPFOTO

the least-cost sites. However, it is not just labour costs that matter. A highly skilled labour force may compensate for slightly higher wage levels through greater labour productivity. Ultimately, the **labour cost per unit produced** is more important than the wage level. This factor is a key aspect of decisions to relocate overseas. Companies such as Marks and Spencer have sourced more of their clothing from Asia because the lower labour costs help to keep prices low and competitive.

Firms basing their location decisions on labour factors also need to consider the **quality and reliability** of the product or service produced. Rolls-Royce, the engine manufacturer, has resisted the temptation to locate its factories overseas because it recognises that the skills of its UK workforce are instrumental in achieving the main requirements of its customers — safety and reliability. Zara still produces its clothing in Europe because this enables it to distribute its products quickly to its main retailers. Rapid distribution is its unique selling point.

Land costs are relatively important for companies requiring large areas, such as wholesalers. For this reason, many wholesalers locate away from town centres to benefit from lower rents. Firms may also be discouraged from locating in areas of expensive land, such as London. In his 2004 budget the chancellor of the exchequer announced plans to relocate a number of government departments from London to the regions, and organisations such as Air Traffic Control have moved away from London.

Land may also be a factor if an industry has **special requirements**. Airports require huge areas of flat land, while hydroelectric power stations require specific geographical conditions. Firms involved in dangerous processes, such as nuclear power stations and toxic waste disposal plants, locate away from densely populated areas.

DID YOU KNOW?

In April 2004, Dixons plc announced plans to close 106 of it 320 town-centre stores. The company blamed high rents compared with out-of-town sites as the key factor behind this decision. It also noted that out-of-town sites provide greater convenience of access for its consumers.

FACT FILE

In April 2004, Shell announced that it was moving thousands of jobs to India in an attempt to cut its £475 million IT budget. Its IT workforce worldwide totals 9,300 and Shell expects to cut over 2,000 jobs. Shell's IT operations are currently based in the UK, the USA, the Netherlands and Malaysia. The site in Malaysia will be retained after a survey showed that it presented cost advantages. In addition to lower costs, India has a vast pool of software engineering. India benefits from time zones too. Engineers in India can carry out work on IT systems while America and Europe sleep.

WHAT DO YOU THINK?

In July 2004, German employees of DaimlerChrysler went on strike in response to managers' demands for longer working hours for the same level of pay. The company has threatened to move around 6,000 jobs from its Sindelfingen plant, which produces the Mercedes C-Class, to South Africa, where wages are much lower.

Public opinion in Germany used to support workers' demands, arguing that workers should benefit from Germany's wealth. However, a recent opinion poll shows that the German people are beginning to believe that the working week should be increased from 35 to 40 hours, in order to improve competitiveness.

This development followed Siemens's success in persuading 8,000 workers to increase their working week from 35 to 40 hours. Siemens had threatened to move production to Hungary.

Should European companies move jobs from Western Europe to low-wage countries?

Resources

The location of **raw materials** is the crucial influence for most primary industries. After all, extractive industries such as mining and quarrying must locate where the materials are found. However, the costs of extraction and transport to the market may determine whether it is economically worthwhile to operate at all.

Heavy industries — notably iron and steel — usually locate in close proximity to their raw material supplies. During the manufacturing process, a significant percentage of the raw materials is wasted. As a result, the final product weighs much less than the raw materials. Therefore, it is cheaper to distribute the finished product to the market than it is to move the raw materials to the place of manufacture. For these **bulk-reducing** or **weight-losing** industries, the least-cost site tends to be close to the raw materials.

For some industries, such as brewing and soft drinks, the ready accessibility of water means that the final product is bulkier to transport than the raw materials. These **bulk-increasing** or **weight-gaining** industries tend to locate closer to the market than the raw materials.

Much of the UK's 'heavy' (weight-losing) industry has declined, so raw material supply has become a less important factor in the UK. Other primary industries in decline include fishing, agriculture and oil extraction.

The location of **suppliers** is still a key factor influencing business location. A manufacturer will reap the benefits of a location that is close to its suppliers, particularly if it is using just-in-time methods. Thus, a region such as Lincolnshire, with its abundance of agricultural suppliers, is an attractive location for a food manufacturer. However, it is more usual for suppliers to decide to locate close to manufacturers than vice versa.

Infrastructure

TERM

infrastructure: the network of utilities, such as transport links, sewerage, telecommunications systems, health services and educational facilities.

Infrastructure is vital for most companies. **Transport links** are the key factor, as the ability to move raw materials and finished products easily is crucial to the success of any business. It is also essential that the labour force can easily access the place of work. Companies also want the basic services that allow them to operate normally, such as sewerage facilities and high-quality telecommunications systems.

INGRAM

The time and cost of transport are more important than distance. In the UK, road is the main form of transport, as it provides flexibility. With the growth of containerisation, roads can be linked to other forms of transport more efficiently too. Thus, the motorway and road network is a major influence on business location in the UK. Improvements in roads can create opportunities for the areas affected, as reduced travelling times lead to lower costs.

In some areas and countries, canals, railway lines and air transport dominate location decisions. Air transport provides speed and, for products requiring high security, airport locations limit the chances of theft. Water and rail transport are effective means of transporting bulky, durable products.

Employees prioritise other aspects of the local infrastructure. They want an acceptable provision of **services** within the local area. Businesses will not locate in a place in which they cannot recruit a workforce to suit their needs. For workers, the quality of educational and health services is important, and facilities such as an excellent shopping centre will also assist recruitment.

INGRAM

The market

For retailers and other service industries, the market is the most important influence on location. As the UK's economy is predominantly based around **tertiary production** (the provision of services), this makes the market a crucial factor in determining the location of many UK firms. Customers expect convenience and easy access, so firms such as electrical retailers, hairdressers and restaurants see this factor as particularly important.

Organisations save transport costs if they locate close to their market. A company supplying raw materials to a manufacturer may find that transport costs represent a large percentage of the final costs. In this case, proximity to the customer may be a key factor.

As just-in-time production grows in popularity among manufacturers, the ability to transport goods quickly becomes a key factor in the choice of suppliers, and so the latter will seek to locate close to their customers.

FACT FILE

For many businesses in sectors such as retailing and financial services, proximity to the customer is still vital, but it is no longer an influence on location. In these businesses, the marketplace is via a telephone line or an internet connection. As a result, local branches are not needed. In the financial services industry, this means that the service is provided through a call centre. The location of a call centre is more likely to be influenced by cost factors such as wage rates, as its geographical situation no longer affects its proximity to the market.

Government intervention

According to the DTI:

> [the UK government's] regional development policy is aimed at improving the economic performance of all the English regions and to reduce the persistent gap in growth rates between regions. If the six least productive regions in England improved their performance to the national average, the average person in the UK would be around £1,000 a year better off...The key [to overcoming disparities between and within regions] is to improve regional productivity, which is driven by five main factors: skills, investment, innovation, enterprise and competition.

Member countries of the European Union must regulate their regional policy within the guidelines established by the European Commission. Assistance can only be provided in specific areas. In England, these are the 'Assisted Areas' (see Figure 32.1); the National Assembly for Wales and the Scottish Parliament provide similar schemes of regional assistance.

KEY TERM

Assisted Areas: parts of England that have relatively low levels of economic activity and high and persistent unemployment.

The financial assistance provided usually takes the form of a grant. The government pays for a certain percentage of the cost of capital investment.

- Firms in areas designated as Article 87(3)(a) (Cornwall, Merseyside and South Yorkshire) are entitled to a maximum grant of 35% of the cost of capital investment.
- Firms in areas designated as Article 87(3)(c) are entitled to a maximum grant of between 10% and 20% of the cost of capital investment.

The European Commission restricts aid according to certain criteria:

- Only certain sectors of the economy qualify, such as iron and steel, coal, synthetic fibres, vehicles, and agriculture and fisheries.

Figure 32.1 Assisted Areas in England, 2000–06

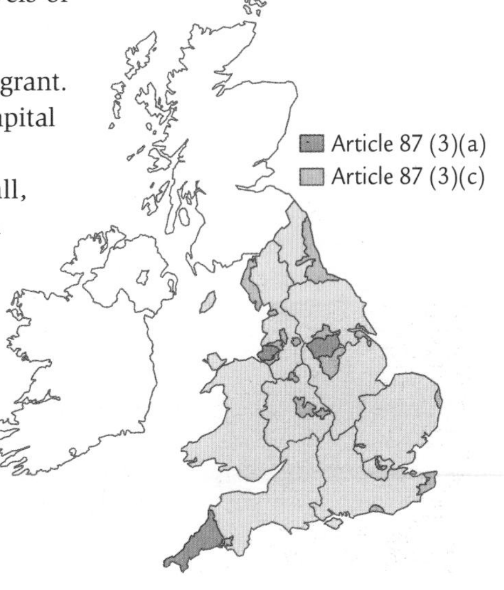

- The project must not lead to overcapacity in its industry.
- The investment must create jobs or introduce new technology, and any jobs must not just be transferred from another Assisted Area. Consequently, local services such as retailing would not qualify.

In England, firms must apply to the DTI for support. Successful applications must satisfy additional criteria, such as scale and future viability.

The UK's regional policy has been most successful in encouraging foreign multinational businesses to locate in areas of high unemployment. Multinational corporations such as Nissan, locating in Sunderland, have helped to regenerate areas that were suffering from high unemployment. Almost half of the grant aid in 2003/04 went to foreign multinationals. DTI forecasts indicate that this portion of the grants provided will create over 8,400 new jobs and safeguard a further 7,900 jobs. Overall, the government estimates that regional policy costs, on average, £6,840 for each job.

FACT FILE

In the UK, applications for regional assistance increased from 723 in 2002/03 to 752 in 2003/04. The number of applications accepted fell from 587 to 557. The total cost of regional assistance fell from £295 million in 2002/03 to £240 million in 2003/04.

From 1 April 2004, the government introduced a new system of regional assistance for England. Regional Selective Assistance (RSA) has been replaced by Selected Finance for Investment in England (SFIE). The main changes are that:
- eligible projects must demonstrate scope for higher productivity
- the majority of jobs created must be at NVQ level 2 or above

Qualitative factors

Ultimately, all business decisions are taken by individuals, often without access to perfect forecasts of the implications of the different choices available. Consequently, directors may base their choices on factors other than business criteria. For example, the Body Shop is located in Sussex because Anita Roddick lived there at the time that she set up the business. Similarly, the Alliance and Leicester plc is based in Leicester because its original founders lived there.

EXAMINER'S VOICE

These are just examples of qualitative factors. If an examination question requires you to consider qualitative factors, look for 'non-quantifiable' factors within the case study. There may also be reference to 'inertia' factors that can be instrumental in persuading the business to stay where it is. These special factors are described in the next section.

The **quality of life** is also a factor that influences location. Entrepreneurs may choose an attractive location that may not be ideal from a 'least-cost' location perspective, but which offers other compensations to the business owner and the workforce. The Met Office outgrew its site in Bracknell in Berkshire and examined alternative locations. The final decision was left to the workforce who, based on personal choice, chose to relocate to Exeter. As a city, Exeter consistently scores highly in 'quality of life' surveys.

TOPFOTO

Industrial inertia

KEY TERM

industrial inertia: the tendency for firms to remain where they are, even though the original reasons for location no longer apply.

Industrial inertia is another factor that can influence location. Once established, firms may be reluctant to *relocate* elsewhere. One reason for this is that established firms can benefit from **external economies of scale**.

KEY TERM

external economies of scale: the benefits gained by a firm as a result of the concentration of an industry in one location.

The main external economies of scale are:

- a labour supply with the skills needed by firms in that industry
- specialist training facilities in the region
- an infrastructure that is geared towards the needs of that industry, such as specialist transport facilities
- suppliers and customers based locally
- the reputation of the area, which may help to sell the product or allow the firm to charge a premium price

EXAMINER'S VOICE

Do not confuse *external* economies of scale with *internal* economies of scale.

Internal economies of scale (often referred to as just 'economies of scale') are the advantages that an organisation gains due to an increase in the size of the organisation. Internal economies of scale are explained in Chapter 29 of the AS textbook.

External economies of scale are benefits to a firm from being part of a large industry that is concentrated in a particular area or region. External economies therefore depend on the scale of the industry, rather than of individual firms within it. Thus a small financial services company will benefit from being located in London because of the concentration of financial services organisations in that location.

Businesses should also be aware of the problems arising from a concentration of firms in an area. These are known as **external diseconomies of scale**.

KEY TERM

external diseconomies of scale: the disadvantages arising from the concentration of an industry in one location.

The main external diseconomies are congestion, pollution and a potential shortage of resources in the area. All of these factors cost a firm in terms of time and money.

- **Congestion.** The concentration of firms in an area increases travelling times and expenses. Where delivery times are an essential factor, this may reduce the competitiveness of an organisation, because transport costs will increase and delivery may become unreliable.

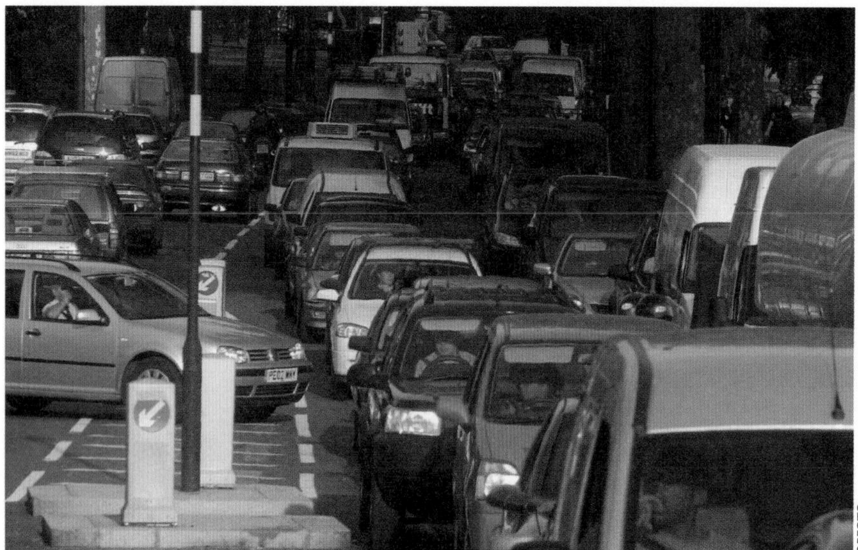
TOPFOTO

- **Pollution.** The social costs created in these areas may be considered excessive by firms that place a high value on their impact on society. Local councils may impose additional costs on firms in order to alleviate this problem.
- **Shortages of resources.** In particular, the cost of land and skilled labour will be inflated by the competition among firms to acquire these resources.

On balance, firms usually find that the external economies of scale outweigh the external diseconomies of scale. This encourages firms to remain in their original location.

In addition, relocation can be disruptive to a firm. Even though, in the long term, a new location may offer lower costs, the short-term inconvenience may be considerable and endanger the future of the organisation.

Other factors that will be considered by a firm if it already has a base and is considering relocation elsewhere are:

- loss of skills developed in the existing workforce
- lower morale and productivity prior to the relocation, as a result of some staff probably losing their jobs
- the break-up of working groups
- finding new suppliers and customers
- the cost of relocation
- redundancy payments
- transitional difficulties while adjusting to the new location and processes
- potential damage to the firm's image caused by these changes

These problems need to be set against the benefits gained from the new location.

The main factors influencing international location

In making worldwide decisions on location, organisations will consider all of the factors discussed in the first part of this chapter, as these apply to nations as well as to regions. In addition, a business might wish to consider the political and economic stability of the country and examine exchange rates to see if there are financial gains to be made from location decisions. Government legislation on employment may also influence location. Countries with more flexible working practices and/or fewer restrictions on levels of pay may be attractive to some firms.

Two factors of particular importance in international location decisions are described below.

Avoiding protectionism

KEY TERM

protectionism: a decision by a country or countries to place restrictions on trade between nations, in order to help (protect) domestic firms competing with foreign companies.

The most common forms of protection are:

- quotas (a limit on the number of imports allowed)
- tariffs (taxes) on imports from other countries, to make imports more expensive
- subsidies on domestic products, allowing these firms to keep their prices low

These approaches 'protect' domestic producers from outside competition. Quotas achieve this by physically preventing more than a certain quantity of imports. Tariffs and subsidies are used to help domestic producers match the prices of external firms.

The **World Trade Organisation (WTO)** is a global organisation that promotes free trade (trade without protection). The WTO tries to eliminate protection, as free trade helps to create free markets and to increase efficiency globally.

More significantly, a number of 'free trade' areas have been formed, such as the European Union, NAFTA (based in North America) and APEC (Asia and the Pacific). These areas are groups of countries that have agreed to remove restrictions on trade between member countries.

TOPFOTO

These areas tend to adopt policies of protectionism against non-member countries. As a consequence, businesses try to locate operations in countries within these areas, so that they can have free access to the other countries in the free trade area. For example, many Japanese companies have set up bases in the UK so that they can access the EU market. A location within the EU provides a firm with free trade access to 460 million people, not just the number living in the country in which the firm is based. The expansion of the EU has made a European location even more attractive to such firms, although the admission of countries from eastern Europe has made the UK less attractive because of travel distances.

Achieving high economies of scale

The UK has a population of 60 million. This has enabled UK firms to expand considerably just by focusing on the domestic market. With 60 million potential customers, firms in the UK can produce on a large scale, achieving high economies of scale. This leads to lower costs of production and greater efficiency for the firm. It has given UK firms an advantage in comparison with firms from smaller countries such as Holland, but they remain at a disadvantage in relation to firms from larger economies such as Japan.

The scope for internal economies of scale is limited by a market's population. In the 1930s, European firms became less competitive than firms in the USA, as the latter were producing on a much larger scale than their European counterparts. The largest European market, Germany, was less than half the size of the USA. After the Second World War, three countries — Belgium, Holland and Luxembourg — decided to form a free trade area (Benelux) that would allow their firms to gain the benefits of a larger market. This led to the formation of the European Union.

FACT FILE

UK companies are moving a variety of activities 'offshore'. Figure 32.2 shows the nature of jobs that are relocating to other countries and the effects that this 'offshoring' is having on UK employment.

The EU allows firms to trade, without restriction, in a market of 460 million. Not only has this helped European companies to grow and gain economies of scale, but it has also encouraged firms from countries such as the USA, Japan and Korea to locate within the EU. The US population is approximately 250 million, so Europe offers greater scope for economies of scale than the USA. However, this is an oversimplification. Language and other barriers mean that the whole of Europe is not always easily accessible, whereas the USA possesses fewer such obstacles.

The world has a rapidly increasing human population, currently totalling 4,300 million people. With over a quarter of the world's population living in China, this is encouraging firms to locate there, particularly as the population of Asia as a whole is expanding rapidly. In industries such as textiles, the opportunities for economies of scale, combined with low wage levels, mean that China, the world's largest textile market, is expected to dominate the global textile industry.

For individual multinational firms, the size of a market is a major factor in deciding on location. Countries with a high gross domestic product, or open access to a free trade area such as the EU, enable these firms to produce on a large scale and transport their goods without trade barriers.

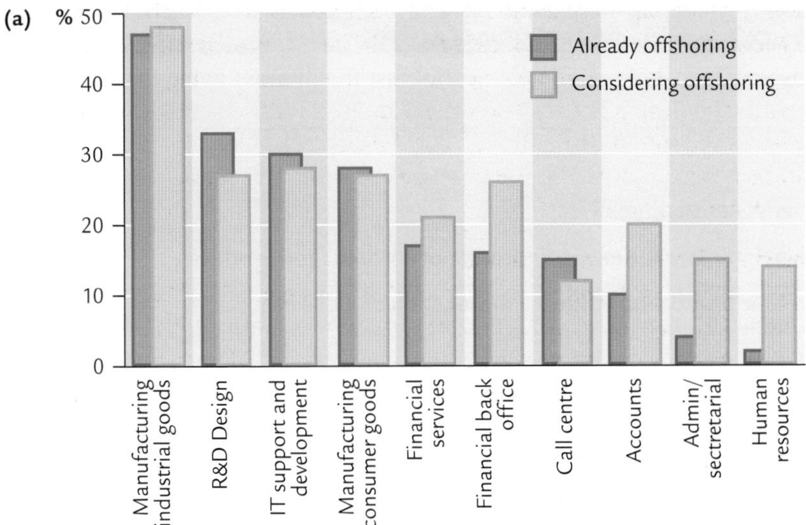

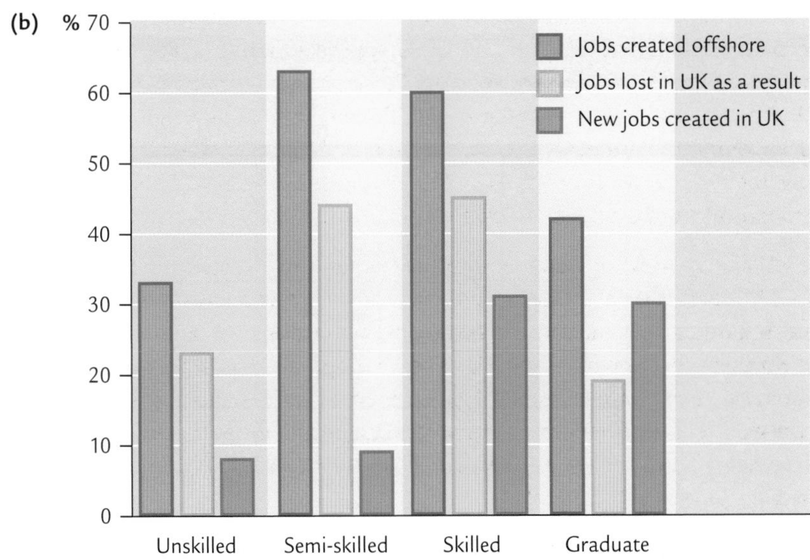

Figure 32.2 *(a) UK companies relocating 'offshore' or considering such a move.*
(b) The effects of offshoring on UK employment.

Source: MORI

DID YOU KNOW?

In December 2004, the Chinese government took the unusual step of announcing that it would be placing tariffs (taxes) on its exports of textiles. A worldwide agreement on quotas expired at the end of 2004. Countries such as the USA were so concerned about the probable dominance of Chinese firms that they put pressure on the Chinese government. Rather than seeing huge taxes imposed on its exports by other countries, China agreed to impose its own taxes to make the goods more expensive. This also means that the Chinese government is able to raise additional tax revenue.

CHAPTER 32 Location

PRACTICE EXERCISE 1

Total: 40 marks (35 minutes)

1 What is meant by the term 'least-cost site'? *(2 marks)*

2 Explain the significance of the term 'weight-losing' or 'bulk-reducing' with reference to the location of industry. *(4 marks)*

3 What is the meaning of the term 'Assisted Area'? *(3 marks)*

4 Analyse four factors that might influence the regional location of a frozen food producer. *(12 marks)*

5 How might the use of just-in-time production influence the location of a business? *(3 marks)*

6 What is industrial inertia? *(2 marks)*

7 Explain the difference between internal economies of scale and external economies of scale. *(5 marks)*

8 How does protectionism influence international location decisions? *(4 marks)*

9 Identify five factors that might be seen as qualitative influences on a decision about where to locate a business. *(5 marks)*

GROUP EXERCISE

Time: 20 minutes

Instructions

A business is seeking to locate a new factory in Squareland.

The map of Squareland shows the location of key resources.

Each square represents an area of Squareland. The factory will incur costs for the transportation of items to and from its factory. Items can only be transported horizontally and vertically (*not* diagonally). The distance travelled is measured in 'squares'. For example, A1 is one square in distance from A2; A1 is three squares away from B3; A1 is 8 squares in distance from E5.

	A	B	C	D	E
1					Raw materials
2		Market	Area of outstanding natural beauty		
3			Area of outstanding natural beauty		
4					
5	Government assistance		Port		Government assistance

Travel costs per square vary according to the item being transported as follows:

- Transport of finished goods from the factory to the market – £50 per product
- Transport of raw materials to the factory – £20 per product
- Transport of items from the port to the factory – £15 per product

In addition, the government has agreed to provide regional assistance to firms locating in areas shown as 'Government assistance'. This is a subsidy of £100 per product.

The government has announced that it will not allow businesses to locate in square B2 because of congestion, or in squares C2 and C3, which have been designated as areas of 'outstanding natural beauty'.

Task

Advise the business on the least-cost site (square) in which it is able to locate.

---

e EXAMINER'S VOICE

In describing section 14.6, 'Facilities', the AQA A2 Business Studies specification states: 'The focus must be on business-based decision-making using methods such as breakeven analysis or investment appraisal (but qualitative factors should not be underestimated).' This section shows how decisions on location can be taken using these quantitative methods.

Location decisions using breakeven analysis

Breakeven analysis lets a firm see how many units it needs to produce and sell in order to avoid making a loss. Market research enables the firm to estimate future sales and to calculate its costs and revenue, in order to see if its sales and output will exceed the breakeven quantity.

Example 1

A restaurant that is seeking a new location. The financial forecasts for setting up and operating the new restaurant are as follows:

- fixed costs — £120,000
- average price — £18 per meal
- variable costs per meal — £8 per meal
- contribution — £10 per meal

The breakeven output is:

$$\frac{£120{,}000}{£10} = 12{,}000 \text{ meals per annum}$$

This represents 1,000 meals per month or approximately 33 meals per day.

If market research indicates that 33 meals per day is a realistic target for the restaurant, the business will go ahead with its decision to locate. In contrast, if the forecast demand falls below 33 meals per day, it will be too risky to locate.

This decision is set out graphically in Figure 32.3.

INGRAM

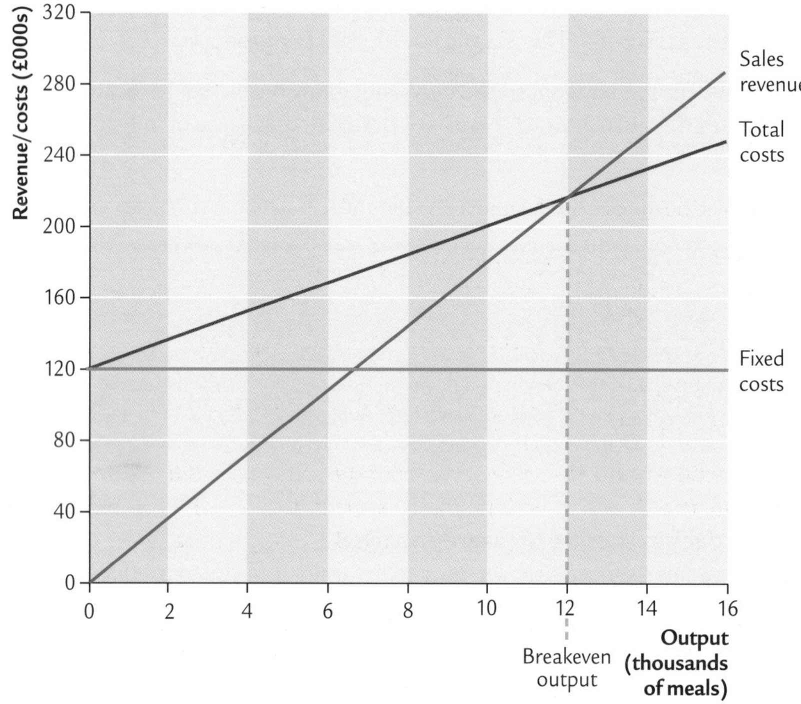

Figure 32.3 *Breakeven analysis*

Breakeven analysis also allows the business to use 'what if?' analysis. The viability of the location can be examined using different prices and costs, to test whether the location is robust. However, there are severe limitations in the use of breakeven analysis to make location decisions. It is most useful when costs and revenue remain the same each year and where only one product is produced, so that revenue per unit and variable costs per unit can be calculated. These conditions are unlikely to apply.

An airline can use this technique to decide between locating in different airports. Airlines pay rent (fixed costs) to the owners of the airports and also pay for variable costs, such as fuel and services for passengers. An airport may offer lower costs to encourage airlines to use it as a base. An example is given below.

Example 2

Flybe.com is wondering whether to set up a base in the northeast. It is examining two location options: Newcastle Airport or Teesside International Airport. Its forecasts for each option are given in Table 32.1.

	Newcastle	Teesside
Fixed costs	£48 million	£47.3 million
Revenue per flight	£17,000	£15,000
Variable costs per flight	£5,000	£4,000
Number of flights	4,400	3,800

***Table 32.1** Forecasts for Flybe.com*

For Newcastle Airport the breakeven output is:

$$\frac{\text{£48 million}}{(\text{£17,000} - \text{£5,000})} = \frac{\text{£48 million}}{\text{£12,000}} = \text{4,000 flights}$$

For Teesside International Airport the breakeven output is:

$$\frac{\text{£47.3 million}}{(\text{£15,000} - \text{£4,000})} = \frac{\text{£47.3 million}}{\text{£11,000}} = \text{4,300 flights}$$

For Newcastle Airport the expected margin of safety is 4,400 – 4,000 = 400 flights. On this basis it is financially worthwhile for Flybe.com to use Newcastle as a base for its flights, although the margin of safety may not be enough.

For Teesside International Airport the expected margin of safety is 3,800 – 4,300 = –500 flights. On this basis it is not financially worthwhile for Flybe.com to use Teesside as a base for its flights, as expected sales are 500 less than the breakeven figure.

Before making a decision, Flybe.com should also consider any qualitative factors. The expected annual return (calculated using the contribution method) is 400 × £12,000 = £4.8 million. Flights above breakeven = 400. Contribution per flight = £17,000 – £5,000 = £12,000. This may not be seen to be a good enough return.

This decision could also be shown using breakeven charts.

Location decisions using investment appraisal

Investment appraisal is necessary to see if a location decision provides a quick payback, yields a high average rate of return percentage (ARR %) or gives a positive net present value (NPV). For most location decisions, investment appraisal is a more useful approach than breakeven analysis, as it is flexible enough to assist decisions for businesses that have many products and where there is not a constant pattern of costs and revenue. An example of the use of investment appraisal in deciding on location is set out below.

TOPFOTO

Example 3

Argos is considering the opening of a new store in Liverpool. The expected initial costs (year 0) are £800,000, as shown in Table 32.2. Future revenue and annual costs for the first 5 years of the store are also shown.

Table 32.2 Forecasts revenue and costs of the new Argos store

Year	Revenue (£000s)	Costs (£000s)	Net return (£000s)
0	0	800	(800)
1	550	350	200
2	750	450	300
3	900	540	360
4	950	560	390
5	950	560	390
Total	**4,100**	**3,260**	**840**

Argos's targets for its new stores are as follows:

- payback — less than 3 years
- average rate of return (ARR %) — greater than 12%
- net present value — positive, based on a 10% discount rate

A new store must achieve all three of these targets in order to be opened. Any revenue or costs after year 5 are ignored.

For detailed information on how to complete the calculations for investment appraisal, see Chapter 18.

$$\textbf{payback period} = 2 \text{ years} + \frac{300}{360} = 2 \text{ years } 10 \text{ months}$$

$$\text{annual return} = \frac{£840{,}000}{5 \text{ years}} = £168{,}000 \text{ per annum}$$

$$\textbf{average rate of return} = \frac{£168{,}000}{£800{,}000} \times 100 = 21.0\%$$

Table 32.3 shows the **net present value** of the new Argos store.

Table 32.3 Net present value of the new Argos store

Year	Revenue (£000s)	Costs (£000s)	Net return (£000s)	Discount factor (10%)	Present value (£000s)
0	0	800	(800)	1.0	(800)
1	550	350	200	0.909	181.8
2	750	450	300	0.826	247.8
3	900	540	360	0.751	270.4
4	950	560	390	0.683	266.4
5	950	560	390	0.621	242.2
Total	**4,100**	**3,260**	**840**		**408.6**

Table 32.4 summarises the decisions on location using investment appraisal.

Table 32.4 Summary of investment appraisals of new Argos store

Method of investment appraisal	Target	Forecast result	Decision (YES/NO)
Payback period	<3 years	2 years 10 months	YES
Average rate of return (%)	>12%	21%	YES
Net present value	>£0	+£408,600	YES
Overall decision			YES

It is crucial that any quantitative decision also allows for **qualitative factors**, such as the impact on personnel and the corporate image, or the possible effect of external changes on the decision.

FACT FILE

One company that is staying in the UK is Rolls-Royce. In 2002 the company's management thought about moving one of its manufacturing plants from Glasgow to the Czech Republic. John Cheffins, chief operating officer, says: 'The simple assumption that low wages will give you a low-cost product just isn't true.' New technology, a skilled workforce and flexible work contracts, including a policy of single status, have all helped to increase productivity by 30%, simply by moving to a new factory in Glasgow. The decision to stay in Glasgow was also helped by a £23 million government grant. Staff have an average salary of £28,000, but the skills that they possess are critical to the success of the firm's products.

Source: adapted from an article by Dominic O'Connell in the *Sunday Times*, 31 October 2004.

DID YOU KNOW?

- 30% of UK companies do part of their manufacturing abroad.
- 10% have more than half their production abroad.
- One in three companies say that they are planning to increase the proportion of foreign production.
- 62% of businesses say that cost is the main reason for moving abroad.

Source: Engineering Employers' Federation.

PRACTICE EXERCISE 2 — Total: 30 marks (40 minutes)

1 A retailer is wondering whether to open a shop in a new location. Its market research suggests that it will attract 500 customers each week. The average price of a product sold is £60 and variable costs are £25 per product.

a If fixed costs are £15,000, is it financially worthwhile to open the new shop? *(5 marks)*

b If fixed costs increase to £15,500 and variable costs rise to £30 per product, should the shop be opened? *(5 marks)*

2 A furniture manufacturer is planning a new factory location. It has gathered together the information shown in the following tables.

Forecast revenue and costs of the new factory

Year	Revenue (£m)	Costs (£m)	Net return (£m)
0	0	25	(25)
1	27	21	6
2	32	22	10
3	29	17	12
Total	**88**	**85**	**3**

Present value of £1 at selected discount rates

	Discount rate		
Year	**5%**	**7%**	**10%**
0	1.0	1.0	1.0
1	0.952	0.935	0.909
2	0.907	0.873	0.826
3	0.864	0.816	0.751

TOPFOTO

a Calculate:

(i) the payback period *(3 marks)*

(ii) the average rate of return (ARR %) *(5 marks)*

(iii) the net present value (NPV), using an appropriate discount rate *(7 marks)*

b Briefly justify the discount rate that you have used in **a(iii)**. *(3 marks)*

c Based on your answers, recommend whether the new factory should be opened. *(2 marks)*

CASE STUDY Call centres

The financial services sector is leading the trend for UK call centres, or contact centres, to relocate. Currently, UK call centres employ almost 800,000 workers. Despite the impression given in the media, the call centre industry in India is only one-fifth of the scale of that in the UK, but it is growing quickly. Most of the high-profile decisions to relocate to countries such as India have come from finance companies.

Among the businesses that have decided to locate their call (or contact) centres in India are Prudential, Abbey, HSBC, GE Capital and American Express.

The Prudential transferred 850 jobs from its call centre in Reading to Mumbai (formerly Bombay) in India. The new call centre costs the Prudential £6 million a year. This represents a large saving as call centre wages in India average £2,250 compared with about £12,950 in the UK. Overall, the Prudential estimates that an equivalent centre in the UK would have cost £12 million a year to run. (This is a greater cost saving than usual. On average, call centre costs in India are 35% lower than the UK, with nearly all of the savings coming from lower wage levels.) The transfer is estimated to have cost Prudential £10 million.

Abbey has also moved work from the UK to India, with 100 IT jobs moving to Bangalore in 2002 and a further 500 at the end of 2003. HSBC was one of the first UK banks to outsource work to India. It has moved 2,000 jobs to Bangalore and Hyderabad and by the end of 2006 another 4,000 jobs will have been transferred to India, Malaysia and China.

For financial services that use an overseas agent, rather than their own set-up, the payback period can be as little as 3 months. However, banks must also keep up quality. Customers most highly value a prompt answer, with the telephone call completed quickly and the problem solved at the first attempt.

Rival firms adopt most changes in the banking industry quickly, but on the issue of call centres the banks are polarising into two camps. Organisations such as HBOS, Nationwide, Alliance and Leicester and the Cooperative Bank have all ruled out going abroad. Nationwide's chief executive, Philip Williamson, says that he receives letters from new customers stating that they are switching accounts into his organisation because their previous bank has transferred jobs overseas. He says: 'There is a view that the quality of service in India is not as good. A number of companies [such as Shop Direct] have transferred jobs back to the UK.' A particular problem in both countries has been the high rate of labour turnover. In the UK, surveys suggest that it costs £2,444 to replace a person who leaves. Furthermore, new agents are only 16% as effective as experienced ones during the early period of their service.

Trade unions are also taking a firmer view on call centres. Bernadette Fisher, national officer of the financial services trade union UNIFI, described Lloyds TSB's decision to move 1,500 jobs to India as 'A callous move. It shows no respect for staff, customers or local communities.' The union is also critical of decisions taken by other financial organisations and is threatening to take industrial action.

Evidence from the Department of Industry confirms this view, to some extent. Table 32.5 summarises some of the key comparisons made in the DTI's study of call (contact) centres.

Table 32.5 *A comparison of UK and Indian call (contact) centres*

Feature	UK	India
Total cost of operations (index)	100	65
Average wage (new operators)	£12,945	£1,502
Labour turnover (%)	15%	29%
Office rents	£303 per square metre	£62 per square metre
Average speed to answer telephone	15 seconds	7 seconds
Perception of suitable accent	100%	70%
Proportion of problems solved through first call	87%	60%
Number of calls answered per operator per hour	15	12
Proportion of call centres using two or more quality assurance methods	81%	66%

Source: Department of Trade and Industry.

A study by the World Bank also highlights India as a greater trading risk for international businesses. Table 32.6 shows the key features included in their study of comparative risk.

Table 32.6 *Comparative trading risk*

International preferred location score	UK	India
Contract enforcement	3	2
Ease of business entry	1	7
Insurance industry sophistication	1	4
Political and economic stability	1	6
Business English proficiency	1	1
Corruption	1	5
Average	1.3	4.2

1 = most favourable rating; 7 = least favourable rating.
Source: World Bank.

Sources: *The UK Contact Centre Industry: A Study* (DTI, May 2004).

Questions

Total: 40 marks (45 minutes)

1 Study the paragraph concerning the Prudential's decision to relocate from Reading to Mumbai in India (lines 12–23).

a Calculate the payback period for this relocation decision. *(3 marks)*

b Calculate the average rate of return (ARR %) for this decision, over a four-year period. *(5 marks)*

c Evaluate the limitations, for the Prudential, of relying solely on the calculations in **1a** and **b** in order to decide on whether to relocate. *(12 marks)*

2 Discuss the main issues that a financial services business needs to examine when deciding whether to locate a call centre in the UK or India. *(20 marks)*

Operations management

Unit 4 consists of a case study built around a 'decision'. The four elements of Modules 4 and 5 are tested equally. Thus, questions totalling 20 marks are based on Marketing. Questions on Accounting and Finance, People, and Operations Management are also worth 20 marks each.

There may be a single 20-mark question or two questions totalling 20 marks, one of which involves some evaluation. It is possible that a single question will test a mixture of two elements. The case study examination will be 90 minutes in duration, of which 10 minutes should be used as reading time. All questions are compulsory.

As Operations Management has just been completed, this case study provides an opportunity to tackle a Unit 4 exam-style case study that is based only on Operations Management and which covers the whole of the A2 Operations Management specification.

CASE STUDY Operations management at AstraZeneca

Two of the world's biggest drug manufacturers have threatened to withdraw new research and development investment from the UK unless the government cracks down on animal rights activists. Sir Tom McKillop, head of AstraZeneca (AZ), warned the government: 'Unless you deal with animal rights issues, we cannot continue.' AZ has doubled the number of its R&D staff in the UK since 1999.

Research and development has always been the key to the success of drugs companies such as AZ. However, alternative drugs pose a threat, especially when patents expire. Sales of Losec, once the world's biggest selling drugs, fell from $3 billion to $2 billion in 2002. Two of its other major drugs suffered declines in sales of over 50% in the same year, after their patents expired.

However, AZ is fighting back. Its R&D work has led to the introduction of ten major new drugs, all with sales forecasts in excess of $300 million a year. Its major hope, Crestor, was expected to achieve annual sales of $5 billion a year, but having passed early safety tests it is now threatened with withdrawal on account of unexpected side-effects. Seven of the top ten new drugs for AZ are predicted to have annual sales in excess of $1 billion — a reward for AZ's commitment to R&D on which the company spends 18.3% of its sales revenue. On average, it costs £400 million to introduce a new drug. Potential returns are outlined in Appendix 1.

The pharmaceutical industry is traditionally the industry that spends most on R&D. The huge

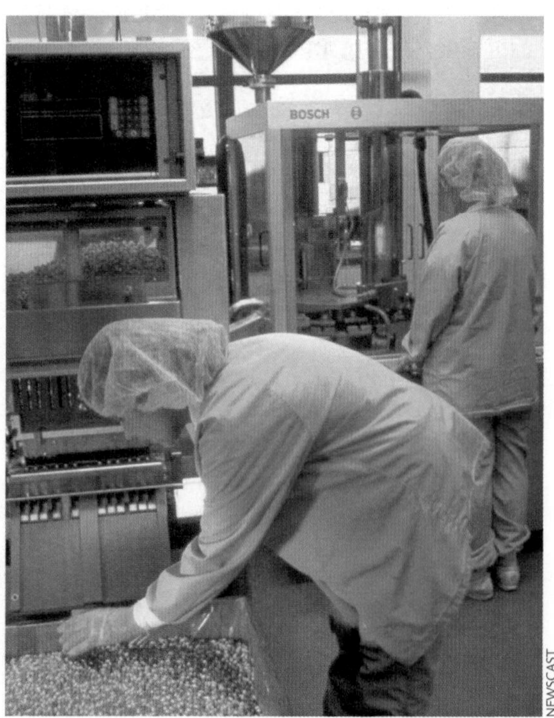

NEWSCAST

worldwide sales opportunities, and the chance to protect inventions through patents, have helped companies like AZ to reap the rewards of their research. The Indian government's decision to tighten up its patent laws, under pressure from other countries, is also helping AZ to limit competition.

Planning the introduction of a new drug is a time-consuming process. In late 2004, three major drugs were reaching the final stages of their development. All three began their development before 1998. In addition, the process is unpredictable. Phase 2 trials of one drug, ZD6126, have caused concern and the drug has been returned to the laboratory for further tests. There is also the risk that a rival will introduce an alternative product before the product is launched. This can cause internal conflict between the desire to achieve early sales and the need for thorough testing. There is also the possibility of setbacks once a product has been launched. Crestor met the requirements of all of its tests during development but has shown unforeseen side-effects since its launch.

The network in Figure 1 shows the stages of the introduction of a new drug. The numbers refer to the number of *months* taken for each stage.

Pharmaceutical companies also spend a lot of money on information technology, which is used to assist much of their initial research. Information can be processed more quickly and simulation of tests can save considerable sums by allowing the company to analyse results without the need to produce the product physically. However, although this has reduced the time taken to release new drugs, the need for thorough clinical tests on volunteers means that it still takes years to release a new drug. Although IT has led to major cost savings, it has not provided the marketing benefits enjoyed by many firms in other industries. In the UK (unlike the USA and many other countries), pharmaceutical companies are prevented from using websites to promote, or even inform people of, their drugs. As a consequence, pharmaceutical companies concentrate their efforts on the doctors who prescribe medicines.

AZ sells 46% of its drugs to the USA and 27% to European countries. However, Asia (and particularly China) represents the highest growth rate of sales. The company employs 11,600 staff worldwide in R&D. The main R&D bases are in the UK, Sweden, France, Japan, India and the USA. According to Nermeen Varawalla, vice president of a testing centre in Mumbai, India is an ideal location for R&D because of the number of graduates with relevant skills and a culture of innovation in drugs. The quality of the workforce and levels of technology are vital to R&D centres.

Some 16,000 staff are employed in the actual manufacturing process. The main manufacturing plants are in the UK, Sweden, France, Puerto Rico, China, South Korea, India and Mexico. Drug production has different requirements to R&D. With high-value-added and physically small products, the proximity to the market is less crucial, while high-quality production is essential. The cost of manufacturing is more important, so production locations are chosen to minimise costs. In some countries, such as France and the UK, government regional assistance has been a major factor. The potential returns of a new manufacturing plant are outlined in Appendix 1.

Figure 1 *Critical path analysis for the introduction of a new drug*

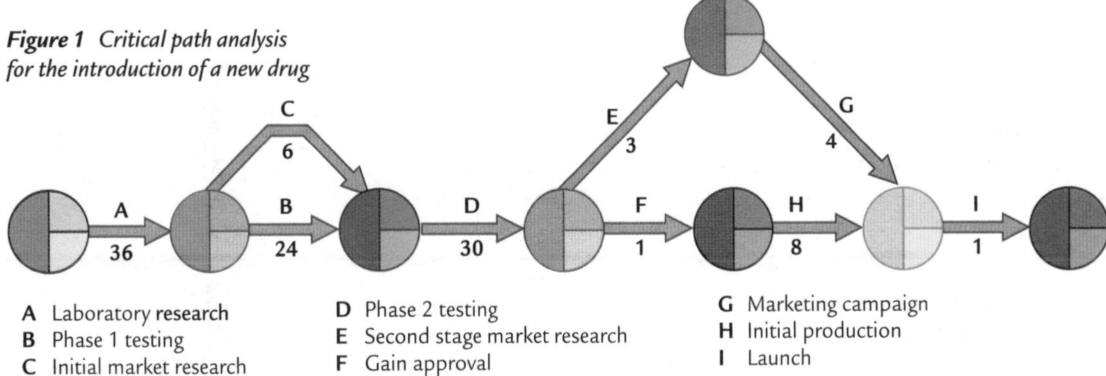

Appendix 1: Financial information on establishing a new manufacturing plant (estimates)

Initial cost of factory:	£5 million
Initial development costs:	£20 million
Annual operating costs (per million bottles):	£200,000
Sales revenue (per million bottles):	£1,950,000

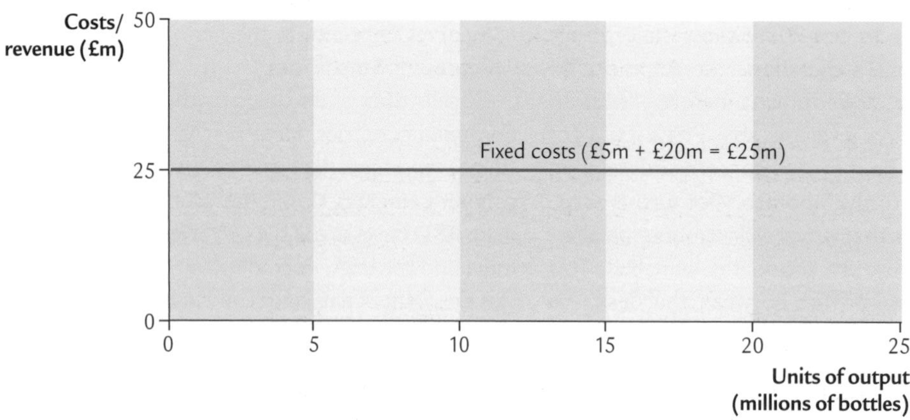

Questions

Total: 80 marks (90 minutes)

1 a Explain two problems facing pharmaceutical companies in carrying out their research and development activities. *(8 marks)*

b Evaluate the factors that are likely to lead to AstraZeneca spending over 18% of its sales revenue on research and development. *(12 marks)*

2 a Copy and complete the breakeven chart in Appendix 1 to show how many units must be sold for the new factory to break even. State your answer to the nearest million bottles. *(6 marks)*

b Discuss the reasons why the countries in which AstraZeneca decides to locate its manufacturing plants are often different from the countries in which it locates its research and development activities. *(14 marks)*

3 a In the UK, pharmaceutical companies are prevented from using websites to promote, or even inform people of, their drugs. Discuss the implications of this ban for AstraZeneca. *(10 marks)*

b Evaluate the main benefits to AstraZeneca of using information technology. *(10 marks)*

4 a Copy and complete Figure 1 to show the network for the introduction of a new drug. Include the earliest start times, the latest finish times and the critical path. *(8 marks)*

b Discuss the reasons why the use of critical path analysis for the release of a new drug is likely to be of limited benefit to AstraZeneca. *(12 marks)*

Unit 4

Unit 4 consists of a case study built around a 'decision'. The four elements of Modules 4 and 5 are tested equally. Thus, questions totalling 20 marks are based on Marketing. Questions on Accounting and Finance, People, and Operations Management are also worth 20 marks each.

There may be a single 20-mark question or two questions totalling 20 marks, one of which involves some evaluation. It is possible that a single question will test a mixture of two elements. The case study examination will be 90 minutes in duration, of which 10 minutes should be used as reading time. All questions are compulsory.

This case study provides an opportunity to test yourself on Modules 4 and 5, using an exam-style case study.

Airbus is a trading name of a business named EADS NV. For the sake of simplicity, the name Airbus is used throughout the case study when any reference is made to the business.

CASE STUDY The Airbus A380

Civil aircraft manufacture is dominated by two firms: Boeing and Airbus. These two firms sell to airlines, such as British Airways and Flybe, so they need to produce aircraft that meet the diverse needs of passengers.

For 40 years, the US aircraft maker Boeing was the market leader, but recently Airbus, its European rival, has gained the largest market share.

The battle between these two giants has intensified with the recent launches of two new aircraft: the Airbus A380 and the Boeing 787 Dreamliner. These planes represent huge gambles. Boeing and Airbus have very different visions of how we will fly in the future.

Airbus's huge double-decker A380 will be limited to flying between the world's major airports, but can carry up to 800 passengers. However, most of the airlines expected to buy the plane will opt for fittings that provide 555 seats and a number of luxury facilities, such as a bar and gym.

Boeing, on the other hand, sees flexibility as the key to success. It is banking on a combination of the old 747 Jumbo (which takes 385 passengers) and the new 787 Dreamliner, which can only take 230–300 passengers, but which can fly directly between more of the world's airports. This reduces the need for passengers to make connecting flights.

The air travel market has been notoriously difficult to predict, although current estimates forecast growth of 5% per annum. Air travel has a high income elasticity of demand, and both business and leisure travel have increased dramatically. However, external factors such as terrorism have caused sudden, unpredictable changes. The nature of the market is also changing, with passengers wishing for greater comfort and more long-distance flights.

Airbus has done everything to ensure that its A380 is suitable. It consulted airlines and 60 airport operators to get their views at the beginning and throughout the design stages. Singapore Airlines,

which has ordered ten A380s, is already advertising the superior comfort of the aircraft as a selling point. Emirates Airlines has ordered 40 A380s. Airport operator BAA estimates that one in eight aircraft landing at Heathrow in 2016 will be an Airbus A380. Per passenger mile fuel consumption is less than that of a small car and Airbus's R&D team has cut costs per seat to 80% of its Boeing equivalent.

Many analysts believe that accurate market forecasts are the key to success, but others believe that research and development is more important. Airbus has spent £6 billion developing the aircraft, with many new lightweight materials introduced to improve fuel consumption.

According to Richard Aboulafia of the Teal Consulting Group, 'Boeing has failed to match Airbus's research and development and fallen behind its rival.' He believes that Airbus has gained market leadership through developing a broad range of aircraft, each serving specific market needs. 'It will take Boeing more than one new aircraft to reverse the tide.' Certainly, Airbus's research and development team has produced a superior aircraft in terms of technical specifications. (See Appendix 1 for a comparison of the features of the Airbus A380 and the Boeing 747 Jumbo.)

Manufacturing the Airbus A380 has also presented problems. As a business, Airbus grew from cooperation between France, Germany, Spain and the UK. The parts of the aircraft are made in five different countries and then assembled in Toulouse in France. Mike Turner, now chief executive of BAE Systems, the British company that supplies the wings, was formerly on the board of Airbus. 'I could not believe what a mess it was. Nobody knew how much money the firm was making.' Although communication has now improved, there are still difficulties in coordinating work between the different countries. These problems have not been helped by the rapid growth of Airbus. Between 2004 and 2006, sales of its aircraft are expected to increase from 400 to 600 per annum.

These changes have affected human resource management at Airbus. Over 11,000 engineers have been involved in the development of the A380 and a 50% growth will put pressure on recruitment of suitable staff. For Airbus the product is a priority, but some of the suppliers, notably BAE in the UK, are separate companies with their own targets. Airbus needs to ensure that companies such as BAE will give priority to Airbus manufacture. This is unlikely as most of BAE's business (and its profit) is in the defence market, supplying entire planes rather than just the wings.

To date, workforce planning at Airbus has been relatively straightforward. Some 10% of the 109,000 employees have been employed in R&D. However, as full-scale production of the A380 Airbus commences, there will need to be a recruitment drive for assembly workers in France and similar requirements in the other countries involved. In the UK and Spain, suitably qualified workers are in short supply, while in France, government moves to abolish the 35-hour week are threatening to cause considerable industrial unrest.

Airbus has received 149 orders so far, still short of the 250 planes that it estimates it needs to reach breakeven. The plane cost £7 billion to develop and needed government loans to keep the project afloat. Long-term profit is by no means certain, but a major concern is the impact of such a project on the working capital and liquidity of Airbus.

There are question marks against the breakeven quantity predicted for the Airbus A380. The A380 has hit the popularity of the Boeing 747 Jumbo to such an extent that the price of second-hand Jumbos has fallen to £30 million. Cathay Pacific is one airline that has decided to buy second-hand Boeing 747s rather than brand new Airbus A380s. This situation may help airlines such as British Airways, which have placed no orders to date, to bargain with Airbus for a lower price on the Airbus A380 than the current price of £155 million per plane.

Airbus faces a critical decision. How can it reach breakeven on the A380 while still continuing the R&D programme that has allowed it to seize market leadership from Boeing?

Appendix 1: Comparison of the features of the Airbus A380 and the Boeing 747 Jumbo

Feature	Airbus A380	Boeing 747 Jumbo
Wingspan	80 metres	70 metres
Number of passengers	555–800	385–420
Fuel consumption	0.145 miles per gallon	0.18 miles per gallon
Cost to buy each aircraft	£155 million	£65 million
Turnaround time at airport*	70–90 minutes	75–120 minutes
Construction lead time	5 months	4 months
Range without refuelling	9,200 miles	8,000 miles
Cruising speed	670 miles per hour	675 miles per hour

*The time taken between touching down at an airport and taking-off again, fully loaded.

Appendix 2: Extract from profit and loss accounts of Airbus

Years ending:	31.12.04 (€bn)	31.12.03 (€bn)
Sales revenue	28.6	30.1
Cost of sales (direct costs)	22.7	24.6
Gross profit	5.9	5.5
R&D expenses	2.1	2.2
Other expenses/overheads	2.2	2.8
Operating profit	1.6	0.5

Appendix 3: Extract from balance sheets of Airbus

	31.12.04	31.12.03
Fixed assets	**(€bn)**	**(€bn)**
Intangible assets	9.8	9.7
Fixed assets	16.0	15.6
TOTAL FIXED ASSETS	**25.8**	**25.3**
Current assets		
Stocks	3.4	3.3
Debtors	3.7	4.0
Short-term investments	8.9	10.7
Prepaid expenses etc.	3.7	3.7
Bank balance and cash	7.8	7.4
TOTAL CURRENT ASSETS	**27.5**	**29.1**
minus		
Current liabilities		
Creditors (less than 1 year)	5.1	5.1
Other short-term liabilities	10.3	10.9
	15.4	**16.0**
equals		
WORKING CAPITAL		
(net current assets)	12.1	13.1
Total assets less current liabilities	**37.9**	**38.4**

Sources: www.airbus.com; www.eads.com; articles by Dominic O'Connell in *The Sunday Times Magazine*, 19 September 2004, and by Charles Bremner in *The Times*, 15 January 2005; and BBC World Service report by Tim Bowler, 10 February 2005.

Questions

Total: 80 marks (90 minutes)

1 a Airbus has experienced communication problems between different plants and different countries. Analyse two ways in which Airbus can improve its communications. *(8 marks)*

b Evaluate the main difficulties facing Airbus in its workforce planning. *(12 marks)*

2 a Discuss the methods that Airbus might use to forecast future sales of its Airbus A380. *(10 marks)*

b What do you consider to be the most important elements of the marketing mix for the Airbus A380? Justify your view. *(10 marks)*

3 To what extent is the success of the Airbus A380 dependent on the quality of Airbus's research and development? *(20 marks)*

4 a In the year ending 2004, Airbus was expecting to increase its operating profit as a result of increased company sales revenue from the Airbus A380. However, the development costs of the aircraft were expected to put pressure on the firm's liquidity. Using the information in Appendices 2 and 3, show whether these expected results actually happened. *(10 marks)*

b Discuss the factors that might cause the financial performance of Airbus to differ from expectations. *(10 marks)*

CHAPTER 33

Unit 5W: the written paper (examination)

Unit 5 tests the whole range of the A2 specification. The AQA specification separates business concepts into modules: Modules 1–3 are AS topics and Modules 4–6 are A2 topics. However, a look at the details of the specification shows that some AS topics are developed further within the A2 modules. Furthermore, the introduction to A2 Module 6 states that 'It builds on all the AS subject content…'. Thus, although there will be a tendency to test A2 subject content in Unit 5, the specification allows questions to be set on any part of the specification from both the AS and the A2 modules. You are advised to revise all of the specification in preparing yourself for the Unit 5 written paper.

Assessment

As indicated in the introduction to this book, every mark that is awarded on an A2 paper is given for the demonstration of a skill. The content of the course (the theories, concepts and ideas) is there to provide a framework to allow you to show your skills — recognising the content on its own is not enough to merit high marks.

The following skills are tested:

- **Knowledge and understanding** — recognising and describing business concepts and ideas.
- **Application** — being able to explain or apply your understanding.
- **Analysis** — developing a line of thought in order to demonstrate its impact or consequences.
- **Evaluation** — making a judgement by weighing up the evidence provided.
- **Synthesis** — recognising the importance and validity of different pieces of information, building the parts of an argument into a connected whole, developing a logical sequence of argument and demonstrating clarity through summarising.

The Unit 5 written paper is an alternative to the coursework option, and is thus assessed in a similar way. The **business report** is a compulsory question, designed to test your ability to synthesise data (recognise the value of specific pieces of information) and then to analyse and evaluate that information. The **essay** provides you with a choice of one from four titles, and enables you to discuss a broad business issue in some depth.

Note that synthesis is only tested in Unit 5. It is classified as a higher-level skill, equivalent to evaluation. Students taking the coursework option must decide on the usefulness and validity of the data that they collect. A similar skill is tested in the business report. In the time allowed, it will not be possible to analyse all the data. Synthesis tests your ability to select the most crucial information and to use it to build a coherent and logical argument.

The business report and essay paper has a much higher weighting for the higher-level skill of evaluation than any paper besides Unit 6 (the case study). Bear this in mind during your preparation and revision for the paper, as you will need to practise developing arguments more fully for this paper. This will be good practice for the case study too, which has a similar, higher weighting for these skills.

The examination paper for Unit 5W has a fixed mark scheme. Marks for each skill in each question are awarded as follows:

Business report — compulsory question

Skill	Weighting	Description
Knowledge	8	How well you understand the terms, theories and ideas
Application	8	How well you can explain benefits and problems, complete calculations, etc. in the context of situations
Analysis	8	How well you apply theory and develop ideas
Synthesis	5	How well you select data and structure the answer
Evaluation	11	How well you judge the overall significance of the situation
Total	**40**	

Essay — one question to be answered from a choice of four essay titles

Skill	Weighting	Description
Knowledge	8	How well you understand the terms, theories and ideas
Application	8	How well you can explain benefits, problems, complete calculations, etc. in the context of situations
Analysis	8	How well you apply theory and develop ideas
Evaluation	16	How well you judge the overall significance of the situation
Total	**40**	

It is worth remembering that, in order to evaluate, you need to demonstrate judgement and the ability to reach a reasoned conclusion. The following sentence structures will help you to evaluate:

- On balance the firm should..............because..............
- The most significant..............is..............because..............
- However, ...would also need to be considered because..............
- The probable result is..............because..............

The structure of the examination

Unit 5 is a 90-minute examination.

There is a compulsory business report followed by four essay titles, *one* of which must be attempted.

Both questions carry 40 marks and are equally weighted in the total for the paper. It is necessary to spend some time reading the data provided for the business report, so you are advised to divide the 90 minutes as follows:

Business report: 45–50 minutes
Essay: 40–45 minutes

Advice on answering the business report

Before answering the business report it is important to remember that it is only half of Unit 5W. Allow yourself enough time to attempt one of the essays. If necessary, you can return to the business report towards the end of the examination, if time permits.

Manage your time carefully

Including reading time you should have 45–50 minutes to complete the business report. Practise answering business reports from past papers or sample reports within this time limit, to ensure that you can produce an appropriately structured and detailed answer.

Use a report format, but do not include unnecessary detail

This is a business report and should be presented in a relevant format. However, whereas an actual business report would include a summary of its findings in the conclusions, this would be wasteful in an examination. Primarily, your report is an examination answer, so you should avoid repeating earlier findings in the conclusions. Furthermore, do not waste time on excessive use of numbered paragraphs, headings and subheadings. A simple report format will save time.

A sample layout is shown in Figure 33.1.

To: xxxxx   From: yyyyy
Date: zzzzz

TITLE OF REPORT

1 ARGUMENTS
(These may be split into suitable subheadings, such as 'Advantages' and 'Disadvantages'.)

2 RECOMMENDATIONS

Signature
Date

***Figure 33.1** Business report: sample layout*

The application and analysis should be presented in section 1. Section 2 (recommendations) should focus on evaluation and should form a substantial part of the answer.

Read the question carefully and plan your answer

Establish the exact requirements of the question in your own mind, and plan your approach. Refer back to this plan to check that you are staying on track.

Keep referring back to the data

On first reading the question, highlight the main points. At this stage, you should also note any links between different appendices. Clarify your logic by mentioning the occasional figure or comparison in your answer. This will help you to respond to the data, as required. But be careful not just to describe the data — you must explain the impact of the data on the decision required in the report.

Remember also that the few lines of introduction at the beginning of the question may include vital information that will help your answer.

Take an overview of the situation

With five appendices (usually) to scrutinise, it is essential to take a broad view. The appendices are like a jigsaw — each element may (or may not) provide you with an insight into the solution, but it is only when they are combined that the full picture can be seen.

Synthesise

Synthesis is the ability to select information that is relevant and useful and distinguish it from that which is marginal or irrelevant. Use the data that allow you to draw the most meaningful conclusion. Do not try to include every piece of information; a selective approach is required.

Integrate the data

Do not use each appendix in isolation. Your answer should match your plan (for example, advantages followed by disadvantages), so the most logical structure is to explain the advantages first and so on. Explaining a factor may need reference to more than one appendix. For example, the significance of a particular strength or weakness, identified in an appendix, may become clearer when compared with data on the firm's competitors that are included in a different appendix.

Explain, analyse and evaluate

During your revision, study the marking scheme for the business report. Check that your answers match the requirements of the Level 4 skills descriptions.

Make a recommendation

The report requires you to make a reasoned decision. Give yourself plenty of time to draw together your main findings in order to provide a recommendation based on evidence. Make sure that you are not just repeating yourself at this stage. Your recommendation should show the key factors that have led to your final decision.

Avoid excessive number crunching

The business report is designed primarily to test your ability to use data. You may need to use a calculator on occasions, but the data are designed to limit the number of calculations required. Invariably, numerical results, such as ratios, will already have been calculated and placed within the appendices. Every moment spent calculating reduces the time available for writing, so you should not need to carry out too many calculations. In most cases, the most appropriate use of the data will be to draw comparisons, particularly with respect to identifying trends.

Advice on essay writing

Advice is given in two sections:

- Section A contains rather general advice, based on material first published by AQA in 1997.
- Section B is an update that presents AQA's current thinking on the best approach to essay writing.

Section A

A useful source of advice on essay writing is from the awarding body itself. In 1997, AQA published 'Ten golden rules' for students on how to tackle the essays in the A-level Business Studies paper. These rules were designed to help candidates avoid the main pitfalls.

1 There is no such thing as an essay about a topic

An essay is a response to a specific title, usually worded so that it cannot be answered by repeating paragraphs from notes. Hence, there is no such thing as the 'communications' essay or the 'marketing' essay, because every answer should depend on the title, not the topic. If the question refers to your favourite topic, do not rush to answer it. Make sure that you understand the question fully before planning your answer.

2 There is no such thing as a one-sided essay

Some questions are deliberately provocative, implying that there is a dominant factor or that it is right to take an action. Do not assume that the examiner is asking you to prove it. If there was just one side to an answer, the question would not be worth asking. Usually, the only questions set are ones that can provoke differing viewpoints.

3 All essays have the same answer

With few exceptions, A-level questions can be answered in two words: 'it depends'. Consequently, the candidate's main task in planning the essay is to consider what the answer depends upon (for example, the objectives of the organisation, internal or external constraints, culture, etc.).

4 Essays need a structure

A logical structure is to present your basic points, explaining and analysing them (using business theories and ideas), and culminating in an overall

weighing up of the evidence in order to create a reasoned conclusion that is supported by the evidence.

5 Most candidates have forgotten the title by their second page

As seen earlier, the key to a good essay is to follow the wording of the title. Discipline yourself by referring back to the question regularly. This is time well spent because it avoids the cardinal sin of irrelevance.

6 Every paragraph should answer the question set

A good paragraph is one that answers a specific aspect of the question set in enough depth to impress the reader. It is recommended that you read over your past essays, asking yourself whether each and every paragraph is directed at the question. You will probably find several that are side-tracks or simple repetition of notes. Do not be tempted to show off irrelevant knowledge — in an examination, such paragraphs gain virtually no marks.

7 Content

Good answers come from the breadth of knowledge and the clarity of understanding that the candidate has shown. Generally, if you analyse the question with care, you will pick up most of the content in passing; consequently, a focus on analysis rather than facts will invariably get you the content marks anyway.

8 Analysis

Analysis means using business concepts to answer questions with precision and depth. The ability to apply business theories and ideas, to break down the question and identify the key issues involved, and to use relevant concepts will lead to analysis marks being awarded. A caution: do not be tempted to force an idea or theory into your answer. This can lead to irrelevance and time wasting.

9 Evaluation — the key to high-mark essays

With 40% of the marks for an essay being awarded for this skill, it is twice as valuable as any other skill that you can show. Evaluation means judgement. For good marks you need to:

- show the ability to examine arguments critically, and to highlight differing opinions
- distinguish between fact, well-supported argument and opinion
- weigh up the strength or relative importance of different factors in an argument, to show which you believe to be the most important, and why
- show how the topic fits into wider business, social, political or economic issues

10 Play the game

Examiners enjoy reading about (relevant) concepts, with appropriate use of terminology. They dislike slang or streetwise language (such as 'on the fiddle') and any suggestion that the issues are obvious or simple. You should keep your work businesslike and relevant, managing your time to ensure that you can write a thoughtful conclusion.

Section B — update

The ten golden rules still apply to current business studies essays. However, there has been a subtle change in the essay titles in recent years. In order to assist students in showing 'application' and 'evaluation', titles are generally broader than they were. The extra detail provided in the titles is intended to give 'hooks' on which students can apply their answers. In turn, this enhanced scope for application makes it easier to make an appropriate judgement (evaluation).

An example of a question containing these 'hooks' is question 4 from the January 2005 examination:

When the company Hutchison Whampoa, an international conglomerate, launched its new 3G technology mobile phones, it set a sales target of 1 million customers in the UK in the first year. Its actual sales in the UK were significantly less than this. Discuss the possible implications for a firm such as Hutchison Whampoa of failing to hit its sales targets for a new product.

This question has been chosen because it illustrates many possible 'hooks'. It is not usual for a question to provide as many 'hooks' as this particular example.

What are the potential 'hooks' for application and evaluation?

- **'International conglomerate.'** This is a very large firm; how important is the UK market to its overall success? When discussing the implications, it is necessary to put the UK market into the overall context of this international business.
- **'New 3G technology.'** How unique is the technology; is failure to reach a short-term target likely to create long-term problems or might it be a temporary 'blip'?
- **'Sales target of 1 million...in the first year**.' This appears to be a very ambitious target. Was it realistic? Was it precise enough? (Hutchison Whampoa has managed to get closer to its target by offering heavily discounted deals on its '3' mobiles.)
- **'Actual sales...were significantly less than this**.' What level is meant by the word 'significant'? This is not a clear description and could cover a huge shortfall or one that is only slightly disappointing.
- **'Possible implications**.' Implications are the consequences; remember these may be problems or benefits. In general, you should try to consider both sides. Although there is not much to be said that is positive about this situation, it may help the business to learn more about the market and to conduct more thorough market research in other markets before launching.
- **'Failing to hit its sales targets.'** Does the firm have contingency plans to ease the extent of its problems? Is this happening elsewhere in the world too?

- **'For a new product.'** Remember this is a new product, subject to the high levels of risk associated with all new products. What established products does the company have? How dynamic is the market? A rapidly changing market will require more success from new products. Are competitors releasing new products too, and are they successful?

You will not need to use every single 'hook' in a question such as this, but it is worth practising on recent past papers. See how well you can apply your answers to recent essay titles. This approach may help you to identify the type of essay title to choose in the examination, and show you the types of title that you should avoid answering.

CHAPTER 34

Unit 5C: the coursework project

This chapter is included to provide guidance to students who are taking the Unit 5 coursework (Unit 5C) option as an alternative to the Unit 5 written paper examination (Unit 5W). We will consider both planning and completion of coursework.

Planning your coursework

Choose your business or study with care

The best projects tend to be those that continue to offer research opportunities throughout the project. Sometimes the initial research throws up a problem or leads to a recognition that further information is needed. In these situations, a business with a continued personal contact, such as a part-time job or a business contact through family or a close friend, is the best choice. Furthermore, firms without personal contact with you or your school/college are less likely to provide you with the information that you need.

If you really cannot get sufficient data from a particular organisation, a feasibility study is almost certainly the best option to choose.

Try to keep the project local

Projects involving national companies are often very challenging. If your best source of information is a large organisation, try to find a title that studies a specific, localised issue.

Choose your title carefully

A good title will look to a future decision. Such a title will require research, analysis of the evidence and its application to the business, and, finally, a judgement or recommendation. Avoid titles that encourage mere description of a business.

Keep a timetable of the plan for your coursework and monitor your progress regularly

- Set specific deadlines for establishing your main objectives, gathering secondary research, undertaking primary research and producing the first, second and final drafts of your project. Make some allowances for delay — set the deadline for your final draft well before the deadline for submission given by your teacher.

- Once you have set your primary objective, think about the secondary objectives — the targets that will allow you to achieve your primary objective. For example, if you are looking at a feasibility study, your secondary objectives should include acquiring forecasts on likely demand, sales revenue, costs and recruitment of staff.
- Record your findings, plans and any ideas as you progress — you should not trust anything to memory.
- Monitor progress so that you know if you are falling behind (and do something about it if you are behind!).

Ensure that you are aware of the marking criteria in your planning

Careful study of the marking scheme will enable you to recognise the skills that you must display. This information will help you to decide sensible objectives, undertake appropriate research and present relevant findings and recommendations.

Be prepared to modify your title

If problems occur in gathering suitable data, it is worth investigating an alternative title. However, you must seek your teacher's advice if you are considering this action.

Make sure that your research meets your needs

If an avenue of research yielded no relevant information, it is best to ignore this line of enquiry, although you may wish to refer to the approach in your section on methodology, if it was a valid approach to plan initially.

Plan your primary research to make sure that it meets all your needs. You may only have one chance to collect some data, especially if you are using an interview as a part of your research. Think carefully about every question in your primary research. Ask yourself: 'Is this question going to help me to achieve my objective(s)?'

For questionnaires, it is worth testing your first draft on a few respondents, to check that the questions are working in the way that you expected.

Completing your coursework

Use the marking scheme descriptors

Use the descriptors for the highest level of each skill in the marking scheme as a guide to your approach. The descriptors for the top level of each skill are set out below, with an explanation of their meaning.

Knowledge and understanding

Includes relevant materials, focused clearly on the project objective(s), fully explained and presented appropriately.

Make sure that the business concepts that you use are helping to solve the problem that you are investigating. Show clearly the purpose of all of your material so that its relevance can be seen. Explain your thinking in some detail, to demonstrate that you understand the business concepts that you are using. The most appropriate presentation is that which explains your ideas most clearly. Diagrams and charts can be an excellent way of clarifying a concept, but it is rare for a diagram or chart to be self-explanatory. You *must* accompany these forms of presentation with some written explanation.

Application of knowledge/methodology

Clear evidence of relevant, valid research drawn from primary and secondary sources — showing a strong grasp of theory and the ability to comment critically on the methods used.

It is vital that you show your sources, so that the assessor can verify that your research is relevant and valid (based on sufficient and unbiased data). It is impossible to gain more than half the marks for methodology without including secondary and primary research.

Plan your research thoroughly. Students who throw in a brief example of secondary data in a project based solely on primary research (or vice versa) will not reach the higher skills levels unless the assessor believes that both the primary and secondary data are relevant and valid. The reason for the methodology used must be explained in the coursework, so that a suitable understanding of theory is demonstrated.

'Critical comment' means an evaluation of the suitability of the methodology used. It does not mean that only criticisms are accepted. Some students produce a faulty, invalid piece of market research (for example, a sample of only 20 people to research potential demand) and then conclude that their research is unreliable because of the sample size. This is not demonstrating 'the ability to comment critically'; it is poorly planned research and will not be rewarded highly. Critical commentary should be based on developments that could not be seen obviously beforehand, such as an unexpected interpretation of a question.

Analysis of evidence

Substantial analysis of the data, selectively using various written and numerate techniques to identify causes and/or possible solutions and showing judgement in the techniques used.

For high marks for this skill, there must be a significant level of analysis of the information that has been gathered. Analysis is 'developing a line of thought' rather than merely describing the data collected. This analysis should be selective (that is, using appropriate techniques), so you must think carefully before choosing your approach: are the financial data suited to a cash-flow forecast; would an investment appraisal be more appropriate or would both help meet the objectives of your coursework? Ensure that you justify the approach taken so that you can be credited with judgement in appropriate techniques. Depending on the project title, your analysis should also identify causes and/or solutions.

Synthesis
Structure well thought through, making it easy to follow the logic, the communication and the recommendations that draw together the most appropriate evidence and arguments.

An index of contents is a great aid in showing the logic behind the project's structure. Check that your information builds in a logical manner, taking the reader through the evidence and the conclusions and recommendations that follow. Present your project as a business report (see Chapter 33) and make sure that you leave enough time and space for recommendations. These recommendations must be based on relevant evidence and arguments.

Evaluation
Appropriate conclusions justified by the evidence, showing an awareness of the most relevant underlying themes or issues and their potential implications for the business concerned.

As stated earlier, the conclusion must be consistent with the evidence presented. Furthermore, you need to demonstrate recognition of the key issues affecting your project (for example, is it being affected by internal problems or does its success depend on certain external factors?). The impact of these themes on the business needs to be included in the project. Underlying themes are the sort of issues that may not be obvious until after the research has been undertaken.

Show the sources of all of your data

If you are forecasting sales or costs, do not just put figures into a chart or table. Explain how you arrived at these figures. Even if you believe that your method was not ideal, it is better than introducing figures that appear to be totally fictitious.

Draw your conclusion at the end of the project, not at the beginning

Match your conclusions to the evidence collected. Do not go into your project with a preconceived conclusion. The best recommendations are those that are a natural conclusion from the evidence submitted.

Seek some advice

You should not feel isolated when completing your coursework. Although your teachers should not initiate suggestions that will improve your project, it is acceptable for some guidance to be given in response to your questions. Think of suitable questions to ask.

Allow plenty of time for the final draft

Remember, it is the final draft that is assessed for your A-level. Coursework is the best opportunity for completing a part of your A-level without a strict time pressure. Use this opportunity well so that you can complete it in a relaxed manner.

Pitfalls to avoid

- Try to avoid over-ambitious targets.
- Do not feel that you have to prove your case. If the evidence of your feasibility study suggests that your proposal is not feasible, do not worry. As long as you have used appropriate information and presented relevant arguments, you will be rewarded accordingly. The coursework project is designed to test your ability to apply the business skills and techniques that you have acquired; it is not a test of whether you can spot in advance a business opportunity or the solution to a business problem.
- Do not be too certain in your conclusions. Most business problems have a number of conflicting factors to weigh up. Ensure that all of these factors are included, even if it makes the final decision less conclusive.
- Avoid including tables, diagrams or charts that have no written explanation. Most data need some written clarification.
- Do not delay your research. In the authors' experience, there is a positive correlation between the final mark and the promptness of starting market research. Try to start your preparation as early as possible.

And finally...

Read your project after final completion, just to eliminate any errors that may have been missed earlier.

UNIT 5W

Total: 80 marks *Time allowed: 90 minutes*

SECTION A

Answer this question. You should spend up to 50 minutes on this section.

Classy Cashmere

Classy Cashmere is a small business selling exclusive cashmere knitwear to middle- and high-income earners. It is based in Harrogate, Yorkshire, and currently sells its products via the internet and small, targeted sales catalogues. It is an established, but small, business and is seeking to expand. Initially the owners decided that expansion should be via the acquisition of another small knitwear retailer, FineKnits, but they are now wondering whether organic growth might be a better option. The following data are available.

1 Produce a report for the owners, analysing the arguments for and against acquiring FineKnits or pursuing organic growth, and recommending which type of expansion Classy Cashmere should pursue.

Appendix A: market information, 2005

	Classy Cashmere	FineKnits
Product	Pure cashmere knitwear	All knitwear
Price range	£80–£500	£30–£150
Average price	£120	£45
Place	Internet and sales catalogues	Six shops throughout the north of England
Direct competition	Two other firms, in the same price range, specialising in cashmere products, which also sell on the internet and via sales catalogues	Numerous high street alternatives
Market	National	North of England

Appendix B: financial information, 2005

	Classy Cashmere	FineKnits
Return on capital	25%	15%
Gearing	10%	50%
Acid test ratio	0.5:1	1.5:1
Fixed assets	£0.25m	£1.5m
Sales turnover	£1m	£2.5m

Appendix C: people and operations information, 2005

	Classy Cashmere	FineKnits
Number of staff	6*	30**
Labour costs (% of turnover)	10%	30%
Location	Unit in a business park in Harrogate	Six shops in the north of England plus HQ in Sheffield
Capacity utilisation	90%	55%
Supplier	Single supplier – batch purchases	Multiple suppliers – bulk purchases

*3 of which work on packing and distribution.
**18 of which work as sales assistants in the shops.

Appendix D: economic and marketing data, 2005

- Income elasticity of demand: Classy Cashmere = 3; FineKnits = 1.5
- Price elasticity of demand: Classy Cashmere = –0.4; FineKnits = –1.2
- Interest rate = 4.75% and forecast to fall.
- Average annual earnings growth = 4.3%

Appendix E: sales growth, 2000–07 (£m)

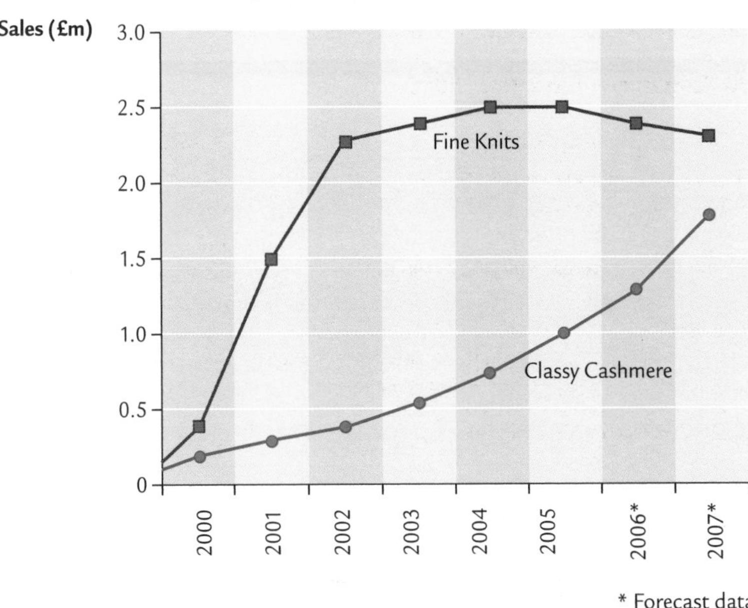

* Forecast data

PLEASE TURN OVER FOR SECTION B

SECTION B

Answer *one* question from this section.

2 If a business has 'pricing power', it is able to pass cost increases on to consumers with ease. Evaluate the nature of businesses with pricing power and the limitations of such power.

3 Many companies are either outsourcing their production and other activities or actually relocating to India and the Far East to take advantage of lower labour costs. To what extent is this simply a good business decision?

4 Bill Gates, founder of Microsoft, said: 'The consumer is always unpredictable. You can only throw products onto the market and then learn from your mistakes.' He was referring to the new improved Xbox 360, which, following investment of £536 million, will be launched in November 2005. Assess how valid his statement is likely to be for the market for such a product.

5 As an organic chocolate company set up to support the Mayan Indians of Belize, Green and Black's became a byword for ethical and enterprising business. On 12 May 2005, it was bought by the giant Cadbury Schweppes. Is it possible for a company such as Green and Black's to maintain its ethical trading objectives as part of a global mainstream confectioner such as Cadbury Schweppes? Justify your answer.

Module 6

External influences

“We have two classes of forecasters. Those who don’t know and those who don’t know that they don’t know.”

J. K. Galbraith

CHAPTER 35

Implications for business strategy of macroeconomic variables

This chapter builds directly upon the macroeconomic issues covered at AS and specifically in Chapters 36–40 of the AS textbook. It is assumed, therefore, that you will know and understand these issues before studying the contents of this chapter. The impact on business strategy of changes in, and the level of, macroeconomic variables, including interest rates, exchange rates, inflation and unemployment, is considered here. The chapter then examines the implications of the business cycle for business decision making and concludes with an analysis of how skills surpluses and shortages in the labour market impact on business.

Implications for business strategy of changes in interest rates

interest rates: the cost of borrowing money and the return for lending money.

Interest rates measure the opportunity cost, to both individuals and firms, of spending money rather than saving it and receiving interest. Since 2000, interest rates in the UK have been relatively low, as shown in Table 35.1.

	2000	2001	2002	2003	2004
Interest rates (%)	6.0	4.0	4.0	3.75	4.5
Source: HM Treasury website. www.hm-treasury.gov.uk/					

Table 35.1 *Annual UK interest rates*

Effects of a fall in interest rates

Changes in interest rates affect business in many different ways. A fall in interest rates can have the following effects.

Increase in demand for consumer goods

The demand for consumer goods is likely to increase for a number of reasons:

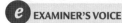

- Saving money is less attractive because less interest is received. This may mean that people prefer to spend rather than save, causing demand for consumer goods to increase.
- The cost of goods bought on credit will fall. In particular, this will affect expensive, durable items such as cars, furniture and electrical goods, and luxuries such as holidays, which tend to be income elastic. People may be encouraged to purchase things that were previously considered too expensive, or to buy replacements more frequently, or to purchase more of a particular item. All of these factors will lead to an increase in demand for consumer goods.
- Variable-rate mortgage payments and other loan repayments will fall, meaning that homeowners will have more discretionary income, which they may spend on more consumer goods.

EXAMINER'S VOICE

Income elasticity of demand is an important concept to consider here. Don't assume that it is only relevant to marketing questions.

Increase in demand for capital goods

Because it becomes cheaper to purchase expensive capital equipment on credit, the demand for capital (investment) goods may increase. Thus firms might bring forward planned future investment or actually increase the level of investment. This is because the return on projects is likely to exceed interest payments that must be made on borrowed funds or that could be received by investing the firm's own funds elsewhere. This results in a rise in demand for capital goods, such as machinery, as firms become more confident.

EXAMINER'S VOICE

Link this argument to investment appraisal. If interest rates fall, the target average rate of return is likely to fall. Similarly, the discount rate chosen in net present value calculations will fall. These changes mean that the probability of a project meeting its financial targets, and thus being accepted, will increase.

Fall in export prices and rise in import prices

If interest rates fall, this will lead to a fall in the value of the pound, which in turn will lead to a fall in export prices and a rise in import prices. Assuming that demand for both exports and imports is price elastic, this is likely to lead to a rise in demand for UK goods at home and abroad because domestic goods are priced more competitively than imported goods, and UK exports are priced more competitively than other products sold abroad. (More detail on the link between interest rates and exchange rates is provided in the section 'Interest rates and their influence on exchange rates', on p. 346.)

EXAMINER'S VOICE

Price elasticity of demand is an important concept to consider whenever analysing pricing issues. Don't assume that it is only relevant to marketing questions.

Fall in costs and rise in profits

A fall in the interest payments on loans will have a beneficial effect on firms that are highly geared. (Highly geared firms are those with a high proportion of their capital employed in the form of long-term loans.) Interest payments are part of fixed costs, so fixed costs for these firms will fall. This in turn will reduce unit costs and the breakeven point. It may also make it possible to

introduce price cuts and therefore adopt a more competitive strategy in the market. Alternatively, it can have potentially favourable effects on profits. As unit costs fall, there will be a rise in profit margins — that is, the difference between unit costs and the price of the product — unless price is reduced.

As a result of a fall in interest rates, the overall increase in demand, for both consumer and capital goods, may lead firms to consider expanding production. As a consequence, more employees may be needed, leading to increased competition in the labour market. This in turn might create skill shortages in certain areas, resulting in increasing wage costs. (Skill shortages are considered on page 358.) Overall, the increasing demand for goods and the possible increasing wage demands may be inflationary. (The impact of inflation on business is considered later on page 350.) Equally, the rise in demand for both consumer and capital goods may increase the rate of economic growth, which can have further effects on business. (Economic growth is considered in Chapter 37.)

> **EXAMINER'S VOICE**
> Note how interrelated so many of the macro-economics issues are. Ensure that you understand the links and can analyse them clearly and fully.

Effects of a rise in interest rates

If interest rates rise, the reverse effects will apply:

- Savings will become more attractive because interest rates earned on savings will rise. This may lead to consumers deciding to spend less of their incomes and save more.
- The demand for consumer goods that are bought on credit, such as cars and furniture, will fall because the interest payments will rise.
- People with high levels of borrowing — for example, on mortgages — have less discretionary income to spend, so there will be an overall fall in spending in the economy.
- Investment in capital projects and machinery may fall because the cost of borrowing will rise — spending will be harder to finance.
- The value of the pound will rise, leading to a rise in export prices and a fall in imports prices, with consequent adverse effects on the competitive-ness of domestic and export markets.
- Overall costs will rise, especially in businesses that are highly geared, and this may lead to a fall in profits for these firms.

In general, falling demand resulting from high interest rates will require firms to operate as efficiently as possible in order to remain competitive and maintain their position in the market.

Interest rates and their influence on exchange rates

When interest rates are low, relative to interest rates in other countries, less investment capital is attracted into the UK. This means that the demand for pounds sterling falls, which pushes its price, or the exchange rate, down. As the exchange rate falls, export prices fall and, assuming price-elastic demand, exports become more competitive and export sales tend to rise. At the same time, import prices rise and imports become less competitive. Assuming imports are price elastic, the demand for imports tends to fall as buyers are attracted by cheaper domestic substitutes. The resulting increase in demand for exports and increase in demand for domestic goods may create upward pressure on output and employment in the UK.

Alternatively, when interest rates are high, relative to interest rates in other countries, capital from abroad flows into this country in order to take advantage of the attractive interest rates. These capital flows increase demand for the currency and tend to push up its price, that is, the exchange rate. As exchange rates rise, export prices rise and exports become less competitive. If demand for exports is price elastic, export sales tend to fall as buyers turn to cheaper substitutes. At the same time, import prices fall and imports become more competitive. If demand for imports is price elastic, purchases of imports tend to rise as buyers are attracted by their relatively cheap price. The resulting fall in demand for exports and increase in demand for imports creates downward pressure on output and employment in the UK.

Implications for business strategy of changes in exchange rates

KEY TERM

exchange rate: the price of one country's currency in terms of another.

There are exchange rates for pounds sterling against all other currencies, although the ones most commonly quoted are the rates against the euro, the US dollar, the Japanese yen and also against a 'basket' of currencies (an average of a number of major currencies).

The annual average exchange rates of the pound against the euro and the dollar since 2000 are given in Table 35.2.

Table 35.2 €/£ and $/£ exchange rates

Exchange rate	2000	2001	2002	2003	2004	2005
€s to the £	1.64	1.61	1.59	1.45	1.49	1.39
$s to the £	1.51	1.44	1.50	1.63	1.82	1.79

Source: HM Treasury website. www.hm-treasury.gov.uk/

The exchange rate of the pound against the Japanese yen in 2005 was £1 = 195.73 yen.

Businesses affected by exchange rates

The level of, and changes in, exchange rates affect businesses in different ways depending upon whether they are:

- businesses that export their goods to consumers in other countries
- businesses that sell their goods in the UK, competing against foreign imports
- businesses that purchase imported fuel, raw materials and components to use in the production of their own goods

EXAMINER'S VOICE

Consider the relevance of each of these three perspectives when analysing the effects of changes in exchange rates.

Effects of an increase in exchange rates

An increase in the exchange rate may increase the price at which exports are sold abroad and reduce the price charged for imports in the UK. This in turn will affect revenue, competitiveness and profitability. The extent to which the changing prices of exports and imports will affect export sales and the purchase of imports depends on the price elasticity of demand.

- If the price elasticity of demand for exports is inelastic, an increase in their price, due to a rise in the exchange rate, will have little effect on sales. Although it is likely to increase revenue substantially in terms of the foreign currency, when converted back to pounds sterling there will be a minimal effect.
- If, on the other hand, the price elasticity of demand for exports is elastic, an increase in export prices is likely to lead to a significant fall in sales volume and in sales revenue.
- If the demand for imports is price elastic and their price falls due to a rise in the exchange rate, consumers are likely to purchase more of them, possibly substituting them for domestically produced goods. This will mean a reduction in demand for UK goods. If, on the other hand, the price elasticity of demand for imports is inelastic — often the case where firms purchase imported raw materials and components — the reduction in price will cause their costs to fall, which could lead them to reduce the price of their finished products or simply increase their profit margins.

EXAMINER'S VOICE

Price elasticity of demand is an important concept in this area, so ensure that you understand the concept and the implications of different elasticities for a firm's revenue.

The above analysis assumes that firms prefer to maintain their profit margins at the same level. If this were not the case — for example, if a firm were prepared to absorb the rise in the exchange rate and reduce its profit margins — it could leave prices unchanged.

It is important to note that sales of exports and of imports are influenced not only by exchange rates and therefore prices, but also by a range of other factors, including reputation and quality, after-sales service, the reliability, design and desirability of the product, the overall packaging provided, and payment terms.

Thus, a change in the exchange rate, by affecting the price of imports and exports, will affect the extent to which a firm remains competitive and profitable in both its overseas and domestic markets. The exact impact will be different for exporters and importers and will also depend on whether price is the main factor when buying a good. In order to determine the most appropriate strategy, firms will need to assess the price elasticity of demand for their products and whether price or other factors are the most important influences on sales.

EXAMINER'S VOICE

Remember that many firms have a competitive advantage based on factors other than price. If a firm has a unique selling proposition, this may override any adverse effects due to changes in the exchange rate or prices.

Problems of fluctuating exchange rates

Because UK exchange rates are determined by supply and demand for the pound sterling, the rate can change from day to day. Businesses that are exporting and importing on a regular basis find fluctuations in exchange rates a source of considerable uncertainty, making it difficult for firms to predict the volume of overseas sales or the price they will receive from these transactions. Such uncertainty affects a firm's ability to plan ahead effectively. In some instances, it can be enough to stop firms developing export markets, especially at times when the exchange rate is rising rapidly, since the loss of competitiveness quickly erodes profit margins.

To overcome some of this uncertainty, firms can make use of **futures contracts**, which are a form of insurance that enables them to buy currency in advance at a guaranteed fixed rate. This reduces the level of uncertainty and risk but is expensive and may reduce profits.

On a more practical level, for an exporting firm, unpredictable exchange rate changes create administrative and marketing problems, such as the costs and inconvenience of continually updating pricing and advertising literature for overseas markets.

FACT FILE

In 1997, UK businesses suffered from very high exchange rates that had significant effects on their markets. There was evidence that many small firms dropped out of the export market while many medium and large firms had to reduce their workforces as sales and profits tumbled. For example:

- Royal Doulton, the china company, axed hundreds of jobs. 'The strong pound has created a difficult trading climate...and it is essential that we aim to keep production, sales and stock in balance,' commented the chief executive.
- Denby Pottery cut jobs. 'The pound's strength was a significant factor in the redundancies. It slowed our international growth and also increased competition in the UK,' said its finance director.
- Corus (formerly British Steel) announced the loss of thousands of jobs as a result of the pound's rise.

TOPFOTO

Summary of the effects of exchange rates on different types of business

For a business that exports its goods to consumers in other countries, a rising exchange rate for the pound means that it must understand how higher prices will affect sales. If sales are likely to fall because foreign buyers switch to competing substitutes whose price has remained the same, it may be better to accept lower profit margins. Staying competitive when the exchange rate is rising is very difficult. Most big businesses want a stable, and low, exchange rate if export markets are important to them.

For a business that exports its goods to consumers in other countries, a falling exchange rate for the pound is a bonus. The value of its product in pounds will rise if the foreign currency price stays the same. It has a choice: it could leave prices the same and accept a higher profit margin, or it could cut the price in the hope of higher sales. The best strategy depends on the price elasticity of demand for its product. A high elasticity — greater than 1 — means that a price cut will bring a disproportionately large increase in sales.

For a business that sells its goods in the UK in competition with foreign imports, a rising exchange rate for the pound will put it under added pressure to improve its efficiency. It may consider increasing investment in labour-saving machinery and reducing the workforce. It may introduce new technologies and organisational strategies. It will increase its marketing efforts. The fight will be on just to maintain competitiveness.

For a business that purchases imported fuel, raw material and components to use in the production of its own goods, staying competitive is more complicated, especially if it then exports its final product, since it will need to think through each of these perspectives when deciding on its strategy.

Thus, for any firm, a decision to enter an export market is influenced by the potential exchange rate risk. A firm that is over-reliant upon one foreign currency because a majority of its sales go to one country could find a rise in the value of the pound to be crippling. On the other hand, for many businesses, selling abroad is absolutely essential if they wish to expand their markets.

Firms in European countries that have adopted the euro, and which trade with other countries in the eurozone, encounter no such risk and have a great advantage over outsiders. (The euro is considered in Chapter 38.)

Implications for business strategy of changes in the rate of inflation

KEY TERM

inflation: an increase in the general level of prices of goods and services within an economy, which means that there is a fall in the purchasing power of money.

The annual average rates of inflation since 2000 are given in Table 35.3.

	2000	2001	2002	2003	2004
Inflation (%)	3.0	1.8	1.7	2.9	2.7

Source: HM Treasury website. www.hm-treasury.gov.uk/

Table 35.3 Annual UK rates of inflation

Some of the effects of inflation can be positive for individual firms or consumers, but in general the effects are negative.

Positive effects of inflation

- Inflation tends to encourage borrowing if interest rates are less than the rate of inflation. For highly geared firms and those with heavy borrowing, inflation reduces the real value of the sum they owe, making it easier to repay the loan towards the end of its life. For example, if a firm borrowed a large sum of money 10 years ago, and if inflation has been increasing such that the average price level is double what it was then, it is likely that the firm's income or revenue has also doubled in this period, so the loan will be much easier to repay towards the end of the 10-year period.

- As inflation rises, so too do property prices and the price of stock. Thus balance sheets tend to look healthier as rising property and stock values boost reserves.
- Consumers become more aware of price differences. Those firms that offer lower-priced products and good service may benefit from the fact that premium-priced brands are perceived as too expensive.
- A firm will find it easier to increase the price of its own products when prices are rising generally, meaning that cost increases can be passed on to the consumer more easily.

Negative effects of inflation

- Higher prices may mean lower sales, depending upon the price elasticity of demand for particular products.
- The producers of major brands that tend to sell at premium prices may suffer as inflation makes consumers more aware of the prices of different products. This increased price sensitivity on the part of consumers may lead them to switch brands towards more competitively priced items. As a result, brand owners will have either to cut their price premiums or to increase their advertising expenditure greatly in order to try to regain customer interest and loyalty.
- Just as consumers become more aware of prices, so workers become far more concerned about the level of their real wages because, unless they obtain a pay rise at least as high as the rate of inflation, their real income will fall. Therefore, industrial action often increases in inflationary periods, as workers and trade unions negotiate for pay increases. As a consequence, industrial relations tend to deteriorate.
- Suppliers may demand higher prices for the goods and services they supply, adding further to a firm's costs and putting more pressure on the firm to increase its own prices.
- If inflation in the UK is relatively high compared with that in other countries, the international competitiveness of UK firms will be reduced.
- As the future is uncertain, forecasts of sales revenue and profits will become very difficult and planning will be less reliable. As forecasting is subject to greater uncertainty, firms will begin to want higher forecast average rates of return on any investments that they undertake. This uncertainty is partly the result of price changes brought about by the inflationary process and partly the result of potential changes to the government's economic policy introduced to combat increasing inflation.
- If the Monetary Policy Committee (MPC) of the Bank of England (the institution that sets interest rates) takes action to reduce inflation by increasing interest rates, this is likely to reduce demand and sales, which will have an adverse effect on business.

- When prices are changing quickly, businesses have more difficulty in keeping track of competitors' pricing strategies.
- Cash flow is squeezed as the costs of new materials and equipment rise.

The effects of a low rate of inflation

A low level of inflation, as experienced in the UK over the last few years (see Table 35.3), can have a number of effects on business strategy:

- Interest rates are likely to be low if the rate of inflation is low, which will benefit most businesses.
- A low rate of inflation relative to other countries is likely to mean that firms become more competitive in their export markets and in their domestic markets against imports.
- In general, low levels of inflation create more certainty in the economy, which means that business is able to plan ahead, because prices (of goods for sale and of supplies) can be predicted more easily.
- Marketing and administrative costs will be lower, as there will be fewer price adjustments to, for example, price lists and advertising information.
- The fact that there is more certainty about short-term pricing decisions means that there should be more time available for long-term strategic decision making.
- Efficient firms survive and inefficient firms disappear. Continually rising prices mean that poorly performing firms can record increasing sales and profits in nominal terms. However, low inflation means that such firms cannot disguise poor sales performance and cannot easily raise prices to cover their own inefficiency.

Implications for business strategy of changes in the level of unemployment

Both high and low levels of unemployment can affect a firm's business strategy.

Implications of high levels of unemployment

As more people are out of work and as pressure on wage levels eases, incomes will fall. In general, this leads to lower sales. This not only reduces revenue and profits but may, in the extreme, lead to redundancies as firms decide to reduce production levels in line with the lower sales.

> **EXAMINER'S VOICE**
> Ensure that your knowledge of income elasticity of demand and of normal and inferior goods is secure, and that you can apply your knowledge in this context.

This analysis applies most significantly to firms that produce income-elastic products: that is, luxury products. Firms that produce **normal goods** will experience a fall in sales that is similar to the fall in incomes in the economy. Firms that produce income-inelastic products, such as food, will find that, despite falling consumer incomes, demand for their products remains more or less the same. Those producing **inferior goods** may find that low incomes actually lead to a *higher* demand for their products.

Workers have less bargaining power as alternative jobs are harder to find, which is likely to mean less pressure to increase wage levels. This is reinforced by the fact that, as jobs are scarce, people may be more willing to work for lower wages in order to get a job. In turn, this will lead to lower costs and possibly reduced prices, enabling the firm to cope better with the decline in demand.

As demand falls, cost-saving strategies may be introduced. Some of these may lead to increased efficiency, but others may be short-sighted, bringing short-term benefits but creating greater problems in the longer term. For example, a firm may decide to reduce its commitment to the training and development of its workforce in order to make cost savings, but in the longer term it may find that this strategy leads to a lack of essential skills and expertise. Similarly, a firm may decide that significant cost savings can be made by delayering the organisation, but may find that as this entails much wider spans of control, it creates longer-term difficulties in relation to management and coordination.

EXAMINER'S VOICE

'On the other hand' is a useful phrase to remember when analysing business issues. Most situations have a whole range of different consequences and businesses can choose from a range of different strategies to deal with them. For example, the above analysis suggests that, as a result of unemployment and the need to reduce costs, a firm might cut training and suffer long-term adverse effects. An alternative analysis might suggest that, because of high levels of unemployment, more skilled and experienced people are available for work. Thus, businesses might benefit from reduced training needs, which in turn reduces costs and the short-term fall in productivity that is inevitable while new employees are being trained.

The reduction in demand is likely to lead to cutbacks or delays in investment projects. This, in turn, may lead to a further decline in employment both in the firms that are reducing investment spending and in other sectors of industry that produce capital goods, for example producers of heavy machinery and construction firms.

The reduction in demand and the need to make cost savings by cutting back on the workforce and investment may cause businesses to consider **rationalisation** as a strategy. Essentially, this means reorganising the business in order to increase its efficiency. The term is used when major savings are required, involving cutbacks in fixed overhead costs that enable the firm to reduce its breakeven point. Rationalisation can be achieved in a number of different ways. For example, it could involve delayering, that is, removing a layer of management. In a multi-site business, rationalisation could involve closing a factory or the administrative or finance departments in each site and creating a single, centralised department. Alternatively, it could involve outsourcing the work, which will inevitably lead to redundancies.

Implications of low levels of unemployment

Unemployment levels since 2000 have been low. In June 2001, unemployment in the UK went below 1 million for the first time since 1975. Annual average rates of unemployment since 2000 are given in Table 35.4.

	2000	2001	2002	2003	2004
Unemployment (claimants) (%)	4.0	3.0	3.0	3.0	2.8

Source: HM Treasury website. www.hm-treasury.gov.uk/

Table 35.4 Annual UK rates of unemployment

Low levels of unemployment affect business strategy in two important ways:

- More people in employment mean that consumers as a whole have more income, and therefore that more spending will take place. This will significantly increase the sales of income-elastic (luxury) goods.
- As more people become employed, the labour market is said to 'tighten': that is, fewer people are looking for work. This makes it more difficult for firms to recruit suitably skilled or qualified individuals. In such a situation, the existing workforce and potential applicants have more bargaining power and firms may be forced to increase wages for existing workers and to offer substantially higher wages in order to attract new workers.

EXAMINER'S VOICE

Remember 'on the other hand'. Low unemployment and the resulting higher levels of consumer income and spending will lead to a fall in demand for inferior goods and will have a relatively minor effect on the demand for income-inelastic goods.

Implications for business strategy of the business cycle

KEY TERM

business (or **trade**) **cycle:** the regular pattern of ups and downs in demand and output, or of gross domestic product (GDP) growth over time. It is characterised by four main phases: boom, recession (or downturn), slump and recovery (or upturn).

EXAMINER'S VOICE

Remember that normal or luxury goods are those for which demand increases as incomes rise and vice versa — for example, fillet steak and other high-quality meat products. Inferior goods are those for which demand falls as incomes rise and vice versa — for example, Spam and other inferior meat products.

Some firms are more vulnerable to changes in the business cycle and GDP than others. Indeed, some are often known as **cyclical businesses** because demand for their products fluctuates very closely in line with the various phases of the business cycle.

The extent to which a business is affected by the business cycle depends on the income elasticity of demand for the firm's products. For example, the construction industry and firms producing machine tools and heavy capital equipment are all very sensitive to changes in GDP, the demand for their products being highly income elastic. In a boom period, when incomes are high and rising, demand for consumer goods is high and this in turn generates a high demand for capital goods. Similarly, high incomes create more demand for house building. On the other hand, the demand for products that are relatively income inelastic, such as flour, soap and paper, is unlikely to be much affected by the business cycle.

Implications for business of a boom

KEY TERM

boom: a period characterised by high levels of consumer demand, business confidence, profits and investment, in line with rising costs, increasing prices and full capacity.

A period of boom is likely to have the following effects on a firm:

- Consumer demand is likely to be greater than supply, creating excess demand, which is likely to lead to increases in the prices of goods.
- The shortage of resources relative to demand means that costs are likely to rise. For example, wages may have to increase in order to attract and/or keep skilled workers, which may in turn lead firms to increase their prices.
- Increased demand may result in firms utilising their production capacity to the full. Such high capacity utilisation may lead firms to consider expansion plans in order to increase output and meet demand.
- Increased demand and high prices may result in an overall increase in profits, allowing for high retained profits and dividends.

FACT FILE

Firms producing capital goods such as machinery and plant tend to suffer most in a recession because other firms cut back on their orders dramatically if they expect to sell fewer items. However, they benefit most in a boom because businesses must buy new equipment etc. in order to keep pace with new demand. In effect, these industries are more likely to experience dramatic changes than businesses producing consumer goods.

Implications for business of a recession (or downturn)

KEY TERM

recession (or **downturn**): a period characterised by falling levels of consumer demand, output, profit and business confidence, with little investment, spare capacity and rising levels of unemployment.

EXAMINER'S VOICE

Remember, when analysing the impact of a particular phase of the business cycle on a firm, to consider the organisation and its products. If a firm is producing and selling inferior goods, for example, it may find that it benefits during a recession as incomes fall.

A recession is likely to have several effects on business:

- Falling demand may result in excess stock and a need to reduce prices in order to sell.
- Falling demand and the need to reduce output may lead to low profits or even losses being made and workers being made redundant. On the other hand, firms producing inferior goods may benefit, as consumers switch from luxury items to low-priced alternatives.
- Liquidations or business closures, as a result of falling demand and losses, may result in fewer suppliers of certain products and also fewer customers for other products.
- As business struggles with falling demand and individuals feel the effects of lower incomes, firms are likely to experience an increase in bad debts. To address this issue, firms may need to introduce tighter credit control procedures, but this may in time lead to less trade.
- A strong balance sheet, sufficient liquidity and low gearing are important requirements for survival during a recession. High unemployment and therefore falling incomes will lead to a drop in demand for some goods and a switch in demand to other (e.g. inferior) goods. This may lead firms

TOPFOTO

EXAMINER'S VOICE

Notice how the analysis of the effects of a recession tends to be circular. For example, falling demand leads to reductions in output, which results in redundancies and more unemployment, which leads to falling income, which leads to falling demand...

facing falling demand to search for new markets. Indeed, one way to survive a recession for a producer of consumer goods is to diversify the product range. In this way the business is not too dependent for its profits on those products that are likely to experience wide variations in demand over the course of the business cycle.

- Low investment, as a result of falling consumer demand, may lead to a serious decline in the output of firms that produce capital goods.
- In order to survive during a recession, businesses need to operate as efficiently as possible. As a result, those that do survive may emerge stronger and better able to compete during the subsequent recovery stage.

FACT FILE

Table 35.5 shows the number of new businesses setting up and those failing or closing down during 2001 and 2002. The net change shows the difference. During 2001, the number of business start-ups was slightly more than the number of business failures, while in 2002 slightly more businesses closed down.

***Table 35.5** Business registrations and deregistrations, 2001–02*

2001			2002		
Registrations	Deregistrations	Net change	Registrations	Deregistrations	Net change
174.6	167.2	7.4	175.8	176.0	-0.2

Source: www.statistics.gov.uk

The table shows the general stability of the UK economy during the time period shown.

Implications for business of a slump

KEY TERM

slump: a period characterised by very low levels of consumer demand, investment and business confidence, with an increasing number of businesses failing and high unemployment.

A slump is likely to have the following effects on business:

- The lack of demand during a slump means that firms are content to charge low prices, concentrating on sales volume rather than sales revenue. It is possible that deflation (falling prices) may occur across the whole economy.
- The low level of demand means that factories are likely to close, leading to large-scale redundancies and unemployment.

Implications for business of a recovery (or upturn)

KEY TERM

recovery (or **upturn**): a period characterised by slowly rising levels of consumer demand and investment, patchy but increasing business confidence and falling levels of unemployment.

A period of recovery is likely to have the following effects:

- Increasing demand for consumer goods may lead to an increase in profits. These favourable conditions may encourage new businesses to be set up.

- The pace of recovery will vary between firms. Some will benefit from the increasingly favourable conditions almost immediately; others will need to await the completion of capital investment before they begin to benefit.
- Business confidence will grow, which may encourage more firms to consider borrowing in order to invest in fixed assets.
- To meet the increasing demand, existing spare production capacity will be used. However, one of the characteristics of a recovery is that shortages, which are almost inevitable as recovery kicks in, may lead to increased costs and potential bottlenecks.

Business confidence

Business confidence can be a key influence on the business cycle. Firms' decisions regarding their labour force needs, investment plans and stock levels are likely to be significantly influenced by their assumptions about potential success and hence by their confidence. Many commentators believe that a high level of business confidence can become a self-fulfilling prophecy — an optimistic outlook leads to higher levels of investment spending and stock building, which in turn causes the economy to grow. For this reason, governments often try to describe the economy in positive terms so that confidence will increase.

Implications for business strategy of changes in the labour market

KEY TERM

labour market: the demand for labour (that is, employers requiring employees) and the supply of labour (those individuals offering themselves for work), which together determine the wage or salary rates paid.

Just as there is a market for every product and service, so there is a market for labour. For every occupation, there is a different labour market and the demand for and supply of people with particular skills determines the wage or salary rates paid in that occupation. Labour markets vary geographically too because the demand for and supply of labour with particular skills differs between areas.

Skills surpluses and shortages

KEY TERM

skills surplus: an excess supply of people with particular skills.

A skills *surplus* usually occurs during a recession when unemployment begins to rise, but may also occur if an industry has declined in importance or is overtaken by new technology, and thus there is less demand for the skills that it uses. For example, the decline of the mining industry in the 1980s meant that there were few jobs available for the large number of skilled miners. Similarly, the introduction of computerised technology in the printing industry led to an oversupply of traditionally skilled printers.

CHAPTER 35 Implications for business strategy of macroeconomic variables

KEY TERM

- **skills shortage:** an excess demand for people with particular skills.

A skills *shortage* might develop because of the rapid growth of an industry, so that demand for labour exceeds supply. This has occurred in the IT industry.

Consequences for business of a skills surplus

- In terms of recruitment and selection of staff, a firm will have more choice. The process might be easier because there are more appropriately skilled employees available.
- Pressure to increase wages will be less because of the surplus of labour that is available. In addition, lower wages can be offered to new employees because of the excess supply of labour.
- Trade union power is likely to be weaker because employers are in a stronger bargaining and negotiation position as a result of the excess supply of suitably skilled labour.
- A firm's reaction to a skills surplus among its own employees may be varied. It may need to make some workers redundant, or it could offer them retraining opportunities if it has skills gaps in other areas of its business. Because it is now in a better bargaining position, it may be able to do this at more favourable wage rates.

Consequences for business of a skills shortage

In general, the impact of a skills shortage on a firm depends on whether the firm needs those particular skills and the seriousness of the shortage.

- With insufficient skilled workers, firms may find it difficult to produce enough output to meet customers' orders.
- Existing skilled employees are in a strong bargaining position because of the shortage of people with appropriate skills, and may thus be able to negotiate increased pay awards. Similarly, firms may have to offer attractive rates of pay in order to attract people with appropriate skills.
- As a result of the better bargaining position of employees, firms are likely to experience increasing labour costs. This in turn might reduce their profit margins or cause them to increase their prices and thus affect their competitiveness.

WHAT DO YOU THINK?

The Learning and Skills Council found that 22% of employers surveyed at the beginning of 2004 were finding skills gaps. Employers were quite literally not able to find suitably competent employees for all of the vacancies on offer. At the same time, earnings in the UK were increasing at an annual rate of 4.4% — the highest for some years. This presents firms with a dilemma — do they absorb the higher wage costs and squeeze their own profit margins, or do they pass these higher costs on to consumers in the form of higher prices?

A firm may try to overcome a skills shortage in several ways — for example:

- offering training to new, relatively unskilled employees or providing retraining opportunities to existing employees whose current skills are declining in value

- recruiting employees from other countries. For example, the National Health Service attempts to overcome the shortage of nurses by recruiting qualified staff from the Philippines, while BUPA Care Homes has recruited carers from Poland, the Czech Republic and Lithuania. First Group, the UK's largest bus operator, has recruited drivers from Poland
- poaching workers from other firms by offering them high rates of pay and fringe benefits
- finding new ways of producing its products or providing its services that are less labour intensive and therefore require a smaller proportion of employees relative to capital equipment. This could involve automating production processes or outsourcing production and other activities such as payroll functions and administration

FACT FILE

It is expected that by mid-2005 there will be 25 **Sector Skills Councils**, covering 85% of the UK workforce. Sector Skills Councils are at the heart of the nationwide drive to improve the UK's productivity. These independent, employer-led bodies will find out what employers need now and will need in the future, assess what resources are already out there, and then create comprehensive deals with supply-side partners to fill skills gaps and shortages. They will draw up Sector Skills Agreements between the demand side (employers) and the supply side (qualification developers, schools, colleges, training providers, universities and bodies that fund them), ensuring that the required numbers of people are skilled in the right ways to meet the needs of UK businesses and public services.

At any point in time there are likely to be either skills surpluses or skills shortages in some labour markets. For example, at present there are shortages in supplies of maths teachers and plumbers. Insufficient maths graduates are deciding to train as teachers, presumably because the pay and conditions are more attractive in other professions. The employer (principally the government) is trying to remedy this by providing financial incentives for those willing to train as maths teachers and for those taking up posts in the profession. Similarly, qualified plumbers are in short supply and are able to charge high prices for their services. As a consequence of this, plumbing has become a highly paid occupation and training courses are inundated with applicants wishing to train.

EXAMINER'S VOICE

Effective workforce planning should assist firms in anticipating future skills shortages or surpluses. Workforce planning was considered in Chapter 26. This link illustrates the fact that business studies is a highly integrative subject. Ensure that you are able to link and integrate your knowledge of different areas of business studies effectively. This topic has strong links with other areas. For example, a firm's strategies in dealing with skills shortages and surpluses may have an impact on methods of production (labour or capital intensive), on recruitment and selection processes and on labour turnover. All of these topics were covered in previous chapters of this book and in the AS textbook.

PRACTICE EXERCISE

Total: 50 marks (45 minutes)

1 Briefly explain two implications for business strategy of a fall in interest rates. *(4 marks)*

2 Compare the impact of an increase in the exchange rate between the pound and the dollar for a company that exports its goods to the USA, a company that purchases inputs from the USA and a company that sells it goods in the UK in competition with imports from the USA. *(9 marks)*

3 Explain two ways in which fluctuations in exchange rates affect business strategy adversely. *(6 marks)*

4 Explain one way in which a low rate of inflation might benefit business. *(3 marks)*

5 Explain two ways in which a low level of unemployment might benefit business. *(6 marks)*

6 Examine the possible implications of a recession for business strategy. *(6 marks)*

7 How might a skills surplus occur? *(4 marks)*

8 Explain the possible impact of a skills shortage on business strategy. *(4 marks)*

9 How might a business overcome a skills shortage? *(4 marks)*

10 Explain how the sales of a product with high income elasticity of demand would be affected by a recession. *(4 marks)*

CASE STUDY Europe's star will rise in the east

Increases in the minimum wage and sterling's rise against the dollar and the euro have made the UK one of the most expensive places in the world for multinational companies to employ people.

The UK now ranks fourth in pay, and fifth overall, with pay and benefits averaging £31,700 a year, in a league of national employment costs produced by Mercer Human Resource Consulting, a specialist in employee benefits (see Figure 35.1). The dollar's weakness, by contrast, has made it cheaper to hire staff in the USA than in any northern European country. But total pay and benefits in the 10 new members of the European Union that were formerly communist countries are typically only a quarter of those elsewhere in Europe.

Mark Sullivan, worldwide partner at Mercer, said: 'There are concerns about whether US companies will continue to invest in the EU. Organisations that do invest are likely to favour eastern European countries.'

Only Belgium, Sweden, Germany and Luxembourg have higher total employment costs than the UK,

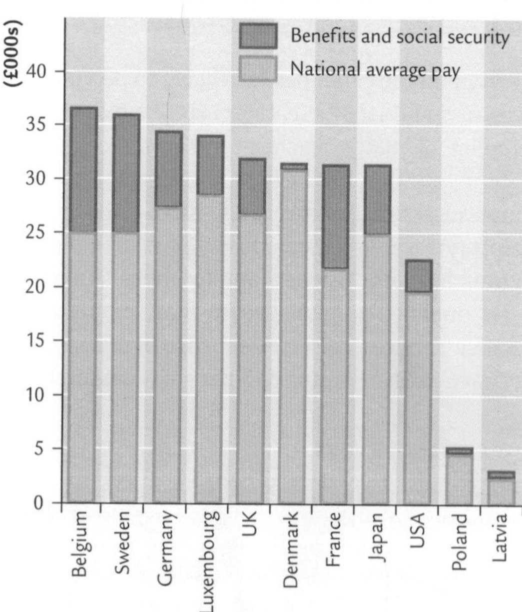

***Figure 35.1** Annual employment costs in selected countries, 2005*

mainly because employers there have to pay higher social security taxes. In the UK and Ireland, however, the cost to employers of voluntary benefits, mostly pensions, is higher than anywhere else. The UK heads a second division in which France, Denmark and Japan have similar employment costs of between £31,000 and £32,000 a year at today's exchange rates.

Worries over the UK's competitiveness will be fuelled by higher pay increases this year, reflecting an acceleration in the cost of living index driven by housing costs. UK pay settlements have averaged 3.3% on deals recorded by Incomes Data Services, the employment research firm. Most higher settlements, which used to be in the public sector, are now in manufacturing and construction (see Table 35.6).

Recent key wage settlements	
AAH Pharmaceuticals	3.7%
Armed Forces	3.0%
BAA	4.0%
British Airways	3.2%
Ford Motor Company	3.0%
Honda UK	3.0%
John Lewis Partnership	3.95%
Network Rail	3.95%

Source: Incomes Data Services.

***Table 35.6** The UK's inflation-busting pay deals*

Source: adapted from an article by Graham SearJeant in *The Times*, 11 April 2005.

Questions

Total: 30 marks (35 minutes)

1 Evaluate the possible impact on the business strategy of UK firms trading in the USA, Europe and the UK of 'sterling's rise against the dollar and the euro' (lines 1–2). *(14 marks)*

2 Discuss the possible strategies that UK firms might adopt if faced with increased pay for employees and a skills shortage. *(16 marks)*

CHAPTER 36

International competitiveness

This chapter considers the main determinants of international competitiveness. It examines the importance of integrating internal issues related to production, people and marketing in order to improve a company's ability to compete internationally, as well as analysing the external factors that influence competitiveness. It also describes the principal methods of controlling imports into the country.

What is international competitiveness?

KEY TERM

international competitiveness: the ability of firms to sell their products successfully both abroad in export markets and at home in competition against imports.

International competitiveness may be based on price competition and/or non-price competition. In general, businesses seek to improve their competitiveness in order to secure a larger market. The more competitive a firm is in relation to its international rivals, the larger will be its potential global market share.

Firms seek to compete in international markets for a variety of reasons. These include:

- avoiding the risks of operating in a single market
- taking advantage of economies of scale and increasing profits
- a desire to increase market share
- a need to compete against international firms in order to safeguard domestic markets

In addition, reductions in trading barriers in the European Union and internationally, and the opening up of extensive markets in eastern Europe and China, have increased competition in world markets and therefore have increased the need for UK firms to be internationally competitive.

Internal factors that influence international competitiveness

Being internationally competitive involves considering factors that are internal to the firm, such as production, human resource management and marketing issues. A firm needs to consider how to improve its efficiency and productivity in order to reduce unit costs and increase the quality of its products. This could mean introducing more capital-intensive means of production and new technology, and generally ensuring that the production process is as efficient as possible in order to increase the rate of productivity. The higher the rate of productivity, the lower unit costs are likely to be and therefore the lower the price that can be charged for the product.

Increasing efficiency could also mean improving the skills of the workforce by training and development, and more generally ensuring that the organisation of human resources is effective and that HRM strategies are linked closely to the needs of the firm.

International competitiveness also involves increasing marketing efforts, ensuring that strategies are appropriate to each of the overseas markets in which the firm intends to operate. To be successful internationally requires that a firm competes with the best companies in the world. Benchmarking against such companies should allow a firm to improve and enhance its procedures and strategies, and therefore its performance.

FACT FILE

On 10 March 2005, the Mars Group, whose products range from chocolate bars to pet foods, announced it was shedding 700 jobs at plants in the UK, as part of a restructuring of its western European operations, aimed at cutting costs and overcapacity. Around 370 jobs would also be lost at plants in France and Germany as part of the same programme. Pierre Laubies, president of the parent company Masterfoods Europe, said: 'The proposals are all about growth and competitiveness. We need to be leaner and more focused.'

Source: adapted from an article in *The Times*, 11 March 2005.

External factors that influence international competitiveness

A firm must take account of the external business environment. Factors to consider include the inflation rate in the UK compared with the rate in the other countries with which it intends to trade, phases of the business cycle in the UK and other countries, the degree of trade protection in the form of import controls, and the levels of exchange rates.

Low inflation in the UK benefits firms that sell their goods in export markets and at home because, in relative terms, their goods are more price competitive than those in other countries and imported goods. A weak pound adds to the benefits of low inflation by reducing further the price of exported goods and increasing the price of imported goods. However, a strong pound might cancel out the benefits of low inflation by increasing the price of exports and reducing the price of imports.

This analysis is further complicated for firms that export their finished goods abroad and use imported raw materials and components in the production of these items. In such a situation, it is important to consider all of the different possible outcomes that might affect a firm.

EXAMINER'S VOICE

Use the knowledge you have already gained about exchange rates and apply it in this context. You should recall that whether export prices are increased following a rise in the exchange rate of the pound depends on the price elasticity of demand for the product and on whether firms decide to accept a lower profit margin. This, in turn, depends upon the aims and financial state of the business.

BMW GROUP PRESS CLUB

EXAMINER'S VOICE

It is important to recognise that businesses compete on a number of fronts. Although price competitiveness may be extremely important for some products, for others, non-price competition may be more important.

In general, the influences on a firm's international competitiveness include the exchange rate, unit costs, the price and quality of the product, prompt delivery and after-sales service. The level of the foreign exchange rate is often seen as the crucial factor in the success of companies competing internationally, but successful exporting countries and companies appear to perform well despite high and rising exchange rates, suggesting that the price of goods is not necessarily the main determinant of competitiveness. Germany and Japan, for instance, have thrived through well-designed, high-quality products such as BMWs and Sony televisions, for which consumers are willing to pay a price premium.

Import controls

Import controls are designed to limit the number of overseas goods entering the domestic market. They take a number of different forms.

Tariffs

Tariffs are taxes imposed on imported goods. In general, the imposition of tariffs leads to an increase in the price of the imported good and, depending on price elasticity of demand, is likely to lead to a reduction in demand, making cheaper domestic goods more attractive to consumers. The importer may seek to keep prices down by cutting profit margins, by becoming more efficient or, in extreme cases, by setting up a production plant inside the country itself. Import tariffs are banned between members of the European Union (EU), but a common external tariff is imposed on imports from non-EU countries.

Two types of tariff can be levied:

- an **ad valorem tax**, which is a percentage added to the price of the imported good, such as 10% added to the price of all imported goods, regardless of whether they are priced at £10 or £1,000

- a **specific duty** added to the price of the imported good, such as £2 per item added to the price of all imported goods, regardless of whether the good is valued at £10 or £1,000

Quotas

Quotas are a form of import protection that limits the sales of foreign goods to a specified **quantity** (e.g. 1 million pairs of shoes), **value** (e.g. £50 million worth of products) or market share (e.g. no more than 10% of the total market for the good).

Non-tariff barriers

Non-tariff barriers are more subtle controls that are imposed by governments because they wish to restrict imports without being seen to do so, perhaps because it would be contrary to international regulation under the World Trade Organization. Such barriers may take several forms, including:

- constantly changing technical regulations, which makes compliance difficult for importers
- forcing importers to use specified points of entry where documentation is dealt with only slowly
- introducing regulations that favour domestic production — for example, packaging and labels that conform to local language requirements

FACT FILE

The **World Trade Organization** (WTO) is a group of over 100 countries that are committed to the encouragement of free and fair international trade through the elimination of barriers.

Embargos

An embargo is an order forbidding trade with a particular country, perhaps imposed by the United Nations against a country that has broken international laws or conventions.

PRACTICE EXERCISE

Total: 35 marks (30minutes)

1 Explain the term 'international competitiveness'. *(3 marks)*

2 Identify two reasons why a firm might wish to compete in international markets. *(2 marks)*

3 Explain two *internal* factors that might influence the international competitiveness of firms. *(6 marks)*

4 Explain two *external* factors that might influence the international competitiveness of firms. *(6 marks)*

5 Distinguish between ad valorem and specific duty tariffs. *(4 marks)*

6 What is a quota in relation to import controls? *(2 marks)*

7 Give two examples of non-tariff barriers, excluding quotas. *(2 marks)*

8 State the purpose of the World Trade Organization. *(2 marks)*

9 How might a fall in the value of the exchange rate influence a country's international competitiveness? *(4 marks)*

10 How is knowledge of price elasticity of demand useful to your answer to question 9? *(4 marks)*

CASE STUDY Clarks left with a sole survivor after closure

Another chapter in UK manufacturing ended yesterday as C. and J. Clark, the shoemaker, closed its last big UK plant. About 70 jobs were lost at the factory near Ilminster in Somerset, which was unable to compete with cheap manufacturers in Asia.

Clarks, which once had more than 20 UK factories, now only has a small site in Cumbria. The factory, near Barrow-in-Furness, makes K Shoes and employs 37 people. Clarks has cut tens of thousands of manufacturing jobs since the early 1980s, and its shoes are now made in China, India, Vietnam, Romania and Brazil.

The company employs about 1,000 people at its headquarters in Street, near Glastonbury. Shoemaking ended there in 1992 and most of the head office jobs are in distribution, IT, accounts and marketing. Former factory buildings were sold and turned into Clarks Village, a collection of shops and restaurants.

In its prime, Clarks was one of the UK's biggest manufacturers, exporting shoes throughout the Commonwealth. The company employed tens of thousands of people in factories across the West Country, and had major sites at Plymouth, Bath, Ilminster and Shepton Mallet.

Competition from abroad took its toll and the first closures occurred in the early 1980s. In 1989, factories closed in Bath and Bridgwater, with the loss of 600 jobs, and in 1995, 360 jobs were lost when a factory in Radstock closed. The factory in Shepton Mallet was sold to R. Griggs, which makes Dr Martens shoes.

Despite the closures, Clarks remained a big employer. As recently as 1999, the company had six UK factories employing 1,000 people. But the shift to cheap overseas producers was inevitable. The closure of a factory in Barnstaple in April last year left only the Ilminster site.

***Table 36.1** Clarks: facts and figures 2003/04*

Pairs of Clarks shoes made each year	39 million
Number of Clarks staff worldwide	13,900
Clarks sales in 2003/04	£943m
Number of UK shops that stock Clarks	1,900

"Before we defeated The Desert Fox
we defeated the desert."
Clarks
THE ORIGINAL
DESERT BOOT

THE ADVERTISING ARCHIVES

Clarks traces its history to 1825 when Quaker brothers, Cyrus and James Clark, began making shoes in Street. By the 1850s, Clarks employed a third of the population of Street. Products such as the Desert Boot and Clarks Wallabee heralded the company's golden years in the 1960s and 1970s. Profits slumped in the face of competition from cheap imports, leaving Clarks vulnerable to takeover. A feud among family members, over whether Clarks should be sold, split the company in 1993.

After deciding to stay private, Clarks aggressively cut costs under Tim Parker, the chief executive from 1996 to 2002. Mr Parker accelerated the factory closures and cut up to 500 head-office jobs in Street. After bringing costs under control, Clarks set about giving itself a younger, 'trendier' image. It embarked on a multimillion-pound advertising campaign with the slogan: 'Act your shoe size, not your age'. The aim was to reduce the age of the typical Clarks buyer from the late 50s to between 35 and 45. For years, Clarks was best known for children's shoes, but the image lost favour and the brand became associated with dull, chunky designs.

Marketing aside, the company is investing some £50 million in a new distribution centre in Street and is introducing a new design for its UK shops. The Oxford Circus store will be the first in London to be revamped with the Global Shop design.

Source: adapted from an article in *The Times*, 2 April 2005.

Questions

Total: 24 marks (30 minutes)

1 Evaluate the possible reasons for Clarks's loss of international competitiveness. *(12 marks)*

2 To what extent are the new, revamped stores likely to be successful? *(12 marks)*

CHAPTER 37

Economic growth

This chapter explains how economic growth is measured and the main indicators used. It considers what determines the level of economic growth and explores the effects of this growth on business and the environment. It highlights the fact that levels of activity or economic growth vary not only between countries but also between regions within a country.

Economic growth and gross domestic product

KEY TERMS

economic growth: an increase in the level of economic activity or real gross domestic product (GDP).

gross domestic product (GDP): the total value of a country's output over the course of a year.

Essentially, economic growth is the extent to which the volume of goods and services being produced increases over time.

If the value of a country's GDP increases by 6% in a year, but the inflation rate is 2%, the increase in actual output of goods and services is approximately 4%. This is the increase in real GDP. Thus, real GDP is a better measure of whether the country is getting wealthier than GDP measured in money. Figures for economic growth are thus based on the percentage increase in *real* GDP.

The growth in real GDP per capita (that is, per head of population) is the main measure of economic growth and measures the growth in average income per person adjusted for inflation.

Measuring GDP

The value of a country's economic activity (GDP) can be measured in three ways:

- The **income method** involves totalling all the income earned in an economy — rent, wages and salaries, interest and profit.
- The **output method** involves totalling the value of all goods (whether these are consumer or capital goods) and services produced in an economy.
- The **expenditure method** involves totalling all spending by consumers, businesses and government plus the balance of export less import spending.

DID YOU KNOW?

Each method gives the same result because it is just a different way of looking at the value of economic activity. For example, from a simplified point of view, if everything that is produced is sold, the total value of output will be the same as the total value of expenditure, and the total expenditure becomes the income of all the factors of production used to create the goods.

Determinants of economic growth

According to Gordon Brown, chancellor of the exchequer, the UK has been enjoying an unprecedented period of continuous economic growth: 'I can now report that Britain is enjoying its longest period of sustained economic growth for more than 200 years; the longest period of sustained growth since the beginning of the industrial revolution' (Budget speech, 17 March 2004). Indeed, the last period of economic contraction, or recession, occurred as far back as 1992.

UK annual economic growth figures since 2000 are provided in Table 37.1.

	2000	2001	2002	2003	2004
Economic growth (% rise)	3.9	2.3	1.8	2.2	2.7

Source: HM Treasury website. www.hm-treasury.gov.uk

***Table 37.1* UK economic growth, 2000–04**

The level of economic growth in an economy is influenced by a number of factors. These include:

- **the exploitation of valuable natural resources.** For example, the extraction and sale of oil in the Middle East and in the North Sea has significantly increased economic growth in these areas.
- **a well educated and highly skilled labour force.** This will improve productivity and generate economic growth.
- **increasing investment and new technology.** This will enable firms to keep pace with other countries and so create economic growth.
- **government policy.** Governments can adopt policies aimed at encouraging economic growth (see Chapter 39).

TOPFOTO

Effects of economic growth on business

The effects of economic growth on business depend on whether the rate of economic growth is rapid, slowing down or actually decreasing. This reflects the various phases of the business cycle. For more detail on this, refer back to the section of Chapter 35 on the implications of the business cycle (pp. 354–57).

Impact on sales

With higher levels of real GDP, real incomes in the economy are higher. This means that consumers' incomes, after adjusting for the effects of inflation, are higher and they can buy more goods and services, which in turn is likely to

EXAMINER'S VOICE

Notice how often elasticity — whether price elasticity of demand or income elasticity of demand — is relevant to the analysis of data on sales.

TOPFOTO

lead to higher retail sales. Higher growth rates are usually recorded for non-food items than for food items. This is probably because many food items are income inelastic and therefore, despite higher consumer incomes, sales in these areas are less positively affected. In contrast, firms producing or selling income-elastic goods and services, such as DVD players, mobile phones and wide-screen televisions, are likely to see sales improve more significantly as real GDP increases. From a strategic point of view, this illustrates the need for businesses to consider the possibility of having some income-elastic products or services in their portfolio.

Stronger periods of economic growth are not necessarily beneficial to all firms. With higher incomes, consumers tend to trade up to higher-priced, branded products, transferring spending away from the low-priced or 'value' items. Theoretically, therefore, retailers such as Next and Boots should gain more significantly during periods of economic growth than 'value' retailers, such as Matalan and Poundstretcher.

Impact on corporate profits

Higher incomes lead to greater demand for goods and services, which provides opportunities for firms to generate higher profits. Not only are sales likely to increase, but in many cases higher demand should provide more opportunities to raise prices as well, helping to boost profit margins. There appears to be a correlation between the UK's improvement in economic growth rates (Table 37.1) and company profitability, as indicated in Table 37.2. With higher profits, share prices are likely to increase and investor confidence should improve, which in turn means that firms should find it easier to raise further funds.

Year	Total	Manufacturing	Services
2002	12.1	6.6	15.4
2003	12.8	7.0	15.6
2004	13.4	6.9	15.8

Source: www.statistics.gov.uk

Table 37.2
Net rate of return by private, non-financial corporations, 2002–04 (%)

Table 37.2 illustrates a clear distinction between the profitability of different sectors of the economy. Despite overall UK corporate profitability improving, the weaknesses in the manufacturing sector are clearly apparent. Manufacturing is suffering the effects of intense international competitive pressure, most notably from lower-wage, industrialising economies, such as China. In recent years, these economies have flooded world markets with low-cost manufactured goods in many low- to middle-technology areas. Domestic firms in the UK, with higher cost structures, have inevitably struggled to compete.

> **DID YOU KNOW?**
> Retained profit is very important as a means of financing investment, providing between 60% and 70% of the funding used for business investment.

Impact on investment

Higher demand for goods and services means that firms are more likely to invest in expanding their operations — for example, seeking larger premises or extensions to existing facilities, or planning to install extra machinery and equipment. Supporting this trend will be the appreciating stock market, which will make it easier for firms to raise funds, and higher profitability, which will mean more retained profits available for reinvestment.

Impact on employment

Businesses seeking to expand production may initially choose to make their existing labour force work harder, by offering overtime to employees, and only recruit more workers once they are convinced that the increase in demand for their products or services is sustainable.

The connection between increasing employment levels and economic growth can be seen in the UK unemployment data shown in Figure 37.1, which indicates that a steady decline in unemployment coincided with the UK economy enjoying economic growth over the same period.

However, falling unemployment can itself pose problems for firms. The labour market is said to 'tighten', meaning that firms may find it more difficult to attract suitably qualified and skilled labour simply because of shortages emerging in certain occupations or geographical areas. The Learning and Skills Council found that 22% of employers surveyed at the beginning of 2004 were finding skills gaps. Employers were quite literally not able to find suitably competent employees for all of the vacancies on offer. If businesses intent on expansion cannot find sufficient skilled employees to meet their demands, it may prevent such firms from growing as quickly as desired and may act as a brake on the rate of economic growth in the UK.

Skills shortages can lead to higher wages, which present further problems. At the beginning of 2004, average earnings in the UK were increasing at an annual rate of 4.4% — the highest for some years. UK firms were therefore

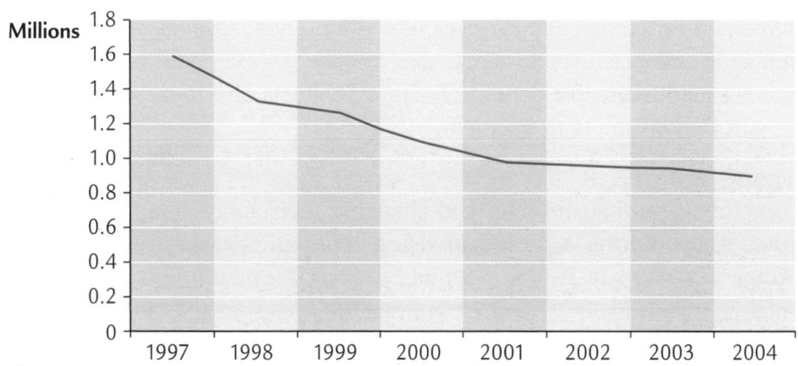

Figure 37.1 *UK unemployment (claimant count), 1997–2004*

faced with rising input costs due to rising wage rates. This leaves them with a dilemma — do they absorb the higher wage costs and squeeze their own profit margins, or do they pass these higher costs on to consumers in the form of higher prices?

DID YOU KNOW?

Just as labour is likely to become more expensive in a fast-growing economy, so firms will find that other resources become scarce and their prices rise. For example, the cost of land and premises is likely to increase significantly, adding to a firm's costs and possibly leading to higher prices.

Impact on business strategy

The impact of economic growth suggests that certain business strategies are better suited to an environment of economic growth.

Expansion

Rapid company expansion is more easily achieved during this period, as a firm may be able to expand production and sales without having to gain sales from rivals. If the market for a firm's products is not growing, the growth in sales of that firm can only come at the expense of falling sales of another — a 'zero sum game', where for one firm to gain, another must lose. In reality, if a firm began an aggressive expansionist strategy in such circumstances, competing firms would be likely to retaliate in an attempt to preserve their customer base, and competition would become intense, with price wars and other hostile strategies being introduced. In a period of strong economic growth, when the demand in the whole market for a product is increasing, firms are able to generate more sales, and even increase their market share, without necessarily having to tempt customers away from rivals. However, expansion and a rapidly growing business can bring their own problems and test a firm's ability to cope in terms of organisational structure, personnel, technology, production capacity and finance.

New products

Economic growth provides new opportunities for firms to update or extend the range of products and services they offer. Thus, strategies based around launching new products have a greater chance of success, as rising consumer incomes lead to greater demand for new products and more willingness on the part of consumers to try them.

Repositioning

Firms intent on repositioning and changing their appeal may also find this policy easier during a period of rising economic prosperity. With higher incomes, consumers are more willing to consider new trends and fashions, which in turn is likely to shorten product life cycles, as the old is substituted for the new. This has encouraged some companies to redefine their image as well as their product offerings, in effect repositioning their brands in the market.

FACT FILE

In March 2004, McDonald's announced a new strategy of offering healthier alternatives to its high-carbohydrate, high-fat range of burgers and fries. It announced the introduction of 'Salads Plus', along with a new range of healthy yoghurts, garden greens, quorn sandwiches and fresh fruit. It allocated £500 million for this rebranding exercise to develop the new dishes and introduce a sustained national promotional campaign. In effect, McDonald's is deliberately attempting to tap into the healthy eating trend, appealing to consumers' awareness about the perceived health benefits of certain food groups. The timing of the strategy is important. McDonald's is more likely to gain trial purchases of its new range of products during periods of economic prosperity, as consumers are prepared to be more adventurous. Clearly, the success of the new strategy will take some time to assess.

Adapted from Andrew Boden, 'Economic Growth', *Business Review*, September 2004.

Thus, economic growth provides ideal conditions for firms that are intent on making changes. Because incomes are rising, consumers are not only better off but also more willing to spend their incomes. If firms can recognise these opportunities and adopt appropriate business strategies, they are likely to benefit from periods of economic growth.

EXAMINER'S VOICE

This analysis suggests that timing the introduction of appropriate business strategies is critical. In order to enable them successfully to schedule their strategic plans well into the future, many firms invest in economic forecasting.

In general, economic growth provides favourable trading conditions and new business opportunities. It means growth and possibly new markets for existing products and market opportunities for new products. High levels of income and spending may even encourage the introduction of what might otherwise have been seen as risky products or business ventures. Economic growth also offers more security and certainty to firms and therefore provides them with more confidence in planning for the future.

Effects of economic growth on the environment

Economic growth and increased wealth do not necessarily produce an increase in welfare and can have serious consequences for the environment. For example, economic growth can result in serious negative externalities, such as pollution, congestion and harm to the environment. This is often apparent in developing countries that undergo rapid industrialisation and also in regional areas that are subject to heavy concentrations of industry. It is important therefore to have sufficient regulation and safeguards in place to minimise such externalities. In the long term, many commentators suggest that it will be impossible to sustain present rates of economic growth as the world's resources are not inexhaustible.

The level of economic activity differs not only internationally between countries, but also between regions within a particular country and between specific areas within a particular region. This has consequences for firms operating in different parts of the country as well as for firms that operate internationally.

PRACTICE EXERCISE

Total: 30 marks (30 minutes)

1 Define the term 'economic growth'. *(2 marks)*

2 State three ways in which GDP can be measured. *(3 marks)*

3 Identify two determinants of economic growth. *(2 marks)*

4 Explain two possible adverse effects that economic growth may have on the environment. *(6 marks)*

5 Explain the possible impact of economic growth on the sales of goods with income-elastic demand. *(5 marks)*

6 Explain how investment in capital goods might be affected by a period of strong economic growth. *(3 marks)*

7 Why might skills shortages occur during periods of economic growth? *(3 marks)*

8 Explain two strategies that companies might adopt to benefit from a period of sustained economic growth. *(6 marks)*

CASE STUDY 1 UK growth is forecast to trail rivals

The UK economy is set to trail behind key EU competitor countries over the next 15 years, with its growth outstripped by the Irish Republic, Spain, France and Portugal, startling new projections suggest.

In a blow to Gordon Brown's hopes to raise the UK's performance in the global race for prosperity, the long-range forecasts from Deutsche Bank indicate that the UK may fall further behind its rivals in the league of global living standards by 2020.

The UK's annual growth between 2006 and the end of the next decade is set to average only 1.9 per cent, according to the long-term projections (see Table 37.3). This would leave the UK lagging behind the USA with average growth of 3.1 per cent, Spain (2.8 per cent) and France (2.3 per cent).

In a league of 32 nations, Britain's forecast growth performance places it in 21st place. Over 15 years, one result would be that Spain's standard of living, measured by national income per head, would leapfrog the UK's. By 2020, Britain's GDP per head is expected to put it nineteenth in the ranking of global living standards, with Spain in seventeenth place. The USA takes first place with GDP per head almost twice that projected for the UK, and with Ireland not far behind the USA (see Figure 37.2).

Table 37.3
Forecast average annual GDP growth, 2006–20

	Growth % per year		Growth % per year
India	5.5	Norway	2.1
Malaysia	5.4	New Zealand	2.1
China	5.2	Austria	2.1
Thailand	4.5	Portugal	2.0
Turkey	4.1	**UK**	**1.9**
Irish Republic	3.8	Sweden	1.8
Indonesia	3.5	Greece	1.7
South Korea	3.3	Denmark	1.7
Mexico	3.2	Italy	1.6
Chile	3.1	Belgium	1.5
USA	3.1	Germany	1.5
Argentina	3.0	Finland	1.3
Spain	2.8	Netherlands	1.3
Brazil	2.8	Australia	1.3
Canada	2.4	Japan	1.3
France	2.3	Switzerland	0.7

Source: Deutsche Bank, *Global Growth Centres 2020*.

Long-term forecasting is notoriously hard, so the figures are controversial. However, Deutsche Bank says they are based on a sophisticated model using key factors that drive growth: population trends, investment levels, workforce skills and nations' openness to trade.

Globally, the forecast shows India as the fastest-growing economy up to 2020, with Malaysia pipping China for second place. Slowing population growth in China is expected to just prevent it eclipsing the USA as the world's largest economy by 2020. By then, the UK is forecast to be the seventh-largest world economy, behind the USA, China, Japan, India, Germany and France.

Source: adapted from an article in *The Times*, 5 April 2005.

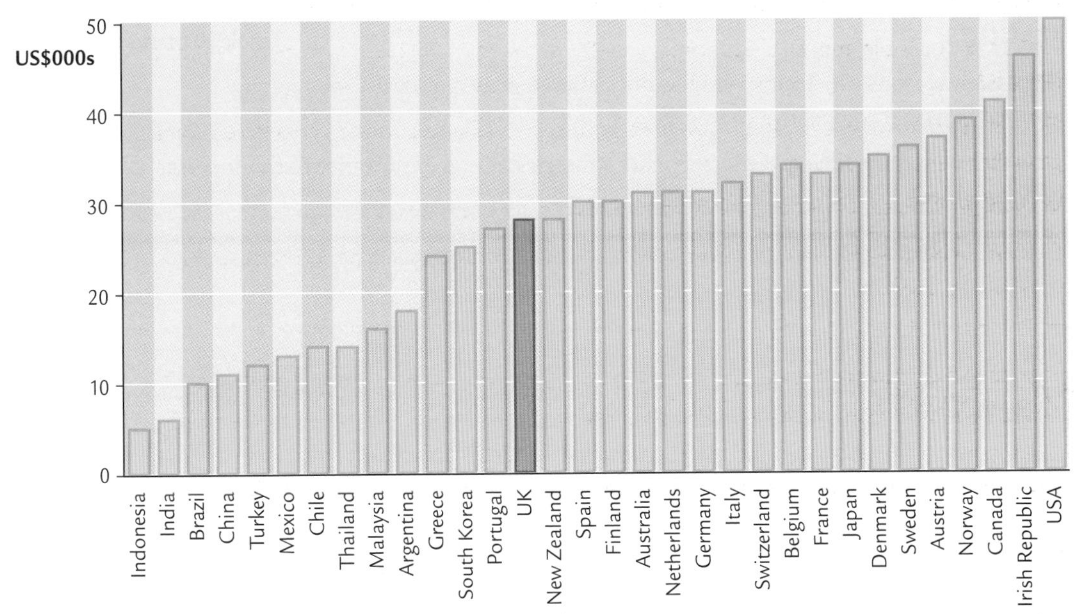

Source: Deutsche Bank, *Global Growth Centres 2020*.

Figure 37.2 *Forecast real GDP per head, 2020*

Questions

Total: 30 marks (35 minutes)

1 Discuss the possible implications of the global GDP projections by Deutsche Bank for a UK company that operates in both domestic and international markets. *(14 marks)*

2 Discuss appropriate long-term strategies for a business to deal with these projections. *(16 marks)*

CASE STUDY 2 Topps Tiles' expansion strategy

Topps Tiles sells a mixture of wall and floor tiles and laminate flooring. Floated on the stock market in 1997, it has grown from just 54 stores at flotation to more than 200 today. For the same period, turnover has jumped from £24.4 million to £120.5 million, with pre-tax profits leaping from £2.5 million to £18.9 million. Its current expansion strategy is set to continue this year, with the opening of a further 24 outlets.

Topps Tiles is taking advantage of the fact that its products are highly income elastic in nature, and have flourished in popularity as rising incomes have propelled the home improvement boom. Over the past

decade, it is estimated that the average semi-detached house has doubled the number of tiles used, partly fuelled by the trend to have bigger kitchens and more bathrooms. Thus, Topps Tiles is successfully penetrating the same market with its products and gaining market share, at the same time as rival operators should also be benefiting from higher sales. Topps Tiles has been able to grow at a faster rate than that of the whole market, without necessarily poaching rival firms' customers.

Source: adapted from Andrew Boden, 'Economic growth', *Business Review*, September 2004.

Questions

Total: 30 marks (35 minutes)

1 Discuss the reasons why Topps Tiles has been able to grow quickly without getting involved in hostile competitive strategies. *(15 marks)*

2 To what extent is the timing of expansionary strategies of vital importance to the success of Topps Tiles? *(15 marks)*

CHAPTER 38

The EU and other overseas opportunities in emerging markets

This chapter explains the European Union (EU) and its major institutions. It considers the impact of the EU on UK business in terms of export opportunities, competition and market access, and examines the implications of the Social Chapter and the single European currency, the euro. It reviews the issues involved in pan-European strategies and also assesses the opportunities provided for UK business in the emerging markets of eastern Europe.

A brief history of the EU

A vision of a new Europe began to emerge at the conclusion of the Second World War in 1945. The objective was to unite the economies of Europe and thereby overcome long-established national rivalries.

The origins of the European Union (EU) lie in the creation of the **European Coal and Steel Community (ECSC)** in 1952. The original members who signed the Treaty of Paris were Belgium, Holland, Luxembourg, Italy and France. West Germany later became a member. The UK participated in the negotiations but refused to join.

In 1957, the Treaty of Rome established the **European Economic Community (EEC)**. The six members of the EEC formed a free trade area with no trade barriers between member states and a customs union in the form of a common external tariff barrier that was levied on goods and services from non-member countries. The six members enjoyed strong economic growth, which encouraged the UK, Ireland (Eire) and Denmark to join this free trade area in 1973.

The next stage of development was a common market with the free movement of all factors of production across national boundaries. In 1986, an agreement between member states of the common market, which by then was known as the **European Community (EC)**, committed them to the creation of a **single market** by the end of 1992.

Key elements of the single market were:

- the creation of common technical standards for EU products

DID YOU KNOW?

Products that meet the technical requirements devised by the EU carry the 'CE' mark, which means that they may be sold throughout the Union.

- the harmonisation of VAT and excise duties, ending tax advantages resulting from locating in a particular EU country
- the free movement of people — EU citizens are allowed to travel, reside, study and work wherever they wish in the European Union
- a reduction in customs posts and the paperwork necessary for trade within the EU
- the free movement of capital, making it possible to invest money anywhere in the EU
- the ending of duty-free sales within the EU in 1999

TOPFOTO

The **Maastricht Treaty** of European Union was signed by all the member states and took effect on 1 November 1993. This treaty created the **European Union** with the aim of developing even greater unity between member countries and, particularly, introducing monetary union and a single European currency. By 1995, there were 15 members of the EU after Austria, Finland, Greece, Portugal, Spain and Sweden had joined.

On 1 January 1999, the **euro** was introduced as the single European currency. On that date, the currencies of the 11 countries adopting the euro were fixed permanently to each other. Greece adopted the euro in 2001. At the same time as the single currency was introduced, the **European Central Bank** took control of interest rates across those countries that had adopted the euro (known as the **eurozone**).

DID YOU KNOW?

BAFFLING PIGS are the initials of those members of the EU that are also members of the eurozone. Of the original 15 countries, those that opted not to join were Denmark, Sweden and the UK.

In May 2004, the EU was expanded to 25 member states (Figure 38.1) when 10 new countries joined, mainly from eastern Europe. The ten new countries were Cyprus, the Czech Republic, Estonia, Hungary, Latvia, Lithuania, Malta, Poland, Slovakia and Slovenia. The previous 15 member countries were: Austria, Belgium, Denmark, Finland, France, Ireland, Italy, Germany, Greece, Luxemburg, the Netherlands, Portugal, Spain, Sweden and the UK.

Bulgaria and Romania are hoping to join the EU in 2006, with Turkey perhaps being considered for membership in 2007.

The institutions of the EU

The EU is managed by its institutions. Currently, these include:

- **the European Commission.** This proposes EU policy and legislation, which is then passed on to the Council of Ministers. All the Commissioners are obliged to act independently of national interest and in the interests of the EU.
- **the Council of Ministers.** This is the EU's decision-making body. It agrees or adopts legislation on the basis of proposals from the Commission. Each member state acts as President of the Council for 6 months.

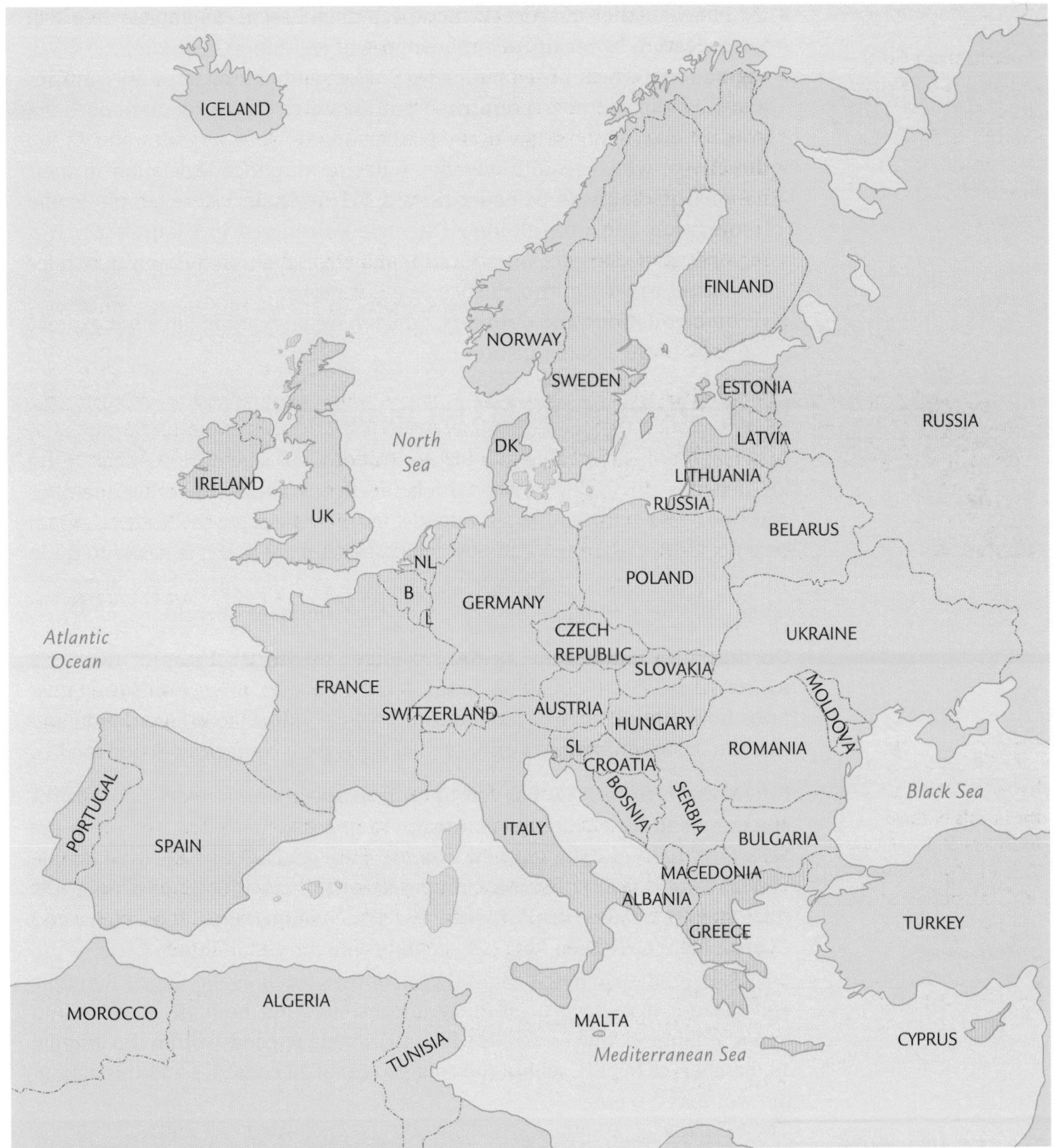

Figure 38.1
The 25 members of the European Union

- **the European Parliament.** This consists of members of the European Parliament (MEPs), who are elected from member states by proportional representation for a fixed period of 5 years. The European Parliament's opinion is needed on any proposals before the Council of Ministers can adopt them. The Parliament votes on the Commission's programmes and monitors day-to-day management of European policies.

The Council of Ministers and the European Commission can impose their will upon the Union by means of various types of legislation, including:

- **regulations**, which have binding legal effect without the need for confirmation by the member countries' parliaments. These regulations have primacy over national law if any conflict arises.
- **directives**, which require member states to introduce legislation in their national parliaments to enact certain EU decisions. An example is the Information and Consultation Directive considered in Chapter 23. If a member state does not introduce the directive, the Commission may refer the matter to the Court of Justice as a last resort.
- **recommendations and opinions**, which have no binding force but express the view of the issuing institution.

Implications of the EU for business

In general terms, the value to a British firm of the UK being a member of the EU depends on the extent to which the firm trades with other member countries and with countries outside the EU, such as the USA. General benefits for British firms of the UK's membership are that it is easier to trade within the EU because there are no barriers and that firms have access to more customers, bringing opportunities for economies of scale.

On the other hand, general disadvantages for British firms of the UK's membership of the EU are that the UK cannot use protectionism against firms from other EU countries, that UK firms are subject to EU legislation and that the UK has to impose tariffs against firms from countries outside the EU.

EU enlargement in 2004 has led to an intensification of competition in UK markets as all the EU countries attempt to improve their position within the EU's tariff barriers. The ten new countries are generally small, for example Latvia, Estonia and Lithuania, and are likely to have little impact upon UK trade and its balance of payments. For some countries, such as Malta and Cyprus, there have been long connections with the UK and trade patterns are not likely to change much. But other countries, such as the Czech Republic and Poland, may have a more significant effect on both UK exports and imports. Table 38.1 gives details of the UK's trade in goods within the original 15 members of the EU, within the enlarged EU of 25 countries and throughout the world as a whole.

***Table 38.1** UK trade in goods, 2004 (£bn, seasonally adjusted)*

	EU (15)			EU (25)			World		
	X	M	B	X	M	B	X	M	B
January	8.5	10.8	-2.3	8.9	11.3	-2.4	14.5	20.1	-5.6
March	8.4	10.5	-2.1	8.8	11.0	-2.2	15.2	19.4	-4.2
May	8.5	11.0	-2.5	8.9	11.4	-2.5	15.3	20.1	-4.8
June	8.7	10.8	-2.1	9.0	11.3	-2.3	15.4	20.4	-5.0

X = exports; M = imports; B = balance

Source: Office for National Statistics.

The ten new members constitute approximately 5% of UK total trade with the EU and have a slightly bigger surplus with the UK than the old members. It will be interesting to see how well UK exports compete in these new markets over the coming years. Much will depend on the agricultural sector, which is generally where the UK is at a disadvantage with the new members. Notice that the EU now constitutes approximately 60% of UK exports and 55% of UK imports.

Positive implications of the EU for UK business

Membership of the EU offers the following benefits to businesses in the UK:

- There is access to a market of 450 million people, which is bigger than Japan and the USA put together.

FACT FILE

Despite the fact that the ten new countries have increased the EU's population by approximately 75 million or 20%, taking it to a massive 450 million people, it is important to put this into perspective. EU GDP has increased by only 5%, with the ten new countries having a combined national income equivalent only to that of the Netherlands, which has a population of just 16 million citizens. These new member states have an average GDP per capita of only 40% of the EU average. If Cyprus, Slovenia and Malta, the richest of the new member countries, are ignored, the remaining seven countries have the equivalent of only 20% of the EU average GDP per person. It would appear at first glance that, economically at least, these new member states have diluted, rather than enriched, the EU.

- The large market provides opportunities for economies of scale, lower costs and increased specialisation.

FACT FILE

In comparison with the EU average GDP per capita of £16,132, Poland, the largest new EU member with a population 38.6 million, has an average GDP of only £5,388. Lithuania, with a population of 3.6 million, has an average GDP of only £4,666 per person. Hence, the markets for goods are much smaller than the relatively large increase in population size of the EU might suggest.

Nevertheless, there is potential for the future, with the expectation of economic growth in the new member countries of between 4% and 6% per annum in the next few years.

- More competition may lead to improved efficiency and therefore lower costs.
- More intense competition can encourage innovation.
- There are opportunities for more European mergers and joint ventures, resulting in synergy and improved efficiency.
- There is encouragement for inward investment from non-EU countries, which increases employment, income and opportunities for supplier industries. The UK has been a major recipient of this, with firms like Toyota in Derby and Nissan in Sunderland establishing themselves within the external tariff wall.

DID YOU KNOW?

If firms such as Toyota and Nissan were simply to import their cars into the EU, they would be faced with the common external tariff barrier, which would make their products less competitive. By locating their production factories in one of the EU countries, they can sell the output from these factories in the EU without the tariffs being levied.

FACT FILE

With the UK experiencing a labour market skills shortage in some areas, there are several instances of UK employers deliberately seeking to take advantage of EU enlargement to solve their recruitment difficulties. For example, BUPA Care Homes has recruited carers from Poland, the Czech Republic and Lithuania. First Group, the UK's largest bus operator, has recruited drivers from Poland.

- There is greater mobility of labour, giving firms a wider labour force to draw on.
- With firms more able to invest anywhere in the EU, there is greater mobility of capital.
- The free movement of factors of production makes it possible for existing EU (and UK) businesses to move to new EU countries where costs are substantially lower. Some firms, such as Volkswagen, have already made this move east.

FACT FILE

The new members of the EU have been deliberately cutting corporation tax rates to create investment incentives for overseas firms. Poland cut its rate from 27% to 19% in 2004, a rate recently matched by Slovakia. Estonia has gone one stage further, abolishing all tax on corporate profitability. This compares with the current headline rate of 30% in the UK, which, until recently, had been at the lower end of the EU league table of corporation tax rates. With such low rates, multinationals may be increasingly tempted to set up operations in these countries, aware that they can retain a greater proportion of the profits they have earned.

Such low profit tax rates also invite the prospect of 'transfer pricing'. Transfer prices are those charged between subsidiaries of the same business. Multinationals in the UK and elsewhere may deliberately seek to distort these prices to ensure that the subsidiary in the country with the lowest corporation tax generates the most profit. This will result if, for example, a subsidiary based in Estonia is charged artificially low prices for supplies obtained from a subsidiary based in a higher corporation tax country, such as the UK. The UK subsidiary apparently makes little profit, but the Estonian subsidiary makes a significantly higher amount of profit. Thus, by transfer pricing, the multinational can minimise its global profit tax commitment. Differential tax rates in the new EU countries are therefore likely to distort investment flows from multinationals.

Negative implications of the EU for UK business

The UK's membership of the EU presents the following difficulties for firms in the UK:

- There is an increase in legislation and the need to meet common technical standards.
- There is increased competition both in Europe and in the domestic market.
- Labour and capital may be attracted to other European countries.
- Low wage rates in countries such as Poland, where average salaries are only 18% of the EU average, will make these new EU members fierce competitors for jobs and they may attract inward investment that might previously have come to the UK.

FACT FILE

Slovakia has succeeded in attracting a significant number of multinationals, ranging from Sony to Volkswagen. Volkswagen already produces 250,000 cars per year in Slovakia, while Peugeot and Hyundai are the latest manufacturers to announce new investment in production there. It is estimated that, by 2007, Slovakia will be producing 850,000 cars per year, making it the largest car producer in the world per capita. However, some economists are suggesting that new investment may now be diverted not to these new members, but to the next wave of EU members currently applying for full membership. Countries such as Bulgaria and Romania may well feature highly in the next round of investments by western multinationals.

The Social Chapter

The Social Chapter is an element of the Maastricht Treaty signed by the 12 members of the EU in 1992. The intention of the Social Chapter is to harmonise working conditions throughout the EU and to ensure that all workers are guaranteed the basic rights to:

- join a trade union
- take industrial action
- be consulted and informed about company plans
- equal treatment for men and women
- a minimum wage and a maximum working week of 48 hours
- a minimum of 4 weeks' paid holiday per year

In addition, the Social Chapter contains provisions relating to redundancies and seeks to encourage employee participation and consultation (see the Information and Consultation Directive on pp. 206–207).

Table 38.2 The Social Chapter: for and against

Arguments in favour of the Social Chapter	Arguments against the Social Chapter
Better worker motivation, improving efficiency and productivity	Rising labour costs as a result of reduced working hours and increasing pay rates
Improved industrial relations as a result of increased participation and consultation	Higher costs make it more difficult to compete against non-EU producers
If all EU countries sign the Social Chapter, there will be a level playing field and none will be at a disadvantage	Firms will be affected differently; some countries have a tradition of shorter working weeks and higher pay

Prior to 1997, the Conservative government in the UK felt that the arguments against the Social Chapter outweighed those in favour. However, in 1997 the Labour government adopted its provisions.

The single European currency — the euro

On 1 January 1999, the euro was introduced as the single European currency. On that date, the currencies of 11 EU countries were fixed permanently to each other. Greece, the twelfth country, joined the euro in 2001. The **eurozone** comprises these 12 countries. (The EU countries that decided not to adopt the euro were Denmark, the UK and Sweden.)

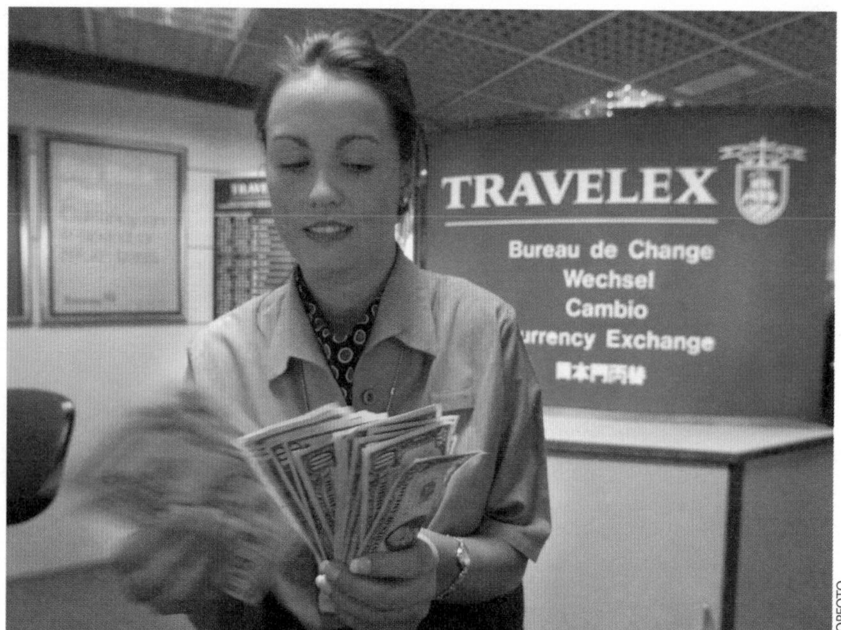

TOPFOTO

If the UK were to adopt the euro, there would be some short-term problems such as the transition costs of new electronic tills, computer software and staff training. However, a single currency and a common interest rate would make trading with the EU much easier and cheaper. UK business might benefit in several ways:

- There would be no exchange rate transaction costs (that is, commission charges when exchanging pounds for euros) in trading within the eurozone, as all countries use the same currency.
- With a common currency, there would be no uncertainty due to exchange rate changes (for example, in relation to export earnings or costs of imported raw materials). This is likely to encourage trade and make financial forecasting more accurate.
- There would be no need to use expensive futures contracts in order to insure against exchange rate changes.
- A common currency would bring price transparency, making it easier for consumers and producers to compare prices within the eurozone.
- A single currency and common interest rates might encourage firms to operate in a wider market, with expansion bringing the benefits of economies of scale.
- New and improved sources of supply, that might previously have been considered too risky, might become viable once exchange rate fluctuations no longer occur.
- Investment from the rest of the world might increase as a result of the move to a single currency, which makes trade with a large market simple and relatively cheap. So far, within the EU the UK is fortunate to have been the

major recipient of direct investment from the rest of the world, but there have been occasional comments from the chief executives of some multinational companies operating in the UK that they would prefer to be located within the eurozone.

FACT FILE

- During 2000, the Japanese car giant Nissan recorded a trading loss of 28 billion yen (£163 million). It was suggested that if undesirable changes in the exchange rate had not occurred, the company would have generated profits in excess of £200 million. In 2001, Nissan warned the UK government that failure to replace the pound with the euro might jeopardise the company's plans to invest further in its factory in Sunderland.
- In 2000, Toyota insisted that its UK suppliers put their invoices in euros. This removed Toyota's exchange rate risk and passed it on to the suppliers, which incurred costs in one currency (pounds) and received revenue in another currency (euros).

Despite these benefits, it must be remembered that at least 40% of the UK's overseas trade is conducted outside the EU (see Table 38.1). This means that there are many firms that, if the UK adopted the euro, would not benefit from the reduced costs of trade with Europe, and which would still face exchange rate issues when they traded with countries outside the eurozone.

Pan-European strategy

A pan-European strategy is an approach that regards all markets within Europe as similar to each other. Thus, a pan-European marketing strategy would assume that there was just one 'European' market. The value of such a strategy depends crucially on whether the markets for particular products are in fact similar across Europe or whether they are very different.

If a pan-European strategy were appropriate for a firm's products, it would create significant economies of scale as a result of being able to produce and operate on a scale that is large enough to meet the needs of 460 million people. However, there is little evidence to suggest that markets across Europe are similar; in fact, most evidence suggests that markets across Europe are differentiated and fragmented. Greece is very different from France, which is very different from Germany — a product that sells very well in Greece may not do at all well in either France or Germany. Similarly, just as markets vary within the UK between, for example, the north and the south, so markets vary within other countries in Europe. A product or service that is very successful in Madrid may not sell well in Mallorca. A key element of success for most firms is their ability to achieve economies of scale while meeting the individual demands of the diverse markets in the various parts of Europe.

Emerging markets: the example of eastern Europe

KEY TERM

emerging market: an international area that has the potential to grow and develop in terms of productive capacity, market opportunities and competitive advantage.

Eastern Europe is a good example of an emerging market. The fall of the communist regimes in the late 1980s and early 1990s and the absorption of ten such countries into the EU in 2004 have had the following implications for UK business:

- Eastern Europe's population is a major new market.
- There are market opportunities for new products and well-established branded products. For example, supermarkets and companies operating in mature markets such as those for chocolate and detergents have seen huge potential for whoever can establish their brand name first.
- Production costs in eastern Europe are lower, with cheaper labour and land rents plus less stringent government controls.
- The introduction of capitalism and the market system in eastern Europe means new competition.

Eastern Europe represents a huge opportunity for UK business, but the transition from an emerging market to a fully developed one does not take place overnight and results in a range of problems:

- The markets in eastern Europe are not wealthy ones, with the average income being approximately one-third of that in the EU. This means that eastern European consumers have relatively little income to spend on the products of EU firms.
- The political systems of many central and eastern European states are still immature and can be unstable, leading to unpredictable decision making and sudden changes in trading conditions.
- High inflation can be a problem. Where this affects confidence in the currency, it may lead to transactions being made in other currencies with more stable values and internationally acceptable status, such as the dollar.
- There may be problems in raising finance in countries where the banking system needs developing or where there is no stock market.
- Relatively poor infrastructure, in terms of transport and communication systems, can be problematic.
- Markets may be less well developed than in western Europe.

FACT FILE

By May 2004, only 2,000 UK firms had established operations in Poland (compared with 8,000 from Germany). Additionally, there seems to be evidence that UK firms are more attracted to Far Eastern destinations, most notably China. In a survey published in *The Financial Times* in April 2004, UK firms ranked China as their 'best location for future investment', whereas 51% of German firms and 41% of French companies opted instead for central and eastern European countries.

PRACTICE EXERCISE

Total: 50 marks (45 minutes)

1 What do the terms 'free trade area' and 'customs union' mean in relation to the EU? *(4 marks)*

2 Explain two features of the operation of the 'single market' within the EU. *(6 marks)*

3 How many countries are members of the EU? *(1 mark)*

4 Explain three positive implications of the EU for UK businesses. *(9 marks)*

5 State three negative implications of the EU for UK businesses. *(3 marks)*

6 What is the Social Chapter? *(3 marks)*

7 Explain three possible benefits for UK firms if the UK adopted the euro. *(9 marks)*

8 What is a pan-European strategy? *(3 marks)*

9 Explain two possible benefits of emerging markets, such as those in eastern Europe, for UK business. *(6 marks)*

10 Explain two possible problems for UK firms attempting to enter emerging markets in eastern Europe. *(6 marks)*

CASE STUDY Tesco plans to open 40 new outlets in Europe

Tesco, the UK's largest supermarket chain, plans to open more then 40 stores in central Europe this year as it seeks growth outside its home market.

Figures obtained by the *Financial Times* show that Tesco – which has about 194 stores across Poland, the Czech Republic, Slovakia and Hungary – intends to increase that number to at least 234 stores.

The retailer declined to comment on its expansion plans ahead of its results announcement tomorrow, when it is expected to report profits of more than £2bn. With a 29.5 per cent share of the UK grocery market, Tesco has to look beyond the UK to drive growth.

In January the supermarket group said that underlying sales in the UK would slow to 3–4 per cent this year as the market became tougher. Underlying sales grew 7.6 per cent in the seven weeks to January 8.

The European expansion is only part of Tesco's international ambitions. It has 200 stores in Asia, operating in China, Japan, Thailand, Malaysia and South Korea. Analysts expect these operations to grow in the coming year. In central Europe, the market has been tough for Tesco.

Andrew Higginson, finance director, said in January that competition in Poland and Hungary from hard discounters, such as Aldi and Lidl, had forced Tesco to cut prices. This had hindered sales growth.

Nevertheless, Hungary – Tesco's first foray abroad in 1994 – is set to be the biggest beneficiary of the European expansion, with 16 new stores planned in 2005–6, taking the total number of stores in the country to 85.

In September Tesco opened its second Hungarian distribution centre on the edge of Budapest. The fresh food depot, which handles 750,000 cases of products a week, is working at 75 per cent capacity, giving the retailer scope to serve up to 20 more stores.

By Elizabeth Rigby, Retail Correspondent
Published: April 11, 2005.

Questions

Total: 30 marks (35 minutes)

1 Discuss the benefits to Tesco of establishing supermarkets in the central and eastern European countries of the EU. *(15 marks)*

2 To what extent might Tesco's success be even greater if the UK were to adopt the euro? *(15 marks)*

Economic opportunities and constraints

Unit 5 of the AQA A2 Business Studies specification comprises a choice between coursework (5C) and a written examination (5W). The written examination consists of a business report and one essay (chosen from four titles).

The business report integrates all six modules of the AQA specification and so the best sources of these reports are the past papers available on the AQA website: www.aqa.org.uk. Advice on how to tackle these reports is provided in Chapter 33 of this book.

The business report below is included for those who may wish to practise one of these reports at this stage of the course. Economic opportunities and constraints often feature as an appendix in the examination reports, as they are an area of the specification that lends itself to interpreting the meaning and significance of numerical data. Therefore, although you will not be required to answer a question based solely on this section of the specification, it is a golden opportunity to practise answering this style of question while a topic is still fresh in your mind. Before tackling this business report, you are advised to read Chapter 33.

BUSINESS REPORT Heart and Soles Ltd — Total: 40 marks (45 minutes)

Heart and Soles Ltd is a UK shoe manufacturer. It has a small but very secure market in the UK for high-fashion, top-quality women's shoes. Given the competition at the top end of the market, it feels that, if it is to expand in this sector, it needs to look abroad – and eastern Europe is looking attractive.

Using the data provided, compile a report detailing the potential opportunities and threats that expansion into particular eastern European countries might provide, and recommending additional information that would be needed before making any decision.

Appendix 1: Population in selected new EU countries

Country	Population (million)
Czech Republic	10.2
Hungary	10.0
Lithuania	3.6
Poland	38.6
Slovenia	1.9

Source: *The Sunday Times*, 2 May 2004.

Appendix 2: GDP per person in selected new EU countries

Country	GDP per person (£)
Czech Republic	8,500
Hungary	7,388
Poland	5,388
Slovenia	10,666

Source: *The Sunday Times*, 2 May 2004.

Appendix 3: UK unemployment rate, 2003–05

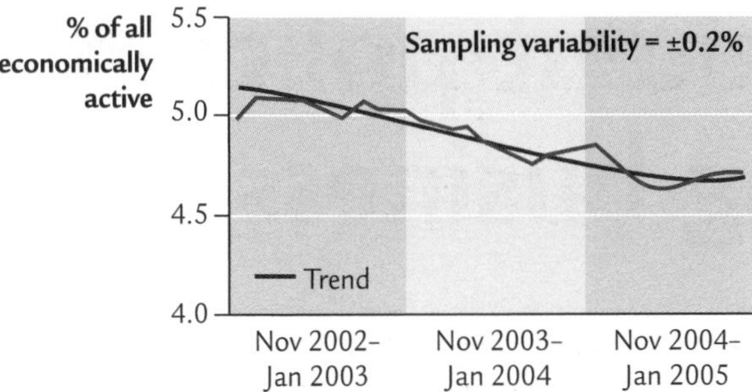

Source: www.statistics.gov.uk

Appendix 4: Real GDP growth rate, 2000–04

	Real GDP growth rate (% change on previous year)				
	2000	2001	2002	2003	2004
EU (25)	3.6	1.7	1.1	0.9	2.3
EU (15)	3.6	1.7	1.1	0.8	2.2
Czech Republic	3.9	2.6	1.5	3.7	4.0
Hungary	5.2	3.8	3.5	3.0	4.0
Poland	4.0	1.0	1.4	3.8	5.3
Slovenia	3.9	2.7	3.3	2.5	4.6
UK	3.9	2.3	1.6	2.2	3.1
USA	3.7	0.8	1.9	3.0	4.4

Source: Eurostat.

Appendix 5: Index of labour productivity, 2000–04

	Index of labour productivity				
	2000	2001	2002	2003	2004
EU (25)	100	100	100	100	100
EU (15)	108.4	108.2	107.9	106.8	106.4
Czech Republic	59.8	61.1	61.5	62.0	63.6
Hungary	61.7	65.0	67.3	67.7	69.5
Poland	51.0	50.3	51.1	58.2	60.1
Slovenia	70.5	72.4	73.4	74.4	76.3
UK	105.4	107.2	109.4	109.0	109.2
USA	134.6	134.9	137.3	139.0	143.8

Source: Eurostat.

CHAPTER 39

Government policies affecting business

This chapter considers government policy and how it affects business. It focuses on economic policies and their implications for business, and in particular analyses the government's use of fiscal and monetary policy. Interventionist and laissez-faire policy approaches are examined, leading to discussion of the process of privatisation that occurred in the UK during the 1980s.

Government policy

Governments seek to control the business environment in order to achieve a range of objectives. These include economic objectives as well as the establishment of an ordered, predictable and equitable (fair) environment in which business can flourish. As economies develop, governments develop a range of policies to achieve these objectives. These include economic policies such as fiscal and monetary policy (discussed below), regulation and legislation.

Regulations enable businesses to operate in an environment that ensures a level playing field: where companies must publish their accounts, where creditors have legal rights if debts are not paid, and so on. Legislation, whether related to employment, consumers, health and safety or competition issues, assists this process. Laws ensure that employees are treated fairly, that products meet health and safety standards, that consumers receive a fair deal and that competition between firms is fair. In this sense, regulation and legislation ensure a more ordered and predictable environment and one that is fairer for all parties concerned.

Economic policy

Economic policy involves efforts by the government to control the economy in order to achieve its objectives. Key economic objectives that most governments try to achieve are:

- encouraging economic growth
- controlling and reducing inflation
- maintaining a satisfactory level of employment
- achieving a satisfactory balance of payments
- maintaining a stable exchange rate

Table 39.1 illustrates the UK's achievement in each of these areas over the last 5 years.

Table 39.1 UK economic indicators, 2000–04

	2000	2001	2002	2003	2004
Economic growth (%)	3.9	2.3	1.8	2.2	2.7
Inflation (%)	3.0	1.8	1.7	2.9	2.7
Unemployment (%)	4.0	3.0	3.0	3.0	2.8
Current balance of payments (£bn)	-24.1	-23.5	-18.0	-26.7	-10.6
Exchange rate (€/£)	1.64	1.61	1.50	1.45	1.49
Exchange rate ($/£)	1.51	1.44	1.50	1.63	1.82

Source: HM Treasury website. www.hm-treasury.gov.uk/

DID YOU KNOW?

The balance of payments is a record of transactions between one country and the rest of the world. It records exports and imports as well as transfers of income and assets.

An important part of the balance of payments is the **current account**, which includes:

- trade in goods (also known as the balance of trade or the visible balance), which records exports of goods minus imports of goods
- trade in services (or the invisible balance), which records exports of services minus imports of services
- the balance of income going to and coming from abroad, such as interest, profits and dividends, together with transfers such as UK government payments to the EU or gifts

The current balance shown in Table 39.1 is the total of the current account. Traditionally, the UK has a deficit on its trade in goods, which is compensated for by a surplus on its trade in services. However, as can be seen in Table 39.1, this has not been the case in recent years.

The problem of managing the economy is the degree of trade-off between these economic objectives. For example, in a boom, GDP and the level of employment will both be growing. But inflation will also be accelerating and the generally high level of demand may suck in more imports. On the other hand, during a recession, inflation will usually slow down and exports may rise as businesses seek foreign markets, but growth will be sluggish and unemployment is likely to rise.

Macroeconomic policy is the government's attempt to influence the level of demand in the economy as a whole: that is, in the macroeconomy. It works primarily through **monetary policy** (such as the impact of interest rates) and **fiscal policy** (that is, the impact of government tax and expenditure changes).

The choice of economic policies depends on the priorities of the government of the day and the particular objectives it wishes to pursue. Since the 1990s, most governments, regardless of their politics, have been concerned to keep inflation down.

A major problem in using economic policy is timing. By the time the government has identified the problem and decided on appropriate policies, the original problem may either have disappeared or have got a lot worse. Thus, in thinking about the effect of economic policies and particularly macroeconomic policies, it should always be remembered that such policies will work with a time lag or delay.

Government policies affecting business

Fiscal policy

TERM

fiscal policy: the use of taxation and government expenditure to influence the economy.

EXAMINER'S VOICE

Injections and withdrawals are part of the circular flow of income that was studied at AS. They are covered in Chapter 36 of the AS textbook.

Taxation allows the government to raise revenue and to influence demand by placing a charge on goods, services or income. It is a withdrawal of money from the economy, in that it tends to reduce total spending and demand. In contrast, government expenditure is an injection of money into the economy and thus tends to increase total spending and demand.

There are two main categories of taxation: direct taxation and indirect taxation. The distinction between a direct tax and an indirect tax is that direct taxation is raised straight from income and profits, whereas indirect taxation is raised when individuals buy goods or services.

Direct taxes are taxes on incomes. Households pay income tax, while businesses pay corporation tax. Direct taxes are usually levied as a proportion of income or profit, so as more income or profit is earned, proportionately more tax is paid. There is also a **progressive** element to these taxes: that is, higher tax rates are levied if earnings are above a certain level. For example, in 2005, small companies paid 19% and large companies paid 30% of their pre-tax profit in corporation tax, while individuals paid 10%, 22% or 40% income tax, depending on the level of their income.

WHAT DO YOU THINK?

In 1978, the highest rate of income tax was 83%, levied on income above £24,000 a year. For people on the highest incomes, for every additional £1 they earned above £24,000, the government took 83p in income tax, leaving them with 17p. What might be the justification for such a rate and what impact is it likely to have?

DID YOU KNOW?

Taxes can be proportional, progressive or regressive:

- A **proportional** tax is one that takes the same proportion of someone's income regardless of how much they earn.
- A **progressive** tax takes a larger proportion of someone's income the more they earn. Income tax is an example of a progressive tax because the rate levied on the lowest income levels is less than that levied on higher incomes.
- A **regressive** tax is one that takes a larger proportion of someone's income the less they earn. Flat-rate taxes, such as VAT, which is set at a fixed rate of 17.5% on most goods, are regressive. For example, an individual earning £1,750 per month who purchases a TV costing £400, on which £70 of VAT is added, is paying 4% of his/her monthly income in VAT. On the other hand, someone earning £7,000 per month who purchases the same product is paying only 1% of his/her monthly income in VAT.

FACT FILE

Tax is levied on cigarettes in three ways: specific excise duty of approximately £100 per 1,000 cigarettes; an 'ad valorem' excise duty of 22% of the total retail price; and VAT at 17.5% of the price including the other taxes. Thus about 80% of the price of a packet of cigarettes consists of taxation.

DID YOU KNOW?

The Inland Revenue collects direct taxes such as income tax and corporation tax, while HM Customs and Excise collects indirect taxes such as VAT and excise duties.

Indirect taxes are taxes on spending. Value added tax (VAT), at the rate of 17.5%, is charged on almost every product and service sold, with the supplier paying this 17.5% VAT to the government. Petrol, cigarettes and alcohol all have an additional tax, known as excise duty, imposed upon them by the chancellor of the exchequer.

Fiscal policy is also known as budgetary policy and is the responsibility of the chancellor of the exchequer.

- A **budget surplus** is where taxation is greater than government spending. Thus, more money is being withdrawn from the circular flow than is being injected into it. As a result, overall spending and demand in the economy will be reduced, leading to a fall in economic activity.
- A **budget deficit** is where government spending is greater than taxation. It means that overall spending and demand are likely to increase, leading to a rise in economic activity.
- A **balanced budget** is when taxation is equal to government spending. Overall spending and demand in the economy remain unchanged, although specific industries and areas may see changes in economic activity.

Initial changes in fiscal policy, such as a change in tax rates or a change in government expenditure, have further **multiplier effects** on business and the economy. For example, an increase in indirect taxation may lead to an increase in the price of goods and a subsequent reduction in demand. This may in turn lead to a cutback in production and, in the extreme, redundancies, triggering a further fall in demand. An increase in income tax will reduce disposable income and thus lower demand.

Governments use fiscal policy in various ways. For example, in a recession, government could try to boost demand in the economy by reducing taxes because this should leave firms and households with more money and so encourage spending. Alternatively, government spending could be increased, which will, in turn, increase demand for goods and services.

The impact of an increase in taxation depends on how much it has been increased, which taxes have been increased and whether consumers and firms are sensitive to such changes and react as expected. Taxes cannot be changed as often or as easily as interest rates, since tax changes are usually announced in the annual budget statement produced by the chancellor of the exchequer. However, compared with interest rates, taxation and government

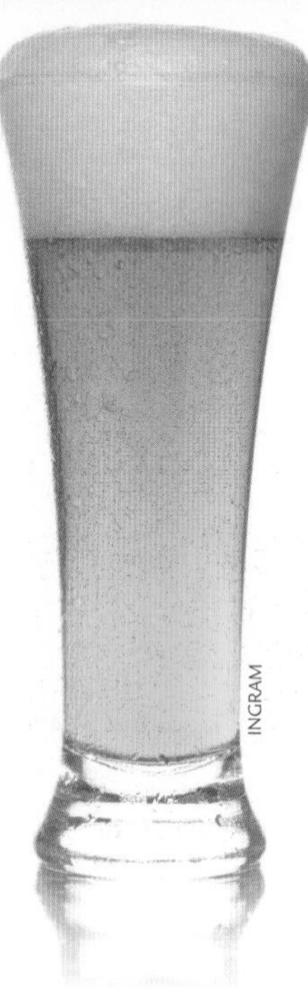

spending can provide the flexibility to target certain products or affect certain types of behaviour more specifically. In this sense, changes in tax and government expenditure can be a very effective way of influencing demand.

FACT FILE

'The duty on spirits has been frozen for the fourth consecutive year to strengthen both the international competitiveness and domestic base of the UK spirits industry.'
(HM Customs and Excise)

'It is generally recognised on all sides that the single most effective policy for reducing tobacco consumption is price. Successive governments have therefore regularly raised excise duty on tobacco products as a means of discouraging consumption.'
(Department of Health, memorandum to Health Select Committee, 2000)

Because a tax increase effectively reduces the spending power of the taxpayers, it can be used selectively to target particular groups of people or types of spending. For example:

- to increase incentives for people to set up their own businesses, corporation tax for small firms could be reduced
- to reduce consumer spending, the rate of VAT could be increased, which will effectively lead to an increase in price
- to deter people from using leaded petrol and thus to reduce environmental pollution, excise duty on leaded petrol was increased, making it more expensive
- to redistribute wealth from the well-off to the less well-off, higher rates of income tax could be increased and the bottom rate could be reduced or the starting point for paying it increased

Monetary policy

KEY TERM

monetary policy: controlling the money supply and the rate of interest in order to influence the level of spending and demand in the economy.

EXAMINER'S VOICE

Refer back to your AS study notes to ensure that you understand fully the possible implications of a change in interest rates.

In recent years, the emphasis of economic policy has been on controlling interest rates. As mentioned previously, interest rates can be changed more easily and more quickly than rates of taxation, with decisions about interest rates being made each month by the Monetary Policy Committee of the Bank of England. In addition, in comparison with taxation and government spending, which can be targeted to influence particular groups, interest rates have a blanket effect on the economy. In fact, a single change in interest rates has a complex array of effects on the economy.

Like fiscal policy, initial changes in monetary policy have **multiplier effects** on business and the economy. Policies needed to stop inflation from rising may throw the economy into recession. Falling demand will cause businesses to cut production. The policies will make people redundant and their incomes will then fall. They will spend less, which will cause demand to fall further in a downward spiral. Before long, the problem of inflation will give way to unemployment and slow or non-existent economic growth. Interest rates then need to fall in order to encourage spending; taxes need to fall and government spending needs to rise.

FACT FILE

TOPFOTO

Whereas the government makes all decisions relating to fiscal policy — that is, the control of tax and expenditure measures — in 1997 the new Labour chancellor of the exchequer, Gordon Brown, made the Bank of England and its Monetary Policy Committee wholly responsible for the setting of interest rates in order to control inflation. The Monetary Policy Committee is a group of government-appointed experts who meet each month to examine the evidence and decide whether any changes in interest rates are needed. The objective is to make the control of inflation independent of political issues. The government's target rate of inflation, as measured by the retail price index (RPI), was originally set at 2.5%. Since December 2003, the main method of calculating inflation has become the consumer price index (CPI) and the target has been adjusted to 2.0%.

EXAMINER'S VOICE

Remember that interest rates have a significant impact on the exchange rate. When interest rates are high, capital from abroad flows into the country to take advantage of the attractive rates that can be obtained on bank deposits. These capital flows increase demand for the currency and tend to push up its price (the exchange rate). As exchange rates rise, export prices rise and exporters lose competitiveness. Export sales will tend to fall off as buyers turn to cheaper substitutes. The resulting fall in demand for exports creates downward pressure on output and employment in the UK.

Impact of fiscal and monetary policies on the economy and business

Tracking through the business cycle illustrates how both fiscal and monetary policies affect the economy and business.

During a period of **recession**, growth can be encouraged by allowing demand to increase. Keeping interest rates down, reducing taxes and increasing government expenditure will all have this effect:

- Low interest rates encourage investment and consumer spending.
- Tax cuts give people more spending power.
- Government spending has multiplier implications throughout the economy. For example, the building of a new hospital involves the employment of builders and eventually of medical staff, who have incomes that they will spend in the local economy. Suppliers of raw materials will receive additional demand that may have favourable effects on their financial position, and so on.

When the economy is **booming**, symptoms of 'overheating' may start to appear, such as high inflation and shortages of skilled labour. Governments, faced with accelerating inflation and rising imports, want to reduce the rate at which demand is growing. They will focus on how to reduce the level of demand by restricting consumer and government spending. Reducing the level of demand to cut inflationary pressures can be done in three different ways, either separately or in combination:

- Interest rates can be increased, which will make it expensive for businesses and individuals to borrow. Businesses will invest less and individuals will consume less, especially if they have mortgages.
- Taxes can be increased, which will reduce purchasing power and consumption generally.
- Government expenditure can be cut, which will reduce demand via the multiplier process.

Of course, reduced demand and a cut in the level of spending will eventually lead to a reduction in investment, which may lead to reduced productivity and competitiveness, and also to unemployment.

Other economic policies

In addition to fiscal and monetary policy, government can introduce other economic policies depending on the economic circumstances:

- **Exchange rate policies.** This is the extent to which the government is prepared to intervene in the foreign exchange market, by buying and selling pounds or by changing interest rates, to influence the value of the currency. The objective of such intervention is to influence the competitiveness of UK firms in export and domestic markets.
- **Protectionism.** This is the extent to which the government uses controls to restrict the amount of imports entering the country. The UK's position on this is determined by its membership of the EU, which has a policy of free trade among member countries and a common external tariff barrier for goods and services coming from non-member countries.
- **Supply-side policies.** Monetary and fiscal policies are known as demand-side policies because they influence the overall level of demand in the economy. Since the early 1980s, most governments have been strongly in favour of encouraging markets to work efficiently at a micro level. Policies to encourage this have become collectively known as supply-side policies. Most supply-side policies focus on particular parts of the economy rather than the economy as whole. Their underlying objective is to make markets work in ways that optimise the level of output. Examples are measures that allow the labour market to function efficiently by reducing the power of trade unions and improving incentives to find and retain jobs. In addition, measures have been introduced to raise the efficiency of business by improving access to education and training, by increasing competition and by privatisation and deregulation (see page 398).

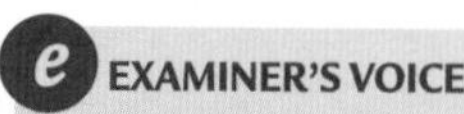

It is important to understand what the various policies are, broadly how they work, and how they affect business.

Intervention versus laissez-faire

KEY TERM

intervention: policy based on the belief that government should exert a strong influence on the economy, rather than allowing market forces to dictate conditions.

Examples of intervention include:

- economic policies (e.g. monetary and fiscal)
- support for new firms and rescue packages for large manufacturing industries

FACT FILE

In April 2005, the government loaned MG Rover £6.5 million to pay workers' wages after the company halted production. Following its collapse, the government announced a £150 million support package to help workers retrain or find other jobs. The support package includes £60 million to help diversify industry in the area and to support the supply chain. There will be another £50 million to fund the retraining and re-skilling of workers made redundant and a further £40 million will be ploughed into statutory redundancy payments. The chancellor, Gordon Brown, said that around £40 million of previously announced money will help with construction of a new industrial park in the region and the government will discuss the prospect of additional help with the EU. Mr Brown said that every Longbridge worker would be interviewed over the next week to be told about opportunities for retraining. They would be given details of the 26,000 job vacancies in the West Midlands.

- regional policies — for example, the provision, via the EU, of funding to help regenerate areas of high unemployment and social deprivation
- policies to influence the exchange rate
- legislation to provide protection for consumers and workers
- competition policies

EXAMINER'S VOICE

Most of these examples have been covered in more detail elsewhere in this module or in the AS textbook.

KEY TERM

laissez-faire: policy based on the belief that the free market will maximise business efficiency and consumer satisfaction; government therefore tries to avoid interfering in the running of business or any other part of the economy.

The extent to which governments intervene in the economy varies from country to country and also changes over time. For example, most eastern European countries, under the communist regime, were extremely interventionist in their approach but have become more laissez-faire as a result of political changes. In the UK, the trend towards privatisation and deregulation in the 1980s and 1990s was a move to a more laissez-faire approach.

Privatisation

KEY TERM

privatisation: when state-run industries and state-owned assets are returned or sold to the private sector.

WHAT DO YOU THINK?

How might the objectives of private sector businesses differ from those of public sector organisations? What effect might these different objectives have on the amount, quality and price of goods and services provided? Is your view supported by the evidence?

The process of privatisation can be viewed as a way of reducing intervention in the economy. A wave of privatisations took place in the UK during the 1980s and 1990s. Examples include:

- contracting out of services, such as refuse collection, which were previously run by government or local authorities, to private sector organisations
- deregulation or the removal of restrictions that prevent competition — for example, in the provision of bus services
- the transfer of nationalised industries such as British Telecom (BT), British Gas, British Airways and British Rail into public limited companies, by the sale of shares to the public
- the sale of government-owned assets

Privatised organisations are owned by shareholders rather than the government, and are therefore likely to pursue different objectives from those of nationalised industries or public-sector organisations.

Arguments for privatisation

- The introduction of competition and the reduction of bureaucracy improve efficiency. The economic performance of the former communist countries of eastern Europe suggests that state decisions on how to distribute factors of production are not the most effective method. Furthermore, the bureaucratic processes involved prevent the achievement of levels of efficiency expected from the market mechanism.
- Competition provides the consumer with more choice. Many state-owned corporations were monopolies that exploited the public. Privatisation introduced competition and gave consumers more choice, better service and, in some cases, lower prices. For example, the provision of telephone services has improved since BT has faced competition from other companies.
- Privatisation encouraged individuals to become shareholders and thus take an interest in the performance of companies. Although many of these original shares have been sold, the process did create a cultural change that increased awareness of the role of business in society. British Gas, for example, still has over 2 million shareholders.

Arguments against privatisation

- Companies may exploit consumers by charging higher prices for the provision of certain basic products. Many state-run enterprises operated in areas where, it might be argued, people had a basic right to enjoy the good or service without price being a barrier. Examples are water and rail travel.
- Many nationalised industries were **natural monopolies**, meaning that the

most efficient means of production was via a single producer or supplier. For example, the creation of regional privatised monopolies has allowed the water companies and others to exploit customers more than ever before, as competition is not realistic in these industries.

Regulation

The impact of privatisation depends on how much competition is created and how well regulated the industry is. Recognising the need for regulation, the government has established regulatory bodies (watchdogs), such as Ofgas, Ofwat and Oftel, to prevent privatised monopolies exploiting their markets. These watchdogs have responsibility for:

- monitoring behaviour and pricing
- setting performance standards
- allowing or forbidding new entrants to the industry

FACT FILE

The opposite of privatisation is nationalisation, which describes the transfer of firms and industries from the private sector to the public sector. Interestingly, most of the nationalised industries that were privatised in the 1980s — for example, the railways, steelmaking and coalmining — were originally failing private sector industries that were nationalised in 1945, at the end of the Second World War. When a whole industry is taken into public ownership, it usually becomes a monopoly. Monopolies face little pressure to stay efficient and may allow their costs to rise more than if they faced strong competition. The losses of nationalised industries are carried by the government and ultimately by the taxpayer.

PRACTICE EXERCISE — Total: 40 marks (35 minutes)

1 List four of the government's main economic objectives. *(4 marks)*

2 Distinguish between the use of fiscal policy and monetary policy in attempting to influence the level of demand in the economy. *(6 marks)*

3 In relation to fiscal policy, explain the following terms and their impact on the economy:
- **a** budget deficit
- **b** budget surplus
- **c** balanced budget *(6 marks)*

4 What is the role of the Monetary Policy Committee? *(4 marks)*

5 Distinguish between interventionist and laissez-faire approaches to government policy. *(6 marks)*

6 Give two examples of privatisation. *(2 marks)*

7 Explain two advantages of privatisation. *(6 marks)*

8 What is meant by exchange rate policy? *(3 marks)*

9 What is meant by supply-side policies? *(3 marks)*

CHAPTER 39 Government policies affecting business

CASE STUDY 1 A consumer slowdown

A chill wind blew down the high street yesterday. Argos, a seemingly unstoppable engine of growth in recent years, had to admit that in the first 3 months of this year its like-for-like sales had slipped by 1%.

There was grim news too from Laura Ashley and Austin Reed, with both reporting a substantial fall in sales: 6% at Austin Reed and almost 14% at Laura Ashley.

The pattern that is emerging is one to frighten almost any shopkeeper. The consumer slowdown that had been predicted for much of last year really does seem to have arrived. Despite the grim projections, Christmas saw a late rush to the shops and, although many stores had been panicked into putting up the 'sale' signs, the festive funds poured into their tills.

But it is now clear that this was a last spree before the purses and wallets snapped shut. Retailers had already had to come to terms with an increased price-consciousness among customers that took its toll on profit margins. Argos said yesterday that it had brought down average prices during the year by a hefty 6%. Earlier this week, Tesco said that, once petrol was taken out of the equation, there was deflation in its prices over the past year.

But Argos is now finding that merely being cheap is not enough to persuade the customer to part with cash. The fact is that people are finding themselves with less disposable income. Gordon Brown will not be shouting about it, but the combination of his hike in national insurance levels, increased interest rates and soaring council tax bills has inevitably taken its toll on the amount of money that people have to spend in the shops.

TOPFOTO

Even among those with plenty of free cash, there is now a lessening of confidence. This results from a number of issues, but particularly the nervousness following the collapse of Rover and the latest government figures showing that the number of people unemployed is edging upwards.

Source: adapted from an article by Patience Wheatcroft in *The Times*, 16 April 2005.

Questions

Total: 30 marks (35 minutes)

1 Evaluate the likely impact of the 'consumer slowdown' on UK retailers and manufacturers. *(12 marks)*

2 Consider how both fiscal and monetary policy might be used to overcome this 'slowdown'. Suggest which might be the most appropriate policy and justify your choice. *(18 marks)*

CASE STUDY 2 MG Rover

Almost 5,000 MG Rover workers are expected to be made redundant and a further 25,000 manufacturing jobs at component suppliers are likely to go, following the collapse of the car maker, which is losing £25 million a month.

If a similar situation had arisen in the 1960s and 1970s, with the closure of a major car factory, then either a Labour or Conservative government would have intervened with subsidies to keep production going. That was done by the Wilson (Labour), Heath

(Conservative), Callaghan (Labour) and Thatcher (Conservative) governments in various sectors. The results were almost universally bad in the medium to long term, as most of the jobs were eventually lost and taxpayers paid out billions of pounds.

But governments no longer pretend they can guarantee specific jobs and in this case there appears to have been a general acceptance that there was no easy alternative on offer. So when the crunch came, the government accepted that closure could not be avoided and concentrated on helping to cushion the immediate pain, while assisting with retraining schemes and helping to create jobs in a new industrial park (see the Fact File on page 397 for more detail).

The closure of Rover is an example of how far UK industry and government policy have changed over the last 30 years.

Source: adapted from an article in *The Times*, 16 April 2005.

Questions

Total: 30 marks (35 minutes)

1 To what extent does the article suggest that government policy has changed from an interventionist to a laissez-faire approach in relation to the support for industry? *(14 marks)*

2 Discuss the extent to which macroeconomic policy could be used effectively to alleviate the unemployment that will be produced by the demise of MG Rover. *(16 marks)*

CHAPTER 40

Social responsibilities

The social responsibilities of business were studied at AS. These were considered in detail in Chapter 42 in the AS textbook and, in relation to stakeholders, in Chapter 50. Before reading this chapter, ensure that you understand these issues and recognise a firm's responsibilities to employees, customers and other stakeholders. This chapter builds upon the coverage of social responsibilities at AS. It examines whether firms should accept their social responsibilities and, if they do, how they might meet them.

Corporate social responsibility

Social responsibilities are the duties of an organisation towards its stakeholders, the environment and society in general. Increasingly, the term used is **corporate social responsibility (CSR)**. Business in the Community defines corporate social responsibility as 'a company's positive impact on society and the environment, through its operations, products or services and through its interaction with key stakeholders such as employees, customers, investors, communities and suppliers'.

The pressure on firms to act in socially responsible ways has increased significantly in recent years, with numerous league tables now produced that rank firms according to their achievements in relation to social responsibility.

What are socially responsible activities?

CSR activities can be divided into two broad categories:

One-off activities

These include straight charitable donations, awards to local youth projects, schools or arts centres, and the company time devoted to community projects by key executives and their staff. Such activities are a matter for the company and its shareholders to decide on a project-by-project basis. If investors think too much money or time is being taken up, they can say so, and the management has the chance to persuade them otherwise at the annual meeting.

Larger issues of policy and strategy

These require CSR to have a major role within a company in order to ensure awareness of the moral, social or ethical environment within which the company operates. This approach allows the company to take account of the views of various interest groups and thus avoid conflict in the future. In this way, management can spot areas where their policies might be in conflict with the views of the world outside. This means that CSR is apparent throughout the operations of the company. For example, in production this could involve making a commitment to use renewable resources and, in relation to employees, having a policy of not paying low wages in its factories in less economically developed countries.

The arguments for accepting social responsibilities

Specific benefits that firms might receive as a result of acting in a socially responsible manner were detailed in Chapter 42 of the AS textbook. The key argument is that social responsibility will improve the performance of companies and, eventually, be reflected in the share price, and that 'irresponsible' companies will be punished by the market. There is some evidence to support this view. For example, the rise in power of the brand means that corporate wrongdoing can immediately be punished in the marketplace by ethically aware consumers.

If social responsibilities are ignored, firms leave themselves open to pressure group action and also may not attract the employees, customers and investors they require. These consequences will ultimately affect all stakeholders, including shareholders.

Concerns about social responsibility

Despite the scandals and horror stories that emerge in the press from time to time, most experts suggest that in the UK strong public and regulatory scrutiny, as well as a major change in attitude among senior managers, has sharply raised the level of responsible business behaviour.

Of greater concern is how to ensure that these standards are maintained when operating outside the UK. China and India are becoming the workshops and back offices of many UK businesses, as more and more companies jump on the outsourcing bandwagon. More than 30% of UK companies are planning to outsource their IT infrastructure or some business processes over the next year. While customers and clients in the West may accept the policy of paying lower wages in Bombay and Shanghai, few will accept that companies should take advantage of lower standards of human and employee rights.

EXAMINER'S VOICE

The issues in Chapters 40, 41, 42, 44 and 45 overlap. For example, socially responsible firms are likely to act ethically and to take their environmental responsibilities seriously. Pressure group activity is likely to be directed at firms that do not take their social responsibilities seriously.

FACT FILE

Mike Rake, international chairman of KPMG and chairman of Business in the Community, suggests:

> Companies need to live by example; they need the determination to apply the highest standards in every country and every market place, even when those you are doing business with don't understand what the fuss is about. A key ingredient of social responsibility is an understanding of the unintended consequences of our investment strategies for developing economies. For example, at one level, moving jobs to developing countries makes sense, but if it disrupts fragile local labour markets by introducing posts that are financially more attractive than, say, working as a doctor, then the law of unintended consequences takes hold. By taking account of such factors, business can play a part in tackling social inequalities at the local level.

PRACTICE EXERCISE

Total: 25 marks (25 minutes)

1 Explain the term 'social responsibility'. *(4 marks)*

2 Briefly explain one example of how a firm might act in a socially responsible manner towards its employees. *(3 marks)*

3 Briefly explain one example of how a firm might act in a socially responsible manner towards its customers. *(3 marks)*

4 Briefly explain one example of how a firm might act in a socially responsible manner towards society. *(3 marks)*

5 State and explain three benefits to business from adopting a socially responsible approach. *(9 marks)*

6 Explain one problem that might face a business that adopts a socially responsible approach. *(3 marks)*

CASE STUDIES Corporate social responsibility in practice

Serco invests in education

Serco has a large, but diverse and decentralised, structure. Its business interests range from running the Docklands Light Railway and speed cameras to leisure centres and education authorities.

Last year, the company said it spent nearly £800,000 on community projects, which is equivalent to 1.4% of the company's pre-tax profits — above the recommended amount for FTSE 100 companies. 'It's very hard to gauge the exact amount we do and its costs,' said Gail Johnson, managing director of corporate social responsibility at Serco. 'Much of it is intangible. But we know that our reputation and standing in the community are vital to our work, so it is very important.'

One big project is the company's Skills for Life initiative, which has been developed to work in conjunction with the government's aim of helping the 4 million UK adults who have literacy problems.

'When we saw these figures we knew some of these people would be our workers,' said Johnson. 'So we decided to set up educational programmes across the group. There is one employee who took up the offer because he had suffered dyslexia for 20 years. Now he is doing an MBA. Communities get to know and like us as a company, while we get a better-trained workforce.'

Serco has similar educational projects around the world, run through the newly established Serco Foundation. An English-teaching school was recently set up in Abu Dhabi. Although the impact on business is difficult to measure, Serco is in no doubt that CSR is good for business, so the company is putting in the structures to monitor it more carefully.

Every part of Serco now has a nominated CSR representative. There is also a full-time manager looking after CSR, who is a member of the Corporate Assurance Group, reporting to the Serco Group board. The manager is supported by a global network of CSR representatives, who are responsible for implementing and embedding the model and process into Serco's business.

Source: adapted from an article in *The Sunday Times*, 2005.

Tesco faces questions over the true value of its computer vouchers

The value of computer equipment claimed by schools through Tesco's Computers for Schools promotion is substantially lower than 6 years ago, analysis by the *Guardian* has established. The fall contrasts with soaring sales and profits at the UK's biggest supermarket in the same period, and despite a steady rise to over 24,000 in the number of schools collecting the vouchers.

Analysis shows that, in terms of pure value of equipment, the scheme peaked in 1999, when schools claimed £10.5 million of equipment. In 2002 and 2003, schools claimed equipment worth only £7 million. The figure recovered to £8 million last year, but Tesco's sales in the UK have grown by 56% since 1999 and its UK profits by 65%.

Tesco will launch this year's Computers for Schools promotion in its stores today, and can be confident that, measured as a slice of sales or profits, the scheme will again cost it less. In 1998 and 1999, the value of computer equipment given to schools equated to 1.14% of the company's UK profits. That ratio has fallen every year since, and was as low as 0.52% last year.

Computers for Schools works by offering customers one voucher for every £10 they spend over a 10-week period. Shoppers donate the vouchers to schools, which can redeem them against a range of products that Tesco sources from RN Group, one of the country's biggest suppliers of computer equipment to schools.

The company describes the scheme as 'the main way Tesco invests in local communities', and its chief executive, Sir Terry Leahy, has called it a 'win-win' for the supermarket and its customers. The principle is that if Tesco's sales increase, more vouchers should be issued and the value of equipment generated for schools should also rise.

Tesco confirmed that, in popularity terms, Computers for Schools is as successful as ever; the percentage of customers collecting the vouchers has been rising steadily through the years. The supermarket may therefore face accusations that the purchasing power of the vouchers in real economic terms – ignoring movements in the retail price of computer equipment – has been gradually reduced.

In a statement to the *Guardian*, Tesco did not directly address the issues of purchasing power and price deflation, but said: 'Computers for Schools remains the biggest and best education initiative of its kind and continues to give millions of pounds worth of equipment to schools every year. Whatever way you look at it, schools are still receiving much-needed equipment that they would not otherwise be able to afford, through a scheme that basically offers something for nothing.'

Source: adapted from an article in *The Times*, 7 March 2005.

BP and Nationwide: building community relations

Building a 1,700 kilometre pipeline through the heart of Asia is bound to have an enormous impact on the many communities it passes on its journey from Baku, in Azerbaijan, through Georgia and Turkey.

BP, the company undertaking the project, known as the Baku–Tbilisi–Ceyhan pipeline, must take account of many issues, not least assessing the effect that the pipeline will have, compensating the communities in its path, employing local firms and workers, and trying to ensure that the revenue it pays to these governments is spent responsibly.

The company can demonstrate several successes in these respects. It is investing in a large agriculture programme to help local communities increase the yields from their crops and is training local firms unused to such large projects to bid for and manage pipeline subcontracting work.

'From a business point of view, it's about creating a sustainable business environment,' said Matt Taylor, BP's corporate responsibility manager. 'You have to make sure local people are getting something out of your business. If you empower local people, they will get more out of it and they will be of more benefit to you as a business. It's also about fostering stability and security, which are the conditions under which business prospers best.'

Managing projects such as these, for the benefit of local communities, is part of a growing realisation among companies that the long-term vitality of their businesses is rooted in the communities they work in.

Volunteer programmes outside the workplace are one of the most important ways of engaging with communities. Such schemes provide a range of benefits, such as creating a sense of employee pride, while improving staff retention and recruitment.

These ideas are familiar to Nationwide staff. The company sees such activities as an inherent part of its business, which is probably one of the reasons staff voted it the best big company to work for in *The Sunday Times Best Companies to Work For, 2005*.

Nationwide encourages staff to take part in volunteer work and will give them time off to do it. 'We are very proud that more than 65% of our staff are involved in one type of volunteering activity or another, whether that has been as reading mentors at the local primary school or as a special constable,' said Andrew Litchfield, Nationwide's head of social and environmental responsibility.

He believes there are many benefits in such an active volunteering programme, apart from improving Nationwide's reputation among potential employees and boosting staff morale.

'We've seen benefits in terms of people's interpersonal skills, their understanding of personal issues and their understanding of our customers. We get nothing but very good feedback from what they do. Our community involvement is firmly embedded in the history of the company as a mutual society and it's a huge advantage for us in so many ways.'

Source: adapted from *The Times Companies that Count, 2005*.

Questions

Total: 40 marks (45 minutes)

1 To what extent might the fact that corporate social responsibility (CSR) is the responsibility of senior management in a company indicate that company's commitment to social responsibility? *(12 marks)*

2 Despite the fact that claims for computing equipment have not kept pace with Tesco's sales, is the Computers for Schools initiative still a good example of a socially responsible activity? Justify your response. *(14 marks)*

3 Study the passage on Nationwide. Evaluate the view of Andrew Litchfield that social responsibility is 'a huge advantage for us in so many ways'. *(14 marks)*

CHAPTER 41

Business ethics

Business ethics was studied at AS and considered in detail in Chapter 43 in the AS textbook. Before reading this chapter, ensure that you understand the meaning of business ethics and the potential conflict between it and profit. This chapter builds upon the coverage of business ethics at AS, examining morality in decision making. It considers the potential conflict of ethics with delegation and the importance of business culture in establishing an ethical approach. It assesses the extent to which ethical decision making is more about public relations and profit than principles.

What is business ethics?

KEY TERM

- **business ethics:** the moral principles that should underpin decision making.

A decision made on ethical grounds might reject the most profitable solution for an organisation in favour of one of greater benefit to society as a whole, or to particular groups of stakeholders. Such ethical decision making is likely to distinguish a business that is behaving ethically from one focused on profit.

Possible ethical stances

Organisations may take different stances in relation to ethics, including any of the following:

- **Viewing shareholders' or owners' short-term interests as their only responsibility.** These organisations are likely to meet only their minimum obligations in relation to other stakeholder groups and to the wider environment.
- **Recognising that well-managed relationships with other stakeholders bring long-term benefits to shareholders or owners.** The approach of such organisations is not dissimilar to the previous stance, but in addition they realise that expenditure on welfare and other provision is sensible, while not seeing it as an ethical duty.
- **Including the interests and expectations of stakeholders in their mission.** Organisations with this stance are likely to go beyond their minimum obligations. For example, they might avoid selling anti-social products or making products in a manner that is considered unethical, and would be prepared to accept reductions in profitability for the social good.
- **Taking an ideological approach and placing financial considerations as secondary.** The extent to which this stance is viable depends on how accountable the organisation is to its shareholders or owners. It is probably easier for a private, family-owned organisation to be run in this way.

FACT FILE

In 1984, an explosion at a Union Carbide plant in Bhopal, India, killed 8,000 people in the world's worst industrial accident. In 1986, the case for compensation was moved from the USA to India. It was settled out of court for just $470 million.

Advantages of ethical behaviour

Over the last 20 years, public expectation that companies will behave ethically has grown. High-profile accidents, such as the explosion in Bhopal, India, in the 1980s and more recent fraudulent activities in the banking and insurance sector have prompted demands for greater ethical accountability.

As consumers become better informed and better educated about products, processes and companies, they demand products and services that do not pollute, exploit or harm. In order to be successful, companies need to respond positively to these demands.

Ethical behaviour can give companies a clear competitive advantage on which marketing activities can be based. Indeed, some companies have developed their ethical behaviour into a unique selling point and base their marketing campaigns on these perceived differences. An example of a high-profile company adopting this strategy is The Body Shop. Not only does the company seek to support relatively poor communities in the less developed world, but it also publicises these actions. By creating a caring image through its marketing, The Body Shop hopes to gain increased sales.

Firms that adopt ethical practices may also experience benefits in relation to their workforce. They may expect to recruit staff who are better qualified and motivated. Employees can be expected to respond positively to working for a business with a positive ethical image and this can lead to greater competition for employment with such companies. Equally, employees may be less likely to leave. All of these factors can help to reduce the employment costs incurred by the business.

On the other hand, ethical decisions might reduce profitability by adding to costs, or might conflict with existing policies.

FACT FILE

Over 80% of FTSE 100 companies now have a code of ethics in place, according to recent research. This is a vast improvement on the situation 10 years ago, when the proportion was only a third. The comparison is highlighted in a report from the Institute of Business Ethics, which sets out a methodology for developing and implementing a code of ethics, indicating the issues that need to be incorporated. These range from environmental responsibility, whistle-blowing and data protection to conflicts of interest, bribery and gifts.

Ethics, business culture and delegation

Organisations have cultures and codes of behaviour that affect attitudes, decision making and management style within them. At the same time, organisations consist of individuals who have their own moral codes, values and principles. To some extent, it depends on which of these two influences is dominant, the corporate culture or the individual culture. If there is any conflict between the ethical position of the organisation and the moral values of the individuals it employs, then delegated decision making may not reflect the ethical position of the organisation.

If only senior managers see ethical practices and behaviour as their responsibility, the risks of delegated decision making not reflecting the ethical stance of the organisation might be higher and junior staff may take decisions that might be regarded as unethical. The potential for this problem to arise can be minimised if the culture of the organisation is one in which all employees understand the firm's ethical position and take responsibility for ensuring that their actions and decisions reflect this. Changing business cultures is not easy to achieve and investment in effective training and communication is important in order to ensure that all staff behave in an agreed ethical manner and that delegated activities are performed on an agreed ethical basis. Of course it may be that employees actually have higher standards than their managers.

There is much evidence to suggest that creating an ethical culture within a business can improve employee motivation and becomes part of a wider policy of employee empowerment.

FACT FILE

Texas Instruments and its policies on ethical business are often used as a benchmark against which other firms measure themselves. Its contention is that, for a business to behave ethically, all of its employees must behave accordingly, which means they must 'know what's right, value what's right and do what's right'. (See Chapter 43 in the AS textbook for more detail on Texas Instruments.)

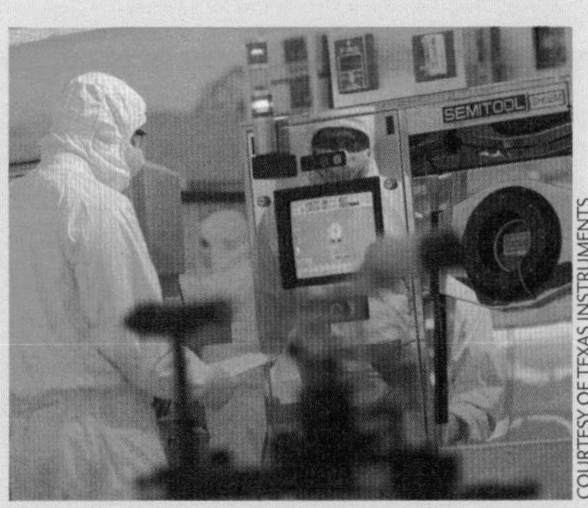

COURTESY OF TEXAS INSTRUMENTS

Ethics or public relations?

KEY TERM

public relations (PR): activities to boost the public profile of an organisation.

Public relations usually involves obtaining favourable publicity via the press, television or radio. Unlike advertising, it is not paid for and there is no control over its content. When a business behaves ethically, it may be good for PR. Indeed, some commentators suggest cynically that good PR is the main reason for ethical behaviour — it can help to enhance the image of a business and is likely to generate more goodwill. This in turn might lead to improved sales and may eventually boost the company's share value.

The case study on Tesco's Computers for Schools on pp. 404–05 is an example of PR. Although the article from *The Times* is implicitly criticising Tesco for the increasing disparity between the value of its sales revenue and the value of its contribution towards the Computers in Schools project, it is nevertheless giving Tesco plenty of free publicity. Regardless of the implicit criticism, readers of the article who knew nothing about the Computers in Schools project might consider shopping at Tesco in order to accumulate tokens.

EXAMINER'S VOICE

Business ethics is an important aspect of all AS and A2 specifications and is an area where you are often required to demonstrate the skill of evaluation. As this topic considers many different values, ensure that you provide well-argued points in your answers to questions about ethics, and avoid the temptation to make value judgements and assertions that are unsupported by argument or evidence.

PRACTICE EXERCISE

Total: 35 marks (30 minutes)

1 Explain the term 'business ethics'. *(3 marks)*

2 Outline two benefits to a business of operating in an ethical manner. *(6 marks)*

3 Explain two possible disadvantages to a firm of operating in an ethical manner. *(6 marks)*

4 Why is there a potential conflict between ethics and delegated decision making? *(4 marks)*

5 How might a business minimise this conflict between ethics and delegated decision making? *(4 marks)*

6 How might business culture influence the extent to which an organisation operates in an ethical manner? *(4 marks)*

7 Define the term 'public relations'. *(3 marks)*

8 How does public relations differ from advertising? *(2 marks)*

9 State three examples of favourable public relations that you have read or seen recently. *(3 marks)*

CASE STUDY Ethics and farming

Ethics is an increasingly important issue in relation to the farming industry. There are a number of reasons for this trend.

- There have been changes in the scale and methods of farming that have raised the profile of ethical issues. For example, intensive production methods have raised serious ethical concerns about rearing animals under 'factory farming' conditions, or growing crops intensively using the latest biotechnology.
- Businesses have seen various changes in the use of technology, many of which have raised the profile of ethical issues. Examples are the increasing use of antibiotics, genetically modified (GM) material, fertilisers and agrochemicals, as well as 'hi-tech' machinery and equipment.
- At the same time, the power of consumers, pressure groups and the media has increased, with the internet now providing huge amounts of information on every topic. Thus, issues related to intensive production and new technology are highlighted more fully and immediately.

One of the major ethical dilemmas in the farming industry is the choice between organic and intensive methods of farming.

Organic farming involves integrating animal and crop production in an economically and environmentally sustainable system, and placing priority on animal welfare. It also involves minimal use of chemicals, including pesticides, fertilisers and herbicides, and a ban on GM inputs and antibiotics. Such conditions may be desirable for the production of food, but organically produced products are more expensive than intensively farmed equivalents.

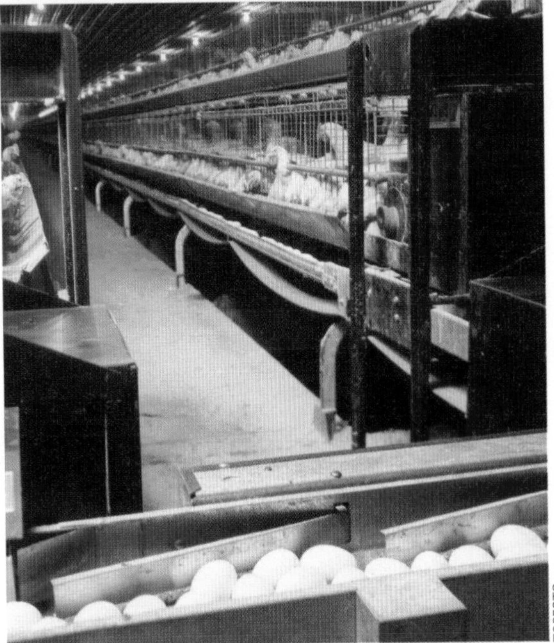
TOPFOTO

Intensive farming uses mass production techniques to increase productivity and therefore profits for farmers, wholesalers and retailers, and to reduce prices for consumers. It uses environmental control to raise production, and antibiotics to prevent disease and increase growth rates. For example, battery hens are kept in cages with no room to behave normally — they cannot stretch, flap their wings or bathe in dust. Because the environment (including lighting, ventilation and heating) is controlled, more eggs are produced than under organic or free-range systems, where hens are not so enclosed or permanently housed. Intensive farming may be ethically undesirable for the production of food, but the products produced in such a manner are less expensive than organic products.

Questions

Total: 30 marks (35 minutes)

1 Most ethical discussion centres on the behaviour of businesses, including producers, wholesalers and retailers. To what extent does the consumer have an ethical responsibility to purchase organic food? *(15 marks)*

2 Pressure from the government, the media and the public has resulted in a substantial change in business practices in the farming industry. If this pressure leads to improved and environmentally friendly farming practices, does it matter whether it is due to market forces or ethical considerations? Justify your answer. *(15 marks)*

CHAPTER 42

Environmental pressures and opportunities

This chapter considers the pressures and opportunities resulting from the environmental issues that face business. It examines the external costs that business imposes on the environment and assesses the tools available to the government in relation to pollution control. Market opportunities and the benefits that business derives from acting in an environmentally responsible manner are analysed as well as the problems that may emerge. Contingency planning as a means of minimising the impact of potential environmental disasters is discussed, together with the importance of effective resource management and the use of environmental audits. The case study at the end of the chapter illustrates the use of taxation as a possible deterrent to environmentally damaging behaviour.

Business and external costs

KEY TERM

externalities: the environmental effects of a firm's activities, which may be positive, such as job creation or providing a pleasing landscape around the factory, or negative, such as polluting the atmosphere with fumes or congesting the roads with lorries.

Negative externalities are also known as **social** or **external costs**. They are costs imposed on society by a firm. The firm does not pay for these costs, which are borne by the public, other organisations or the government. Essentially, therefore, firms fail to pay for the full cost of their actions and make private profit at the cost of social welfare.

Individuals also create external costs. For example, by travelling to work by car rather than bus, an individual creates higher levels of pollution and congestion.

Cost–benefit analysis is a method used in making decisions about large-scale investment projects, such as new roads or airports, that are likely to have an impact on the environment. This method involves costing all aspects of a project and weighing up the financial and social costs and benefits. Only if the benefits outweigh the costs should the firm consider going ahead with the project.

DID YOU KNOW?

In 2004, it was estimated that the total cost of noise at all airports in the UK was £25 million, based on the effect on house prices close to runways. A European Commission study found that air pollution from UK flights cost £119–236 million a year, which includes, among other things, the impact in terms of the NHS costs of treating respiratory illnesses.

Pollution control

In a market economy, because the external costs that a firm creates do not directly affect the profit of that firm, there is no direct incentive for the firm to minimise the external costs. This is a form of market failure that requires government intervention in order to influence the behaviour of firms and individuals. Types of intervention include:

- legislation to ban or control certain activities
- licences that allow a certain level of activity to be undertaken
- taxation to make the polluter pay and encourage firms and individuals to select options that have less impact on the environment (the case study at the end of this chapter provides an example of environmental taxation)
- fines to penalise those who carry out undesirable actions

The extent to which a firm is concerned about the external costs it creates depends on the degree of government intervention in this area, pressure group action (discussed in Chapter 44) and the extent to which the firm takes its environmental responsibilities seriously.

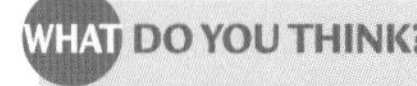

WHAT DO YOU THINK?

Should passengers have to pay for the pollution they generate by flying?

EXAMINER'S VOICE

The key issue in analysing questions on this subject is to consider both costs and benefits. In many cases, a particular course of action that may have environmental benefits may also have other social costs, such as unemployment.

WHAT DO YOU THINK?

Is it right to make 500 workers redundant because the factory they work in is polluting the environment? It is important not to ignore one side of the argument in favour of another.

The opportunities provided by environmental responsibility

Taking account of environmental responsibilities can be beneficial for business as well as for the environment.

Marketing opportunities

A good reputation in relation to environmental issues can act as a positive marketing tool that encourages consumers to choose one brand over another. As a result, many firms have spent time and money building up a 'green' image as an integral part of their marketing strategy. Examples are the

Co-operative Bank (considered in Chapter 42 of the AS textbook) and The Body Shop. In addition to increased sales and possibly stronger brand loyalty, a 'green' firm may be able to charge a higher price for its products. Many different products, from shampoos to coffee to banks, trade on the environment as a unique selling point. However, the increasing significance of the whole area of corporate social responsibility (CSR), which includes social and environmental responsibility, suggests that, eventually, a 'green' image will not be a unique characteristic of certain products, but a requirement for all.

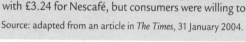

FACT FILE

Sales of Cafédirect, one of the UK's leading fair-trade brands, have been increasing rapidly in an otherwise static market. Sales of its best-known brand, Cafédirect 5065 (named after the altitude in feet at which the best beans are said to grow), rose by just under 40% in 2003. Sales of Teadirect were up by more than a third in 2003, while the tea market as a whole declined by just over 2%. Cafédirect aims to pay producers in the developing world a better price for their commodities, and farmers receive a large premium over the market price. In 2004, suppliers of robust coffee, for example, received about $1.06 for a pound of beans compared with the market price of about $0.35. The coffee sold for a higher price than other regular brands. A 200 g jar of 5065 coffee cost £4.71 at Tesco, compared with £3.24 for Nescafé, but consumers were willing to pay this premium.

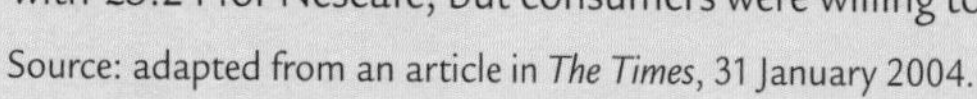
Source: adapted from an article in *The Times*, 31 January 2004.

CAFÉDIRECT

Financial advantages

Firms may find it easier to gain finance if they are able to point to a solid record of helping rather than damaging the environment. There are now a number of banks, most notably the Co-operative Bank (considered in Chapter 43 of the AS textbook), that will not invest in firms with a proven reputation for damaging the environment.

Human resource opportunities

A reputation for damaging the environment can have adverse effects on employees' perceptions of a firm and its products, leading to a demotivated workforce and adversely affecting the ability of the firm to attract high-quality applicants. An organisation that is keen to improve its overall environmental reputation and performance needs its employees to be committed and to behave in a way that is consistent with the firm's environmental stance. This commitment is likely to come from good communication and training.

Production dilemmas

Business faces dilemmas about low-cost production versus environmentally responsible production. For example, in relation to the use of raw materials and energy, firms have choices about whether to use finite resources such as coal and oil, or to use renewable resources. In many cases, the finite resources are cheaper, but their continued use will deplete supplies. In some cases, their use may also cause additional environmental damage.

INGRAM

Another environmental choice involves waste and by-products generated by production processes. Waste and by-products need to be disposed of in some way. Gases may be released from large chimneys into the environment, while liquid waste may be pumped into rivers. Solid waste is likely to be taken away and buried in a landfill site. All of these methods of disposal are harmful to the environment. In addition, disposal of waste safely is often expensive for firms and the alternative — changing methods of production in order to reduce waste — may be even more costly. Governments can tax or fine firms that pollute the environment, but it might be cheaper for the firm to pay the fines and continue polluting than to find a better way to dispose of its waste.

FACT FILE

As the EU tries to reduce its electrical goods scrapheap, now growing at 6 million tonnes a year, recent legislation agreed by the European Parliament requires manufacturers to recycle all unwanted electronic appliances. This means that individual companies have to pay to recycle their electrical products once consumers no longer have any use for them. Similar measures, requiring motor manufacturers to cover the cost of scrapping old cars, are already on the EU's statute book. Manufacturers estimate that new fridges will increase in price as a result. However, it is hoped that the new requirements will give companies an incentive to design the most environmentally friendly equipment possible.

WHAT DO YOU THINK?

Should firms operate at the lowest cost or should they operate at the most environmentally responsible level, regardless of costs?

Environmental responsibility and contingency planning

KEY TERM

contingency planning: planning for unexpected, often unwelcome events in order to minimise their risks and costs.

The aim of contingency planning is to minimise the risks and costs of an environmental disaster, such as a leakage or spillage of dangerous substances, by limiting its immediate impact and its long-term consequences for the company in terms of reputation and demand. Many large companies have environmental policies aimed at minimising any damage that their activities might cause to the environment. If a firm is prepared, it should be in a better position to manage any crisis that occurs. The following Fact File indicates how Severn Trent, the water, waste and utility services group, tries to anticipate and manage climate change in order to minimise the potential risks and costs to the business. Contingency planning is considered in detail in Chapter 54.

FACT FILE

Climate change is no longer a distant environmental issue for Severn Trent. The water, waste and utility services group sees global warming as a reality that it must tackle today if its business is to prosper tomorrow. The reason it is taking climate change seriously now is that it expects to be one of the first companies to be affected by it, according to Andy Wales, Severn Trent's group head of corporate responsibility. 'Climate change is by far the most important environmental issue for us,' he said. 'The probability of extreme drought or flooding occurring in any given year is rising. Drier summers would put more pressure on the group's water resources, and wetter winters would mean flooding, which would threaten sewerage systems,' said Wales. The group must also take account of factors such as how higher temperatures affect the rate at which waste degrades and produces landfill gas.

'Anticipating and managing the effects of climate change would help minimise the risks and costs to Severn Trent's business,' said Wales. 'We've done a lot of thinking about the kind of risks we face and we have identified 150 potential climate hazards.'

As well as making sure it deals with the effects of climate change, the group, which has a turnover of £2 billion, is trying to limit the impact its activities have on global warming. 'We generate 0.3% of the UK's greenhouse-gas emissions, so it is something we have to take responsibility for and act on.' The group is reducing this share by developing and generating renewable energy — for example, by capturing and using methane gas from landfill sites — and optimising the energy efficiency of its operations. Last year it increased its renewable electricity generation capacity by 10% to more than 100 MW, equivalent to 43% of its own electricity requirements.

Severn Trent sees climate change as the single most pressing environmental issue facing businesses today.

Source: *The Sunday Times, Companies that Count*, 2005.

If an environmental disaster occurs, the firm's image will be under serious threat. Successful public relations will often form a vital part of the management of the crisis. This means that the firm needs to communicate with its consumers, directly and clearly: for instance, using a wave of informative advertising designed to get a clear message across. This can be an expensive solution, since the advertising will undoubtedly be required to reach as many consumers as possible, as quickly as possible. Alternatively, traditional public relations methods, such as press releases and press conferences, can be used. These involve few costs, but leave the message in the hands of the journalists. So it is vital that the firm manages its press releases and press conferences as clearly and openly as possible.

Resource management

KEY TERM

resource management: the way in which firms utilise their resources or inputs in the production process, involving the integrative management of time, people, materials and money.

Effectively managed resources result in increased efficiency and are likely to reduce costs and increase profit margins. Systems such as lean production, covered at AS, assist in this process by minimising wastage of all resources. More competition, both in domestic markets and abroad, means that there is an ever-increasing need to control costs. This, together with the growing importance of considering the impact of actions on the environment, means that better resource management is vital for a firm to survive and to prosper.

Environmental resource management aims to ensure that a business has a comprehensive overview of any project it is involved with and considers its wider impact. (See Fact File on page 403 and the article on the BP pipeline on page 405.)

Environmental audits

KEY TERM

environmental audit: an independent check on a firm's polluting activities, such as emissions, wastage levels and recycling.

An environmental audit is an organisation's key to environmentally responsible behaviour. It:

- identifies the ways in which the business interacts with the environment
- establishes priorities in tackling environmental issues
- establishes policies and procedures
- identifies responsibilities
- commits the organisation to train staff on environmental matters
- establishes standards of monitoring performance

An increasing number of companies have been publishing annual environmental audits for years; however, there is no legal obligation to do so. As a result, firms that perform poorly in this area are unlikely to publish the results of any audit.

A starting point might be a SWOT analysis, concentrating on environmental **s**trengths, **w**eaknesses, **o**pportunities and **t**hreats. Figure 42.1 provides the environmental SWOT analysis for an imaginary company.

Strengths	**Weaknesses**
• Public image for 'greenness' • Recycling activities • Staff involvement in green activities • Environmentally friendly products	• Continuing emissions into the atmosphere • High energy use • Toxic waste • High dependence on road transport
Opportunities	**Threats**
• Scope for waste reduction • Continuing rise of the green consumer • R&D advantages in developing green products	• Potential legislation • Rising energy and landfill costs • Potential accidents and their impact on image

Figure 42.1 *SWOT analysis for an imaginary company*

PRACTICE EXERCISE

Total: 40 marks (35 minutes)

1 How do external costs differ from other costs? *(4 marks)*

2 Give two examples of external costs. *(2 marks)*

3 Explain the meaning of 'cost-benefit analysis'. *(3 marks)*

4 Identify two examples of investment projects for which cost-benefit analysis might be used. *(2 marks)*

5 Explain two ways in which acting in an environmentally responsible way might benefit a firm. *(6 marks)*

6 Explain two problems a firm might face as a result of acting in an environmentally responsible way. *(6 marks)*

7 What is contingency planning? *(3 marks)*

8 How might effective PR minimise the impact of an environmental disaster for a firm? *(4 marks)*

9 Explain why resource management can benefit a business. *(4 marks)*

10 State three ways in which government could encourage business to reduce pollution. *(3 marks)*

11 What is an environmental audit? *(3 marks)*

CASE STUDY Air travellers may be charged for climate damage

Airline passengers may be forced to pay higher fares because they are not covering the cost of the environmental damage done by their flights, the government said yesterday.

The aviation industry is facing an annual bill of £1.4 billion to compensate for the global warming caused by carbon emitted from aircraft, according to Treasury calculations.

Passengers on long-haul flights are likely to see the sharpest increases in fares if the government imposes a green tax on air travel.

Yesterday's paper calculated that a Boeing 747 travelling 3,700 miles, the distance from London to Miami, would emit 171 tonnes of carbon. The cost of the environmental damage caused by the flight is put at £12,000. The cost per passenger would therefore be £40, based on British Airways' current record of selling 300 seats on a 400-seat 747.

The paper also measures the climate change costs of the 8 tonnes of carbon emitted by a Boeing 737 flying 600 miles, the distance from London to Nice. Each passenger would pay about £4, based on an average of 135 seats sold on the aircraft.

TOPFOTO

A Treasury consultation paper, 'Aviation and the Environment', concluded: 'Full environmental costs are not currently factored into the prices paid by those who benefit from aviation. Hence there is a case for the government to intervene.'

The paper considers the cost of air pollution and noise caused by aviation, but concludes that these are negligible compared with carbon emissions.

The industry argues that it already contributes some £800 million a year in air passenger duty, but the Treasury has previously made clear that the air passenger tax is not an environmental tax.

The paper said that forcing passengers to pay the environmental cost of their flights would reduce demand by 10%. This suggests that passenger numbers may grow to only 450 million by 2030, meaning the southeast would require only two new runways, not three.

Mike Toms, BAA's planning director, said that a new charging structure was needed that more closely reflected the environmental cost of each flight and gave the industry an incentive to purchase quieter, less polluting aircraft. 'We are not arguing that taxes should be used to stop people flying, but we would want people to fly in the most environmentally efficient way,' he said.

Source: adapted from an article in *The Times*, 15 March 2003.

Question

Total: 15 marks (20 minutes)

Discuss the possible impact on airlines of the plan to charge passengers prices that reflect environmental as well as general business costs.

CHAPTER 43

Political change

This chapter considers how political change in a country can create new opportunities as well as constraints for business. Chapter 38 examined changes resulting from the addition of ten new countries to the EU and particularly those from central and eastern Europe. This chapter revisits some of the issues discussed there and develops the analysis further.

The impact of political change in the UK

Political change can create new opportunities for business as well as introduce new constraints. The election of governments in the UK, whether Conservative or Labour, usually has relatively little impact on the business environment. However, the election of a Conservative government, led by Margaret Thatcher, in 1979 had a huge impact on the economy and the business environment, and significantly changed business conditions.

The changes placed a much greater emphasis on the market with the introduction of an extensive policy of privatisation and deregulation, and legislation to reduce the power of trade unions and 'free up the labour market'. Despite the election of a Labour government in 1997, there has been no return to the previous, more interventionist, government policy.

The impact of political change in central and eastern Europe

The fall of the communist governments in central and eastern Europe (CEE) in the late 1980s and the 1990s had major implications for businesses in the UK and the rest of Europe. In most cases, the new governments wanted to replace the old centrally planned systems, which were thought to be inefficient, with market-based systems. As a result, many of these countries have undertaken huge privatisation policies and, in the early years of this process, recruited experts from the UK and other western economies to advise on the transfer of assets from the public to the private sector.

Opportunities

Opportunities available to UK businesses include:

- The CEE countries have a combined population of over 100 million and a wide range of resources. As a result, they offer new **market opportunities** for companies that face mature and often saturated markets in western Europe. For example, chocolate and detergent producers, as well as supermarkets, have been eager to establish their brands there.
- **Wages and salaries** are much lower in central and eastern Europe. For

example, the average annual salary in Estonia is only £4,100, meaning that unit costs there are low compared with operating in western Europe.

- **Rents** are lower than in western Europe and, because there are fewer stringent **controls on production**, the associated costs of, for example, pollution control are also lower, again contributing to lower unit costs.
- In many cases, governments are keen to attract western European businesses to locate in these economies and do this by providing **tax advantages and government funding**. For example, in Estonia some company taxes are as low as 0% in order to attract foreign investment, and in Slovakia government subsidies of over £200 million were provided to US Steel when it located in the country.

FACT FILE

Germany's Chancellor Gerhard Schroeder has said that Estonia's 0% company taxes are driving jobs away from Germany. But the Estonian Prime Minister, Juhan Parts, defends his policies by saying: 'We are trying to encourage business to come to Estonia and to motivate entrepreneurs, both domestic and foreign. The tax system is very effective and it is trying to create jobs here.'

Businesses in the EU have sought to take advantage of the CEE markets in a number of ways:

- **Joint ventures** — where EU firms contribute cash, machinery and management skills, while the host country provides land, buildings and labour. As wages and rents are lower, and in some cases controls on production and pollution are less stringent, EU firms gain a low-cost means of production and access to a relatively untapped market (see Figure 43.1).
- **Technical cooperation** allows some co-production, short of a formal joint venture. Such agreements might encompass joint assembly of products or the creation of assembly plants in the host countries near to potential markets, as with Volvo cars in Hungary. This reduces production costs for western producers, while offering eastern firms technical expertise.
- **Selling technology and expertise** to producers in CEE countries, often in the form of licences to produce particular products. For example, Coca-Cola has granted a licence to allow manufacture in Bulgaria, which provides a cheap method of extending its market.

Enterprise Russia

Does your company want a hassle-free way to get its products onto the Russian market?

We specialise in locating Russian companies looking for joint ventures and manufacturing under licence agreements.

Does your company have trade waste of surplus production?

Remember: 'one man's waste is another man's gold!'

If you think we can help turn your expansion plans into reality or turn your waste into gold, e-mail us NOW!

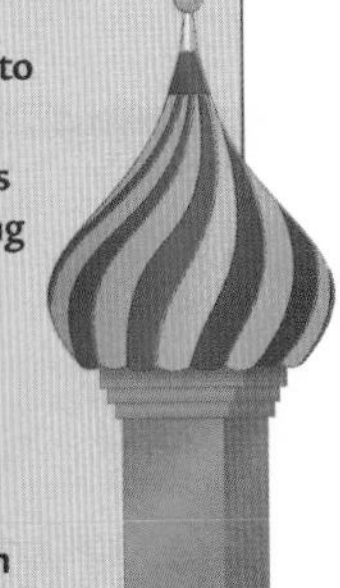

Figure 43.1 *Advertisement for Enterprise Russia*

Constraints

- **Average incomes** in CEE countries are much lower than in the EU (see Appendix 2 on p. 388). It was mentioned earlier that the average annual salary in Estonia is only £4,100, which means that consumers have relatively little income to spend on the products of EU firms.
- The **political systems** of many CEE countries are relatively immature, so trading conditions may be unpredictable or uncertain. However, the situation

is changing quickly, especially in those countries that have joined the EU.

- Excessive **bureaucracy** is a feature of planned economies and is a characteristic that the CEE countries are working hard to reduce. From a business perspective, bureaucracy can mean delays in receiving planning permission to build new premises, or permission to employ local people. However, again the situation is changing quickly: for example, the World Bank in 2004 suggested that Slovakia had improved its business climate the most by cutting the time needed to start a business, reducing red tape and making it easier for firms to collect debts (see the case study at the end of this chapter).
- In theory, under a planned economy, inflation does not exist because prices are set by the state. Following the liberalisation of their markets, the former planned economies experienced **high inflation rates** — in some cases as high as 1,000% — but by the late 1990s these had been brought under control. An effect of high inflation was that some businesses reverted to bartering for resources, exchanging their products for other goods or services, or for currencies with more stable values, such as the dollar.
- Changing from a planned economy to a market economy does not take place overnight. From a business point of view, short-term but significant problems are bound to emerge as a result of the **lack of a commercial infrastructure** that in western Europe we take for granted. For example, businesses will have problems raising finance due to a lack of commercial banking institutions that are able to loan money and the absence of a stock market where shares in a company can be sold to raise finance. Transport, communications and markets for buying and selling goods will not be ready for the level of business activity that will take place under a market system, resulting in late deliveries, a lack of information and a restriction in selling opportunities.

DID YOU KNOW?

The control of inflation was a condition that had to be met for those countries that joined the EU in 2004.

WHAT DO YOU THINK?

What does a rate of inflation of 1,000% actually mean for a consumer, for an employee and for a business?

PRACTICE EXERCISE

Total: 35 marks (30 minutes)

1. How might a greater emphasis on the importance of the market in an economy affect business? *(4 marks)*
2. Give two examples of the privatisation and deregulation strategy undertaken by the government in the UK during the 1980s. *(2 marks)*
3. Explain how reducing the power of trade unions might 'free up' the labour market. *(3 marks)*
4. Distinguish between a centrally planned system and a market-based system. *(4 marks)*
5. Identify and explain two advantages for UK businesses of the political changes that have taken place in central and eastern Europe. *(6 marks)*
6. What is a joint venture? *(2 marks)*
7. Explain two other ways in which UK businesses have tried to take advantage of the opportunities in central and eastern Europe. *(6 marks)*
8. Briefly explain two consequences for business of a poor commercial infrastructure. *(4 marks)*
9. Explain two consequences for business of very high inflation rates. *(4 marks)*

CASE STUDY Slovakia

In 1998, Slovakia's economy lagged behind its neighbours', and reforms were badly needed. Now, things have changed almost beyond recognition. A report from the World Bank in 2004 suggested that Slovakia was one of the countries that had improved its business climate the most during 2003. It had cut the time needed to start a business, revamped labour laws, reduced red tape and made it easier for firms to collect debts. As a result, growth had picked up and the black economy had shrunk.

Helping to drive the reform in Slovakia, as well as in a number of other European nations, was the lure of European Union membership. One of the ten new entrants that joined in May 2004, Slovakia needed to bring its domestic regulation in line with EU standards and ensure that companies were prepared for the increase in competition that was likely to follow. It now has foreign companies rushing to take advantage of its low labour costs and well-educated workforce.

Among the pioneering foreign firms that have established themselves in Slovakia are the American giant US Steel and the German car-maker Volkswagen. Both can lay a strong claim to have played a major role in transforming Slovakia's image abroad.

Volkswagen first turned up in the region in 1991, before Slovakia had won its political independence. In the years that followed, it turned a decaying and obsolete Skoda car parts factory near Bratislava into a huge, state-of-the-art production line, employing 8,000 people. The company now accounts for over 25% of Slovakia's exports, sending gleaming new Volkswagen Polos and Touaregs to markets in North America and Italy.

Its success has prompted its rivals Peugeot Citroën and Hyundai to start setting up their own factories there. Slovakia's economic fortunes are now so closely tied with those of the automotive sector that some analysts are becoming concerned. If there is a slowdown in the industry, Slovakia could be badly hit. But, according to Ludovit Ujhelyi of Slovakia's Automobile Industry Federation, the offer of more investment was simply too good to turn down. 'To concentrate our industry only in the automotive sector is a big risk,

but it's also a big chance for us,' he says. 'Really, we have no other choice but to be in the European market, and there was no one else investing here.'

At the opposite end of the country, in the poorer eastern region of Kosice, US Steel has its own production base — an enormous factory that churns out tens of thousands of tonnes of steel every day. The US giant bought the plant in 1999, after the collapse of the state-owned Eastern Slovakian Iron Works. The deal was sweetened by government subsidies worth some £280 million over 10 years — later reduced to £240 million after protests from the EU. In exchange, US Steel Kosice has agreed to safeguard the jobs of the 16,000 workers it inherited in the deal. The company is now the largest employer in Slovakia, and in a region where unemployment exceeds 20%, its presence is vital.

It is clear that both Volkswagen and US Steel enjoy the benefits of very low labour costs and low taxes in Slovakia, as well as growing markets in eastern Europe. In fact, wage costs are only half the levels in the neighbouring Czech Republic. A cynic might say that this is the only reason for doing business in Slovakia. But there are strong signs that both firms take their responsibilities seriously, and believe that their interests are best served by Slovakia's increased prosperity.

Volkswagen has deliberately recruited from outside the relatively wealthy Bratislava region, bussing in workers every day from less prosperous areas up to 200 kilometres away. It has also chosen to take on a great many younger workers, aged between 20 and 35.

US Steel Kosice, as the dominant economic force in the eastern region, also takes an interest in general welfare. It sponsors badly needed educational and infrastructural projects throughout Kosice and the surrounding countryside. It has also spent significant amounts of money reducing the pollution caused by the plant's ageing mills, investing heavily in new, more efficient technologies. All this has helped win the companies a degree of popular support in Slovakia.

There is no doubt that US Steel Kosice and Volkswagen have done well out of their investments in Slovakia. Both companies say their plants are now very profitable. In return, there is equally no doubt that their presence helped to tip the balance in favour of Slovakia's entry into the EU — and has provided a lead that other foreign companies are now eagerly following.

Source: adapted from an article at www.bbc.co.uk

Questions

Total: 30 marks (35 minutes)

1 Discuss the opportunities and constraints that political changes in Slovakia and other central and eastern European countries might offer to a UK manufacturer of car components. *(12 marks)*

2 To what extent are Volkswagen and US Steel operating as socially responsible companies or as profit-maximising companies? *(18 marks)*

CHAPTER 44

Pressure group activity

This chapter considers pressure group activity. It examines the characteristics of successful pressure groups and their activities in putting pressure on consumers, firms and governments, such as by lobbying and taking direct action against a company's image.

Pressure groups

pressure group: an organisation formed by people with a common interest or shared goal, who join together to further their interests or achieve their goals by putting pressure on the general public, governments or businesses.

Pressure groups include single-issue pressure groups, such as a group against the construction of a particular road or building project, and those with ongoing concerns. Examples of the latter are:

- environmental groups such as Greenpeace
- employee groups such as trade unions
- consumer groups such as the Consumers' Association
- employer groups such as the Confederation of British Industry
- animal rights groups such as the National Anti-Vivisection Society
- human rights groups such as Amnesty International

Pressure group activity usually aims to change legislation, the actions of businesses or public opinion.

Activities of pressure groups

The activities of pressure groups include:

- lobbying politicians and other influential people
- boycotting products (that is, persuading consumers not to buy the products of a particular company)
- publicity activities to attract media attention and alert the general public (for example, organising demonstrations, approaching the media directly and getting articles or letters published, and publishing information in the press or on the internet about particular issues)
- organising demonstrations outside business premises or on a large national scale
- direct action, ranging from passive observation to causing actual damage (for example, by releasing minks into the wild) or threatening employees of particular organisations

'Consumer power scored a victory following the announcement from electronics giant Samsung that it plans to phase out hazardous chemicals in its products. Seeing its brand-name products graded red (i.e. containing hazardous chemicals) on the Greenpeace database prompted the company to do the right thing on dangerous chemicals.'

Source: Greenpeace website, 17 June 2004. www.greenpeace.org

Characteristics of successful pressure groups

- **Financial resources for public relations (PR) activities.** A well-financed pressure group is more likely to achieve success in both marketing and organisational terms. Large pressure groups, such as Friends of the Earth and Greenpeace, run marketing campaigns in the same way that a large business might do, commissioning market research companies to help them identify the most appropriate target audience for their cause and then running large-scale, expensive advertising campaigns. Large financial resources enable pressure groups to use direct mail shots to raise awareness and attract new members, and to stage publicity-grabbing events that help public relations. To a large extent, the financial resources of the pressure group are determined by the number of members and their organisational and negotiating skills.
- **A good reputation.** The public, the media and politicians are likely to take the words and actions of a pressure group more seriously if it has a good reputation. Credibility is vital to pressure groups. Where relevant, the scientific data they provide to back up their arguments will be accepted as reliable only if their reputation is good.

FACT FILE

In 1995, Greenpeace called for a boycott of Shell over its plans to sink its oil-storage platform, Brent Spar. As a result, Shell's sales in Germany fell dramatically and the company backed down. However, subsequent fears that the new method of disposing of the platform was even less environmentally friendly damaged the credibility of Greenpeace.

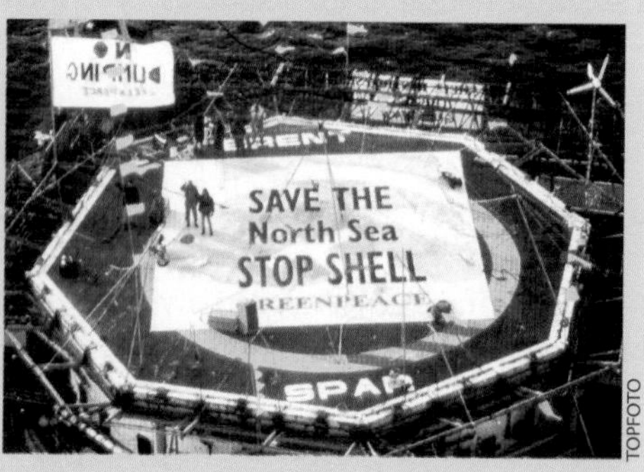

- **Public sympathy for its cause.** Some behaviour attracts more support than others, while some types of action (such as threatening employees of a medical research establishment), although gaining publicity, obtain little sympathy or support from the general public. The ideal position for a pressure group is to be campaigning for changes that the general public fully supports. In such a situation, the pressure group can act as a focus for public backing, and can more easily bring pressure to bear on politicians or companies, rather than having to battle to achieve support. Where a pressure group campaigns for causes that the public either disagrees with or simply does not know or care about, it faces a much more difficult task. It first has to raise public awareness of the issues and then persuade people of the validity of their arguments. Getting the message through is likely to take time and resources in terms of advertising, mail shots and media coverage.

FACT FILE

'Thanks to years of pressure from environmental groups, the consumers, our cyber-activists and Greenpeace, we can celebrate a victory for the environment following the announcement by Monsanto that it would suspend further development or open-field trials of its genetically engineered Roundup Ready wheat. Monsanto stated that it was deferring all further efforts to introduce the crop and that it was discontinuing breeding and field-level research of the wheat. This follows a similar announcement in 2003 when the company announced its withdrawal from the development of pharmaceutical crops.' (11 May 2004)

'Following the controversial UK government approval of genetically engineered (GE) maize for commercial planting, the only company authorised to grow GE maize withdraws its application. In a victory for activists and consumers across Europe, who lobbied for tougher legislation and boycotted GE products, Bayer CropScience, a German company authorised to plant a herbicide-resistant variety of maize known as Chardon LL, said regulations on how and where the crop could be planted would make it "economically non-viable". Chardon LL was the crop pulled up by Greenpeace UK activists in 1999. The activists were acquitted of charges of criminal damage when the court agreed they were acting in the interest of protecting the environment.' (31 March 2004)

'Bayer conceded to Greenpeace India that *all* its projects on genetically engineered (GE) crops have been "discontinued" in a letter sent by Aloke V. Pradhan, head of Bayer's corporate communications in India. This announcement followed earlier actions by Greenpeace outside Bayer's head office in Mumbai.' (4 November 2004)

Source: Greenpeace website, 31 March, 11 May and 4 November 2004. www.greenpeace.org

- **Access to politicians.** The key objective of many pressure groups is to force a change in the law — hence lobbying of politicians is often crucial. In this context, lobbying involves putting a viewpoint across to government ministers and MPs (or any individual with power and influence), who can then vote on particular pieces of legislation or encourage new laws.
- **Access to the media.** A considerable amount of pressure group activity involves using the media as a mouthpiece via public relations exercises. Some pressure groups have more success than others in attracting media attention, but as a free form of advertising it is vital for success, especially where marketing budgets are limited.

Possible responses to pressure group activity

Companies, governments and the public can respond in a number of ways to pressure group activity:

- **Companies agreeing to change.** In some situations, companies may actually agree with pressure groups and introduce the changes demanded. Such a decision could be motivated by genuine ethically, socially or environmentally responsible beliefs, by a desire to protect the image of the company, or simply by a wish to avoid the costs that might be incurred in doing battle with a pressure group. A compromise is often reached, following negotiations between the company in question and representatives of the pressure group.

- **Companies resisting pressure group demands.** Companies may launch a PR campaign that aims to counter and discredit a pressure group's claims. The fact that firms often have far more financial resources at their disposal than pressure groups means that this response can be successful. Alternatively, trade associations often have good access to government and this type of lobbying can be an effective way to ensure that a pressure group campaigning for changes in the law is defeated.
- **The government imposing change by passing new laws.** If pressure group activities are successful, the government could require firms to change their operations in some way. For example, in the case of tobacco companies, it could mean a ban on advertising on television and in other media, while in the case of a chemical company, it could involve technical requirements to reduce emissions.
- **The public changing its approach.** Pressure group activity could persuade people to change their approach to the consumption or disposal of certain products, or the pollution that accompanies certain activities. For example, environmental groups might be keen to promote the sales of reusable, organic or fair-trade products. In some instances, such a change has been viewed successfully by companies as an opportunity rather than a threat.

FACT FILE

The world's longest-running, high-profile consumer action concerns the Swiss-based company Nestlé. Many consumers have boycotted its wide range of products because of the company's policy of promoting and selling baby milk powder in less economically developed countries. The main concerns of the pressure group Baby Milk Action are that Nestlé persuades poor families to buy the product when most mothers could feed their babies naturally and that, because of poor sterilisation of babies' bottles, over 1.5 million babies a year die from diarrhoea. According to the World Health Organization, where water is unsafe, a bottle-fed child is up to 25 times more likely to die as a result of diarrhoea than a breast-fed child. Although the campaign began in 1977, Nestlé has continued to sell its product in less economically developed countries.

Pressure groups as stakeholders

Some might argue that the job of a business pressure group is to become accepted as a valid stakeholder. Where a pressure group is seeking changes in the objectives or strategy of a business, it must convince the business of its claim to be a valid stakeholder. In order for this to happen, the pressure group must persuade the firm that it represents the views of people affected by the actions of the business. If a pressure group succeeds in gaining acceptance as a stakeholder, it is in the interests of the business to listen to its views.

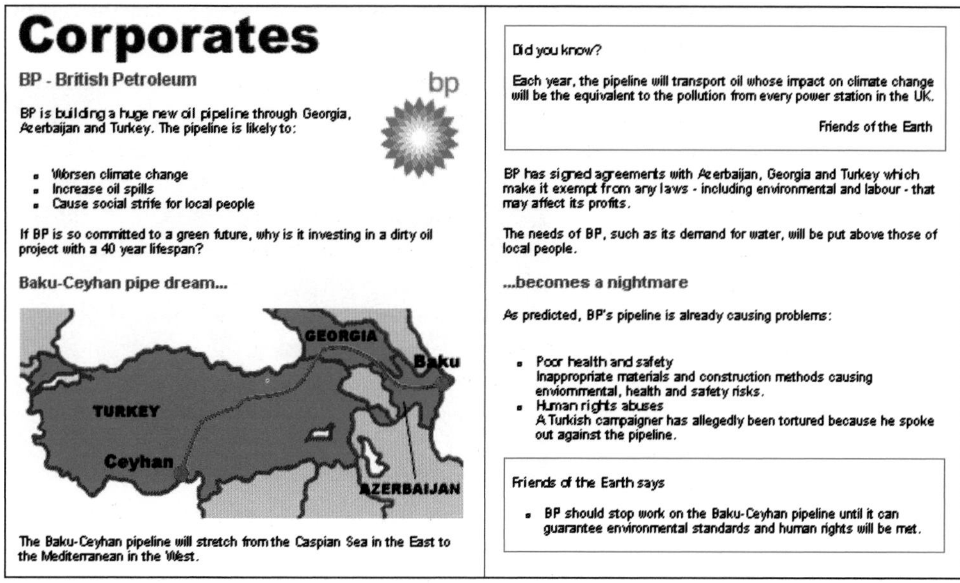

Corporates

BP - British Petroleum

bp

BP is building a huge new oil pipeline through Georgia, Azerbaijan and Turkey. The pipeline is likely to:

- Worsen climate change
- Increase oil spills
- Cause social strife for local people

If BP is so committed to a green future, why is it investing in a dirty oil project with a 40 year lifespan?

Baku-Ceyhan pipe dream...

The Baku-Ceyhan pipeline will stretch from the Caspian Sea in the East to the Mediterranean in the West.

Did you know?

Each year, the pipeline will transport oil whose impact on climate change will be the equivalent to the pollution from every power station in the UK.

Friends of the Earth

BP has signed agreements with Azerbaijan, Georgia and Turkey which make it exempt from any laws - including environmental and labour - that may affect its profits.

The needs of BP, such as its demand for water, will be put above those of local people.

...becomes a nightmare

As predicted, BP's pipeline is already causing problems:

- Poor health and safety
  Inappropriate materials and construction methods causing enviornmental, health and safety risks.
- Human rights abuses
  A Turkish campaigner has allegedly been tortured because he spoke out against the pipeline.

Friends of the Earth says

- BP should stop work on the Baku-Ceyhan pipeline until it can guarantee environmental standards and human rights will be met.

Figure 44.1 *Campaign against the Baku–Tbilisi–Ceyhan pipeline* Source: www.foe.co.uk

Different perspectives

One of the case studies in Chapter 40 (see p. 405) referred to the BP project to build the Baku–Tbilisi–Ceyhan pipeline. This was discussed in the context of a company that was making great efforts to ensure that it met its social responsibilities in relation to the project. Pressure groups such as Friends of the Earth are very much against this project and are working hard to put pressure on BP and the governments concerned either to halt or to modify the scheme. The information in Figure 44.1 comes from the Friends of the Earth website.

WHAT DO YOU THINK?

On the basis of your reading so far, do you think the construction of this pipeline should go ahead? Follow the progress of this debate in the press and on the internet.

PRACTICE EXERCISE — Total: 40 marks (35 minutes)

1. What is a pressure group? *(3 marks)*
2. Identify three different types of pressure group. *(3 marks)*
3. What is meant by 'a single-issue pressure group'? *(3 marks)*
4. Explain two different activities that a pressure group might use in order to achieve its aims. *(6 marks)*
5. Identify and explain three characteristics of successful pressure groups. *(9 marks)*
6. What does lobbying mean? *(2 marks)*
7. Explain three possible responses that a business might make to pressure group activity. *(9 marks)*
8. Why are public relations important for a pressure group and how might they be encouraged? *(5 marks)*

CASE STUDY Extremists are driving drugs firms out of the UK

Evidence that animal rights extremists are driving drug companies out of the UK emerged yesterday, with figures revealing a collapse in investment in new laboratories and the first fall in research spending in the UK for 15 years.

Capital spending in 2003 fell by nearly a fifth to £753 million — the steepest decline in more than a decade. Spending on research fell by £100 million to £3.2 billion — the first fall since records began in 1990, according to the Association of the British Pharmaceutical Industry (ABPI).

The new data, which cover 2003, come as a bill targeting animal rights extremists is listed for its third reading in the House of Lords today.

The legislation, the Serious Organised Crime and Police Bill, will outlaw 'unwarranted targeting' of people involved in the drugs industry, as well as 'economic harassment' of businesses or institutions with links to pharmaceuticals companies.

Extremists face a 5-year prison sentence if convicted under the new law, expected to receive royal assent by tomorrow.

The pharmaceutical industry association said that instances of abusive or threatening phone calls from extremists had risen fourfold over the past 2 years to more than 100, while cases in which campaigners had inflicted damage to personal or company property had almost tripled to 177 between 2002 and 2004.

Vincent Lawton, president of the trade body, said that the UK's traditionally strong position in pharmaceuticals was being threatened by violent animal rights campaigners. 'It is clear that the continuing threat posed by animal extremists is a contributory factor,' he said.

The UK investment figures are at odds with estimates for global research and development spending. According to Pharmaceutical Research and Manufacturers of America, the US trade association, global spending surged 11% to £118.3 billion in 2003.

Mr Lawton said that growing rivalry from China, India and eastern Europe and mounting red tape were also discouraging drug companies from investing in the UK.

Mr Lawton said the UK's leadership in drug development was increasingly being challenged by new centres of research in emerging markets, where companies often enjoy significant tax breaks.

Source: adapted from an article in *The Times*, 6 April 2005.

Questions

Total: 30 marks (35 minutes)

1 Using information from the case study and your own knowledge of pressure groups, answer the following question. To what extent do pressure groups ensure that the 'right' business decisions are made? *(12 marks)*

2 a Consider the characteristics and actions that are likely to make a pressure group successful. *(8 marks)*

b Discuss whether these characteristics and actions have been successful in the case of the pharmaceutical industry. *(10 marks)*

CHAPTER 45

Social auditing

This chapter focuses on the purpose and implementation of social audits and emphasises their use in providing non-financial measures of efficiency. The chapter revisits the issue of the social costs created by business activity, the market failure that this entails and the approach of government in dealing with the issue. Environmental audits, which were first encountered in Chapter 42, are discussed as an integral part of social auditing.

Purpose of social auditing

social auditing: the process by which a business attempts to assess the impact of the entire range of its activities on stakeholders and society in general.

Businesses are becoming more aware of the need to try to meet the expectations of different groups of stakeholders. At AS, consideration was given to the differing objectives of the various stakeholder groups and the fact that it may never be possible to reconcile all of these different objectives (see Chapter 50 in the AS textbook). Social auditing goes some way towards assisting businesses to address this issue and to meet their social responsibilities.

The process of social auditing is part of the move towards more scrutiny of business practices and increased availability of information for stakeholders, whether employees, consumers, pressure groups, the local community or the government. Social audits are much broader than environmental audits, which tend to investigate the impact of a business on the local environment and which are *part* of a social audit. (See Chapter 42 for more detail on environmental audits.)

DID YOU KNOW?

Social auditing is now more commonly known as corporate social responsibility (CSR) reporting.

Implementation of social auditing

Social auditing involves each of the following stages:

- identifying social objectives and ethical values
- defining stakeholders
- establishing social performance indicators
- measuring performance, keeping records and preparing social accounts
- submitting accounts to independent audit and publishing the result

The process is described in more detail below:

1 Corporate social responsibility takes in the environment, employees, customers and the local community. However, there is no fixed list of issues

in CSR. It should embrace all the non-financial impacts of the company, which are broadly in three areas: ethics, interactions with people inside and outside the company, and how the company affects the environment.

2 The company needs to set priorities. It should decide what issues matter for the organisation by talking to employees, customers and investors.

3 The company should weigh up its values. A CSR policy cannot be created in isolation from the values of the company. CSR is about the behaviour of the company and the only way this can be judged effectively is against the values that the company has set itself.

4 The company needs to find where it is at by conducting an internal audit to check what CSR activities are already carried out — for example, measuring waste output or contributing to the local community. Big organisations should start by sampling just a small proportion of their locations.

5 The board of directors needs to be supportive. It is vital to secure backing from the top, so that CSR is embedded in the corporate business strategy rather than simply an add on.

6 Targets need to be set and methods of monitoring and measuring introduced. The company needs to measure its impacts and set itself targets to demonstrate progress. Some areas are more conducive to numerical targeting than others. For example, it is relatively straightforward to set targets and measure waste output, but in the safety arena it would be very difficult to set a target for fatalities, so other ways of measuring progress need to be established.

7 In order to ensure that CSR is more than a PR exercise, companies need to be open and transparent and be able to acknowledge their weaknesses and explain how they are going to improve.

8 The report needs to be published and available. A common format is to include a concise summary in the company's annual report, backed up by a much more detailed report available online.

Business in the Community (BIC) was formed 23 years ago when a group of UK companies decided to improve the way that business affects society. It now has 750 member companies, including 72 of the FTSE 100, and a further 2,000 participate in its programmes and campaigns. In 1998, it created the Corporate Responsibility Index when it decided that companies needed a way to measure and report on responsible business practice.

Non-financial measures of efficiency

A social audit results in the production of a set of social accounts that attempt to evaluate performance against a set of non-financial criteria. Just as financial ratios allow a firm to judge and compare financial management and performance over time and within and between companies, social ratios can be used to examine how well a company is performing in relation to a range of 'social' issues.

BIC suggests that an audit might be divided into four sections, each of which explores a particular area of responsibility that a business needs to consider. The four sections are:

- **The workplace.** In this area, a business needs to consider:
  - how well it is treating its employees and how well it values them
  - how well it monitors health and safety-related accidents and the strategies it has in place to reduce accidents
  - the range of salaries in the organisation from the highest to the lowest
  - whether it is respecting human rights
  - the extent to which it is employing individuals from minority ethnic groups
- **The marketplace.** Here a business needs to consider:
  - the extent to which it is responding to its customers' needs and concerns
  - the extent to which it trades with ethically sound suppliers
- **The environment.** Here a business needs to consider:
  - the extent to which it is using renewable raw materials and recycling inputs
  - how effectively it is monitoring the pollution and emissions it creates and the waste it generates
  - whether it is setting targets in this area and the extent to which it is reaching them
  - whether it is talking to pressure groups
- **The community.** In this area, a business needs to consider the extent to which it is communicating with, helping and giving something back to the community.

The value of social audits

Social auditing or CSR reporting, if done seriously and effectively, is beneficial both for business and for stakeholders.

Research suggests that graduates and, in particular, post-graduates with MBA (master of business administration) degrees favour companies that are able to demonstrate high levels of social responsibility.

A social audit provides information to all the stakeholders of a business about the extent to which it is meeting its non-financial objectives. Evidence suggests that consumers increasingly prefer to purchase their goods and services from 'responsible' businesses. Social audits enable consumers to be more informed about which firms to purchase from and which firms to avoid. They enable pressure groups to gain access to valuable information, which may inform their campaign against a particular firm or minimise their complaints against it. They also assist government in monitoring the behaviour of firms and identifying the need for legislation or regulation in certain sectors of business.

Social auditing

FACT FILE

British American Tobacco (BAT), the major cigarette manufacturer, produces CSR reports. The anti-smoking group ASH calls the whole idea laughable. BAT's CSR report defines targets for reducing energy use, water consumption, CO_2 emissions and waste production, and commits itself to enlightened employment practices. This is at odds with what many see as BAT's ruthless marketing to entice young people to smoke, as illustrated by the situation when BAT employees were caught on television handing out packets of Benson and Hedges to teenage volleyball players in the Gambia. BAT helped to draw up the International Tobacco Products Marketing Standards, intended to bring worldwide marketing in line with UK restrictions. However, it does not fund, for example, anti-smoking campaigns among the young.

WHAT DO YOU THINK?

How useful is a social audit? Can a company such as BAT, which produces an arguably lethal product, be socially responsible? Can an organisation such as BAT reconcile its business interests with people's health?

A social audit provides employees with information about the non-financial performance of the whole organisation rather than simply the department or office they work in. It ensures that senior management has a complete view of the impact of the firm's activities on all of its stakeholders, thus identifying areas for improvement and encouraging more informed decision making. This is particularly important for large organisations and multinational companies, such as BP, which have businesses in many different locations worldwide.

By opening up its activities to public scrutiny, a social audit might deter future criticism of a firm, which in turn might reduce the actions of pressure groups. This is more likely to be the case if the social audit is carried out by independent consultants or is independently scrutinised and published in full. Just as financial audits are carried out by independent experts who check to make sure that the financial performance of the business, as shown in its accounts, is accurate, so an independent audit, carried out against widely accepted standards, ensures fairness and comparability in the results.

Of course, undertaking social audits may highlight areas that need improving and that will incur high costs. Firms may be reluctant to pursue developments that will incur these costs, but pressure from stakeholders and more responsible competitors is likely to mean that, eventually, they will have no choice.

FACT FILE

'Issues that many managers think are soft for business, such as environment, diversity, human rights and community, are now hard for business,' says David Grayson, a director of Business in the Community (BIC). 'They are hard to ignore, hard to manage, and very hard for businesses that get them wrong. However, managed well, these issues can be a source of competitive advantage.'

Social costs and market failure

As mentioned in previous chapters, the social or external costs of a firm's activities constitute a form of market failure. For example, assume that the social costs of certain business activities are air and water pollution. Such pollution might produce chest infections and other illnesses, which in turn add to the costs of the NHS. The NHS is funded by the government and thus the public. If the principal cause of pollution is the activities of business, the market mechanism is failing because, although business is bearing the financial costs of its activities, it is not bearing the full cost(financial and *social*). Market failure often leads to a need for government intervention.

To date, the government has stuck to a policy of encouraging compliance in relation to social auditing. 'The voluntary nature of CSR is its strength. Regulation would put a dead hand on innovation, creativity and imagination,' said Stephen Timms, the CSR minister in 2003. However, many believe that the voluntary approach has failed and there has been growing pressure to make it compulsory for firms to engage in some level of social auditing. As a result of such pressure, from April 2006, under the Department of Trade and Industry's 'Operational and Financial Review', all public limited companies (plcs) must provide information on the environmental, social and ethical risks and opportunities faced by the business. Private limited companies (ltds) will be exempt, but it is hoped that they may wish to consider introducing similar procedures because of the benefits mentioned above.

Most commentators are in favour of this move and few stakeholders are against it. However, critics of the trend towards full social auditing suggest that companies that pursue social goals could be neglecting shareholder interests and taking decisions on behalf of others about what they think is right. One of the most cogent statements of their case came from the free market economist Milton Friedman in 1962: 'If businessmen do have a social responsibility other than making maximum profits for stockholders, how are they to know what it is? Can self-selected private individuals decide what the social "interest" is?'

WHAT DO YOU THINK?

To paraphrase Milton Friedman, do you think that business has a social responsibility other than making maximum profits? If so, why? Should self-selected private individuals or the government decide what the social 'interest' is?

PRACTICE EXERCISE 1 Total: 40 marks (35 minutes)

1. Explain the purpose of a social audit. *(3 marks)*
2. What is meant by an 'environmental audit'? *(3 marks)*
3. What is meant by 'non-financial measures of efficiency'? *(3 marks)*
4. Identify the four sections that Business in the Community suggests should be included in a social audit. *(4 marks)*
5. Give three examples of what a firm might review in each of the four sections (12 examples in total). *(12 marks)*

6 Explain the value to the government of businesses producing social audits. *(3 marks)*

7 Define the term 'social cost' and give two examples. *(5 marks)*

8 Explain the term 'market failure' in relation to this topic. *(4 marks)*

9 What additional information are all public limited companies required to provide from April 2006? *(3 marks)*

PRACTICE EXERCISE 2

Total: 30 marks (30 minutes)

1 Assess the difficulties that an organisation might face if it were required to produce a social audit of its activities. *(12 marks)*

2 Which is more important for a business, financial reporting or social reporting? Justify your answer. *(18 marks)*

Module 6

Objectives and strategy

> "Even if you are on the right track, you'll get run over if you just sit there."
>
> Will Rogers

CHAPTER 46

Financing growth

This chapter examines sources of finance, both external and internal, the effects of growth on cash flow and the risks of overtrading. Sources of finance were considered in detail at AS (see Chapter 14 of the AS textbook). Here the emphasis is on the importance of sufficient and appropriate forms of finance, whether for start-ups or growing firms.

Reasons for the growth of firms

Growth is usually seen as a natural development for a company. It can provide benefits and opportunities for a business and for its stakeholders. At a basic level, growth enables a company to reach breakeven and make profit. It provides more opportunities for a company to take advantage of economies of scale, and a growing and dynamic company is more likely to remain competitive. Growth by diversification allows a company to spread risks, and a large company with plenty of assets and diversified activities will find it easier to cope with recession and fluctuations in the business cycle.

Despite this, growth can be risky if it is not managed well and, in particular, if its finances are not well planned. A growing company requires financial resources that are both sufficient and appropriate for its situation.

Sources of finance

The sources of finance considered at AS, listed in Table 46.1, are categorised into external and internal and short-term and long-term sources.

***Table 46.1** Sources of finance*

	External sources of finance	
Internal sources of finance	**Short term**	**Long term**
Retained profit	Trade credit	Share capital
Controlling working capital	Debt factoring	Bank loan
Sale and leaseback of assets	Bank overdraft	Debentures
Asset sales	Hire purchase	Venture capital
	Leasing	Grants

EXAMINER'S VOICE

Even though no interest is paid on internal sources of finance, there is an opportunity cost in using them.

EXAMINER'S VOICE

Ensure that you are familiar with the sources of finance listed in Table 46.1, which were originally studied at AS.

Internal sources of finance are likely to lead to relatively slow growth, but the lack of interest payments means that growth is less costly. On the other hand, external sources of finance allow for more rapid growth, but at a cost in terms of interest payments and the risk, depending on the state of the economy, of increases in interest rates.

Factors determining the most appropriate source of finance

The source of finance must be appropriate and the level of finance sufficient to meet the needs of the particular situation. This depends upon a range of factors:

- **The type of business** — whether it is a sole trader, private limited company (ltd) or public limited company (plc).
- **The stage of business development** — whether it is a new or an established business. In general, a new business will find it more difficult to obtain finance than an established business with a good reputation.
- **The success and financial strength of the business.** Adequate collateral and a good track record will encourage lenders and investors.
- **The state of the economy and the stage of the business cycle.** Boom conditions will encourage confidence and a willingness to invest in businesses that might appear too risky in less prosperous times.
- **The attitude of shareholders.** There may be a conflict of interest between shareholders and the company's long-term interests. Shareholders may want an immediate return on their investments in the form of high dividends, whereas a company's growth strategy will benefit from more retained profit and lower dividends.
- **The cost of finance.** This includes not only interest rates for loans, but also the costs of advertising and administration involved in share issues and rights issues.
- **The use of funds** — whether for fixed assets (**capital expenditure**), in which case long-term finance is required, or for working capital (**revenue expenditure**), in which case short-term finance is required.
- **The timing of the finance.** Short-term finance is usually for less than 1 year and includes bank overdrafts and trade credit. Medium-term finance is usually for 1–5 years. Long-term finance is usually for more than 5 years and includes equity (ordinary share capital), debentures, loans and venture capital.

TOPFOTO

> **EXAMINER'S VOICE**
> Note the importance of integration in business studies and the value of being able to apply knowledge gained in different modules. Refer back to Chapters 10–16 and review your knowledge of ratio analysis and gearing in particular.

- **The effect on the balance sheet and financial ratios** — particularly the effect on the gearing ratio and what implications this has for the business. A company that is already highly geared may prefer to raise more finance by issuing shares, thus avoiding the risk of an increase in interest rates on its long-term loans.
- **The level of risk versus the level of control.** Borrowing increases the gearing of a company and therefore the level of risk associated with the possibility of a rise in interest rates. On the other hand, the issuing of share capital, or of extra share capital, dilutes control and ownership in the company.

Table 46.2 provides examples of imaginary business growth scenarios requiring finance that are matched with the most appropriate source of finance. The matching takes into account the factors noted above.

Table 46.2 Finance requirements and sources of finance

Business scenario requiring finance	Source of finance
The company is earning high profits and wishes to expand further in a steady manner. Its shareholders are agreed on its expansion strategy.	Retained profit
As part of its expansion plans, the firm is purchasing a new office block that will eventually return the initial investment. It then intends to repay the sum needed.	Debentures
The firm is large and is seeking to undertake a major expansion programme. Currently, interest rates are very high and this has reduced business activity. However, the organisation is confident that the programme will start to produce good returns in 5–10 years' time and eventually reap very high rewards.	Ordinary shares
A small retailer is hoping to expand and increase its stocks of confectionery items and newspapers, but has no money to purchase them.	Trade credit
An established firm is hoping to update its computer network to facilitate its expansion plans and has calculated a 3-year payback on the investment.	Bank loan
A small business is involved in a very high-risk, but potentially very profitable, activity. The current owners are prepared to share the ownership of the business, if necessary.	Venture capital

> **EXAMINER'S VOICE**
> Selecting and justifying a source of finance for a particular business need allow you to demonstrate the skill of evaluation.

Cash flow and overtrading

In practice, most of the financial problems that accompany business growth are related to overtrading and cash-flow difficulties.

Cash flow

Cash-flow planning (considered in Chapter 13 of the AS textbook) is as important for a growing business as for a business start-up. New assets need to be purchased or hired, and adequate working capital is needed for extra raw materials and labour costs. Thus, a growing business needs to forecast its future needs by estimating the value and timing of the additional *sales* it is intended that growth will bring, as well as estimating the value and timing of the additional *costs* that growth will generate. Obtaining this information enables the business to produce a cash-flow forecast to ensure that the necessary working capital is available.

If expansion involves a specific investment project, such as new production facilities, a business should also undertake an investment appraisal (see Chapter 18) to make sure that the return from the expansion project is acceptable. It should then ensure that sufficient and appropriate funding is available to cover both fixed and working capital needs, and is available for long enough to repay any loans out of the profits generated by the growth of the business.

EXAMINER'S VOICE

Ensure that you understand the difference between cash and profit and their impact on a business.

Overtrading

 TERM

overtrading: where a business fails to obtain the appropriate finance to fund its growth and as a result experiences liquidity problems from growing too fast.

Overtrading is a major problem for a growing business. Failure to obtain appropriate finance places enormous strain on working capital and can force a firm into liquidation. It is therefore vital to arrange finance in advance in order to ensure there are sufficient funds to meet short-term financial commitments.

Overtrading is the cause of many business failures and is more likely if there is an ineffective budgeting system and if the rate of growth is too fast for the skills and experience of managers. It is often the unfortunate outcome of unplanned growth, such as in a situation where demand for a product increases suddenly and significantly. Because growth has not been planned for, existing stocks and production capacity are likely to be inadequate. In trying to meet demand, the firm manages to increase production but only by raising costs. In the process, because of a lack of planning, its only source of finance is likely to be its overdraft. If the business is one where debtors take time to pay, the firm will find that cash flows in more slowly than it flows out. With insufficient revenue coming in and an overdraft at its limit, a demand for payment from a creditor may force the firm into liquidation.

DID YOU KNOW?

Although growth is seen as a major objective for most companies, it is not always the best strategy. Indeed, many businesses are refocusing on their 'core business' and getting rid of costly sections acquired in earlier, often ill-planned and hasty, attempts to grow.

FACT FILE

Although it was growing steadily and profitably, the Giffen Group, which carries out electrical contracting work for railways, was being held back by the reluctance of its bank to extend its funding facilities. Yet growing to a certain scale was becoming increasingly important to the company's survival as contracts grew in size, said its chairman, Jonathon Giffen. 'In our industry, it's not unusual to have long payment terms on contracts and this was putting considerable strain on our cashflow.' The group is now sustaining its growth by using debt factoring. Giffen said: 'We were initially concerned that there would be a negative impact on our profits but the benefits far outweigh the cost.'

Source: adapted from an article in *The Sunday Times*, 3 March 2005.

PRACTICE EXERCISE 1 — Total: 40 marks (40 minutes)

1 Give three reasons why a business might wish to expand. *(3 marks)*

2 State two external sources of finance and two internal sources of finance. *(4 marks)*

3 State two short-term and two long-term sources of external finance. *(4 marks)*

4 Explain three factors that might influence the most appropriate source of finance for a growing business. *(9 marks)*

5 Why might its level of gearing influence the source of finance that a business seeks when planning expansion? *(3 marks)*

6 Explain the term 'overtrading' and state the circumstances that might lead a growing business to experience it. *(6 marks)*

7 What is the difference between cash and profit, and why is this distinction important for a growing business? *(6 marks)*

8 Examine the importance of cash-flow planning in facilitating the growth of a business. *(5 marks)*

PRACTICE EXERCISE 2 — Total: 40 marks (40 minutes)

1 Discuss the possible reasons why small firms in particular find it difficult to raise finance to fund their expansion plans. *(14 marks)*

2 Assess the extent to which financing growth by the issue of share capital or the use of retained profit is always preferable to the use of loan capital. *(12 marks)*

3 To what extent is poor financial planning rather than a lack of finance likely to be the main problem facing a small growing business? *(14 marks)*

CASE STUDY Bridging the equity gap still a headache for small firms

Many small businesses, trying to raise between £500,000 and £2 million, find themselves squeezed in an equity gap. While £500,000 is more than banks are usually willing to lend, less than £2 million is often not enough to interest venture capitalists.

One alternative is to use debt factoring (see the Fact File on p. 441 for an example) and asset-based lending, where loans are secured against the firm's assets. These methods are becoming increasingly easy to organise, said Gerry Hoare of Enterprise Finance Europe. 'Some businesses still think debt factoring and asset-based lending are for struggling companies, but that's a misconception; it is for growing ones. In fact, we would turn away struggling companies.'

One possible way to find capital is to seek a private placement, where ordinary shares are just offered to a particular individual, as there are a lot of interested private investors who are willing to invest £500,000 and more. This is a good route for small, growing businesses rather than start-up companies, whose products are still in the development stage.

Alternatively, a new exchange has been set up to help growing firms to drum up money from private investors, and even institutions. AngelBourse, which was founded last year, has just launched a national, low-cost, online trading service in unlisted companies. It aims to help find funding of between £200,000 and £2 million from professional investors for small firms with high growth potential.

AngelBourse's managing director, John Blowers, said:

Most promising businesses are looking for private investors to put together six-figure equity investments, but until now they haven't had a smart way of reporting progress or letting shareholders sell out if they choose to. If the business is growing fast, winning contracts and hiring key staff, the AngelBourse trading facility allows investors and the wider market to follow progress and trade shares based on this progress.

Question

Total: 12 marks (15 minutes)

To what extent might the new exchange, AngelBourse, improve the opportunity for small businesses to finance their growth?

CHAPTER 47

Management reorganisation during growth

This chapter examines the managerial problems encountered as an organisation grows. It identifies the particular problems of adjustment from boss to leader/manager, including the risk of loss of direction and control, and discusses the changes required in the management structure and hierarchy within an organisation. Most of the issues considered here have been covered at AS and it would therefore be useful to review areas such as organisational design and delegation (Chapters 17 and 19 in the AS textbook) before reading this chapter.

Managing growth

Growth is a difficult process to manage, especially if it is rapid. It often means that an individual owner, who has been in complete control of all aspects of a business, has to plan for, and then adjust to, handing over responsibility to others. In comparison to the boss of a small business, the leader of a large business tends to have a less hands-on approach and needs to delegate more. Equally, in a large business, the task of controlling and coordinating activities is more difficult. Many find this transition from being the boss to being a leader and a manager very difficult, but for a business to grow successfully, such a transition must be managed effectively.

Without strong and effective management, growth can result in a loss of direction and control. The demands placed on a leader/manager in relation to managing and motivating a larger team require very different skills from those needed in a business start-up situation. Introducing a solid organisational structure, having an effective management team and carrying out detailed financial and operational planning and forecasting, are vital.

There are a number of issues to consider when a business grows and the boss becomes the leader/manager:

- **Management structures and hierarchies** will need to change so that the business is better positioned to achieve its objectives. Very small start-up businesses may find that they need to create a formal structure. A business may replace its simple and clear functional structure with a complex matrix structure or, depending on the nature of the business, a product-based or region-based structure. Spans of control are likely to increase and new layers of authority and departments will need to be created. The whole process of management becomes more complex.

- There will be more **delegation**. The original owners are likely to lose much of the direct contact they had with customers, suppliers and staff, and will take on more of a managing and leading role. Professionals in finance, marketing and personnel will need to be recruited to take on growing specialist responsibilities, and an effective management team will need to be created.
- **Staff responsibilities** will need to be changed. In a start-up business, staff numbers tend to be small, with everyone taking on multiple roles. As the business and workload grows, employees will need to focus on what they do best; jobs will become more clearly defined, with job descriptions, training and development plans, and appraisal systems being introduced.
- **Staff motivation** may decline, at least in the short term, as the changes that result from growth begin to have an impact, which may in turn affect customer service. For example, in the past staff might have been used to dealing directly with the owner/boss of the business, and the additional layers of management that will be introduced as the business grows may be resented. Managing and motivating a larger team successfully will require a democratic leadership and management style. This is very different from the style of many small business owners, which tends to be rather autocratic simply because they have been used to being responsible for everything.

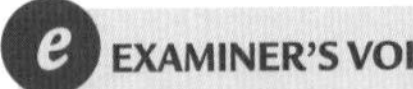

When answering questions about the problems associated with business growth, try to take an integrated approach and consider financial, marketing, operations management and human resource issues.

Bringing in a management team

As mentioned above, as a business grows it will need structuring. In most instances, the expertise to build and manage that structure will come from outside the business. A bigger company needs managers to take control of

FACT FILE

James Murray, co-founder of the telecommunications services provider Alternative Networks, wanted to expand the business but had little time to do so. 'As a board we were getting to the size where we needed a senior management team to deal with day-to-day issues. The board had five members which, with eight departments to look after, were spread too thinly and getting bogged down by nitty-gritty activities. We weren't getting the opportunities to look away from the business and work on strategy. We needed to bring people in to look after these areas and then report to the board,' says Murray. In support of its corporate objective to double existing sales of £40 million over the next 2 years, Alternative Networks appointed an HR director, a head of IT, a finance controller, a head of marketing and a client management director. While still being fully integrated into the company, Murray claims, the board has already felt the benefits of its new management structure. 'It has allowed the board to focus on new ideas, new products, strategy, acquisitions and the overall direction of the business.'

Source: www.growingbusiness.co.uk

WHAT DO YOU THINK?

Michael Dell, of Dell Computers, once said: 'If you limit a company by its structure or by the people in the company, you will, by definition, limit the full potential of that business.' Do you agree?

departments and a hierarchy that has the expertise and the time to drive it forward. The Fact File on p. 445 and the case study of Friends Reunited at the end of this chapter provide examples of how growing businesses can benefit from outside expertise.

Private investors and venture capital firms evaluate management structures and expertise before committing funding, and often insist on recruiting new or interim management. This can be seen as a way of taking control away from the founder, but it is often a means of protecting their investment by ensuring that any skills gaps are plugged and that the necessary structures and experience are in place.

DID YOU KNOW?

Interim managers are employed for a specific task or set period. They can oversee a period of development or setting up of a new structure, or can come in to run departments until existing members of staff have developed the skills to take over.

PRACTICE EXERCISE 1 — Total: 30 marks (30 minutes)

1 Explain two differences between being the boss of a small business and being the leader/manager of a large business. *(6 marks)*

2 Explain two types of change that are likely to take place in the organisational structure of a growing business. *(6 marks)*

3 Distinguish between a functional and a matrix structure. *(4 marks)*

4 Why might growth lead to a loss of direction and control? *(6 marks)*

5 Explain one advantage of increasing delegation in a growing firm. *(4 marks)*

6 Why might the owner of a growing business be reluctant to delegate? *(4 marks)*

PRACTICE EXERCISE 2 — Total: 40 marks (40 minutes)

1 Does every entrepreneur who successfully starts and establishes a company have the skills to make it a larger company? Justify your answer. *(12 marks)*

2 Assess the extent to which management and leadership style should change as a business grows. *(14 marks)*

3 To what extent does the role of the boss of a small business differ from that of the chief executive of a large business? *(14 marks)*

CASE STUDY Friends Reunited

Steve Pankhurst, founder of Friends Reunited, realised that he had a business with plenty of potential, but without the expertise to exploit it. 'We quickly became aware of the true value of the company, but we were ideas people and developers who, all of a sudden, had this massive company on our hands. We had a go at growing it ourselves and had taken on 10 people who were mostly friends and family, but we were struggling. We knew we were missing opportunities, such as global expansion, where we simply didn't have the experience.'

Friends Reunited's appointment of a new management team to drive the expansion came from an assessment of their long-term objectives for the business. They received a number of takeover offers. 'The offers we received were tempting and we listened to what they had to say. But it became clear that by selling or giving away some of the company, the site would have become over-commercialised and lost its core values. We didn't want that, so decided to keep control and bring someone in who shared our beliefs.'

Pankhurst and his co-founders appointed former *Financial Times* chief operating officer Michael Murphy as chief executive. 'We liked him because he was down-to-earth and shared our entrepreneurial feelings about not over-commercialising the site and he had the experience to grow the site internationally. Michael then brought in someone to take care of the marketing side of the company and made several other management appointments.'

Friends Reunited now operates additional businesses under the umbrella of Happy Group Ltd, with the original founders instead focused on developing new ideas.

'Bringing in management has allowed us to step away from the running of the business. It's helped stabilise the business and take it to the next level.'

It can be difficult to accept criticism about a business you've sweated blood over building. While Pankhurst says the introduction of Friends Reunited's management team went smoothly, it wasn't without its teething problems. 'When Michael came in we were still a bit hands-on, particularly on the technology side, and we were the only people who knew how certain things ran. Initially, Michael wanted to change things, such as the design, and when you've got so close to something, you can become blinkered and defensive about it. You have to learn to take a step back and accept that's why you've brought these people in.'

Source: www.growingbusiness.co.uk

Question

Total: 15 marks (20 minutes)

Discuss whether Friends Reunited was right to use outside expertise to build and manage the company as it grew.

CHAPTER 48

Problems of transition in size

This chapter considers the problems of transition in size faced by firms. It focuses on the transition from private to public limited company status, and from national to international markets, and the problems of retrenchment. As with many of the topics covered in the Objectives and Strategy section of Module 6, the emphasis is on integration and the application of knowledge gained earlier, particularly in relation to the legal structure of business, cash-flow management, management structure and operational efficiency.

From private to public limited company

EXAMINER'S VOICE

The different legal structures of business were covered at AS. Ensure that you are familiar with the characteristics and implications of private and public limited companies.

For many firms, problems arise when growth involves changing from private to public limited company status.

Going from a private limited company to a public limited company usually means floating shares on the stock market. Companies join the stock market all the time and the more optimistic the economic climate, the more new issues of shares there are. The value of a stock market listing is that a company has a higher profile and access to a large pool of capital. This can provide a more balanced capital structure, especially for highly geared firms.

Table 48.1 illustrates the fact that the number of fully listed companies has declined sharply in recent years, from almost 1,600 in 1997 to only 910 at the end of 2003.

	1997	1998	1999	2000	2001	2002	2003
Firms at the start of the year	1,593	1,570	1,474	1,315	1,227	1,120	1,016
Going private or foreign acquisition	24	37	40	86	50	33	29
Firms at the end of the year	1,570	1,474	1,315	1,227	1,120	1,016	910

Source: *The Sunday Times*, 2 May 2004.

***Table 48.1** UK companies fully listed on the London Stock Exchange, 1997–2003*

A drawback of flotation is that public companies are answerable to their shareholders and investment analysts will scrutinise the company prospectus closely. Once the company is floated on the stock market, shareholders may simply be interested in generating quick profits at the cost of longer-term success. The shareholders of a private company tend to be 'in it for the long run': for example, happy to agree to high levels of research spending and accepting relatively low dividend payouts. However, once the shareholder base is widened, the firm comes under severe pressure to generate record levels of profit year by year, even if the 'right' thing to do is to spend heavily on research in the hope of generating future success.

FACT FILE

In 1998, Google began trading as a company. In August 2004, it was successfully floated on NASDAQ. (NASDAQ is the largest US electronic stock exchange.) The flotation was structured so that the two founders will retain a major influence, owning one-third of what are referred to as 'class B' shares. These shares (which cannot be sold to the public) carry ten times the voting rights of normal class A shares. This move is as clear an indication as any that the founders still wish to run the business in the way in which they have always intended.

From public to private limited company

A number of companies have changed back from public to private limited companies. Private limited company status has the advantages of more privacy and less pressure on management resulting from share price movements. This allows management to take a longer-term view. Firms go private because, in general, there is a lack of interest in private firms. In such instances, the benefits of being listed are outweighed by the cost of meeting regulatory requirements and by the time that needs to be spent with analysts and fund managers and generally communicating with the market. The trend for turning plcs into private limited companies is growing, mostly in the form of management buyouts (see Chapter 49).

FACT FILE

Michael Fort felt he had finally made it when in 1988 Pronuptia, the bridal business of which he was chief executive, floated. 'The stock market was booming. I was 29 years old and it was all red braces and handkerchiefs. I felt really proud.' But it soon became obvious to him that the company had made a mistake. 'We were operating in a declining market where sales and profits were difficult to get. At the same time we were trying to increase our market share and kept trying to raise money to make acquisitions.' The business kept issuing more shares in an effort to raise more cash but could never increase profits to the kind of level that shareholders expected. 'We were entirely reactive, constantly trying to push up the share price and failing to focus on the running of the company,' Fort recalls. Eventually the company went private at a price well below its float price.

Source: *The Times*, 18 November 2003.

TOPFOTO

DID YOU KNOW?

Virgin was floated in the 1980s, but in 1984 Richard Branson took it back into private ownership. Branson blamed the short-termism of city investors who, he felt, might damage the long-term interests of the business. The Body Shop is another organisation that went from private to public limited and back again for similar reasons. Arcadia, Selfridges, Harvey Nichols, Hamleys, New Look, Debenhams and Pizza Express are among many well-known firms that have been taken private in the past few years. In the fitness club sector, Fitness First, Cannons and Esporta have all dropped from the quoted market.

FACT FILE

In 2003, the family-owned shoe repairer Timpson bought Minit UK, which owns Sketchley cleaners, Supasnaps and Mister Minit. Timpson now controls more than 1,000 retail outlets nationwide. John Timpson, the group's chairman, said at the time of the purchase that he was in the process of integrating the various divisions but added: 'We only have one firm plan, which is that we will not float the business. We think staying private is the best way to run the business.'

From national to international markets

Where opportunities for growth in the UK market are limited, firms may consider expanding into international markets. In addition, government competition policy may mean that further domestic growth, if it increases market share, could lead towards monopoly and provoke intervention by the Competition Commission.

International expansion is frequently a difficult process. For example, neither The Sock Shop nor Laura Ashley was successful in the USA, and Marks and Spencer has not been particularly successful abroad. Firms often make the assumption that what works in the UK will also work elsewhere. However, there is often a lack of understanding of issues such as local markets, consumer tastes and attitudes, and the best location for sales outlets, all of which can cause problems. In addition, there may be problems with control and the delegation of authority to local management.

Retrenchment

KEY TERM

- **retrenchment:** the cutting back of an organisation's scale of operations.

Just as companies encounter problems when becoming larger, so there are problems when they reduce the scale of their operations. Retrenchment can take a range of forms, each of which is likely to have different effects on various stakeholder groups and on the organisation. The overarching problems include possible damage to morale, to relationships and to trust as a result of the inevitable job losses.

Types of retrenchment

- **Halting recruitment or offering early retirement or voluntary redundancy.** Using this strategy might lessen the feelings of job insecurity among existing employees, as any actions on their part would be voluntary. On the other hand, staff who choose to retire early or take voluntary redundancy may be key people in the organisation and, if they leave, their skills and experience disappear. Cutting back in this way may provide less opportunity for the organisation to introduce change and to restructure.
- **Delayering.** Removing a layer of management from the organisational hierarchy has less impact on operations at shop-floor level and hence on production. It may empower or enrich jobs at the lower level of management, which will have to take on more responsibility. However, the workload of the remaining management team will increase, which can add to stress levels and reduce motivation. Motivation might be further affected due to loss of promotion prospects as a layer of opportunities vanishes.
- **Closing a factory, outlet or division of the business.** The effect of this for the business is to reduce overall fixed costs and hence the breakeven point. In addition, depending on the nature of the closure, capacity utilisation may rise in other factories, outlets or divisions. However, this strategy is difficult to reverse if there is an upturn in the economy. Closure will mean a loss of many good staff with valuable skills.
- **Making targeted cutbacks and redundancies throughout the business.** This strategy should allow the company to reorganise to meet objectives — for example, putting more emphasis on e-commerce. It also enables the company to get rid of less productive staff members, which might improve the overall performance of all staff. It will, however, create feelings of job insecurity and lack of trust among the remaining staff.

PRACTICE EXERCISE 1

Total: 40 marks (40 minutes)

1 Explain the benefit of a stock exchange listing for an organisation. *(3 marks)*

2 Distinguish between a private limited company and a public limited company. *(4 marks)*

3 Explain two problems that may occur for a growing firm that changes from private limited to public limited status. *(6 marks)*

4 Explain one reason why a firm might change back from plc to private limited status. *(3 marks)*

5 Why might a UK firm wish to expand into international markets? *(4 marks)*

6 Explain why a UK firm might not be able to repeat, in international markets, the success it has had in the UK. *(5 marks)*

7 Define the term 'retrenchment'. *(3 marks)*

8 Explain two types of retrenchment. *(6 marks)*

9 Explain one positive and one negative effect of retrenchment on an organisation or its stakeholders. *(6 marks)*

PRACTICE EXERCISE 2

Total: 45 marks (45 minutes)

1 Refer back to the Fact File on Google (p. 449). Now that the company has floated as a plc, will the original owners be able to run the business in the way they have always intended? Justify your answer. *(14 marks)*

2 Under what circumstances might it be in the best interests of a public limited company (plc) to consider becoming a private limited company (ltd)? *(15 marks)*

3 Assess the effect of different types of retrenchment on a business and on its stakeholders. *(16 marks)*

CASE STUDY 1 Making it on the market

Almost 2 years on from the flotation of his company, the Wigmore Group, Peter Hewitt, chief executive, feels confident being at the helm of a quoted business.

Since he listed the company, which does building maintenance and construction work, Hewitt has raised funds twice more to enable him to make acquisitions. However, he warns other companies not to underestimate the challenges involved in such a move. 'There is no doubt that going public puts the business on a whole different plane,' he says. 'It is like moving from a two-dimensional to a three-dimensional world.'

For Hewitt, the biggest change has been adapting to the world of investor relations. 'You have to remember that the shareholders are your customers and can buy and sell your shares,' he says. 'As a consequence, you are not only having to run the business and make it viable — you also have to go out and sell the business to them and market it in a way that is far beyond the normal trade marketing. That includes everything from meeting investors to lunching the financial journalists.'

Company owners can gain a picture of market sentiment towards their business by reading the literature in which investors look for information. 'Read the magazines and the websites and keep abreast of what people are saying about your business,' he says.

Being in the public eye also means that any mistakes a company owner makes are far more visible. As a result, Hewitt says, company owners need to plan carefully. 'Bear in mind the saying, "Prior planning and preparation prevents poor performance",' he says.

Source: adapted from an article in *The Times*, 18 November 2003.

Question

Total: 15 marks (20 minutes)

Discuss the arguments for and against the flotation of a company such as the Wigmore Group.

CASE STUDY 2 Caffè Nero looks to Europe and the Middle East

Caffè Nero, the coffee bar operator, has opened its 200th store — opposite King's College in Cambridge — and expects at least to double in size to more than 400 outlets over the next 4–5 years. In the next 2 months, the group will open new stores in Edinburgh, Manchester, Wakefield, Bury St Edmunds, Maidstone, Huddersfield, Halifax and Stockton.

Gerry Ford, chairman, who founded the company in 1997, said that although a move outside the UK was 'off the agenda' at the moment, he strongly believed Caffè Nero had the potential to become an international brand. 'This year is about rolling out the UK, though next year we'll probably spend a bit more time looking at what our best strategic options are,' said

Dr Ford, who cited northern Europe and the Middle East as the two areas on which Caffè Nero would probably focus first.

In Europe, where it is expected to consider opportunities in Germany, Scandinavia and the Benelux countries, it would seek a joint venture partner with local knowledge, while in the Middle East the company would probably adopt the same approach as Whitbread's Costa chain and appoint a master franchisee. 'If we can open up another country and show it can work, we could add a lot of value to this company,' he said.

The group is looking to appoint a UK managing director, a move that would give Dr Ford, who remains executive chairman, time to investigate such opportunities. However, he said that the UK remained the priority, particularly as softening rent levels meant that 'this is a great time to be buying sites'.

Source: www.growthcompany.co.uk

Question

Total: 15 marks (20 minutes)

Discuss the extent to which a successful UK firm, such as Caffè Nero, can repeat its success by operating in international markets.

CHAPTER 49

Change in ownership

This chapter considers the risks, rewards, benefits and problems resulting from the external growth of business organisations. It focuses on takeovers and mergers, including horizontal, vertical and conglomerate integration, and also on management buyouts.

EXAMINER'S VOICE

Growth, via takeover and merger, is part of a company's strategy and is pursued with specific objectives in mind. Consequently, link this area to the later sections on business objectives (Chapter 50) and business strategy (Chapters 51–54).

Types of growth

Growth is an important objective, and is sometimes the only way to ensure that a firm survives. Growth can be achieved either internally or externally. The choice of which type of growth is best suited to a particular organisation depends on a trade-off between the costs involved, the level of risk and the speed of each method of development.

Internal growth

TERM

internal (or **organic**) **growth:** when a firm expands its existing capacity or range of activities by extending its premises or building new factories from its own resources, rather than by integration with another firm.

Internal growth can result from repeating the success of existing products or processes in other markets, by exploiting the firm's own technological superiority (like Dyson) or its own marketing and customer relations superiority, or by seeing gaps in the marketplace more clearly and sooner than its competitors. Finance for the investment and expansion accompanying this type of growth usually comes from the retained profit resulting from existing activities, from borrowing or by attracting new investors. As a result, this process of growth tends to be relatively slow, but less risky than external growth.

Internal growth may be pursued by a firm for a number of reasons: for example, when its product is in the early stage of its life cycle and is not yet fully established in the marketplace, or when its product is highly technical and the firm needs to gain experience of dealing with it, ensuring that any problems can be ironed out. If the costs of growth need to be spread over time, internal growth is likely to be pursued. For many firms, internal growth is the best option because there are no suitable acquisitions available.

FACT FILE

HBOS, the UK's fourth largest bank by market value, was formed by a merger between Halifax and Bank of Scotland in 2001. At the bank's annual general meeting in 2005, James Crosby, its chief executive, said: 'We're happy with our plans to continue to grow organically. As we have become a larger bank, it has been harder to find acquisitions that make sense.'

External growth

KEY TERMS

integration: the coming together of two or more businesses via a merger or takeover.

merger: where two or more firms agree to come together under one board of directors.

takeover (or **acquisition**)**:** where one firm buys a majority shareholding in another firm and therefore assumes full management control.

External growth tends to be via the integration of two or more companies and can occur by merger or takeover (usually known as acquisition). Mergers occur when two businesses believe and jointly agree that they can increase their combined profit by merging their businesses. Takeovers or acquisitions are accomplished by the acquiring firm offering cash or shares (or both) to the shareholders (that is, the owners) of the firm that is being taken over. In practice, the difference between takeovers and mergers is not very clear, as both tend to use the same techniques.

External growth is usually the fastest way to achieve growth, but given the problems of integrating two separate organisations, it can be risky.

DID YOU KNOW?

Any buying or selling of shares on the stock market results in a change in the ownership of a company. These changes are usually only very small and do not significantly affect the control of the business. If, however, an individual or organisation buys up at least 51% of shares, this means they will be able to win all votes taken at an annual general meeting (AGM), and thus control moves to this individual or organisation. In practice, control can be gained with ownership of much less than 51% of shares because most shareholders, probably owing to inertia, do not attend AGMs and do not vote.

Takeovers can be hostile or friendly. A hostile takeover is where the attention of the predator company (the company wishing to take over the other company) is not welcome. The company being targeted recommends that its shareholders do not accept the bid, as was the case in the unsuccessful bids by Philip Green, owner of BHS, for Marks and Spencer. In contrast, a friendly or recommended takeover is where the company being targeted welcomes the takeover and recommends shareholders to accept the bid.

External growth, whether by merger or takeover, friendly or hostile, can be classified into three broad types of integration — vertical, horizontal and conglomerate — each of which is discussed below.

Vertical integration

vertical integration: the coming together of firms in the same industry but at different stages of the production process.

COREL

An example of a firm using vertical integration is BP, which has grown by integrating with firms at all points in the chain of production, from oil exploration, extraction and refining, to distribution and retailing via petrol stations. Another example is the Thomson Travel Group, which owns Thomson Holidays, Britannia Airways and Lunn Poly travel agency. The Thomson Travel Group was itself acquired by TUI AG in 2000. TUI AG is a business whose aim is to cover all stages of the tourism chain. It is the largest tourism operator in Europe, providing a wide range of products and services related to tourism, including tour operators, travel agencies, aviation, destination services, and hotel and resort bookings.

This type of integration can occur by one firm vertically integrating *backwards*. A manufacturer might integrate with the supplier of its raw materials or components: for example, a car assembler owning a component supplier or an oil distribution company owning oil wells. On the other hand, vertical integration can also occur by one firm vertically integrating *forwards*: for example, where a manufacturer integrates with a retailer that sells its finished product.

Backward vertical integration means that the resulting organisation is in a position to control the supplies of raw materials and components in terms of price, quality and reliability, while forward vertical integration means that it is able to control the marketing and sale of products to the final consumer. In both cases, integration:

- enables internal planning and coordination of processes to be substituted for the uncertainty of dealing with external suppliers and retailers
- facilitates cost savings in both technical and marketing areas
- builds barriers to the entry of new competitors
- enables the use of transfer pricing for intra-firm trading
- enables the resulting organisation to absorb the profit margins of suppliers and/or retailers.

FACT FILE

Shanghai Automotive Industry Corporation (SAIC), the Chinese company that chose not to buy MG Rover in 2005, is a state-owned company with a very ambitious goal of selling more than 3 million cars per year by 2020. In 2004, it sold 850,000 cars and it hopes to sell more than 1 million in 2005. Its rapid growth has been the result of vertical integration and the boom in car sales in its domestic market. It has expanded from tractor making into a major automotive group involved in car retailing and leasing as well as car loans.

In practice, mergers or takeovers designed to achieve vertical integration are relatively few in number; the vast majority are designed to achieve horizontal integration.

Horizontal integration

KEY TERM

horizontal integration: the coming together of firms operating at the same stage of production and in the same market.

Firms involved in horizontal integration are usually potential competitors, such as Nestlé and Rowntree, Wal-Mart and ASDA, and Morrisons and Safeway. Horizontal integration is likely to create significant economies of scale, resulting in lower unit costs because duplicate and/or competing facilities can be closed down. However, diseconomies are possible if the integration results in poor communications and coordination.

TOPFOTO

Horizontal integration will reduce the amount of competition in the market and thus mean that the resulting organisation has an increased market share. But if, as a result of the takeover, market share is likely to reach or exceed 25%, it might be referred to the Competition Commission, which may either ban the takeover or set various conditions.

FACT FILE

Here are some more examples of takeovers in practice.

Morrisons and Safeway
Morrisons, a medium-sized but fast-growing UK supermarket chain, took over its rival Safeway in 2004. The combined firm, with 598 stores and a market share of 16%, aims to be able to compete with ASDA, Sainsbury's and Tesco — giants of the UK supermarket sector. Morrisons was looking for a way to grow quickly and could afford to fund an acquisition to achieve that goal. The Office of Fair Trading allowed the takeover to go ahead on condition that Morrisons sold off 52 stores following its takeover of the Safeway chain.

TOPFOTO

FACT FILE

Sony and BMG

The European Commission reported that the planned £3 billion merger of Sony Music and BMG might limit consumer choice and reinforce alleged anti-competitive behaviour among the main music companies. Sony and BMG are the companies behind pop stars such as Britney Spears and Beyoncé. The merger might reduce the number of large record labels from five to four, controlling 80% of the market, and create the world's second-largest music company, with a market share of about 25%. It is forecast to yield annual cost savings of just under £200 million.

Following extensive investigation, however, the merger was permitted. The newly merged company is called SonyBMG.

Conglomerate integration

KEY TERM

conglomerate integration: the coming together of firms operating in unrelated markets.

The General Electric Company (GE), founded by light bulb inventor Thomas Edison, is a conglomerate. Throughout the 1980s and 1990s, it transformed itself from a simple maker of electrical appliances into a giant conglomerate with interests in sectors from aircraft engines and power generators to financial services, medical imaging, television programmes and plastics.

Conglomerate integration results in diversification and thus helps the resulting organisation spread its risks, which is in the long-term interest both of shareholders and employees. It can also lead to a sharing of good practice between different areas of business. However, in some instances, management may have little or no expertise in the newly acquired business area. Studies of corporate growth through conglomeration seem to indicate that unrelated diversification is the fastest route to the growth of sales, but not to the growth of profits. The latter is more likely to come through growth in existing fields.

FACT FILE

Mercedes and Chrysler

Since 1998, Mercedes (known as Daimler-Benz) has been gradually making its $38 billion takeover of the US company Chrysler work. It struggled but was successful in blending the two firms' contrasting business cultures. Besides products, the two firms complement each other in their markets as well. Chrysler is bigger in the US market than Mercedes, while the German firm has much more presence in Europe and Asia. But even when both companies sit side by side in the same country's car market, they operate in different segments. DaimlerChrysler shows how two firms can come together and exploit synergies for their mutual benefit: that is, they enjoy greater benefits from operating together than they would have done separately.

Conglomerates, by buying up companies, can grow to giant proportions. However, the popularity of the conglomerate form of growth has declined and there have been a number of demergers of conglomerate divisions, often as a result of unsuccessful takeovers and the subsequent need for companies to focus more clearly on their core activities.

FACT FILE

Hewlett-Packard and Compaq

In 2002 the US computer giant Hewlett-Packard completed a merger with Compaq. At the time, there was talk of huge benefits, including greater synergies, economies of scale, improved market share and improved profit margins. The merger resulted in a loss of 15,000 jobs (about 10% of the new company's workforce). The combined group's shares remained stubbornly low and the expected benefits were not realised.

DID YOU KNOW?

Synergy, which means that the whole is greater than the sum of the parts (1 + 1 = 3), is often claimed to be a major advantage of takeovers. The evidence suggests that it happens less often than is claimed.

Motives for takeover

- A large company entering a new market may not have the technical expertise and may thus acquire smaller companies with that expertise. In the mid-1990s, Sony did this when it entered the entertainments industry with its PlayStation. While it had the ability needed to produce the hardware, it did not have sufficient software programmers. Its purchase of smaller software producers allowed it to gain a suitably skilled workforce.
- The costs of acquisition or integration may be more favourable than the costs of internal growth, and the speed of growth might be a high priority.
- Brands are expensive to develop, in terms of both time and money, and therefore acquiring companies with prominent brand names is a way to avoid such expense. This was one of the main reasons for Nestlé's takeover of Rowntree.
- The resulting organisation can exploit any patents owned by the company it has acquired. This is particularly the case in takeovers in the pharmaceutical and computing industries.
- An organisation may have identified that the market value of a particular company is considerably less than its asset value. Once the company has been acquired, its valuable assets can be sold and the loss-making aspects of the business wound up. This technique is known as **asset stripping**.

FACT FILE

BMW and Rover

When BMW took over the Rover Group in 1994, it claimed it wanted to get a share of the small car market. True, the marriage spawned the successful new Mini, but this was launched 7 years after the takeover. In 2002, when BMW sold Rover to the Phoenix Consortium for £10 (which apparently still has not been paid), Rover was losing £2 million a day. All told, BMW's mistake cost it £2,560 million. Great though the Mini may be, it is definitely not worth that much. There were two reasons why the BMW Rover deal failed: BMW did not do its homework on the business culture and operational problems inside Rover; BMW's motive was to stop Honda getting Rover.

Do takeovers work?

Theory suggests that growth via mergers and takeovers will produce synergies, economies of scale, lower unit costs, higher profit levels and increased market share. However, research in the UK and the USA tends to suggest that most takeovers lead to disappointing results.

Many studies show that the majority of takeovers damage the interest of the shareholders of the acquiring company, while rewarding the shareholders of the acquired company, who receive much more for their shares than they were worth before the takeover was announced. Professor Mark Sirower, an adviser to the Boston Consulting Group, in his book *The Synergy Trap: How Companies Lose the Acquisition Game* (Simon and Schuster, 2000), says that surveys have repeatedly shown that about 65% of mergers fail to benefit the acquiring company, whose shares subsequently underperform in their sector.

America Online and Time Warner

AOL Time Warner was the result of a merger between America Online (AOL), one of the world's largest internet companies, and Time Warner, the ITS media group that owns Warner Bros film studios, the Warner Music record company, the CNN television news channel and *Time* magazine. The merger in 2001 was, at the time, the largest corporate merger in history and resulted in the world's largest media and entertainment company.

The merger was attractive to AOL as it enabled the company to keep its place as the top internet service provider. To do this, it needed access to a rapid distribution system; and as Time Warner owned one of the USA's largest cable television networks (reaching into 13 million homes), this allowed AOL to offer fast internet services, via cable modems, to millions of households. Owning Warner Bros, one of Hollywood's most powerful studios, plus Warner Music, one of the world's largest record companies, also gave AOL a wealth of content.

The merger was the culmination of AOL's ambition to create a vertically integrated company that would offer consumers everything they need in the interactive world of the future, from media to films and music. Rupert Murdoch, chairman of News Corporation, applauded the deal, saying: 'Vertical integration is the way forward. AOL is a distribution company that ... took the chance of getting a huge chunk of content.'

However, the internet bubble burst and AOL Time Warner failed to meets its targets. Many of AOL's senior management team failed to cope in the corporate culture of Time Warner and the company failed to exploit many of its advantages. In 2003, shareholders argued that the merger had been a 'grandiose' waste of their money. The company dropped AOL from its corporate name in 2003 and at the same time got rid of most of AOL's management team in an effort to demonstrate that it still valued its core assets. Since then it has sold off non-strategic businesses and assets, and begun to focus more on its core activities.

Analysts suggest that to some extent the merger failed because the claims made for the combined company were foolish, based on wishes rather than any realistic assessment of the market and the world.

The majority of failed mergers suffer from poor implementation and the fact that, in a significant proportion of cases, senior management fails to take account of the different cultures of the companies involved. Merging corporate cultures takes time, which senior management does not have, particularly immediately after a merger. The nature of the problem is not so much that there is direct conflict between the two sides, but that the cultures do not merge quickly enough to take advantage of the available opportunities.

Many consultants refer to how little time companies spend before a merger thinking about whether their organisations are compatible. The benefits of mergers are usually considered in financial or commercial terms rather than human and organisational terms.

If 65% of mergers fail to benefit shareholders, what are the conditions that allow the remaining 35% to be successful? Consultants suggest that the combined organisation has to deliver better returns to the shareholders than they would separately — the synergy element. In addition, the merging companies need to decide in advance which partner's way of doing things will prevail — the culture element. Finally, the combined organisation must generate advantages that competitors will find difficult to counter.

Management buyouts

management buyout (MBO): where the managers of a business buy out the existing shareholders in order to gain ownership and control of the business or part of the business.

Finance for buyouts

Finance for management buyouts comes from managers' personal funds, bank loans and investment funds obtained by selling shares to employees, but more usually it comes from either venture capitalists or private equity firms. Venture capitalists and private equity firms work by lending the MBO the cash it needs and by taking a stake in the company for a return of about 25–30% on their investment over 3–5 years.

Glenshee ski centre

In 2004, one of Scotland's main ski centres was saved by a management buyout. The Glenshee resort was put up for sale after suffering a drop in business because of a lack of snow. Its sister centre at Glencoe was sold in June. The group that took over was led by the resort's operations manager, Graham McCabe. The deal secured six full-time jobs and up to 120 seasonal posts, and ensured the continuation of skiing at Glenshee. The resort operator, the Glenshee Chairlift Company, which also ran the Glencoe centre, went into receivership in May. The resorts, which were put up for sale in February, suffered combined losses of approximately £1 million in 2002/03 and 2003/04.

Reasons for buyouts

- A large business might sell off a small section to raise cash, refocus the business or get rid of an unprofitable activity. The management team of the parent company's unwanted section might feel it could be successful with a different approach or more finance.
- Owners of a family business who wish to retire might prefer to sell to the management team in the hope of maintaining employment and continuity in the community.
- The firm might be in the hands of the receiver, who must try to keep it going in order to raise money to pay off creditors. One way of doing this is to sell part of it to the management team.

Rewards of buyouts

- Management and employees have more motivation and responsibility.
- Objectives may be clearer because there is no owner–manager conflict.
- There is likely to be less bureaucracy in the form of a head office that might hinder progress.
- Profits will not be diverted to another part of the organisation.
- If successful, the possibility exists of floating the company on the stock market or selling shares in a takeover offer.

Risks of buyouts

- If unsuccessful, personal losses are felt by the new owners or investors.
- The original owners might have been correct in assessing that the business was fundamentally unprofitable.
- There may be little access to capital.
- They often involve considerable rationalisation and job losses, with adverse effects on staff morale.

ClarityBlue

ClarityBlue was founded by an MBO. The software systems of this hi-tech company allow a number of blue-chip firms, from Lloyds TSB to Vodafone, to monitor and develop their interactions with their customers. Before its successful MBO in 1993, it was part of a US company, but today it is wholly UK owned. 'Basically it got to the stage where we outgrew our American parent company,' says ClarityBlue chief executive Duncan Painter. 'We were by then representing 80% of the business, and it became obvious that it was no longer sensible for them to keep control of us. We needed a lot more investment than was possible to continue to grow and develop.'

Once ClarityBlue's parent decided to let the business go, Mr Painter and his fellow directors immediately faced tough competition. No fewer than three outside companies expressed an interest in buying the firm. The US parent firm was not going to choose Mr Painter's team simply out of loyalty. 'Our proposal had to be competitive, the best possible,' says Mr Painter. 'We had to pay a fair price...In the end I think the company went with us — both because we offered a very good financial deal, but also because we would continue to be one of their main customers.'

Source: www.bbc.co.uk, January 2005.

- Managers have immediately to learn a whole range of new skills, particularly if they have bought out from a large company. Suddenly, they have to do everything that before they took for granted, such as looking after the IT infrastructure, human resources and payroll.

Are buyouts a good thing?

According to figures from the Centre for Management Buy-Out Research at Nottingham University Business School, 314 MBOs were completed in the first half of 2004 — the equivalent of 12 a week — at a total value of £7.6 billion.

Some institutional investors are critical of such deals, suggesting that if management sees value in a business, it should deliver this value to existing shareholders of the plc and not wait until the division has been hived off in a buyout before exploiting such value. Historically, the main method for management to realise investments in a buyout is to float it on the stock market again.

Some commentators argue that workers may be more at risk with a management buyout than if the company had been purchased by a large organisation. If the company is not successful, workers and managers share the loss, but if the company is successful, it is really only the managers who benefit. Others argue that managers are the real risk takers and that workers' jobs might have disappeared if there had been no management buyout.

PRACTICE EXERCISE 1 — Total: 40 marks (40 minutes)

1 Distinguish between organic growth and external growth. *(4 marks)*

2 Explain the difference between a merger and a takeover. *(4 marks)*

3 Distinguish between vertical and horizontal integration. *(4 marks)*

4 Explain the term 'conglomerate integration'. *(3 marks)*

5 State one example of horizontal integration and one example of conglomerate integration. *(2 marks)*

6 Give one example of forward vertical integration and one example of backward vertical integration. *(2 marks)*

7 Explain one possible motive for each of the following types of external growth:
- **a** horizontal integration *(3 marks)*
- **b** forward vertical integration *(3 marks)*
- **c** backward vertical integration *(3 marks)*
- **d** conglomerate integration *(3 marks)*

8 Define the term 'management buyout'. *(3 marks)*

9 Explain one risk and one reward for management and the workforce that might result from a management buyout. *(6 marks)*

PRACTICE EXERCISE 2

Total: 45 marks (45 minutes)

1 On the basis of the information in this chapter, assess the implications for a firm of organic growth as compared with external growth. *(14 marks)*

2 The Fact Files on pages 459–460 support the research that suggests 65% of mergers fail to benefit shareholders. Discuss why the other 35% are successful. *(15 marks)*

3 With reference to the information in this chapter, evaluate the extent to which stakeholder groups, other than the management team, benefit from a management buyout. *(16 marks)*

CASE STUDY Integration and diversification on the high street

The days when UK clothing retailers manufactured their own garments are long gone. Now only a few retailers, among them Pringle and Jaeger, own factories and control the whole supply process. Even Austin Reed, the epitome of gentlemanly tailoring, has not been in manufacturing since 2000. Laura Ashley still makes curtains and fabrics for soft furnishing, but is no longer a clothing manufacturer.

It was not always thus. In the early postwar years, many high street stores manufactured products. In fact, many of the biggest names in retail started life as tailors – opening shops almost as an afterthought, to improve distribution.

Montagu Burton, the founder of what became Burtons, part of the Arcadia Group, made off-the-peg suits before his move into shopkeeping, as did Hepworth, the menswear retailer, which transformed itself into Next, now the UK's third largest clothing retailer.

Richard Hyman of Verdict, the research consultancy, says that in bygone days it made more sense for retailers to make their own clothes. Labour was cheap, the high street was not so competitive and merchandising was less of an art form.

How that has changed. The UK textiles industry has crumbled in recent years because of high production costs. Increased competition means that retailers need all of their skills simply to lure shoppers past the window displays.

Even those that still boast manufacturing capabilities cannot do so with much fervour. Jaeger, the troubled women's-wear company that has been put up for sale, has closed three of its four factories. It is now left with just one knitwear factory in Derbyshire.

Likewise, Pringle of Scotland has just one knitwear factory, which produces all of the group's cashmere and most of its other woollen products. Marks and Spencer, the UK's biggest retailer, has overhauled its supply chain, dropping some dedicated manufacturers along the way.

Roger Jennings, chief executive of Austin Reed, which once owned four factories, says: 'Vertically integrated retailing can be detrimental to flexibility, in terms of the cost of the supply chain and adapting quickly to new styles.'

Richard Ratner, of Seymour Pierce, the broker, adds: 'Owning your own factories is normally a disaster. Apart from the cost of labour, you have to worry about keeping the factories and the staff occupied during quiet periods.'

In Europe there is one exception to the rule that vertically integrated retailing does not work – Zara, the cutting-edge Spanish fashion chain. Like many UK retailers, Zara was a clothing producer long before the first store opened in 1975. But, unlike its UK rivals, Zara managed to transform the manufacturing arm into a highly efficient machine, able to cater to the needs of customers, rather than trying to dictate to the market.

Fifty per cent of the retailer's garments and accessories are made up in wholly owned factories in Galicia and Portugal, and later finished at La Coruña. As a

result, company executives claim that Zara can translate a catwalk design into high street fashion within 3 weeks, which means that the company does not have to second-guess what will be fashionable up to 9 months ahead. However, industry observers say that the Zara model cannot readily be transported to the UK.

Kien Tan, of Crédit Lyonnais Securities, says: 'The manufacturing base is completely different. Spain has lots of cheap factories.' Others speculate about what might happen to the model should Spanish labour costs rise.

Integration still takes place on the high street. Arcadia Group is the result of a number of examples of horizontal integration, bringing together Burton, Topshop, Topman, Outfit, Miss Selfridge, Evans, Dorothy Perkins and Wallis. Recently it was acquired by Philip Green's BHS group.

For some retailers, diversification is the way ahead. Sensing its vulnerability to growing incomes in the UK, Woolworths took the decision to move into new areas. B&Q (DIY), Comet (electrical products) and MVC (CDs and related items) were all set up as part of Woolworths' diversification programme.

Questions

Total: 24 marks (30 minutes)

1 'Vertically integrated retailing can be detrimental to flexibility, in terms of the cost of the supply chain and adapting quickly to new styles' (lines 42–45). Discuss this statement in relation to the fashion industry. *(12 marks)*

2 Evaluate the reasons why BHS and Arcadia Group have chosen to expand through horizontal integration, while Woolworths chose diversification. *(12 marks)*

CHAPTER 50

Mission and organisational culture

This chapter introduces mission statements, why they are used and the problems associated with them. The concept, sources and types of organisational culture are considered. The chapter also examines the impact of culture on an organisation and the difficulties involved in cultural change.

Mission statements

EXAMINER'S VOICE

Review mission statements, corporate aims and objectives, as introduced in Chapter 49 of the AS textbook.

Before an organisation can start to address the task of planning and setting objectives, it must have a clear understanding of its overall purpose. This is expressed as a **mission** and is communicated via a **mission statement**. The mission of an organisation is its essential purpose, and the mission statement a means of communicating to key stakeholders (for example, shareholders, employees, suppliers and customers) what the company is doing and what it ought to be doing. It should set out clearly the primary purpose of the organisation, its values and distinctive features, and provide a rationale for its strategic plan. It should be presented in as clear, concise and memorable a way as possible.

DID YOU KNOW?

The mission statement for Pizza Express is 'high-quality produce and authentic food, served in stylish surroundings at value-for-money prices'.

Disney's vision or mission statement (the two terms can be used interchangeably) is 'to make people happy'. The mission of 3M, the inventors and producers of Post-It Notes, seems appropriate: 'to solve unsolved problems innovatively'. Boeing's mission is 'to push the leading edge of aviation, taking huge challenges, doing what others cannot do', while British Airways describes itself as 'the world's favourite airline'. Other examples are BT, which aims 'to provide world-class telecommunications and information products and services...', and ASDA, which intends 'to be Britain's best-value fresh food and clothing superstore, meeting the weekly shopping needs of ordinary working people and their families, who demand value'.

Why use a mission statement?

If a company is small, employing, say, 100 people, all the employees are likely to know exactly what the business does and will have a reasonable idea of what its goals are. In a small company, everyone is involved, but in a large company, employing thousands or even tens of thousands of people, this is not the case. An organisation such as a large public limited company may have a varied range of activities, with plants and offices in different locations.

There is no reason to expect a manager from a manufacturing division in Scotland to share a sense of mission with the board of directors, who are hundreds of miles away in the head office in London, or with the human resource manager of a retailing division in the USA. So, for a large, diversified company, a mission statement is useful for defining what the company is trying to do in a way that all staff can understand and identify with.

DID YOU KNOW?

Monsoon's mission is 'to provide an experience that is distinctively different, in terms of both product offering and levels of customer service. Monsoon recognises that its people, and in particular its continuing ability to inspire, motivate and reward them, are critical to the achievement of this aim'.

Factors to consider in producing a mission statement

One difficulty with drawing up a mission statement for a large organisation is that it can tend to ignore parts of the business. How, for example, do you write a single-sentence mission statement for a supermarket that is also a bank? To counter this, companies such as The Body Shop and Imperial Tobacco produce mission lists, while others produce mission booklets. While these tend to cover all of a company's activities, they are less memorable than a single sentence.

In general, when producing a mission statement, a company should start from the top and get everyone involved in thinking about what the statement is going to be. Once the statement is defined and understood by senior management, it needs to be disseminated effectively throughout the organisation, ensuring that everyone within the company understands what the organisation is doing and what it wants to do. The statement can then be communicated to other stakeholders, such as customers and suppliers.

Once a mission statement has been written and communicated effectively in a company, it needs to be continually monitored and altered as the nature of the business and its goals change. Over 20 years ago, Microsoft supplied the operating system for a major mainframe provider; its early vision was 'a computer on every desk and in every home'. Today, its range of activities has grown to encompass the internet and related technologies and its mission now is:

> At Microsoft, we work to help people and businesses throughout the world realize their full potential. This is our mission. Everything we do reflects this mission and the values that make it possible.

Problems with mission statements

- Some mission statements have been criticised for containing idealistic values that have no meaning in practice and are simply part of a PR strategy to promote the company to the public. This criticism has arisen because many mission statements fail to show how the high ideals they express are to be put into practice.
- Some mission statements fail to have any impact on company performance because they do not provide a clear signal as to how the purpose, values and strategy should guide employees' standards and behaviour.
- Mission statements do not necessarily add value and can do serious harm if, for example, employees recognise that the values and behaviour

DID YOU KNOW?

Scott Adams, in his office satire *The Dilbert Principle*, describes mission statements as 'long, awkward sentences that demonstrate management's inability to think clearly'.

standards mentioned in the statement are different from their own. When a high-profile petroleum company issued a mission statement that included an appeal for a balanced home and work life, many of the hardest workers in the company started to ridicule the document.

- Mission statements need to match what is actually happening in the company and should be checked for any hidden meanings or negative implications before being placed into the public domain. This was clearly not the case when the former British Rail, noted for delays and cancellations of train services, launched its 'We're getting there' mission statement.

Mission statements and organisational culture

A major reason for introducing mission statements is the desire to provide a common purpose among employees, which is above individual or departmental needs. If this can be achieved, a strong organisational culture will be developed that matches the purposes established for the organisation and its strategic approach.

Organisational culture

KEY TERM

organisational culture: 'the way we do things around here' — a result of tradition, history and structure.

A key role of organisational culture is to differentiate an organisation from others and to provide a sense of identity for its members: 'who we are', 'what we do' and 'what we stand for'. It is an acquired body of knowledge about how to behave and the shared meanings and symbols that help everyone interpret and understand how to act within an organisation. An organisation's culture shows what it has been good at and what has worked in the past. These values are often accepted without question by long-serving management and employees. Although an organisation can have subgroups with different cultures and with varying agendas, a strong organisational culture is one that is internally consistent, is widely shared, and makes clear what is expected and how people should behave.

Every organisation has its own unique culture. It will have been created unconsciously, based on the values of the founders, senior management and core people who built and now direct the organisation. Over time, the culture may change as new owners and senior management try to impose their own styles and preferences on the organisation or because of changing marketplace conditions. Thus, culture influences the decision-making processes, styles of management and what everyone sees as success. Interpreting and understanding organisational culture is therefore a very important activity for managers because it affects strategic development.

Just as there is no ideal style of management or organisational structure, so there is no preferred culture. What is important is that the culture is suited to the environment in which the firm operates, allowing it to react appropriately to market and other changes.

Sources of organisational culture

- **Company routines** — the way everyday decisions and tasks are undertaken. In some organisations, managers regularly walk around and talk to staff; in others, management is rarely seen. In some organisations, managers communicate and consult with their staff on a routine basis; in others, staff are only informed once decisions have been made.
- **Formal controls** — the rules and procedures governing employee actions. In some organisations, employees have autonomy and independence, and entrepreneurial activity is encouraged; in others, employees are expected to follow procedures closely.
- **Organisational structures** — the way management is organised both vertically, by layers of hierarchy, and horizontally, by functional areas. Some organisational structures are decentralised and place emphasis on delegation; others are more hierarchical and centralised.
- **Power structure** — the interrelationship between individuals or groups who take decisions about how the organisation's resources are allocated. In some organisations, challenging management's views is encouraged; in others, this would be considered disloyal. Some organisations encourage cooperation between different groups, while others encourage a level of competitive rivalry.
- **Symbols** — the emblems representing the organisation's culture. For example, in the professions, the language or jargon that is used can effectively exclude others and thus reinforce professional cultures. Other emblems include the range of pay scales from the highest to the lowest, which indicate status within the organisation, the size and location of managers' offices and whether they have their own secretaries, and whether there are separate canteens, entrances and car parks for management and workers.
- **Rituals and myths** — the patterns of behaviour that have become formalised in the everyday life of the organisation, and the stories that are told of its history. For example, it may be that in a particular organisation, the only training that is considered worthwhile is on-the-job and employees are not seconded to college courses, perhaps because the owner is 'self-made' and values experience over education.

Classifying organisational cultures

Organisational culture has been classified in many different ways. At the simplest level, it is possible to distinguish between a 'them and us' culture in an organisation where strict divisions exist between management and workers, and a more equitable culture in an organisation that tries to reduce barriers, with emphasis being placed on teamwork and more equal treatment of all. Three further approaches to the classification of organisational culture are considered here.

Charles Handy's classification system

Charles Handy, in *Understanding Organisations* (Penguin, 1981), identified four different types of organisational culture: power, role, task and person. Each culture is determined by different assumptions about the basis of power and influence, what motivates people, how people think and learn, and how change should occur.

TOPFOTO

- **Power culture.** This is where a powerful individual or a small group determines the dominant culture. Power culture is like a web with a ruling spider. Those in the web are dependent on a central power source. Rays of power and influence spread out from the central figure or group. Examples of such an organisation are small, entrepreneurial companies, where power derives from the founder or top person, and a personal relationship with that individual matters more than any formal title or position. However, in some large companies, a charismatic leader like Virgin's Richard Branson (left) can do much to define the culture.
- **Role culture.** An organisation with a role culture is often referred to as a bureaucracy. Such organisations are controlled by procedures and role descriptions. Coordination is from the top and job positions are central. Such organisations value predictability and consistency and may find it hard to adjust to change. Such a culture creates a highly structured, stable company with precise job descriptions, and is often based on a single product.
- **Task culture.** This is where the organisation's values are related to a job or project. Task culture is usually associated with a small team approach. It indicates a network organisation or small organisations cooperating to deliver a project. The emphasis is on results and getting things done. Individuals are empowered with independence and control over their work. Such an organisation is flexible and adaptable, and the culture emphasises talent and ideas and involves continuous team problem solving and consultation.
- **Person culture.** This culture occurs in universities and in professions, such as accountancy and legal firms, where the organisation exists as a vehicle for people to develop their own careers and expertise. The individual is the central point. If there is a structure, it exists only to serve the individuals within it. Those involved tend to have strong values about how they will work, and they can be very difficult for the organisation to manage.

WHAT DO YOU THINK?

Which of these four cultures best applies to your school or college, or to other organisations with which you are familiar? Try to justify your answer.

Bureaucratic/entrepreneurial cultures

Organisational culture can also be classified as either bureaucratic or entrepreneurial. Examples of **bureaucratic organisations** are government departments, universities, banks and building societies. Their characteristics include some or all of the following:

- an emphasis on roles and procedures (rather like the role culture noted above)
- risk averse and anxious to avoid mistakes

- generalised and non-commercial goals
- precisely defined responsibilities and roles
- a hierarchical structure

In general, these characteristics result in organisations that survive for long periods of time, whose staff are unsuited to a dynamic environment and which often have a culture where making the right decision is less important than making decisions in the right way.

Bureaucratic cultures tend to be found in large, mature businesses or public-sector organisations. Such organisations are likely to discourage risk-taking and even penalise managers who introduce unsuccessful projects. As a result, individuals will fear failure and seek to minimise its likely occurrence. Such behaviour may lead to the rejection of interesting or exciting projects because they are judged too risky or uncertain.

Entrepreneurial organisations are found in smaller businesses, profit-centred organisations and conglomerates with local management control. The characteristics of an entrepreneurial culture include:

- an emphasis on results and rewards for individual initiative (rather like the power culture noted above)
- risk taking
- quantitative and financial goals
- a task culture with flexible roles
- a flatter and more flexible structure, giving more local control

In general, these characteristics result in organisations that have high business mortality (that is, they are less likely to survive in the long term than organisations with bureaucratic cultures) and are focused on commercial results and profit.

An entrepreneurial culture often applies to businesses in their early years of development. Such a company may encourage risk taking and the acceptance of occasional failure, on the basis that large gains may be achieved when there is success. Such behaviour may lead to maximum returns on investments if good decisions are made.

YOU KNOW?

Polaroid's mission statement is 'to provide the best imaging technology to consumers and professionals everywhere'.

Marketing/production/technological orientation

Cultures can be categorised according to whether organisations are marketing, production or technology orientated. Marketing orientated organisations, such as Virgin, place heavy emphasis on meeting the needs of their customers and are continually alert to changes in the market. Production orientated firms place an emphasis on good engineering and high quality in production, for example Dyson. A technology-driven firm tends to define itself in terms of the technology it exploits — for example, Polaroid with its instant picture technology, which it has championed for almost 40 years.

The impact of culture on the organisation

Organisational cultures determine how firms respond to changes in their external environment. Though intangible, culture has an important bearing on an organisation's behaviour and performance. A production- or engineering-based culture can lead to a neglect of marketing skills and financial controls. Similarly, an over-concern with financial controls can undermine product development, leaving the firm increasingly exposed to competition from products that are technologically superior.

Organisational culture and change

The values of an organisation affect the way it behaves or operates. Indeed, information may be ignored or downgraded if it does not accord with how the organisation views the world. Hence, organisational culture can be a barrier to change. When the dominant culture is challenged, this can produce strong resistance within the organisation because the fundamental values of staff are under threat. When the external environment alters — for example, the market becomes more competitive — the organisation's values may no longer be appropriate. They may hinder the ability of the organisation to adapt.

DID YOU KNOW?

'Organizational culture is the key to organizational excellence...and the function of leadership is the creation and management of culture' (Edgar Schein, *Organizational Culture and Leadership*).

By contrast, changing organisational culture can be a way to change the organisation's performance. A change in the external environment may require profound changes in the way things are done.

The importance of leadership in culture change

In bringing about culture change, the role of the leader or senior management is crucial. Leaders and senior management act as role models. For example, if a firm needs to introduce tighter controls on expenditure, senior management should set an example by practising financial restraint.

Similarly, senior management can support the case for change by allocating the necessary resources to bring it about. They can promote and demote staff to signal the desired change. They can communicate the case for change and introduce the necessary training and recruitment policies. Where the organisational structure acts as a barrier to change — for example, where a hierarchical structure may constrain entrepreneurial flair and risk taking — management can restructure the business to help bring about the change in culture.

EXAMINER'S VOICE

In studying the culture of an organisation, focus not on what the organisation says, but on what it does.

If senior managers say one thing and do the opposite, no one will take the culture change seriously and it will quickly lose all credibility.

Conclusion

There is no 'right' or 'wrong' culture, since the appropriate approach depends on the nature of the business and the environment in which it operates. However, when mergers and takeovers occur, firms with very different cultures, even though they might be operating in similar markets and with similar technologies, are brought together, often leading to managerial confusion and failure (see Chapter 49 for examples of this). Differences in culture can be an important explanation of why so many promising mergers fail. Putting it another way, a successful business needs a culture that is appropriate for the environment in which it operates. Failure is often traceable to an inappropriate culture.

PRACTICE EXERCISE 1

Total: 35 marks (30 minutes)

1 What is a mission statement? *(3 marks)*

2 Explain one advantage for an organisation of having an effective mission statement. *(3 marks)*

3 What is meant by the term 'organisational culture'? *(3 marks)*

4 Name Charles Handy's four different cultures. *(4 marks)*

5 Distinguish between a bureaucratic culture and an entrepreneurial culture. *(6 marks)*

6 How might an organisation's culture influence its attitude to risk taking? *(4 marks)*

7 Explain two ways in which management might achieve a change in culture. *(6 marks)*

8 Explain how organisational culture might influence an organisation's ability to cope with external change. *(6 marks)*

PRACTICE EXERCISE 2

Total: 30 marks (30 minutes)

1 To what extent would you expect the culture in a public sector body (such as the Local Education Authority or your school or college) to be different from that of a private sector company operating in a highly competitive market? *(15 marks)*

2 Refer back to the discussion of mergers and takeovers in Chapter 49. To what extent does it appear that conflicting organisational cultures play a part in the failure of many takeovers to achieve the success they anticipate? *(15 marks)*

CHAPTER 51

Decision making to achieve objectives

This chapter considers decision-making models. Scientific decision-making modelling is examined with specific reference to the marketing model, introduced in Chapter 3. Ansoff's matrix is explained and its use as a tool for strategic decision making is analysed.

Decision making

Decision making in any business is very important and takes place at every level of the organisation. It varies from short-term to long-term, and from functional and tactical to strategic and corporate. Decisions are usually constrained by both internal and external factors — for example, by the finance available, the skills of the workforce, competitor activity or government policy. Most decision-making includes an element of risk and this is certainly the case with strategic decisions. Just because something is risky does not mean that it should not be pursued. It does mean, however, that careful analysis of the balance of risk and reward should be carried out. Most successful businesses have become successful by taking risks in order to gain first-mover advantages in the marketplace.

EXAMINER'S VOICE

Review your understanding of opportunity cost, which is an important concept to consider in relation to strategic analysis. It refers to the real cost of a decision in terms of the next best alternative.

A number of decision-making models are available to assist firms in this difficult but important process.

Scientific decision making

A scientific approach involves using a systematic process for making decisions in an objective manner. Such a procedure removes the practice of decisions being made on the basis of a 'hunch' (or feeling or instinct) and also removes, as far as possible, bias and subjectivity by ensuring that decisions are made on the basis of well-researched, factual evidence. It therefore reduces risk because decisions are based on hard data, and it allows actions to be reviewed and the most effective course of action to be decided. This does not mean that the decisions made will always be the right ones. Scientific decision making can be criticised as being a rather slow process and one that lacks creativity, and which therefore may fail to lead to innovative and different approaches.

A scientific decision-making model similar to that in Figure 51.1 is widely used. The model can be explained by reference to the following hypothetical decision. Assume that a firm is faced with falling demand for its existing product and wishes to cut production of that product and to build up production of an alternative aimed at a different market. It can close down one of its existing factories, making the workforce redundant, and open a new factory abroad. Labour is cheaper abroad, but the workforce is relatively unskilled in relation to the new product and there is poor infrastructure and relatively weak links with suppliers, customers and distributors. Alternatively, the firm can retrain its existing skilled workforce and switch production at its current factory to the new product. The decision is whether to retain its existing workforce and maintain production in the UK or to move production overseas. The steps in the decision-making process are as follows:

1 Set objectives

The firm must set objectives in relation to what it wants to achieve and where it wants to be within a given time scale, ensuring that this fits well with the corporate mission statement. In relation to the decision, the firm wants production to take place in the most cost-effective location, taking account of long-term training costs, infrastructure costs, building up relationships with customers, suppliers and distributors, etc.

2 Gather data

Data on costs, demand, location and logistics, available workforce, reputation, etc. will be needed and may be gathered through primary and secondary research methods.

3 Analyse data

Data that have been gathered need to be analysed in order to provide a recommendation. Various quantitative decision-making techniques or tools are available to do this, such as investment appraisal, cost–benefit analysis, critical path analysis, ratio analysis, elasticity of demand and decision trees (the latter are considered in Chapter 52).

4 Select a strategy

The decision as to which strategy to pursue should be made on the basis of the recommendations that emerge from the data analysis.

5 Implement and review the decision

Implementation will itself involve numerous decisions on tactical and operational issues. Reviewing the decision involves looking at how well the outcome has succeeded in achieving the initial objective. For example, if the decision was to retain the existing workforce but it transpires that unit costs are too high and so competitiveness is reduced, the decision not to move abroad may need to be re-examined.

The marketing model, explained in detail in Chapter 3, provides a scientific decision-making model for use with marketing strategy. It is not dissimilar to the

Figure 51.1 *Scientific decision-making model*

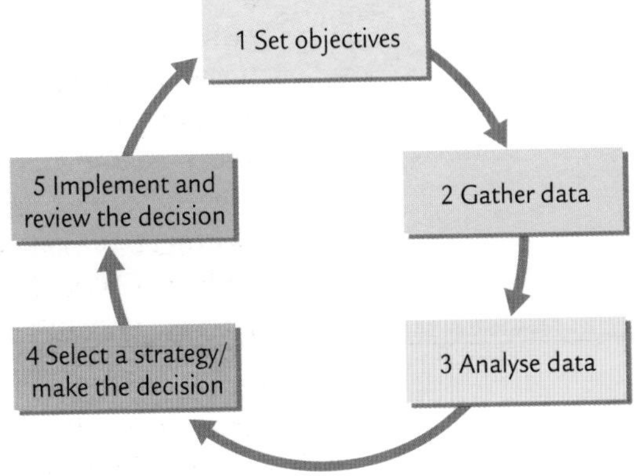

EXAMINER'S VOICE

Refer to Chapter 3 of this book in order to revise your understanding of the marketing model. In Unit 6 it is used as an exemplar of a strategic decision-making technique.

model provided above and can also be applied more generally to assist managers in planning and executing strategy.

Ansoff's matrix

Ansoff's matrix is another decision-making model or tool for corporate planning. It was created by Igor Ansoff and first published in his article 'Strategies for Diversification' in the *Harvard Business Review* in 1957. Ansoff's matrix provides a useful framework for analysing a range of strategic options in relation to risks and rewards.

EXAMINER'S VOICE

In looking at the strategic options available in Ansoff's matrix, draw upon your understanding across all of the functional areas and external influences. Try to take an integrative view of business when using Ansoff's matrix.

Ansoff's matrix consists of four cells that provide a company with a range of options or strategic choices, each with a different degree of risk attached (see Figure 51.2). We will examine each of these choices in turn.

Figure 51.2 Ansoff's matrix

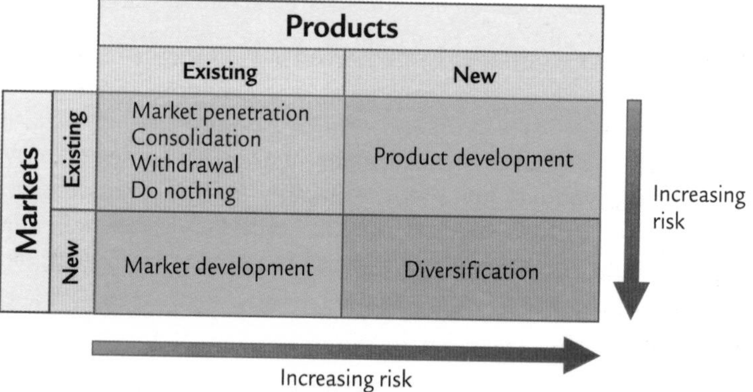

Products
Existing
New
Markets
Existing
New
Market penetration
Consolidation
Withdrawal
Do nothing
Product development
Market development
Diversification
Increasing risk
Increasing risk

Existing products, existing markets

In this situation, the company has the choice of whether to penetrate the market further, consolidate its present position, withdraw from the market altogether or simply do nothing. Providing existing products in existing markets is a low-risk strategy because the firm is working in areas in which it has both knowledge and experience. This is known commonly as 'sticking to the knitting'.

- **Market penetration** — promoting growth in existing markets with existing products. Several different tactics can be employed: increasing brand loyalty in order to reduce customers' purchases of substitute products; encouraging customers to use the product more often, and therefore make more frequent purchases; or encouraging customers to use more of the product on each occasion — for example, by promoting the sale of larger packs. In highly competitive markets, taking customers from rivals may result in short-term

FACT FILE

Hornby plc, the classic toy train and Scalextric producer, has been facing tough competition in a world where children are more interested in playing computer games than spending hours setting up an elaborate new train set. Commentators in the toy industry suggest that the company should market nostalgia more aggressively and aim either at the thirtysomethings or at an even older potential market among both fathers and grandfathers: 'People are retiring earlier, going back to their old hobbies and renewing their interest in toy trains and Scalextric sets. They are the ones with the disposable income.'

Source: *Business Review*, April 2005.

gains, but competitors are likely to fight back. As a strategy, market penetration has its limits and once the market approaches saturation, another strategy must be pursued if a firm is to continue to grow.

- **Consolidation** — concentrating activities on those areas where the firm has established a competitive advantage or competence, and focusing its attention on maintaining its market share. If this strategy is prompted by falling profits, then some form of retrenchment, such as redundancies or the sale of assets, might be needed. This could, in the longer term, lead to improvements in the firm's cost structure, more emphasis on quality and increased marketing activity.
- **Withdraw** — through the sale of all or part of the business. This might be appropriate if: there is an irreversible decline in demand; the firm is overextended; the firm is adversely affected by competitive pressure and environmental change; or opportunity costs are such that a better return can be earned if resources are used elsewhere.
- **Do nothing** — that is, continue with the existing strategy. This might be appropriate in the short term when the environment is static or the firm is waiting to see how a situation develops, but it is not realistic or beneficial in the long term.

FACT FILE

Opened in Seattle in 1971, Starbucks now has over 7,500 stores located in over 31 countries. In the USA, it has ten times the number of stores of its nearest competitor, and this market has now reached saturation point. In terms of Ansoff's matrix, Starbucks has pursued a strategy of market development and its success is based on a number of factors. It has a powerful brand name that is recognised around the world and it has sought to ensure customer satisfaction by speeding up service and introducing a range of new drinks. But the main reason for the company's growth has been its ability to repeat a winning formula throughout the world, with stores from Chile to China and Hong Kong to Hawaii. However, it has pulled out of the coffee bar market in Israel as a result of a number of external factors, including risks over security and the fact that Israel has been suffering from an economic recession, resulting in sluggish sales. Starbucks has also struggled in Japan.

Source: *Business Review*, April 2005.

FACT FILE

Costa Coffee and Caffè Nero have also built their success around a strategy of market development. Costa Coffee has developed a successful store model, with Costa stores in partner outlets, such as Homebase, WH Smith and Abbey (formerly Abbey National). Meanwhile, Caffè Nero has expanded by opening stores in suburban high streets and city centres and inside department stores, such as Selfridges. Opening coffee shops within existing retail outlets is a good way of keeping overhead costs down – particularly the cost of city-centre rents – in order to remain competitive.

Source: *Business Review*, April 2005.

Existing products, new markets

Here the strategy of **market development** is followed to extend market penetration into new areas. Examples are seeking new geographical territories, promoting new uses for the existing product, or entering new market segments. The development of new markets for the product is a good strategy if a firm's core competencies are related more to the product than to its experience with a specific market segment. Market development is more risky than market penetration because the firm will not be familiar with the needs and wants of the new market.

New products, existing markets

Here a **product development** strategy is followed, which may involve substantial modifications or additions to a product range in order to maintain a competitive position. This strategy is particularly useful in competitive markets where firms need to maintain product differentiation. In some instances, products are changed completely, while in other cases, 'spin-offs' are developed, such as Mars Ice Cream and Kit Kat Kubes. This strategy might need extensive research and development funding, but the company has the advantage of operating from the security of its established customers. Product development is appropriate if a firm's strengths are related to its customers rather than a specific product. Like market development, product development is more risky than simply trying to increase market share.

FACT FILE

Coffee Republic has managed to stem losses by pursuing a strategy of product development. The company has adopted a 'me-too' approach by copying the success of Pret A Manger. The business will be relaunched as Coffee Republic Deli, with its coffee bars becoming US-style deli bars, selling sandwiches and hot food. In this respect, it is at a significant disadvantage compared with Pret A Manger because, in the eyes of the consumer, Pret A Manger will be seen as the 'original'. Coffee Republic has been careful to test the new-style stores before launching nationwide. Refurbishing stores is expensive, and the advantage of using a test market is that the company can find out what customers think of the new formula before a full-scale launch.

Source: *Business Review*, April 2005.

EXAMINER'S VOICE

Remember that there are disadvantages in using test marketing. In the case of Coffee Republic, it would provide rivals with an opportunity to see what the company is planning and give them time to develop a similar product or service before the full-scale launch. Second, it might produce misleading results. For example, if it used a particular area as a test market, rivals could increase promotional spending in this area in order to give Coffee Republic the impression that its new business proposition would not be successful.

New products, new markets

The strategy of launching new products in new markets is known as **diversification**. It is a high-risk strategy because it requires both product and market development and may be outside the core competencies of the firm. Despite this, it may be the right choice if high risks are balanced by the chance of a high rate of return. Diversification could take place by means of organic growth, or it could involve a move into new but related markets by vertical or horizontal integration, or into new and unrelated markets by conglomerate integration. Nokia moved from being a producer of car tyres in the early 1990s to become a major player in the mobile phone market 10 years later.

FACT FILE

Oxfam is another recent entrant into the coffee bar market, with a chain of shops called 'Progresso'. It is pursuing a strategy of diversification. As Richard Davies of BANC Public Relations, which represents Oxfam, said: 'We have 753 stores, including 60 bookshops and specialist music shops. So the old image of being a retailer of second-hand jumpers is disappearing rapidly. This is a different market and we're targeting people who don't usually use our shops.' Oxfam hopes that an emphasis on fair trade — which guarantees a fair price to producers — will give it a niche in the coffee market. The fair trade market is worth £100 million per year, but some analysts are sceptical of Oxfam's ability to diversify successfully and compete against well-established rivals that have greater marketing muscle and expertise in this industry.

Source: *Business Review*, April 2005.

EXAMINER'S VOICE

When analysing possible strategies in a Unit 6 case study, use Ansoff's matrix if one or more of the four strategies is being implemented. This will show your ability to analyse strategic situations in a theoretical way.

Ansoff's matrix is a useful tool for deciding on strategic direction, but it does not take account of what competitors are doing or what they are planning for the future; nor does it take account of how competitors will react to the selected strategy, and in what timescale.

PRACTICE EXERCISE 1 — **Total: 40 marks (35 minutes)**

1 Identify the five main stages involved in a scientific decision-making model. *(5 marks)*

2 State three quantitative decision-making tools. *(3 marks)*

3 Explain two advantages of scientific decision making. *(6 marks)*

4 Explain two disadvantage of scientific decision making. *(6 marks)*

5 Identify the options available to a business that is following a strategy of 'existing product/existing market'. *(4 marks)*

6 Distinguish between the market development and product development strategies in Ansoff's matrix. *(4 marks)*

7 Explain the diversification strategy in Ansoff's matrix. *(3 marks)*

8 Which strategic option from Ansoff's matrix is a risk-averse firm likely to follow and why? *(5 marks)*

9 Explain one weakness of Ansoff's matrix in helping a firm to develop a successful strategy. *(4 marks)*

PRACTICE EXERCISE 2

Total: 30 marks (30 minutes)

Refer to the Fact Files on coffee bars and oxfam in this chapter.

1 Discuss why diversification might be considered high-risk in the case of Oxfam's strategy of moving into the coffee bar business. *(14 marks)*

2 To what extent is market development rather than product development the most appropriate strategy for the coffee bar business? *(16 marks)*

CASE STUDY 1 Hornby

Despite generally difficult trading conditions in the wider UK retail sector, Hornby's ranges, particularly model railways, have performed well. The robust characteristics of the collectable and hobby market have resulted in continued strong consumer demand. The new product ranges launched in early 2004 have proved to be very popular. The ranges of Live Steam model trains and historic Scalextric racing cars have strengthened the company's position in the hobbyist and enthusiast market. There is evidence that these new product lines have helped to attract a number of customers new to the hobby.

One of the main factors behind this growth was the company's network of in-store concessions. Hornby now operates 120 concessions, which are proving popular with enthusiasts and collectors, who often prove to be loyal, repeat customers. The company has also made good progress on improving its relationship with the major national retailers. Many are recognising the attractions of products associated with the hobby and collectable market, and Hornby has proved that the popularity of its product ranges is a long-term trend.

TOPFOTO

Hornby's Spanish subsidiary, Electrotren, has also continued to perform well. It has launched more locally oriented products into its core markets. As the company predicted at the time of the acquisition, Hornby is also utilising its existing network to drive sales growth in slot-car racing systems into the Spanish market. It is making good progress in winning market share. During 2003, the company secured the worldwide exclusive licence to produce slot cars associated with the Renault Formula 1 team. Given the popularity of Spanish driver Fernando Alonso, sales in Spain have been excellent.

The board remains aware that continued innovation and maintenance of a strong pipeline of new products is an important aspect of its business, and underpins the company's future strategy for growth. Hornby has also given attention to its younger customers. The 'Thomas the Tank Engine' range has been revitalised and the feedback from retailers gives the company confidence that this will prove to be a popular product range. In Scalextric, the company has been boosted by the impact of a number of important international licences that will help to generate further sales growth. Hornby has secured a licence with Ferrari and Mattel to produce a number of slot-car models based on current and historic Ferraris. The company has also agreed a licence with Warner Bros to launch a range of products associated with the *Batman Begins* movie, which is expected to be launched in mid-2005. The continued focus on high-quality product development is a proven formula that can be expected to continue to drive sales growth. Hornby's chief executive states:

> I am delighted to report on our recent trading, which continues to reflect the successful product development and marketing strategies being pursued in all sectors of the business. Our strategy continues to be to develop the Hornby and Scalextric brands as market leaders that appeal to the broadest possible consumer base. Coupled with this, our international acquisitions provide an excellent platform to replicate our UK success story in other major markets. We therefore remain confident of the future growth potential of the business.

Source: Hornby plc *Trading Update*, 31 January 2005.

Question

Total: 15 marks (20 minutes)

Using the information in the case study and the Fact File on p. 477, assess which of the strategic options in Ansoff's matrix have benefited Hornby.

CASE STUDY 2 Dyson's magic carpet ride

It took 5 years and 5,127 prototypes for James Dyson to come up with his first bagless cleaner, which started selling in Japan in 1986. Since then, Dyson has expanded the business to 37 countries, shifting his factory from England to Malaysia. The company continues to develop the technology and about a quarter of the 1,300 employees at Dyson's headquarters in England work in research and development.

Within two-and-a-half years of its introduction to the English market, the Dyson vacuum cleaner became England's bestseller. Recently, Dyson announced a new milestone. Three years after its US debut, the Dyson had become the market-leading upright cleaner, according to 2004 sales figures. Selling 891,000 units, up 350% from the previous year, Dyson captured 21% of the US market based on value, beating traditional leader Hoover, which claimed less than 16%. The company said around two-thirds of its sales now came from overseas. Worldwide sales in 2004 grew by 54% to £426 million (with sales in Europe up by 35% and sales in Russia and Japan doing very well), and profits more than doubled to £102.9 million.

What lies behind the success of the Dyson cleaners, especially given that they are anything but cheap? Priced from $399 to about $590 in the USA, a Dyson costs more than twice as much as most rival models, which tend to retail at $60 to $389. Moreover, the marketing campaign for the cleaners has stayed decidedly low-key. Straightforward television commercials feature the 57-year-old Dyson in his lab, calmly explaining how his frustration with ordinary vacuum cleaners prompted him to create a better machine.

According to Dyson, superior technology explains his brainstorm's popularity. Because there is no bag or filter to clog, his cleaners stay powerful. 'They maintain constant, maximum suction,' he says. 'All the time it's working to full efficiency, cleaning your home.'

The Dyson has developed an intensely loyal following. The company's research in the UK found that 70% of all users bought the machine after recommendation from friends. Even a brief look at Dyson users' reviews on Amazon.com reveals, in many cases, a level of enthusiasm rarely associated with household appliances. Among the headline comments are: 'I LOVE this vacuum!', 'Believe the hype!' and 'WOW!'

Tim Calkin, a US professor of marketing, says that Dyson has succeeded by bringing something new and innovative to a market that had focused exclusively on price. 'They certainly have set themselves up as a superior vacuum cleaner,' says Calkin. 'They've almost made it an aspirational purchase, but people who buy Dysons really like them. People take pride in their vacuum when they own a Dyson.'

Indeed, Dyson cleaners have benefited from some glamorous associations. They have appeared in episodes of television shows such as *Will and Grace* and *Friends* (used by Courteney Cox's compulsively clean character Monica) and were included in the presenters' gift bag at the last Academy Awards ceremony.

Dyson, however, wants to expand. Last month in the UK, Dyson unveiled 'the Ball', a new vacuum that will eventually roll out in the USA and which replaces wheels with a ball to allow easier movement. Its starting price will be $600 (in the UK it sells at £319.99 for the basic 'all floors' model and up to £349.99 for the extra-clean 'allergy' and 'animals' versions). It took nearly 4 years, 182 patents and £25 million to get the 'Dyson DC15 The Ball' from scribbled sketch into department stores. 'We have no sales target, but personally I believe the Ball will account for 50% of all upright vacuum cleaners we sell,' Mr Dyson said.

Dyson shifted production of its vacuum cleaners from Malmesbury in Wiltshire to Malaysia in 2002, resulting in a loss of 865 manufacturing jobs. At the time, Mr Dyson said he had been forced to shift offshore because of lower costs. He also cited the fact that both component suppliers and some of the cleaners' biggest markets were based in the region. This was followed by an announcement in 2003 that production of Dyson's washing machines would also be transferred to Asia. The move to Malaysia boosted profits and allowed the company to grow and expand in the USA, where it became market leader in just 2 years. But going to the stock market to fund further expansion is not on the cards, says Dyson. 'If we would go public, I would have to spend time in the City; right now I can continue doing what I do best – tinkering with technology.'

Source: adapted from articles on Business Week and BBC News websites, April 2005 (www.businessweek.com www.bbc.co.uk).

Questions

Total: 50 marks (60 minutes)

1 Assess Dyson's development in terms of the strategic options available in Ansoff's matrix. *(12 marks)*

2 Evaluate whether further opportunities for the business are likely to lie in market development or product development. *(12 marks)*

3 To what extent does the business and its owner, James Dyson, benefit from remaining as a private limited company? *(12 marks)*

4 Assess the extent to which a scientific decision-making model might have benefited the company in deciding upon its production move from England to Malaysia. *(14 marks)*

CHAPTER 52

Decision trees

This chapter explains how to construct simple decision tree diagrams based on business choices and probabilities, and how to calculate and evaluate the outcomes. It examines the value and limitations of using decision trees as a decision-making technique.

Business decision making

Businesses make decisions all the time. Some are hugely important, one-off strategic decisions, while others are more routine, tactical decisions. The former are made by senior management; the latter may be delegated to staff further down the hierarchy.

In small firms, hunch and personal judgement are often the main approaches to decision making. The owner-manager knows his or her customers, competitors and staff, and can make decisions quickly and effectively without the need to justify them to others. Even here, however, it is important to have a logical approach to decision making that considers all options thoroughly.

In larger firms, decisions are likely to be more complex and to involve more individuals. Furthermore, decisions need to be justified to superiors, to shareholders and possibly to other stakeholders. In this situation, it is vitally important that the decision-making process is logical, thorough and transparent. Decision-makers must be able to explain why particular decisions were taken, especially if they go wrong.

Decision trees

A number of models and tools are available to assist businesses in their decision-making processes. For example, investment appraisal can be used to decide between alternative investment projects, while Ansoff's matrix may help to provide strategic direction for a business. The focus of this chapter, decision tree analysis, is usually applied to problems for which the probability of different consequences and the financial outcomes of decisions can be estimated.

Decision tree analysis provides a pictorial approach to decision making — the diagram used resembles the branches of a tree. It maps out the different options available, the possible outcomes of these options and the points where decisions have to be made. Calculations based on the decision tree can be used to determine the best option for the business to select.

Some argue that decision making is most effective when a quantitative approach is taken: that is, when the information on which decisions are based and the outcomes of decisions are expressed as numbers. A decision tree does just this. However, as with all quantitative models, caution must be exercised when considering the nature of the information used and the results themselves.

Constructing and evaluating a decision tree: example

We will now use a business scenario to demonstrate how to construct and evaluate a simple decision tree using the stages identified above.

A business wishes to invest in a new plant in order to extend its range of products. It has to decide whether to use the new plant to make product A or product B. Making product A will require a much higher investment (£7 million) than that required for product B (£2 million), but the business estimates that the financial returns look higher for product A than product B. Its estimates are as follows:

- If product A is produced and demand is high, the payoff will be £16 million. However, if demand is low, the payoff will only be £6m. The probability of a high demand for product A is 0.7 and that of a low demand is 0.3.
- If product B is produced and demand is high, the payoff will be £12 million. However, if demand is low, the payoff will only be £4 million. The probability of a high demand for product B is 0.6 and that of a low demand is 0.4.

EXAMINER'S VOICE

Remember that, in a decision tree, squares represent decisions and circles represent uncertain outcomes.

Constructing the decision tree

1 Start with a small square, to represent the decision, towards the left of your sheet of paper.

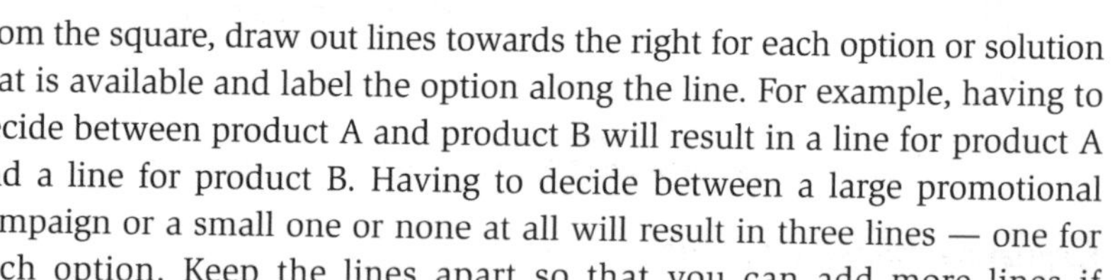

2 From the square, draw out lines towards the right for each option or solution that is available and label the option along the line. For example, having to decide between product A and product B will result in a line for product A and a line for product B. Having to decide between a large promotional campaign or a small one or none at all will result in three lines — one for each option. Keep the lines apart so that you can add more lines if necessary. Remember to add a 'Do nothing' option if this is an alternative.

3 At the end of each line, consider the results. If the result of taking that decision is uncertain, draw a small circle. For example, if production of product A may be successful or may result in failure, this is an uncertain outcome. If a promotional campaign might result in success or failure, this is an uncertain outcome. If the launch of a product may or may not result in a competitor launching a rival product, this is an uncertain outcome. If, on the other hand, the result of a particular option is not uncertain,

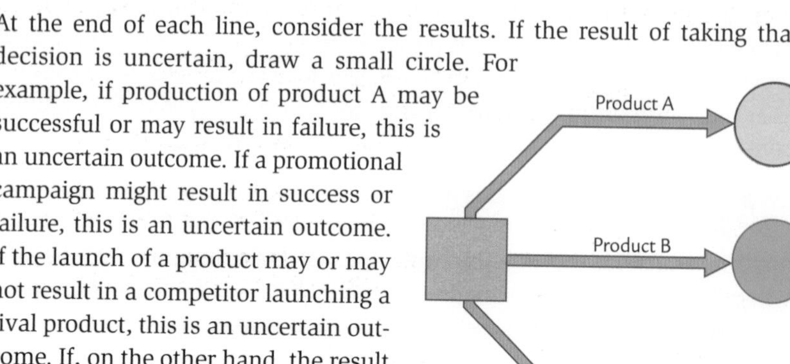

as is the case with the option 'do nothing', extend the line to the far right. Insert the financial outcome (payoff) of any certain, final outcome.

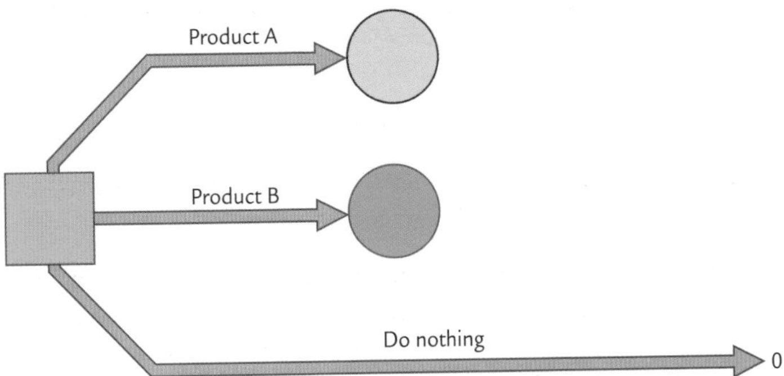

4 From any circle(s), draw lines to the right representing possible outcomes and above each line label the outcome (for example, success or failure, competitive launch or no competitive launch). Review your tree diagram and see if there are any options or outcomes that you have missed. If so, draw them in.

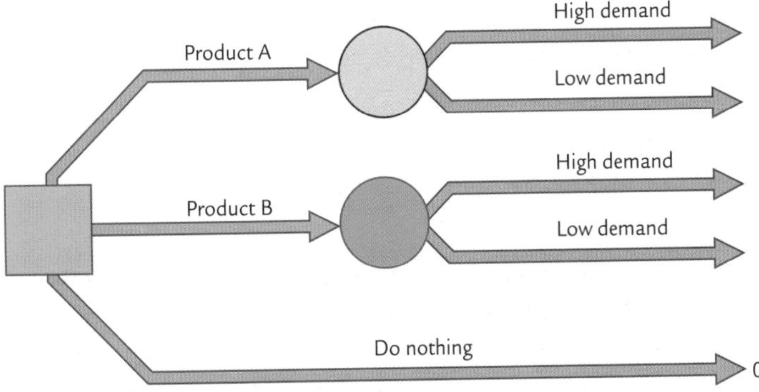

Evaluating the decision tree

This is where you work out which option is financially better.

5 At the end of the line, insert the financial result (payoff) of each outcome.

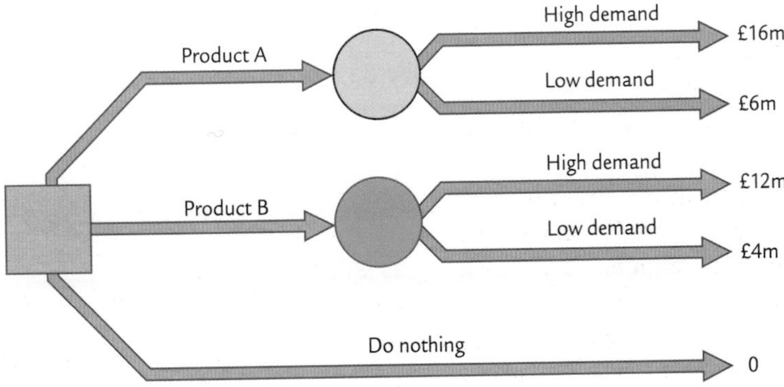

6 Note the probability of each outcome occurring immediately below the line showing that outcome. This will be calculated by considering data on similar events in the past and what experts and forecasts predict. If percentages are being used, the total for each option must add to 100%; if decimals or fractions are used, the total for each option must add to 1.

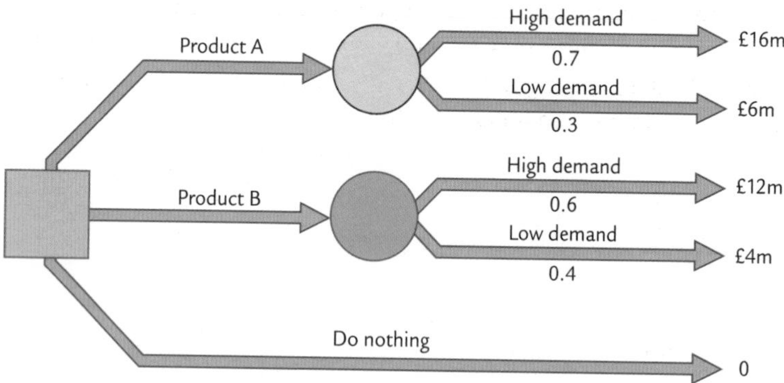

7 If there is a cost involved in selecting a particular option, note this under the line labelled with the option.

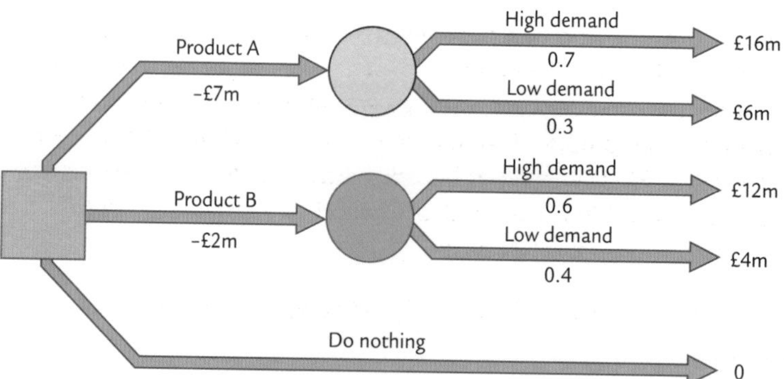

8 Calculate the expected values for each outcome and option. Start on the right-hand side of the decision tree. First calculate the expected monetary value of the uncertain outcomes by multiplying the value of the outcome by its probability. Then add the expected monetary values of all the uncertain outcomes of a particular option. Subtract any cost of that option. This gives you a value that represents the benefit of that particular decision or option (the net expected value).

Product A: high demand	0.7 × £16m	= £11.2m
low demand	0.3 × £6m	= £1.8m
		£13.0m
		−£7.0m
		£6.0m

Product B: high demand 0.6 × £12m = £7.2m
low demand 0.4 × £4m = £1.6m
£8.8m
−£2.0m
£6.8m

> **EXAMINER'S VOICE**
> Always include all of your workings when answering questions on this area — remember the 'own figure rule'.

9 When you have calculated the net expected value of each option, add them to the diagram and cross through any rejected decisions with two small diagonal lines, leaving untouched the line representing the decision that provides the largest financial benefit.

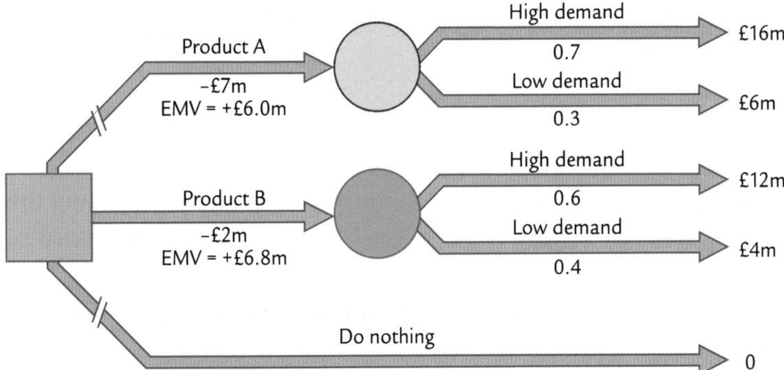

10 Taking into account your decision tree and any non-quantitative (qualitative) factors that might be important, make a final decision on the best approach for the business to take. If quantitative factors only were taken into consideration, product B would be produced, as it has the highest net expected value. However, the relatively narrow difference between £6.0 million and £6.8 million means that qualitative factors will probably be very important in the final decision.

Constructing and evaluating a decision tree: a summary

The construction and evaluation of a decision tree can be broken down into a number of steps:

1 Identify the options available to a business. Squares represent the decision nodes: that is, the points where management decisions about alternative options must be made.

2 Estimate the costs associated with particular options.

3 Assess the likely outcomes of each option or decision. Circles represent outcome nodes or points and show the possible outcomes of a particular option or decision.

4 Estimate the likely probability of each outcome occurring. This can be given as a percentage, fraction or decimal. The probabilities for a particular option or decision will always add up to 100% or 1.

5 Estimate the likely financial return from each outcome.

6 Once you have drawn and labelled the decision tree, start on the right and work from right to left, calculating the expected monetary value by multiplying its likely financial return by its probability. (Note that the expected monetary value does not reflect what will actually happen. It is simply an average or expected value and is influenced by the probability that has been estimated for the outcome. If the probability of a particular outcome is 0.6 or 60%, this means the outcome is likely to occur six times out of ten but, equally, four times out of ten it is unlikely to occur.)

7 For each option or decision, add together the expected monetary values of each outcome.

8 Calculate the net expected value of each option by deducting any costs from the expected monetary values calculated in step 7.

9 Take into account non-quantifiable (qualitative) factors before making the final decision. The following questions are examples of factors to consider once a decision tree solution has been produced:
- How reliable are the figures used? For example, how were the estimated costs, probabilities and financial returns arrived at? Who provided them? When? What was their original purpose?
- What market research has been done and how effective is this?
- Are there other non-quantifiable factors that might affect the decision? For example, are competitors likely to enter the market, is the economy heading for a recession, what will be the impact on the brand image, will employees' morale be adversely affected?

10 Select the option or decision that generates the highest expected value, unless significant, non-quantifiable issues strongly suggest that an alternative choice should be made.

Benefits of using decision trees

Decision tree analysis is a useful tool to use when choosing between several options. It provides an effective structure within which to set out the options available and to investigate the possible outcomes of choosing those options. It also helps to form a balanced picture of the risks and rewards associated with each option.

Most decisions cannot be taken with 100% certainty of the outcome. The fact that decisions are rarely based on perfect information means that some risk is usually present. This could be because the business has limited information on which to base the decision, or because the outcome of the decision is uncertain. For example, launching a new product in a new market will be risky, especially if a firm has no experience of selling in that market and if, despite market research, it is unsure about how consumers will react. A given level of risk is not a bad thing if it is balanced by acceptable rewards. Most successful businesses have had to take risks in order to succeed, such as entering a new market in order to gain first-mover advantages.

One of the advantages of decision tree analysis over other decision-making tools, such as investment appraisal, is that it takes into account uncertainty and risk, and tries to quantify these by estimating the probability of a particular outcome occurring. This estimation may be based on past experience, market research or informed guesswork.

By highlighting the issue of uncertainty, decision trees emphasise the fact that every decision can result in a range of possible outcomes, and they ensure that managers make more carefully considered decisions. In addition, using a quantitative approach should ensure a more objective decision-making process than the 'gut reaction' type of decision making based on a hunch.

When faced with a number of different options, a business will usually want to choose the option that gives the highest financial return. When the outcome of each option is uncertain, decision trees can be used to help reach a decision that balances risk and financial return.

Table 52.1 summarises the main advantages and disadvantages of using decision trees.

Table 52.1 Advantages and disadvantages of decision trees

Advantages	Disadvantages
They set out the problem clearly and encourage a logical approach to decision making	They ignore the constantly changing nature of the business environment
They encourage careful consideration of all alternatives	It is difficult to get accurate and realistic data in order to estimate probabilities
They encourage a quantitative approach that may improve the results and also means that the process can be computerised	It is quite easy for management bias to influence the estimates of probabilities and financial returns, and for managers to manipulate the data
They take risk into account when making decisions and encourage a quantitative assessment of such risk	They are less useful in relation to completely new decisions or problems and one-off strategic decisions or problems
They are useful when similar scenarios have occurred before, so that realistic estimates of probabilities and financial returns can be made	Few decisions can be made on a purely objective basis; most include a subjective element based on managerial experience and intuition
They are useful when making tactical or routine decisions rather than strategic decisions	They may lead to managers taking less account of important qualitative issues

Limitations of decision trees

As with all quantitative models, caution must be exercised when considering the nature of the information used. For example, the figures used might be biased or may have been manipulated in order to gain a particular outcome.

It is therefore important to consider who produced the figures and to assess their objectivity.

Decision trees are least useful when decisions do not involve clear-cut alternatives, when there are many individuals involved in the decision-making process, when circumstances are very uncertain or changing rapidly, and when completely new or one-off situations exist. In the last two instances, it would be almost impossible to estimate in any realistic or reliable way the probability of a particular outcome occurring.

Because of the disadvantages of using decision tree analysis (see Table 52.1), it should only be *part* of the decision-making process. Other non-quantitative factors should be taken into account before a final decision is made.

'What if?' or sensitivity analysis

'What if?' or sensitivity analysis can be applied to decision trees by changing either the estimated probabilities of options or the estimated financial returns of outcomes. This type of analysis can be used to answer questions such as: 'How small does the probability of the most optimistic outcome need to be before the other option gives a greater expected monetary value?'

FACT FILE

Weather Sensitivity Analysis is a specialised service designed to uncover and quantify the precise relationship between the weather and a business's performance. This comprehensive resource from the Met Office offers a valuable insight into how weather affects consumer behaviour and demand for products or services. A firm's historical sales and marketing data are gathered along with specific weather data provided by the Met Office. This collated information is analysed and a report produced that documents the effects of the weather on a particular industry and the correlation between sales performance and specific weather activity.

The Met Office has found that, in the majority of cases, the most important weather variable for explaining sales history is not the first one considered by the client.

The benefits of this system to firms are that it helps them to:

- understand the types of weather that have most impact on their business
- ensure availability of products and services to meet customer demand
- control costs
- plan the timing of promotional activity
- manage inventories and stock levels effectively
- deploy staff and other resources
- schedule maintenance work

'One of our retail customers wanted to analyse the sales of hot meals and the impact of temperature levels. They discovered that hot meal sales declined by £70,000 a day each time the temperature rose by one degree over 20°C.'

Source: Met Office website (www.metoffice.gov.uk).

This more detailed analysis helps to reduce the risks involved in the decision-making process by providing a thorough review of each possible outcome, from the most optimistic to the most pessimistic. Sophisticated computer packages are available for this kind of complex procedure — they are able to produce tree diagrams and an array of 'what if?' solutions, once the data have been input.

By using data such as those provided by the Met Office (see the following Fact File), businesses can estimate probabilities (for example, the chances of bad weather) and their likely financial outcome. When the organisers of Formula 1 racing changed the date of the British Grand Prix from July to April a few years ago, the owners of Silverstone used data of this type to argue successfully for shifting the date back to a time of year in which rainfall was likely to be much lower.

EXAMINER'S VOICE

Try to get lots of practice in handling decision tree analysis and make sure that you understand the procedures and calculations involved. Be aware of the shortcomings of the method and the fact that the qualitative factors involved in any decision must not be ignored simply because the numbers look convincing. The qualitative factors that need to be considered will be similar to those that you considered in investment appraisal and ratio analysis – the impact on the company's image, its workforce, short-term liquidity and the views of the organisation's stakeholders.

PRACTICE EXERCISE 1

Total: 40 marks (35 minutes)

1 What is a decision tree? *(3 marks)*

2 Explain two advantages of using decision trees in a business context. *(6 marks)*

3 Explain two disadvantages of using decision trees in a business context. *(6 marks)*

4 Why might decision trees be less useful in making decisions that concern new situations? *(3 marks)*

5 Explain three qualitative (non-quantifiable) factors that might be important in making a business decision. *(9 marks)*

6 If the probability of success is 0.6, what is the probability of failure and why? *(2 marks)*

7 A particular outcome has a 40% chance of earning £40,000 and a 60% chance of earning £100,000. What is its expected value? *(4 marks)*

8 Explain one advantage that decision tree analysis has over investment appraisal. *(3 marks)*

9 What is sensitivity analysis? *(4 marks)*

PRACTICE EXERCISE 2

Total: 10 marks (10 minutes)

A chocolate manufacturer is faced with a decision of whether or not to add a new chocolate bar to its existing range of products. If it goes ahead, the launch will cost £1.2 million, whereas choosing to do nothing will cost nothing. If it decides to go ahead with the launch, the probability of a competitor introducing a new, similar product at the same time is estimated to be 0.7. If it decides to do nothing, the probability of the competitor introducing a new product is estimated to be 0.4. The payoff from introducing the product is likely to be £1.5 million if the competitor introduces a product at the same time or £2.5 million if the competitor does not introduce a new product. The payoff from doing nothing is likely to be a loss of £0.4 million if the competitor introduces a new product or a return of £0.6 million if the competitor does not introduce a new product.

TOPFOTO

Construct a decision tree to determine which option should be pursued.

PRACTICE EXERCISE 3

Total: 20 marks (20 minutes)

A business is about to launch a new product and has to decide on whether it needs a promotion campaign and, if so, on what scale. It is considering whether to conduct a small promotional campaign costing £300,000 or a larger campaign costing £2 million. It estimates the likely success or failure of each option as follows:

	Probability of success	Probability of failure
£2 million promotional campaign	0.6	0.4
£300,000 promotional campaign	0.4	0.6
No promotion	0.1	0.9

Whichever option the business chooses, it expects to gain a return of £8 million profit if it succeeds, or to suffer a £3 million loss if it fails.

1 Construct the decision tree for this situation and calculate the expected value for each of the three options. *(10 marks)*

2 Which course of action is most desirable on financial grounds? *(2 marks)*

3 Explain two qualitative factors that the business might need to consider before it makes its decision. *(8 marks)*

PRACTICE EXERCISE 4 Total: 20 marks (25 minutes)

Lynne Lilley has been making crafts in her small studio in Skipton for approximately 10 years. Her products include handmade greeting cards, beeswax candles, pottery and potpourri, most of which she makes herself and much of which she sells to larger shops and stores in Skipton and the surrounding area. The studio is rented and she employs another person on a part-time basis to assist at weekends and during holiday periods. Profit over the years has been reasonable, but during the last few years costs, and in particular rents, have started to rise. Skipton, a market town in Yorkshire, attracts many visitors and there have been more businesses setting up in competition with Lynne. As a result of the increased competition, cost increases cannot be passed on to customers through higher prices and thus Lynne has found her profit falling steadily. Lynne believes she has two options available to her — to continue as she is at present or to move to cheaper premises.

- If she continues as she is, she envisages three possible outcomes: there is a 30% chance of a downturn in the economy, resulting in a loss of £10,000; there is a 40% chance that the economy will stay the same, resulting in a profit of £30,000; and there is a 30% chance of an upturn in the economy, resulting in a £40,000 profit.
- Lynne could move to premises in a less prominent area of the town, where rents are much cheaper. She has built a good reputation and therefore assumes that local customers will still find her, but she realises that she would be less accessible for the tourist trade. Lynne believes it would cost £4,000 to refurbish the premises she is considering and to cover the cost of advertising that would be needed to alert the tourist trade to the presence of the new premises. Again, she faces three possible outcomes: a downturn in the economy, the economy staying the same, or an upturn in the economy. Each of these outcomes has the same probability of occurring as described above, but the expected values are different: if there were a downturn in the economy, she would expect profits of £5,000; if the economic situation stayed the same, she would expect a profit of £35,000; if there were an upturn in the economy, she would expect profits of £50,000.

1 Draw the decision tree and calculate the expected values. *(9 marks)*

2 Which option should she choose and why? *(2 marks)*

3 How useful is a decision tree to Lynne in helping her to make this decision? *(9 marks)*

CHAPTER 53

Corporate planning in the medium to long term

This chapter discusses business strategy, considering strategic versus tactical decisions and examining the role of corporate planning in pursuing objectives. It introduces Michael Porter's generic strategies model as a tool for evaluating strategic options. The material covered in this chapter is closely linked with other parts of the specification, drawing upon the knowledge and understanding gained across the functional areas, external influences and other aspects of objectives and strategy. In particular, it draws upon material covered in Chapter 50 of this book and Chapters 35, 49 and 51 of the AS textbook.

EXAMINER'S VOICE

Strategic analysis requires you to bring together many of the concepts and content covered elsewhere in the course — marketing, finance, people, operations — so revise all of these issues, particularly the material on SWOT analysis (Chapter 51 of the AS textbook).

What is a corporate plan?

KEY TERM

corporate plan: a strategy detailing how a firm's aims and objectives will be achieved, comprising both medium- and long-term actions.

EXAMINER'S VOICE

Don't allow different terms to confuse you. In this area, many terms are used interchangeably and essentially mean the same thing. For example, corporate plan, strategic plan and corporate strategy all refer to the broad corporate-level plans that business has in order to achieve its objectives.

A firm's mission statement and corporate aims and objectives dictate its future direction. The corporate plan attempts to achieve these aims and objectives and to ensure that the firm's actions match its mission statement. Aims and objectives start off broad at the corporate level and become more detailed at the level of each functional area, thus encouraging a coordinated approach.

The same approach is used in determining the corporate plan or strategy that will be put in place to achieve these aims and objectives. This will have an impact at every level of the firm, from the corporate level to the functional, departmental or operational level. Functional plans will set out what the different functions of the business (including marketing, production, human resource and finance) will do to contribute to the corporate plan and hence the achievement of corporate objectives.

A corporate plan thus clarifies the role of each department in contributing to meeting the aims and objectives of the organisation. As a result, it allows for better coordination of activities within a business. In addition, it helps to identify the resources required by the organisation and so makes it easier to raise finance by providing a clear plan of action, indicating how and why investment is required. Its success depends on a number of issues, including whether it is the right plan for the business in its present circumstances, whether there are adequate financial, human or production resources to implement the plan, the probable actions and reactions of competitors, and how changes in the external environment are likely to affect the plan and the business.

EXAMINER'S VOICE

Try to read a newspaper, listen to the news or log on to the BBC News website regularly so that you are aware of changes taking place in the business environment and are able to identify the dynamic nature of the external environment and how this influences corporate plans.

Strategic decisions

Strategic decisions, which result in the corporate plan, concern the general direction and overall policy of the firm and are likely to influence its performance. These decisions have significant long-term effects on the firm and therefore require detailed consideration and approval at senior management level. They can be high risk because the outcomes are unknown and will remain so for some time.

Strategic decisions often involve moving into new areas and this requires additional resources, new procedures and retraining. Strategic decisions might be about whether the firm should consider expansion by acquisition or organic growth in order to achieve its corporate goal of, say, market dominance. They might also be about how the firm will compete in a way that distinguishes it from its competitors — for example, on the basis of quality and uniqueness or in terms of cost leadership and low prices.

EXAMINER'S VOICE

Just as any decision has an opportunity cost, so choosing one strategy rather than another involves an opportunity cost.

Tactical decisions

In contrast to strategic decisions, tactical decisions tend to be short to medium term and are concerned with specific areas rather than overall policy. Unlike

strategic decisions, tactical decisions are calculated and their outcome is more predictable. For example, if a product's sales are below target, a firm may make tactical decisions to remedy this — for example, cutting the price of the product and/or running a sales promotion. Tactical decisions may be used to implement strategic decisions and are usually made by middle management.

Corporate planning process

The corporate planning process involves the following stages:

- **Mission statement.** This stage sets out the purpose of the organisation and its corporate aims (discussed in Chapter 50).
- **Objectives.** This stage breaks down the corporate aims and indicates how they can be achieved in terms of functional objectives (discussed in Chapter 49 of the AS textbook).

To produce a plan of action, the company needs to gather information about the business and its market. Such information comes from internal and external sources.

- **Internal environment.** This stage reviews the organisation's different functional areas, including marketing, finance, operations and human resources, in order to assess its core competencies, what its key resources are and how successful it is in the markets in which it operates. It is through sensible resource utilisation and a focus on its core competencies that a business is best able to take advantage of opportunities in its environment.
- **External environment.** This stage assesses the key changes that are taking place in the organisation's external environment and makes use of PEST analysis and Porter's five forces competitor analysis (discussed in Chapter 35 of the AS textbook).
- **SWOT analysis.** This stage identifies the key internal strengths and weaknesses of the organisation and its external opportunities and threats. It analyses what the organisation needs to do to counter threats, to seize opportunities, to build on its strengths and to overcome its weaknesses (covered in Chapter 51 of the AS textbook).
- **Strategic choice.** This stage identifies a range of options available to the organisation using, for example, Ansoff's matrix (covered in Chapter 51 of this book), the marketing model (Chapter 3 of this book) and Porter's generic strategies (see page 497).
- **Strategic implementation.** This stage puts a strategy into effect, creating a framework and responsibility for carrying out the strategy at the functional or departmental level. This is where strategies are translated into policies, rules, procedures and operational targets within the different functional areas.
- **Control and evaluation.** This stage monitors and reviews the success of the strategy and assesses actual performance against what was intended. It

enables modifications to be made to the mission, aims and objectives, SWOT analysis, strategic choices and implementation strategies. It is therefore not only a control device but also a means of continuous improvement.

EXAMINER'S VOICE

Note how almost all of these stages have been covered at AS, in other A2 modules and in earlier sections of Module 6. Ensure that your knowledge and understanding of all of these areas is sound and that you can apply your understanding of corporate planning effectively, and in an integrated manner, to a given situation.

Figure 53.1 Map of the corporate planning process

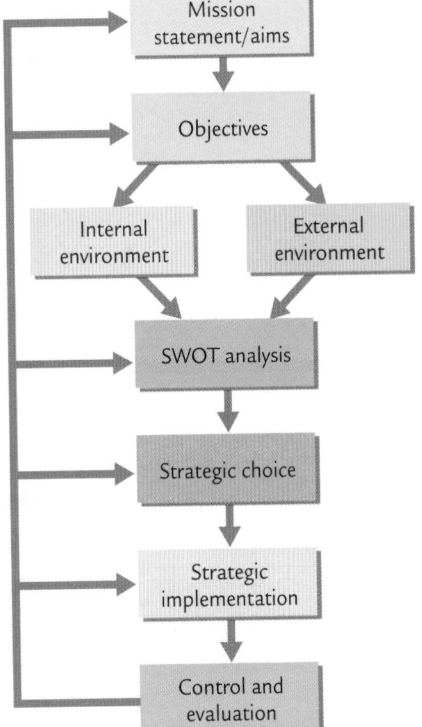

Figure 53.1 illustrates the whole process of corporate or strategic planning and demonstrates how each aspect is linked.

Porter's generic strategies

If a successful firm's winning formula is easy to copy, its superior returns will not last long. Rivals will offer either a better price or a better product, and profitability will be driven downwards. Only if the winning formula is 'special' in some way, and difficult to imitate, will superior profitability be sustainable. A formula of this kind represents a competitive advantage.

Every business strategy needs to find a basis for competitive advantage that can be defended against the forces of competition. This means that business strategy must involve the analysis of **Porter's five competitive forces** (covered in Chapter 35 of the AS textbook). Five forces analysis considers new entrants, substitute products, the power of buyers and sellers, and rivalry between firms. Thus, if customers can see acceptable alternatives, or if suppliers can find alternative markets, the firm's competitive advantage will weaken. Relevant questions for a firm to consider include: Is this an attractive industry in which to compete? How can we protect ourselves from the threat of these forces? How can we build our competitive advantage so that it will be resilient in the face of such threats? Successful companies build highly distinctive products and services for which there is no ready substitute. The perils of a business strategy that ignores competition may seem obvious, but established companies such as Marks and Spencer, Sainsbury's and WH Smith have lost ground over recent years as a result of complacency and a failure to maintain competitive advantage.

TOPFOTO

Michael Porter's work suggests that firms that achieve 'sustainable competitive advantage' do so through one of three generic strategies — cost leadership, differentiation and focus (see Figure 53.2), each of which is explained below.

Figure 53.2 *Porter's generic strategies*

		Strategic advantage	
		Low producer cost	High customer value
Strategic target	Mainstream market	Cost leadership	Differentiation
	Niche market	Focused cost leadership	Focused differentiation

Cost leadership

By pursuing a strategy of cost leadership, a firm sets out to become the lowest-cost producer in its industry. It does this by producing on a large scale and gaining economies of scale, by automating production and by reducing overheads. Its products will tend to be standard and mass produced, perfectly adequate but fairly average.

KINGFISHER PLC MEDIA CENTRE

The key to success with this strategy is to achieve the lowest costs in the industry, but with prices that are close to the industry average. A problem with this strategy occurs if customers perceive the quality/value of products to be lower than that of competitors, which may then force the company to reduce prices and thus profits. Moreover, if competitors are able to reduce their costs to match the firm's levels, cost leadership will be lost. Examples of firms following this strategy are B&Q and ASDA.

Differentiation

By pursuing a strategy of differentiation, a firm sets out to have a valuable, unique selling point, which provides it with the opportunity to charge high prices. Differentiation, also known as **value leadership**, can be based on a number of characteristics, such as superior performance, better-quality styling, product durability, after-sales service or simply a more appealing brand image.

TOPFOTO

The key to success with this strategy is to try to reduce costs in areas that do not affect the uniqueness of the product and to identify the features that add value to the product without leading to significant increases in costs. Problems occur if the extra costs incurred in achieving differentiation outweigh the additional revenue generated by the higher prices. Examples of firms following this strategy are Next and Thorntons.

Focus

Cost leadership and differentiation have so far been applied to firms in mainstream mass markets. Porter also identified the comparable approaches of firms operating in niche markets where a strategy of focus on one or more market segments is applied. This focus may depend on cost leadership or on differentiation and is the basis of success for most smaller and medium-sized enterprises.

By pursuing focus as a strategy, a firm picks a segment of the market that is poorly served by the main players in the industry and then adopts either a cost leader strategy or a differentiation strategy to target the segment or niche. The key to success here is that the particular strategy selected, whether cost leadership or differentiation, is aimed at a particular market segment.

Porter suggests that a firm must make a conscious choice about the type of competitive advantage it seeks to develop. If it fails to choose one of these strategies, it risks being stuck in the middle, trying to be all things to all people, and ends up with no competitive strategy at all (see Figure 53.3).

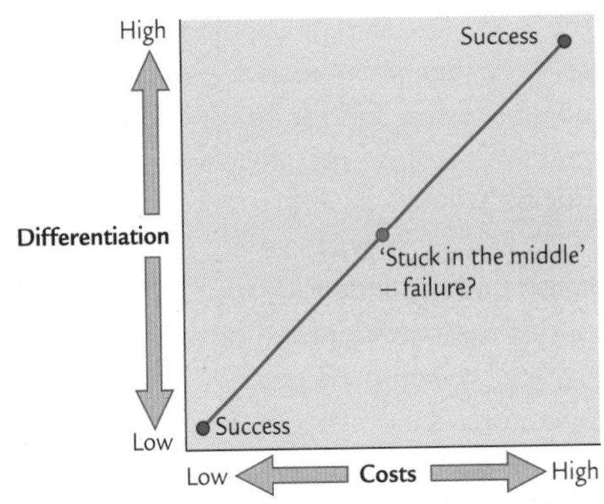

Figure 53.3 *Porter's generic strategies and firms that are 'stuck in the middle'*

DID YOU KNOW?

Not all commentators agree with Porter's view that a company must make a choice about the type of generic strategy to pursue. But it is interesting to note that, while Sainsbury's was still the UK's number one supermarket, Porter argued against its compromise strategy of 'Good Food Costs Less at Sainsbury's'. Since then, Sainsbury's has been struggling and it is now in third place.

PRACTICE EXERCISE

Total: 50 marks (45 minutes)

1. What is a corporate plan? *(4 marks)*
2. Explain one advantage of a corporate plan for a business. *(3 marks)*
3. Identify six stages involved in the corporate planning process. *(6 marks)*
4. Explain two reasons why a corporate plan might fail. *(6 marks)*
5. Briefly explain the four elements of a SWOT analysis. *(8 marks)*
6. Identify Porter's five forces. *(5 marks)*
7. Distinguish between strategic and tactical decisions. *(5 marks)*
8. Porter's generic strategies model is a tool for assisting business to identify strategic options. Explain his three recommended strategies. *(9 marks)*
9. Why does Porter suggest that 'being stuck in the middle' of the generic strategies model is likely to lead to failure? *(4 marks)*

CHAPTER 53 Corporate planning in the medium to long term

CASE STUDY 1 Ryanair

In the early 1990s, the Ryan family was considering closing down the loss-making Irish airline Ryanair. As a last resort, a new young chief executive, Michael O'Leary, was hired and sent to the USA to see how Southwest Airlines was becoming a rising star. O'Leary learned well, and returned to Ireland convinced that the Southwest Airlines approach was right – focus solely on minimising costs in order to deliver the lowest possible price, and set up routes going directly from point to point, so that people do not need to change flights.

TOPFOTO

O'Leary, as a graduate of business studies, understood that the underlying strategy was to take Ryanair out of the centre ground of the Ireland–UK market. Instead it would be positioned as the lowest-cost operator in a niche market. From then on, every aspect of the Ryanair operation was geared to minimising costs – to provide enormous pricing flexibility. The success of this approach is shown in a few figures. Whereas British Airways and low-cost EasyJet need a capacity utilisation level of 75–80% to break even on a flight, Ryanair needs less than 55% – yet Ryanair's actual utilisation rates are above 80%.

O'Leary set about the task of building up Ryanair's position in a number of ways:

- Extreme minimisation of overhead costs; staff work in cramped surroundings and are expected to work extremely hard.
- Minimising aircraft costs (depreciation and interest charges) by purchasing second-hand Boeings.
- Minimising maintenance costs by buying just one model (the Boeing 731), so that stocks of spares are minimised and the maintenance staff know the planes backwards and can therefore service and repair them quickly.
- Minimising landing charges: that is, the price that airports charge to allow a plane to land and to 'rent' time on the ground at the stand, waiting to take off again. Ryanair pioneered the use of secondary airports, flying from Stansted to unheard-of airports such as Alghero (Sardinia) and Dinard (Brittany). Airports keen to build business were willing to offer cheap deals to an airline that could bring in so many passengers.
- 'Sweating' the key asset – the planes – by ensuring that they operate many more times per day than rivals. The key is the turnaround time. Ryanair takes little more than 20 minutes to get passengers off the plane, clean it, refuel it and get new passengers seated. So the plane spends the maximum time in the air – earning revenue.
- 'Sweating' the staff. A Ryanair pilot flies around 80–90 hours per month – twice the British Airways equivalent. Cabin crew are similarly hard-worked. For example, in the first 6 months of 2003, Ryanair flew 24 million passengers with 2,000 staff; Lufthansa flew twice as many passengers, but with more than 30,000 staff. Ryanair has achieved this partly through ruthless treatment of unions; the compensation is that it pays well and gives staff share options that have proved very valuable as its share price has risen.

Ryanair's marketing mix has also been rooted in cost minimisation. O'Leary learned from Southwest Airlines that low airline prices are newsworthy – they can be showbusiness. So Ryanair launched by painting its telephone ticket sales number in huge letters on the planes, refused to sell through travel agents (saving 10–15%) and relied on news reports of its unprecedented low prices and word-of-mouth advertising from customers.

O'Leary's other ace was to follow Richard Branson's example by manipulating the media. He staged stunts such as the May 2003 'attack' on EasyJet's Luton headquarters. O'Leary hired a tank, dressed himself and other staff in army uniform, and drove up to the EasyJet HQ waving banners saying 'Ryanair blasts 50% off EasyJet's fares'. The newspapers and television cameras lapped up the story, giving Ryanair masses of free promotion.

The basic marketing rule for airlines has always been to encourage repeat business by looking after the passengers. Ryanair, by contrast, lays down rules that it will not break, such as 'no refunds'. If you are booked on to a Ryanair flight and are rushed into hospital that morning, do not waste time asking for a refund.

Part of the company's cost-cutting approach is that there is no customer service section at all. Bizarrely, O'Leary even created some terrible publicity by reneging on a promise that his one millionth customer would have free flights for life. Yet despite tut-tuts from the media, investors recognised that O'Leary's passion for cost cutting could be good news, while customers were reminded again that Ryanair means low costs and low fares.

British Airways (BA) and the other main European airlines have been left gasping as the Ryanair strategy (copied largely by EasyJet) has stripped their scheduled services of passengers. And Ryanair has a much stronger balance sheet than BA, meaning that there is no possible threat from a price war or even from excessively rapid growth.

Source: adapted from Ian Marcousé, 'Strategic marketing', *Business Review*, November 2003.

Questions

Total: 30 marks (35 minutes)

1 Assess the effectiveness of Ryanair's corporate strategy in achieving its objectives. *(14 marks)*

2 Using Ryanair as an example, discuss Porter's view that a firm must make a conscious choice about the type of competitive advantage it seeks to develop or it risks being stuck in the middle, trying to be all things to all people, and ends up with no competitive strategy at all. *(16 marks)*

CASE STUDY 2 J Sainsbury plc

Sir Peter Davis became chief executive officer (CEO) of Sainsbury's in March 2000 in what was seen as an attempt by the company to regain market position. During his term, however, Sainsbury's was demoted to third in the UK grocery market and the decline in performance relative to its competitors led the group to make its first ever loss in 2004. Davis also oversaw an almost £3 billion upgrade of stores, distribution and IT equipment.

J. SAINSBURY PLC MEDIA LIBRARY

In March 2004, Davis was replaced as CEO by Justin King, who joined Sainsbury's from Marks and Spencer plc. King was previously a managing director at ASDA. King ordered a direct-mail campaign to 1 million Sainsbury's customers as part of his 6-month business review, asking them what they wanted from the company and where the company could improve. This reaffirmed the commentary of retail analysts that Sainsbury's was not ensuring that shelves were fully stocked. The retailer's supply chain was badly disrupted by problems stemming from the introduction of new IT and delivery systems by Peter Davis.

On 18 October 2004, all store managers gathered in Birmingham where King unveiled the results of the business review and his plans to revive the company's fortunes. This was made public on 19 October and was generally well received by both the stock market and the media. Immediate plans included laying off 750 headquarters staff and recruiting around 3,000 shopfloor staff to improve the quality of service and overcome the firm's main problem of stock availability. At the same meeting, Lawrence Christensen, the newly appointed supply chain director, highlighted the reasons for availability problems and his plan to address them. Immediate supply chain improvements included the reactivation of two distribution centres. Another significant announcement was the halving of the dividend to increase funds available to finance price cuts and quality improvements.

13.01.05 update from www.bbc.co.uk

Mr King warned that trading in the first quarter of 2005 would be 'challenging', but expressed confidence that customers would notice the improvements made to its stores. Sainsbury's has cut prices on 6,000 products over the past year in an effort to generate more business. It has also taken action to improve product availability.

According to sales data released on Wednesday, Sainsbury's market share has recently stabilised after declining for much of 2004. Mr King said that the retailer's 3-year recovery plan, which aims to raise its sales by £2.5 billion by 2007/08, was on track. By the end of 2005, Sainsbury's sales should be growing in line with the market, Mr King stressed. 'We said this is a 3-year turnaround. Being successful in this marketplace means you have to be a very good business because we have very good competitors.'

26.03.05 update from www.bbc.co.uk

Sainsbury's like-for-like sales increased by 3.7% during the 12 weeks to 26 March against a year earlier. More impressively, Sainsbury's sales increased by 7.2% during the 3-month period against the previous 3 months, as the group managed to make more products available to shoppers. The UK's third-biggest supermarket added that, while price cuts had not drawn more shoppers into its stores, they had helped to lift sales revenue per customer. 'We recovered well from the Christmas and New Year peak trading period,' said chief executive Justin King.

Analysts were encouraged by the performance, saying the group may now have turned the corner. 'They've gradually improved market share in the last few months; the tough bit now is converting that to profit.' Mintel retail analyst Neil Mason added: 'Basically, it comes down to product availability. Before Christmas they had big problems with the supply chain and now they're adopting the right strategy.' However, he added that, while price cuts had lifted sales, they could hit the group's profits.

Despite the improvement, King warned that the group continued to battle in a competitive environment, adding that 'in these circumstances we are particularly pleased that we have seen an improving trend in sales'. 'Our major focus on availability is beginning to show results with both colleagues and customers noticing improvements in store,' King added. He also said that the group was confident of achieving its sales targets for 2005/06 despite fierce competition.

Questions

Total: 60 marks (70 minutes)

1. Discuss the value of a corporate plan such as Sainsbury's '3-year recovery plan' in assisting a company to achieve its objectives. *(14 marks)*
2. To what extent are the decisions made by Sainsbury's senior management team strategic or tactical? *(14 marks)*
3. To what extent is Sainsbury's using Porter's generic strategies in order to achieve its aims? *(16 marks)*
4. Using Sainsbury's as an example, discuss why broad corporate objectives and strategies need to be broken down into functional objectives and strategies if an organisation is to be successful in meeting its aims. *(16 marks)*

CHAPTER 54

Contingency planning

This chapter examines contingency planning and the constant need to question current methods and assumptions. It distinguishes between predictable, quantifiable risks and unexpected crises, and considers corporate responses to each. The related topics of sensitivity analysis and risk management are examined too.

Crisis in business

In a business context, a crisis is any unexpected event that threatens the well-being or survival of a firm. It is possible to distinguish between two types of crisis: those that are fairly predictable and quantifiable, and those that are totally unexpected and have massive implications for business. This is the difference, for example, between sudden fluctuations in exchange rates and natural disasters such as the Asian tsunami. The former can be dealt with by contingency planning and the latter must be dealt with by crisis management.

Examples of crises include:

- physical destruction due to a natural disaster such as the Asian tsunami in December 2004
- environmental disasters, such as an oil spillage that adversely affects coastal areas
- fraudulent activities of employees, such as scandals involving Enron and other financial services organisations
- health scares such as SARS, BSE and MRSA
- major customers withdrawing their custom or becoming bankrupt — for example, the impact on component suppliers of the closure of Rover
- pressure group activities or unwelcome media attention, such as animal rights activists picketing pharmaceutical companies and their laboratories, or revelations about child labour used in the production of products for high-profile companies such as Nike
- faulty or dangerous products, such as Coca-Cola's Dasani water, Microsoft's Xbox leads and the illegal dye Sudan 1 in foodstuffs
- strikes by the workforce, such as those by postal workers and London Underground staff
- hostile takeover bids, such as the attempted bid for Marks and Spencer by Philip Green

TOPFOTO

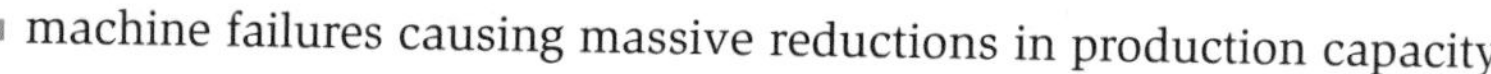

- machine failures causing massive reductions in production capacity
- competitors launching new products
- a severe recession or slump in demand
- changes in exchange rates
- sudden changes in demand

In the list above, the unexpected crises are towards the top and the more predictable and quantifiable risks are at the bottom.

TOPFOTO

FACT FILE

Coca-Cola

Dasani purified bottled water is the second biggest brand in the USA with sales of 1.3 billion litres a year. It was introduced in the UK in February 2004, ahead of a planned pan-European launch. However, the launch proved a major marketing disaster, as it emerged that some bottles in the UK had more than the recommended level of bromate, a potential carcinogen. In addition, the product was exposed in the media as simply being purified tap water, as opposed to mineral water. The media were quick to criticise the brand, especially as it was launched at a premium price. As a result, Coca-Cola recalled all of its stocks and abandoned its plans for the European markets.

Source: adapted from an article in *The Times*, 14 April 2005.

Contingency planning versus crisis management

KEY TERM

contingency planning: preparing for unexpected and usually unwelcome events that are, however, reasonably predictable and quantifiable.

crisis management: responding to a sudden event that poses a significant threat to a firm.

Contingency planning aims to minimise the impact of foreseeable yet non-critical events. In relation to such events, the organisation usually has weeks in which to prepare and respond. Contingency planning normally involves gathering detailed information on predictable situations and using computer models that provide systematic opportunities to ask and answer 'what if' questions.

Crisis management normally involves damage limitation strategies and places a heavy emphasis on PR and media relationships. It emphasises the need for a flexible response to any situation and the selection of a crisis team to deal with situations as they arise.

Effects of crises on functional areas

Crises can have effects on marketing, finance, operations and personnel aspects of a business, and each function needs to be able to respond and manage the situation.

FACT FILE

Microsoft

In February 2005, Microsoft had to recall 14 million power leads for its Xbox game console after a defect scorched carpets and burned some users.

Source: adapted from an article in *The Times*, 14 April 2005.

- **Marketing.** When a firm's public image is under threat, successful public relations often forms a major part of managing a crisis.
- **Finance.** Crisis management usually requires immediate cash expenditure, whether on advertising campaigns, environmental clean-up campaigns or a response to a hostile takeover bid.
- **Operations.** Contingency planning is important in this area, so that customers' needs can be met, especially if the company is reliant on just-in-time production systems.
- **Personnel.** A crisis usually requires direct, authoritarian-type leadership in order to issue instructions and make quick decisions. In addition, effective internal and external communication systems are required. Internal communication should be direct, rapid and open; external communication should be informative, truthful and controlled.

FACT FILE

MG Rover

MG Rover's high-profile collapse into administration has highlighted the need for small and medium-sized suppliers to shield themselves from their customers' financial woes.

Martin Dean, director of membership services at the Engineering Employers' Federation in the West Midlands, says: 'Today, most suppliers are diversified so that they are not reliant on one customer. Over 100 of our members supply to Rover, relying on the company for between 5 and 10 per cent of their turnover and, with the exception of one, will only have to lay off a handful of employees. But if this had happened 5 years ago, when most suppliers relied on a single large company for 70–80% of their turnover, the situation would have been considerably worse — all those companies would have had to go to the wall.'

Mr Dean points to 2000, when BMW sold Rover. 'It was then that suppliers started looking around at where else they could sell their products,' he says.

If a large customer goes into liquidation, small suppliers are third in the queue behind preferred creditors such as employees who are owed wages, and secured creditors such as banks.

AP Smith, a 35-year-old family-owned business, is among the hundreds of small and medium-sized firms hit by the fallout from MG Rover's financial woes. But the situation could have been far worse for the Birmingham-based metal pressings company. Eight years ago it relied on Rover for 30% of its business; today it has got that figure down to 8%.

Tony Parr, managing director, says: 'We realised at the time that if Rover went bust, we would be in a lot of trouble. We knew that we needed to diversify and to find businesses to work with which were non-automotive.'

Source: adapted from an article in *The Times*, 14 April 2005.

Stages in contingency planning

If a firm is prepared for a crisis, it should be in a better position to deal with it. Contingency planning involves the following steps:

- Recognising the need for contingency planning. Without such recognition, a firm is unlikely to be prepared to deal with a crisis.
- Distinguishing between issues that are critical for the future of the business and those that are not critical but will still have an adverse impact. In relation to the former, the business has no choice but to do everything possible before the issues arise. For the latter, it is likely that these problems will be dealt with as and when they occur. For example, if the crisis is a computer crash, banks cannot risk losing records of customer accounts and hospitals cannot close down intensive care facilities; hence, both need back-up facilities at all times. On the other hand, disruption to computerised invoice systems may hit cash flow but is not as critical and could be resolved in the short term by correcting mistakes by hand.
- Listing all possible crisis scenarios and then using sensitivity analysis (see p. 507) and 'what if' questions — for example, 'What if the workforce doesn't accept the pay offer and decides to take industrial action?', 'What if a machine failure causes a 35% reduction in capacity and cannot be fixed for the next 12 hours/12 days/12 weeks?', 'What if our largest competitor launches a new product that is more attractive than ours?' and 'What if our firm is the target of a hostile takeover bid?'
- Searching for ways to prevent each crisis: for example, using extra quality checks and relying less on a single buyer or supplier.
- Formulating plans for dealing with each crisis. This should include planning access to the necessary resources — human, financial and physical. A contingency fund should be established.
- Simulating each crisis and the operation of each plan. This is usually a computer-based activity, but it can also take the form of role-play exercises.

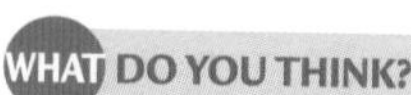

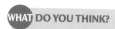

WHAT DO YOU THINK?

This highlights an interesting evaluative question: should a firm spend £1 million now in order to avoid a crisis that, if it occurs, might cost the firm £1,000 million, but which might never happen? Justify your answer.

Costs of contingency planning

Contingency planning is a costly activity. In large firms, it can involve huge numbers of highly qualified staff in assessing risk and planning what to do if things go wrong. Like any other form of insurance, it reduces risk but may seem like a waste of money if nothing ultimately goes wrong. The millennium bug was a case in point (see the following Fact File). For many firms, the potential problems of the millennium bug became very expensive in terms of time and money spent searching for appropriate solutions and strategies. For example, the situation gave rise to an increase in demand for the services of IT and management consultants. In addition, as many firms outsourced all of the work connected with the millennium bug, the fees of computer programmers rose dramatically.

INGRAM

FACT FILE

The problem of the millennium bug stemmed from computer programmers reducing the space needed for their programs by using shorthand versions of dates. Thus, 31 December 1999 appears in a computer program as 31/12/99. The following day, 1 January 2000, appears as 01/01/00. It was feared that computers would not accept this date as valid because they would be looking for a number in the 'years' space and would not recognise '00' as a year. If a program did not recognise '00', it was feared that the program or even whole computer systems might crash.

It was only in the early 1990s that computer experts identified this problem. Between then and 2000, many programs and operating systems were amended so that they would continue to work as normal on the first day of the year 2000 ('Y2K'). However, some programs, because of their size and complexity, had not been made fully compliant.

At one extreme, as many aircraft are largely controlled by computers, there were fears that the millennium bug could cause widespread disasters as planes fell out of the sky. Other companies were expected to face large bills for the cost of rewriting their computer software or replacing their IT operating systems. Even a company with little or no IT, or whose complete IT package was recent enough to be fully 'Y2K compliant', feared being affected by the bug as their suppliers or customers faced problems that might have knock-on effects.

Thus a potential crisis had been identified, but there was no certainty as to when problems might arise, the exact form they might take or their severity. The millennium problem therefore demonstrated a clear need for detailed contingency planning and preparation so that, when or if problems arose, a firm would know how to respond to minimise the adverse effects.

Sensitivity analysis

As we saw in Chapter 52, sensitivity analysis is a technique used to try to reduce uncertainty in decision making. It takes the estimates used in the decision-making process and considers what would happen if the figures were different. It enables managers to evaluate how sensitive the calculations are to changes affecting the inputs to a decision. It asks the question: 'What if?'

Two main methods of applying sensitivity analysis are used. The first asks the question: 'How will the results be affected by a change in each of the variables?' For example, how much will a 10% reduction in sales or a 20% increase in raw material costs affect the expected results?

The second method asks the question: 'What change in the variables will result in the project becoming unacceptable?' This method looks at each of the variables within the calculation and works out how much each of these would have to change to make the project unacceptable. The percentage change in value that makes the project unacceptable is called the **sensitivity margin**. For example, in an investment appraisal, a firm might calculate how much costs and revenues would have to change in order to reduce the net present value (NPV) of a particular project to zero.

Sensitivity analysis is a valuable tool in contingency planning. It gives managers more information to aid decision making and enables them to take a wider view of the risks and to be more prepared for changes. It helps to quantify some of the uncertainties that inevitably accompany business decisions. The results obtained by the sensitivity analysis need to be supported by further analysis and judgement. Managers can see the impact of a 10% reduction in sales, but they also need to be able to judge the probability of that situation occurring and whether the risk is worth taking.

Risk management

TOPFOTO

Business is fraught with risk, and rehearsing the many ways in which things can go wrong is an important management activity. From small start-ups to established global corporations, all companies have to incorporate risk management in every aspect of their business or run the risk of ruin.

Even the smallest slips can have far-reaching consequences. In 1991, jewellery retailer Gerald Ratner (left) gave a speech in which he described some of his company's products as 'total crap'. In doing so, he committed one of the major PR crimes. It ruined his business and he is still trying to shrug off the stigma 14 years later. That type of obvious PR disaster can be easily avoided.

Others problems can occur after great planning and consultation, and even government endorsement. For example, Cadbury Schweppes, voted 'Most Admired Company' at the *Management Today* awards in 2004, suffered a severe backlash to its 'Get Active' promotion, in which chocolate wrappers could be redeemed for school sports equipment. Initially, the government's sports minister backed the scheme. But then teachers and health watchdogs criticised the company for linking chocolate consumption with fitness at a

FACT FILE

Diageo, the international drinks company, employs thousands of staff simply to assess risk and plan what to do if things go wrong. Joan White, Diageo's global supply governance director, has a degree in risk management. 'We have a robust risk-assessment process to capture strategic and operational risk. We have developed a matrix that allows us to assess potential events in terms of likelihood and impact,' she said. 'All aspects of the business are subject to this assessment, from the risk of a fire in a European brewing plant to the potential impact of new European legislation. A lot of time is spent developing practical policies that grass-roots staff can implement when things go wrong.'

In January 2005, two European directives — known within the industry as 'track and trace' — came into force, stipulating how companies must identify their products and track their movements around the globe. White says that the implications of failing to comply with this legislation were so serious for a global drinks retailer like Diageo that a special team spent 18 months preparing for it. 'It has cost us several million pounds,' said White. 'But we are very confident we can comply now.'

Source: *Personnel Management*, February 2005.

time of increasing concern over childhood obesity. As a result, the promotion was dropped.

Once a company's reputation has been damaged, it can take years to restore it because a snowball effect exaggerates the problem. Talented people are less likely to apply for jobs or remain loyal to the company and, as a result, management and morale may suffer. Low staff morale can lead to poor customer service. All of this can have adverse effects on company profits. As a consequence, large companies make risk management a priority.

Some risks are specific to particular industries. For example, mobile phone operators have come under scrutiny over the potential health risks of mobile phone use. At the moment, there is no conclusive evidence that electromagnetic radiation from mobiles causes ill health, but if such a link were to be established, it would devastate the industry. Mobile operators are managing this risk by spending millions on independent research into the potential health effects of mobiles and phone masts.

V. CRUDGINGTON

All businesses face risks. But those that assess and manage risk the best are likely to survive the longest.

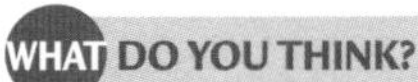
WHAT DO YOU THINK?

Given that all businesses face risks, is the alternative for those businesses that fail to assess and manage risk simply to hope for good luck?

FACT FILE

A planned ad for Pepsi, with David Beckham, Ronaldinho and Thierry Henry, among others, has been delayed indefinitely following the tsunami in Asia. Press releases sent out only a few hours before the tsunami happened contained images of the football heroes posing in front of a giant wave. 'If we had a crystal ball, we would never have sent out these images,' said a Pepsi spokesman. 'The image was taken from the commercial, which had a surfing theme, and was meant to be humorous, but it looks frightening now after the disaster.' Pepsi had scheduled a glitzy promotional event in Madrid to introduce the ad, the latest in a celebrity-studded campaign employing David Beckham and other athletes and entertainers. 'In light of the recent tragedy in Asia, we at PepsiCo International have taken the decision to put our 2005 surf-themed football campaign on hold for the foreseeable future,' the company said in a statement.

TOPFOTO

Other firms took similar action. Unilever, the makers of Marmite, ordered the withdrawal of advertisements on London buses. The adverts, which featured people fleeing a huge blob of Marmite, complemented a television campaign as part of Marmite's main winter promotion. The television campaign was virtually finished when the tsunami struck in December, but the campaign on London buses was to have continued into the New Year. American Express, the credit-card provider, decided to withdraw television and cinema advertisements featuring Laird Hamilton, a surfer, talking about the thrill of riding powerful waves.

PRACTICE EXERCISE

Total: 55 marks (50 minutes)

1. Distinguish between contingency planning and crisis management. *(6 marks)*
2. Compare the differences in how a firm should deal with a real crisis and with a fairly predictable and quantifiable risk. *(8 marks)*
3. Explain how the marketing function of a firm needs to be able to respond to a crisis. *(4 marks)*
4. Explain how the operational function of a firm needs to be able to respond to a crisis. *(4 marks)*
5. Identify six steps involved in contingency planning. *(6 marks)*
6. Explain, with an example, the difference between critical and non-critical issues and activities, in the context of contingency planning. *(5 marks)*
7. What is sensitivity analysis? *(4 marks)*
8. Briefly explain two approaches to sensitivity analysis. *(6 marks)*
9. What is risk management? *(4 marks)*
10. Because things rarely go wrong, can the costs of contingency planning be justified? Explain your answer, using examples where possible. *(8 marks)*

CASE STUDY Food alert

A large consignment of red chilli, purchased by Premier Foods, was found to contain the illicit dye Sudan 1. The red chilli was used in a vast range of foods, including Crosse and Blackwell Worcester Sauce, in which it was initially found. As a result, millions of food products have been recalled from supermarket shelves over concerns that they may be contaminated with the illegal and health-threatening dye. The recall affects all large supermarket chains including Tesco, Sainsbury's, Marks and Spencer, ASDA and Waitrose, as well as the fast-food chains McDonald's and Pret A Manger.

The UK supplier of the contaminated food products faced very bad PR and a huge bill, although insurers are expected to cover the cost of product recalls, which is estimated at tens of millions of pounds.

The supermarkets acted quickly and by the time shoppers began dropping their weekend groceries into trolleys last night, the poisoned products had long been plucked from supermarket shelves. Most of the leading chains sent out an alert early on Tuesday morning sending stackers into a frenzy of activity before the doors opened for business.

Wayne, who looks after the refrigerated ready-meal shelves at ASDA in Longsight, Manchester, said: 'It is the biggest recall we have had in all the time I have worked here. It has never happened like that before. We got the list very early in the morning, around 6.45 a.m., and we managed to get them all off the shelves before the store opened. Nobody in Longsight will be poisoned. That's a promise.'

The same kind of operation swung into action at the large Tesco superstore near Wilmslow, in Cheshire, as soon as the emergency product withdrawal notice arrived from head office. Instead of food, many shelves contained red notices saying 'Sorry, temporarily out of stock'. A duty manager said: 'There are checks and cross-checks to make sure these things happen properly. Be assured, whenever we get notification, we don't hang around. We deal with it as a matter of urgency.'

One manager at Marks and Spencer said: 'The products were off the shelves as soon as we heard about it. We had a red alert. All stores are notified at the same time and in the same way. We reacted to this extremely quickly. At the end of the day, we will be assuring customers we have reacted swiftly to the first news of this. If any customer believes they have bought one of these products, they will receive a full refund.'

The worry for Premier Foods, the owner of Crosse and Blackwell, is whether the damage to the brand will be serious. Such worries are understandable in the light of previous health scares. Coca-Cola abandoned its Dasani water in the UK last year when it was found to contain illegal levels of the carcinogen bromate.

In 1990, bottles of Perrier, the carbonated mineral water, were found to be contaminated with benzene, a poisonous liquid linked with cancer. It later emerged that the water was not naturally carbonated and sales halved.

But it is possible to emerge from a crisis with credit. In 1982, seven people in Chicago died after consuming a capsule of Johnson and Johnson's Extra-Strength Tylenol. The capsules had been tampered with and were contaminated with cynanide. Johnson and Johnson recalled $100 million worth of Tylenol, a painkiller, and advised consumers not to use any type of the product. This earned the company praise for putting the consumer first, and subsequently the drug rapidly recovered its sales.

Source: adapted from an article in *The Times*, 19 February 2005.

Questions

Total: 30 marks (35 minutes)

1 Discuss how effective contingency planning on the part of supermarkets is likely to limit any adverse effects on demand for their products. *(14 marks)*

2 To what extent does the response of supermarkets to the Sudan 1 food scare suggest that rapid operational responses are more important than public relations and strong leadership in a crisis situation? *(16 marks)*

Unit 6

Read the case study and answer the questions that follow.

CASE STUDY Aga Foodservice Group

Aga range cookers have been around for a long time. Aga was once part of Glynwed, which in January 2001 sold its metals and pipes businesses to Etex, a Belgian company, for £786 million in cash. It then changed its name to Aga Foodservice Group, with two main operations: a consumer business, selling cookers and fridges; and a commercial business, supplying equipment to hotels, bars and restaurants.

Since then, the management has steadily used the cash it received from Etex to make acquisitions. Early examples included Fired Earth, the paint and tiles company, and Elgin and Hall, a fire surrounds business. Another acquisition was Domain, a US home furnishing retailer. On the commercial side it owns Belshaw, a US maker of doughnut equipment, and Bongard, a French bakery equipment manufacturer. 'If you go to France and buy a baguette, there's over a 70% chance that it's cooked in an oven that we've supplied,' says William McGrath, the chief executive. Recent acquisitions include La Cornue, the French maker of expensive cookers, and Northland-Marvel, a US maker of refrigeration appliances. And there is still £20 million cash left from the sale to Etex.

The plan is to build on the group's consumer strengths while reducing the over-reliance on the UK. This strategy is based on the idea that a strong brand can open doors to anything. McGrath says, 'The group was a good, solid business, but not really brand-oriented. The idea was to bring Aga to the centre and build the business around that.'

Aga cookers are part of a wide consumer product range, with price as the determining factor. Rangemaster begins at £1,200, Rayburn comes in at about £4,500, Agas range from £5,500 to £10,000 and La Cornue cookers sell for up to £20,000 each.

TOPFOTO

Celebrity La Cornue owners include Brad Pitt, Jacques Chirac and Silvio Berlusconi. In the UK, Fired Earth rounds off the portfolio. Aga, with a 50% market share of range cookers in the UK, is associated with quality, reliability, traditionalism and Britishness, and is said to set the standard for competitors. 'This is our effort to pull together a whole lifestyle brand,' says McGrath. Like Aga, Fired Earth and La Cornue are premium niche brands, whose products have pricing power and are able to pass on cost increases to consumers easily.

Management's initial priority was to change Aga's image and to appeal to a younger, more urban, audience. McGrath set a target of raising sales of Aga cookers from 8,000 a year in 2001 to 10,000 a year in 2004. Sales were boosted by opening new retail outlets and a £3 million advertising campaign. Aga comfortably hit its target of 10,000 cookers a year and is now aiming for 15,000 a year by 2006.

There have been some well-documented disaster stories involving UK companies trying to break into the US market, but McGrath says that he 'did his homework' in selecting Domain as a platform for the group's US ambitions. The company is beginning to compete effectively in the USA and in Europe in an attempt to rebalance the business and make it less dependent on the UK consumer market.

The non-consumer side of the business has had a tough couple of years, although it has recently won the refrigeration contract for the new Wembley stadium. Along with commercial refrigeration and bakery services, the group is pinning its hopes on a fashionably 'green' product – the 'Infinity Fryer'. The fryer is aimed at fast-food outlets. It claims to use a third less oil than conventional fryers and the oil lasts longer. Whitbread, the UK's largest restaurant chain, signed a deal to install the fryer as its units come up for renewal over the next 3 years. McGrath says: 'We want to crack the QSR – quick service restaurant – market: McDonald's, KFC and Burger King, which we've never really been in.'

A corporate social responsibility report commented favourably on the Infinity Fryer, noting that it supports healthier eating by reducing the fat content of fried food and thus helps to address obesity concerns. It went on to say that it provides greater energy efficiency, improves operator working conditions and helps the environment through energy efficiency from the reduced use of cooking oil. The latter point is particularly important given that the UK implemented the EU Animal By-Product regulation on 31 October 2004. This prevents used cooking oil from being used in animal feeds: a route by which over 90% of used cooking oils were previously disposed. These factors also give it a significant economic advantage in cooking oil and fuel usage.

The company has been able to weather the storm in a sector consistently exposed to fluctuations in customer spending and confidence. McGrath notes that the business is cyclical: '2002 was a great year; 2003 more difficult; 2004 saw a rebound and we would hope that growth will continue through this year. Consumer confidence is a key thing for us. Certainly we've always recognised that, at some point, there could be a cycle within the UK – interest rates could increase and consumer markets could slow down.'

In 2005, the company hopes that the work done to turn Aga into an international brand and to boost its related premium products (the range cookers) succeeds. The French and North American markets are the main targets. On the bakery side, they feel that the business is very much aligned to some of the important trends of the moment – interest in food and health – and hope to see good growth in this area. Furthermore, publicity for the Infinity Fryer has been good and the product is expected to play a significant role in the group's portfolio.

Appendix 1: Aga Foodservice Group turnover by segment, 2004

	UK and European consumer	US consumer	UK and European commercial	US commercial	Total
Turnover	40%	15%	35%	10%	**100%**

Appendix 2: Performance of Aga Foodservice Group, 2004

Segment	Turnover (£m)	Operating profit (£m)	Cash flow (£m)	Net assets (£m)
UK and European consumer	166.3	20.3	18.4	86.8
US consumer	62.2	1.2	4.4	19.8
UK and European commercial	140.3	8.1	4.9	133.1
US commercial	39.8	4.5	2.0	31.8
Total	408.6	34.1	29.7	271.5

Sources: adapted from an article in *The Times*, 21 February 2005, and the AFG website (www.agafoodservice.com).

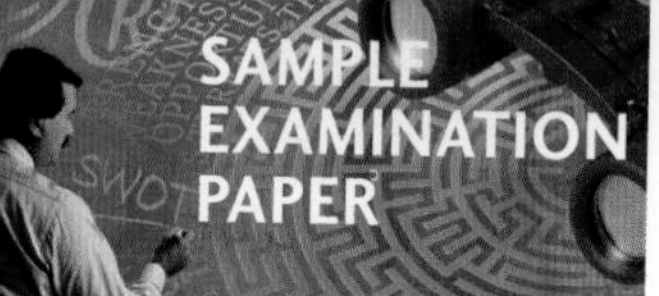

Unit 6

Questions

Total: 80 marks (90 minutes)

1 Assess whether a rise in interest rates is likely to affect a business such as Aga Foodservice Group adversely. *(14 marks)*

2 Evaluate whether Aga Foodservice Group should try to break into the US market. *(16 marks)*

3 Discuss the benefits and problems for Aga Foodservice Group of accepting its social responsibilities. *(16 marks)*

4 To what extent have Aga Foodservice Group's acquisitions brought risks and rewards to the business? *(16 marks)*

5 Using Ansoff's matrix, evaluate the possible success of Aga Foodservice Group's growth strategy. *(18 marks)*

Index

Page numbers in **red type** *refer to key term* **definitions.** *(Where the definition appears more than once, the first entry is referenced.)*

P

Q

R

S